Bering Sea

Novosibirsk Ilds.

Kolyma

ARCTIC CIRCLE

KAMCHATKA

Khatanga

Lena

OKHOTSK

PETRO PAVLOVSK

Sea of Okhotsk

YAKUTSK

KURILES

S O C I A L I S T   R E P U B L I C

SAKHALIN

Amur

Lena

KHABAROVSK

IRKUTSK

Lake Baykal

M A N C H U R I A

NNU TUVA

CHARBIN

VLADI– VOSTOK

J A P A N

M O N G O L I A

MUKDEN

K O R E A

I I N A

PEKING

PORT ARTHUR

THE 15 SOVIET SOCIALIST REPUBLICS:

1. ESTONIAN S.S.R.	6. MOLDAVIAN S.S.R.	11. KAZAKH S.S.R.
2. LATVIAN S.S.R.	7. GEORGIAN S.S.R.	12. UZBEK S.S.R.
3. LITHUANIAN S.S.R.	8. ARMENIAN S.S.R.	13. KIRGIZ S.S.R.
4. BYELO-RUSSIAN S.S.R.	9. AZERBAIDZHAN S.S.R.	14. TADZHIK S.S.R.
5. UKRAINIAN S.S.R.	10. TURKMEN S.S.R.	15. RUSSIAN S.F.S.R.

Scale: *1000 Miles*

Second Edition

RUSSIA

A Short History

MICHAEL T. FLORINSKY

The Macmillan Company
Collier-Macmillan Limited, London

Library of Congress catalog card number: 69-18818

THE MACMILLAN COMPANY
COLLIER-MACMILLAN CANADA, LTD., TORONTO, ONTARIO

Printed in the United States of America

PREFACE

To the Second Edition

The present volume endeavors to present between two covers the history of Russia from the very beginning to the second half of 1968. This is an ambitious undertaking that raises difficult problems of organization and selectivity. Information available on the earlier part of Russia's history, as well as on the age of the Soviets, is grievously incomplete. In deciding what "facts" and interpretations should be included or left out, value judgments, which are necessarily subjective, have to be made. It was my purpose to write a book that would provide what I believe to be essential information on Russia, with enough detail to convey something of the feeling of each period. I do not believe that history is made by impersonal economic and social forces, although, of course, they have a part in the historical process. A history that would omit the personal element would be as dull as it would be remote from reality.

The first edition of this book (1964) brought the story to the middle of 1963, that is, a period when Khrushchev was seemingly at the height of his power and held a central place on the international political stage. The present edition extends the narrative to the autumn of 1968; it covers the eclipse of Khrushchev and four years of the Brezhnev-Kosygin "collective leadership." The post-1963 developments are presented in the new Chapter 27 and in the revised sections of the chapter on letters, arts, and science (now Chapter 28). There are also additions to the Bibliography. Except for this new material the book remains unchanged; in my judgment, neither recent publications on pre-revolutionary Russia and the Soviet Union nor the post-Khrushchev

[v]

trends in Soviet ideology and policies call for a revision of the interpretation that I have advanced.

A warning must be given concerning the calendar. Until February 14, 1918, Russia adhered to the Julian (Old Style, O.S.) calendar, which in Catholic countries was superseded in 1582 by the Gregorian (New Style, N.S.) calendar introduced by Pope Gregory III. The Julian calendar was adopted in Russia in 1699, replacing the old Muscovite calendar that reckoned time from the somewhat uncertain date of creation. In the seventeenth century the Julian calendar was 10 days behind the Gregorian; in the eighteenth, 11 days; in the nineteenth, 12 days; and since March 1, 1900, 13 days. The discrepancy was the source of much confusion. For instance, the "October" revolution of October 25, 1917, O.S., occurred on November 7, N.S. A decree of January 26, 1918, introduced the Gregorian calendar: February 1, 1918, became February 14 and the difference between the Russian and Western calendars disappeared. In this book dates are given in accordance with the Russian calendar in force at the time, except when otherwise stated, usually in the case of international events.

The Russian alphabet presents difficulties. It is derived from the Cyrillic alphabet and consists of 33 letters. There are various systems of transliteration, none of them satisfactory. The transliteration I have used is that of the Library of Congress, with some simplifications. I have deliberately departed from the Library of Congress rules in using what I believe to be the accepted form of well-known Russian names and terms; for instance, I have written Rachmaninoff (not Rakhmaninov), Tchaikovsky (not Chaikovsky), *boyar* (not *boiar*).

It is my pleasant duty to express my gratitude to my publishers, The Macmillan Company of New York, for their patience, encouragement, and interest in my work. Dr. Paul Avrich of Wesleyan University read Chapters 11 through 26, and most of Chapter 28, made valuable suggestions, and expertly advised us on maps and illustrations. Miss Grace H. Gerberich has ably assisted me on editorial matters, and Mrs. Lyn Scott was most helpful in preparing the manuscript for the press; I gratefully acknowledge their assistance. The research librarians of Columbia University, especially Miss M. Eleanor Buist, have solved for me a number of seemingly insoluble puzzles. To them, too, I am most grateful.

I wish also to thank the administration of *Bibliothèque cantonale et universitaire,* of Lausanne, whose hospitality and courtesy have greatly facilitated my work.

Vevey, Switzerland   M. T. F.

CONTENTS

PART THREE *1696–1801*

PART FOUR *1801–1917*

Constitution of the RSFSR / Civil War, Intervention, and Independence Movements / Economic Policies / End of an Era

MAPS

PART ONE

862-1533

CHRONOLOGY OF PRINCIPAL EVENTS

Third century B.C.– eleventh century A.D.	Great migration in Black Sea steppes
862	Riurik arrives in Novgorod
End ninth – second half twelfth century	Kievan period
987–988	Conversion to Christianity
1019–1054	Yaroslav I of Kiev
1147	First reference to Moscow
1169	Andrew Bogoliubsky plunders Kiev
Late twelfth – early fourteenth century	Rostov-Suzdal-Vladimir period
End twelfth century	Formation of the principality of Galicia-Volynia
c. 1200	German knights land on Baltic littoral
1237–1240	Mongol invasion
Middle thirteenth century	Formation of grand duchy of Lithuania
1252–1263	Alexander Nevsky grand duke of Vladimir
1300	Metropolitan see transferred to Vladimir
1307 – early fourteenth century	Russian borderlands annexed by Lithuania
1325–1341	Ivan I Kalita of Moscow

[1]

1328	Ivan I becomes grand duke of Vladimir
c. 1330	Metropolitan see transferred to Moscow
1359–1389	Dimitry Donskoy grand duke of Moscow
1380	Kulikovo battle
1389–1425	Vasili I grand duke of Moscow
1425–1462	Vasili II grand duke of Moscow
1448	Breach with the patriarchate of Constantinople
1453	Fall of Byzantium
1462–1505	Ivan III grand duke of Moscow
1474	Moscow annexes Rostov
1478	Moscow annexes Novgorod
1480	End of Mongol rule
1485	Moscow annexes Tver
1497	Code of Ivan III
1502	Golden Horde destroyed
1503	Moscow annexes Chernigov
1503–1520	Moscow annexes Riazan
1505–1533	Vasili III grand duke of Moscow
1510	Moscow annexes Pskov
1514–1522	Moscow annexes Smolensk

1

The Kievan State, IX-XII Centuries

The Land

Geography and the Nation. Geography is a powerful factor in shaping the destinies of nations. The Russian state originated in the ninth century as a small principality on the Dnieper River. From this modest beginning grew the Muscovite tsardom, then the Russian empire, and finally the Union of Soviet Socialist Republics, one of the largest and most populous states in the world. In modern times the boundaries of Russia stretch from the Arctic Ocean to the Black Sea, India, and China, and from the Baltic Sea to the Pacific Ocean. This vast territory comprises a variety of climatic and botanical conditions ranging from the icy wastes of the tundra within the arctic circle to the sun-drenched subtropical growths of the Crimea, the Caucasian littoral, and Turkestan. Three geographical factors exercised a strong influence on the history and territorial expansion of the Russian state: the basic unity of the Russian plain, the character and distribution of its rivers, and the division of the land, from the botanical standpoint, into the belt of forests in the north and the steppes in the south.

Mountains, Rivers, and Forests. A striking feature of Russia's topography is the level character of her territory. The lofty mountain chains of the Caucasus, in European Russia, and of Verkhoiansk, Altai, Tian Shan, and

[3]

Saian, in Siberia, and the high plateaus of Armenia and Pamir are situated in the remote and politically unimportant border regions. The Ural Mountains, that traditional divide between Europe and Asia, are but a glorified chain of hills rising some 1,500 feet above sea level; topographically, the division of Russia into Europe and Asia has little to commend itself. The absence of natural barriers emphasizes the unity of the Russian plain.

The distribution of Russian rivers, like that of the mountains, is of considerable importance. The principal rivers of European Russia—the Volga, the Dnieper, and the Western Dvina—originate at the foot of the Valdai tableland in central European Russia; their leisurely courses take them over vast distances before they reach, respectively, the Caspian, the Black, and the Baltic Seas. The proximity of the issues of these rivers and the large number of their tributaries form a complex and almost interlocking system of waterways which favored trade, internal migration, and political unification. Moreover, it encouraged Russia's eastward expansion: the Kama, a tributary of the Volga, is within easy reach of the system of the Ob River in western Siberia. Internal waterways were extensively used by the Cossacks, whose exploits in the sixteenth century led to the annexation of Siberia and, eventually, to the establishment of Russia on the shores of the Pacific.

The physical unity of the Russian plain had important consequences: it offered no obstacles to foreign invasions, worked against the formation of independent states, and contributed to the advancement of political unification. The character of the rivers, these highways of the ancient world, tended to exercise a similar influence, especially by promoting the movement of settlers. There is a superficial resemblance between the eastward march of Muscovy and, later, the Russian empire, and the westward movement of the American frontier. Rivers, perhaps, had a decisive part in shaping the early history of the Russian state.

The significance of the rivers, however, was minimized by the fact that for centuries Russia did not control their outlets to the free seas. The Caspian, which was reached in the sixteenth century, is a closed sea, and it was not until the eighteenth century that Russia established herself on the shores of the Baltic and the Black Seas; even then her coastline remained small in relation to the extent of the hinterland. Most of the coastline, moreover, is in the inhospitable regions of the extreme north. This geographical limitation retarded contact with the West.

During the early part of Russian history the broad belt of forests comprised most of northern and central Russia and extended southwards, roughly, to the line of Kiev-Kazan. Further south were the Black Sea steppes, which, through a gap between the Urals and the Caspian Sea, merged with the steppes of Siberia. Asiatic invaders, who came in successive waves and against whom the Russians fought until the end of the eighteenth century, held the steppes most of the time. Fortunately for the inhabitants of the woodlands, the Asiatic nomads seldom penetrated the forest belt, which was the principal arena of Russian history. From the sixth century B.C. to the eighteenth century A.D. the southern steppes remained a no-man's land; but they were also a haven for those—and their number was surprisingly large— who endeavored to escape Muscovite oppression.

The People

The Great Migrations. Little is known about the early inhabitants of the territories which later became Russia, and the contents of the following paragraphs are of necessity speculative and conjectural. The earliest references to these regions appear in the writings of the Greek authors of the seventh century B.C., when Greek colonies were established on the northern shores of the Black Sea. The natives, with whom the Greeks carried on an animated trade, were known as the Scythians. In the third century B.C. they were overcome by another nomadic tribe, the Sarmatians, who in the third century A.D. were superseded by the Goths. A warlike Germanic tribe, the Goths kept in a state of terror the eastern territories of the Roman empire and reached the pinnacle of their strength in the middle of the fourth century, but they were soon forced to withdraw westward under the pressure of new invaders from the east, the Huns, founders of a powerful state that stretched from the Volga to the Danube. However, after the death of their leader Attila (453), their empire disintegrated. In the seventh century the Khazars, a tribe keenly interested in trade, established themselves in the region of the lower Volga and gradually extended their dominion over the Black Sea steppes, reaching the zenith of their power in the ninth century. Early in the eleventh century, however, the Khazars were superseded by another Asiatic tribe, the Patzinacs (also known as Pechenegs), who probably first appeared in the southern steppes in the ninth century and were themselves followed, in the later part of the eleventh century, first by the Turks and then by the Cumans (Polovtsy), and, in the thirteenth century, by the Tatars.

Except for the Goths, who presumably came from the region of the Baltic Sea, the great migration of nations in arms that for a millennium swept over the Black Sea steppes originated in the uplands of Asia and was caused by the obscure political and social turmoils of that continent. As already noted, it was the good fortune of the inhabitants of the forest belt that the Asiatic nomads seldom ventured behind the protective line of the forests where were found the political and ethnographical elements of the future Russian state.

The Slavs. The origin of the Slavs is as obscure and uncertain as is that of the Asiatic invaders. References to Slavs, under various names, have been identified in documents of the first and second centuries A.D. In the sixth century A.D. their settlements were presumably in the region of the Carpathian mountains. It was probably in the seventh century that the mass of the Slavs became subdivided (perhaps, in part, as a consequence of the fall of the Hunnish empire and the invasion by the Avars, another Asiatic people) into three separate groups, which shifted to new places of settlement: the southern or Balkan Slavs, the western Slavs (Czechs, Moravians, Poles), and the eastern Slavs, later known as Russians. It is believed that the eastern Slavs reached the Dnieper in the seventh century. In the middle of the ninth century they held both banks of that river, controlled the upper course of the Western Dvina, and extended as far north as the southern shores of Lake Ladoga. In the northeast the Slavs reached the upper course of the Volga, the Moscow River, and the Oka. Northward expansion brought them in conflict with the Lithuanians and the Finns, who formerly held these territories. The Lithuanians were pushed back into the region of the Niemen River and the lower Western Dvina, while the Finns were forced further north, although they retained the shores of the Gulf of Finland. Divided into a number of tribes whose names need not be recorded here, the eastern Slavs provided the bulk of the population of future Russia.

The Varangians. The appearance of the Varangians, or Norsemen, to whom tradition ascribes the leading part in the founding of the Russian state, was a consequence of the character of the Russian rivers. The territory that later became Russia was traversed by two important water routes which were extensively used by foreign and native traders as early as the eighth and ninth centuries. One was that of the Volga–Western Dvina, which linked the Baltic Sea with the Caspian and the Arabic east; the other comprised the Neva, Lake Ladoga, Volkhov, Lake Ilmen, the Lovat, and the Dnieper, and led "from the Varangians to the Greeks," that is, from the Gulf of Finland to the Black Sea and Constantinople. As already noted, the Khazars, whose capital Itil was on the lower Volga, were actively engaged in trade, an interest that has sometimes been explained by the large number of Arabs and Jews in their midst. The influence of the latter was sufficiently strong to cause the Khazar ruler (*kagan*) and a number of his subjects to embrace Judaism. It was during the period of Khazar dominion, from the seventh to the tenth century, that trading along the Volga–Western Dvina route reached its full development. Trade relations with Byzantium were quite important but came somewhat later.

The Varangians were Scandinavian traders, pirates, and soldiers of fortune, and their raiding parties began to appear in Europe in the eighth century. They came to Russia as traders, mercenaries, and sometimes conquerors, and mixed freely with the upper stratum of the native society. Their alleged part in the establishment of the Russian state will be discussed presently, but it may be stated here that they soon became assimilated by the Slavs and left no lasting imprint on the social and political structure. The one exception is the country's name, *Rus*—Russia—which many historians believe was derived from *Ros* or *Rhos,* a term originally applied to bands of Norsemen. This "Norman" theory of the origin of Russia's name is prevalent but not universally accepted, and in recent years it has been challenged anew, as derogatory to national dignity, by Soviet historians of the Stalin era.

Beginnings of the Kievan State

The Chronicles. The basic source for the study of early Russian history is the chronicles, a monumental record that covers a long stretch of centuries, from the ninth to as late as the eighteenth. Some of the chronicles comprise an account of the events of 862, which led to the establishment of the Russian state. The earliest available manuscript containing this compilation is the so-called Laurentius Chronicle, dating back to 1377; an analysis of this text has revealed an earlier chronicle allegedly written in 1039. Yet even this restored version is separated by some 170 years from the events which it purports to describe. Its authority, therefore, is open to serious doubt. Moreover, the chronicles, contrary to what their name implies, are not merely accounts of happenings of which their authors were contemporaries, but are collections of miscellaneous information derived from various sources. The use and interpretation of the chronicles present other major difficulties. The business of keeping these records was in the hands of the Church, and each copyist considered himself free to edit the text according to his predilections and the political exigencies of the day. Inevitably, errors as well as baffling linguistic and paleographical difficulties are numerous in ancient scripts which were copied by hand many times in the course of centuries. The systematic collection and publication of the chronicles did not begin until the nineteenth century.

Sources other than the Russian chronicles are extensively used in the study of medieval Russia. These are foreign chronicles, writings of Byzantine and Arab authors, folklore, and archaeological, ethnographical, and linguistic data. Although helpful and, indeed, necessary, these sources have to be used with skill and caution. The findings of archaeology and linguistics, on which recent historians lean heavily, are particularly inconclusive and controversial. To sum up: information on the early centuries of Russia's history is untrustworthy, fragmentary, and lacking in precision.

The City-States. In the ninth century and perhaps even earlier, city-states made their appearance along the rivers of the Russian plain. The founding of these communities was due presumably to two main causes: the gradual involvement of the leaders of the Slavic tribes in trade with the Arabic East and Byzantium, and the necessity of defense against the Asiatic nomads and other warlike neighbors. According to tradition, the city-states were at first ruled by Norsemen. What the Varangians and the Slavs contributed to trade were slaves and the products of the forest—furs, wax, honey, amber; these commodities were obtained by conquest and by collecting tributes from the subjugated population. In this manner the territories adjoining the commercial cities gradually came under their control. It was in the interest of the ruling group in the cities to protect from the external enemy the areas which they governed.

Novgorod and Kiev. One of the earliest city-states was Novgorod, an important trading center in northwest Russia. According to the traditional version of the founding of the Russian state that appears in the chronicle under the year 862, the Slavic and other tribes of Novgorod ejected their Varangian rulers but were soon forced by internal disorders to call in other Norsemen to govern their land. Riurik, a Scandinavian *konungr* (prince, Russian *kniaz*), accepted the invitation, arrived accompanied by two brothers and the customary retinue, and became prince of Novgorod and founder of the dynasty that was to rule Russia until the end of the sixteenth century. While this romantic tale is generally discounted as the invention of a later writer, it is believed that it contains an element of truth, namely, the existence in the northwest of Russia, prior to 862, of a state controlled by Norsemen.

The chronicle relates that two members of Riurik's retinue, Askold and Dir, went southward along the Volkhov-Dnieper waterway and established themselves in Kiev. They subdued the local Slavic tribes and fought success-

Kievan Russia

ful wars against the Asiatic nomads, but about 880 they were murdered by one of their countrymen, Oleg, who ruled Kiev for the next 30 years. From the end of the ninth to the second half of the twelfth century, Kiev was the principal political center of the land populated by the eastern Slavs which gradually came to be known as Russia. The rise of Kiev to national leadership was presumably due to its position on the Dnieper, the main trade route to Byzantium, and to its importance as a bulwark against the nomads roaming the southern steppes. The same geographical factors contributed to Kiev's undoing in the changed conditions of the twelfth century.

The Early Kievan Princes. The early Kievan princes belong to the twilight zone where history merges with legend and popular fancy. The authors or the subsequent editors of the chronicles have surrounded these rulers of the nascent Russian state with the romantic aura of national heroes. Oleg is represented as a great and successful soldier. It was during his reign that the first commercial treaty with Byzantium was concluded (907). In 912 he was succeeded by Igor (allegedly a son of Riurik), who was murdered in 945 while on an expedition for the collection of tribute from the subjugated Slavic tribes. Sviatoslav, the young son of Igor, became his successor under the regency of Olga, Igor's widow and the only female ruler Russia knew until the end of the seventeenth century. Olga was converted to Christianity probably some time before 957, when she visited Emperor Constantine Porphyrogenitus in Constantinople. Sviatoslav, like Oleg, is pictured by the chronicle as an ambitious and daring warrior. He is said to have fought the Bulgars living on the Kama, the Khazars, and the Patzinacs, as well as the Bulgars living on the Danube. His first Balkan campaign (967) was in alliance with Byzantium; four years later he again invaded the Balkans, but this time the Greeks fought successfully against his armies. Sviatoslav was forced to withdraw and on his way home was killed in an ambush by the Patzinacs (972). His death was followed by a struggle for power among his descendants, and the rule of Yaropolk I, his son and successor, was brief and stormy. In 978 Yaropolk was murdered by his half-brother Vladimir I, who became the prince of Kiev. Vladimir was a robust and seemingly unrepentant heathen; nevertheless, he embraced Christianity, established Greek Orthodoxy as Russia's official faith, and was eventually canonized by the Russian Church. His death in 1015 was the starting point of severe strife among his many sons; from this struggle Yaroslav emerged victor in 1019. According to tradition, he was a gallant military leader, an able administrator, the author of Russia's first collection of laws, a great church builder, and a patron of enlightenment and the arts. These claims, especially the last, rest on the flimsiest foundation. Yaroslav was the last Kievan ruler to exercise direct control over the entire realm. With his death in 1054 the history of Kievan Russia entered into a new phase.

Political Structure to the Middle of the Eleventh Century. The policies of the early Kievan princes pursued a two-fold objective: the subjugation of the neighboring Slavic tribes, a process which presumably was not completed until the end of the tenth century, and the maintenance of the control of Kiev over the other city-states. The Kievan rulers of the ninth through the twelfth centuries are usually referred to as grand dukes (*velikii kniaz,* literally "great prince"), although the terms "grand duke" and "grand duchy" were not applied to Kiev in the early chronicles. In the context of Russian history of this period the term "grand duchy" suggested the "seniority" or leadership of Kiev in relation to the other city-states, which were known as principalities. One manifestation of Kiev's supremacy was its relations with Byzantium. Although regulated by several commercial agreements (of which the first, it will be remembered, was concluded in 907), they were not always friendly: Kievan Russia is known to have organized six or seven military expeditions against Byzantium, the first of which took place in 860 and the last in 1043. At times, as under Sviatoslav in 967, the Russians fought in alliance with the Greeks.

In constitutional theory Kievan Russia was a loose federation of city-states which were themselves still in a process of expansion. The unity of the federation was maintained through the appointment by the Kievan grand duke of a relative or member of his retinue as *possadnik* (governor) of each principal city. Vladimir I had 12 sons and each of them was governor of a city-state. Thus the dynastic element permeated the constitutional arrangements, that is, the unity of Kievan Russia found its expression in the kinship of the rulers of the principalities (city-states) and in the fact of their appointment by the grand duke of Kiev, who was also the senior member of the Riurik dynasty. The constitutional framework of Kievan Russia—in so far as one can speak at all of constitutional framework with reference to this period—was the adaptation to political ends of the principles governing the property of the clan: either recognition of paternal authority (exercised in this case by the grand duke of Kiev) and the indivisibility of the Russian land as the hereditary domain of the house of Riurik; or, after the death of the patriarch, the division of the estate among the heirs—in effect, the breaking up of the national territory into independent and quasi-independent principalities. Until the death of Yaroslav in 1054 the former principle of unification prevailed, although it was frequently violated.

From the Middle of the Eleventh to the Middle of the Twelfth Century

Yaroslav's "Testament." The pre-eminence of Kiev among the Russian principalities made it a coveted prize and focal point of princely feuds, but the opposite tendency manifested itself during the century after Yaroslav's death: the desire of the junior princes to emancipate themselves from the rule of Kiev. What may be called today political separatism was viewed in eleventh-century Russia as the issue of family *versus* clan ownership, that is, the breaking up of the estate jointly controlled by the clan into separate estates owned by individual families, members of the clan. Emancipation from the rule of the grand duke of Kiev, however, inevitably led to the dismemberment of the Kievan state, and this ran contrary to the vaguely recognized need for national unity dictated by political considerations—chiefly those of defense and protection of trade routes. It is the conflict between these two tendencies—unitarian and disruptive—that permeates the political and constitutional history of Kievan Russia and that of the Russia of the twelfth to the fifteenth century.

Yaroslav's "testament" (1054), which appears in the chronicle in the form of an appeal by the dying Yaroslav to his sons, is an important landmark in the constitutional evolution of the Kievan state. Yaroslav divided his realm among his five sons and one grandson whose father had died in Yaroslav's lifetime. This partition was a departure from the policy of unification followed by his predecessors. Iziaslav, the eldest son, received Kiev and was enjoined by his dying father to protect Yaroslav's other sons should they suffer injustice, while the latter were urged to obey Iziaslav as they had obeyed their father. These admonitions notwithstanding, the testamentary dispositions of Yaroslav basically changed the constitutional relationship. Iziaslav, unlike the earlier Kievan grand dukes, was not the natural head of the princely family but merely the senior brother and as such only "first among equals" (*primus inter pares*). Moreover, henceforth the junior princes ruled their respective principalities not by virtue of appointment by Iziaslav, as grand duke of Kiev, but as heirs of their father, Yaroslav.

Feuds Among Yaroslav's Heirs. The 1054 partition of Russia brought no peace to the land. Iziaslav, indeed, found it increasingly difficult to enforce his authority as the senior member of the dynasty. For some 14 years he succeeded in maintaining a measure of national unity and in suppressing minor movements of disaffection through the cooperation of two of his brothers—Sviatoslav, prince of Chernigov, and Vsevolod, prince of Pereiaslavl. In 1068, however, the three princes were decisively defeated by the Cumans, and a popular uprising in Kiev forced Iziaslav to flee to Poland. There followed an extremely bitter and complicated feud, in the course of which Iziaslav, supported by the Poles, returned to Kiev (1069), was compelled to flee again (1073), returned once more to Kiev with Polish help in 1076 (from 1073 to 1076 Kiev was ruled by Sviatoslav of Chernigov, who died in the latter year), and was finally killed (1078) in a war against his nephews, who fought in alliance with the Cumans.

Iziaslav was succeeded as Kievan grand duke by his brother, Vsevolod I, whose rule, which lasted for 15 years, was filled with intermittent struggle with other Russian princes. During this period the disruptive tendencies inherent in Yaroslav's testamentary dispositions gained strength. Following the partition of 1054 the sons and grandsons of Yaroslav came increasingly to look upon their principalities not as integral parts of the Kievan state but as the exclusive property of their families, that is, of themselves and their issue. The gradual transformation of the princes and the members of their retinues from soldiers of fortune into landed proprietors tended to strengthen local ties. Vsevolod endeavored to counteract these disruptive tendencies by imposing his sons and nephews as rulers of the principalities held by the weaker princes, a policy which met with resistance and led to strife.

The Liubech Decisions. Vsevolod I's immediate successor as grand duke of Kiev was not his son Vladimir Monomakh, but his nephew Sviatopolk (son of Iziaslav). In 1097, shortly after his accession, representatives of the main branches of the dynasty met in Liubech and confirmed the principle of patrimonial succession which had been in effect for some time; that is, the princes were to rule over the territories which their respective fathers had received from Yaroslav in 1054. This principle was applied, at least at that time, to the succession of the grand duchy of Kiev as well as to that of the other principalities. Thus the conference confirmed Sviatopolk as grand duke of Kiev, not because he was the senior member of the dynasty but because his father Iziaslav had ruled over that land.

The formal recognition of the exclusive right of each princely family to the territory it governed was a further step towards the dismemberment of the Russian state. Yet the notion of national unity was not abandoned; it survived in the solemn promise of the members of the conference to observe the agreement and to refrain from feuds. The decisions of the conference, however, made no provisions for safeguarding the authority of the senior member of the dynasty—the grand duke of Kiev—such as were contained in Yaroslav's "testament." The former rule of the clan was thus being transformed into a federation of independent or quasi-independent principalities held together by political exigencies, dynastic ties, and a tradition of national unity. With the eclipse of Kiev later in the twelfth century the function of national leadership devolved upon the conferences of princes which met at irregular intervals.

The principle of patrimonial succession and the right of each member of the princely family, at the death of the patriarch, to a share in his estate applied (with a few exceptions which will be noted later) throughout the land. This meant in practice that in due time a domain was to be carved for every adult member of the local dynasty, with the result that with the passing of generations the national territory became subdivided into a continuously increasing number of political units (principalities) while the area of each was getting smaller. In the eleventh and twelfth centuries the more important city-states which grew to be principalities were Kiev, Novgorod, Chernigov, Galicia, Pereiaslavl, Polotsk, Riazan, Rostov-Suzdal, Smolensk, and Volynia. The multiplicity of the principalities, loosely held together by the uncertain ties of inter-princely agreements, and the weakness of the central authority were the chief characteristics of the "appanage" (*udelnyi*) period of the Russian history, which lasted from the twelfth century to the unification of Russia under the rule of Moscow in the fifteenth century.

It was but slowly and gradually that the long-range effects of the customary law which found its expression in the Liubech decisions made themselves felt. Meanwhile conflicts among princes persisted, the promises made at Liubech notwithstanding. Sviatopolk, who was married to the daughter of a Cuman khan, fought numerous wars against both Russian princes and the Cumans. He died in 1113 and was succeeded, in contravention of the Liubech decisions, not by his son but by his nephew, Vladimir II Monomakh.

Vladimir Monomakh. Under the rule of Vladimir II Monomakh, who died in 1125, and during the brief reign of his son Mstislav, the disruptive forces were kept in check and Kiev reached the height of its power. Vladimir, reputedly a wise and enlightened leader, dealt sternly and successfully with the Cumans and maintained the unity of the Kievan state, as did his predecessors in the tenth and in the first half of the eleventh century, by imposing a son or nephew as *possadnik* (governor) of each of the more important principalities. These authoritarian policies led to conflicts with local rulers, but Vladimir had the upper hand and, in spite of the many wars, his popularity allegedly remained unimpaired.

The Decline of Kiev. Mstislav continued these policies, but after his death in 1132 the disruptive forces came to the fore with great violence. The Cumans resumed their attacks on the Russian land. Between 1132 and 1169 the Kievan throne changed hands 16 times. The final and fatal blow to its authority was dealt in 1169 by Andrew Bogoliubsky, prince of Rostov-Suzdal. His armies took Kiev by assault, pillaged and burned it, and drove away much of its population, which was reduced to slavery. This was an unprecedented disaster: never before was Kiev treated by a Russian prince as a conquered city. Moreover, Andrew returned to the principality of Rostov-Suzdal, where he established his capital. Kiev was put under the rule of his younger brother Gleb and rapidly sank into political insignificance. Meanwhile the center of political authority was shifted northeast to the land of Suzdal-Vladimir.

Social and Economic Conditions

Evolution of the Social Structure. Little information is available on Russia's social structure during the early period of her history. It is believed that the majority of the population were freemen enjoying approximate equality of status; slaves were presumably few and were drawn from among the subjugated tribes. A process of stratification, however, set in, and towards the end of the twelfth century there appeared several social classes: princely dynasties, an upper class that evolved from the *druzhina,* or military retinues of the princes, burghers or townsmen, a free peasantry, and slaves.

Princely Dynasties. As already noted, princely dynasties all claimed descent from Riurik, but from the middle of the eleventh century they became identified, to the exclusion of the other branches of the clan, with the principalities over which the immediate forbears (father and grandfathers) of the local princes had ruled. A notable feature of the political organization of this period was the frequent transfer of princes from city to city. The reason for this mobility, which was discontinued in the thirteenth century, is a source of much disagreement among historians. It was presumably due to the rule of customary law entitling each member of the dynasty to participation in government. This was not, however, an absolute right, and its implementation depended on a number of factors among which the consent of the governed, expressed through the *veche* (popular assembly), was particularly important. Nevertheless, from the middle of the eleventh century every principality except Kiev and Novgorod acquired its own dynasty. In the case of Kiev the exception is explained by the unique position of that city as the traditional center of political authority; somewhat similar considerations, as will appear later, account for the failure of Novgorod to obtain a permanent dynasty.

The chief duties of the princes were military leadership and administration of justice, which, however, were often exercised through appointed representatives of the princes. Their revenue consisted of war booty, proceeds of trade operations, tribute from the subjugated peoples, and judicial fines. Probably as early as the tenth century the princes began to appropriate landed estates, which became their private property. This development was fostered by the decline of foreign trade which followed the destruction of the Khazar empire and later, in the eleventh century, the cutting off by the Cumans of the trade routes to the Arabic East and Byzantium. The transformation of the princes from soldiers of fortune into landed proprietors forged an important economic link between the rulers and the principalities which they governed and discouraged the practice of princely transfers.

The Upper Class. The princes depended, particularly in the earlier period, on the support of their *druzhina,* or military retinue. Members of the *druzhina,* like the princes, were at first Varangians, but eventually the *druzhina* came to include native Slavs as well as foreigners other than the Norsemen—Lithuanians, Poles, Finns, and others. Originally the members of the *druzhina* were supported by grants from the princely treasury and shared in war booty, judicial fines, and proceeds of trade ventures. Their influence rested on princely favors, tenure of high offices, and wealth. At an early stage the new ruling class became subdivided into a number of groups, of which the more important were the boyars. They filled the principal offices of state and formed a council known as the boyar *duma,* over which the prince presided. Apparently the boyar *duma* had no formal constitution or definite membership; nevertheless, as a matter of both custom and expediency, the princes and later the Muscovite tsars found it necessary to consult with it on important state issues. The boyar *duma* survived well into the seventeenth century.

During the earlier part of the period when princely transfers were common (eleventh and twelfth centuries), it was customary for the *druzhina* to follow the prince from city to city. This was not an obligation, however, and it is believed that the practice declined in the eleventh century. The boyars, like the princes, turned to land as a source of revenue, and by the twelfth century, again like the princes, they were no longer mere soldiers of fortune and administrators: the aristocracy of the sword was being transformed into a landed aristocracy and became an element of stability in the shifting world of Kievan Russia.

Townsmen and the Veche. The urban population consisted of freemen —merchants, traders, artisans, and the common people—but no reliable information about them exists. The political influence of the cities, however, was considerable and was exercised, under the leadership of the wealthier citizens, through the *veche,* or popular assembly. The origins of this institution are not known, but they may be traced, quite speculatively, to the meeting of the clan elders in prehistoric times. The *veche* was an assembly of the adult male population of a city and its dependencies and could be summoned by the prince, the *possadnik,* or any citizen. Like the boyar *duma,* it had no formal constitution, no definite jurisdiction, no franchise requirements, and no rules of procedure. Yet its functions were important. The *veche* entered with the princes into agreements which determined, sometimes in great detail, their rights and duties, and not infrequently it ejected the princes of whom it did not approve and invited new ones. With two minor exceptions, the *veche* is not mentioned in the chronicle prior to the middle of the eleventh century. It reached its greatest influence in the second half of the eleventh and in the twelfth century because of the instability of the princely governments, the multiplicity of inter-princely feuds, and the emancipation of the principalities from a weakened central authority. With the decline of the commercial cities and the Mongol invasion, the *veche* lost much ground and, with the exception of Novgorod and Pskov, ceased to function in the fourteenth century. Crude and imperfect as it was, the *veche* was the nearest approximation to popular government that Russia has ever known.

The Peasantry. The peasantry formed the bulk of the free population. Members of this group paid tribute to the prince, served in the army, and lived by hunting, bee-keeping, and agriculture. Quite early, perhaps in the ninth and tenth centuries, farming became a major pursuit. Originally the peasants owned their plots, but in the eleventh and twelfth centuries, with the spreading of the large estates held by the princes, the boyars, and the Church, the situation changed and there came into being a large group of tenant farmers. In some cases, the wealthy and powerful lords appropriated the land formerly owned by the small-holders; in other cases, the farmers themselves settled on the large estates in order to secure the protection and financial assistance which the lords could provide. The tenants were often in debt to their landlord, and economic dependence brought personal dependence in its wake. Moreover, many peasant farmers deemed it advantageous to trade their precarious freedom for the protection of a powerful secular or ecclesiastical lord. Thus there came into existence a class of people, known by various names, who were neither freemen nor slaves but were on the borderline between the two. This relationship, which eludes precise definition, proved one important source from which Russian serfdom eventually developed.

The Slaves. The status of a slave was acquired by birth, marriage, bankruptcy, voluntary agreement, and in a few other ways; it was also the fate of prisoners of war. Authorities differ as to whether Russian slaves were looked upon as chattels and deprived of all personal rights. There is substantial agreement, however, that the number of slaves was not large and that slavery was not an economically significant factor.

The Church

Introduction of Christianity. Prior to their conversion, the eastern Slavs were heathens and worshiped crude images representing the forces of nature. It is likely that Christianity was known in the territory of future Russia in the ninth century and perhaps earlier. As already noted, the Grand Duchess Olga became a Christian in the middle of the tenth century, but the establishment of Greek Orthodoxy as Russia's official faith took place in 987 or 988, in the reign of Vladimir I. While the formal breach between the Eastern and the Western Church did not occur until 1054, the schism was well advanced at the time of Russia's conversion. The reasons why Vladimir turned to Byzantium rather than to Rome can be only surmised; presumably the geographical proximity of Constantinople and old-established ties with Kiev were the determining factors. Russia's conversion is represented in the chronicle as an act of public authority that took the form of mass baptism, although there is disagreement in the sources whether the rites were performed in Kiev or elsewhere and whether the converts were immersed in the waters of the Dnieper or in those of its tributary, the Pochaina. It is clear that strong official pressure was brought to bear upon the Russians to make them embrace the new faith; the result was that the acceptance of Christianity was in many instances formal rather than a matter of inner conviction, and heathenism survived for centuries in the religious practices of the Russian people side by side with Christian doctrine and observances. The slow and unsatisfactory progress of Christianity may be explained in part by the character of the Russian church organization and the complexion of the clergy.

Church Administration. The significant feature in the organization of the Russian Church was its dependence on Constantinople. The whole of Russia constituted one metropolitanate, governed by a metropolitan who was both nominated and consecrated by the patriarch of Constantinople. The patriarchate exercised the general right of supervision over the Russian Church and was the higher court in all ecclesiastical matters and in cases bearing on Church administration. The metropolitanate was subdivided into several dioceses which were administered by bishops who, according to the canons, were elected by a council of bishops (but were actually often nominated by local princes) and were consecrated by the metropolitan. As Russians trained for the sacerdocy were at first unavailable, the higher and many of the lower clergy during the earlier period were Greeks and Balkan Slavs, but in later years the ranks of the clergy, including the bishops, were filled with native Russians. The patriarch of Constantinople, however, strove to retain control over the Russian Church; prior to the Mongol invasion in the 1230's only two metropolitans were native Russians, and the appointment of foreigners to the highest office in the Russian Church continued, with interruptions, until the breach between Moscow and Constantinople in 1448.

There was a marked difference in the social and economic status of the higher and the lower clergy. The bishopric was lucrative and honorable. Bishops received the proceeds of a special tax levied on the laity as well as various fees and charges paid by the lower clergy (for consecration, permission to perform marriages, and so on). Another source of revenue was judicial fees, the jurisdiction of the Church being both comprehensive and broad. It also appears that at an early date Church dignitaries and institutions acquired large landed estates. Members of the higher hierarchy were well provided for, lived in ease and luxury, and zealously defended Church properties and privileges against the secular power.

The lower clergy enjoyed none of these advantages. At the beginning of Russia's Christian era village priests received a small stipend (*druga*), but this was soon discontinued; their only privilege was exemption from the land tax and other taxes. Their income was derived from donations of the believers and fees charged for services rendered, such as marriages, baptisms, funerals, and so on. It was also customary to grant the priests the use of small parcels of land. Out of this modest income the lower clergy was called upon, as has already been noted, to contribute to the support of their ecclesiastical superiors.

With some exceptions, the intellectual standards of the clergy were low. Byzantium, which in the tenth century had entered a period of political decadence, was reluctant to send to Russia, a distant and barbaric country, her more high-minded churchmen. The Russians who later succeeded the Greeks were seldom qualified for the performance of the duties of the higher ecclesiastical offices. The education levels of the lower clergy were—and remained for centuries—deplorable. Few of the village priests were fully literate, while a large proportion could neither read nor write and merely committed to memory the more important prayers and services. This complexion of the clergy may well explain the high place held in Russian piety by external observance, and the relative indifference to dogma and the inner meaning of the Christian faith. This aspect of Russian Christianity had important consequences in the subsequent history of the Russian Church.

Monasticism. Monasteries deserve special mention in an account of medieval Russia. Two principal types of monasteries existed in Russia in the eleventh century. Some, like the Kievan Monastery of the Caves, were founded by men of ascetic disposition who dedicated themselves to meditation and prayer and strictly observed the rules of the monastic orders; others were established by princes and wealthy boyars and had as their primary object to minister to the spiritual needs of their benefactors and, after their death, to pray for the peace of their souls. The remarkable increase in the number of monasteries and the rapid growth of their wealth may be traced to the already mentioned attachment to external observance which is characteristic of Russian piety. Monasteries, by virtue of their organization, were in the position to assure perpetual prayers for the dead, which were regarded as essential to gain eternal salvation. These could be secured by appropriate gifts. Salvation could also be achieved, according to the then prevailing view, by taking monastic vows at the close of a perhaps sinful life. The practice was common among the princes and wealthy people. Taking of the vows, moreover, was a prerequisite for the bishopric, a requirement which led to the invasion of monastic cells by ambitious candidates awaiting consecration. The demand for the services which the monasteries alone could provide led to the great increase in their number but was accompanied by frequent disregard for monastic rules (equality of all members of the order, poverty, charity, chastity, strict discipline). The landholding of the monasteries, too, extended rapidly; it is believed to have been modest in the thirteenth century (a period for which no precise information is available), but in the sixteenth century the Church owned about one-third of the total area under cultivation. The discovery of miracle-working icons and "unperishable" remnants of saints which many monasteries claimed to possess added to their popularity and brought pilgrims and donations.

The Church and the State. The expansion of Church landholdings eventually led to conflicts with the state. Most of the time, however, the Church, following Byzantine tradition, lent its authority to the support of the secular power. The position of the Church as a large landowner and the fact that it was administered as a single metropolitanate made it a champion of national unification in the midst of inter-princely feuds, while the appointment of the metropolitan by the patriarch of Constantinople gave the Church a degree of independence in its relations with the Russian authorities.

Cultural Developments

The Letters. The Church laid down the foundation of Russian enlightenment. It is believed that prior to Russia's conversion the eastern Slavs had no written language. In the latter part of the ninth century Cyril, a Greek missionary, evolved from the Greek alphabet the Church-Slavonic alphabet for the use of the western Slavs, and his brother Methodius translated the Bible into the Church-Slavonic language. Church-Slavonic came to Russia *via* Bulgaria and until the eighteenth century was Russia's literary language. The modern Russian alphabet was derived from the script devised by Cyril.

Early Russian literature consisted of translations of Greek originals or slavish imitation of Byzantine models. It was predominantly religious in character and consisted of lives of saints, sermons, and polemics against Roman Catholicism. The chronicles were kept in monasteries but, of course, dealt with many non-religious matters. The outstanding example of the lay literature of this period is the *Tale of the Host of Igor,* a poetical account of a Russian campaign against the Cumans in 1185. It was not discovered until the end of the eighteenth century; its authenticity, which was at times questioned, would seem to be well established by now.

A notable product of Kievan learning is the collection of legal enactments known as *Russian Truth (Russkaia Pravda).* It was once regarded as a code of laws enacted by Yaroslav of Kiev, but this theory has been put aside, and the prevalent view is that *Russian Truth* was the work of several generations, although there is no agreement among the authorities whether it was an official code or a private collection of no official standing. In spite of the many uncertainties surrounding *Russian Truth* it is the principal source for the study of early Russian social and economic institutions.

Kiev in the eleventh and twelfth centuries is sometimes represented as an important center of enlightenment. The Grand Duke Yaroslav in the middle of the eleventh and the Grand Duke Vladimir II Monomakh in the first quarter of the twelfth century are pictured as well-educated men, lovers and collectors of manuscripts. The Grand Duke Vsevolod (1078–1094) is said to have had command of five languages. These assertions, however, rest on flimsy evidence. A few Russians must have known some Greek, otherwise Greek hierarchs could not have performed their duties, but it is unlikely that learning went much further, and there is no real ground for speaking of Kievan enlightenment.

The Arts. What has been said about the letters applies to the arts. The most important monuments of Kievan Russia were the churches built by Vladimir I and Yaroslav. They were erected by Greek architects and artisans and were decorated by Greek artists. Foreign influence, especially Byzantine, is unmistakable. Attempts based on archaeological data have been made recently, particularly in the 1940's and 1950's, to prove that arts and crafts reached a high degree of development in Kievan Russia. The evidence yielded so far by archaeology, however, is controversial and inconclusive and does not justify the broad claims of a flourishing Kievan civilization which are sometimes made.

The Fall of Kiev

A Recapitulation. Kievan Russia, in the words of a famed historian, was "a federation based on the fact of the kinship of the rulers, a union involuntary in origin and not really binding in its effects, one of those medieval social formations where political relationships have evolved from the norms of private law." One reason for the decline and fall of Kiev was its location —its proximity to the steppes and the impairment of its position as the leading commercial city on the water route "from the Varangians to the Greeks." With the appearance of the Cumans, trade relations with Byzantium became difficult and lost much of their former importance, especially in the second quarter of the twelfth century, while new commercial ties were established between northwestern Russia and western Europe. The breaking up of the clan rule and the partition of the country into quasi-independent principalities governed by separate dynasties tended to increase the attraction of regional capitals, and the spreading of princely and boyar landownership strengthened these local ties. Although the idea of national unity survived in the conferences of the princes, its economic base—the political hegemony of the commercial cities and their common interest in foreign trade—was gone. Moreover, the supremacy of Kiev was undermined by inter-princely feuds which led to its sacking in 1169 by the troops of Andrew Bogoliubsky, who removed the center of political power northwards to the land of Rostov-Suzdal. From this blow Kiev never recovered.

2

The Cleavage:
XII-XIII Centuries,
Southwest and Northeast;
Novgorod and Pskov

Kiev's Successors

Economic Decay. The eclipse of the political supremacy of Kiev which followed the events of 1169 was prepared by the decline of the Eastern and Byzantine trade, the pressure of the Cumans, and incessant inter-princely feuds. The state of political turmoil that prevailed in Kievan Russia had its repercussions on the economic conditions of the land. Organization of defense was among the principal duties of the early Russian rulers and, presumably, one of the reasons for the establishment of the Kievan state. In the second half of the twelfth century, however, the grand dukes of Kiev not only failed to protect their people from foreign invaders but even brought upon them the calamity of war as a result of the inter-princely strife, in which the Cumans and other external enemies often participated as allies of the warring princes. Moreover, in those days defeat in war was a major disaster, for it usually meant both economic ruin and the reduction of the conquered people to slavery.

Flight of the Population. Confronted with this prospect the inhabitants of the territories of the Kievan state which were the object of frequent invasions gave up their settlements and sought salvation in flight. Contemporary Russian records and accounts of foreign travelers have preserved a vivid picture of the depopulation of these regions. Some of the refugees went westward to Volynia and Galicia, while others made their way to the wooded wilderness of the northeast, to the principalities of Smolensk, Murom-Riazan, Tver, and Rostov-Suzdal. The shift of the population was presumably at least in part responsible for the shift of political power. The appearance towards the end of the twelfth century of two new political centers—Galicia-Volynia, in the southwest, and Rostov-Suzdal-Vladimir, in the northeast—was of considerable importance. They became the immediate successors to Kiev's vanishing supremacy, while their diverging fate left a profound imprint on the subsequent course of Russian history.

The Southwest

Galicia and Volynia. The ancient lands of Galicia and Volynia formed the southwestern outpost of the Russian world. Their geographical location accounts for the peculiarities of their development. On the one hand, their relative remoteness from the Black Sea steppes offered them a degree of protection from invasion by the Cumans and, later, by the Tatars and explains why the harassed populations of the more exposed regions sought refuge within the borders of these principalities. On the other hand, proximity to Hungary, Poland, Lithuania, and the German knights brought Galicia and Volynia into close contact with these Western or Westernized countries and exposed them to political, economic, cultural, and religious influences different from those experienced by the other Russian principalities, except perhaps Novgorod. The multiplicity of Western ties tended to minimize the dependence of Volynia and Galicia on Kiev and, later, on the new Russian political centers in the northeast—Vladimir and Moscow—paving the way for their eventual absorption by Lithuania and Poland. Galicia and Volynia carried on an extensive trade with their Western neighbors as well as with Russia, although their relations with these countries were often stormy. One source of the wealth of Galicia and Volynia was the important deposits of salt which supplied the Russian markets. Both principalities had powerful and ambitious boyars, who, through the *veche* (popular assembly) and the selection of and control over the princes, actively participated in government.

Galicia and Volynia emancipated themselves from the direct rule of Kiev and became independent principalities late in the eleventh century. At the end of the twelfth century they were merged and formed the principality of Galicia-Volynia under the leadership of Roman, a prince of Volynia. Roman, reputedly a powerful and able ruler, fought against Kiev and the Lithuanians and was killed in 1205 in a war with the Poles. His death was followed by a period of extreme confusion, the throne of Galicia-Volynia changing hands nine times in the course of 33 years. Among its shadowy occupants were two Hungarian princes. The Russians, the Poles, and the Hungarians all contributed to the political disorder, and it was not until 1238 that Roman's son Daniel, who was four years old at the time of his father's death, finally succeeded in establishing himself on the throne. Two years later the Tatar invasion swept over the principality. Daniel, according to tradition a gallant soldier and a wise statesman, swayed uneasily between the necessity of making obeisance to the Mongols, whose vassal he now was, and the desire to restore the independence of his land. He made plans for a war of liberation in alliance with the Holy See, Poland, Hungary, and Lithuania, but nothing came of it. Daniel, indeed, was forced to comply with the order of the Tatars to destroy all fortifications in his principality. In spite of this setback Galicia-Volynia enjoyed considerable prestige and authority during that period. After Daniel's death in 1264, however, it entered into an era of decline which finally led to the loss of its independence and its annexation by Poland and Lithuania in the middle of the fourteenth century.

The German Knights. In the thirteenth century two new influences came to bear on Russia's western borderlands. These were the German knights and the grand duchy of Lithuania. In the 1180's German missionaries led by the monk Meinhard, later bishop of Livonia, landed on the Baltic littoral in the region of the Western Dvina and proceeded to conquer the adjoining lands and to convert the Lettish population to Roman Catholicism. Meinhard's successor was killed by the Letts, who repudiated their conversion, but a new German expedition under Bishop Albert landed in 1200. Albert founded the city of Riga and in 1202 established the Order of the Knights of the Sword, which was dedicated to the spreading of Catholicism. Another German order, that of the Teutonic Knights, was founded further west on the Baltic littoral in 1226; ten years later the two were reorganized as the Livonian Order without, however, losing their identity. Although the number of knights was never large, the order, as an instrument of militant Germanism and Catholicism, exercised—until its dissolution in 1561—a major influence in the affairs of that region.

The Grand Duchy of Lithuania. While the German knights were newcomers, the Lithuanians, who lived in the basin on the Niemen and the Western Dvina, were Russia's old neighbors and prior to unification presented no special problem. In the middle of the thirteenth century, however, the Lithuanians formed under the leadership of Mindovg a strong state which became known as the grand duchy of Lithuania. At the end of the fourteenth century (1385) Lithuania, by virtue of the so-called union of Krevo, was incorporated in the kingdom of Poland. It speedily recovered its independence, but the link between the two states was maintained, with short interruptions, through a personal dynastic union until 1569, when, by the Act of Lublin, Lithuania was finally merged with the Polish Crown, although it retained its administrative identity.

These developments were of considerable import to the western Russian principalities. Throughout the fourteenth and early in the fifteenth century a number of these lands were annexed by Lithuania and Poland. The first to be annexed was the principality of Polotsk (1307); it was followed by Vitebsk, Galicia, Volynia, Chernigov, Kiev, and Smolensk. The eastward expansion of Lithuania-Poland was made possible by the political fragmentation of Russia and her weakening under the Mongol rule; the moving power behind it was the ambition of the Lithuanian princes (Viten, Gedymin, Olgerd, Yagailo, Vitovt), and it was probably facilitated by a certain community of interests between the upper class in the western Russian principalities and their conquerors, which made foreign rule more palatable if not actually welcome. According to a distinguished Russian authority, the annexation of Russia's western principalities by Lithuania was a process similar to that of the unification of the city-states under the rule of Kiev in the tenth and eleventh centuries.

It should not be overlooked, however, that while a certain homogeneity of political, social, and economic conditions prevailed in Kievan Russia, the influences to which the Russian lands annexed by Lithuania-Poland were subject were Western, not Russian. The social structure and the institutions of the aristocratic constitutional monarchy of Lithuania-Poland differed sharply from those of Muscovite absolutism. The ascendency of Poland in the union meant the dominance of Roman Catholicism, which eventually became the religion of the Lithuanian upper class, while Greek Orthodoxy remained the faith of the peasantry and was looked upon as a mark of social inferiority.

The Russian lands absorbed by Lithuania-Poland did not return to Russian rule until centuries later. Kiev, which was annexed by Lithuania in the 1360's (probably in 1362 or 1366, the exact date is not known), reverted to the Russian Crown at the end of the seventeenth century, 300 years later. Other Russian principalities (Polotsk, Vitebsk) remained under Polish domination until the partitions of Poland in the second half of the eighteenth century. The western borderlands, therefore, had no part in the building up of the unified Russian state that emerged from the confusion of the thirteenth and fourteenth centuries. The elements of this new political formation, as well as the leadership, came from the northeast.

The Northeast

The Land of Rostov-Suzdal-Vladimir. The real successor to Kiev as Russia's political center was not Galicia-Volynia but the principality of Rostov-Suzdal, on the northeastern fringe of the Russian world. An ancient land, Rostov was among the cities distributed by Riurik to the members of his retinue on his arrival in Novgorod in 862. Little, however, is known about the history of Rostov until the twelfth century, when Yuri Dolgoruky, a son of Vladimir II Monomakh of Kiev, became the founder of a separate Rostov dynasty. It was under his rule (he died in 1157) that the city of Suzdal was raised to the dignity of regional capital. Vladimir Monomakh is said to have visited this borderland and to have founded the city of Vladimir-on-Kliazma, to which the senior Rostov princes eventually transferred their residence. The changes in the status of its three major cities may explain why this territory is referred to in the chronicle as the principality of Rostov, Suzdal, Rostov-Suzdal, and Suzdal-Vladimir, or, finally, as the grand duchy of Vladimir—after its rulers assumed the grand-ducal title in the second half of the twelfth century.

A combination of factors may account for the ascendency of Rostov-Suzdal-Vladimir. It is believed that by the middle of the twelfth century this principality had reached an advanced stage of economic development, which is attributed to its trade with the Arabic East. It will be remembered that the Volga-Western Dvina trade route, which traversed the Rostov territory, was known and used perhaps as early as the eighth century. The princes, boyars, and merchants of Rostov-Suzdal were linked by common interests with the military and trade communities of the other Russian lands—Kiev, Novgorod, Chernigov, Galicia. The cultural and economic progress of the northeastern principality is suggested by the character of the Rostov, Suzdal, and Vladimir churches: built in the twelfth century of stone which was imported from the Kama region, they were the work of Western or Byzantine architects, artists, and craftsmen and rank among the outstanding examples of early Russian art. These monuments, as well as the existence in Rostov, Suzdal, and Vladimir of a powerful boyar class, confirm the view that economically, socially, and culturally the northeast had kept pace with Kiev and may be regarded as its legitimate successor. The influx of settlers from the south, which augmented the human resources of the northeastern territories, and the ambition and determination of the Rostov-Suzdal-Vladimir princes were perhaps other reasons why, after the eclipse of Kiev, national leadership passed to Vladimir. It would be unwise to ascribe to the early Russian princes reasoned statesmanship and capacity for long-range political planning. Yet the pillage of Kiev by the troops of Andrew Bogoliubsky, a prince of Rostov-Suzdal, and his subsequent policy of associating his principality with the notion of "seniority" among the Russian lands may not be entirely due to accident.

"Seniority" of the Grand Duchy of Vladimir. The basic difference in the constitutional arrangements of the grand duchy of Vladimir and those of the grand duchy of Kiev was that the former had, and the latter had not, a firmly rooted local dynasty. This meant in practice that the grand dukes of Vladimir, unlike their Kievan predecessors, were primarily concerned with the advancement of the interests of their hereditary domain, the land of Rostov-Suzdal-Vladimir; to these local interests were subordinated the broader national interests associated with the notion of "seniority" which gave a measure of unity to the Kievan state. In some respects, however, the Kievan tradition was continued by the grand dukes of Vladimir. Control over Novgorod, the trading metropolis of northwestern Russia, came to be looked upon as the necessary condition of leadership in the Russian world. The grand dukes of Kiev had jealously maintained their dominion over Novgorod through the appointment of its princes, subject, however (as will appear later in this chapter), to approval by the Novgorod popular assembly (*veche*). The grand dukes of Vladimir established a similar relationship with Novgorod. It was a contest over that city that led to the raid on Kiev by Andrew Bogoliubsky in 1169, and when in the fourteenth century national leadership passed into the hands of Moscow, the latter lost no time in asserting its dominion over Novgorod. An other major objective of Vladimir's policy was to prevent Kiev from regaining its supremacy. To achieve this aim the grand dukes of Vladimir endeavored to control the appointment of Kievan princes.

The dynastic policies of Yuri Dolgoruky and his successors called for the retention of the principality of Rostov-Suzdal in their family and for the defense of its all-too-recent claim to leadership among the Russian lands. The involvement of Rostov-Suzdal in Eastern trade made imperative the protection of the trade routes, while the requirements of security dictated a watchful or even an aggressive attitude towards the Cumans and other warlike neighbors. Novgorod did not submit readily to domination by Rostov-Suzdal, and conflicts with that dependency were frequent. Close association with Novgorod, moreover, brought the Rostov-Suzdal princes in contact with the West and led them to participate in Novgorod's campaigns on its western borders as well as in the north, where it held a vast domain.

These far-flung interests forced Yuri Dolgoruky to fight the Kama Bulgars and to impose his sons and nephews as princes of Novgorod. A similar policy was followed by Yuri's son Andrew Bogoliubsky, who, too, fought the Kama Bulgars (1162 and 1172) and compelled Novgorod to accept his sons and nephews, as well as by his brother and successor Vsevolod III (1184–1212). Vsevolod transferred his capital to Vladimir and assumed the title of grand duke. Like his brother, he fought the Kama Bulgars (1184 and 1186) and subdued Novgorod to obedience by the force of arms. It was under his rule that, after considerable resistance, Novgorod formally accepted the leadership of the grand dukes of Vladimir. The princes of Rostov-Suzdal and the grand dukes of Vladimir showed no particular interest in southern Russia, except for intermittent warfare with the Cumans and the endeavor to retain control over Kiev. Kiev, in spite of repeated devastations, was still a valuable political and cultural asset. It remained the see of the head of the Russian Church until 1300, when the metropolitan chair was transferred to Vladimir.

The idea of "seniority"—that is, leadership among the Russian lands—survived the fall of Kiev and in the second half of the twelfth and in the thirteenth century was attached to the grand duchy of Vladimir. Like their Kievan predecessors, the princes of Rostov-Suzdal and later the grand dukes of Vladimir continued to refer to themselves as "senior in the brotherhood of Russian princes," even though they were chiefly concerned with the advancement of narrow local interests. Nevertheless some of their policies, for instance defense against the Cumans and other external enemies, may be interpreted as serving the needs of Russia as a whole. Broadly speaking, the other Russian princes acknowledged the "seniority" of the grand dukes of Vladimir and, although not always readily, lent their support to policies designed to achieve common objectives. This tradition was firmly established by the beginning of the thirteenth century and was maintained during the reign of Vsevolod III's son and successor, Yuri II, who perished in 1238 in the Mongol invasion.

Social Conditions. The social evolution of Rostov-Suzdal-Vladimir followed the lines which were clearly discernible in Kievan Russia. The principle of "patrimonial" succession, that is, the association of the princely fam-

ily with a specific territory and the right of each male descendant to share
in the family estate, was in operation in Rostov-Suzdal as in other Russian
principalities. The inevitable consequence of this system was the breaking
up of the territory into an ever increasing number of small quasi-independent
political units over which the grand dukes of Vladimir exercised general
supervision.

Another significant development was the rise of the boyar class. The decline of foreign trade in the second half of the twelfth century and the
gradual transformation of the members of the princely retinue from soldiers
of fortune into landed proprietors had a two-fold consequence: the weakening of the commercial cities and of the influence of the *veche,* and the growing independence of the boyars as a class. In the twelfth century Rostov,
Suzdal, and Vladimir had developed their own boyar aristocracy, which
found itself in frequent conflict with the princes. Boyar opposition led Yuri
Dolgoruky to transfer his capital from Rostov to Suzdal, and similar reasons
later forced Vsevolod III to abandon Suzdal in favor of Vladimir. The boyars,
as a rule, supported the local dynasty, for the arrival of new princes accompanied by their boyars was likely to infringe on the prerogatives of the local
aristocracy, but they opposed the breaking up of the principality into smaller
units, which followed inexorably from the application of the principle of
"patrimonial" succession. This was a frequent source of conflict. The testamentary dispositions of Yuri Dolgoruky to divide after his death his domain
between his two sons were set aside, and he was succeeded by his elder son,
Andrew Bogoliubsky, who, however, eventually fell victim of a boyar conspiracy (1174). It was not until three years later that Vsevolod III emerged,
after a bitter feud, as prince of Rostov-Suzdal. His death in 1212 was followed
by another outburst of princely strife. However, clashes between the princes
and the boyars were common during this period and occurred also in the
other Russian lands—in Kiev, Chernigov, Galicia, Volynia, and so on.

Novgorod the Great

Western Trade. The history of Novgorod—whose people, according to
tradition, were the actual founders of the Russian state by inviting Riurik
"to rule over them"—differs in some essentials from that of the other Russian
lands. Situated within easy reach of the Gulf of Finland and on the Volkhov,
which was a part of Russia's ancient trade route, Novgorod was one of the
earliest military and trading outposts established by the Varangians and the
Russian merchant-princes. Like Rostov-Suzdal it benefited by its remoteness

from the southern steppes but had the additional advantage of access to the Baltic Sea, which led to a flourishing trade with the Swedish island of Gotland and later with the Hanseatic League. While the beginnings of Novgorod's Western trade cannot be precisely dated, it is known to have reached considerable volume by the twelfth century. Early in the thirteenth century Novgorod became involved in complicated relations, at times friendly and at times hostile, with its Western neighbors—the German knights, Lithuania, and Sweden. Trade, especially foreign trade, was by far the most important pursuit of the leading groups in Novgorod and the source of its influence and wealth. The chief articles exported were the products of the forest—furs and wax. The desire to secure supplies of these commodities led to the annexation by Novgorod of large territories in the northeast which in the thirteenth century extended to the White Sea, the upper Volga, and the Urals.

Western trade, which acquired particular importance with the dwindling of commercial relations with Byzantium and the Arabic East, was largely in the hands of German merchants who formed in Novgorod a closed corporation patterned upon the medieval guilds. Relations between the members of the corporation and the Novgorod authorities were regulated by written agreements which conferred upon the Germans important privileges but also imposed upon them far-reaching restrictions. The Germans were required to reside within a compound known as the German Settlement, which was administered by elected officials, who also tried cases involving the Germans alone. Members of the corporation were exempt from arrest by the Russians, and cases involving both Russians and Germans were litigated by a mixed tribunal composed of representatives of both parties. The length of stay of the German merchants was limited to the time necessary to sell their wares, the value of which was not to exceed 1,000 silver marks, that is, they were not permitted to settle down in Novgorod. They could not form partnerships with the Russians, were excluded from the retail trade, and were not allowed to engage in business outside the city limits. The normal method of business was barter; cash sales were tolerated but credit transactions were specifically prohibited. The enforcement of these regulations led to much friction, which, however, did not unduly interfere with the flow of commerce. The principal articles imported were woolens, beer, wine, salt, sweetmeats, metalware, linen, needles, thread, yarn, and grain. Since Novgorod was not a seaport and had no merchant marine, the export-import trade was carried in foreign bottoms, and Russian merchants seldom went abroad.

Self-Government. During the early part of its history Novgorod, like the other Russian lands, paid tribute to Kiev and was governed by a prince assisted by a *possadnik* (governor). Both were appointed by the grand duke of Kiev, whose kin the prince usually was. The *veche,* as in other principalities, had a part in the administration of public affairs but enjoyed no special powers. By the twelfth century the structure of the Novgorod government underwent substantial changes. Novgorod's prominence as a trading center had two important consequences which determined the course of its subsequent development: the failure to obtain a separate dynasty, and the ascendency of the *veche* at the very time when elsewhere in Russia it suffered a decline. Control of Novgorod came to be looked upon, in Kiev and later in Vladimir and Moscow, as the necessary condition for the supremacy of the grand-ducal throne. Novgorod, too, needed the leadership of the more powerful among the Russian princes, that is, the "senior" grand dukes (several grand duchies existed in Russia in the thirteenth and fourteenth centuries), in its many military enterprises and, moreover, was dependent for its supply of grain on the lands south and east of its borders. This situation was well known and provided the grand dukes of Vladimir and Moscow with a powerful weapon which they occasionally used to bring Novgorod to terms.

The enhanced role of the Novgorod *veche* may be traced, on the one hand, to the spirit of independence of its sizable well-to-do urban community and, on the other, to the weakening of the authority of Kiev. Frequent changes of the occupants of the Kievan throne after the death of Vladimir II Monomakh (1125) resulted in great instability of the upper levels of the Novgorod administration (which was appointed by the Kievan grand dukes) and encouraged trends towards autonomy which took the form of increased control by the *veche* over the prince and the appointment of higher officials. Beginning with the second quarter of the twelfth century the *possadnik* and other higher administrative officers were elected by the veche; from 1156 on, the bishop, too, was elected by the *veche* (he was formerly appointed by the metropolitan of Kiev) and then consecrated by the metropolitan. Thus, both lay and ecclesiastical officials were brought under local control. The acceptance of the principle of election basically altered the character of the Novgorod administration: formerly representatives of the grand-ducal power in its dealings with Novgorod, the *possadnik,* bishop (later, archbishop), and other dignitaries became the spokesmen of Novgorod in its relations with Kiev, Vladimir, and Moscow.

The powers of the prince were drastically curtailed. It was customary for the *veche* in Kievan Russia to conclude with the princes agreements which were designed, by defining the sources of princely revenue, to protect the population from excessive exactions. The Novgorod agreements went considerably further. Under their terms the prince was bound to exercise his judicial and administrative powers jointly with elected officials whom he could not remove from office. He and his retinue were debarred from owning land or holding mortgages within the Novgorod territory, were prohibited from interfering with the German Settlement, and could deal with the German merchants only through Novgorod intermediaries. The prince in Novgorod, like the Varangian rulers in the early city-states, was primarily the hired military leader and organizer of defense. His residence, Gorodishche, was outside the city limits.

The *veche,* theoretically the sovereign organ of the Novgorod government, was an anarchistic institution unrestrained by any constitutional provisions or rules of procedure. It comprised all male citizens; the initiative in calling the *veche* usually came from the prince or the *possadnik,* but any citizen could summon it by striking the *veche* bell. The meetings, which were held in public squares, were often stormy. Not infrequently two *veches* would be held simultaneously, one on each bank of the Volkhov, which traversed the city, and the disputed issues would be settled in a free-for-all fight that would take place on the bridge. This was hardly a satisfactory method of framing the policies of a great commercial city, metropolis of a vast colonial domain. In actual fact the affairs of Novgorod were administered by a handful of officials, of whom the most important was the *possadnik,* and a council of notables, an assembly of some 50 members which included the archbishop, the higher officials, and the leading citizens. It was in fact this oligarchy and not the tumultuous and unruly *veche* that governed Russia's "northwestern democracy."

Social Conditions. Except for the existence of an ambitious and wealthy urban class, the social structure of Novgorod was, broadly speaking, similar to that of the other Russian lands. The upper level of the social pyramid was formed by the boyars, who, as elsewhere, derived their influence from landholdings and tenure of high offices. Landed estates were important because they provided commodities for export. Immediately below the boyars were the *zhityi liudi* (prosperous men), whose status did not differ substantially from that of the boyars, although they did not belong to the aristocracy. Next came the merchants, an important and powerful group which in the second half of the twelfth century was organized into guilds. It would seem, however, that the merchants operated largely with funds borrowed from the boyars, which tended to make their business less profitable while increasing boyar revenue and authority. The lower stratum of the urban community consisted of tradesmen, artisans, and laborers. The rural population was comprised of free peasants and slaves (*kholopy*), but the former were by far the more numerous and lived on the land they owned or on estates held by the Church, the boyars, and others. In Novgorod, as in other Russian principalities, the thirteenth to the fifteenth century was a period of the rapid growth of large landholding and of curtailment of the rights of the free peasantry. In other words, freemen—both smallholders and tenants—fared no better in Novgorod than they did, for instance, in Suzdal-Vladimir. This situation may help to explain the relative ease with which Novgorod was absorbed in the unified Russian state of the fifteenth century.

The Fall of Novgorod. The history of Novgorod from the twelfth to the fifteenth century presents a confused and bewildering picture of internal discord and frequent clashes with its western and eastern neighbors. A system of government under which the popular masses forming the *veche* were the instrument—even though not always a docile one—in the hands of a small and divided aristocracy offered no guarantee of stability. The multiplicity of Novgorod's political and economic interests worked against the emergence of an integrated national policy. For economic and other reasons some of the competing boyar groups gravitated towards Vladimir and Moscow, others towards Kiev and Smolensk, still others towards Lithuania and Poland or the German knights. While two elements in the situation—pre-eminence of the Western trade and dependence on Muscovy for supplies of grain—were quasi-permanent and not subject to change, the actual policies followed by the Novgorod government were determined by the predilections and interests of the boyar group in power. The progressive deterioration of the status of the once-free peasantry weakened the social bias of resistance to aggression from either east or west. Autonomy and representative institutions, however imperfect, were incompatible with Russia's fifteenth-century absolutism, while Novgorod's avowedly pro-Lithuanian sympathy offered a plausible pretext for Muscovite intervention. The long drawn-out struggle culminated in the latter part of the fifteenth century in the defeat of Novgorod by the Muscovites, the abolition of the elective organs of government, and the incorporation of the once-free city in the Muscovite state. The *veche* bell, symbol of Novgorod's ancient liberties, was removed to Moscow (1478).

Pskov

Novgorod's Colonial Domain. The territories constituting Novgorod's colonial domain may be divided, according to their form of government, into three groups: territories enjoying a degree of autonomy, territories administered by permanent appointed officials, and territories (especially in the far north) which had no permanent administration but were visited annually by military detachments for the collection of tribute. The self-governing territories were grouped into five regions (*piatina*), which were subdivided into townships (*volost*). The administrative center of a region had a *veche* and an appointed *possadnik,* paid tribute to Novgorod, and contributed men to its armed forces.

Pskov and Its Undoing. Pskov was an ancient dependency of Novgorod situated west of the metropolis near the Lithuanian border. Its geographical location may explain why, beginning in the middle of the thirteenth century, Lithuanian influence was strong in Pskov, while its relations with Novgorod became increasingly strained. Pskov intermittently accepted Lithuanian princes as its rulers, and early in the fourteenth century its *veche* elected its own *possadnik,* who carried on the business of government jointly with a *possadnik* appointed by Novgorod. In 1347, after much friction, Novgorod finally recognized the independence of Pskov and the adjoining territories and withdrew from the administration of their affairs.

The government of Pskov was similar to that of Novgorod and consisted of a *veche,* a prince invited by the *veche* and endowed with limited powers, a council of notables, two elected *possadniks,* and other officials. The social structure of Pskov and Novgorod had much in common. In Pskov, as in Novgorod, Western trade was the chief concern of the upper class, and the free tenants were inexorably driven, again as in Novgorod, into a state of near-serfdom. The fate of Novgorod's "younger brother," as Pskov was referred to in the chronicle, duplicated that of its former metropolis, except that the absorption of Pskov by Moscow came somewhat later and was achieved without resorting to warfare. In 1510 the Pskov *veche* and elected officials were abolished, Pskov was formally incorporated in the Muscovite state, and its *veche* bell was carried away to Moscow. The inconclusive experiment in "democracy" thus came to an end.

The absorption of both Novgorod and Pskov by the Muscovite state was accompanied by the mass eviction of their leading citizens, who were given estates elsewhere in service tenure, while their landed properties in Novgorod and Pskov were confiscated by Muscovy and were distributed, also in service tenure, to men foreign to the tradition of the two principalities.

The Three Branches of the Russian People

Great Russia, White Russia, and the Ukraine. The divergent historical fortunes of the Russian people and the variety of the ethnic influences to which they were subject account for the division of the once homogeneous mass of the eastern Slavs into three distinct nationalities: the Great Russians, in the center and north; the White Russians (Byelo-Russia), in the west; and the Little Russians, or Ukrainians, in the south and southwest. The terms "Great Russia" and "Little Russia" have been traced back to documents of the fourteenth century, and all three (Great, Little, and White Russia) were used as part of the tsar's title in the middle of the seventeenth century. The existence of the terms, however, proves little, for they might have been used in a purely geographical sense. Russian historians, both pre-revolutionary and Soviet, place the split, that is, the formation of the Ukrainian and the White Russian nationalities, between the fourteenth and the sixteenth centuries. But at what stage does an ethnic group become a nation? And what are the attributes of nationhood? These are not easy questions to answer.

Politically Great Russia—or what later became Great Russia—dominated the Russian state. The Ukraine achieved precarious statehood for a brief time in the seventeenth century, and White Russia for but a few ephemeral weeks after the revolution of 1917. Their historical claims to nationhood rest chiefly on the emergence of national consciousness and their participation in the struggle against Poland, Lithuania, and the Ottoman empire. This approach, however, is inconclusive, because medieval national and political movements in a contested region, such as the tormented borderland between Russia and Lithuania-Poland, are difficult to interpret.

The Linguistic Approach. Philologists sometimes hold that a separate language is the earmark of a nation. The basis of the literary Russian language is Old-Russian thoroughly permeated with Old-Church-Slavonic, which came to Russia shortly after her conversion to Christianity. The interaction of the literary Old-Russian, Church-Slavonic, and the popular east Slavic dialects, and some influence of foreign tongues, resulted in the formation of the Russian (Great Russian) literary language, while the Ukrainian and the White Russian languages grew from popular dialects, developed into literary languages considerably later, and therefore were unaffected by the Old-Church-Slavonic (which was also the South-Slavic language). The principal foreign influences in this process were: on the Russian language—Old-Church-Slavonic, Greek, Iranian, Old-Norse and Gothic, Turko-Tatar, and Finno-Ugrian (the Old-Church-Slavonic, Greek, and Old-Norse influences were particularly pronounced in the literary language); on the Ukrainian language—in addition to the common Slavic heritage—Polish, German, Turko-Tatar, Turkish, Latin, and Lithuanian; and on the White Russian language—Polish, German, Yiddish, Lithuanian, Russian, and Ukrainian. According to the prevalent view in modern linguistics, the Russian and the Ukrainian dialects became distinct national languages in the seventeenth and eighteenth centuries, and the White Russian as recently as the nineteenth. The philologists thus differ from the historians as to the time when the split into the three nationalities occurred. Moreover, there is no agreement among the philologists themselves. For instance, it is claimed by Ukrainian nationalists that the Ukrainian language originated in Kievan Russia and by far antedates both the Russian and the White Russian tongues. The supporters of this view invert the traditional and widely-accepted terminology and substitute "Ukrainian" or "Old-Ukrainian" for "Old-Russian."

3

Russia and the Mongols, XIII-XV Centuries

The Conquest

The Mongol Empire. The destinies of nations, like the fates of individuals, are sometimes profoundly affected by events over which they have no control. The conquest by the Mongols, in the thirteenth century, of a large portion of the then known world, including Russia, is a good instance of the decisive part which the contingent and the unforeseen play in human affairs.

The Mongols were an Asiatic people of mixed descent inhabiting the territory which bears their name (Mongolia) and lies north of China and east of Siberia. Accomplished horsemen and fierce warriors, they lived chiefly by cattle raising, and the necessity of providing for their large herds determined their nomadic way of life by forcing them to move from place to place in search of grassland. In 1206, according to tradition, the chiefs of the heretofore scattered Mongol tribes foregathered and reached an agreement establishing the Mongol empire under the leadership of Temnuchin, who assumed the title of great khan and the name of Chingis Khan. For reasons which are not clear the new empire embarked at once on a vast program of conquest. In 1207 southern Siberia was conquered; then followed protracted wars with China and Khorezm (Turkestan). At the time of

Chingis Khan's death in 1227 his empire comprised Mongolia, north China, southern Siberia, central Asia, and Trans-Caucasia.

Prior to his death Chingis Khan, who was succeeded as great khan by his son Ugedei, divided his realm among his descendants, subject to their acceptance of the supreme authority of the great khan. Each territorial share was known as an *ulus,* and that of Chingis Khan's eldest son Djuchi comprised the still unconquered territories west of the Urals, that is, Russia. Djuchi, however, died shortly before his father, and the conquest of the new domain was undertaken a few years later by his son Batu. Meanwhile, the Russians received a foretaste of what was in store for them when in 1223 several Russian princes, fighting in alliance with the Cumans, were decisively defeated on the River Kalka by a flying detachment of Mongol horsemen. The invaders, however, were not yet ready for the main thrust and withdrew as suddenly as they had appeared. The great onslaught of the Mongols, or Tatars (Tartars), as the Russians usually called them, was not to occur until 13 years later.

Batu's Russian Campaign. In 1236 a large Mongol army commanded by Batu crossed the Yaik River in the Ural region and invaded and devastated the state of the Kama Bulgars. Unlike the 1223 incursion of horsemen, the massive advance of the Mongol horde in 1236 was no mere military campaign: the warriors were accompanied by wagons which carried their wives and children and by herds of cattle—clearly they had no intention of returning to their native steppes. This being the case, it is all the more notable that at first the conquerors treated the subjugated people with extreme harshness and mercilessly destroyed and burned their cities, towns, and settlements.

It is likely that the Russians did not immediately realize the magnitude of the peril confronting them. Next to nothing was known about the Mongols—their empire, the strength of their army, and the object of their sudden appearance in the Russian plains. Disunity among the Russian princes, which was a characteristic of this period, precluded any effective organization of defense, although it is probable, in view of the almost unbroken record of Mongol victories in their encounters with other nations, that the defeat of the Russians was a foregone conclusion.

Having disposed of the Kama Bulgars, Batu crossed the Volga and turned against the Russians. The princes of Riazan, the first Russian land to be invaded, pleaded vainly for assistance from the grand duke of Vladimir. The city of Riazan was captured in December 1237, pillaged, and burned. A similar fate befell Kolomna, Moscow, Suzdal, Vladimir, Rostov, Yaroslavl, and Tver. The Mongol advance was particularly rapid in the spring of 1238.

In February of that year at least 14 Russian cities were seized by the enemy.

The case of the capital city of Vladimir was typical. The Grand Duke Yuri II withdrew from it in order to raise additional troops, but his family and members of his household remained in the besieged capital. It was captured by Batu in February 1238, and Yuri's wife and children, as well as the local bishop and many other notables, were massacred by the invaders. Shortly thereafter, in March, Yuri himself was killed in a battle on the River Sit. Meanwhile, the Mongols, after capturing and pillaging Torzhok, turned north and advanced towards Novgorod, but reversed their course before reaching that city and marched south to the Black Sea steppes. The Novgorod campaign was presumably abandoned because of the difficulties presented by the forests which cover that part of the country.

In the later part of 1238 and in 1239 Batu was chiefly occupied with destroying the Cumans and conquering the Crimea; he then reverted to the northwest, devastated Pereiaslavl and Chernigov, and in December 1240 occupied Kiev, which put up a brief but stubborn resistance. Galicia-Volynia and Poland were overrun next. Some of the Russian cities and their rulers fought gallantly what was clearly a losing battle; many of the princes were killed in action, while others fled westwards to Poland and Hungary.

The Mongols and Western Europe. Late in 1241 Batu crossed the Carpathian Mountains and invaded Hungary, Silesia, Moravia, Croatia, and the Dalmatian littoral. In spite of the spirited resistance of the Czechs, his progress continued unimpeded, and his advance appeared to be threatening western Europe when, in the spring of 1242, he suddenly turned back and retreated through Serbia and Bulgaria to the Black Sea steppes. The death of Ugedei at the end of 1241 and the resulting uncertainty concerning the future of the Mongol empire were presumably the reason for Batu's change of heart. Western Europe, except for its southeastern fringe, was spared the distressing experience of Mongol invasion and, perhaps, the protracted occupation which was to be the fate of Russia for the next 240 years.

The Golden Horde

The New Mongol State. At the end of his western campaign Batu did not return to Asia but remained in the Black Sea area and founded the autonomous Mongol state of the Golden Horde; its capital was Sarai, a newly-built city on the lower Volga. The territory of the Golden Horde comprised the Russian principalities, the land of the Volga-Kama Bulgars, the Black Sea steppes inhabited by the Cumans, the northern Caucasus, and—in Asia

—western Siberia and Khorezm (Turkestan). The Golden Horde was an *ulus,* or province, of the Mongol empire. In the thirteenth century the central government of Mongolia exercised effective control over its dependent territories; this is why the Russian princes, who after the conquest became the vassals of the Golden Horde, had at times to journey to Karakorum, the capital of the great khan in distant Mongolia, to comply with imperial summonses or in order to secure confirmation in office or the redress of grievances. Dissension among the Mongol leaders and conflicts between the central authority and the dependent territories led to the weakening and eventual breakdown of the Mongol empire and then to the disintegration of the Golden Horde, which split into several autonomous warring states. This process of political decline was not a continuous one, that is, periods of internal strife alternated with periods of consolidation, but with the passing of the years, especially in the fifteenth century, the inability of the Mongols to control their vast domain became patent. During the same period (fourteenth and fifteenth centuries) the Russians gradually succeeded in overcoming their ancient disorders and in building up, under the leadership of Moscow, a unified state. Their endeavor was unwittingly prompted by the Mongols. The concurrence of these two closely interrelated developments—disintegration of the Golden Horde and the consolidation of Muscovy—culminated in what is traditionally known as "liberation from the Tatar yoke," an event that took place towards the end of the fifteenth century.

The Mongols, as a nation, were notably free from racial and religious exclusiveness. They mixed willingly with the Chinese, absorbed and assimilated the Cumans and other nomadic peoples whom they had conquered, and in the fourteenth century officially embraced Islam. With the weakening of the Golden Horde, many Tatar chieftains and dignitaries entered the Russian service and were eventually merged with the Russian nobility.

The Army. The khans of the Golden Horde were stern masters. The principal objective of their Russian policy was recruitment of men for the army and the raising of revenue to meet the costs of administration and imperial expansion. Russian soldiers are known to have fought in the ranks of the conquerors. There is no agreement among the historians, however, as to the method by which these contingents were raised. The Mongol army was organized on the decimal principle, that is, the country was divided into military districts corresponding in size and number to army units and comprising, respectively, 10, 100, 1,000, and 10,000 (the Mongol *tümen*) men, each district being placed under the command of an appointed leader of appropriate rank. The decimal system also provided the framework of the administrative structure. It is sometimes held that this system was imposed by the Mongols on the conquered countries, including Russia. To ensure obedience the leaders of each district or army unit, from the "ten" up, are said to have been Mongols. The sources, however, do not justify this dogmatic assertion. Moreover, it is unlikely that a uniform decimal system could have been applied over the vast and sparsely populated territory controlled by the Golden Horde or that any such scheme actually could have been enforced if the attempt had been made. How could an army unit or administrative district as small as a "ten" function properly under a foreign leader who was unable (at least during the initial period) to communicate with the men under his command? There is no reference in the sources to levies of Russian troops by the Golden Horde in the fourteenth and fifteenth centuries. Nevertheless, the fact remains that the Mongols used Russian soldiers. The reasonable explanation would seem to be that Russian princes continued to draft men into their armed forces as they did before the invasion but that under the Mongol rule these troops were largely at the disposal of the khan. This theory is in keeping with the Mongol policy not to interfere unduly with Russia's established administrative practice.

Taxation. Exaction of tribute was the chief concern of the Golden Horde in dealing with its Russian dependency. There was a variety of new taxes, and their assessment was based on censuses taken by the Tatars in different Russian lands at different times, approximately between 1245 and 1275. According to Russian sources no census was taken after the latter date. The collection of the tribute was at first in the hands of Mongol officials known as *baskaks,* but this office was abolished at the end of the thirteenth and early in the fourteenth century, when the function of tax collection was assumed by the Russian grand dukes and princes. The most important direct tax was *vykhod;* its total amount was determined by the Mongols and was then assessed by the local grand duke among the princes under his jurisdiction, who made the final allocation and were in charge of the collection of the tribute. The political and social consequences of this function of the princes will be examined presently.

Direct extortions were heavy, but their actual amount cannot be ascertained with any degree of accuracy. Of the indirect levies an onerous one was the obligation to provide means of transportation, lodgings, and maintenance for Mongol officials. No less burdensome were the frequent journeys to Sarai and, in the early years of the conquest, to Mongolia which the Russian princes were compelled to undertake. On these journeys they were usually accompanied by their wives and court dignitaries and were expected to provide suitable presents for the khan, his family, and Tatar notables.

Government. While the devastation wrought by the invasion was great, the conquerors made surprisingly few formal changes in the pattern of the Russian government. One change, however, was basic and unmistakable: the source of all power was now the sovereign will of the khan of the Golden Horde (except when he was superseded by the great khan). This meant in practice that the Russian princes had to be confirmed in office by their new suzerain and that all major issues were referred to the Golden Horde. Hence the frequent pilgrimages of the princes to Sarai. A tangible reminder of Mongol watchfulness was the installation of the princes in office by an envoy of the khan. The Mongols, however, seldom used their absolute powers in an arbitrary fashion; as a rule, they showed respect for Russian traditional institutions and confirmed in office the princes who appeared to be entitled to it by precedent and custom. In the instances, however, when there were contesting claims, the decision inevitably rested with the khan. In this connection, the transfer of the tax collection function to the grand dukes and princes was of paramount importance. At first sight, the substitution of Russian hereditary rulers for Tatar officials as agents for the performance of this distasteful task may be interpreted as a move potentially beneficial to the people, whose interests the Russian princes might be expected to protect. This, however, was not necessarily the case. In the contest over a disputed grand duchy or principality the promised increase in the amount of the tribute was a powerful argument which the claimants seldom overlooked, because the khans tended to favor the higher bidder. The results were, in a sense, unfortunate. The dynastic position of some of the ruling families, as for instance the princes of Moscow, was strengthened by increasing the financial burdens of the people whom they governed. In many instances the princes came to be looked upon, not as spokesmen of local interests before the Mongol power, but as agents of the khan enforcing his edicts at the expense of the local people.

The total dependence of the princes on Sarai undermined the constitutional position of the *veche.* After the conquest the *veche* was deprived of its traditional powers of making agreements with the princes and of expelling and inviting them. This loss of authority, combined with the devastation suffered by the commercial cities and the decline of trade during the opening decades of the Mongol rule, was presumably responsible for the eclipse of the *veche,* which, with the exception of Novgorod and Pskov, ceased to meet in the middle of the fourteenth century.

With the above reservations—and they are not unimportant—Russia continued to be governed as she had before the invasion. This apparent continuity of the historical tradition has led some historians, including eminent ones, to argue that the Mongol domination had little effect upon the course of Russian domestic development. Even a cursory survey of Russo-Mongol relations suggests that this contention is contrary to evidence.

The Church. The Church fared poorly during the invasion: monasteries and houses of worship were pillaged and burned, and bishops and priests were butchered. After the conquest, however, the policies of the Golden Horde towards the Church were tolerant, humane, and politically expedient. The status of the Church was determined by *yarlyks* (decrees) of the khan. The members of the higher Church hierarchy, like the princes, were confirmed in office by the khan, and the Church assumed the obligation to pray publicly for the Mongol ruler and his family. In return, Russian clerics and their kin were granted immunity and exemption from taxation; ecclesiastical estates and the population living on them were exempt from taxes and the obligation of military service. Derogatory references to the Greek Orthodox faith were made punishable by death, and Mongol agents were specifically directed to protect the Church from any violation of its privileges. These generous provisions led to an unexpectedly close cooperation between the Church and the Golden Horde which was prompted by the temporary eclipse of the metropolitan of Kiev, the titular head of the Russian Church. Metropolitan Joseph perished in the attack on Kiev in 1240, and his successor Cyril was not appointed until 1246 and did not return to Russia from Byzantium until 1249 or 1250. He found Kiev largely destroyed, spent much of his time in the grand duchy of Vladimir, and, being involved in the abortive plans of Prince Daniel of Galicia for a crusade against the Mongols, was unpopular with the Golden Horde. It would seem that in the 1260's and 1270's the actual leadership of the Russian Church was exercised by the bishop of Sarai, an office created in 1261 or 1262 and held at first by Mitrofan. His successor (since 1269) Theognost was on good terms with the Mongol rulers and visited Constantinople as the envoy of both the Russian metropolitan and the khan.

The understanding between the Church and the Golden Horde proved mutually beneficial. On the one hand, harmonious relations with the Orthodox hierarchy facilitated the task of the Mongols in governing a hostile country. On the other hand, exemption from taxation and military service of the population of the ecclesiastical estate contributed to the rapid expansion of Church landholding, which, however, eventually led to a serious conflict between Church and state.

Trade. The invasion brought about the destruction of all the principal Russian commercial cities except Novgorod and dealt a severe blow to Russian commerce. This setback, however, proved of but passing significance. By the middle of the fourteenth century Russian trade had largely recovered. The Mongols, their nomadic mode of life notwithstanding, were a trading nation, and Sarai grew rapidly into an important commercial center which maintained extensive relations with East and West. Other commercial cities were restored and new ones were founded. Trade with western Europe was carried on chiefly through Novgorod, which was an outpost of the Hanseatic League. Information on commerce during this period is slight, but it is reasonable to assume that although much of the Russian trade was in the hands of the Mongols, native traders had a share of the profits. It is known that Russian merchants visited Sarai frequently and that some of them resided there permanently.

From Defeat to Liberation

"The Tatar Yoke." While the formal changes which the conquerers introduced in Russian government and administrative practice were relatively few (especially after the withdrawal of Mongol tax officials at the end of the thirteenth century), the "Tatar yoke," as the Mongol rule is traditionally known, was no mere figure of speech but a stern reality that permeated every aspect of Russian life. We know that pre-Mongol Russia was not, as it is sometimes imagined, a progressive country endowed with democratic institutions (a common but much too generous interpretation of the *veche*) and enjoying high technical, cultural, and economic standards. Indeed, the opposite was the case, and it is therefore unreasonable to claim that the invasion destroyed a flourishing Russian civilization: such a civilization simply did not exist. Yet the conquest did untold harm and left a lasting imprint on the subsequent course of Russian history.

A warlike nation, the Golden Horde relied largely on the use of its armed might in its dealings with the subjugated peoples. According to an authoritative estimate, Russia suffered no fewer than 48 Tatar invasions between 1236 and 1462, and on numerous other occasions Mongol troops came in as allies of warring Russian princes. Threats of military action and frequent armed clashes form the somber background of Russo-Mongol relations. The Golden Horde was primarily interested in exacting the greatest possible financial advantage from its Russian dependency, while the Russian princes endeavored to use the authority of the khan in order to attain their own political and dynastic aims, which, as often as not, were in conflict with the aspirations of other Russian princes.

Alexander Nevsky. With the establishment of the Golden Horde and of the regime of occupation the Russian princes hastened to Sarai in order to secure confirmation in office. The case of the grand duchy of Vladimir, the leading principality in northeast Russia, presents special interest. The grand duke Yuri II was killed in battle in March 1238. He was succeeded by his brother Yaroslav I, who was confirmed by Batu in 1243 and died three years later in Karakorum, the capital of Mongolia, where he was attending the festivities on the occasion of the accession of a new great khan. According to rumors, Yaroslav was poisoned. Two of his sons, Andrew II and Alexander (known as Nevsky because of his victory over the Swedes in a battle fought on the banks of the Neva River), went at once to the Golden Horde to pay homage to Batu, who directed them to report to the great khan. They journeyed to Karakorum and were appointed—Andrew, grand duke of Vladimir, and Alexander, prince of Kiev. Soon, however, Andrew ran into difficulties with his suzerain. He had married the daughter of Prince Daniel of Galicia and became involved in his father-in-law's plans for a crusade against the Tatars which was sponsored by the pope. When in 1251, in connection with another change in the leadership of the Mongol empire, Russian princes were ordered to appear at the Golden Horde, Alexander Nevsky complied at once, but Andrew demurred, brought upon himself a punitive Tatar expedition, was defeated, and fled to Sweden. Alexander, unlike his brother, rejected any idea of collaboration with the Holy See and military action against the Mongols. In 1252 Batu rewarded Alexander by appointing him to succeed Andrew as grand duke of Vladimir.

Batu's confidence was justified: Alexander proved a faithful and dependable executor of his wishes. In 1257–1258 the Golden Horde decreed in its Russian domain a census which met with widespread resistance. Alexander, however, used the authority of his office and armed force to ensure compliance with Mongol orders. When Novgorod at first refused to admit census officials and then rebelled against them, Alexander took stern measures: he removed from office his son Vasili, prince of Novgorod, executed the latter's advisers, and suppressed the rebellion with an iron hand. To the policy of compliance with Tatar wishes Alexander remained faithful to the end. He died in 1263 on his way home after a protracted stay at Sarai.

The story of Alexander Nevsky is significant because it shows the total dependence of the Russian princes on the conquerors. To repeat, the khan of the Golden Horde or the great khan was the arbiter of Russian affairs.

Policies such as were pursued by Alexander in Novgorod inevitably caused resentment, bitterness, and disaffection among the people, but careful subsequent editing of the texts has largely succeeded in expunging these sentiments from the chronicles and other contemporary records. In Russian historiography Alexander Nevsky lives as a great national figure. Historians usually touch lightly on the less palatable aspects of his rule and emphasize with some justification that his submissive attitude towards the Tatars saved Russia from much needless suffering. The Orthodox Church espoused the cause of Alexander. His allegedly imperishable remains were discovered at the end of the fourteenth century, and he was canonized in the middle of the sixteenth. On a less exalted level, the significance of Alexander's reign rests in the fact that he established a pattern of relationship between the Russian authorities and the Mongol power which has been followed, with but a few defections, by his successors for over 200 years.

Dimitry Donskoy. Other instances of Mongol involvement in Russian affairs will be noted in Chapter IV. The khans were at times ruthless and cruel. Quite a few of the Russian princes were executed by order of the khans, but in many cases the true cause of their ruin was the intrigues of other Russian rulers. And, again, devastating Tatar invasions were frequently the consequence of inter-princely feuds the participants of which came to look upon the use of Mongol troops as the legitimate method of achieving dynastic and national (or quasi-national) ambitions.

The internal strife that developed in the Mongol empire towards the end of the thirteenth century and continued intermittently until its final disintegration offered the Russian princes opportunities to reassert, at least temporarily, their independence. A situation of this nature obtained in the closing decades of the fourteenth century. In the 1360's a rebellion in southern China led to the severance of that territory and the breakdown of the Mongol empire. About the same time the Golden Horde was temporarily split into two political entities, the western (Russian) portion being controlled by Mamai, a powerful military leader. Mamai confirmed in office the youthful grand duke Dimitry of Moscow, but friction soon developed. Dimitry had secured a reduction in the amount of the customary tribute and presumably withheld all payments after 1375. He was emboldened by the difficulties experienced by the Mongol rulers and also by his success in bringing temporarily under the control of Moscow important Russian lands, including the principality of Tver. The conflict entered an acute stage in August 1378, when Dimitry defeated a punitive Tatar detachment on the Vozh River (a tributary of the Oka). This was of purely local significance, but it caused Mamai to take decisive action. He concluded an alliance with Yagailo, grand duke of Lithuania, ordered the resumption of the payment of the Russian tribute (which was to be substantially increased), and when these demands were refused, marched his troops into Russia to the region of the Don, where they were to be joined by a Lithuanian corps.

The Russians had no choice but to fight. Dimitry issued a call to arms, to which, however, several lands failed to respond. Novgorod, Pskov, Suzdal, Nizhni-Novgorod, and Tver stayed away, while Prince Oleg of Riazan endeavored to remain on good terms with both sides, with the result that while his army took no part in the war, his principality was invaded and devastated first by the Tatars and then by Dimitry. The encounter between the Russians and the Mongols took place on September 8, 1380, in the Kulikovo plain, in the proximity of the Don (hence Dimitry's surname of Donskoy); the Lithuanians failed to arrive and the battle resulted in the total defeat of the invaders. This was all the more unexpected because, according to trustworthy accounts, the general feeling in Russia on the eve of Kulikovo was one of unrelieved gloom and despondency. The Kulikovo battle was the first and only major Russian victory over the Golden Horde; it stunned contemporaries, and its significance has been grossly exaggerated by later commentators, although it probably added to the stature and luster of the grand dukes of Moscow.

Aftermath of the Kulikovo Battle. From the standpoint of the victors the immediate consequences of Kulikovo were unrewarding. The Muscovites were under no illusion that the Tatars would accept defeat. Mamai, on his return to the Golden Horde, was in the midst of preparations for another expedition against Russia when he was overthrown by Khan Tokhtamysh, who, however, carried out the war plans of his predecessor. In 1382 Tokhtamysh invaded Russia and plundered Moscow and other cities. The Russian princes hastened to Sarai to pay homage to their new suzerain. Dimitry sent to the Golden Horde his son Vasili, was confirmed in office by Tokhtamysh, and to his death in 1389 dutifully complied with the orders of the Mongol ruler. Vasili I, son of Dimitry Donskoy, was installed in office as grand duke of Moscow by an envoy of the khan. The Russo-Tatar relations had returned to the pre-Kulikovo pattern.

This situation obtained throughout the long reign of Vasili I (1389–1425), and Mongol intervention in Russian affairs became even more pronounced in the stormy reign of his son and successor, Vasili II (1425–1462). The principal elements in this relationship were the same as during the earlier period: acceptance by the Russian princes of the supremacy of the khan, payment of tribute, occasional cooperation with the Mongols in the struggle against Lithuania (for instance, in 1406), and attempts to avoid the obligations of vassalage whenever the situation seemed propitious, followed by punitive Tatar expeditions. The death of Vasili I was the starting point of a protracted feud over the right of succession between the supporters of his son Vasili II (a boy in his teens) and Vasili I's brother, Yuri. The dispute came before the khan and was decided in favor of Vasili on the plea of his representative Vsevolozhsky, who argued that precedents and custom on which Yuri based his case were irrelevant because in Russia the sovereign will of the khan was the sole source of power. This theory was unreservedly endorsed by the Metropolitan Photius. Appropriately, Vasili II, like his predecessors, was inducted into office by an envoy of Sarai.

In the second quarter of the fifteenth century the Golden Horde entered a period of acute political crises which led to its disintegration. Minor secessions of Mongol hordes occurred in the earlier part of the fifteenth century, but the power of the Golden Horde was not seriously impaired until the establishment of the autonomous Tatar kingdom of Kazan in 1445 and of the kingdom of the Crimean Tatars in 1446 or 1449. From these developments, which were favorable to Russia, Moscow and the other Russian principalities derived no immediate benefit. Vasili II of Moscow became involved

Sovfoto

Battle of Kulikovo (1380), by Victor Vasnetsov

in a disastrous dynastic conflict with his uncle Yuri and the latter's sons Vasili and Dimitry Shemiaka.[1] This family feud led Vasili II to inject himself, in a most unfortunate manner, in the disorders which beset the Golden Horde. In 1445 he was made prisoner by Khan Ulu Mehmet and regained his freedom only by assuming heavy financial and other obligations towards his captors; some of them the Russian chronicler deemed it wise not to spell out. Vasili returned to Moscow accompanied by a large number of Tatar officials who were appointed to important positions and granted large estates. These unpopular policies were an element in Vasili's overthrow by Dimitry Shemiaka, but in 1450 Vasili, who was blinded, was restored to the Moscow throne with the assistance of his Tatar supporters. It was presumably in fulfillment of his undisclosed obligations towards the Golden Horde that he established in the early 1450's the semi-independent kingdom of Kasimov on the lower Volga. The new state, it is believed, was created for Kasim, son of Ulu Mehmet. There is much uncertainty about the nature and purpose of the kingdom of Kasimov; some historians believe that its true object was to check the ambitions of the Kazan Tatars. In spite of the conciliatory attitude of Moscow, Tatar raids continued throughout the reign of Vasili.

"Liberation from the Tatar Yoke." The second half of the fifteenth century saw the strengthening of Muscovy and the further decline of Mongol power. Yet the traditional and by then firmly rooted relationship of vassal and suzerain continued. The leading Russian prince of this period was Ivan III of Moscow (1462–1505), son of Vasili II; the Golden Horde was ruled from 1460 to 1480 by Khan Akhmad. Friction, presumably resulting from Russia's failure to provide tribute, led to a major Mongol invasion in 1472 which was accompanied by the destruction and burning of a number of cities. Two years later Moscow was visited by a large Tatar embassy and a huge trade delegation comprising some 3,000 merchants. New difficulties between the two governments arose soon thereafter, and when negotiations, the nature of which is not known, failed, Akhmad concluded an alliance with Casimir, king of Poland and grand duke of Lithuania, and in 1480 invaded Russia. Ivan was reluctant to accept the challenge but was finally prevailed upon to assume the command of the troops. The two armies found themselves facing one another across the Ugra River, a narrow stream that formed the boundary between Russia and Lithuania. For months neither side took action, but in November Akhmad suddenly retreated. His unexpected withdrawal may be explained by the failure of his Polish-Lithuanian ally to send troops and by the attack of a rival Tatar chieftain on the en-

---

[1] See below, p. 63.

campment occupied by Akhmad's wives and family. Soon thereafter he was assassinated by one of his countrymen. In this undramatic and unheroic fashion the "Tatar yoke" came to an end, officially in 1480. The Golden Horde survived until 1502, when the Crimean Tatars dealt it the final blow which terminated its existence as a state. In view of the record of the Russo-Mongol relations it was probably no accident that Russia had no direct part in that momentous event. Curiously, after the elimination of the Golden Horde, Muscovy continued to pay tribute to the Crimean Tatars. This khanate was conquered by the Turks in the 1470's and became a dependency of the Sublime Porte.

Mongol Influence

Political and Social. Two and one half centuries of foreign rule are bound to leave a profound imprint on a subjugated nation. We have seen that throughout most of this period the khans of the Golden Horde were the actual masters of Russia and effectively intervened in Russian affairs. The influence of the Mongol tradition may be traced in the crude methods by which Russia's unification was achieved in the fifteenth century and in the character of the absolutist government that was to rule her for over 300 years.[2] The conditions created by the invasion were probably instrumental in bringing about the destruction of the *veche,* although there is no assurance that this rudimentary form of democracy would have survived and would have grown into an institution of truly representative government even if the Tatars had never come to Russia.[3] Imaginative historians have detected traces of Mongol institutions in the military organization and administrative practice of Muscovy. That such influence made itself felt is probable, even though the sources shed little light on this subject.

The social effects of the Mongol rule are clearly discernible. There was a great deal of intermarriage and social intercourse between the Russian princes and members of the Russian upper class, on the one hand, and their opposite numbers in the Golden Horde, on the other. Moreover, as the fortunes of Sarai declined and those of Moscow rose, an increasingly large number of Mongol notables transferred their allegiance to Muscovy. As stated above, in the middle of the fifteenth century Vasili II returned to Moscow from Mongol captivity accompanied by numerous Tatar officials who entered the Russian service and were given landed estates. With the

[2] See Chapter IV.
[3] It will be remembered that the *veches* of Novgorod and Pskov continued to function under the Mongols and were suppressed not by them but by Muscovy.

The Trinity, icon by Andrew Rublev, c. 1400

breakdown of the Golden Horde and, later, the conquest by Russia of the kingdom of Kazan and other Tatar kingdoms, the influx of the Tatars into the Russian army and administrative services became even greater. According to an eminent historian, at the end of the seventeenth century about 17 per cent of the Russian upper class were of Eastern, chiefly Mongol, origin.

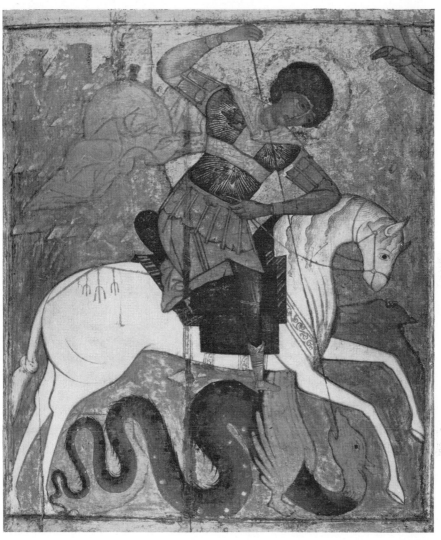

St. George and the Dragon, sixteenth-century icon

Moreover, after the disappearance of the Golden Horde its seceding states—the kingdoms of Kazan, the Crimea, and Astrakhan—continued to harass Russia's eastern and southern borderlands. The resulting perennial struggle was not over until the end of the eighteenth century. It imposed a heavy burden on the nation and had far-reaching social repercussions: the subjugation of the nobility by the Crown and the reduction of the once-free peasantry to a state of serfdom were, to some extent, the results of this situation.

Cultural and Economic. Mongol domination retarded Russian cultural development. It did not destroy an earlier Russian civilization, which, as we know, did not exist, but it delayed for at least two centuries any contact between Russia and western Europe, which was at that time the only fountain of progress and enlightenment. The Russian Middle Ages were barren of achievement in any field of creative endeavor, except perhaps that of icon painting, which reached high standards in the fifteenth century.

In the economic field the most spectacular development was the impact of the invasion. It took time before the Russian economy recovered from the devastation wrought, although the extremely low technical and economic levels prevalent during this period facilitated the task. Foreign trade, which came to a standstill with the conquest, revived substantially thereafter. There was little progress in agriculture and industrial arts, but there is no evidence that these pursuits sank below their modest pre-Mongol level. As with cultural endeavor it was a case of stagnation and arrested development rather than of deterioration and decline. The Russian economy, however, was severely affected by two manifestations of the Mongol rule: exaction of tribute, often exorbitant ones, and warlike action that took the form either of invasions of Russia or of foreign wars in which the Russians were forced to participate side by side with their masters.

To sum up: the Mongol domination had a profound effect upon Russia's conditions in the thirteenth to the sixteenth century and on her subsequent development.

4

Unification Under Moscow, XIV-XV Centuries

Decline of the Grand Duchy of Vladimir

The Morrow of the Tatar Invasion. The unification of Russia under the rule of Moscow unfolded itself against the background of the Mongol rule. In the thirteenth century, however, Moscow was still a minor city, and leadership in northeastern Russia was exercised by the grand duchy of Vladimir. It will be recalled that Yuri II, grand duke of Vladimir, was killed in the invasion but that his brother Yaroslav I and the latter's sons—first, Andrew II and then Alexander Nevsky—were confirmed by the khan as successive occupants of the grand-ducal throne. Alexander Nevsky, a major historical figure, complied unwaveringly with the orders of the khan whose vassal he was.[1] These policies, which manifested themselves, among other ways, in the increased burden of the tributes and in the suppression of the anti-Mongol movements, could hardly be popular in Russia, though they might have been expedient and even necessary to protect the people from the worst Mongol excesses. The benevolent attitude of the Golden Horde was essential for the preservation of the position of leadership or "seniority" among the Russian lands, which the grand dukes of Vladimir had held in the past and to which they continued to aspire.

[1] See above, p. 46.

[55]

In the lifetime of Alexander Nevsky (he died in 1263), and sporadically for several decades thereafter, the grand dukes of Vladimir, in spite of their submissiveness towards the Mongols, endeavored to follow policies which were designed to serve the interests of Russia as a whole. Thus they were the leaders in the armed struggle with Sweden, the German knights, and Lithuania, and they strove to retain control over Novgorod, which was essential to the supremacy of the grand-ducal throne. In 1240 Alexander, then prince of Novgorod, repulsed with heavy losses an invading Swedish army on the banks of the Neva River—hence the surname of Nevsky—and two years later he inflicted a disastrous defeat on the German knights on the ice of Lake Peipus. In the second half of the thirteenth century Vladimir was again at war with Sweden, the German knights, and Lithuania. These campaigns originated in attacks by those foreign powers on the territory of Novgorod and Pskov, which it was the duty, and also the interest, of the grand dukes of Vladimir to defend.

Causes of the Decline of Vladimir. The political eclipse of Vladimir which took place in the last quarter of the thirteenth and in the first quarter of the fourteenth century may be traced to a variety of causes. The Tatar invasion wrought great devastation on the territory of the grand duchy, checked its eastward expansion and colonization, and dealt a severe, albeit temporary, blow to trade. The drying up of the resources of the grand-ducal treasury made it difficult for Vladimir to carry on its broader national policies. Beginning in the later 1260's Novgorod and Pskov showed an increased tendency to emancipate themselves from the tutelage of Vladimir, which gradually lost the function of military leadership. There were recurrent conflicts among antagonistic boyar groups and frequent changes in the occupants of the grand-ducal throne. The death blow to the political authority of Vladimir was dealt in 1328, when Ivan I of Moscow was appointed grand duke of Vladimir by the khan but continued to reside, in this new capacity, in the city of Moscow.

The Rise of Moscow

Why Moscow? The rise of Moscow admits of no simple and conclusive explanation. It was first mentioned in the chronicle under the year 1147, but next to nothing is known about its subsequent history until the end of the thirteenth century when it was still an insignificant territory comprising but three urban settlements: Moscow, Zvenigorod, and Ruza. Daniel, son of Alexander Nevsky, was the first prince known to have ruled Moscow. He died in 1303 and was succeeded by his son Yuri.

A combination of factors helps to account for the political ascendency of Moscow. They were its position in the geographical center of Russia, which offered a degree of protection from invasions from both south and west; the location of Moscow on the river of that name, which was a link in the network of Russian waterways and made Moscow a participant in trade; the growth of the population due to the influx of settlers fleeing from the exposed border regions; and, as a consequence of these conditions, the "strategic" position of Moscow in the broader meaning of the term, which tended to make it the rallying point of the movement for national unification. The dynastic and personal ambitions of the Muscovite princes and their unscrupulous reliance on the Mongol power were essential elements in the process that secured their victory over their many rivals.

In the fourteenth and fifteenth centuries Russia was divided into several independent or quasi-independent political units. The more important among them were, in addition to Moscow and Vladimir, the grand duchies of Tver, Riazan, Yaroslavl, Nizhni-Novgorod, and, perhaps, Pronsk (a component of the grand duchy of Riazan). Novgorod and Pskov loomed large in the political and economic life of this period, as did occasionally some of the smaller principalities. There was keen competition for supremacy among the more powerful political formations, especially between Moscow and Tver, and the final ascendency of the Muscovites was achieved by imposing their leadership on the other Russian lands, which were gradually deprived of their independence. The process of unification was tortuous and painful, and the final outcome was often uncertain. It is in this setting of the struggle for power that the rise of Moscow must be examined and explained.

The Appanage System. The appanage system, the origins of which go back to the Kievan era, reached its fullest development in the fourteenth and fifteenth centuries. Stemming from the application to territorial constitutional arrangements of the principles governing the right of succession under the regime of family or clan property, the appanage system resulted in perpetuating independent and quasi-independent principalities which became more numerous—and smaller in size—with the passing of generations. The idea of national unity was at a low ebb but survived, nevertheless, chiefly through the instrumentality of the inter-princely agreements.[2] The conflict between the two tendencies—disruptive and integrating—is inherent in the appanage system and colors the entire history of this period.

Moscow's part in bringing about the unification of Russia involved two distinct processes: (1) the consolidation of the principality of Moscow, its amalgamation with the grand duchy of Vladimir, and the resulting emerg-

[2] See above, p. 13.

The growth of Moscow, 1300–1533

ence of the "Grand Duchy of Moscow, Vladimir, and All Russia," and (2) the imposition of the authority of this new grand duchy upon other Russian lands.

Moscow's Bid for Supremacy. Moscow entered the road of territorial expansion in 1301, when it secured the city of Kolomna, at the confluence of the Moscow River with the Oka; a year later Prince Daniel of Moscow inherited the principality of Pereiaslavl. These acquisitions added substantially to the resources and status of Moscow, but the annexation of Pereiaslavl led to a sharp conflict with the powerful princes of Tver, who considered themselves entitled to that principality. When Andrew III, grand duke of Vladimir, died in 1304, Prince Michael of Tver and Prince Yuri of Moscow both aspired to succeed him, journeyed to the Golden Horde, and appealed to the khan. The appointment went to Michael; he was duly installed and held the grand-ducal throne from 1304 to 1318, while Yuri continued to intrigue against, and occasionally to fight, his successful rival. His machinations were unwittingly favored by the unwise and tactless conduct of Michael, who antagonized the newly-appointed Metropolitan Peter, thus forfeiting the valuable support of the Church, and who became involved in a protracted conflict with Novgorod, which for a time was held by Yuri. In this fratricidal war Michael was assisted by the Tatars, and both parties intermittently suffered onerous and humiliating defeats.

In the meantime Yuri of Moscow made protracted stays at Sarai, married the khan's sister, and was appointed grand duke of Vladimir. His attempt to take over the grand duchy, although supported by a Tatar force, met with the resistance of Michael. Eventually both princes returned to Sarai, where Michael was tried on a variety of charges, convicted, and executed (1318). Yuri was confirmed as grand duke of Vladimir but soon ran into new difficulties. His victory over Michael was purchased at the price of higher tributes to the Tatars, which the population resented. In 1322–1324 he fought several costly wars in the defense of Novgorod, while his relations with Tver continued to be highly strained. Prince Dimitry of Tver, Michael's son and successor, took advantage of the inability of Yuri to meet in full his financial obligations towards the Golden Horde, denounced him to the khan, and secured a *yarlyk* for the grand duchy of Vladimir. After some unsuccessful attempts at resistance, Yuri went to Saria, where he was murdered by Dimitry (November 1324). For this bloody deed Dimitry was executed by order of the khan. Moscow, however, derived no immediate political benefit from the staggering blow that befell its antagonist: Dimitry's brother, Alexander of Tver, succeeded him as grand duke of Vladimir.

A remarkable change in Moscow's political status occurred in the reign of Ivan I Kalita (literally "Moneybag"), who became prince of Moscow in 1325, following the murder of his brother Yuri. In 1327 a Tatar emissary and his suite were massacred in Tver. Ivan went at once to Sarai, took charge of a Tatar punitive expedition against Tver, and was rewarded with the office of grand duke of Vladimir (1328). This was the beginning of the fateful association between Moscow and the grand duchy of Vladimir that was to last, with but short interruptions, until the completion of the process of Russia's unification.

Meanwhile Alexander of Tver fled to Pskov and then to Lithuania but in 1335 returned to Russia and made his peace with the khan. The Muscovites were properly alarmed and took characteristic defensive measures. When in 1338 Alexander was induced to visit Sarai, he was confronted with charges instigated by Ivan and was tried and executed, together with his son.

Such was the bloody and slippery path that led to Moscow's first important victory in the struggle for political supremacy.

The Ebb and Flow, 1325–1425. The notion of the "Grand Duchy of All Russia" was inherited by Ivan I from his predecessor, Michael of Tver, who was the first to use this appellation during his tenure of the Vladimir throne (1304–1318). It took some time, however, before this high-sounding title acquired a definite, if rather forbidding, meaning.

Ivan I is traditionally represented as the founder of Muscovy's future greatness through a policy of enlightened frugality and wise investments which led to the expansion of his domain by extensive land purchases. There is little substance in these contentions. Acquisitions of territory, if they actually took place, which is doubtful, were of small consequence in the building up of the authority of Moscow, which stemmed from the growth of its political power. The source of the latter was primarily the fact that the Moscow grand dukes were the chief agents for the collection of Tatar tribute and, in this capacity, the intermediary between the Golden Horde and the other Russian princes. The strengthening of Lithuania under the rule of Gedimin (1316–1341) was an important factor in the situation. Pro-Lithuanian sympathies were common in Russia's western borderlands and were stimulated by the desire to escape the payment of the Tatar tribute which the acceptance of Lithuanian suzerainty appeared to promise. Both the grand dukes of Moscow and the Golden Horde opposed this trend; the resulting community of interests made their collaboration easier, but it did not enhance the standing of Moscow with the other Russian lands.

Ivan did not openly attempt to amend the rules of the appanage system, which worked against the unity of the grand duchy of Moscow and of Russia as a whole. His testament (he died in 1341), however, somewhat limited the application of these rules by providing for the readjustment of the territorial shares of his heirs if the territory of Muscovy had suffered diminution; in other words, the traditional arrangements were made more flexible. The integrating elements, that is, policies aimed at protecting and promoting territorial and political unity, were reflected in the provisions of Ivan's will that entrusted the administration of the city of Moscow and the collection of the Tatar tribute jointly to his three surviving sons.

In the grand duchy of Moscow, as in other Russian lands, the relationship between the senior prince and the junior members of the dynasty was regulated by inter-princely agreements. The prerogatives of the grand duke, as defined in these instruments, usually comprised the leadership of the armed forces and the collection of the Tatar tribute. The agreements, on the other hand, sought to safeguard the rights of the junior princes and their issue in the principalities which they held and to protect them from arbitrary interference by the head of the princely house. As time went on, the Moscow grand dukes tended to ignore the precedents bearing on territorial arrangements (to which reference was invariably made in the inter-princely agreements) and to substitute for them their own decisions. Thus there came into being a new source of princely territorial rights—the grand-ducal grants. The first recorded instance of such a grant was in 1389, the last year of the reign of Dimitry Donskoy, who in his testament disregarded the traditional distinction between the principality of Moscow and the grand duchy of Vladimir and disposed of both as his "patrimony."

The rule of Ivan I's successors—his sons Simon and Ivan II, his grandson Dimitry Donskoy, and his great-grandson Vasili I—was filled with foreign wars and domestic strife. Simon (1341–1353) secured the *yarlyk* for the grand duchy by the usual method of raising the amount of the Tatar tribute. The collection of these heavier levies brought him in conflict with Novgorod and the other Russian lands, which, far from submissively accepting the leadership of Moscow, strove to improve their own political status. It was during these decades that Nizhni-Novgorod and Riazan styled themselves grand duchies. The influence of Lithuania was strong in Novgorod the Great, Tver, and Riazan, and in the 1340's Pskov was ruled for several years by a Lithuanian prince. The right of Ivan II (1353–1359) to succeed his brother Simon as grand duke of Vladimir was unsuccessfully challenged by Constantine, prince of Nizhni-Novgorod and Suzdal. After the death of Ivan II, Constantine's son Dimitry of Suzdal contested the right of Dimitry (Donskoy) of Moscow (1359–1389) to succeed his father Ivan II. This was a period of considerable confusion in the Golden Horde, and both Dimitry (of Suzdal and of Moscow) obtained conflicting *yarlyks* for the grand-ducal throne from rival khans. There followed a war between the two pretenders which ended in the victory of Moscow. In the early 1370's Khan Mamai twice appointed Michael of Tver to the throne of Vladimir, thus contributing to the bitterness of the Tver-Moscow armed conflict which was in progress from 1366 to 1375 and resulted in the recognition by the prince of Tver of the "seniority" of his Moscow rival. Moscow also fought Riazan and became involved in a protracted war with Lithuania which led to the annexation by that country of Russia's western borderlands. How precarious was Moscow's leadership is indicated by the failure of several lands (Novgorod, Pskov, Nizhni-Novgorod, Tver, Riazan) to be represented in the army led by Dimitry Donskoy against the Tatars on the Kulikovo plain in September 1380. The surprise victory gained by the Russians had no immediate effect on their relations with the Golden Horde, whose vassals they remained for another hundred years, although it probably added to the prestige of the Moscow dynasty.[3]

On the morrow of the Kulikovo battle Dimitry Donskoy fought a lengthy war with the prince of Riazan, who was finally compelled to acknowledge the "seniority" of Moscow, as Tver had done a few years earlier. In spite of this success the hold of Moscow over the Russian lands in the 1380's was faltering. Tver, Novgorod the Great, Nizhni-Novgorod, and Riazan, their agreements with Moscow notwithstanding, resumed direct relations with Lithuania and the Golden Horde, while Michael of Tver went further and, following a raid on Russia by Khan Tokhtamysh in 1382, made another unsuccessful attempt to supersede Dimitry Donskoy as grand duke of Vladimir.

Vasili I (1389–1425), Dimitry Donskoy's son and successor, inherited from his father a most difficult political situation and exercised little actual control over the destinies of the nation. He began his reign by obtaining from Khan Tokhtamysh, in return for a large payment, a *yarlyk* for the principality of Nizhni-Novgorod, together with the city of Gorodets and territories along the Oka River. Boris, the last prince of Nizhni-Novgorod, was deported and died in Suzdal, presumably in captivity. Political disorders at the Golden Horde at the end of the fourteenth century temporarily eased Moscow's dependence on the Tatars, and an improvement in the relations with Lithuania, albeit only a passing one, followed the marriage of Vasili to the daughter of Vitovt of Lithuania (1391). In 1406, however, Vasili, assisted by

---

[3] See above, p. 48.

the Tatars, was at war with Lithuania, but towards the end of his reign relations with that country were again improved. Meanwhile the control of
Moscow over Novgorod the Great, Pskov, Riazan, and Tver was notoriously
weak, these lands conducting their foreign relations very much as they
pleased.

This show of independence, however, was the last manifestation of a
political order which was about to disappear. The introduction of grand-
ducal grants as a source of territorial princely rights had dealt a severe
blow to the appanage system.[4] The former quasi-immutable rules governing
princely succession were superseded by bargaining and exchange of territories in which the final decision rested with the senior prince. In the fifteenth
century the powers and resources of the grand-ducal throne of Moscow,
Vladimir, and All Russia, in spite of the numerous setbacks that institution had suffered, were much greater than those of its competitors, and its
authority was gradually substituted for that of the local senior princes (those
of Tver, Suzdal, Riazan, and so on). Moreover the breaking up of the once-
sovereign principalities into small territorial units tended to destroy their
sovereign character and reduced them to the status of landed estates held in
service tenure. Eventually their princely owners became merged in the mass
of boyar landowners.

Unification Under Vasili II. The immediate cause of the triumph of unification and Muscovite absolutism was one of the longest and cruelest feuds
in the history of the Russian Middle Ages. Vasili II (1425–1462) succeeded
his father, Vasili I, but his right was challenged by his uncle Yuri, who, as
the senior member of the dynasty, considered himself entitled to the grand-
ducal throne. The dispute came before the khan and was decided in favor
of Vasili; nevertheless, Yuri and later his sons Vasili and Dimitry Shemiaka
carried against their successful rival a bitter struggle which lasted for a
quarter of a century and in the course of which the grand duke was blinded.[5]
It was the support of Tatar troops who entered Vasili's service in large numbers that brought about the final defeat of Dimitry Shemiaka in 1450.

Once firmly established in Moscow, Vasili II proceeded, with almost unex-
ampled ruthlessness, to exterminate all potential centers of opposition. His
primary aim was to enforce total obedience within his hereditary domain—
the grand duchy of Moscow and Vladimir—by eradicating all vestiges of
sovereignty or even autonomous government in its component parts. The
extensive use of *hired* Tatar troops was an unprecedented feature in the

---

[4] See above, p. 61.
[5] See above, p. 50.

policy of liquidating the Yuri-Dimitry Shemiaka revolt. Having achieved his immediate objective, Vasili turned to other Russian lands. In 1456 a Muscovite army invaded Novgorod the Great and drastically curtailed, but did not yet destroy, its ancient liberties. Riazan, while still ranking as a grand duchy, was virtually reduced to the status of a vassal of Moscow. Of the principalities of northeastern Russia Tver alone retained a semblance of independence. Nevertheless, its prince was brought to acknowledge the "grand-ducal throne of Moscow and Novgorod the Great" as the patrimony of Vasili and his heirs and to promise that his foreign policy, especially relations with Lithuania and the Tatars, would be coordinated with that of Vasili. Such undertakings were not in themselves novel but, unlike the earlier princes, Vasili II and his heirs were in a position to enforce them. Following Byzantine precendents Vasili appointed as his co-ruler his eldest son and heir, the future Ivan III, a boy in his teens. The share of Ivan III in his father's estate comprised the principal lands of the grand duchies of Moscow and Vladimir, which came to be looked upon as an indivisible whole. They formed the territorial base of the unified Muscovite state.

Such were the remarkable changes in the position of Moscow which took place in the brief span of 12 years from 1450 to Vasili II's death in 1462. They were prepared by the earlier course of Russian history, but were hastened by the ruthlessness and cruelty displayed by Vasili and resented by his contemporaries. If the sources have preserved but few criticisms, it is because of subsequent editing by Muscovite schoolmen who regarded unification under Moscow as a preordained task, the wisdom and beneficial effects of which could not be questioned. This belief has left a profound imprint on Russian historiography and is still shared by many historians.

The Church

The Church and Unification. The Church consistently favored unification. From the administrative point of view the Russian Church was a dependency of the patriarchate of Constantinople. It inherited from Byzantium the tradition of universality (catholicism) and of close cooperation with the secular power. The Russian Church, moreover, was organized as a single metropolitanate, except for the brief periods when a separate metropolitan was appointed for the southwestern regions under Lithuanian rule. As a large landowner with properties scattered through the various principalities, the Church was vitally interested in the prevention of inter-princely feuds. It was fortunate for the grand dukes of Moscow that by a historical accident some of the Church leaders during the period of the acute struggle for power were partisans of Moscow and of its claims to supremacy.

As a rule the higher Church hierarchy, including the metropolitan, tended to lend authority to the senior princes, who ostensibly carried on the tradition of national unity and represented Russia as a whole. It was no mere accident that the see of the metropolitan was in the capital of the senior prince most of the time. During the Kievan era the metropolitan resided in Kiev, which remained nominally the center of Church administration for 130 years after the pillage of that city by Andrew Bogoliubsky in 1169. The metropolitans, however, were frequently away from their official residence, especially after the devastation of Kiev in the Tatar invasion in 1240. They made protracted stays in the city of Vladimir, to which Metropolitan Maxim, the first titular head of the Church to use the title of "Metropolitan of All Russia," transferred the metropolitan see in 1300.

Cooperation with Moscow. Maxim died in 1304 and was succeeded by Metropolitan Peter (1308–1326), whose fitness for office was challenged by Michael of Tver, then grand duke of Vladimir. A trial of Peter by a representative of the patriarch on charges brought by Michael ended in his exoneration. Yuri of Moscow sided with the accused prelate and won his lasting gratitude. Peter spent much of his time in Moscow, was buried there in the Uspensky Cathedral, and was eventually canonized and became Moscow's patron saint. The estrangement between Peter and Michael of Tver was an element in the undoing of the latter,[6] who, curiously, was also canonized. Peter's successor, Metropolitan Theognostus, transferred the metropolitan see from Vladimir to Moscow.

Cooperation between the Church and the Moscow authorities was particularly close during most of the reign of Dimitry Donskoy. Metropolitan Alexis (1354–1378), a native Russian like his predecessor Peter, came from an old Moscow boyar family and was a militant partisan of the dynastic and political ambitions of the Muscovite princes. He regarded a defection from Moscow as a crime against the Church, and he used the ecclesiastical weapons of interdicts and excommunications against the Russians who refused to bow to Dimitry's dictations. These policies were of real service to Muscovy, especially in combating the pro-Lithuanian sympathies which were strong in the western borderlands. On the other hand, the long-range effects of the identification of the interests of Church and state were unfortunate. The Church thought differently, and Alexis' services received recognition in his canonization.

[6] See above, p. 59.

Break with Constantinople. An important change in the status of the Russian Church occurred in the middle of the fifteenth century. Byzantium had studiously cultivated and successfully implanted in the Russian Church profound distrust of and, indeed, hatred for Roman Catholicism. It so happened, however, that beginning in the second half of the thirteenth century the leaders of eastern Christianity and the Byzantine emperors found it necessary to negotiate with Rome for a reunion of the Churches; these policies were distasteful to the Russians, who considered them as predatory.

In the reign of Vasili II, Isidor, a Greek or a Bulgarian, was appointed Russian metropolitan by the patriarch of Constantinople. After a brief visit to Moscow the new head of the Russian Church went to the Ferrara-Florence Church Council (1438–1439), which after protracted and stormy deliberations proclaimed the reunion of the Churches. For his part in securing this result Isidor was rewarded with the title of cardinal and papal legate. He returned to Moscow in this new capacity in March 1441 and announced the reunion of the Churches at a mass celebrated in the Uspensky Cathedral. On his way to Russia Isidor had spent several months in Lithuania, where the union was favorably received. Although information about the decisions of the Ferrara-Florence Council and the part played in them by the Russian metropolitan had presumably reached Moscow before his return, the announcement of the union of the Churches, according to the chronicle, took the Russians by surprise. Isidor was locked up in a monastery and was tried and condemned by a council of Russian bishops, but in spite of threats of burning at the stake, he refused to repudiate the union. In September 1441 he escaped and fled abroad, presumably with the connivance of his jailors.

The elimination of the troublesome prelate did not remove the difficulties confronting the Russian Church. The patriarch of Constantinople was a Uniate, while most of the Russian clergy and churchmen rejected the union. For several years the Russians did not quite know what to do, but they finally decided to break with Constantinople. In 1448 a council of Russian bishops and higher clergy elected Jonah to the metropolitan see. The dependence of the Russian Church on Byzantium, which for a long time had been largely nominal, was thus formally brought to an end. The capture of Constantinople by the Turks and the fall of the Byzantine empire five years later (1453) were interpreted by Russian theologians and political leaders as conclusive evidence of their own wisdom and of the decadence of their former mentors: captivity by the infidels was clearly a manifestation of divine wrath for the betrayal of the true faith.

On a lower plane, the breach with Constantinople was significant. The elimination of the patriarch of Constantinople from participation in Russian affairs removed the last safeguard, frail as it was, which protected the Church from interference by the secular power. At the very time when Muscovite absolutism was gaining ground, the Church found itself at the mercy of the lay authorities. Henceforth whenever the Muscovite grand dukes and, later, tsars did not approve of a metropolitan, they removed him from office. The breach with Constantinople was an important landmark on the road to the subjugation of the Church by the state which reached its full development early in the eighteenth century.

The State and Social Groups

The Boyars. Russia's upper class, the boyars, were—like the Church—partisans of political unification. Originally the power of this group was derived from its membership in the princely retinue (*druzhina*) and tenure of high offices, but beginning in the twelfth century or perhaps earlier its influence came to rest primarily on the ownership of landed estates. These properties being often scattered through several principalities, it was to their owners' advantage to prevent the devastating inter-princely feuds. An important office was *kormlenie* (literally "feeding"). The holder of this position was the chief administrative, tax, and judicial officer of a city or province and retained for his own use a portion of the revenue and judicial fines which he collected on behalf of the government. The avowed object of *kormlenie* —and hence its name—was to provide the appointee with the opportunity of amassing a comfortable fortune. A *kormlenie* was usually given for a short time, but there were exceptions and instances are known when this office was hereditary. The origins of *kormlenie,* an institution deservedly unpopular with the governed, go back to the Kievan era; it was widely used in the fourteenth and fifteenth centuries and survived into the seventeenth. It would probably be a mistake, however, to interpret boyar policies exclusively in terms of narrow class economic interests. Some of the members of this group, especially in the larger and politically conscious principalities (Kiev, then Rostov-Suzdal-Vladimir, Tver, Moscow, Riazan), probably believed in the ideal of national greatness, the road to which led through unification, and they tended to identify their personal and class interests with those of the nation.

By the twelfth century the boyars had largely emancipated themselves from princely authority. The two pillars of their liberties were (1) the contractual character of their relations with the prince, that is, the right to take service under a ruler of their own choice and to sever this relationship if they so wished, and (2) the ownership of hereditary landed estates (*otchina, votchina*) unencumbered by any obligation of service. Both these rights suffered curtailment and finally disappeared during the period of Russia's unification under Moscow.

The Right of Free Service. The right of free service stemmed from immemorial tradition. It was customary for the boyars to enter the service, usually army service, of a prince, but they did so of their free will and could shift their allegiance to another ruler. Inter-princely agreements contained provisions guaranteeing immunity from seizure to the estates of the boyars who had availed themselves of this right. Since the principalities were often at war, the resulting situation presented obvious inconveniences from the standpoint of the princes. To obviate this difficulty some of the inter-princely agreements prohibited the princes and the boyars from acquiring estates within the territory of the contracting party, but such restrictive clauses were not common practice. So long as the princes were weak and had to rely on boyar support, the distasteful privilege was tolerated; but with the strengthening of the central authority, violations of the free-service rule became frequent, especially in the case of the boyars who went over to the enemy. The Church aligned itself with the princes in combating boyar defection. In the second half of the fourteenth century Metropolitan Alexis inflicted the penalty of excommunication on the noblemen who had repudiated their allegiance to Moscow.[7] Formal measures to restrict the right of free service, however, were few and of limited application. The privilege gradually ceased to be used in practice, although it survived in theory until the completion of Russia's unification in the sixteenth century. The change was of great practical importance: the once-free landed aristocracy was reduced to the status of a servant of Muscovite absolutism.

Pomestie, or Service Tenure. The second pillar of boyar liberties was the ownership of estates involving no obligations except that of paying taxes. The origin of this form of landownership, known as *votchina*, was presumably occupancy and purchase. It became customary to confer upon the owners of estates the privilege of collecting taxes from, and administering justice among, the free population (tenants) living on their land. Letters patent conferring the above privileges were issued chiefly to large ecclesiastical and secular landowners, although some of the recipients were smallholders of modest social standing. This practice can be traced to the beginning of the fourteenth century, but it is believed to have existed even earlier. The exercise of tax and

[7] See above, p. 65.

judicial powers, which were usually granted for a term of years, enhanced the position of the landowner by imparting to his rule an element of public authority. There were also economic advantages. The tenants of an estate could well benefit by the reduction of taxes and other privileges conferred upon the owner. These considerations, as well as the general protection which a powerful lord could give his tenants, may explain why tenancy appeared attractive to many smallholders.

Princely grants, the appearance of which cannot be precisely dated, became in the fourteenth century an important means of acquiring land. The granting of estates to ecclesiastical and secular lords brought under cultivation wasteland, thus creating new sources of revenue for the princely treasuries. Under these grants the use of land was sometimes made conditional on the performance of specific services, chiefly army service. Estates thus held in service tenure were known as *pomesties;* their owners, like those of *votchina,* might be given the privilege of collecting taxes and administering justice. Although basically a personal grant, a *pomestie* could be transferred by inheritance, provided the heirs performed the obligations stipulated in the original grant. Landholding of the *pomestie* type presumably existed in the thirteenth century; its importance increased considerably in the fourteenth and the fifteenth centuries, and in the sixteenth century the difference between *votchina* and *pomestie* disappeared and all landowners became liable to the obligation of service.

The Peasantry. In the fourteenth and the fifteenth centuries the position of the peasantry continued to evolve along lines which were discernible during the earlier period, that is, it was characterized by the transformation of the once-independent peasant farmers into tenants living on the land of ecclesiastical and secular lords and by the curtailment of their personal and property rights. There were two main reasons why tenancy tended to supersede independent peasant farming: appropriation of the land of the smallholders by a powerful lord, and voluntary change of status because of the advantages in taxation and other matters which a lord could extend to the population living on his estate.[8] With mounting tax burdens under the Mongol rule, the latter consideration became particularly important, especially in the case of Church estates, which were exempt from taxation.[9] Since land was plentiful and labor scarce, landowners had good reasons to make tenancy appear attractive, at least in the initial stage.

The relationship between landlord and tenant was regulated by agree-

[8] See above, p. 17.
[9] See above, p. 44.

ments which defined the rights and obligations of each. At the expiration of the term of the agreement or, under certain conditions, while it was still in force, the tenant was free to move away; the landlord had the corresponding right to dismiss a tenant or not to renew his lease. From the standpoint of the tenant, a vital element in this relationship was that, so long as he performed his part of the contract, tenancy did not restrict his right to leave or impair his status as a freeman. It is arguable that a farmer is linked with the soil on which he toils by innumerable ties which make the abandonment of the allotment unlikely. Russia's population in the Middle Ages, however, was in a state of continuous flux, and the eagerness of the landowners and the government in devising measures to prevent the moving away of the tenants supports the view that the danger of the depopulation of the estates was real.

The indebtedness of the tenants to their lord was, as in the earlier period, an important factor leading to their loss of freedom. It was customary for the tenants to borrow from their lord funds which were used to improve their farms. The rate of interest was high and the debtors frequently found themselves unable to meet their obligations. At first the existence of the debt did not in itself prevent the tenant from leaving, although the creditor retained his claim and could enforce it through the courts. A delinquent debtor, however, was bound over to his creditor and was to work for him until the debt was paid off, which usually meant for life.

The Muscovite government had compelling reasons for discouraging and, later, preventing the movement of the farming population. A taxpayer could elude taxes and other obligations towards the state (such as military service) unless he was firmly attached to a community. The Muscovite military establishment depended largely on the ability of service people, holders of *pomesties,* to perform their duties. A *pomestie,* that is, an estate held in service tenure, was cultivated by tenant farmers, and their wandering away threatened to destroy the economic base of the service class. It is not surprising therefore that the central authority should intervene, at first timidly and haphazardly, in the relationship between tenant and landlord and should endeavor to restrict the freedom of movement of the peasant farmer. Restrictive legislation on a national scale was not applied until the very end of the fifteenth century, and the earlier measures of this nature were tentative and of local significance. For instance, in the middle of the fifteenth century the grand duke of Moscow prohibited the tenants of certain ecclesiastical estates from leaving until they had settled the debts owed by them to their lord. At first the authorities endeavored not to abrogate the right of free movement but to make the exercise of this right more difficult. Some of the agreeme which were concluded by the grand dukes of Moscow and other princes con tained the reciprocal obligation not to accept peasants coming from the estates of the contracting parties. Similar provisions concerning peasants living on grand-ducal estates were included in some of the letters patent granting estates or conferring tax and other privileges. In the middle of the fifteenth century tenants living on certain monastic estates were permitted to relinquish their tenancy only during the week preceding and the week following St. George's Day (November 26). This, again, was a purely local measure at first; however, it was given general application at the end of the fifteenth century. In the middle of that century tenant farmers could still move from one landowner to another, but they were far less free to do so than they had been one or two centuries earlier.

A Summary

Inroads of Absolutism. National unification under the leadership of Moscow took place within the framework of the Mongol rule and was accompanied by the destruction of the autonomous communities of medieval Russia. In the process of unification the Church and the leading social groups—the boyars and the free peasantry—were deprived of many of the liberties, limited as they were, which they had enjoyed in the past. The political and social evolution that brought into existence the Muscovite state was well advanced by the time of the death of Vasili II (1462). It was completed in the reign of his successors Ivan III and Vasili III.

5

Muscovite State, 1462-1533

Consolidation of Moscow's Authority

An Outline. Vasili II laid down the foundation of a unified centralized state. The evolution of Moscow in the direction of an autocracy continued under his immediate successors, Ivan III and Vasili III, and reached its full development in the reign of Ivan IV the Dread. The principal elements in the process of political and territorial unification and of the building up of monarchical absolutism were the subjugation by Moscow of the other Russian principalities, the annexation of the former Russian territories held by Lithuania-Poland, the emergence of a theory of Moscow's political supremacy, the creation of agencies of centralized government, and the elimination or curtailment of whatever independence was still enjoyed by the existing institutions and social groups: the Church, the princely dynasties, the landed aristocracy, and the free tenant farmers. The power of Moscow, which in the second half of the fifteenth century was much greater than that of its competitors, insured its ascendancy and final triumph.

Ivan III. The policy of extending and consolidating Moscow's control over the other Russian lands was continued by the son and heir of Vasili II, Ivan III (1462–1505). The details of this process have been expunged from the record.[1] For reasons which are no longer discernible but of which Musco-

[1] See above, p. 64.

vite pressure was presumably the chief one, the rulers of Russian principalities proceeded one after another to transfer their hereditary rights to the grand duke of Moscow, whose service they entered. The circumstances varied from case to case, but the result was invariably the same: the former sovereign or semi-autonomous principalities were reduced to the status of provinces of Moscow, while their princes joined the ranks of the service nobility. Such was the fate of the ancient lands of Vereia, Yaroslavl, Rostov, Tver, and Viatka. In some instances (Tver, Viatka) armed force was openly used. Novgorod the Great, which showed strong pro-Lithuanian sympathies, was besieged by Muscovite troops in 1470 and paid a heavy indemnity; shortly thereafter its dependent territory of Perm was annexed by Moscow, and in 1478 Novgorod capitulated to Ivan's army, was deprived of its autonomous institutions, and was incorporated in the Muscovite state. In Novgorod, Yaroslavl, and Viatka, the loss of independence was accompanied by mass deportations of boyars and other landowners, who were given estates elsewhere to hold in service tenure. The land owned by the deportees was confiscated and distributed, also in service tenure, to men coming from other parts of the country. Not a few of those who opposed Muscovite expansion were imprisoned or executed.

Vasili III. Vasili III (1505–1533), son and heir of Ivan III, completed the process of political and territorial unification. In 1510 Pskov was deprived, without a war, of its organs of self-government and became a province of Moscow. The turn of the grand duchy of Riazan came next. Its prince was accused of treasonable relations with the Crimean Tatars and was thrown in prison; its territory was absorbed by Moscow. In both Pskov and Riazan, as earlier in Novgorod and some of the other newly-acquired lands, the leading citizens were deported and their estates were resettled with Moscow's trusted supporters. Towards the end of Vasili's reign Moscow annexed the principality of Sever, allegedly because its princes were engaged in treasonable negotiations with Poland.

Moscow and the Fall of Byzantium. The Muscovites, however, were no longer satisfied with imposing their rule upon the former independent Russian principalities. The broader program formulated by Ivan III provided for the return to Russia of the territories which had been taken over by Lithuania in the fourteenth century and early in the fifteenth. This ambition was prompted by international developments. In 1453 the Byzantine empire was overthrown by the Turks, who established themselves at Constantinople. The substitution of a warlike aggressive Moslem power for a weak decadent Christian Byzantium eventually confronted Moscow with a situation of utmost gravity, especially since Turkey, being firmly entrenched on the Bosphorus, held (and still holds) the keys to the Black Sea. For nearly 500 years the Russians have intermittently fought the Turks, and there were periods, especially in the nineteenth century, when the Eastern Question, that is, the fate of Constantinople and the Ottoman empire, dominated Russian and European politics. These future complications, however, were not foreseen in the fifteenth century, when Russia was not yet a Black Sea power. Muscovite princes and the leaders of the Russian Church, indeed, viewed the fall of Byzantium with complacence which had a touch of malice. At the Ferrara-Florence Council of 1438–1439 Byzantium had accepted the union of the Eastern and the Western Churches,[2] a decision regarded by the Russian hierarchy as the betrayal of the only true faith. The catastrophe that overtook Byzantium shortly thereafter was interpreted by Russian theologians and political leaders as a manifestation of divine justice. It was also held that, with the seizure of Constantinople by the Turks, leadership of Eastern Christianity passed into the hands of Moscow. These doctrines, which will be examined later in this chapter, added to the feeling of self-importance and encouraged the political aspirations of Moscow.

Meanwhile the Tatar rule became less stringent and was officially terminated in 1480.[3] Although the part taken by Ivan III and the other Russian princes in this event was unimpressive, the fact that Russia regained the status of a sovereign power was clearly of paramount importance.

Annexations from Lithuania. The union of the Churches, by fomenting internal strife in Lithuania, favored Moscow's plans of territorial expansion. Measures for the implementation of the union were resented by the members of the Orthodox Church living in that land; friction increased in intensity in the second half of the fifteenth century when a Uniate prelate was appointed metropolitan of Lithuania, especially after the enactment of a decree in 1481 which prohibited the building and renovation of Orthodox churches. A number of princes and boyars of the Orthodox faith who resided in Lithuania sought the protection of Ivan III; their requests were granted and Moscow claimed sovereignty over the "hereditary estates" of the petitioners, although such shifts of allegiance by Muscovite and Lithuanian landowners were specifically forbidden by treaties concluded by the two countries. Nevertheless, the Lithuanian government deemed it expedient to comply with Muscovite demands. In this manner a wide stretch of territory along the Russo-Lithuanian border was transferred at the end of the fifteenth century to the sover-

---

[2] See above, p. 66.
[3] See above, pp. 50–51.

eignty of Moscow. In spite of dynastic ties, which were strengthened by the marriage of Ivan III's daughter Helen to Alexander, ruler of Lithuania and Poland, the two countries were at war most of the time from 1500 to 1522. By virtue of peace and armistice settlements concluded during this period, Moscow secured from Lithuania extensive areas, including the city of Chernigov (1503) and the city of Smolensk (1522).

The aggregate territorial gains were considerable. Between 1462 and 1533 the area directly controlled by the grand duchy of Moscow increased by some 40,000 square miles, that is, it was nearly four times as large at the end as it was at the beginning of this period.

Internal Unification. The newly-established unity of Muscovy continued to be threatened by the survival of the traditional constitutional doctrine stemming from the notion of family property: the territory of the grand duchy was still looked upon as the joint property of the Moscow princely house, in which each male heir of the grand duke had a share. This theory, if logically applied in practice, would have led to the dismemberment of the Muscovite state. We have seen that Vasili II and his predecessors had taken steps to ensure the supremacy of the grand-ducal throne. The policy of curtailing the rights of the junior princes was pursued by Ivan III and Vasili III. Ivan III had four brothers, who at different times and by different means strove to increase the territorial shares allocated to them at their father's death. Ivan III suppressed these attempts. To achieve his object he used primarily the traditional method of inter-princely agreements which he concluded with his brothers. By virtue of these instruments the junior Moscow princes acknowledged the right of Ivan and his issue to the grand duchy of Moscow, the area of which was so defined as to include, in addition to the ancient lands of Moscow and Vladimir, the territories of Novgorod, Tver, and Pskov. The grand duke was recognized as the leader of the national armed forces and was empowered to conduct foreign relations to the exclusion of the other members of his house. These concessions were exacted from Ivan's kinsmen by pressure, and when this was not enough, stronger measures were used. For instance, Ivan's brother Andrew Senior (*Bolshoi*), who resisted the encroachments on what he regarded as his rights, was charged with plotting with the Tatars and was thrown into prison, where he died.

The gains of the grand-ducal throne were consolidated and expanded in Ivan III's testament, which, however, according to custom divided the territory of the grand duchy among his five sons; but the share of the Grand Duke Vasili III was much larger than those of his brothers. Moreover, the testament provided that if a junior prince died without issue, his domain was to revert to the grand-ducal throne. The prerogatives of the latter were extended to comprise the right of coinage and jurisdiction in the more serious criminal cases—functions formerly exercised by the junior princes. The testament and the accompanying inter-princely agreements, their traditional phraseology notwithstanding, were a significant move in the direction of political absolutism.

Customary beliefs and administrative practices, however, are inflexible, and it took time before the junior princes became reconciled to the diminution of their position. Accordingly, the reign of Vasili III was filled with conflicts with his brothers. A historical accident contributed to the defeat of the forces inherent in the appanage system which worked for the dismemberment of the Muscovite state. Vasili III was survived by two infant sons, the future Ivan IV and George. In conformity with custom, Vasili divided the grand duchy between these two heirs, but George died without issue, his share reverted to Ivan, and the two portions of the Moscow territory became once more reunited. Vasili III's testamentary dispositions were the last instance in which the principles of the appanage order were embodied in a major state document. Fifty years later, at the end of the reign of Ivan IV, the breaking up of Russia into autonomous principalities such as had existed from the twelfth to the fifteenth century was no longer within the realm of possibility.

Foreign Relations

The Tatars. Political unification and the changes in the international situation had significant repercussions on Russia's international position. The formal termination of the Tatar rule in 1480 and the destruction of the Golden Horde by the Crimean Tatars some 20 years later did not end the Mongol threat. Moscow continued to battle—and to negotiate—with the Tatar succession states: the kingdoms of Kazan and Astrakhan, on the Volga, and of the Crimea, on the Black Sea peninsula. To the Crimean khanate, a vassal of Turkey, Russia paid a regular tribute.[4] Meanwhile separate Tatar hordes roamed in the Black Sea steppes south of Muscovy's ill-defined boundary line and frequently invaded Russian territory. These unsettled conditions, which taxed Russian military and financial resources, lasted until nearly the end of the eighteenth century.

Europe, Turkey, and India. As indicated in an earlier section of this chapter, the Lithuanian wars of Ivan III led to the westward expansion of Russian territory and brought Muscovy into closer contact with Europe. Dip-

---

[4] See above, p. 51.

lomatic relations with Hungary, the Holy See, Denmark, and the Holy Roman Empire were established in the 1480's and the 1490's. In most cases these contacts were perfunctory and were limited to exchanges of embassies. Russia and the Western countries still had few interests in common. The Muscovites, for instance, would have nothing to do with the crusade against Turkey which Pope Alexander VI endeavored to organize. The Russo-Danish alliance, however, had a concrete practical purpose and was directed against Sweden. Fruitful, on a different level, were the relations between Muscovy and Venice, which supplied Ivan III with architects, artists, and craftsmen employed in the rebuilding of the Russian capital.

The diplomacy of Vasili III followed similar lines. He negotiated an anti-Polish alliance with the Holy Roman Empire, made similar overtures to France, concluded a long-term armistice with Sweden, re-established with the Hanseatic League relations which had been broken when Ivan III annexed Novgorod, and exchanged envoys with Pope Leo X. These diplomatic moves had few practical results. The Holy Roman Empire and France kept aloof from the Russo-Polish quarrels, while Muscovy showed no interest in the union of the Churches and the eviction of the Turks from Europe, which were advocated by the Holy See.

The first steps were taken to bring the Near East and the Far East within the purview of Russia's diplomatic action and her sphere of commercial interests. In the 1490's Moscow established direct relations with Constantinople, then capital of the Ottoman empire, and somewhat earlier (1467–1472) an enterprising Russian merchant from Tver, Athanasius Nikitin, made his way to India. He left a diverting account of his adventures.

These were modest beginnings; yet Russia was no longer entirely cut off from the outside world.

Doctrine of Muscovite Absolutism

"Moscow—The Third Rome." The broader field of diplomatic action was in keeping with Moscow's newly-acquired sense of self-importance. The emancipation of the Russian Church from the control of the patriarch of Constantinople, the fall of Byzantium, and the collapse of the Golden Horde—momentous events packed within the brief span of three decades—gave a powerful stimulus to Moscow's political ambitions. From the time of its conversion to Greek Orthodoxy to the middle of the fifteenth century Russia held a subordinate place among the countries of Eastern Christianity. With the Turks in control of the Bosphorus and of the Balkans,

Moscow found itself projected into a position of prominence which only recently had seemed beyond its reach, and the restoration of its status as a sovereign nation which followed the elimination of the Tatar rule was another evidence of the ascendancy of Moscow at the very time when both its spiritual mentor and its secular master—Byzantium and the Golden Horde —vanished from the historical stage.

This remarkable sequence of events greatly impressed Russian ecclesiastical and lay leaders. Early in the sixteenth century there came into circulation a doctrine evolved by Filotheus, a monk in a Pskov monastery. According to this theory Rome, the first capital of the Christian world, failed because it had betrayed true faith by accepting Catholicism; Constantinople, the Second Rome, became a victim of the Turks because it, too, had betrayed true Christianity in agreeing to the union of the Churches; Moscow, the Third Rome, was the new center of the Orthodox world and would go on for ever: there would be no Fourth Rome.[5]

The notion that Muscovy was the successor of Byzantium gained easy acceptance among Russian theologians—the only literate Russians of that period—but the tenuous nature of the link between Moscow and Constantinople created uneasiness. Sophie Paleologue, niece of the last emperor of Byzantium, who had been killed in the Turkish invasion, was the second wife of Ivan III and mother of Vasili III, but these all-too-recent dynastic ties provided no foundation for Moscow's far-reaching claims. To remedy the situation, imaginative Russian schoolmen traced the ancestry of the Muscovite grand dukes to Roman caesars and spread the legend that a crown and royal vestments were presented early in the twelfth century to the Kievan Prince Vladimir Monomakh by the Byzantine Emperor Constantine Monomakh. It was also held that Russia was converted to Christianity not through Byzantium but directly by "Andrew, brother of Peter the Apostle." The Muscovite rulers of the sixteenth century appear to have taken no small pride and pleasure in these fanciful historical schemes in which they probably believed.

The Church and Absolutism. The Church was consistently a supporter of unification. Faithful to the Byzantine tradition and influenced, perhaps, by considerations of expediency—after the breach with Constantinople, the Russian Church was more than ever dependent on the secular power—the Church unreservedly upheld the claims of the Muscovite throne. It was the Church

[5] This doctrine was devised in the fifteenth century in the Balkans, from where it was borrowed by Russian schoolmen. In the original version Tyrnowo, the capital of Bulgaria, held the place later assigned to Moscow.

that provided the dynasty with a decorous, albeit imaginary, genealogy. In the reign of Ivan III the most influential and articulate group among the clergy was led by Joseph Sanin, abbot of the Volokolam monastery. According to the theologians of this ultra-conservative school, Muscovite absolutism was of divine origin, and unwavering obedience to the grand duke (and, later, to the tsar) was the sacred duty of both clerics and laymen.

There was, however, one major issue on which the Church and the government were not in agreement: ecclesiastical estates. By the end of the fifteenth century the monasteries and other ecclesiastic bodies had accumulated vast landholdings which in the past were recognized and protected by the princes and the Golden Horde. This attitude appeared to be changing in the later part of the fifteenth century, when the Muscovite government found itself short of improved land for distribution in service tenure, land which constituted the economic basis of the armed force. The sequestration of some of the monastic estates in Novgorod at the time of its annexation by Moscow greatly disturbed the churchmen of the Joseph of Volokolam school. They argued, not very convincingly, that the wealth of the monasteries was used exclusively for the relief of the poor (of which practice there was little evidence). Another and more practical argument was that since the taking of monastic vows was the prerequisite for the bishopric, monasteries should be properly endowed in order to provide for the requirements, as Joseph put it, of "the honorable and noble monks," candidates for the higher ecclesiastical offices. Monasteries, according to this view, were not places for meditation and prayer away from the perturbations of a sinful world, but rather training schools for church officials.

Dissension Within the Church. The views of Joseph of Volokolam and his disciples were not universally shared. In the fifteenth and the sixteenth centuries there appeared several dissenting movements within the Church. The more important among them were the so-called "Judaizers," a sect established in Novgorod in the 1470's; the "hermits beyond the Volga," a movement which originated about the same time and was founded by Nil Sorsky, a protagonist of the hermitage type of monasticism;[6] and in the first half of the sixteenth century an informal group of religious thinkers who gathered around Maxim the Greek, a learned monk who for a time was in charge of the correction of Russian Church books. Without going into the details of the teachings of the dissenters, who differed among themselves in some essentials, the significant elements which they had in common may be briefly

[6] Nil Sorsky and his followers established hermitages in the wooded wilderness east of the Volga, hence the name of the movement.

summarized. The doctrines of the Judaizers, Nil Sorsky, and Maxim were tinged with a rationalism that was reminiscent of Protestantism in western Europe. Unlike Joseph of Volokolam and the official Church, the dissenters held that the essence of faith was not external observance but an understanding of the principles of Christianity acquired through the critical study of the Scriptures; and they took a dim view of Russian monasticism and advocated the secularization of ecclesiastical estates. This latter aspect of their teaching, which pleased the authorities, and the fact that the dissenters had supporters in high places, including the grand-ducal court, explain the unusual tolerance which they enjoyed for a while. But the view of the official Church prevailed in each case. Some of the leaders of the rationalists were fortunate enough to die before the outbreak of persecution; those who did not were tried and suffered punishments ranging from burning at the stake to incarceration in ecclesiastical prisons.

The basic issue—that of Church estates—remained unresolved and continued to be a source of conflict between Church and state until well into the eighteenth century, when secularization finally took place.

Central Government

The Grand-Ducal Power. Political unification wrought far-reaching changes in the position of the grand duke and in the mechanics of the Muscovite government. Unlike their predecessors, Ivan III and Vasili III were no longer "first among equals" in their relations with the other Russian princes but the depository of the supreme authority the like of which did not exist anywhere else in the Russian land. Many of the former sovereign princes (and their boyars) flocked to the capital, held offices under the Muscovite crown, and received estates in service tenure. The Russian rulers of yesterday were therefore no longer the peers of the grand duke but his subordinates. Under the influence of Sophie Paleologue the Muscovite court adopted a rigid etiquette which contrasted with the easy-going informality of the earlier days. The two-headed eagle of Byzantium became Russia's coat-of-arms, and on occasion Ivan used the title of "tsar and autocrat." The appearance of the capital underwent a change. Prior to the middle of the fifteenth century Moscow had few stone buildings: even the grand-ducal palaces were unpretentious frame structures. This situation may be partly explained by the fact that skilled masons were still rare in Russia. Ivan III undertook an extensive reconstruction of the Kremlin, which was surrounded by a massive stone wall. The planning and execution of this work was done by foreign artists and craftsmen; among them was the noted Italian architect Rodolfo (Aristotle) Fioraventi, who designed and built the Uspensky Cathedral in the Kremlin.

The Boyar Duma and Central Departments. The boyar *duma* (council) [7] continued to meet under Ivan III and Vasili III but was shorn of much of its former authority. The *duma,* as we know, never had a formal constitution or definite competence. It was consulted by the grand dukes so long as they needed the willing cooperation of the boyars. With the diminution of the status of the landed nobility the reasons for seeking its advice and consent lost much of their urgency. After unification the possibility of refusal by the boyars to comply with the orders of the grand duke no longer arose, except in the relatively rare and extreme cases of defection to the enemy. Ivan III and Vasili III convoked the *duma* but seldom and showed little respect for its members.

The concentration of political authority in the hands of Moscow, accompanied as it was by the destruction of indigenous administrative institutions, necessitated the creation of new central departments. Thus there came into existence the *prikazy* (singular, *prikaz*), which were purely bureaucratic agencies. Some of them were in charge of a branch of government, for instance, foreign relations or the judiciary; others administered specified territories. The earliest known *prikaz* was organized in 1512; by the end of the sixteenth century their number increased substantially and is variously estimated at from 40 to 60. They became the stronghold of a huge centralized bureaucracy and the mainstay of the Muscovite administrative machine. The *prikazy* functioned until the eighteenth century, when they were superseded by institutions of a different type, but bureaucracy continued to grow and remains to this day the principal element of the Russian government.

Social Conditions

The Upper Class. The changes in the position of the upper class which were noted in the earlier part of the fifteenth century reached their logical development under Ivan III and Vasili III. The independence and political power of the landed nobility rested on the right of free service (that is, the right to transfer allegiance from one ruling prince to another) and the right to own estates unencumbered by any obligation of service.[8] With the unification of Russia the former right lost all practical significance because the op-

---

[7] See above, p. 16.
[8] See above, pp. 67–69.

portunities for exercising it no longer existed: by the end of Vasili III's reign all autonomous Russian principalities were absorbed by Muscovy. The one avenue of escape still available led to Lithuania and Poland, but such shifting of allegiance came to be looked upon as treason and brought upon the noblemen who chose that course confiscation of their estates and other penalties. That flight from Muscovy had its attraction is indicated by the measures devised by Ivan III to prevent it. He inaugurated a system of mutual guaranties under which the leading boyars were liable to heavy fines if other noblemen for whom they were induced to stand surety left the service of Moscow. The first known arrangement of this nature was in the 1470's; it was extensively used by Vasili III and especially by his son Ivan IV, under whose rule the conflict between the Crown and the boyars entered an acute stage. The right of free service was never formally abolished, but by the end of the fifteenth century it ceased to operate.

Erosion was again the fate of the *votchina* form of landholding, that is, ownership of landed estates which did not involve the obligation of service. With the growth of Muscovite armed forces in the fifteenth and the sixteenth centuries the granting of estates of the *pomestie* type (held in service—usually military—tenure) became increasingly common. The owners of both *votchinas* and *pomesties* were sometimes granted by the Crown the privilege of collecting taxes and administering justice on their estates. In law, the conferring of these privileges had nothing to do with the ownership of the estates, but gradually the grand-ducal grants came to be regarded as the sole dependable titles to land. Such grants were given in return for accepting the obligation of service. The result was that the once-clear distinction between hereditary ancestral estates (*votchina*) and estates held in service tenure (*pomestie*) became blurred and finally disappeared. No law or decree making service obligatory for all landowners was ever enacted. In the reign of Vasili III there was still much confusion and uncertainty about the service obligation of estate owners, and it is believed that some of them succeeded in avoiding it; but there was a clear tendency to make service compulsory for all landowners, and this was enforced with increasing thoroughness.

The Muscovite government went to considerable length to prevent the possibility of resistance to the policy of unification. The holdings of the leading citizens of Novgorod, Pskov, Yaroslavl, Viatka, and Riazan were confiscated, and their owners were deported and received estates elsewhere in service tenure. Similar measures were applied to former sovereign princes. Some of them, even after unification, continued to reside in their former principalities and enjoyed a measure of autonomy, including the right to keep private armies. Under various pretexts Ivan III and Vasili III withdrew these privileges. The princes were removed from the land which they and their ancestors had once ruled and were given estates in service tenure in other parts of the country. The possibility of separatist tendencies was thus effectively checked.

The Nobility and the Crown. The policies outlined above produced a profound change in the position of the landed nobility by reducing it to the status of a servant of the Muscovite crown. The question naturally arises: why did not the Russian noblemen endeavor to secure a charter of liberties— a Magna Charta—from the Muscovite grand dukes while Russian absolutism was still in its infancy? One basic reason for the lack of concerted action was

New York Public Library, Slavonic Division

Three Horsemen, drawing by Herberstein, early sixteenth century the heterogeneity of the service class: it comprised men of widely divergent economic and social standing, ranging from former sovereign princes and great boyars to holders of small plots and slaves of yesterday. A group thus constituted could hardly be expected to evolve a common policy.

Another reason for non-resistance to the encroachments of the Crown was the tenuous and gradual nature of official policies. Neither Ivan III nor Vasili III made a frontal attack on the privileges of the landed nobility. It was, to repeat, a process of erosion which offered few opportunities for organized action by its victims.

In this connection mention should be made of *mestnichestvo* (from *mesto,* place), a curious ancient institution which provided for the arrangement of the members of the aristocratic families in a hierarchical order that determined their position in the service and at court and social functions. The essence of *mestnichestvo* was the interrelationship of the offices held by the various families, which was to be preserved, that is, *mestnichestvo*—unlike feudalism in western Europe—did not create hereditary claims to offices but was supposed to maintain the hereditary relationship of the various families with reference to the offices held by their members. In other words, what mattered was the relative position of officeholders, not the office itself. The working of this system required exceedingly involved computations and was enmeshed in a maze of obscure and all-but-unintelligible rules. Genealogical tables and service records of the aristocratic families were kept by special departments. The conflicting interpretations of these data, in which the Muscovite nobility took passionate interest, led to murderous feuds. To be appointed to a position which the prospective holder regarded as inferior to the one to which he believed himself entitled in the light of his ancestral record was deemed an unspeakable disgrace. *Mestnichestvo* was retained until the end of the seventeenth century. Meanwhile the leading boyar families spent in futile genealogical quarrels much of the energy that might have been used to protect their vital interests from the arbitrariness of the Crown.

Finally, the service class was deeply concerned with retaining the services of the peasant population living on its estates. The simplest and seemingly safest way of attaining this objective was to attach the farmers to their plots, that is, to reduce them to the state of serfdom. The Moscow government, for reasons of its own, moved in the same direction. The resulting community of interests between the Crown and the landed nobility may help to explain the submissive attitude of the latter.

The Onward March of Serfdom. Under Ivan III and Vasili III the evolution in the position of the peasantry, like that of the service class, was the continuation of a process that had begun during the earlier period.[9] Its main aspect was the curtailment of the tenants' freedom of movement. There were various reasons for this development: the desire of the tenants for greater security, which led them to seek closer dependence on a powerful lord; the debtor-creditor relationship growing from the indebtedness of the tenants to their landlord; and the policy of the government, motivated by fiscal, police, and military considerations but designed to achieve the same objective—the immobilization of the rural population. Two developments of this order may be noted. From the middle of the fifteenth century the notion of *starozhiltsy,* or "old-timers," gained acceptance. *Starozhiltsy* were tenant farmers who, by maintaining their tenancy for a specified period (the length of which cannot be determined by available information) forfeited the right to leave. It is believed that this rule applied both to state peasants, that is, farmers living on state-owned land, and to tenants living on private estates. According to some of the authorities, *starozhiltsy* were the first Russian serfs.

The second development was the extension of the application of the St. George's Day rule. Originally, by this rule the right of the *tenants residing on specified estates* to renounce their tenancy was limited to a week preceding and a week following November 26 (St. George's Day). The code of 1497, Russia's first legislative collection since the eleventh century, applied the St. George's Day rule to *all tenants,* making it illegal to release tenancy at any other time. This was a long step towards serfdom; yet—except for the *starozhiltsy*—the tenant farmers were still freemen, although it became increasingly difficult to maintain that status.

A Summary

Muscovite Absolutism. In the 1530's, when Vasili III died, Muscovite absolutism was firmly established. The appanage order, with its multiplicity of small sovereign rulers, was gone, and the supreme authority was centered in the hands of the occupant of the Moscow throne, who occasionally used, and was soon to assume formally, the title of tsar. The once-autonomous principalities became provinces of Muscovy. The Mongol domination which had lasted for nearly two and a half centuries was terminated, and with the conquest of Byzantium by the Turks Moscow proudly proclaimed itself its successor. The territory of Russia, now a unified state, was greatly expanded, and some of its western borderlands which were under Lithuanian-Polish rule were brought within the fold of Muscovy. A massive machinery of

[9] See above, pp. 69–71.

bureaucratic government came into being. The Church allied itself unreservedly with the Muscovite autocracy which it had powerfully contributed to build, but the vexing and disputed question of ecclesiastical estates loomed ominously as a potential source of conflict. The social structure underwent a truly revolutionary change. Both the former sovereign princes and the great boyar landowners lost their independent status and became servitors of the Muscovite Crown, holding estates in service tenure, while the once-free peasantry was driven along the path that inexorably led to serfdom.

The Muscovite absolutism that grew out of the political unification was not merely the territorial merging of autonomous principalities into a national state. It was also the emergence of a highly centralized administrative and social system from which all manifestations of self-government, public initiative, and independence were rigorously excluded.

PART TWO

1533-1696

[87]

1606, May – 1610, July	Tsar Vasili Shuisky
1607, June – 1610, December	The second Pretender
1609, September	Beginning of Polish intervention
1610, November	The Poles occupy Moscow
1611, July	The Swedes occupy Novgorod
1611, October	Beginning of liberation movement under Minin and Pozharsky
1612, October	Capitulation of the Poles in Moscow
1613–1645	Tsar Michael Romanov
1617	Peace of Stolbovo, with Sweden
1618	War with Poland; armistice of Deulino
1632–1634	War with Poland
1645–1676	Tsar Alexis
1648	Uprising in Moscow
1649	Code of Tsar Alexis
1649	Uprising of "voluntary slaves"
1650	Uprisings in Novgorod and Pskov
1652	German Settlement in Moscow re-established
1652–1666	Patriarch Nikon
1654	Russia incorporates the Ukraine
1654–1667	War with Poland; by the armistice of Andrusovo, Russia annexes Smolensk, Seversk, the left-bank Ukraine, and Kiev
1654–1666	Correction of Church books
1656–1658	War with Swedes; peace of Cardis (1661)
1662	"Copper rebellion" in Moscow
1667	Excommunication of the dissenters: the schism
1667	The New Statute of Commerce
1667–1671	Uprising of Stenka Razin
1676–1682	Tsar Fedor (Romanov)
1676–1780	War with Turkey; armistice of Bakhchisarai confirms Moscow's control over the left-bank Ukraine
1682–1696	Tsars Peter I and Ivan V, co-rulers
1682–1689	Regency of Sophie
1682	*Mestnichestvo* abolished
1686	"Eternal peace" with Poland
1687	The Slavono-Greek-Latin theological academy established
1687–1689	War with the Crimean Tatars
1689	Treaty of Nerchinsk with China

6

Ivan IV the Dread, 1533-1584

Ivan and the Historians

Political Prejudice and Paucity of Information. There is much disagreement among Russian historians concerning the interpretation and the very facts of Ivan IV's reign. Ivan was both a tyrant and a reformer, and his policies and their results have been invoked by historians in support of widely divergent theories of government and social change. Stalin took a favorable view of Ivan IV, and the Soviet historians of the 1930's and the 1940's, obedient to the wishes of the dictator, exerted themselves to represent Ivan as a wise, far-sighted, and enlightened ruler. Not a few nationalistically-minded Russian scholars residing outside the USSR have espoused this line of argument. The resulting studies of Ivan IV display imagination and inventiveness but show little familiarity with the sources and often do violence to common sense.

The notorious paucity of information on the Russian sixteenth century is another major source of confusion, but this is seldom mentioned in print, except in the more specialized studies. The truth of the matter is that gaps in the sources are great. There are long stretches of years for which no information is available on the doings of Ivan, and many of the basic documents bearing on his policies, including the more important ones, have not been preserved. Thus, conjectures and theories are substituted for factual studies. Generalizations resting on so uncertain a foundation are necessarily frail and must be treated with caution.

The First Tsar

The Boyar Rule. When Vasili III died in 1533, his son and heir, Ivan IV, was three years old. With the Muscovite throne occupied by an infant, the separatist ambitions of the former sovereign princes, including Ivan's kin, which had been kept in check by his father and grandfather, came again to the fore. However, the brewing revolt against the rule of Moscow was successfully resisted by Helen, mother of Ivan and a member of the Glinsky family, who with the assistance of a group of boyars governed the country in her son's name. Many of the representatives of the Muscovite nobility, among them two of Vasili III's brothers, were arrested; others were deported or executed. In 1538 Helen died—it was rumored that she was poisoned—but the struggle among the warring boyar groups continued for another 10 years. In this strife the contesting parties displayed great ruthlessness, and acts of brutality were sometimes performed in the presence of young Ivan. On ceremonial occasions he was treated with all external manifestations of extreme deference, but, if his well-known letters to Prince Kurbsky are to be trusted, he was spared no indignities in his day-by-day relations with his advisors and mentors. Gradually, however, Ivan emancipated himself from the influence of the leading boyar families. In January 1547 he was crowned Tsar of All the Russias, assuming officially the title which for decades had been informally used by his predecessors. It is probable that the coronation was engineered by Metropolitan Macarius (1542–1563), a disciple of Joseph of Volokolam and a believer in the principles of semi-theocratic absolutism.

Soon thereafter a fire of undetermined origin swept over Moscow and destroyed much of the city, including portions of the Kremlin. This untoward occurrence was used by the enemies of Ivan's kin, the Glinskys, to bring about their downfall. An angry mob, incited by rumors that the Glinskys had caused the fire, plundered the capital and apprehended and murdered the suspected incendiaries. The elimination of the Glinskys, who were influential in the Moscow government, proved an important turn on the road that led to the undoing of the boyar aristocracy. Shortly after the revolt Ivan appointed a "selected council" which was largely dominated by men of modest social standing and whose advice he followed closely for the next 10 or 12 years.

Ivan the Dread, a contemporary engraving

A Characterization. Ivan IV is a sinister and arresting figure in the history of the Russian Middle Ages. The surname of *Groznyi* (The Dread or The Terrible) by which he is known is fully deserved. Boundless suspicion, insatiable cruelty, and extreme depravity were perhaps his outstanding characteristics and became apparent while he was still an adolescent. Intellectually Ivan was markedly above the level of his contemporaries, and he ranks indeed as one of the most literate of the Russian rulers. His voluminous writings, among which the better known are his messages to Prince Kurbsky, disclose considerable literary ability and familiarity with the theological literature of the day, which he presumably owed to Metropolitan Macarius, his close associate for over two decades. Like the head of the Church, the tsar firmly believed in the doctrine of "Moscow—The Third Rome" and in monarchical absolutism by the grace of God. His writings on this subject qualify him, according to some authorities, as one of the few authors who have made contributions to Russian medieval political theory. Ivan's exalted view of autocracy did not prevent him, however, from seeking election to the Polish-Lithuanian throne when it became vacant after the death of Sigismund II Augustus (1572); simultaneously Ivan promised to maintain, and if necessary to extend, the traditional liberties of the Polish nobility. The Poles and the Lithuanians remained unimpressed.

A devout churchman, Ivan scrupulously observed the complex ritual of Orthodox services and was active in Church affairs. Yet the metropolitans who succeeded Macarius found their tenure of office precarious; some of them (Athanasius, Herman) were merely removed, but others suffered a worse fate; Metropolitan Philip, for instance, was assassinated. Members of the clergy were frequently subject to grievous indignities, as was the case during the punitive expedition against Novgorod in 1570, when churches were desecrated and priests were flogged and tortured. Under the regime of the *oprichnina* (which will be discussed later in this chapter) the tsar's residence of Aleksandrovskaia Sloboda was converted into a lewd and revolting travesty of a monastic order, with Ivan holding the center of the stage.

The family affairs of Ivan were highly irregular. The exact number of his marriages is uncertain but is usually given as from five to seven. His unfortunate spouses either died—Ivan claimed that they were poisoned—or were forced to take the veil. All of them were Russians, but the tsar was eager to establish dynastic ties with the European ruling houses and carried on protracted negotiations towards this end, first with the court of Poland and later with that of England. He was particularly anxious to secure an English bride; nothing, however, came of these efforts.

About 1560 Ivan abruptly dismissed the "selected council" and, obsessed by the notion of treason which he suspected everywhere, instituted a regime of political terror. A very large number of men drawn from every social class, including many who at various times were close to the tsar, perished from untold tortures. Ivan kept lists of his victims and distributed money to churches and monasteries to pray for the rest of their souls. The lists which have been preserved, and which are probably incomplete, contain over 4,000 names. In 1581 Ivan, in a fit of rage, murdered his son and heir, Tsarevich Ivan. The tsar himself died three years later and, according to custom, on his deathbed took monastic vows.

Many ingenious theories have been advanced to explain the fantastic vagaries of Ivan's behavior, yet much of it remains irrational and should be recognized as such.

The Reform

Central Government. The 1550's and the early 1560's brought important changes in the mechanics of the Muscovite government. The initiative for most of these reforms is ascribed to the influence of the "selected council" created by Ivan after the rebellion of 1547 and dominated by the court chaplain, Sylvester, and Alexis Adashev, who came from the service class but was not a member of the boyar aristocracy. The council was in no sense a revolutionary body. It is believed that Metropolitan Macarius, a prelate of unimpeachable conservatism, and Prince Andrew Kurbsky, spokesman for the

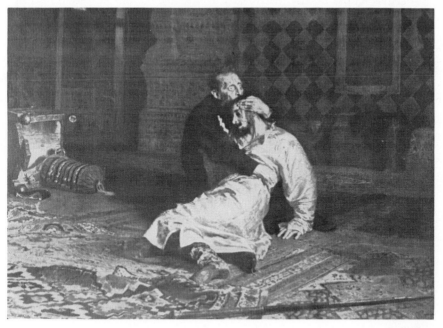

Sovfoto

Ivan the Dread and His Son, by Ilya Repin

great aristocratic landowners, were prominent in this inner circle. Lack of reliable information largely accounts for the variety of interpretations of Ivan's reforms.

Three developments which took place during this period had a bearing on the character and functions of the central government: the alleged limitation of the powers of the Crown introduced by the Code of 1550, the institution of the *zemskii sobor* (consultative assembly), and the rapid growth in the number of *prikazy* (central administrative agencies).

The Code of 1550, which superseded the Code of 1497, was primarily a manual of judicial procedure. Although based largely on the provisions of its predecessor, the Code of 1550 endeavored to discourage the use of customary law in the courts and to substitute for it the wider application of statutory law. The revision of the Code of 1497 was made mandatory by the reform of local government, which will be examined in the next section. The Code of 1550 contained the controversial Article 98, which stated that amendments of the code required examination and approval by the tsar and the affirmative decision of "all boyars." The literal interpretation of this provision would mean the limitation of the legislative power of the Crown, which, to be effective, would require the consent of "all boyars," but no curtailment of the Crown's privileges actually resulted. The Code of 1550 remained in force for 100 years (the next code was adopted in 1649), but no indication of any restriction on autocracy can be detected in the constitutional practice of Ivan after 1550 or in that of his successors. In other words, Article 98 was a mere restatement of the customary rule which provided for the traditional consultation with the boyar *duma* but imposed no constitutional limitations on the Crown.

The story of the *zemskii sobor* is equally controversial. This institution was a consultative assembly of representatives of various social groups convoked by the government in emergencies. It is often said, although without adequate ground, that the first *zemskii sobor* was held in 1550 in connection with the preparation of the new code. According to better-founded opinion, the first and only *zemskii sobor* in Ivan's reign was summoned in 1566 to pass on the peace proposals for the settlement of the war with Lithuania which was then in progress. The *sobor* consisted of representatives of the clergy, the boyar *duma,* the service class (*dvoriane*), and commerce and trade. Somewhat similar consultations were held by the government during the earlier period, although they did not include spokesmen of commerce and trade. The *sobor* functioned in an advisory capacity; its members were not elected but were appointed by the authorities. The *sobor* therefore was not a representative popular assembly and was not entitled to speak on behalf of local interests; it was a gathering of government agents brought together to provide information, tender advice, and carry out decisions. Thus, the *zemskii sobor* did not have in it the beginnings of popular representation, although, of course, it might eventually have evolved in that direction. As will appear later, the *zemskii sobors* which met in the earlier part of the seventeenth century reflected local feelings more accurately than their predecessor; yet this institution never reached the status of an authoritative popular assembly endowed with legislative powers, and it ceased to function at the end of the seventeenth century. To sum up: neither the provision of the Code of 1550 concerning the consent of "all the boyars" nor the convocation of a *zemskii sobor* imposed any limitations on the powers of the Crown or broadened the basis of government.

The territorial expansion of Muscovy, the emergence of a highly centralized form of government, and the destruction of local centers of authority and local institutions called for the establishment of new administrative agencies operating on a national scale. These agencies were bureaucratic bodies known as *prikazy*. They made their appearance early in the sixteenth century and by the end of that century numbered several scores.[1]

Local Government. In the first half of the sixteenth century the administration of provincial Russia consisted of a system of governorships known as *kormlenie*.[2] The holders of this office were appointed by the Moscow grand dukes and later by the tsars and were vested with comprehensive fiscal, administrative, police, and judicial powers, but the Code of 1497 contained few provisions as to how they were to be exercised. The resulting situation invited spoliation and malfeasance and was one of the reasons for the revision of the Code of 1497. Several measures were taken early in the sixteenth century to limit the discretionary powers of the governor, especially in fiscal matters.

The general breakdown of law enforcement suggested the necessity of a drastic change of policy. An important innovation was the transfer of the governor's police and judicial functions to officials elected by the free population of the county (*uezd*). At first the right to elect judicial and police officials was conferred upon the communities which petitioned for and secured a special charter (*gubnaia gramota*),[3] but gradually this practice was extended to the entire land, that is, the election of judicial and police officials ceased to be a privilege granted at the request of the local people and became an obli-

---

[1] See above, p. 81.
[2] See above, p. 67.
[3] The earliest recorded instance of the issuance of such a charter was in 1539.

gation. The community was made jointly responsible for damage that might result from the action of its judicial and police officers, even if (as it sometimes happened) they were appointed by the government and not elected. The communities were also subject to fines in case a local resident was convicted of a crime. The object of these measures was to enroll the population at large—without any cost to the government—in fighting lawlessness, especially banditry.

In 1550-1552 a new form of local self-government, the *zemstvo,* was introduced in the northern provinces, subject to local option. The pertinent legislation provided for the election in each rural locality of several officials, headed by the *zemstvo* elder and vested with fiscal, policy, and judicial powers. *Kormlenie* was officially abolished but actually survived until the end of the seventeenth century. The principal functions of the *zemstvo* officials were collection of taxes and maintenance of peace and order. Local residents were jointly responsible for the performance of the officers whom they elected. Malfeasance of *zemstvo* officials was punishable by death and confiscation of property, and if the latter was insufficient to meet the claims brought against the delinquent officeholder, the community was to make good the deficiency. Many aspects of the *zemstvo* reform are not clear, and the text of the law has not been preserved. Nevertheless, it is reasonably certain that the sixteenth-century *zemstvos,* although elected, were not institutions representing local interests and ministering to local needs. They were rather a crude and burdensome device for collecting tributes and for carrying out the policies of the central government.[4]

The Service Class. One consequence of the unification of Russia was the rapid growth of the service class, which came to be known, collectively, as *dvorianstvo,* usually translated "the nobility." [5] By the beginning of the sixteenth century the distinction between hereditary ancestral estates (*votchina*) and estates held in service tenure (*pomestie*) had disappeared, and all estate owners became subject to the obligation of service.[6] There was, however, much confusion and lack of uniformity in the administration of this system, which the legislation of the 1550's, especially a decree of 1556, attempted to remedy. These enactments endeavored to make precise the obligations of service: the number of men to be provided for the armed forces and their

---

[4] The tendency of Russian historians to idealize the sixteenth-century *zemstvos* may be explained by the fact that the *zemstvo* institutions which were created in 1864 played in the closing decades of the empire a leading part in the promotion of social and cultural welfare as well as in the advancement of liberal and revolutionary ideas (see below, pp. 304-306, 339). These later *zemstvos* had little in common with their sixteenth-century namesake.

[5] *Dvorianin* is singular for a member of this group, *dvoriane* is plural.

[6] See above, p. 82.

equipment were to be determined by the total landholding of the *dvorianin*. Land grants were supplemented by monetary allowances, an arrangement that perhaps antedated the decree of 1556, which confirmed the hereditary character of both the ownership of estates and the obligation of service: the two were interrelated, and failure to serve destroyed the right to the land. The decree of 1556 consolidated much of the earlier legislation and provided new detailed regulations concerning the length, nature, and form of service which a *dvorianin* was expected to render.[7] These obligations remained in force, with but relatively minor modifications, for 200 years, until in 1762 they were done away with by Emperor Peter III.

The concern of the government with the well-being of the service class, which formed the bulk of the armed forces, was reflected in the tightening of the control exercised by the estate owners over the peasant population living on their land. Among the provisions of the Code of 1550 was the confirmation of the rule of the Code of 1497 which restricted the right of the tenants to give up their tenancy to a brief period before and after St. George's Day.[8] It is believed that legislation enacted in the early 1580's, the text of which has not been preserved, went further and abrogated the right of the tenants to relinquish their tenancy during a period known as "forbidden years" (*zapovednyia leta*), the length of which cannot be determined because of the incompleteness of available information. It should be noted, however, that the meaning of the above term is unclear, and there is no agreement on this matter among the authorities.

The Church. The ambitions of Ivan and Metropolitan Macarius inspired by the doctrine of "Moscow—the Third Rome" (and its ecclesiastical counterpart, "Moscow—The Second Jerusalem") account for the intensive activity displayed by the Russian Church during this period. Elated by Moscow's newly-acquired importance as the alleged center of Eastern Christianity (which was assumed to be the consequence of the fall of Constantinople and Byzantium) Macarius embarked upon a comprehensive program designed to eclipse the Church of Rome. An element in this endeavor was the mass canonization of Russian saints which was carried on by several Church councils, beginning with that of 1547. The number of saints added to the calendar was very large, indeed unprecedented in the annals of Christianity.

---

[7] The above legislation might have been influenced by the writings of Ivan Peresvetov, a soldier of fortune born into a Russian family in Lithuania and later enrolled in the Muscovite armed forces. A man of literary ability, Peresvetov believed in monarchical absolutism and was a champion of the service class and an enemy of the boyar aristocracy. In 1549 Peresvetov submitted to the tsar petitions dealing with the reorganization of the army along the lines followed by the legislation of the 1550's.

[8] See above, p. 85.

The tsar and the metropolitan were less successful in implementing the second part of their program—the raising of the avowedly exceedingly low standards of the clergy. This matter was taken up by the so-called "Hundred Chapters" Church council, which met in 1551. The proceedings of the council disclosed the shocking conditions prevailing in the Church and among the clergy: illiteracy, drunkenness, debauchery, indifference to the spiritual and physical welfare of the parishioners, to mention but a few. The council deplored and condemned this situation but did nothing to remedy it except to adopt resolutions which were never acted upon.

The vital issue of ecclesiastical estates remained unsolved. So long as Macarius was alive, he succeeded in protecting Church properties against encroachment by the secular power, although he was compelled to accept the rule that the Church should not acquire new estates without the consent of the tsar. After the death of Macarius in 1563 the position of the Church was weakened. A twice-enacted law (1573 and 1580) prohibited the expansion of ecclesiastical landholding under the threat of confiscation, but this rule was not enforced and the growth of Church and monastic estates continued throughout the seventeenth century.

Mention must be made of the establishment in Moscow of a printing press, which published its first book in 1564; the book's appearance, however, caused a riot in which the press was destroyed. Shortly thereafter a new press was set up by Ivan at his residence of Aleksandrovskaia Sloboda.

Oprichnina

The Tsar Gives Up His Realm. About 1560 Ivan dismissed the "selected council." Adashev was appointed to a minor army command in Livonia, where he soon died: it was rumored that he had committed suicide. The priest Sylvester was exiled to the Solovetsky Monastery on an island in the White Sea. Macarius, who continued to enjoy the confidence of the tsar, died in 1563, and a year later Prince Kurbsky deserted to Lithuania, with which Russia was at war. The explanations of the rise and fall of the "selected council" are many, but none of them is entirely satisfactory. The simplest and least incongruous one, perhaps, is the acceptance of the view that the creation of the council was due more or less to accident and that it fell victim to Ivan's suspicious disposition. It is arguable that the mental condition of the tsar was aggravated by the death in 1560 of his first wife Anastasia Zakharin-Yurev, to whom he was greatly attached and who he believed had been poisoned. Whatever the reason, the severity of Ivan's rule, which was stern enough during the earlier part of his reign, increased markedly after 1560: a great many people, especially members of the upper class, perished at the hand of the executioner. It was during this period that the system of sureties and mutual guarantees of "non-departure" was extensively used.[9] The defection of Kurbsky—a great landowner, high military commander, and trusted advisor of the tsar—is conclusive evidence that the charges of boyar disaffection and treason were not entirely figments of Ivan's imagination. That the Russian nobility should be reduced to such extremes is a telling comment on the conditions prevailing in Muscovy under the rule of Ivan the Dread.

In December 1564, in a dramatic move, the tsar, accompanied by his family and members of his household, left Moscow, ostensibly never to return. The royal caravan, however, did not travel far and settled down in the nearby Aleksandrovskaia Sloboda, which was to serve as Ivan's official residence until the end of his reign. Shortly thereafter Ivan, in messages to the Muscovites, announced his intention to abdicate. He bitterly attacked the boyars and the clergy, whose failings had allegedly forced him to renounce his royal status, but he exonerated the merchants, artisans, and the common people from all responsibility. The not-unexpected result of this curious maneuver was the prayerful request of the Muscovites to Ivan to reconsider his decision and to resume his duties on his own terms. This he agreed to do; the price was a large indemnity to defray the cost of the royal flight, the surrender and execution of the leading boyars, and the creation of *oprichnina,* a royal domain directly controlled by the tsar.

Organization and Meaning of Oprichnina. An ancient term, *oprichnina* signifies an entailed domain and was used to describe the estate settled on the widow of a sovereign prince. The choice of the term was presumably Ivan's own: he liked to think of himself as an orphan or a widower. Under the new dispensation the territory of the nation was split into two parts: *zemshchina* and *oprichnina.* The former was administered by the traditional institutions, from the boyar *duma* down; *oprichnina,* the personal domain of the tsar, had its own administrative agencies independent of those of *zemshchina.*

Oprichnina presumably had two main objectives: the first, of a passing nature, was the extermination of treason; and the second, of lasting significance, was the elimination of the political influence of the landed aristocracy. In pursuit of the former goal the *oprichniki* (as the members of *oprichnina* were called) were actually agents of the security police. This function was emphasized by their appearance; the emblem of their authority was a broom

[9] See above, p. 82.

and a dog's head attached to their saddles. The second objective—the destruction of the influence of the landed aristocracy—was achieved by a mass transfer of the population, a familiar policy used extensively by Vasili II, Ivan III, and Vasili III. The territories assigned to *oprichnina,* including streets in Moscow and other urban centers, were cleared of property-owners and occupants and resettled by the *oprichniki.* The dispossessed owners, among them many boyars and descendants of former sovereign princes, were given estates in service tenure elsewhere, preferably in distant border regions. There was nothing very new in this policy except the magnitude of the scale on which it was applied. The resulting elimination of the influence of the landed aristocracy and the mass transfer of land were the chief political, economic, and social consequences of *oprichnina.*

It must be emphasized again that information on *oprichnina* is fragmentary and that the pertinent legislation has not been preserved. The picture is further blurred by the fact that the sharp distinction between *zemshchina* as the stronghold of the old traditional boyar Muscovy and *oprichnina* as an institution dominated by the new blood of the service class—a distinction stressed in this discussion—is not entirely valid. A great many members of the boyar aristocracy served in the ranks of the *oprichniki,* while Ivan displayed a truly terrifying impartiality in executing, with refined cruelty, both the *zemshchina* boyars and the leading *oprichniki,* including his favorites of yesterday (Alexis and Fedor Basmanov, Prince Athanasius Viazemsky). Aleksandrovskaia Sloboda, Ivan's residence after 1564, was organized along the lines of a quasi-monastic order. In this fortified enclave the tsar and his henchmen divided their time between Church services, on the one hand, and orgies and the torture chamber, on the other. This fantastic state of affairs lasted for years. In 1574 Simeon Bekbulatovich, a Tatar prince converted to Christianity, was installed by Ivan as the Russian tsar. He was crowned and enjoyed the external attributes of power, while Ivan assumed the title of Prince of Moscow. Simeon never exercised any real authority and was eventually deported to Tver. The whole puzzling episode, presumably a comedy, is not easy to reconcile with the exalted view of monarchical absolutism held by Ivan. It is difficult to escape the conclusion that many of Ivan's activities were irrational, the product of a deranged mind.

Was Oprichnina *Abolished?* Oprichnina being what it was—the reshuffling of landed proprietors on a huge scale—it is practically self-evident that the undoing of what was done, that is, the turning back of the wheel of history and the return of the confiscated estates to their former owners, would be an enormous and probably an impossible task. Nevertheless the view was advanced and gained wide acceptance that *oprichnina* was abolished in 1572 and that the sequestrated properties were ordered restored to their pre-1565 owners. Since no legislation abolishing *oprichnina* was ever found, the above opinion is based on conjectures and circumstantial evidence, of which the principal, although not the only, one is the total absence of references to *oprichnina* in the sources after 1572.

The theory that *oprichnina* was dismantled was formulated by reputable Russian historians shortly before World War I, although some of them took the view that the restoration of the pre-*oprichnina* pattern of landholding was a slow process which extended over many years. These reservations were largely dropped by later writers, and references to the abolition of *oprichnina* were made in many studies published in the USSR and in the West during and after the 1930's. In so far as the Soviet historians are concerned, the acceptance of the above theory was presumably an element in the campaign for the rehabilitation of Ivan IV which, it is believed, was instigated by Stalin. *Oprichnina* has traditionally an unsavory connotation, and educated Russians are inclined to take a dim view of this institution. By representing it as a temporary policy used by a far-sighted tsar to destroy the power of wicked and selfish feudal lords in order to achieve political unification on which depended Russia's future greatness, the reputation of Ivan was enhanced. Other historians who profess to admire Ivan IV took the position that the elimination of the old landed aristocracy was dictated by the exigencies of the international situation and that *oprichnina* was a beneficial policy that could not be abandoned. According to the authoritative statement that appeared in a leading Soviet publication (in 1955), "*oprichnina* in its development went through two stages: from 1565 to 1572, when it existed under the name of *oprichnina;* and from 1572 to 1584, when for the appellation of *oprichnina* was substituted that of *dvor.*" The first stage was characterized by stern measures for the suppression of the reactionary boyars and clergy. "The second stage brought about the extension of the *oprichnina* institutions to the entire country. The experience of the *oprichnina* administration and of its organization of the armed forces was applied everywhere." [10] Thus *oprichnina,* far from being scrapped in 1572, was extended over the entire territory of the nation. It is doubtful whether this theory, any more than the opposing one, could be documentally "proved," but the more recent interpretation has the advantage of recognizing that the basic changes wrought by

---

[10] Article on *Oprichnina* in *Bolshaia Sovetskaia Entsiklopediia* (*Large Soviet Encyclopedia*) (Moscow, 1955), vol. 31, p. 92. See also R. Iu. Vipper, *Ivan Groznyi* (*Ivan the Dread*) (Moscow: Institute of History, USSR Academy of Science, 1944), pp. 80, 90, 102-105.

oprichnina were not, and presumably could not be, obliterated by subsequent government orders.

Territorial Expansion, War, and Diplomacy

Kazan, Astrakhan, and the Crimean Tatars. Ivan IV was engaged in numerous wars which were not uniformly successful. Under his rule Moscow acquired by the force of arms important territories in the east, extending its dominion to and beyond the Urals, but it failed to check the Crimean Tatars or to implement the ambitious plans of expansion in Lithuania and the Baltic region. In the first half of the sixteenth century there was intermittent warfare between Moscow and the Tatar successor states—the kingdom of Kazan on the middle Volga, which was established in the 1440's, and the kingdom of Astrakhan on the lower Volga, which was founded after the final disintegration of the Golden Horde. Inner dissensions were rife in these Oriental principalities and were fostered by the Russians. In the late summer of 1552 a large army commanded by Ivan invaded the territory of Kazan and besieged its capital city. The Tatars put up a spirited resistance, and the siege lasted for several weeks; finally, however, Kazan was taken by assault and was incorporated in the Muscovite state. Astrakhan was conquered and annexed in 1556. The dissolution of these two Mongol states did not end the conflict, however, and the struggle for the subjugation of the outlying sparsely-populated regions which were formerly ruled by Kazan and Astrakhan continued for years. The sacrifices involved in these wars were heavy, but the results, measured in terms of territorial aggrandizement, were impressive: the entire basin of the Volga was brought under Muscovite control and gave a powerful stimulus to further expansion. The conquest of Astrakhan also established Muscovy on the littoral of the Caspian Sea, in the proximity of Persia. The long-range effect of the eastward advance of Muscovy was gradually to bring Central Asia and the Middle East within the Russian sphere of interest.

The annexation of Kazan and Astrakhan eliminated the danger of invasion from the east, but the Mongol threat in the south remained. The Crimean Tatars, who were entrenched on the Black Sea isthmus, made frequent raids into the border provinces of Muscovy, Poland, and Lithuania, occasionally penetrating as far north as the Russian capital. What the raiders were after was booty and especially prisoners of war, whom they sold on the slave markets of Asia Minor. Protection against these incursions was a vital task of the Moscow government. To check the invaders a line of fortifications and

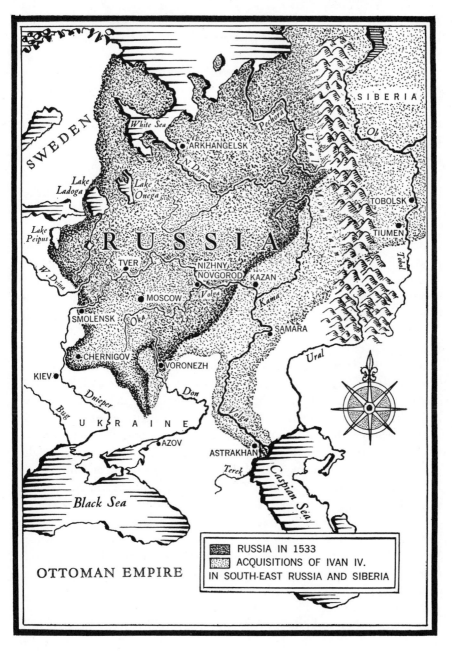

Russian expansion under Ivan IV, 1533–1584

military outposts was thrown along Russia's uncertainly traced southern border. At times Moscow hired, as frontier guards, the Cossacks who lived in the no-man's land of the still unconquered expanse of the Black Sea steppes. The earliest mention of the term "Cossacks" appears in the Russian sources towards the end of the fifteenth century; it was used to describe the shifting group of outlaws, partly of Turkish and Mongol extraction but chiefly fugitives from Russia, Poland, and Lithuania, who were loosely organized into semi-military formations and made a precarious living by brigandage, by fishing and hunting, and by hiring themselves out to whoever cared to pay them. Moscow's competitors for the services of the Cossacks were the other states bordering on the steppes—Poland-Lithuania and Turkey. The protection offered by the Cossack troops was of doubtful efficacy, and their enrollment in the service of Moscow did not remove the danger of Mongol raids. In 1571 the Crimean Tatars invaded Russia, besieged and partly burned Moscow, and drove away perhaps as many as 150,000 prisoners. Another major raid, which, however, was checked before it reached the Russian capital, took place in 1572. Ivan at that time was engaged in a war of conquest in the west.

The Livonian War. Ivan IV shared the ambition of his father and grandfather to restore to Muscovy the western territories which had been annexed by Lithuania. These aspirations were one cause of the continuous friction between Russia and her Western neighbors. In the middle of the sixteenth century the Livonian Order of the German knights, which for over 300 years had held an important section of the Baltic littoral, experienced extreme difficulties which were due to a variety of causes, including the rapid progress of the Protestant Reformation. Ivan and his advisors, who coveted the Baltic ports held by the Germans, judged the moment opportune, and in 1558 the Russian armies invaded Livonia. The Muscovites did well in the opening stage of the campaign, occupied Narva, Dorpat, and other important centers, and besieged Reval. In 1561 the knights, in a desperate plight, dissolved the Order and divided its territory among the neighboring states—except Russia. Kurland became a fief of the Polish Crown, the southern provinces (Livonia proper) went to Lithuania, Estonia was given to Sweden, and the island of Oesel was annexed by Denmark.

With this partition the character of the war was altered, and Russia was confronted with a coalition of Western powers that requested her to withdraw her troops from their recently-acquired territories. This she refused to do, and the war was resumed in the new international setting. Not all the Western countries involved, however, participated in the fighting all the time. At first the principal theater of war was in Lithuania. In 1563 the Russians took Polotsk, the much-coveted capital of the principality of that name, but the next year they suffered a major defeat, and their commanding officer, Prince Kurbsky, fled to Lithuania. A Lithuanian peace proposal requesting Russian withdrawal from Livonia was examined and rejected by the *zemskii sobor* of 1566. The war dragged on, with interruptions, for another decade and a half. Meanwhile the Act of Lublin (1569) converted the personal dynastic union of Lithuania and Poland into a "real" union by merging the grand duchy of Lithuania with the Polish Crown.[11] Russia's principal Western antagonist thus gained in inner coherence and military strength.

However, the death of the Polish king Sigismund II Augustus in 1572 was followed by a period of political turmoil. Ivan was among the unsuccessful candidates to succeed Sigismund. With the election in 1576 of Stephen Batory, prince of Transylvania, as the ruler of Poland-Lithuania, the Livonian war entered into a new phase. Hostilities, which had been temporarily in abeyance, were resumed in 1577. Batory, a capable military leader, won several resounding victories, although he failed to take Pskov. Both countries were exhausted by the long struggle. In January 1582 a Russo-Polish armistice, which was negotiated by the papal envoy Antonius Possevinus, was concluded on the basis of the *status quo ante bellum*. The terms of an armistice with Sweden that followed in 1583 were even less favorable to Moscow. Russia renounced all claims to Estonia and surrendered to Sweden the stretch of the littoral of the Gulf of Finland (from Narva to Lake Ladoga) that she had held prior to 1558—her only foothold on the Baltic. Such were the unrewarding results of the Livonian war that had lasted for a quarter of a century.

Relations with England. It is often held that the true purpose of the Livonian war was to terminate Muscovy's isolation from the West. This objective, however, was achieved—at least in part—several years before that war broke out. In 1553 one of the three ships sent by the Fellowship of English Merchants for the Discovery of New Trades to investigate the possibility of a northern route to India was blown by the arctic gales into the White Sea and landed its crew on the Russian shore. Richard Chancellor, the leader of the expedition, made his way to Moscow, was received by Ivan, and on his return to London became one of the founders of the Muscovy Company, which was given by the tsar valuable trade privileges and the monopolistic right to exploit the northern route. This was the first sustained effort, except

[11] See above, p. 26.

for the Novgorod trade, to maintain commercial relations between Russia and the West. Not everything went smoothly, yet the trade link with England proved rewarding and lasting. Ivan took a strong fancy to the English and pressed Queen Elizabeth and her advisors for a treaty of alliance as well as for an English bride for himself (presumably, she was to be his eighth wife). In these endeavors he did not succeed.

Annexation of Western Siberia. Expansion in western Siberia stands alone (except, perhaps, for Alaska) in the history of Russian colonization because it was achieved in its initial stage by private endeavor with no intervention by the state. The wealthy and powerful Stroganov family had vast trading interests in northeastern Russia and was granted large tracts of land in the upper basin of the Kama River, in the Ural region; they also maintained a private army recruited among the Cossacks. Since the middle of the sixteenth century the rulers of the Siberian nomadic tribes had owed a nominal allegiance to the Muscovite Crown, although their acceptance of Russian rule was tenuous. In 1581 the Stroganovs sent beyond the Urals a detachment of their Cossack mercenaries under the leadership of Ermak Timofeevich. The expedition met with little resistance and by using firearms conquered by 1583 the whole of western Siberia. Ermak's campaign was at first watched with marked disapproval in Moscow as a source of friction with the Siberian natives, but recognition came with success, and the Cossack leader was acclaimed as a great empire builder. The people of Siberia were not at first reconciled with the Muscovite rule: Ermak himself perished in an ambush in 1584. Yet resistance was suppressed, and Russian control over Siberia was maintained and led eventually to expansion in the Pacific area and in Central Asia.

Conclusion

The Price of Unification. The reign of Ivan the Dread was the logical culminating stage of the process of historical development that began with the rise of Muscovy in the early fourteenth century and gained momentum under Vasili II in the middle of the fifteenth. The basic political aspect of this process was the emergence of a unified centralized state governed by an absolute monarchy. The social structure was thoroughly remodeled. The landed aristocracy lost its independence and was reduced to the status of a service class holding estates at the pleasure of the Crown, while the once-free tenant farmers were gradually but inexorably deprived of their precarious freedom and were forced into the position of serfs, although in the closing decades of the sixteenth century they still retained some of the characteristics of freemen. The newly-born Russian absolutism found its theoretical justification in the doctrine of "Moscow—The Third Rome" and "Moscow—The Second Jerusalem," the secular power ruthlessly extending its dominion over the Church. This transformation—and it was a great transformation—was achieved at the price of the destruction of the political and social institutions of medieval Russia which, although imperfect, were the depository of immemorial custom and century-old administrative practice. Viewed against this background *oprichnina* acquires its real significance.

Ivan the Dread, his theories and policies, reflected accurately the final stage of the process of unification and of the establishment of unbridled monarchical absolutism. The tsar's morbid imagination, a product perhaps of an unbalanced mind, gave a sinister twist to many of his activities, but essentially he remained faithful to the historical tradition from which he stemmed. The changes wrought by Ivan IV and his immediate predecessors were revolutionary, and by shattering the political and social framework of the nation they unwittingly contrived the great upheaval that was to overcome Muscovy at the turn of the seventeenth century.

7

The Great Upheaval,
1584-1613

The Background

Social Unrest. The three decades following the death of Ivan the Dread were an exceptionally stormy and eventful period in the life of the nation. It began innocuously enough with the accession of the colorless and insignificant Tsar Fedor but moved rapidly to a dramatic climax with a Polish prince on the Moscow throne and the country torn by civil war and overrun by foreign troops. The very continuation of Muscovy as a national state appeared to hang in the balance, yet Russia survived the ordeal, succeeded in overcoming her disorders, freed herself from foreign invaders, and regained a measure of stability by electing to the throne Michael Romanov, founder of a dynasty that was to last for 300 years.

These tormented decades are known in Russian historiography as *smutnoe vremia;* the accepted English equivalent is "the time of troubles," which, however, is not a good translation. An expression conveying the feeling of bewilderment, unsettlement, and puzzlement connoted by the Russian term would have rendered better the meaning of the original and would have described more accurately the events which took place.

The true cause of the great revolutionary outbreak was the disintegration of the political and social texture of the state brought about by the painful process of unification under Moscow and the Mongol rule. The advent of Muscovite autocracy was accompanied by the destruction of local institutions and far-reaching changes in the position of all social groups. The transformation that took place in the status of the upper class—the former appanage princes, the boyar aristocracy, and the service people—was not strictly comparable to that of the free peasant farmers living on the estates owned by the Crown and large landowners, yet the two developments had important elements in common. In both cases the fourteenth and the fifteenth centuries brought about a marked loss of independence: the landed nobility, including the once-sovereign princes, were reduced to the position of servitors of the Crown dependent on the pleasure of the tsar, while the small tenant farmers lost the right to relinquish their tenancy and were soon to be finally deprived of their status as freemen.

The cumulative deterioration in the position of every social group was aggravated by developments which took place in the reign of Ivan IV: the *oprichnina,* with its mass shifting of landed proprietors and reign of terror, and the crushing financial burdens resulting from the long and futile Livonian war. Faced with mounting restrictions and exactions, the peasants, burghers, and some of the service people sought salvation, as their forefathers had done before them, in flight to the still sparsely-populated eastern territories or to the no-man's land of the southern steppes, where they joined the free communities of the Cossacks.[1] These disaffected and uprooted elements were to play a major part in the revolutionary events of the opening years of the seventeenth century.

Tsar Fedor and Boris Godunov

The Son of Ivan the Dread. Ivan IV was succeeded on the throne by Tsar Fedor (1584-1598), his son by his first wife. A bigot and a retiring and dull-witted man, Fedor made no imprint on the course of Russian history, except that he left no heir, his only daughter having died in infancy; the Moscow branch of the Riurik dynasty thus came to an end. In his reign the strife among the boyars which had been kept within narrow bounds by Ivan IV came again to the fore and led to the disgrace and banishment of several leading aristocratic families, among them the Mstislavskys and the Shuiskys; the Metropolitan Dionysius was removed from office and locked up in a distant monastery. Fedor, however, was prevented by his mental condition from conducting the business of government, and the administration of the affairs

[1] See above, p. 104.

of state was actually in the hands of his brother-in-law Boris Godunov, to whose sister Irene Fedor was married.

Boris Godunov. Boris Godunov came from a family which was close to the Moscow court but did not belong to the old aristocracy. Although not an *oprichnik* he was a favorite of Ivan IV and had reputedly amassed a vast fortune. In the reign of the feeble-minded Fedor, Boris built for himself a position of unchallengeable leadership; his name appeared in official documents next to that of the tsar, and foreign relations were conducted jointly in their name. Often referred to as regent, Boris is believed to have controlled completely the machinery of the government, especially the security policy. It was not surprising, therefore, that after Fedor's death, the head of the Russian Church, who owed his office to Boris, offered him the crown on behalf of the nation. This Boris refused to accept and insisted on the convocation of a *zemskii sobor,* which met in 1598 and duly elected him to the throne; he thus became Russia's first elected tsar.

In spite of the depletion of Moscow's military and financial resources at the end of the reign of Ivan IV, warlike operations continued on the various frontiers. The death in 1586 of Stephen Batory, king of Poland, removed one of Russia's implacable enemies, permitted the conclusion of a 15-year armistice between Muscovy and Poland, and made vacant the Polish throne. The candidacy of Tsar Fedor was advanced but met with no support, and Sigismund III, of the Swedish house of Vasa, was elected king of Poland (1587). Five years later he succeeded his father John II as king of Sweden, thus bringing about the dynastic union of Poland-Lithuania and Sweden, a contingency that Moscow particularly dreaded. However, Sigismund proved exceedingly unpopular in Sweden and was shortly forced to withdraw to his Polish kingdom. The resulting estrangement between Poland and Sweden appeared to favor Moscow. In 1590 the Russians became engaged in a war with Sweden that lasted until 1595 and resulted in the recovery by Moscow of the territories on the shores of the gulf of Finland lost under Ivan IV, but Sweden retained the port of Narva, which was the real object of Russian ambitions.

The advance in western Siberia, where the Cossacks had suffered some reverses in 1584, was resumed as Moscow's hold over this vast territory had been strengthened by the establishment of new military and trading outposts. Raids by the Crimean Tatars into Russian territory continued but were less frequent than in the past; in 1591, however, the invaders reached the outskirts of Moscow before they were repulsed. Russian infiltration in the north Caucasus, which began with the annexation of Astrakhan (1556), continued, and in 1598 Moscow established relations with Georgia.

Significant developments took place in domestic affairs. In the middle of the fifteenth century the Russian Church had emancipated itself from the control of the patriarch of Constantinople.[2] It was felt, nevertheless, in Russian Orthodox circles, especially since the acceptance of the doctrines of "Moscow—The Third Rome" and "Moscow—The Second Jerusalem," that the Russian Church should be headed, like the other Orthodox Churches, by a patriarch rather than by a metropolitan. The Orthodox patriarchs living under the Turkish rule depended largely on Russian bounties and were anxious not to antagonize their benefactors, but they showed no enthusiasm for the establishment of a Russian patriarchate when proposals to this effect were made by Godunov. Taking advantage of the visit to Moscow by Jeremiah, patriarch of Constantinople, who came to Russia in quest of alms, Boris obtained his consent to the elevation of the head of the Russian Church to the rank of patriarch. Job, a nominee of Godunov, was elected by a Russian Church council as the first incumbent of the new office (1589). The Eastern patriarchs, although unconvinced of the canonical validity of the procedure adopted by the Russians, deemed it wise to sanction the change but, contrary to the wishes of Moscow, relegated the new patriarch to the fifth—and last—place among his peers. The creation of the patriarchate was of small practical significance: the Russian Church had long been independent of Constantinople, and the tsars showed no more respect for the patriarchs than they did for the metropolitans who preceded them.

The government was concerned with the mass flight of the population which was a consequence of the political and economic crisis. The Code of 1550 confirmed the provisions of the Code of 1497 extending to the entire peasant population the St. George's Day rule; furthermore, according to some authorities, legislation enacted in the early 1580's suspended altogether the right of the tenant farmers to move away during the so-called "forbidden years" (*zapovednyia leta*). The latter contention is based in part on the provisions of a decree of November 1597, which disallowed action for the recovery of *fugitive* peasants after the lapse of five years. During the famine of 1601–1603 this rule was suspended in so far as it affected tenants living on small estates, a measure which was presumably intended to benefit the smallholders.[3]

During his regency and the first year or two of his reign Boris Godunov

[2] See above, p. 66.
[3] See above, p. 85. The issue of the "forbidden years" is highly controversial. It is possible that by "fugitive" peasants the decree of 1597 meant tenants who had left in contravention of the St. George's Day rule, or without having settled their obligations towards their landlord, or in violation of other regulations. In other words, the reference to "fugitive" peasants in the decree of 1597 is not conclusive evidence that an earlier decree definitely attached the tenants to their plots. It is well to remember that no legal text depriving the tenants of the right to move away has been preserved.

was a popular and seemingly benevolent ruler—accessible, considerate, and kindly. His elevation to the Muscovite throne after the death of Fedor would seem to have been a foregone conclusion, although there were other candidates, among them Fedor Romanov and Bogdan Belsky. In spite of the unanimity of the assembly (*zemskii sobor*) which elected Boris, his position was not too secure. The election of a tsar was an unprecedented occurrence, and there were many members of the Muscovite aristocracy who felt that they had a stronger claim to the throne than did Boris. During the interregnum of 1598 that followed Fedor's death, Godunov showed great nervousness, which was increased by the machinations of the rival boyar groups and outbursts of popular unrest. Opposition continued after the election, and gradually Boris came to suspect subversion and treason everywhere round him and proceeded to exterminate them ruthlessly. Belsky and Romanov were among the first victims of the revival of political terror. The former was tortured and locked up in a distant prison, while Fedor Romanov, accused of sorcery, was forced to take monastic vows and was sent to a remote monastery. His wife took the veil, and his son, Michael, the future tsar, as well as the other members of the Romanov clan, were exiled. Other persecutions followed, the government making extensive use of private informers and, especially, encouraging slaves to spy on their masters. The state of unrest was aggravated by the famine of 1601–1603, which wrought untold ravages and forced more people to take to the road. Many slaves were set free either because the estates of their masters were sequestrated or because their owners could no longer provide for them. The distribution of supplies organized by the government failed to bring real relief, with the result that Godunov's tottering authority was further undermined. At that tragic juncture the harassed Moscow government was confronted with what proved to be a formidable threat: the appearance of the Pretender who claimed to be Tsarevich Dimitry.

The First Pretender

Tsarevich Dimitry. Tsarevich Dimitry was the son of Ivan IV by his seventh wife, Maria Nagoi. In May 1591 he died at the age of nine in the town of Uglich, where he lived with his mother under the surveillance of Boris' agents. According to the official version, which was confirmed by a contemporary investigation carried on by Prince Vasili Shuisky, Dimitry had cut his throat by accident in an attack of epilepsy. There were, however, persistent rumors both in Russia and abroad that the boy had been murdered by orders of Boris, who wished to remove a possible obstacle between himself and the throne. For several years these rumors did not seem to affect Godunov's position or impair his popularity. They certainly did not influence the *zemskii sobor* which elected him to succeed Tsar Fedor in 1598.

The Pseudo-Dimitry. In 1603 there appeared in Poland a young man calling himself Tsarevich Dimitry and claiming to have escaped assassination. Known in history as the first Pretender or the pseudo-Dimitry, he was identified by the Moscow government as Grishka Otrepev, an unfrocked monk and a former bondsman of the Romanov family; however, it was never established who this adventurer actually was. He was well-spoken and well-mannered, knew Polish and Latin, and held his ground well among the Polish aristocracy. The Polish government recognized him as the true Dimitry, lawful heir to the Muscovite throne, and provided him with troops, funds, and the opportunity to organize his movement. Meanwhile the Pretender resided most of the time at the castle of Sambor, on the Dniester River, which was owned by the Polish nobleman George Mniszek. Early in 1604 the Pretender embraced Roman Catholicism; he also became engaged to Marina Mniszek, his host's attractive daughter. His many Polish affiliations and the patronage extended to him by King Sigismund III of Poland and by several Polish magnates suggest that the Pretender might have been primarily the instrument of aggressive Polish policy in the struggle for the domination of Russia. Some of the Polish leaders thought in these terms. Yet it is more likely that the appearance of the pseudo-Dimitry was engineered by Boris Godunov's Russian enemies, probably the disaffected boyar aristocracy led by the Romanovs. The remarkable albeit brief success of his movement in Muscovy indicates that it was basically a Russian phenomenon.

In October 1604 the Pretender, at the head of a small army of some 3,000 to 4,000 men in which Polish soldiers of fortune predominated, crossed into Russia, with Moscow as his objective. He suffered several military reverses at the hands of government troops, but these failed to check his advance, which assumed the character of a triumphant progress. All the social elements hostile to Godunov—and their range was exceedingly wide—hastened to welcome the Pretender as their leader, even though their own aspirations were mutually incompatible. The Cossacks and the runaway peasants who were soon to constitute the bulk of the Pretender's force craved for land and freedom; the service class demanded larger land grants, higher pay, and stricter control over the servile population; and the boyar aristocracy agitated for the return of the good old days and the restoration of its patriarchical rule. The confusion of programs and issues contained the elements of inevitable conflict. Meanwhile the death of Boris Godunov in April 1605 favored the progress of the insurrection. His son and successor, the youthful Fedor Godunov, was murdered a few weeks later in a popular uprising. Vasili Shuisky, reversing his attitude of 1591, as well as many leading boyars, hastened to welcome the Pretender as the true Dimitry. Government troops went over in large numbers to the insurgents. The struggle was over. In June 1605 the Pretender entered Moscow amidst scenes of wild rejoicing.

As the Pretender was unable to reconcile the conflicting aspirations of his heterogeneous following, his popularity proved ephemeral. The Orthodox clergy and laymen resented his Roman Catholicism, tepid as it was, and there was much friction between his Russian and Polish supporters. The aristocratic exiles of the Godunov regime were recalled to the capital, and the monk Filaret—formerly Fedor Romanov—was elevated to the dignity of Metropolitan of Rostov. Vasili Shuisky, his endorsement of the Pretender notwithstanding, became involved in an obscure intrigue which led to his condemnation to death. This sentence, however, was commuted to banishment, and he was soon permitted to return to Moscow. In March 1606 the Pretender married Marina Mniszek, who had arrived in the Russian capital with a large suite of Polish noblemen and Catholic clergy. Shortly thereafter a popular uprising, instigated presumably by the boyars, broke out, and on May 17, 1606, the Pretender was murdered.

Tsar Vasili Shuisky

The Boyar Tsar. Two days later (May 19, 1606) Prince Vasili Ivanovich Shuisky was proclaimed tsar. There was no *zemskii sobor* and no pretense at an election. Shuisky based his case on dynastic grounds as the senior member of a family tracing its descent from Riurik. The announcement of his accession won the tumultous approval of a casual gathering of the Moscow populace summoned by his supporters. The policies of the new government were ultra-conservative. It is unlikely that the vaguely worded promises to refrain from arbitrary persecution made by Tsar Vasili at the time of his accession constituted an actual limitation of his absolute powers or offered a real safeguard to the nobility. Shuisky realized, however, that the murder of the Pretender had solved nothing. Attempts were made to prevent at least the appearance of new impostors. Reversing again his stand on the Uglich events, Tsar Vasili officially confirmed that Dimitry had died in 1591. His "unperishable" remains were found, not without difficulty, in Uglich, and his name was added to the calendar of Russian saints. To believe that the

Pretender was the true Dimitry was to challenge the authority of the Church.

The country rallied around Shuisky far less unanimously than it had a year earlier around the Pretender. There was much friction among the boyar aristocracy, some of its members being heavily compromised (although none more than Shuisky himself) by their support of the pseudo-Dimitry. The removal or demotion of office holders, inevitable as it probably was, created enemies for the new government. Filaret (formerly Fedor Romanov) was made patriarch, but his appointment was immediately rescinded, and he was relegated to his former status of Metropolitan of Rostov; the patriarchate went to Hermogen. The head of the Romanov family and his kin and retainers resented this reduction in rank and tended to side with the enemies of Shuisky.

The Cossacks. The chief opposition to the new regime, however, came from below. Tsar Vasili was cordially disliked by the *dvoriane* and was hated by the Cossacks and the fugitive peasants, who had nothing to expect from a boyar tsar except the knout and forcible return to their masters.

About half of the country refused to recognize the new government, resistance centering in the eastern and southern provinces, while the northern and, to a lesser extent, the western territories sided with Moscow. Peasant uprisings took place in southwestern Russia and elsewhere, and the non-Russian tribes rebelled in the Volga region. Most of these outbreaks were of local significance and were easily suppressed, but the movement, led first by the disgruntled nobleman Prince Gregory Shakhovskoy and later by the Cossack and former slave Ivan Bolotnikov, assumed major proportions. Bolotnikov's sizable Cossack army was joined by detachments of the *dvoriane* commanded by the brothers Zakhar and Prokopi Liapunov. In October 1606 this combined force advanced towards Moscow, which it failed to take by assault and which was besieged. Meanwhile Bolotnikov issued inflammatory proclamations inciting the peasants and slaves to rise against their masters. These appeals met with wide response, but they also frightened the *dvoriane,* who, as landowners and slaveowners, were no supporters of social revolution. The Liapunov detachments, therefore, went over to Shuisky. In December 1606 Bolotnikov and his Cossacks were defeated by government troops and were forced to withdraw, first to Kaluga and then to Tula. Hostilities continued; the insurgents fought with desperate courage, but with the fall of Tula in October 1607 they were compelled to surrender; both Bolotnikov and Shakhovskoy were made prisoners. Shuisky's armies overran the insurgent provinces, wiping out with extreme harshness local centers of disaffection. Somewhat earlier measures were taken to discourage the flight of the peasantry. A decree of March 9, 1607, extended to 15 years the time during which action could be brought for the recovery of runaway peasants [4] and imposed heavy fines for the harboring of fugitives. These provisions were a major concession to the wishes of the smallholders among the *dvoriane*.

The Second Pretender. The policies outlined above were an attempt to quell public unrest by armed force and police measures, but they did nothing to remedy the causes of the ferment and therefore failed to attain their objective. The spectacular, even though short-lived, success of the first Pretender invited emulation. A number of impostors masquerading under fancy names made their appearance during these troubled years. They were easily disposed of and, with one exception, left no imprint on Russian history.

The exception was the so-called second Pretender, who appeared in Poland in the summer of 1607 and claimed to be the Dimitry who had escaped assassination in Moscow in May 1606; nothing is known about his identity. Although his story was generally disbelieved, he was recognized by Marina as her husband [5] and found many adherents, his movement being launched at an opportune moment. King Sigismund of Poland was angered by the misadventures of his countrymen in Moscow and was determined to teach the Russians an exemplary lesson. He had just succeeded in defeating the dissenting factions of the Polish nobility and had consolidated his own rule. The protracted Polish civil war had left in its wake a large body of uprooted men eager to join almost any military venture. A campaign in Russia appeared to many as providential. The second Pretender, unlike his predecessor, depended chiefly on Polish troops. His army comprised large well-trained and well-equipped units commanded by the Polish magnates Jan Sapieha (7,500 men) and Prince Roman Rozynski (4,000 men). His Russian following consisted at first of the remains of the Bolotnikov force, other Cossack detachments under Ivan Zarutsky, and various disaffected elements organized by Alexander Lisowski.

The Pretender, at the head of these troops, crossed into Russia in the spring of 1608, inflicted a defeat on government armies at Bolokhov, and after an unsuccessful thrust at Moscow, established his headquarters within easy reach of that city, at the village of Tushino. Located on the high bank of the Moscow River, Tushino for the next two years played the part of Russia's second capital. While the siege of Moscow, which was never fully effective, continued, the insurgents overran the northern provinces, which had been previously spared by the civil war. The depredations of the Cossacks and

---

[4] It was formerly five years; see above, p. 111.
[5] Marina Mniszek was detained in Russia after the assassination of the first Pretender.

the Poles provoked a strong movement of resistance and led to the formation of a popular militia (*opolchenie*) which by the spring of 1609 largely succeeded in clearing the invaders from the northern and the eastern territories. Meanwhile Tsar Vasili Shuisky signed with Sweden (February 1609) an agreement by virtue of which Moscow ceded to that country the Russian-held areas on the shores of the Gulf of Finland in return for Sweden's promise of military support against the Pretender. In fulfillment of this agreement a foreign corps of some 15,000 men drawn from many countries (Sweden, the German principalities, England, Scotland, France) and commanded by a Swedish general was dispatched to Novgorod, where it joined a Russian army under the orders of Prince Michael Skopin-Shuisky (a nephew of Tsar Vasili). In the spring of 1609 these troops advanced towards Moscow, restoring on their way the control of the central government over the territories formerly held by the insurgents.

The inconclusive character of the Pretender's military campaign and the agreement between Moscow and Sweden, whom the Polish government regarded as its enemy, were responsible for direct Polish intervention. In September 1609 a large Polish army led by King Sigismund entered into Russian territory and besieged Smolensk, which, however, resisted enemy pressure with great fortitude for 21 months. The entry of Poland in the war precipitated the disintegration of the Pretender's movement. Sigismund directed the Polish commanders and troops at Tushino to join the Polish army that was besieging Smolensk. Some of the Poles serving with the Pretender had only recently fought against Sigismund in the Polish civil war, and not all of them complied with the king's request. Nevertheless, friction between the Pretender and his Polish supporters mounted, and in January 1610 he abandoned Tushino and with the Cossacks and some Polish troops withdrew to Kaluga, while the bulk of his Polish followers went over to Sigismund.

The Dethronement of Shuisky. As the crisis deepened and the ineptitude of the Shuisky rule became patent, the idea of a Polish tsar gained ground. Negotiations for the accession to the Muscovite throne of Wladyslaw, son of Sigismund, were initiated by Russian boyar circles in 1605. Nothing was done about it, however, until February 1610, when a group of Tushino notables led by Filaret Romanov, whose position was somewhat equivocal (he was simultaneously a "prisoner" of the insurgents and their revered patriarch), concluded with Sigismund an agreement that bestowed the Russian crown on Wladyslaw but provided for the continuation of Muscovite state and Church institutions. The removal of Shuisky was clearly the prerequisite for the implementation of the agreement. Sigismund being detained by the siege of

Smolensk, the Polish hetman Stanislas Zolkiewski was assigned the task of subjugating Moscow.

In spite of these ominous developments the position of the Shuisky government in the spring of 1610 appeared to be improved. Sigismund was bogged down before Smolensk. Prince Michael Skopin-Shuisky and the Swedish expeditionary corps freed the western provinces from the insurgents and in March made a triumphant entry into Moscow. Prince Michael enjoyed extraordinary popularity that might well have proved his undoing: he died in April of a mysterious ailment, and it was rumored that he was poisoned. Muscovy lost an able commander, and the large Russian-Swedish army that was to stop Zolkiewski's Polish legions was led by Prince Dimitry Shuisky, a brother of Tsar Vasili and reputedly a mediocre soldier. Under his undistinguished leadership the Muscovites and their allies, in spite of their numerical superiority, suffered a rout in the battle of Klushino (June 24, 1610). The foreign mercenaries at first gave a good account of themselves but, finding no support from the Russians, went over to the Poles, the Swedes withdrawing eventually to the Novgorod region, which they occupied. In one stroke (or nearly so, for there were negotiations between the Swedes and the Russians) Tsar Vasili lost both his army and his allies. The road to Moscow lay open. Zolkiewski and the Pretender, who abandoned his Kaluga quarters, advanced to the capital, which was in the throes of political turmoil. Filaret had been in Moscow since May. He was intercepted by government troops while making his way from Tushino to Sigismund's camp near Smolensk and was feted by the Muscovites as a distinguished prisoner liberated from captivity. He and other boyar leaders had a part in instigating the uprising of the Moscow populace which forced the abdication of Tsar Vasili: on July 17, 1610, he was compelled to take the vows and was incarcerated in a monastery in the Kremlin; his wife became a nun and his brothers were arrested. A boyar *duma* (council) of seven members presided over by Prince Fedor Mstislavsky was constituted as a provisional government.

The Poles in the Kremlin

A Polish Tsar. The provisional government, with the Pretender and Zolkiewski on its doorsteps, was faced with the prospect of fighting simultaneously a civil war and an international war, but it had no troops and saw little chance of raising an army. Thus the choice was to be made between a Polish tsar, who would presumably adhere to the traditional ways, and the Pretender, who represented the forces of discontent and social change. Even the most skeptical and cynical among the Muscovite boyars probably believed that a foreign tsar was the lesser evil. (It is well to recall that nationalism was a far less potent social and political factor in the sixteenth and seventeenth centuries than it is today and that it was customary to have foreign rulers on the throne; nowhere was the practice more prevalent than in neighboring Poland.) The Pretender was clearly an impostor; no good could be expected from him and his Cossacks, and no national leader of any stature had emerged from the great turmoil. It was not surprising therefore that the boyars decided in favor of a Polish ruler. After that, events moved swiftly. A *zemskii sobor* of a kind met in the capital, and after electing Wladyslaw to the throne, the oath of allegiance to the new tsar was administered to the Moscow populace. A Moscow-Polish agreement of August 1610 confirmed and extended the guaranties for the preservation of Russian institutions accepted by the Poles in the February agreement with Tushino leaders.[6] Zolkiewski fulfilled his part of the bargain: he defeated the Pretender and forced him to withdraw again to Kaluga, while the Polish troops occupied Moscow.

Here, however, the real difficulties began. A huge Russian delegation of over 1,200 members headed by Filaret and other prominent Muscovites journeyed to Sigismund's camp near Smolensk to make arrangements for the arrival of Wladyslaw and to secure the acceptance of additional conditions, including Wladyslaw's conversion to Greek Orthodoxy. After the excesses of Ivan IV and years of civil strife the Moscow aristocracy was longing for a self-effacing and pliable foreign monarch who would interfere as little as possible with Russian affairs. The tsar-elect, a boy of fourteen, fitted well into the part which was intended for him, but his father had very different plans for Muscovy's future. Sigismund wished to govern Russia himself; he requested that the election of Wladyslaw be put aside and that he be elected in his place. The members of the delegation who refused to comply with this demand were roughly handled and were deported to Poland; Filaret was among them. Zolkiewski was replaced in Moscow by Alexander Gosiewski, a Polish proconsul of stern mettle. He displayed total contempt for Russian institutions and customs and unceremoniously dismissed Russian officials, whom he replaced with men of his choice. The inevitable consequence of these policies was the awakening of anti-Polish sentiment. Patriarch Hermogen encouraged resistance by forbidding the believers to take the oath of allegiance to a Roman Catholic tsar. He was imprisoned by the Poles and died in captivity, or was murdered, in January 1612.

The Anti-Polish Movement. The second Pretender was assassinated in

[6] See above, p. 117.

Kaluga in December 1610. His death eliminated one obstacle to the unification of the anti-Polish forces, although the tradition of social revolution survived among those Cossacks who transferred their allegiance to the Pretender's infant son Ivan, born to Marina soon thereafter.

The origins of the movement for the ejection of the Poles cannot be
traced with precision. Messages of Patriarch Hermogen denouncing the
Polish rule and first circulated in the middle of 1610 exercised considerable
influence. An early center of resistance was Riazan, where in January 1611 the
local governor (*voevoda*) Prokopi Liapunov proceeded to form detachments
of the militia consisting chiefly of the *dvoriane*. He endeavored to broaden
the social base of the movement by appealing to the Cossacks, the peasantry,
and the slaves, to whom he promised redress of their grievances. These ex-
hortations struck a responsive chord. Liapunov established friendly relations
with the former Tushino Cossacks led by Prince Dimitry Trubetskoy and
with other Cossack groups commanded by Zarutsky. The example of Riazan
was emulated in other localities, and gradually there came into being a broad,
informal, and loosely-knit federation of Russian cities united by the desire
to get rid of the Poles. By the middle of March 1611 the bulk of the militia detachments converged upon Moscow. In spite of a popular uprising, of a huge
fire that destroyed much of the capital, and of some sanguinary fighting, the
Russians were unable to dislodge the small Polish garrison entrenched in the
walled section of the city. The attempt to take Moscow by assault was not
renewed, the militia marking time and wrangling with insoluble domestic
issues. The outcome of long-drawn acrimonious negotiations was the so-
called "Decision" of June 30, 1611, which established a provisional government consisting of Liapunov, Trubetskoy, and Zarutsky. This curious document, which was never made fully effective, was imbued with the spirit of
rigid conservatism and distrust of the masses. The nobility was to retain its
privileges, the peasants were to be returned to their lords, and the Cossacks
were to be put under the control of the *dvoriane*. The "Decision" was thus
the negation of Liapunov's promises to the Cossacks and to his peasant followers. Retribution came quickly: on July 22 Liapunov was murdered by the
Cossacks. This was the signal for the disintegration of the movement. The
dvoriane, forgetting about the struggle for liberation from the foreign yoke,
hastily returned to their estates, and although Trubetskoy, Zarutsky, and their
Cossacks continued the siege of Moscow, the nation-wide crusade against the
Poles appeared to be over.

A consequence of the civil war was severe setbacks which endangered
Muscovy's territorial integrity. Pskov, rebelling against Tsar Vasili Shuisky,

proclaimed its independence. Early in June 1611 Smolensk finally surrendered to Sigismund, and in July of the same year Novgorod, which was occupied by the Swedes, broke off its ties with Moscow and accepted Swedish sovereignty. The partition of Russia among its Western neighbors became a distinct possibility.

Eviction of the Poles. In the summer of 1611 the outlook for the movement of liberation was unpromising. Yet the experience of Liapunov in 1606 and again in 1611 had taught the would-be Russian national leaders a useful lesson, namely, that collaboration between the proprietary groups and the Cossacks was not feasible.

The collapse of the Liapunov militia, discouraging as it was, spurred the country to fresh efforts. The beginnings of the new liberation movement, which was to prove fruitful, were exceedingly modest. In October 1611 Kuzma Minin, a Nizhni-Novgorod butcher and local government official, pleaded with his fellow townsmen to take common action for the restoration of order. Minin was a man of ability, conviction, and perseverance, and his preaching was surprisingly successful. The object of the movement was to free the land of both the Poles and the Cossacks and, eventually, to elect a Russian tsar. To achieve this purpose Minin and the Nizhni-Novgorod burghers and *dvoriane* proceeded to organize a militia which was provided with an adequate political and financial backing. Prince Dimitry Pozharsky, a soldier wounded in a recent encounter with the Poles, became commander of the troops, but Minin retained control over the financial and civilian administration. The initiative of Nizhni-Novgorod met with support in the eastern and northern provinces, where the intrusions of the Poles and the Cossacks were greatly resented, and later in other parts of the country as well. By the beginning of 1612 the movement acquired a nation-wide character.

Restoration of order as interpreted by the proprietary groups was not a program that would commend itself to the Cossacks. One of their leaders, Zarutsky, relinquished his encampments near Moscow and advanced with his men towards Yaroslavl in an attempt to cut off communications between Nizhni-Novgorod and the northern provinces. He failed in this endeavor, but civil war, that is, fighting between the militia and the Cossacks, was resumed. From March to August 1612 Yaroslavl was held by Minin and Pozharsky, and the militia extended its control over the northern provinces while the Cossacks continued the siege of Moscow. A *zemskii sobor* convened in Yaroslavl, and plans were made for the election of a new tsar without waiting for the liberation of Moscow, when it became known in August that Hetman Jan Chodkiewicz at the head of a Polish corps was approaching the Russian capital to rescue his besieged countrymen. Pozharsky realized that the lifting of the siege and the strengthening of the Polish hold on Moscow might well prove fatal to his own enterprise. Without making peace with the Cossacks he advanced with his troops to the besieged city, where, side by side, the two hostile Russian forces faced the common enemy.

The resulting highly confused situation led to the breakdown of the Cossack front. The more intransigent Cossack elements under Zarutsky withdrew first to Kolomna and then to Riazan and Astrakhan. The Cossacks who continued the siege of Moscow were commanded by Prince Trubetskoy. Chodkiewicz's first attempt at getting men and supplies into the Kremlin was successful partly because Trubetskoy hesitated to support the militia. An agreement between Pozharsky and Trubetskoy, which was concluded late in September or early in October, brought about a measure of cooperation between the two factions, but it never worked satisfactorily and frequent conflicts continued. In the meantime the Poles, reduced to extremes by siege, were at the end of their rope and finally surrendered on October 22, 1612. Sigismund's belated attempt to recapture Moscow in December was repulsed by the Russians. The capital, if not the borderland, was freed of the invaders. It may be noted that while the militia dealt effectively with bands of marauders, it took but a minor part in fighting the Poles, which was largely done by the Cossacks.

Election of Michael Romanov

What Next? Important as was the reconquest of the capital, the capitulation of the small, exhausted Polish garrison did not signify the end of Muscovy's troubles. The Poles were still in Smolensk, the Swedes in Novgorod, and the rulers of these two countries had claims or designs on the Russian throne. The Cossacks were unmanageable and unruly, and much of the land was in a state of rebellion or near-rebellion. Public authority everywhere was in abeyance. The militia, having fulfilled its immediate task—liberation of Moscow—disintegrated, and its members returned hastily to the provinces. This was the situation with which the ramshackle government of Pozharsky, Minin, and Trubetskoy that took over the conduct of public affairs on the morrow of the Polish defeat had to deal. Its immediate endeavor was the restoration of a central authority clothed at least with the appearance of power.

The New Dynasty. After some delays due to the disinclination of the provinces to send delegates, a *zemskii sobor,* believed to be the most representative assembly of this kind ever to foregather in the Russian capital, convened in Moscow in January 1613. There were numerous candidates: several foreign princes—Polish, Swedish, and German; Ivan, the infant son of the second Pretender and Marina, who had the backing of the Cossacks; and an array of Russian noblemen, including Pozharsky, who appeared eager to secure election. In spite of the multiplicity of the candidates the deliberations of the assembly were relatively brief: Michael Romanov was elected on February 7 and was proclaimed tsar a fortnight later. His election bore the earmark of a compromise, as foreign princes and the candidates of the extreme conservative and the extreme radical groups were unacceptable to the majority of the assembly. The Romanov family was long associated with the Moscow court and was related by marriage to Ivan IV. These considerations won for Michael the support of conservative delegates. On the other hand Filaret, Michael's father, was on good terms with the left-wing faction of the insurgents: he was made metropolitan of Rostov by the first Pretender and patriarch by the second Pretender and had lived long in Tushino, the second Pretender's capital. The Cossacks therefore were willing to support his son. The fact that at the time of the election Filaret was detained in Poland worked to Michael's advantage. Imprisonment conferred an aura of martyrdom upon the senior member of the Romanov family and, what was more important, provided the guarantee of his non-interference with the affairs of state at least for some time to come. The strongest argument in favor of Michael was his insignificance. A timid and physically backward boy of sixteen, he was unlikely to exercise any personal influence on the conduct of the business of government. This is exactly what the constituent assembly of 1613, like its predecessor which elected Wladyslaw in 1610, desired.

Michael's whereabouts were not known at the time of his election. Discovered, not without difficulty, in a convent where he lived with his mother, he accepted election in March and was crowned in Moscow on July 11, 1613.

Some Conclusions

The Revolution That Failed. Perhaps the most striking aspect of the dramatic events through which Russia lived at the turn of the sixteenth century was their failure to leave any lasting imprint on her political, social, and economic structure. The powers of autocracy suffered no diminution. The service class (*dvoriane*), which for some time had been merging with and superseding the old landed nobility, retained and consolidated the leading position that it had attained in the previous centuries, while the masses of the farmers found themselves in a state of dependence on the landlords that was greater than before and was soon to be formalized in serfdom.

The Cossacks, who seemingly held the destinies of the nation in their hands, gained nothing, except that a small minority among them was permitted to organize into semi-autonomous communities on the southern and eastern fringe of the Russian world. But the vast majority, unless they succeeded in escaping into the no-man's land of the southern steppes, had to share the fate of fugitive peasants and were turned over in bondage to landowners.

Oddly, the great upheaval aggravated the conditions which brought it about. By 1613 the uprising, which had the elements of a peasant war, was suppressed or petered out, but the social and economic inequities which had caused it remained; so inevitably did their consequences. Peasant unrest expressing itself in sporadic revolts forms the somber background of Russian history in the seventeenth, eighteenth, and nineteenth centuries and was probably the decisive factor in the revolution of 1917.

8

The Seventeenth Century,
I

The Tsars Michael, Alexis, and Fedor

Mediocrity of Leadership. The first tsars of the House of Romanov, who had to face the formidable task of reconstruction after the great upheaval, had in common certain traits which may help to explain the drab and uninspiring character of this period. Like two of their immediate predecessors on the Russian throne—Fedor Godunov and Wladyslaw—Michael Romanov and the monarchs who followed him in the seventeenth century were, on their accession, adolescents or children; and with the exception of Peter, whose reign began at the very end of the century, they were men of exceedingly limited gifts, devoid of intelligence, vision, ambition, or ability to conduct the affairs of state. They were mere figureheads, the business of government being carried on in their name by their favorites, who seldom held authority for any length of time. The unenlightened and casual nature of leadership accounts, in part, for the absence of any real progress in the art of government or of any betterment in the economic conditions and cultural standards during this period.

Tsar Michael. Tsar Michael (1613–1645), a shy and unprepossessing youth of sixteen, received hardly any education and manifested no inclination to exercise the functions of his office. During the opening years of his reign he was under the domination of his mother (known as Sister Martha after she was forced to take the veil by Boris Godunov) and her numerous relatives, who used power for enrichment and advancement of personal ambitions. In 1619 Michael's father Filaret was released from Polish imprisonment and returned to Moscow. He was elevated to the patriarchate, an office that he had held under the second Pretender but which officially had remained vacant since the death of Hermogen in 1612. Unlike his son, Filaret was ambitious and authoritarian. With his return to Moscow Martha and her kin were relegated into the background, Filaret assuming the conduct of public affairs. He used the title of "Majesty" (*velikii gosudar*) and was designated as Michael's co-ruler and the leading member of the governing diarchy. His position was analogous to that of Boris Godunov under Tsar Fedor, but his powers were even greater, and the fact that the dominant member of the diarchy was not only the tsar's father but also the head of the Russian Church gave the government the appearance of a theocracy and, indeed, contributed to the legend of "Holy Russia." Such an interpretation, however, is unwarranted. Filaret was not a statesman, he cared little about the Church, and like the favorites who preceded and those who followed him, his main concern was securing petty personal advantages and favors for his proteges. With Filaret's death in 1633 the diarchy came to an end. The kin of Sister Martha returned to power, and the new patriarch, Joasaph, was a compliant servitor of the Muscovite Crown. The notion of the supremacy of the spiritual over the temporal power, which seemingly found its embodiment in the Michael-Filaret diarchy, was alien to Russia's historical tradition. The short-lived ascendancy of Filaret was but a historical accident. An attempt to duplicate this situation under Tsar Alexis ended, as we shall see, in the defeat of the Church.

Tsar Alexis. Michael was succeeded by his only son Alexis (1645–1676), a boy of sixteen. Although the youthful tsar received but the most rudimentary schooling, which ended when he was ten, he was literate as well as literary-minded and even tried his hand, admittedly without much success, at writing poetry. An extreme conservative, a devout churchman, a firm believer in the divine origin of his power, often exceedingly coarse in his relations with others, Alexis was kind-hearted and capable of generous impulses and at times displayed surprising tolerance, especially with people tried by misfortunes. His palace, an untidy establishment, was crowded with dwarfs, giants, and other freaks of nature; he was particularly fond of a mild variety of imbeciles, known as *iurodivyi,* who are revered by pious Russians as enjoying special divine protection. His rigid conservatism notwithstanding, Alexis adopted, under the influence of his favorites, innovations which were departures from the tradition of the Kremlin. He permitted the installation of foreign furnishings, maintained an orchestra and a theatrical company, allowed the tsarina and his daughters greater freedom than was customary in the past, and entrusted the education of his children to Simeon Polotsky, a cleric known for his liberalism and learning. A conscientious ruler, Alexis endeavored to fulfill the duties of his office, but he was interested only in the external attributes of kingship, and, as a historian of this period put it, the tsar's time was fully occupied by the performance of the complex Church and palace ritual as prescribed by custom. Meanwhile the machinery of government was run by the bureaucracy, with occasional guidance from an ambitious or public-minded favorite.

Tsar Fedor. Alexis died suddenly at the age of 47. He was married twice, first to Maria Miloslavsky and after her death to Nathalie Naryshkin, and was survived by three sons and six daughters. The two elder sons, Fedor and Ivan, were by his first wife, and the youngest, Peter, the future emperor, by the second. Alexis was succeeded by Fedor (1676–1682), a boy of fourteen whose age and delicate health precluded his taking an active part in the business of government. The country was ruled again by favorites, whose position was made all the more precarious by the struggle for power between the rival Miloslavsky and Naryshkin families. With the death of Fedor this struggle came to a head.

The Regency of Sophie

The Two Tsars. Old Muscovy had no law of succession, but custom pointed to the eldest son of the deceased tsar or, if none were available, to the nearest senior male relative as the next ruler. Fedor died childless and was survived by a brother, Ivan, aged fifteen, and by a half-brother, Peter, aged ten. Ivan was feeble-minded and an invalid, while Peter showed physical strength and mental vigor far beyond his age. These physical and mental traits mattered little, however: the Miloslavskys rallied to the support of Ivan and the Naryshkins to the support of Peter. An unprecedented development was the appearance at the center of the political stage of Tsarevna Sophie, daughter of Tsar Alexis by his first wife and therefore a member of the Miloslavsky clan. Sophie, like her brother Tsar Fedor, was a pupil of Simeon Polotsky and, according to the standards of her time, was an exceptionally well-educated woman. Twenty-five years of age at the time of Fedor's death, she was physically very unattractive, intelligent, and immensely ambitious. She was infatuated with Prince Vasili Golitsyn, an intimate of the Tsars Alexis and Fedor, and it is believed that this passion largely accounts for her determination to assume power.

Taking advantage of the confusion that prevailed after Tsar Fedor's death (April 27, 1682), the Naryshkins engineered the accession of the boy Peter, which was confirmed by a *zemskii sobor* of a most questionable complexion. That the claims of Ivan were set aside created consternation in the Miloslavsky camp, which dreaded the advent of the Naryshkins. Expecting persecution and exile the Miloslavskys decided to fight and found their leader in Sophie, who feared, with good reason, that she would be incarcerated in a convent if the Naryshkins had the upper hand. Sophie and her confederates used as their weapon the *streltsy*,[1] a medieval semi-military formation whose members nursed real or imaginary grudges against the government. In the middle of May the *streltsy*, instigated by the agents of the Miloslavskys and spurred by promises of reward, repeatedly invaded the Kremlin and assassinated most of the members of the Naryshkin family, as well as their political associates, although Tsarina Nathalie and Peter were not molested. The movement exceeded the bounds of a palace revolution, however, and for a while assumed the character of a mass popular uprising directed against the upper class. These excesses notwithstanding, Sophie kept her promises and showered gifts of money and honorary distinctions on the mutinous soldiery. At the end of May a casual assembly represented as a *zemskii sobor* revised the decision of its predecessor: Ivan was made *the first* and Peter *the second* tsar, an arrangement allegedly inspired by Providence and based on Egyptian and Byzantine precedents. Simultaneously Sophie, at the request of the *streltsy*, agreed to accept the regency until the boy-tsars were of age. Her road to power was inglorious and bloody, but she achieved her immediate major objectives.

The Rule and Fall of Sophie. Great as was Sophie's triumph, it contained important elements of weakness: her tenure of office depended on the uncertain support of the *streltsy* and was to end when Ivan and Peter reached maturity, that is, within a few years.

The *streltsy* were restless, violent, and poorly disciplined. Many of them were deeply involved in the movement of the old-believers that split the Russian Church and had far-reaching political and social repercussions.[2] The easy success of the mutiny of May 1682 tended to give the *streltsy* an exaggerated opinion of their importance and made them particularly exacting and unmanageable. Conflicts between the government of Sophie and the military

[1] See below, p. 140.
[2] See below, pp. 152–154.

force on which its power rested began at once and continued throughout the entire period of the regency, which lasted for seven years. Both concessions and stern measures of repression were tried but with little success: the *streltsy* remained unruly and rebellious. It was their defection that finally brought about Sophie's fall.

The difficulties inherent in the position of the regent were aggravated by the general state of popular unrest prevailing during this period and by the government's ill-advised and unfortunate domestic and foreign policies. The first three Romanovs did nothing to improve the conditions of the masses and to check the growth of discontent caused by the advancement of serfdom, which was the true cause of the great upheaval at the turn of the century. Schism in the Church which began in the reign of Alexis added another powerful strain to the suppressed but ever-present movement of rebellion. Although Prince Vasili Golitsyn, Sophie's principal advisor, was reputedly one of the best-educated men in Russia and an avowed supporter of Western ideas, no liberal influence can be detected in the domestic policies of the regency. In dealing with the momentous issues of the day—peasant unrest and schism in the Church—Moscow fell back on the familiar methods of police control and the knout. The campaigns of 1687 and 1689 against the Crimean Tatars, in which the Russian troops were commanded by Golitsyn, were failures, and Sophie's efforts to represent them as great victories merely contributed to the unpopularity of the government at home and created embarrassment abroad. The predilection of Golitsyn for Western ways, especially his association with the Jesuits, antagonized conservative and traditionalist circles.

Sophie's provisional status as regent and her determination to retain power were bound to bring her in conflict with her brother and half-brother. Although Ivan was the older of the two, he caused little concern, because he was an invalid and a moron and, like Sophie, belonged to the Miloslavsky clan. The case of Peter was different. Physically developed far beyond his age, he showed surprising vigor and initiative. After the bloody events of May 1682 he was left largely to his own devices and most of the time lived with his mother in the village of Preobrazhenskoe, near Moscow. His schooling was perfunctory, and he spent his time in quasi-military exercises with a band of adolescents known as *poteshnye,* who in the early 1690's (that is, after the fall of Sophie) were reorganized as the regiments of the guards. There was much hostility between Sophie and her supporters on the one hand and Tsarina Nathalie and the surviving members of the Naryshkin family on the other.

Sophie was determined to get rid of the nominal regime of Ivan and Peter and have herself proclaimed Muscovy's autocratic ruler. In August 1689 she endeavored to organize a *coup d'état* with the assistance of the *streltsy* but met with little response. Peter was forewarned and escaped to the fortified Troitsko-Sergievsky Monastery near Moscow, where he was joined by his *poteshnye,* loyal troops, and Church and civil dignitaries. The *streltsy* leaders and others who sided with Sophie were arrested and executed, Golitsyn was dismissed and deported, and the regent was incarcerated in a convent.[3]

With the elimination of Sophie the control of public affairs passed into the hands of the Naryshkins, as Peter was still too young and inexperienced to impose his leadership. Formally, the diarchy continued to function until 1696, when Ivan died. With his demise Peter became the sole occupant of the Russian throne.

Foreign Relations

The Morrow of the Great Upheaval. The capitulation of the Moscow Polish garrison in October 1612 and the election of Michael Romanov to the throne some three months later marked a turning point on the road leading to the restoration of order and stability, but there was still a long way to go before Muscovy's relations with neighboring foreign powers recovered a degree of normalcy. In 1613 Poland held Smolensk and Sweden held Novgorod, and princes of the ruling houses of these two countries had claims on the Russian throne. There was also much domestic unrest, especially among the Cossacks and the peasants.

The Swedish Wars. The process of liquidation of foreign intervention proved protracted and costly. In dealing with Sweden Moscow was helped by the failure of the Swedish attempt in 1615 to take Pskov and especially by the fact that King Gustavus Adolfus of Sweden became engrossed in vast plans of conquest in central Europe and was therefore anxious to wind up the Russian war. Negotiations initiated through the intermediary of England and Holland led to the peace of Stolbovo, which was concluded in 1617. Russia paid an indemnity and ceded to Sweden the littoral of the Gulf of Finland, but recovered Novgorod, and Prince Philip of Sweden, brother of Gustavus Adolfus, formally renounced his claim to the Russian throne.

Hostilities between the two countries were resumed some 40 years later in connection with the struggle over Poland-Lithuania, in which both Tsar Alexis and King Charles X of Sweden were involved. The Russians deemed

---

[3] In 1698, in connection with a new *streltsy* uprising, Sophie was forced to take the veil. She died in 1704.

the time opportune to recover the territories on the shores of the Gulf of Finland lost to Sweden by the peace of Stolbovo. A Russo-Swedish war began in 1656 but proved inconclusive and was ended in 1661 by the peace of Cardis, which confirmed the pre-war territorial arrangements, that is, Moscow failed to secure access to the Baltic Sea.

Struggle with Poland. Throughout much of the seventeenth century Russo-Polish relations were overshadowed by the aftermath of the Polish intervention. During the reign of Michael the Polish government was not reconciled to the defeat of 1612, while the Muscovites resented the loss of Smolensk and other territories which were held by Sigismund. Hostilities, however, were not resumed until 1618, when a sizable Polish army comprising Cossack contingents and commanded by Wladyslaw advanced towards Moscow but was successfully resisted by the Russians. Neither side seemed to be keen on fighting, and military operations were brought to an end late in 1618 by signing of the armistice of Deulino, which was to last for 14 years. Its terms were onerous to the Russians; Poland retained the lands of Smolensk, Chernigov, and Seversk, and Wladyslaw did not so much as renounce his claim to the Russian Crown. In 1632, at the expiration of the armistice, which happened to coincide with the death of Sigismund III of Poland, a Russian army led by Michael Shein, hero of the Russian defense of Smolensk in 1609, besieged that city. This operation, to which Moscow attached high hopes, proved extremely unfortunate. A raid of the Crimean Tatars on Russia's southern borderlands led to the mass desertion of the *dvoriane* whose estates were in the invaded or threatened provinces. Meanwhile Wladyslaw IV, who was elected to succeed his father Sigismund III as king of Poland, approached Smolensk with a large army and forced the ignominious capitulation of the Russians and the surrender of their entire artillery. Under the provisions of a treaty of "eternal peace" signed in 1634, Poland retained Smolensk and the other disputed territories, but Wladyslaw at last abandoned his claims to the Russian throne. Michael Shein, on his return to Moscow, was executed.

The incorporation in 1654 of the Ukraine, a dependency of Poland, into the Muscovite state [4] precipitated another Russo-Polish war which lasted, with interruptions, for 13 years. Supported by the Cossacks, the Russian troops occupied Smolensk and portions of Lithuania and Poland, including the cities of Vilna, Kovno, Grodno, and Lublin. In 1656 King Charles X of Sweden entered the war, seized Warsaw and Cracow, and proclaimed himself king of Poland. The conflict of Russian and Swedish ambitions in that country led to a temporary suspension of the hostilities between Russia and

[4] See below, p. 136.

Poland and the inconclusive Russo-Swedish war (noted at the beginning of this section). Fighting between Russia and Poland was resumed but was terminated in 1667 by the armistice of Andrusovo, which was concluded for 13½ years and transferred to Russia Smolensk, Seversk, and the left bank of the Ukraine (that is, the Ukrainian territories east of the Dnieper) and Kiev on the right (western) bank of the river. That city, however, was to be evacuated by the Russians within two years, a provision that was not carried out.

The invasion of the Ukraine in 1672 by Mahommed IV, sultan of Turkey, resulted in a war between that power and Poland and, later, a war between Turkey and Russia. By the peace of Zurawno (1676) Poland ceded to Turkey a large portion of the right-bank Ukraine. The Russians were more fortunate: the Russo-Turkish armistice of Bakhchisarai (1681) confirmed Moscow's control over the left-bank Ukraine and Kiev, although the Russians had to resume the payment of an annual tribute to the Crimean khan, a vassal of the sultan.

International recognition of the annexation by Russia of the eastern Ukraine and Kiev followed soon thereafter. In the 1680's King Jan Sobieski of Poland espoused the plan of a crusade for the ejection of the Turks from Europe. Russia's participation was considered essential to the success of the vast enterprise, and Sobieski had to accept the terms insisted upon by the Moscow government: a treaty of "eternal peace" between Russia and Poland and the final cession of the territories held by Moscow by virtue of the Andrusovo armistice. An agreement to this effect was signed in 1686. The outcome of both the crusade and Russia's part in it proved disappointing. The Turks were not evicted from Europe, and the two campaigns against the Crimean Tatars conducted by Prince Vasili Golitsyn in 1687 and 1689 ended in disaster and, indeed, contributed to the fall of the regency of Sophie.

Expansion in Asia. Expansion in Siberia, which began under Ivan IV, continued throughout the seventeenth century. Vast territories stretching to the Arctic Ocean and the North Pacific came under the more or less nominal control of Muscovy. Penetration in Siberia was due chiefly to the initiative of private hunters and traders who by the middle of the century had advanced towards the Amur River and the Chinese border. The resulting friction with the Chinese was resolved in 1689 by the treaty of Nerchinsk, which excluded the Russians from the Amur basin. By the end of the seventeenth century Siberia was largely conquered but for decades remained a dormant asset: her economic development had hardly begun at the end of the nineteenth century and did not gain momentum until after World War II.

Diplomacy. Tsar Michael and his successors were active in establishing diplomatic relations with European courts. The insistence of Sobieski and his allies on Russia's participation in the Turkish crusade was an indication that her traditional isolation was breaking down. For good or ill Muscovy was preparing to take her place in the quarrelsome family of European nations.

Incorporation of the Ukraine

The Ukraine and Its People. The most important single feature of Russia's territorial expansion in the seventeenth century was the incorporation of a part of the Ukraine in the Russian state. In the broadest sense the Ukraine, which literally means "borderland," included the territories comprising the Black Sea steppes from the Urals to the Carpathian Mountains. In the late sixteenth century the term "the Ukraine," and its Russian counterpart "Little Russia" (Malorossiia), were used to describe the southern provinces of Poland-Lithuania, that is, the lands situated north of the Black Sea and the Sea of Azov but not bordering on them, roughly from the Dniester River in the west to the Donets River in the east. Within the uncertain boundaries of this vast area lived a shifting population known as the Cossacks; it will be remembered that in the reign of Ivan IV they conquered eastern Siberia for the Russian Crown and later took a leading part in the revolutionary events at the turn of the seventeenth century. The Cossacks were a group of mixed ethnic origin, consisting chiefly of fugitives from Muscovy, Lithuania, and Poland, with a large admixture of Turks, Mongols, and various nomadic tribes. War and brigandage were their chief occupations, but they also engaged in peaceful pursuits such as hunting, trapping, fishing, bee-keeping, cattle-raising, handicrafts, and occasional farming. Under the relentless pressure of Muscovite and Polish colonization the Cossacks moved further and further south and during the earlier centuries presumably led, like their many predecessors in the steppes, a nomadic existence. In the middle of the sixteenth century or perhaps even earlier the Cossacks gradually settled down in autonomous semi-military communities situated on the principal Ukrainian rivers and organized on lines of crude democracy. The better-known were the communities of the Don Cossacks, on the river of that name, and the *Zaporozhskaia Sech* or *Zaporozhie*, on the Dnieper island of Khortits, near the rapids which cut that river.[5] Towards the end of the sixteenth century the *Sech*, whose origins may go back to the later part of the fifteenth, was

---

[5] Hence the name of *Zaporozhie*, which literally means "beyond the rapids."

a military brotherhood headed by an elected hetman. All important issues were decided by a general assembly of the members, who also elected the officials. The *Sech* was a military camp teeming with activity in the spring and summer, when the Cossacks prepared for or were engaged in military raids, but largely deserted in winter except for small detachments in charge of military stores. Women were not admitted in the *Sech,* and the married Cossacks lived on the mainland, some of whom were engaged in farming.

The geographical location of the Cossack settlements, in the frontier region between the Turks and the Crimean Tatars, on the one hand, and Poland-Lithuania and Muscovy, on the other, accounts for the military character of their organization and determined the part they were called to play in the tangled political relations of this tormented area. Both Poland-Lithuania and Muscovy coveted the Ukrainian Cossacks as a frontier guard for the defense of their southern borders and as ancillary troops in their perennial tug-of-war. The Cossacks were rebellious and unreliable and at times transferred their allegiance to their enemies of yesterday and fought Moscow or Poland on the side of the Turks or the Crimean Tatars. In the course of the sixteenth century Poland-Lithuania and, to a lesser degree, Muscovy consolidated their hold over the Ukrainian Cossacks. In 1570 the Don Cossacks assumed the obligation to serve Ivan IV. Meanwhile Poland extended her authority over the western Ukraine and the Dnieper Cossacks. By the union of Lublin (1569), which merged Lithuania with Poland,[6] the latter acquired the Ukrainian lands of Volynia, Kiev, and Chernigov. This expansion gave a strong stimulus to Polish colonization on both the western and the eastern banks of the Dnieper, where large tracts of land were granted to the Polish magnates Zolkiewski, Potocki, and others. To protect their estates the Polish landowners organized the frontiersmen into a guard known as "registered" Cossacks, a status that brought with it important privileges and resulted in social stratification among the Cossacks. There were but a few hundred "registered" Cossacks in the 1570's; 50 years later they numbered several thousand. The privileged minority formed the ruling class—the "elders" (*starshina*)— and assumed a position of leadership, while the liberties of the masses tended to disappear because of the encroachment of serfdom which the Polish landowners enforced on their Ukrainian estates.

Revolt Against Poland. For a number of reasons the Polish-Ukrainian partnership did not work well. There was the religious issue. Poland was Catholic, while most of the Cossacks belonged to the Greek Orthodox Church. At first, however, the frontiersmen showed little interest in religious ques-

[6] See above, pp. 26, 105.

tions: the *Sech* had no churches or priests, and in their expeditions the Cossacks plundered with impartiality houses of worship irrespective of their denomination. The situation changed after the union of Lublin (1569), when Catholicism was on the ascendancy in the newly-merged Polish-Lithuanian state. The Jesuits, alarmed by the success of the Reformation, arrived in large numbers and were particularly active in Lithuania and the Ukraine. They made many converts among the landed nobility of these regions, with the result that membership in the Greek Orthodox Church came to be looked upon as a mark of social inferiority. In 1595 a group of the Lithuanian Orthodox clergy negotiated a union between the Western Russian Church and the Church of Rome. This brought a cleavage in the Western Russian Church, many of the clergy and laymen refusing to accept the union, which was recognized and upheld by the Polish government and the Catholic hierarchy. There followed a bitter feud between the opponents of the union and the Uniats supported by the Catholics for the control of Church properties. Both sides displayed great ruthlessness. In 1623 the Uniat bishop Joasaphat Kuntsevich, who was later canonized by the Catholic Church, was murdered in a popular uprising. These developments shook some of the Cossacks out of their state of religious indifference and aligned them against Poland.

Another major source of discontent was the vagaries of Poland's military policy in the Ukraine and their impact on the social conditions in that borderland. The Polish government encouraged the military organization of the Cossacks enrolled in its service but endeavored to prevent their incursions into the Crimea and Turkey, which embittered Poland's relations with her southern neighbors but which the Cossacks took as a matter of course. The establishment of a privileged group of "registered" Cossacks led to much friction. The Cossack leaders insisted on the expansion of this force, but the Polish government at times attempted a reduction, a policy which influential Cossack circles sternly resisted. Moreover, the pay of the "registered" Cossacks was often in arrears, and the other obligations assumed by Poland were but loosely observed. The advancement of serfdom, a concomitant of Polish rule and colonization, was presumably the chief cause of the growing disaffection among the frontiersmen, who attached little importance to such abstract formal notions as allegiance to the Polish Crown.

Numerous anti-Polish uprisings took place in the Ukraine in the later part of the sixteenth and in the first half of the seventeenth century and were suppressed by the better-organized and better-led Polish troops. In 1638, following a Cossack mutiny, the autonomy of *Zaporozhie* was abolished, and the elected hetman was replaced by an appointed Polish official. Ten years later a Cossack revolt led by Bogdan Khmelnitsky, acting jointly with the Crimean Tatars, succeeded in defeating the Poles and was terminated by the peace of Zborov (1649), which restored the autonomy of the *Sech* and raised the number of "registered" Cossacks to 40,000. The armed conflict with Poland was resumed the following year; this time the fortunes of war were on the side of Poland. Bogdan Khmelnitsky, who had become hetman of *Zaporozhie,* was abandoned by his Tatar allies and was forced to accept vexatious peace terms which provided, among other things, for the reduction by half of the number of "registered" Cossacks. The Ukraine was again in a state of extreme ferment. In 1651 Khmelnitsky turned to Moscow and requested Tsar Alexis to take the Ukraine under his protection.

Moscow Incorporates the Ukraine. Moscow hesitated, partly because the tsar and his advisors did not wish to become embroiled again with Poland and partly because they did not like Khmelnitsky's plan for an autonomous Ukrainian duchy under the suzerainty of the Russian Crown. It was not until January 1654, after Khmelnitsky had threatened to go over to the Turks or the Crimean Tatars, that the Moscow government agreed, with the approval of a *zemskii sobor,* to the incorporation of the Ukraine into Russia. Simultaneously the Cossacks took the oath of allegiance to the tsar. The Ukraine retained its autonomous institutions, the hetman being given the power to carry on foreign relations except with Poland and Turkey. The number of "registered" Cossacks was increased to 60,000.

The immediate consequences of the incorporation of the Ukraine into Russia were civil war in that country and the protracted Russo-Polish war that resulted in the annexation by Muscovy of the left-bank Ukraine and the city of Kiev on the right bank of the Dnieper, although these acquisitions were not made final until 1686.[7]

Civil war and partition were but a part of the price paid by the Ukraine for Khmelnitsky's acceptance of Russian suzerainty. He and his successors thought nothing of repudiating their allegiance to Moscow, and for over a century the Ukraine remained a bone of contention among Russia, Poland, and Turkey. The Ukrainians who cherished the ideal of national independence or autonomy had good reasons to regret the decision of 1654. The subsequent history of Russo-Ukrainian relations is the disheartening record of relentless infringements of Ukrainian liberties by the Moscow–St. Petersburg government, culminating in the abolition of Ukrainian national institutions in the second half of the eighteenth century.

[7] See above, p. 132.

Central Government

Autocracy and the Boyar Duma. The Muscovite government under the first Romanovs differed little from that of Ivan IV and of his immediate predecessors. The theory that is sometimes advanced that the powers of Tsar Michael were made subject, on his accession in 1613, to constitutional limitations imposed upon him by the leading boyars is not supported by evidence and is contrary to the subsequent practice of the Muscovite Crown. In law and in fact Michael, Alexis, and Fedor were as absolute monarchs as were before them Ivan III, Vasili III, and Ivan IV. With the exception of the brief episode of the *zemskii sobor,* which will be examined presently, the machinery of the central government remained largely intact, as if no revolutionary outbreak had taken place. The fullness of power was vested in the Crown. The boyar *duma,* an informal body of the tsar's councillors,[8] continued to meet in an advisory capacity but had little influence on official policies.

Central Administrative Agencies. The business of government was conducted, as in the sixteenth century, by the *prikazy,* central bureaucratic agencies through which the Crown exercised its authority.[9] The resulting administrative structure which had evolved haphazardly and inadvertently over many decades was uncoordinated, cumbersome, and untidy. It will be remembered that some of the *prikazy* were organized on the functional principle, that is, they administered a specific branch of public activity, such as the judiciary or the distribution of estates (*pomestie*) to the service people; other *prikazy* governed specific territories—Siberia, the Ukraine; still others were in charge of groups of the population, for instance, the *streltsy.* The administration of public finance was dispersed among several departments, and there was no clear delimitation of the various executive functions. For example, the *posolskii prikaz*—Muscovy's ministry of foreign affairs—both conducted foreign relations and collected taxes in territories assigned to its jurisdiction. In the seventeenth century the number of *prikazy* varied from about 40 to 60. Attempts to bring some order in this unwieldly structure were made from time to time, and a degree of simplification and coordination was achieved towards the end of the century, although new *prikazy* continued to appear. Centralization and bureaucratism remained the salient fea-

[8] See above, pp. 16, 81.
[9] See above, pp. 81, 95.

tures of the Muscovite government, as they had since Russia's unification in the fifteenth century.

The Zemskii Sobor. The possibility of a change in administrative methods was suggested by the revival of interest in the institution of *zemskii sobor*. The first known *zemskii sobor* met in the reign of Ivan IV and was an advisory assembly consisting of representatives of the clergy, the boya *duma,* the service class, and commerce and trade. The delegates were not elected but were appointed by the authorities.[10] The *zemskii sobor* met during the stormy events at the turn of the seventeenth century to elect to the throne, or to confirm the election of, Boris Godunov in 1598, Wladyslaw in 1610, and Michael Romanov in 1613. The collapse of central authority during this period forced provincial Russia to organize and created the need for a representative assembly that would participate in national affairs. A *zemskii sobor* actually functioned in connection with the Minin and Pozharsky liberation movement which led to the defeat of the Poles.[11] It is impossible to say definitely how these various assemblies came about and what exactly their functions were. It would seem that they were elected and that at least in one instance, the *sobor* of 1613, the peasants were represented.

The fate of the *zemskii sobor* after the election of Michael Romanov is of particular interest. From 1613 to 1622 the *sobor* was continuously in session. It was convened again in 1632, 1637–1638, and 1642 (that is, at considerable intervals) when relations with Poland and Turkey deteriorated. During the reign of Alexis the *zemskii sobor* met four times: in 1645, to confirm the tsar's accession; in 1648–1649, to examine the new code; in 1650, in connection with the rebellion in Pskov; and in 1651–1653, to approve the incorporation of the Ukraine. With the 1651–1653 meeting the history of the *zemskii sobor* was virtually closed. None was summoned in connection with the accession of Tsar Fedor in 1676, and it is unclear whether the two assemblies which in the spring of 1682 went through the motions of electing to the throne Peter and Ivan could properly be regarded as *zemskii sobors*.[12]

The above list is tentative. Information on the *zemskii sobor* is fragmentary and offers no ground for well-founded generalizations. It would seem, nevertheless, that except for the opening decade of Michael's reign, when the government was notoriously weak, the *zemskii sobor* were convened only in emergencies and the delegates usually returned home with the unwelcome news of new imposts which their fellow townsmen had to meet. The function of the *zemskii sobor* was not so much to advise the government as to

[10] See above, pp. 94–95.
[11] See above, pp. 121–122.
[12] See above, p. 128.

shoulder fiscal burdens and carry out directives emanating from the central authorities. The assembly never attempted to impose any limitation on the powers of the Crown. There was no uniformity in the complexion of the *sobor,* but it would seem that the *dvoriane* predominated. Some of their criticisms were quite outspoken, and this was presumably the reason why an institution that might have contained the seeds of representative government functioned for only a few decades and was discontinued in the 1650's.

Local Government

Crown Officials and Self-Government. Throughout the seventeenth century local government, like the central administration, adhered closely to the traditional pattern and, again like the central administration, showed the growing impact of centralization and bureaucratism. The highest official in the provincial administration was the *voevoda,* or governor, appointed by the Crown. His authority was practically unlimited. He was supposed to differ from his fifteenth- and sixteenth-century predecessors, holders of *kormlenie,*[13] in not being permitted to divert for his own use any part of the public revenue the collection of which he supervised. Moreover, the governors were repeatedly enjoined not to acept bribes. These were clearly unenforceable rules which ran contrary to the deeply-rooted custom of Muscovite officialdom. Whatever illusions might have existed on this score should have been dispelled by the denunciations of the malfeasance and abuses of local government officials voiced by the delegates at the *zemskii sobor.*

The *zemstvos,* that is, the institutions of local self-government established by Ivan IV,[14] continued to carry out their unexciting duties under the watchful eye of the appointed governor. Their jurisdiction in matters pertaining to the advancement of local interests was limited to the election of a few minor officials (including the priest) and similar perfunctory matters. The chief function of the *zemstvo* officials was the collection of taxes; their integrity and efficiency in the performance of this distasteful task were guaranteed by the joint responsibility of the communities which elected them. The seventeenth-century *zemstvos* therefore were not elected institutions, spokesmen of the interests of the electorate; they were rather a body of unpaid public officials in charge of the collection of revenue for whom the community was jointly responsible. This was the only kind of self-government the Muscovite bureaucracy would tolerate.

[13] See above, pp. 67, 95.
[14] See above, p. 96.

Armed Forces

The Dvoriane *Militia.* The protracted wars of the sixteenth and the seventeenth centuries imposed a severe strain on Muscovy's military establishment. The basic component of the army was the *dvoriane* militia, which was mobilized only in emergencies. We know that the *dvoriane* were compensated for their services by the granting of *pomesties* (landed estates), which were farmed first by peasant tenants and later by serfs. The *dvoriane* were required to provide their own arms, horses, and equipment as well as a specified number of fully equipped soldiers recruited from the servile population of their estates. The strength of these detachments and the nature of the arms and equipment the *dvoriane* were obliged to supply varied according to the size of the landholding of each and were actually determined at reviews which were held at irregular intervals and which all *dvoriane* were expected to attend. The *dvoriane* received monetary compensation which, however, was in the nature of allowances to defray the costs of service rather than regular pay. The type of arms used varied a great deal, from muskets to arbalests and bows and arrows. The militia was poorly disciplined and poorly trained, its fighting capacity was low, and evasion of service was prevalent. The evaders were flogged and deprived of their *pomesties,* but the deterrent effects of cruel punishments appear to have been slight.

Other Troops. The unimpressive showing of the militia led the government to seek alternative forms of military organization which would come closer to the pattern of a standing army. The earliest formations of this nature were the "registered" Cossacks and the *streltsy.* The former were the frontiersmen enrolled in the service of Muscovy. The *streltsy* were peasant-soldiers who received regular pay and land allotments which they farmed themselves. They lived in special settlements, chiefly around Moscow, and engaged in trades and handicrafts. They carried firearms which, together with other equipment, were supplied by the state. They were subject to a more thorough and systematic training than the *dvoriane,* but they were not full-time soldiers. Their officers were usually native Russians.

There was still another type of military formation. Some of the foreign soldiers who participated in the Swedish and Polish intervention in the opening years of the seventeenth century [15] eventually entered Russian service and formed the nucleus of new Muscovite regiments known under foreign names —*soldaty, reitary, draguny.* These regiments were captained by foreigners,

[15] See above, p. 117.

were organized and trained according to the Western model, and retained their foreign names although their manpower was drawn from the Russian countryside. It is believed that in the 1680's some 60 regiments accounting for more than half of the Russian army (excluding the Cossacks) were of the "Western" type.

Military service was compulsory for all social groups. The *dvoriane,* who lived on the proceeds of their estates, were individually liable to serve with the forces. The other classes—burghers, merchants, and peasants—were required to provide a specified number of recruits from each rural or urban community, that is, in their case army draft was a group and not a personal obligation.

9

The Seventeenth Century, II

Social Conditions

Aftermath of the Great Upheaval. The state of confusion and uncertainty we have observed in Muscovy's foreign relations on the morrow of the accession of Michael Romanov was fully matched by the conditions of domestic instability and popular unrest, which at times verged on open rebellion. Some of the Cossacks led by Zarutsky abandoned the siege of Moscow before the capitulation of its Polish garrison in October 1612[1] and made their way to the Astrakhan region, in the delta of the Volga. Zarutsky was accompanied by Marina, the ill-fated spouse of the pseudo-Dimitry, and her infant son Ivan, who was known as *vorenok*—"The Little Brigand."[2] Their Cossack following soon melted away, however, and in the summer of 1614 they were apprehended by government troops. Zarutsky and the boy Ivan were executed, and Marina died (she might have been murdered) soon thereafter. With the fall of Zarutsky the organized Cossack movement disintegrated, although sizable Cossack bands were still numerous, defied control, and frequently eluded the punitive expeditions sent against them.

[1] See above, pp. 121–122.
[2] *Vorenok* is the dimunitive of *vor*—brigand; the name was applied to the Pretender by his opponents.

Perhaps the greatest difficulty that the government had to face at home was the high mobility of the population. This situation was not new, but with the passage of time its consequences became increasingly grave. Complaints concerning the flight of peasants and burghers were frequently voiced at the *zemskii sobor*. A factor that stimulated the urge of people to give up their domiciles was Muscovy's fiscal system.

Taxation. The principal taxes levied by the Muscovite government were of the "apportioned" type, that is, a central agency determined the desired yield of the tax and apportioned it among the administrative subdivisions, which, in turn, re-assessed their respective quotas among the taxpayers. The basic unit of assessment was the *sokha,* which consisted either of a specified area of farm land or of a stipulated number of households. *Sokha* was an ancient term used for tax purposes [3] as early as the thirteenth century. The number of *sokhas* in a locality was deemed to be indicative of its wealth, and the tax thus levied was a property tax. Censuses (*soshnoe pismo*) taken at more or less regular intervals determined the actual number of *sokhas* in each region, on which the total assessment depended. In the seventeenth century the basis of taxation was gradually shifted from the *sokha* to the *dvor* (household), that is, the latter was made the unit of assessment. The transition was practically completed in the 1680's. The change was significant because it altered the nature of the tax. The household tax was levied not on property (as in *sokha*) but on the labor power of the household members. Thus, the property tax became a tax on the ability of the people to earn a living. The next logical step was the introduction of the poll (head) tax, which was actually enacted in 1723.

The essential and significant element in both the *sokha* and the *dvor* methods of taxation was the joint responsibility of the community for the total amount of the impost which it was assessed, as well as for the integrity of the tax officials whom it elected. We know that, except for the *dvoriane,* army service—like taxation—was a group, not a personal, obligation.[4] There were important practical consequences from the resulting legal situation. On the one hand, a taxpayer, by changing his domicile, could evade his fiscal and service obligations until he was caught anew in the net of the census-taker. On the other hand, both the state and the community were vitally interested in preventing the elusive peasant or burgher from wandering away: the state, because it needed taxpayers and soldiers; the community, because its remaining members had to shoulder the burden of those who had left.

---

[3] *Sokha* also means a plow.
[4] See above, p. 141.

This explains much in the legislation and social history of the seventeenth century.

"Voluntary" Slavery. Another way of evading state exaction was provided by the ancient institution of "voluntary" slavery (*kabalnoe kholopstvo*), which gained great popularity in the first half of the seventeenth century. The official consideration for becoming a "voluntary" slave was a loan which, it is believed, was often fictitious. The actual reason for the change of status was that "voluntary" slaves, like all slaves, were exempt from taxation, army service, and other obligations borne by freemen. The protection of a powerful lord, who enjoyed a variety of privileges and might be concerned with the well-being of the servile population living on his estates, appeared to many as worth the sacrifice of the uncertain advantages of personal liberty. Among those who sold themselves into "voluntary" slavery were men coming from every social class, including the *dvoriane.*

The Code of 1649. The code of laws of Tsar Alexis, which was examined and approved by a *zemskii sobor* held in 1648-1649, consolidated the existing legal and social institutions and largely determined their subsequent evolution for nearly 200 years and, in a smaller degree, until the end of the empire. The *sobor* was convened on the morrow of a particularly tumultuous popular rebellion and was dominated by the *dvoriane.* It is a moot question, however, whether its complexion was actually reflected in the provisions of the Code. We know that the decisions of the *sobor* were not binding on the Crown, and, since about half of the members of the 1648-1649 assembly were illiterate, it is likely that many of them took no active part in legislative work. The Code followed the pattern of the Lithuanian Statute of 1588, and although inferior to its model (by then 60 years old), it was a marked advance over the earlier Muscovite legislative collections—those of 1497 and 1550—which were but manuals of procedure. The Code of 1649 was Russia's first comprehensive attempt at codification and remained the law of the land until 1833, although it was amended and in part superseded by later enactments.

The Russian legislators of the seventeenth century adhered to a principle which was the direct opposite of the one written into the American Declaration of Independence. The Muscovites held fast to the doctrine prevalent in medieval Europe that all men *are not* born equal. Accordingly, the population of Russia was divided into hereditary classes or "estates" (*soslovie,* the French *état*) whose members had specific rights and duties and, as a rule, were attached to their place of residence.

The Dvoriane. In the seventeenth century the highest estate of the realm was the *dvoriane,* or service class, with whom the descendants of the former appanage princes and ancient landed aristocracy, the boyars, had by then fully merged. The principal duty of the *dvoriane* was army service, for which they received *pomesties,* that is, landed estates farmed first by free peasant tenants and later by bondsmen. After Russia's unification the once-sharp distinction between the patrimonial estates unencumbered by the obligation of service and the *pomestie* disappeared, and service became compulsory for all landowners employing tenants or servile labor.[5]

The *dvoriane* militia was the backbone of the armed forces, and the government was vitally concerned with maintaining its fighting capacity, which, in part, depended on the economic well-being of its members. Legislation enacted in the seventeenth century, especially the Code of 1649, strove to achieve these objectives. To prevent the weakening of the militia the *dvoriane* were debarred from selling themselves into "voluntary" slavery, since this change of status would remove them from the service rolls. The *dvoriane* had long complained of the small size of the *pomesties,* which was attributed to the depletion of the land reserve through the expansion of Church landholding and to the admission to their ranks of men drawn from other social groups. Measures were taken to remedy this situation. The Church was enjoined from acquiring new landed properties, although those it owned were not secularized. The right of ownership (by private individuals) of *pomesties* and other estates farmed by servile labor was restricted to the *dvoriane,* their kin and descendants, thus conferring upon the future Russian nobility its most valuable privilege. The authority of estate owners over the servile population was vastly extended. On the other hand, *mestnichestvo,* the archaic institution which controlled the relative position of the members of noble families in government service,[6] was abolished in 1682, removing a vexatious restriction on the power of the Crown to make appointments.

The Serfs. The long drawn-out process of enslavement of the once-free peasantry living on the land of the *dvoriane* and the Church reached fruition in the middle of the seventeenth century. It must be emphasized again that national defense and security depended on the *dvoriane's* ability to perform their duties, which was closely related to the condition of their estates. In the seventeenth century land was still abundant (even though complaints were heard about the smallness of the *pomesties*), but labor was scarce and the mobility of the population, including the rural population, was high. The efforts of both the *dvoriane* and the government, whose interests in this matter were intertwined, were to ensure that the farmer would stay on the job. The

---

[5] See above, pp. 82, 96.
[6] See above, p. 84.

simplest way to attain this objective was to attach him to his plot. After the Time of Troubles the tenant's right to relinquish his tenancy is no longer mentioned in the sources, while administrative and legal restrictions to check mobility multiplied. A freeman who took service under a lord for three months was requested to issue a *kabala,* that is, to renounce his status as a freeman. Similarly, tenancy contracts came to contain provisions obligating the tenant to cultivate his allotment until his death. This relationship was known as *krestianskaia krepost:* literally, the peasant was "fast" to the land, and presumably it gave serfdom (*krepostnoe pravo*) its name. The landowners had agitated for years for the removal of restrictions limiting the time during which action could be brought for the recovery of runaway peasants.[7] The Code of 1649 gave them full satisfaction by abolishing the time limit and by providing heavy fines for harboring the fugitives.

Serfdom, however, did not mean merely the attachment of the peasants to their allotments. In the seventeenth century and, indeed, until the emancipation of 1861, the legal and economic status of the serfs was and remained highly ambiguous: they were not slaves, but they were also not freemen and seemed to possess the disadvantages of both. Serfs, like slaves, were at the mercy of their master and were at times treated like chattels. They could be exchanged for other serfs, sold without the land, pledged for loans, and given away. But like freemen the serfs paid taxes, served in the armed forces, and had some family rights. The law made no provision concerning the property rights of the serfs, nor was there any legal limit as to services and other exactions which their master could demand from them. The powers of the landowners, moreover, had an element of public authority: they were government agents responsible for the performance by the servile population living on their estates of fiscal and other obligations towards the state.

The State Peasants. Not all peasants were serfs. A large number of farmers, perhaps half of the rural population, lived on state-owned land and were known as state peasants (*gosudarstvennye krestiane*). They were organized in village communes whose members were jointly responsible for the payment of taxes and the performance of other obligations towards the state. In the sixteenth and seventeenth centuries the state peasants, like the serfs, became attached to the land which they farmed, as the government was anxious to maintain the paying capacity of the communes and to prevent evasion. The communes enjoyed a degree of rudimentary self-government under the supervision of Crown officials. Unlike the serfs the state peasants could not be removed from the land.

[7] See above, p. 116.

The Burghers. Progress of urban life in the Muscovy of the sixteenth and seventeenth centuries was slow, and many of the so-called towns—*gorod* or *possad*—were but military outposts which differed little from villages. The burghers (*possadskie liudi*), who lived in urban settlements, were engaged in commerce and handicrafts and paid a special tax. In the second half of the sixteenth century it became customary to appoint as government tax collectors the more affluent among the local merchants. These officials were personally responsible for the collection of the imposts and were rewarded with the title of *gost* and with exemption from taxes and the jurisdiction of ordinary courts. The rank and file of the burghers resented these privileges of the wealthy few, especially since the share of taxation borne by the merchants prior to their enrollment as government agents had to be made good, after their appointment, by their fellow townsmen. There were other reasons for discontent. The position of the burghers was undermined by the competition of people who did not pay the business tax but actually carried on trading and other business activities; some of these interlopers were *dvoriane,* but the majority were the tenants, slaves, and bondsmen of powerful ecclesiastical and lay lords who established near the towns trading settlements (*sloboda*) where their retainers kept shops or worked as craftsmen. The competition of these "unlicensed" merchants and artisans put the burghers at a disadvantage and forced many of them to close their enterprises and move away. These developments aggravated the general unsettled conditions and led to a massive flight of the burghers. As an eminent historian put it, the towns of Muscovy were dying a slow death. The depopulation of the towns led to loss of revenue, alarmed the authorities, and invited restrictive policies.

The earlier measures designed to immobilize the burghers were provided by the Code of 1550. These proved ineffectual and were repeated in later years. Searches for "fugitive" burghers (including those who had sold themselves into "voluntary" slavery) and their forcible return to their former place of residence were ordered in 1619 and 1638. The Code of 1649 consolidated previous legislation and laid down the rule that no burgher was permitted to change his domicile, even to move to another town. Severe penalties, including the knout and deportation to Siberia, were to be applied to the violators of the law; yet infringements must have been frequent, because a decree of 1658 instituted capital punishment for the above offense and a decree of 1682 allowed the burghers who had unlawfully changed their place of residence to remain where they were but retained the prohibition of further changes of domicile.

Simultaneously with these restrictive and deterrent measures, attempts were made to eliminate some of the conditions which were responsible for the flight of the burghers. The Code of 1649 decreed the sequestration of the trading settlements (*sloboda*) inhabited by the *dvoriane,* bondsmen, and others who did not pay the business tax but engaged in business activities. Henceforth the population of such settlements was to pay this tax, and the establishment of new *slobodas* was prohibited. Commerce and industry became the burghers' exclusive preserve: members of other social groups were not permitted to own commercial and other business enterprises. Russian traders also gained protection against competition by foreigners. First, foreign merchants were deprived of some of their privileges and their taxes were raised, and then the New Statute of Commerce (1667), an act imbued with mercantilist ideas, denied them the right to participate in retail trade. "Buy from the Russians" became the law of the land.

Popular Uprisings

Under Tsar Michael. The policies of regimentation outlined above were both the cause and the effect of the deep-rooted popular unrest that was responsible for the great upheaval at the turn of the seventeenth century. The restoration of central authority with the election of Michael Romanov did not eliminate the conditions which brought about the crisis and, indeed, probably worsened them. During much of Michael's reign, the Cossack bands, their ranks replenished by runaway serfs and army deserters, roamed about the country. The cost of frequent unsuccessful wars aggravated economic hardships and fostered the mood of discontent and disaffection. The highly unpopular measures enacted by the government towards the middle of the century provided the focal point for the rebellious impulses of the masses and led to violent outbreaks.

The Middle of the Century. The accession of the youthful Tsar Alexis in 1645 brought to power his intimate advisor and former tutor, the boyar Boris Morozov, who was married to a sister of Tsarina Maria Miloslavsky, Alexis's first wife. The tsar and his government were faced with a grave financial situation. The protracted war with Poland had taxed to the limit the financial resources of the Muscovite treasury, which had not yet recovered from the disorders of the Time of Troubles. To meet the emergency the government resorted to ill-advised measures: a drastic increase in the rates of the salt tax and of the excise on tobacco, and the debasement of currency through the substitution of copper for silver coins. The resulting sharp rise in the cost of living was particularly felt by the poorer section of the urban population and was presumably the immediate cause of the revolt which broke out in Moscow in June 1648 and which had repercussions throughout the land. Alexis, unceremoniously buffeted by angry crowds, was forced to surrender to the rebels two of his trusted councillors, Leonid Pleshcheev and Peter Trakhanitov—both of them kin of the tsarina—who were then murdered; but Morozov, who was also sought by the crowd, escaped unhurt, although he was compelled to retire to a remote monastery. The movement, however, was not directed against the Crown, even though the tsar had to endure grievous personal indignities. A by-product of the revolt was the Code of 1649, which gave some satisfaction to the wishes of the *dvoriane* and the burghers. It also became the cause of severe unrest among the "voluntary" slaves, who protested against the forcible restoration to their former status.

In 1650 Novgorod and Pskov rebelled against Moscow. The latter city demanded, among other things, the right to have its representatives participate in the administration of justice by the appointed governor. The situation was judged serious enough to warrant the convocation of a *zemskii sobor*. The insurgents were defeated after a stubborn struggle, as Pskov was able to hold back government troops for nearly three months. The so-called "copper rebellion," allegedly a belated protest against the substitution of copper coins for silver coins in the middle 1650's, broke out in July 1662 but was actually due to the iniquities of the regime. On this occasion, as in 1648, the tsar was roughly handled, although his authority was not seriously challenged. The movement had ramifications all over the country and was suppressed with great severity.

Stenka Razin. As was to be expected, the onward march of serfdom and its enshrinement in the Code of 1649 added fuel to the smouldering flames of peasant revolt. The lavish distribution of landed estates to the members of the service class and to the favorites of the day, especially in the reign of Tsar Michael, reduced large groups of state peasants to the status of serfs, which meant greater exploitation and heavier financial burdens. Peasant disturbances flared up here and there throughout the earlier decades of the seventeenth century and reached their zenith in the movement of Stenka Razin, a Cossack leader who made his appearance in the region of the upper Don in 1667. He met with considerable success in the Ukraine and in the territories along the Volga, which were teeming with disaffected elements. Razin, however, sailed on the Caspian Sea and carried out raids on Persia. In 1669 he was back in the Ukraine, took Astrakhan, and in the following year opened military operations against Muscovy. Like the leaders of other popular movements of this period, he claimed that he was fighting the boyars and the landlords but not the Crown. Razin made triumphant progress along the Volga and was acclaimed as their savior by Russian peasants and by the native tribes (the Bashkir, Mordva, Kalmyk, Cheremiss, and others). His army, however, was poorly organized and poorly equipped, and in October 1670 it was defeated near Simbirsk by government troops. Razin withdrew to the Don, where he was arrested by the conservative Cossack leaders, was surrendered to the Russian authorities, and was executed in Moscow in June 1671. The peasant war, as Razin's revolt is sometimes called, thus came to an end, but unrest among the local tribes continued into the 1680's.

Meanwhile cleavage in the Church added another strain to the subdued but powerful movement of revolt.

The Patriarch Nikon and the Schism

The Background. The state of disorder prevailing in the Church under Ivan IV and condemned by the Church council of 1551 [8] continued throughout the next 100 years. It was probably inevitable that ritual, prayers, and other religious observances should suffer changes with the passage of time. The prevalence of illiteracy among the clergy and its low intellectual levels favored this unintentional and unwanted transformation. Errors inexorably crept into religious texts which had once been translated from the Greek—perhaps not very satisfactorily—and had since been copied by hand many times. The visiting Greek hierarchs repeatedly drew the attention of Muscovite authority to the widening gap between the Russian and Greek practices. Assuming that it was desirable to remove the irregularities which had gained acceptance, the obvious thing to do would have been to compare the Russian religious texts with the Greek originals, to make the necessary corrections, and to restore the old ritual. The execution of this program, however, met with formidable difficulties.

First and foremost was Muscovy's traditional attachment to external observances. Ritual, as understood by seventeenth-century Russians, was the very essence of Christianity. Any change in the accepted practice, however trivial, was regarded as an abandonment of true faith. Another reason for the resistance to the revision of the books was doubts about the Orthodoxy of the Greek Church. Since the fall of Byzantium and the espousal of the doctrine of "Moscow—The Third Rome" and "Moscow—The Second Jerusalem," the Russian hierarchy tended complacently to assume its own infallibility and looked with suspicion upon its former mentors: Were the Greek

[8] See above, p. 98.

patriarchs to be trusted? Did they preserve intact, under the rule of the infidels, the purity of the ancient faith? These suspicions were deemed to be
all the more warranted because the Byzantine Church had first accepted and
then repudiated the union of the Churches proclaimed by the Ferrara-
Florence Council which was anathema to the Russian theologians.

Attempts at correcting the Church books were made in the first half of
the sixteenth century but met with no success. They were in part responsible
for the undoing of Maxim the Greek,[9] who was tried twice by a council of
bishops and spent long years behind the bars of an ecclesiastical prison. Yet
agitation for the correction of religious texts continued and in the middle
of the seventeenth century found ardent supporters in a group of influential
laymen and clerics led by Patriarch Nikon.

Patriarch Nikon. Nikon was a born reformer, a man of imagination, conviction, energy, and vast ambition. He came of peasant stock, received little
or no formal education, and took the vows while still young, monastic status
being the prerequisite for the elevation to the bishopric and other higher
Church offices. A forceful and eloquent preacher, Nikon commanded a devout following that included highly-placed persons who introduced him to
Tsar Alexis. The pious, youthful, and impressionable Alexis fell under the
spell of the authoritarian Churchman and for a time blindly accepted his
guidance. The patriarchal see being vacant, Alexis secured in 1652 Nikon's
election to that office by a Church council. Conforming to tradition, the
patriarch-elect went through the motions of withholding his consent but
finally agreed after being promised complete obedience and the powers to
restore order in the Church.

Nikon was much concerned with the conditions prevailing in the Church
and was animated by the sincere desire to get rid of the irregular practices,
but the revision of the Russian ritual to make it conform to that of the Greek
Church assumed the superior authority of the Greek patriarchs which Nikon
had once challenged. His espousal of the cause of the Greek Church had,
in part, political motivation. He believed in the supremacy of the spiritual
power over the secular power and endeavored to enhance the political authority of the Church by reviving the dual form of government (diarchy)
such as had existed in Russia in the reign of Michael, when Patriarch Filaret
actually ruled the country.[10] Nikon, like Filaret, adopted the style of "Majesty" (*velikii gosudar*), and his name appeared next to that of the tsar in
official documents. Although a signatory of the Code of 1649, Nikon de-

[9] See above, pp. 79–80.
[10] See above, p. 126.

nounced it because it imposed restrictions on the Church. Not only did the Code prohibit the expansion of ecclesiastical landholding, but it curtailed the judicial powers of the Church by providing that a lay department (*monastyrskii prikaz*) should try the civil and criminal offenses committed by members of the clergy. By upholding the authority of the Greek Church with its long tradition of supremacy of the spiritual power, Nikon hoped to advance his political plans for Muscovy.

On taking office Nikon, on his own initiative and without consulting a Church council, ordered the revision of certain generally accepted practices. He directed the use of three instead of two fingers in making the sign of the cross, the reduction in the number of genuflections performed during the recitation of certain prayers, and so on. Icons, which are revered by pious Russians, were to conform to the approved Byzantine pattern. Ownership of icons which deviated from the model sanctioned by the patriarch became an offense. Homes were searched for the offending images, which were publicly destroyed. The faithful were aroused and some resisted. The patriarch retaliated by imposing on the dissenters severe penalties: anathema, excommunication, deportation.

Correction of the Books. The correction of religious texts was ordered by a Church council and began in 1654. This attempt was more promising than its predecessors in the sixteenth century, because the earlier editors, as a rule, did not know the Greek language. In the second quarter of the seventeenth century, however, Peter Mogila, metropolitan of Kiev, founded in that city an Orthodox theological academy organized along the lines of Jesuit colleges. Greek and Latin were among the subjects taught at the academy. Some of its graduates went to Moscow and took a leading part in the revision of the Church books. About 500 Greek texts were assembled in the Russian capital, but the vast majority of this collection had no bearing on the proposed reform: allegedly only seven items dealt with church ritual. The apprehensions of the conservative elements were strengthened by the knowledge that the reform rested on so flimsy a documentary foundation. Nevertheless, a revised manual of Church services was issued in 1655 and was approved by a Church council; other textual revisions, accompanied by prohibitions of irregular practices, followed. With the expansion of the scope of the reform the resistance of the clergy and laymen mounted and was unwittingly fostered by official policies. For over a decade no general measures against the dissenters were enacted, although individual offenders were punished with extreme harshness. It was known, moreover, that the condemned practices had adherents among important persons, including Tsarina Maria, and were tolerated in the tsar's palace, a situation that could not but encourage resistance.

The Fall of Nikon. Meanwhile the position of Nikon was being shaken. He was unpopular with the clergy, whom he treated in a curt and arrogant manner, and he made many enemies in every class of society. Alexis grew tired of the overbearing ways of the patriarch, who wished to usurp the powers of the Crown but denied the tsar any participation in the affairs of the Church. The notion of the supremacy of the spiritual power over the temporal power had no roots in Russian tradition, and Nikon's insistence on making it effective proved his undoing. The breach between the tsar and the patriarch occurred in 1658 over a trivial matter of court etiquette. Nikon left the capital in a fit of temper, but contrary to his expectation he was not asked to return. His position as head of the Church remained unclear until 1666, when he was tried by a Russian Church council with the participation of two Greek patriarchs (those of Alexandria and Antioch), deprived of the patriarchal see and the rank of bishop, and exiled to a remote monastery. His meteoric career was over, but his work survived his downfall.

The Schism. While the fate of Nikon hung in the balance, resistance to the reform gained momentum and became a nation-wide movement. Dismayed and confused, the Muscovite government in the spring of 1666 convoked a purely Russian Church council which addressed itself to three familiar issues: Were the Greek patriarchs truly Orthodox? Could the Greek books be trusted? Were the decisions of the Church council of 1654, which ordered the revision of the religious texts, valid? The answer to each question was in the affirmative. The government's next step was to summon another Church council—this time with the participation of two Greek patriarchs—which met in the autumn of 1666 and continued in session into 1667. It was this council that condemned Nikon; it approved his work, however, and made a decision of momentous consequence to the Church and the nation: those who refused to use the corrected books and to adhere to the revised ritual were anathematized. This edict basically altered the situation. What was a dispute—admittedly a passionate one—over trivialities became a formal cleavage, a schism or *raskol*. It must be emphasized again that no question of principle or dogma was involved. The disagreement was exclusively about inconsequential minor points such as the correct spelling of the name of Jesus, the direction to be followed by religious processions (with or against the sun), the repetition of the exclamation *alleluia* two instead of three times, and the like. Ironically, both sides ostensibly sought to preserve the old faith: the reformers wished to purge the books and the ritual of the irregularities which had inadvertently crept in; to their opponents, however, the alleged restorations of ancient rites and texts were damnable innovations. Historical tradition had decided the contest, at least formally, in favor of the dissenters (*raskolniki*), who are usually referred to as old-believers or old-ritualists. With the anathema of 1667 they were expelled from the fold of the official Church.

The intransigence of the government and the ecclesiastical authorities was matched by that of the dissenters. Neither would consider a compromise. Nationalistic-minded Russians were outraged by the notion of the superior authority of the Greek hierarchy which had been so unexpectedly proclaimed. Rigid formalism had been traditionally a characteristic of the Russian Church. Interference with the customary practices, therefore, was all the more resented and led to indignant rejection. The schism added greatly to the ferment throughout the country. There were many people who believed that a wretched government was deliberately attempting to deprive them of what they most treasured—the hope of eternal salvation. The more extreme dissenters saw in the revised ritual and the corrected books the work of the anti-Christ and held that to escape this abomination no sacrifice was too great. The Solovetsky monastery, on an island in the White Sea, rejected the reform and for nearly ten years withstood a siege by government troops. The priest Avvakum, a fanatical advocate of resistance, was burned at the stake. This penalty for the leaders of the opposition to the reform was specifically provided by a decree of 1684 issued by Tsarevna Sophie, whose regency marked the high tide of persecution. The deterrent effect of this cruel edict, however, was not great. In the wooded wilderness of northern and eastern Russia, where many dissenters had fled from their tormentors, there developed a movement of mass suicide by self-burning. At least 37 human holocausts involving some 20,000 people took place between 1672 and 1691, when persecution subsided.

The schism showed remarkable vitality and had adherents throughout the land, although it thrived particularly in the areas of recent colonization —the Ukraine and the eastern and northern provinces. All efforts of the Church and the government to stamp it out failed. The legal status of the dissenters was altered many times during the subsequent 250 years, but legal disabilities were not finally removed until the beginning of the twentieth century. Nevertheless the number of old-ritualists remained large and, indeed, continued to increase.

Muscovy Looks West

Conservatism and Change. Unbending conservatism was the characteristic feature of seventeenth-century Muscovy. Even the cleavage in the Church, the most potent social movement of this period, was basically a conflict in which the contesting parties vied in proclaiming their devotion to immemorial tradition. Contacts with the outside world were still few, and departures from the customary ways were looked upon with suspicion and dislike. However, the force of necessity and, later in the century, the influence of a few highly-placed people succeeded in denting Muscovy's rigid traditionalism. Reference has already been made to the creation of a Westernized army to implement the unwieldy and ineffectual *dvoriane* militia.[11] A combination of the pressure of events and individual initiative occasionally succeeded in breaking through the ramparts of hostility, inertia, and bureaucratic complacency by fostering the acceptance of untried policies. Signs of change, haphazard and hesitant, could be observed in the evolution of the nascent Russian industry and in the timid beginnings of schools and literature.

Handicrafts and Industry. Western influence contributed to the growth of Russian handicrafts and industry. Articles of mass consumption—metalware (tools and utensils), woodwork (especially spoons and buckets), linens, woolens, pottery, felt boots, bark shoes, leather goods, sheep skins, and so on— were produced by the methods of cottage (domestic) industry, either as a part-time occupation by peasants living in the villages or by residents of urban settlements, who had largely severed their connection with farming. Handicrafts were well-established and progressive pursuits and remained until the end of the empire a major source of supply for a wide range of articles. Specialization of handicrafts on a geographical basis, especially in the Moscow region, came in the seventeenth century. The villages of Pavlovo and Vorms, for instance, became centers of metal-working; Lyskovo, of linens; and Murashkino, of sheep skins and mats.

Foreign artisans had a part in the development of handicrafts and the promotion of new skills. They were familiar figures in Kievan Russia. In the post-Mongol period the custom of importing foreign craftsmen goes back to the reign of Ivan III, that is, the end of the fifteenth century. In the middle of the sixteenth century Moscow had a sizable German Settlement (to the Russians all foreigners were Germans) where foreigners were expected to reside. It was wiped out during the great upheaval at the turn of the century

[11] See above, pp. 140–141.

but was reconstituted in 1652, partly because friction developed between the natives and the foreign residents. The German Settlement was quite large; its population comprised many skilled artisans—glass makers, weavers, masons, watchmakers, smelters, ironmasters, painters, chemists, even doctors and astrologers. It was their duty to train the Russians in their respective trade; in return, the government allowed the foreigners considerable freedom by not interfering with their customs and by tolerating foreign churches and schools. It was in the taverns and in the less reputable establishments of the German Settlement that the youthful Peter I, the future Tsar-Reformer, gained his first taste of European culture.

Manufactories, that is, large-scale industrial enterprises operated by manual labor, began to appear in Muscovy in the seventeenth century. A pioneer in this field was the Dutch merchant Andrew Vinius, who in 1632 was granted a concession for the exploitation of the iron ore deposits near Tula; he became the founder of important armament works which were later taken over by the government. Several manufactories producing glass, metalware, woollens, and paper goods were established near Moscow in the second half of the seventeenth century. Some, like the Tula works, were owned by foreigners, others by the state and by Russian noblemen (the boyar Boris Morozov) and merchants. Such enterprises were few. They employed either servile labor or hired workers drawn from the poorer section of the urban population.

Schools, Literature, and the Arts. Little needs to be said about cultural developments. Prior to the 1650's Muscovy had no schools, and any smattering of literacy acquired by the children of a few noblemen and priests was due to the ministrations of private tutors, usually low-ranking clerics whose own ability to read and write was questionable. The vast majority of even the nobility and the clergy were illiterate. A change occurred in the middle of the seventeenth century. The theological academy which was established in Kiev, when the Ukraine was still under Polish rule,[12] became an important educational center. The children of Tsar Alexis—the future Tsar Fedor and Tsarevna Sophie (but not Peter)—were taught by Simeon Polotsky, an eminent representative of Kievan learning and a man of letters of some distinction. The example set by the tsar was followed by some of the noblemen, who entrusted the education of their children to the graduates of the Kievan academy. In 1649–1650 the boyar Fedor Rtishchev founded in a monastery near Moscow, which he had built and endowed, a school patterned after the Kievan institution. Another theological school, which emphasized the study

[12] See above, p. 152.

of Latin and was headed by Simeon Polotsky, was established in Moscow in 1666. There followed a stubborn and obscure controversy between the supporters of Latinism and Hellenism. The dispute was resolved by establishing in 1687 the Slavono-Greek-Latin Academy, which, however, was more concerned with maintaining the purity of Greek Orthodoxy than with imparting knowledge to its students. The Academy was given dictatorial powers over the teaching of Greek, Latin, and modern foreign languages, as well as over questions of faith. Offenses against its edicts were punishable by deportation to Siberia and, in cases of alleged heresy, by burning at the stake. In the phrase of a famed historian the Academy became "a terrifying inquisition." Fortunately, its influence declined notably in the middle of the 1690's. The number of students enrolled in the Moscow schools just mentioned remained insignificant; yet the appearance of these institutions must be recorded as Russia's first advance along the thorny path of learning.

The spread of the art of book printing gave a stimulus to the development of science and literature, but the achievements were meager. The study of mathematics was hindered by the use of Slavonic characters instead of Arabic figures, which did not gain general acceptance in Russia until the eighteenth century. Other branches of knowledge, too, fared poorly. The available manuals of algebra, trigonometry, astronomy, rhetoric, dialectics, philosophy, and other subjects were pedestrian and clumsy translations (or mistranslations) of European scholastic treatises of the twelfth and thirteenth centuries. No Russians were qualified to make independent contributions to scientific studies.

The record of literature was somewhat brighter. While much of it was dreary and followed slavishly the didactic pattern of medieval scholasticism, some of the popular collections, both translated or written by native authors, displayed the welcome tendency to enlighten, entertain, and amuse rather than to uplift and educate. Although the prevalence of illiteracy restricted the circle of readers, such stories enjoyed considerable popularity and contributed to the gradual evolution of the literary language in the direction of greater simplicity, the traditional Old-Slavonic being reserved for writings dealing with religious subjects. The emancipation of a literary language, however, was not achieved until the eighteenth century. Of considerable interest were the writings of several contemporary Russians who took a dim view of existing conditions. The better-known among these authors were the eccentric Prince I. A. Khvorostinin (died in 1625) and Gregory Kotoshikhin, a disgruntled government official who in 1666 fled to Sweden, where he wrote a bitter indictment of his native land.

There is nothing to say about the arts, except perhaps architecture. Some of the seventeenth-century buildings, especially churches, are outstanding examples of the Russian baroque, which, however, was the adaptation of a style borrowed from western Europe.

Some of the Westerners. The departures from the sacrosanct tradition and the acceptance of Western ideas and practices did not actually amount to much: two or three theological schools with a handful of students; Westernized army units; some liberalization of lay literature; new skills among the artisans and the appearance of the first manufactories; modification of social customs, such as the relaxation of the seclusion of women; use of imported articles of dress and furniture; and the establishment of a court theatrical and ballet company. The beneficiaries of these changes were a tiny group of the upper class. The more notable supporters of modernization were high court officials—Boris Morozov, Fedor Rtishchev, Athanasius Ordyn-Nashchokin, Artamon Matveev, and Prince Vasili Golitsyn, eventually Tsarevna Sophie's favorite and advisor. Oddly, the true source of innovation was Tsar Alexis himself, although he had never aspired to be a reformer and firmly believed in the immutability of the Muscovite tradition. The changes which he accepted were those contributing to his comfort and pleasure. Further he would not go. If some of his councillors, as it is alleged, harbored more ambitious plans for reform, nothing came of them. The Code of 1649, with its ruthless regimentation and immobilization of every class of the population, was a representative document of the seventeenth century: it laid down a program which the government did its best to enforce.

The views of the Muscovite "Westerners" of the seventeenth century had no direct influence on the policies of Peter I, who was soon drastically to change the course of the Russian ship of state. Nevertheless, they are helpful to place the events of the eighteenth century in their true historical perspective.

PART THREE

1696-1801

CHRONOLOGY OF PRINCIPAL EVENTS

1721	Decree on "possessionary" peasants
1721	Peter assumes title of emperor
1722–1723	War with Persia
1721	Table of Ranks
1722	Law of succession
1723	Poll Tax
1724	Tariff act
1725–1727	Empress Catherine I
1725	Academy of Science established
1726–1730	Supreme Privy Council (central executive agency)
1727–1730	Emperor Peter II
1730–1740	Empress Anne
1731–1741	The cabinet (central executive agency)
1733–1736	War of Polish Succession
1734	Commercial treaty with England
1735–1739	War with Turkey
1736, December	Manifesto shortening and easing terms of government service
1736	Judicial powers of the landowners over the serfs extended
1740–1741	Emperor Iván VI; Anna Leopoldovna regent
1741–1761	Empress Elizabeth
1741–1743	War with Sweden
1743	Peace of Abo; Russia annexes strip of Finland
1747–1748	Russia's participation in War of Austrian Succession
1753	Removal of internal customs barriers
1754	Founding of Commercial Bank
1754	Founding of State Nobility Bank
1754–1762	St. Petersburg Winter Palace built by Rastrelli
1755	Publication of *Monthly Essays*, first Russian journal
1755	University of Moscow founded
1756–1762	Conference advisory to the Crown (central executive agency)
1756–1763	Seven Years' War
1757	Academy of Arts founded
1760	Estate owners empowered to deport serfs to Siberia
1761–1762	Emperor Peter III
1762	Peace with Prussia and withdrawal from Seven Years' War
1762, February 18	Manifesto freeing nobility of obligation of compulsory service

1762–1796	Empress Catherine II
1763	Beginning of Russian armed intervention in Poland
1764	Alliance with Prussia
1764	Secularization of Church estates
1765	Further extension of the juridical power of estate owners over serfs
1766	Tariff act
1767	"Confederation" of Radom
1767–1768	Legislative Commission
1768	"Confederation" of Bar
1768–1774	War with Turkey
1769	First Russian foreign loan, floated in Holland
1769	Paper currency introduced
1769–1796	Advisory council to the empress (central executive agency)
1770, June	Russians defeat Turkish fleet at Chesme (Tchesme)
1772	First partition of Poland
1773–1774	Pugachev's peasant uprising
1774, July	Peace of Kuchuk-Kainardzhi
1775	Law on the administration of provinces
1775	Freedom of establishing industrial enterprises proclaimed
1779	Founding in St. Petersburg of the Russian ballet school
1780	Declaration of Armed Neutrality
1780–1786	Abolition of central administrative agencies ("colleges")
1781	Suppression of autonomous institutions in the Ukraine
1782	Comedy *The Minor* by Fonvizin
1782	Tariff act
1783	Annexation of the Crimea
1783	Poll tax introduced in the Ukraine
1785	Charter of the Nobility
1785	Charter of the Towns
1786	Attempted school reform
1787	Catherine's inspection of southern provinces
1787–1792	War with Turkey
1788–1790	War with Sweden
1790	Prosecution of Radishchev
1791, May 3	New Polish constitution
1792, January	Treaty of Jassy
1792	Port of Odessa founded

1792	Prosecution of Novikov
1792	"Confederation" of Torgowica
1793, January	Second partition of Poland
1793–1796	Restrictive foreign trade policies
1794	Kosciuszko leads Polish resistance to partition
1795–1797	Third partition of Poland
1796	Attempt at invasion of Near East and India as part of the "Oriental Project"
1796–1801	Emperor Paul I
1797	Law of succession
1798, October	Paul elected grand master of Maltese order of knights of St. John of Jerusalem
1798–1799	Russia participates in the anti-French coalition
1799	Russian American Company established
1799	Russian Black Sea fleet occupies Ionian Islands and Corfu
1799	Suvorov crosses St. Gotthard Pass, Switzerland
1800, December	Second Armed Neutrality League
1801, January	Annexation of Georgia in the Caucasus
1801, March 11	Murder of Emperor Paul

10

Russia Becomes an Empire: Peter I, 1696-1725

The Tsar Reformer

Youth and Training. The reign of Peter I as Muscovy's sole ruler began in 1696, after the death of his half-brother and co-ruler, Ivan V.[1] Peter received little formal schooling, and, especially after the advent to power of his half-sister Tsarevna Sophie (1682), he was allowed to spend his time very much as he pleased. It was during these formative years of adolescence and early manhood that he developed a passionate interest in the army, the navy, and in the Western European technology and way of life which he mistook for European culture. Although all three interests began more or less inadvertently, they largely determined the character of his reign and the destiny of Russia. During the regency of Sophie, Peter lived most of the time in the village of Preobrazhenskoe, near Moscow; his favorite pastime was sham warfare, in which he engaged in the company of boys of his own age who were organized along military lines and were known as *poteshnye*. The center of their manoeuvres was the miniature fortress of Presburg, on the Yauza River. The chance discovery of a ramshackle English sailboat in a barn in the nearby village of Izmailovo proved the starting point of the crea-

---

[1] Events which followed the death of Tsar Alexis in 1682 and led to the accession of Peter are related in Chapter 8, pp. 127–130.

tion of the Russian navy. Peter experimented with this craft, first on the Yauza River, and then on Lake Pereiaslavl, where (and later at Archangel, on the White Sea) he proceeded to build boats with the assistance of Dutch sailors.

Associates and Pleasures. Peter's genuine craving for knowledge and concern with nautical matters, about which the Russians knew nothing, were presumably responsible for his early contacts with the foreign expatriates who lived in Moscow's German Settlement. One of them, the Dutchman Franz Timmermann, taught Peter arithmetic, geometry, artillery, and fortification, although his own notion of these subjects was hazy. Among the other foreigners who became Peter's close friends the better-known were the Scotsman Patrick Gordon and the Swiss Francis Lefort. Both were considerably older than the young tsar, but they had great influence over him during the opening years of his reign. Peter had unbounded admiration for Gordon and Lefort, who were to him the living embodiment of the mysterious and all-powerful Western civilization. Actually, however, his foreign mentors were men of questionable ability and low moral standards.

The Russian associates of Peter were drawn from every class of society. Some of them came from the old Muscovite aristocracy, others from families of modest or even humble standing. Alexander Menshikov, one of the most powerful personalities of the reign, began in life as a street peddler and could barely sign his name, but he rose rapidly to the dignity of prince of the Holy Empire and field marshal, held many high offices, and assembled a vast fortune. The tsar had seemingly boundless affection for Aleksashka, as the favorite was called by his intimates, and overlooked his many misdeeds.

Peter was a conscientious and indefatigable ruler and at times displayed a breadth of interest that is surprising in view of the limitations of his upbringing. Basically, however, he was crude and uncouth, sentimental and savagely cruel. His chief recreations in the midst of exacting military campaigns and far-reaching administrative and social reforms were the festivities held by the "All Drunken *Sobor* of Fools and Jesters," which he founded about 1690 and which continued to function until the end of the reign. The *Sobor* was organized on the hierarchical principle and was a gross and obscene parody on the institutions and ritual of the Russian Orthodox and the Roman Catholic Churches. Its chief object was the staging of monstrous drinking bouts interspersed with masquerades and pageants which lasted for several days and invariably provided for the display of fireworks manufactured, in part, by Peter himself. Throughout his life the tsar took a passionate interest in these festivities; he planned them carefully and wrote for them detailed, elaborate, and usually lewd instructions. No political implications should be read into the activities of the *Sobor:* they were but one manifesta-

PETRUS PRIMUS
RUSSORUM IMPERATOR

Peter the Great, engraving by Jakob Houbraken

tion of Peter's quaint sense of humor, exuberance, tireless energy, and craving for action.

First Visit to Europe. His inborn curiosity, stimulated by contacts with foreigners, was responsible for Peter's decision to visit Europe. The first Muscovite tsar to leave his realm on a peaceful mission, he traveled incognito as a member of an embassy headed by Lefort whose object it was to investigate the possibility of an alliance of Christian states against Turkey and to enroll foreign craftsmen in Russian service. The embassy left Moscow in March 1697, visited Kurland, Prussia, Holland, and England, and then proceeded by slow stages to Vienna. Plans for a visit to Italy had to be abandoned because of a *streltsy* uprising that forced Peter to return hastily to Moscow in August 1698. The tsar's incognito was loosely observed, and he was entertained in a manner befitting his rank by foreign rulers. His real purpose, however, was to learn, and he is said to have studied shipbuilding, architecture, engineering, fortification, book printing, drawing, engraving, natural history, anatomy and even dentistry. He also visited government and scientific institutions, churches, museums, factories, and shipyards, and participated—with his customary verve—in social activities of a wide range, from receptions by crowned heads to informal gatherings in waterfront taverns. Whether so crowded a program permitted Peter to gain a real grasp of the many subjects which he wished to study is doubtful, but he obtained some first-hand impressions of Europe and engaged hundreds of artisans and craftsmen in the service of Moscow. This first visit to western Europe was followed by many others, which were dictated by the exigencies of the Northern War and Russia's involvement in European affairs.

The Streltsy Uprising. Peter's European travels were interrupted by an uprising of the *streltsy.* After the fall of Sophie (1689) the *streltsy,* resenting the loss of their influence, continued to display a spirit of insubordination and were particularly incensed by the resettlement in the region of Azov (annexed in 1696) of their regiments which were formerly quartered in and around the capital. Some of these regiments mutinied in the summer of 1698 and marched towards Moscow but were stopped by loyal troops under Gordon. Peter, nevertheless, hastened to return home and assumed in person the direction of the investigation, which aimed at linking Sophie with the rebellion. Her complicity, however, was never established, and she was forced merely to take the veil. The mutinous soldiers were dealt with severely, Peter as well as Menshikov and the tsar's other intimate collaborators actually carrying out the executions, which are said to have exceeded 1,000. The *streltsy* regiments stationed in Moscow and Azov, where the mutiny originated, were disbanded, but other *streltsy* formations survived until 1705, when, following another mutiny, they were finally abolished.

The Two Marriages. In 1689, while still sixteen, Peter married Eudoxie Lopukhin, daughter of a palace official. The union was not a happy one; after a few weeks of marital life Peter abandoned his bride and returned to his military games and to the less innocent pleasures provided by his friends of the German Settlement. Ten years later (1699) he forced Eudoxie to take the veil, which was the traditional Muscovite way of terminating marriage bonds. About 1703, after several liaisons of a passing nature, Peter became enamoured of Catherine, an illiterate servant girl of Polish or Lithuanian origin and a former mistress of Menshikov. He married her in 1712, after she had borne him several children, and in 1724 had her crowned empress of Russia, after Peter himself had assumed the dignity of emperor in 1721. Catherine was the great feminine influence in Peter's life, although, as it will appear later, her affection failed him shortly before he died.

Tsarevich Alexis. Tsarevich Alexis, born in 1690, was Peter's first child by Eudoxie. Although Muscovy had no formal law of succession, the eldest male descendant of the tsar was traditionally regarded as heir-apparent. There was, however, no affection between father and son, and their relations became openly hostile after Peter's marriage to Catherine. Alexis, unlike his father, was of delicate health but, like his father, was given to heavy drinking. Historical tradition represents him as the leader of the opposition to the Petrine reforms and as the standard-bearer of the old Muscovite tradition, but there is no real ground for these contentions, although those who disapproved of Peter's policies naturally turned with hope to his son, whom the tsar was known to dislike. In the autumn of 1715 Alexis' wife, a German princess, died in giving birth to a son, the future Emperor Peter II. Almost simultaneously Catherine also gave birth to a son who, too, was named Peter. The appearance of these infants changed the dynastic situation by seemingly assuring the male succession to the throne, irrespective of what might happen to Alexis. Meanwhile the tsar made up his mind to disinherit his eldest son. Alexis escaped abroad but was prevailed upon, by promises of forgiveness, to return. On his arrival in St. Petersburg, however, he was brought before a special court of high ecclesiastical and civil officials, was charged with high treason, and was sentenced to death, but actually died after he was put through the torture chamber the third time (June 1718). The tsar himself conducted the investigation and witnessed his son's torments.

The Petrine Wars

Their Significance and Nature. The policies of Peter were largely shaped by the exigencies of war. Wars indeed were the great determining element of his reign. Between his accession in 1689 and his death early in 1725, the year 1724 alone was entirely free from war; during the preceding 34 years, periods of peace were few and far between, aggregating perhaps 13 months. These wars were not dictated, as is often alleged, by "historical necessity"; they were rather brought about by Peter's arbitrary and capricious decisions.

The Two Campaigns of Azov. Tired perhaps of the limited scope offered to his nautical ambitions by experimentation with boats on the Yauza River and Lake Pereiaslavl and at Archangel, Peter turned his attention to Azov, a Turkish port situated on the sea of that name at the mouth of the Don River. From the Sea of Azov egress to the Black Sea could be gained through the Straits of Kerch, which, however, were controlled by the Turks. The outcome of the 1687 and 1689 Russian campaigns against the state of the Crimean Tatars, a dependency of Turkey, was not encouraging,[2] but the tsar was young, reckless, and war-minded. In the spring of 1695 some 30,000 Russian troops marched south and besieged Azov; the operation was unsuccessful, partly because the fortress continued to receive supplies by sea. The Russians withdrew and spent the following months building light ships at Voronezh, a city on the upper course of the Don. This enterprise proved surprisingly rewarding. In the spring of 1696 a reorganized Russian army, supported by a flotilla of some 30 galleys which sailed down the Don, appeared again before Azov and besieged it—this time both by land and sea. The fortress capitulated in the summer, and, although the state of war continued for three more years, Azov was finally ceded to Russia (July 1700), an annexation that proved ephemeral. Peter was the mastermind of the Voronezh shipbuilding program and fought in both Azov campaigns as one of the rank and file.

Beginnings of the Northern War. The two Turkish campaigns were a mere curtain raiser. War with Sweden, known as the Northern War, lasted from 1700 to 1721 and was the principal and the most onerous of Peter's wars. It is likely that he became converted to the idea of a Swedish war during his European tour and that this plan took shape in 1698 in the course of a meeting with Augustus II, king of Poland and elector of Saxony, who was committed to recover certain former Polish provinces which were then held by

[2] See above, pp. 129, 132.

Sweden. Peter's warm friendship for Augustus, an unreliable ally and a sinister political figure, was an element in the subsequent course of events. In the autumn of 1699 Russia, Poland, and Denmark concluded a secret alliance against Sweden. Poland and Denmark began naval action early in 1700, but Russia was not to participate in the hostilities until the conclusion of peace with Turkey. Charles XII, the youthful king of Sweden (he was born in 1682), had a reputation as a great general, and his small but well-trained and well-equipped army was rated as the best in Europe.

The allies made a poor start. The unexpected landing of Charles in Denmark forced that country to withdraw from the coalition at the very time (August 1700) when Peter, after having at last received the news of the signature of the peace treaty with Turkey, was invading Swedish Livonia. Augustus met with severe reverses and failed to take Riga, while soon thereafter (November 1700) some 40,000 Russians were routed at Narva by a Swedish army 8,000 strong. Hordes of prisoners, vast military stores, and the entire Russian artillery fell to the enemy. Peter fled, abandoning his troops, and for a time had but one thought—peace at any price. He soon regained his composure, however, and during the next few years displayed remarkable determination and perseverance in reorganizing the army and creating an artillery and a fleet.

The Russian endeavor was greatly facilitated by Charles himself, who, paying no further attention to the Muscovites, became involved in a protracted war with Augustus, upon whom he inflicted crushing defeats. Augustus was deposed as king of Poland (1704) and, reduced to extremes, concluded with Sweden a secret agreement in which he repudiated his Russian alliance (1706). These were ominous developments, but Peter, taking advantage of the reprieve granted to him by Charles, conquered Livonia and Ingria where—in the bleakness of the Finnish marshes—he founded in 1703 the city of St. Petersburg. Yet the Russians were uneasy and in 1707 made an unsuccessful attempt to negotiate, through the intermediary of England, a peace settlement with Sweden.

Defeat of Charles XII. Meanwhile Charles, having disposed of Augustus, turned against the Muscovites. At the end of 1707 his troops crossed the Russian border and in the summer of 1708 advanced to Mogilev, on the Dnieper. The road to Moscow appeared to lie open, but Charles bode his time: he was waiting for the arrival from Sweden of reinforcements, supplies, and munitions. In September 1708, however, the Swedish relief corps under General Löwenhaupt was intercepted and routed by the Russians near the village Lesnaia, on the left bank of the Dnieper. This was a serious setback which forced Charles to revise his plans and to march his soldiers into the Ukraine, where food supplies were reported to be ample and where he could count on the support of Ivan Mazepa, hetman of the Ukraine, with whom he had a secret agreement.

To Peter, as well as to nationalistically-minded Russian historians, Mazepa was a traitor. His duplicity and tortuous policies were as reprehensible as they were ill-advised, but his appraisal of the Russo-Ukrainian relations was basically sound: an experienced Ukrainian national leader, he was convinced that the continuation of the Ukraine under Russian sovereignty was incompatible with the retention of her autonomous institutions. Subsequent events proved him to be right. Mazepa, however, grossly overestimated the intensity of the anti-Russian feeling among the Ukrainians. When in October 1708 he went openly on the side of Charles, he was followed by merely some 2,000 Cossacks, while the mass revolt against Muscovy which the Swedish king was led to expect failed to materialize. In the meantime Baturin, the hetman's capital, was captured and destroyed by the Russians, and Ivan Skoropadsky, a partisan of Muscovy, was elected hetman to succeed Mazepa.

Charles had to contend with other disappointments. The winter of 1708–1709 was an exceptionally severe one, and the epidemic-ridden Swedish army, bogged in a hostile country miles away from its bases, experienced extreme privations. In April the Swedes began the siege of the fortified town of Poltava; it was in this locality, on the banks of the Vorskla River, that the decisive battle took place in which the Swedes were overwhelmingly defeated (June 27, 1709). Charles, who was suffering from a wound received in a previous encounter, witnessed from a stretcher the rout of his troops. He, Mazepa, and a few of their followers succeeded in escaping by crossing the Dnieper and took refuge in Turkish territory, where the hetman died soon thereafter. The bulk of the Swedish army found its avenues of retreat cut off by the Dnieper and were made prisoners by the Russians.

Although the total number of Swedish soldiers in Russia did not exceed 20,000, the defeat and flight of Charles XII produced a deep impression both in Muscovy and abroad. War with Sweden was not over, but the climate of European opinion had undergone a marked change. Augustus II was restored to the throne of Poland and in October 1709 concluded with Russia a new alliance against Sweden, which was joined by Denmark and Prussia, the latter, however, in a purely defensive capacity. Meanwhile Russian troops resumed operations along the littoral of the Baltic Sea and the Gulf of Finland and in 1710 occupied several important ports (Riga, Reval, Viborg).

Setback in Turkey. The presence of Charles XII in Turkey became the source of discord between that country and Russia. The Swedish king, aided and abetted by the French, intrigued against Moscow; Peter peremptorily demanded his expulsion and when Constantinople refused to comply, Russia and Turkey found themselves at war (November 1710). The tsar, counting on the uprising of the Orthodox Slav population of the Ottoman empire, invaded Turkey early in the summer of 1711 and advanced to the Pruth River. His army numbered some 40,000. The anticipated revolt of Turkey's Christian subjects, however, was not forthcoming, and the Russian army, which was commanded by Peter and accompanied by Catherine and the ladies of the Russian court, was encircled by a vastly superior Turkish force. To escape seemingly inevitable defeat and the unattractive prospect of joining Charles XII in Turkish captivity, the tsar hastened to make peace on Constantinople's own terms: the Turks recovered Azov, and Russia agreed to raze the fortifications erected in that region, not to interfere with Poland and the Cossacks, and to guarantee the passage of Charles XII through her territory (July 1711). Peter was prepared to accept much more onerous terms and was delighted by Turkey's unexpected moderation, even though the peace settlement of 1711 obliterated the gains of the two Azov campaigns and did not enhance his military reputation.

End of the Northern War. Charles XII did not return from Turkey until the end of 1714; meanwhile the war by land and sea continued, the Russians conquering the Baltic littoral from Finland to Pomerania. Particularly impressive was the victory won by the young Russian fleet over the Swedes at Hangö, Finland (June 1714). The European governments, including Russia's allies, watched with apprehension and misgivings the progress of the Muscovites. This uneasiness was increased by the establishment of dynastic ties between the Russian ruler and some of the European princely houses. Peter's nieces Anne and Catherine (daughters of his half-brother and erstwhile co-ruler, Ivan V) were married, the former in 1710 to the Duke of Kurland, and the latter in 1716 to the Duke of Mecklenburg. The Duke of Holstein-Gottorp, pretender to the Swedish throne, became engaged to Peter's daughter Anne and married her in 1725 after her father had died. The attempt to find among the French royal princes a husband for the eldest daughter of the tsar, Princess Elizabeth, proved unsuccessful. The dynastic alliances with petty German courts had important political consequences. They enmeshed the Russian government in the light-hearted plans of expansion and nebulous political schemes stemming from the territorial and dynastic ambitions of some of Europe's most unworthy and foolish rulers. The involvement of Peter in the affairs of his new or prospective relatives prolonged the Northern War and made the final settlement more difficult.

The anti-Swedish coalition, which was restored after Charles XII's defeat at Poltava, carried on the war for the conquest of the German provinces of Sweden and had considerable success. Its original membership—Russia, Poland, Saxony, and Denmark—was extended to include Hanover, Prussia, and eventually England, whose King George I occupied simultaneously the throne of Hanover. There was, however, little unity among the allies, whose territorial claims were often in conflict. Russia's high-handed interference in the affairs of Kurland, Mecklenburg, Holstein, and Poland caused much concern among the other members of the coalition, for whom Peter, too, had little liking. At one time he became converted to the idea of an agreement with Sweden which would allow Russia to retain her territorial conquests but would compensate Sweden at the expense of the other allies, especially Hanover and Denmark. Russian troops were to be used, at the discretion of Charles, in achieving Swedish annexationist aims. Negotiations to this effect were in progress at the Aland Islands when Charles XII was killed in action (December 1718); they were broken off a few months later. Charles XII was succeeded by his younger sister Ulrica Eleonora.

The death of Charles XII was the signal for the disintegration of the wobbling coalition. Hanover, Saxony, Denmark, and Prussia hastened to make peace with Sweden, securing slices of her continental domain. Russia continued military and naval action and in 1719, 1720, and 1721 landed Cossacks on the southern shore of Sweden. Some of the raiding parties made their way to within a short distance of Stockholm.

Ulrica Eleonora abdicated in 1720 in favor of her husband, Frederick I, who had none of Charles XII's zest for fighting. The Russo-Swedish peace negotiations began in April 1721 and were concluded in August of the same year. Under the treaty of Nystadt Russia acquired the provinces of Livonia, Estonia, and Ingria, a portion of Karelia (which is part of Finland) with the city and district of Viborg, and the islands of Oesel and Dagoe. Most of Finland, however, which was held by the Russians, reverted to Sweden.

The Northern War was exceedingly costly, but Russia emerged from it as a European power established on the shores of the Baltic Sea. Peter felt justified to assume at the end of the struggle the title "Father of the Country, Emperor, and Great."

The Persian War. Since about 1715 the Russian government had shown interest in Persia, particularly in the possibility of developing trade in the region of the Caspian Sea. As conditions in that part of the world were chaotic, war and annexation were regarded as the proper method of safeguard-

European Russia at the death of Peter the Great, 1725

ing Russian interests. In the spring of 1722 Peter led an expeditionary corps some 100,000 strong into the Persian provinces bordering on the Caspian Sea. There was little organized resistance, but shortages of supplies, including foodstuffs and fodder, inflicted grievous losses on the invaders. A treaty with Persia (September 1723) ceded to Russia the southern shores of the Caspian Sea with the cities of Baku and Derbent. Muscovy's hold over these territories proved short-lived: ten years later they were restored to Persia to ensure her friendly attitude during an impending war with Turkey.

Administrative Reforms

Their Origins and Character. The origin and character of most of the Petrine reforms, administrative and others, may be traced to two principal sources: the imperative demands of the Northern War and the tsar's predilection for Western institutions and Western ways.

The Army. The upholding of Russia's newly-acquired status as a great power, which was the consequence of Peter's victory over Charles XII, called for an armed force much larger than that maintained in seventeenth-century Muscovy. The protracted Northern War had a profound effect upon the size of the army, the length of service, and the methods of recruitment. As early as 1690 or 1691 Peter's former playmates (*poteshnye*) were reorganized as two regiments of the guards (to which a third regiment eventually known as the Horse Guards was added in 1719) but, although they were soon to play a decisive role in the political and social history of the nation, their effectives remained few (about 3,000) and were a minor factor in warfare. During the initial stage of the Northern War the Russian army numbered some 40,000 and consisted of the *dvoriane* militia and volunteers drawn from every social group, including the slaves. Soon thereafter the volunteer system was superseded by the draft, groups of households (their number varied) being required to provide a recruit. The draftees received some military training and served for protracted periods with the regiments to which they were assigned. The militia was thus gradually transformed into a standing army, which was provided with a statutory framework by the Army Regulations of 1716. By the end of Peter's reign the regular army numbered 200,000 men; there were also 100,000 Cossacks and a large but undeterminable force of native troops from Russia's eastern borderland.

The Navy. Prior to the eighteenth century Russia had no navy and, indeed, no seaports except Archangel, on the rather inaccessible White Sea. Peter, therefore, is legitimately regarded as the founder of Russian sea power.

Peter at the Shipyards, by V. A. Serov

Battle of Hangö, 1714

Early attempts at building sea-going naval vessels were made in 1695–1696 at Voronezh in preparation for the second Azov campaign and in 1702 at Archangel. After the conquest of Ingria Peter established shipyards on the Svir River, and in 1704 the first Russian man-of-war was launched in the Baltic Sea. By 1725 the Russian naval establishment in these waters consisted of some 800 vessels of various types manned by 28,000 men. In several encounters with the Swedes the young Russian navy gave a good account of itself, but contrary to expectations Russia did not become a major naval power: a decade after Peter's death the number of seaworthy naval vessels in the Baltic had dropped to 15. The merchant marine, too, made little progress, and until the end of the empire Russian sea-borne trade was carried predominantly in foreign bottoms.

Administrative Decentralization. Administrative reforms were the by-product of the desire to increase revenue and to introduce some order in public finance. According to a plan adopted in 1699 this was to be achieved by consolidating the receipts in a central agency. Financial disorders persisted, however, and were all the more disturbing because of the urgent need for funds created by the war. Centralization having failed, decentralization was tried: groups of taxpayers were to provide directly—that is, without the intermediary of a central department—for the maintenance of specified army units. To attain this objective, legislation enacted in 1708–1711 divided Russia into eight provinces (their number was increased to 12 in 1719), each headed by an appointed governor. Army units then were allocated among the provinces, which provided for them. It was expected that by eliminating the rapacious and cumbersome central agencies the service of supply would be greatly improved. These expectations were not fulfilled, but the provinces furnished a durable administrative framework which was retained, with modifications, until the end of the empire. The principal divisions of the provincial government, each under an appointed official, were finance, grain collection, armed forces, and administration of justice. Provinces were subdivided into counties, which were administered by appointed officials vested with military, fiscal, judicial, and police powers.

The financing of army units directly from the proceeds of taxes collected by the provincial governors contributed to the disintegration of the central administration by transferring to local authorities functions formerly exercised by central departments (*prikazy*): some of the latter were abolished or became extinct. There were other signs of the decline of the central authority. The boyar *duma,* which had been losing influence since Russia's unification, did not meet after the opening years of the eighteenth century and was not replaced by any formally constituted body. Moreover for a decade or longer Russia had no real capital: Moscow was being rapidly deprived of this status but was not entirely superseded by St. Petersburg until the closing years of Peter's reign. The tsar himself, that fountain of power, made but rare and brief appearances at the seat of government.

The Senate. The decay of the machinery of central government proved but a passing phase. The reconstruction of central institutions, like their decline, came about in a casual and haphazard manner. In 1711, before leaving for the Pruth campaign, Peter appointed the "Governing Senate," a 9-member body which was to exercise supreme authority during his absence. It was an organ of administrative, primarily financial, control as well as the highest court, but the judicial function was not vested in the Senate until somewhat later. At the time of its establishment the Senate was directed to ensure the financing of the armed forces and to supervise the collection of taxes by the provincial governors, thus restoring a measure of unification in financial administration. Located at first in Moscow, the Senate was transferred to St. Petersburg in 1714. Although intended as a provisional institution for the duration of the Turkish war, the Senate actually outlived the empire and was not abolished until a month after the advent of the Bolsheviks to power. Contrary to the terms of the 1711 decree, however, it was not a supreme body, its powers being exercised under the supervision of officials appointed by the Crown. After 1722 the Senate was narrowly controlled by the procurator-general, who was responsible directly to the tsar. This arrangement was retained until the fall of the monarchy.

Administrative Colleges. The creation of the Senate was but the first step in the reconstruction of centralized government. The multiplicity of the central departments (*prikazy*) in the seventeenth century and their uncoordinated and overlapping jurisdictions resulted in much confusion and waste. Unlike the other Petrine reforms, the remodelling of the central administration was preceded by extensive planning and protracted deliberations. Peter was greatly impressed by the government of his life-long antagonist, Sweden. Swedish institutions embodied the collegial principle, that is, the power of decision rested not with individual officials but with administrative boards or "colleges," an arrangement designed to minimize arbitrariness and to prevent abuses. After some inconclusive preliminary experimentation, Peter in 1715 entrusted the preparation of pertinent legislation to an erudite German advisor, who made a detailed study of the Swedish administrative system; and since few Russians were qualified to serve in the reconstructed departments, some 150 Germans as well as a number of Swedish prisoners of war were recruited for this purpose. The constitution of the nine administrative colleges which were to replace the existing *prikazy* was formally announced in 1717, but they were not actually organized until 1719. Contrary to the Muscovite tradition, their functions were sharply delimited. Each college was in charge of a separate branch of government: foreign relations, revenue, expenditure, state control, justice, army, navy, extractive industry and manufactures, and commerce. A college was headed by a board of 11 members, including a president, a vice president, and a foreign advisor; decisions were arrived at by majority vote.

While the re-distribution of administrative functions according to an orderly plan was an improvement of the conditions prevailing during the earlier period, the collegial principle, which was the essence of the reform, did not prove viable. In 1726, soon after Peter's death, the membership of the collegial boards was reduced from eleven to six—"to facilitate the reaching of decisions." In practice, moreover, college presidents were far more important officials than the members of their respective boards and ruled their departments very much as the heads of the *prikazy* had done previously. The college of extractive industry and manufactures was soon closed as unnecessary.

Local Government. The division of Russia into provinces was followed by an extensive remodelling of the local government. The object of the earlier measures was the creation of a direct link between army units and the taxpayers who provided for them. To achieve a more equitable distribution of the tax burden, there was introduced in 1715 a new administrative-territorial subdivision, the *dolia,* which was to comprise 5,536 taxable households. Regiments were to be re-allocated according to the number of *dolia* in each province. This scheme failed and was superseded in 1718 by the attempt to transplant to the Russian soil the institutions of Swedish local government. The *dolia* was dropped and was replaced by the county. Confusion resulting from the implementation of this reform was aggravated, with the termination of the Northern War, by the billeting on rural areas of the troops, for which the local taxpayers were to provide. This arrangement led to the formation of a new administrative-territorial unit, the "regimental district," which cut across all other administrative subdivisions and was run largely by the military. The taxpayers found themselves in a truly desperate plight from which they were rescued only by the transfer of the troops to urban settlements in 1727. Simultaneously the cumbersome and costly institutions of local government modelled on those of Sweden were discarded. An instruction of 1728, which was to remain the law of the land for nearly 50 years,

retained the Petrine administrative-territorial framework but conferred plenary powers upon appointed provincial governors as well as officials in
charge of the smaller administrative subdivisions—counties and towns. For
all practical purposes this was a return to the administrative practice of
the seventeenth century.

Municipal Government. The municipal reform was as haphazard, confused, and ineffectual as that of the provincial and county government. Legislation enacted at the turn of the seventeenth century endeavored to substitute
elected representatives of the well-to-do merchants for Crown officials in charge
of urban affairs. No real self-government emerged from this experimentation,
which, moreover, was soon permitted to peter out. A more ambitious program
was tried between 1718 and 1724. It aimed at the introduction in Russia of
municipal institutions patterned after those of Riga and Reval, ancient Germanic cities recently conquered by Russia from Sweden. Under the new dispensation the urban population was organized, according to professional and
property qualifications, into three distinct groups or corporations: the first
guild, the second guild, and the "common people." Executive powers were
exercised by the town council elected by the two guilds but on which only
the members of the first guild were eligible to serve. In theory the highest
organ of the city government was the town meeting, an assembly of all taxpayers. These institutions proved stillborn. The corporate organization which
had developed organically in the prosperous German commercial cities could
not be re-created in the hopelessly poor and backward Russian urban settlements. The town meeting met seldom and exercised no real authority, and
in 1727 the municipal councils were formally subordinated to appointed
Crown officials, that is, the ill-conceived experiment in municipal self-government came to an end.

Finance, Industry, and Trade

The Poll Tax. War is always an expensive business. Much of the state
revenue, which between 1680 and 1724 increased from 1.4 million rubles to
8.5 million rubles, was spent on the army and the navy. At the time of Peter's
death, about three-quarters of the total receipts were used for the maintenance of the peacetime armed forces. As the government was incessantly
harrassed by the shortage of funds, a variety of measures to deal with the
ever-recurrent emergency were tried. Currency was repeatedly debased by
reducing the amount of silver in the coins in circulation, with the result that
during the reign of Peter the ruble lost about 50 per cent of its metallic con-

tent and much of its purchasing power. A special service of the so-called "profit-makers," an unpopular branch of financial administration, concerned itself exclusively with devising new sources of revenue. Everything taxable was taxed. Beards, for instance, were taxed according to the status of their owners, the annual rate being as high as 100 rubles for wealthy merchants. Bearded peasants were exempt from the tax so long as they remained in their villages but had to pay one copeck every time they entered or left an urban settlement. The sale of salt, tobacco, tar, chalk, fish, oil, potash, caviar, bristle, and several other commodities became government monopolies; their financial returns, however, often proved disappointing, especially because of loose enforcement and the prevalence of evasion. In 1719 freedom of private trading in most of the articles just mentioned was restored, but the state salt monopoly was retained until nearly the end of the nineteenth century.

The decline in the yield of the household tax, the principal direct tax, caused much concern. The dwindling of the revenue from that source was due to the decrease in the number of households, as revealed by the censuses which were taken at irregular intervals. Gradually the authorities concluded that the shrinkage in the number of households was the consequence not so much of the flight of the taxpayers, as was formerly believed, as of the merging of households for the very purpose of evading the household tax. The obvious remedy was to shift the basis of assessment and to substitute the poll (head) tax for the household tax. Accordingly, the decree of January 9, 1723, made the entire servile male population, irrespective of age, subject to the poll tax, thus eliminating the former distinctions between the serfs and other ill-defined groups of bondsmen. The rate of the tax was 74 copecks a year for serfs living on privately owned estates (they had to pay in addition a tribute to their owners) and 1.20 rubles for state peasants.[3] The immediate financial results of the reform were highly satisfactory: the yield of the household tax had been 1.8 million rubles a year, while that of the poll tax was estimated at 4.6 million rubles. The poll tax, although the earmark of servile status, survived the emancipation of 1861 and was not abolished until the 1880's.

Industry. Russian industry made some progress in the seventeenth century, as its development was fostered by mercantilist policies.[4] Conditions prevailing during the first quarter of the eighteenth century accelerated the pace of industrial development. The Northern War and the revolutionary changes wrought by Peter in the dress and social customs of the upper class created a new demand which the existing industrial enterprises were unable to meet.

[3] See above, p. 143.
[4] See above, pp. 148, 155–156.

Imports were hindered by the dislocation caused by the war and by the treasury's perennial shortage of funds. Moreover, the mercantilist doctrine discouraged imports. The alternative that commended itself to the tsar and his advisors was the expansion of domestic industries. Like his predecessors Peter imported foreign artisans and sent young Russians abroad to be trained in arts and crafts. Geological surveys undertaken by the government led to the discovery of important deposits of industrial minerals. As the most urgent need was for army and naval stores, foundries and munition works were started, as well as enterprises producing arms, cloth, cordage, canvas for sails, and so on. Other establishments were engaged in manufacturing silks, brocades, linens, velvets, woollens, paper, hosiery, and other consumers' goods. The new enterprises were usually set up by the government and then transferred to private ownership, which was made attractive by conferring upon the industrialists various privileges: subsidies; exemption from taxation; exemption from government service for the owners, their children, and skilled workers; duty-free imports of machinery and raw materials; free supply of labor; high tariff protection or even exclusion of competing foreign articles; and in some cases the monopoly of the domestic market.

The bulk of the new industrialists came from the merchant class, although several of the higher officials (for instance, Prince Menshikov) were owners of, or partners in, a number of enterprises. The source and volume of industrial investments is a disputed matter. The better-founded view would seem to be that the amount of capital available for investment, including "commercial" capital (that is, capital owned by the merchants), was small; government participation, therefore, especially in the initial stage, was practically a necessity.

Some of the enterprises were large and employed several hundred or more workers, but production was carried on by the method of "cottage" industry, that is, in the workers' own homes. The recruitment of industrial labor presented formidable difficulties, because the Code of 1649, which endeavored to assign each social group to specific tasks, made no provision for employment in industry.[5] There were two main sources of industrial labor: the servile population, and the dregs of society, such as criminals, beggars, prostitutes, and the like. The practice of assigning serfs to industrial enterprises was formalized by a decree of 1721 which established the so-called "possessionary" works. Serfs were permanently attached to such establishments and could not be employed anywhere else. The rule of the Code of 1649 which made the ownership of estates populated by serfs the prerogative of the *dvoriane* did

[5] See above, p. 144.

not apply to possessionary works, which could be and were owned by members of other social groups, especially the merchants. The government exercised over the enterprises of this category an extensive control that in time proved highly restrictive. Possessionary works continued to exist until the emancipation of 1861, but their record was one of technical stagnation and declining output accompanied by recurrent labor disturbances. Attachment to possessionary works was indeed one of the harshest forms of serfdom.

It is easy to exaggerate Russian industrial gains during the reign of Peter. By the time of his death the number of large industrial enterprises was about 200. The greatest advance was scored in the smelting and iron industry: throughout most of the eighteenth century Russia was, by a narrow margin, Europe's leading producer of pig iron.[6] Other industries fared less well. The quality of the goods produced remained low and, a number of large enterprises closed their doors before the middle of the century. Industrial progress under Peter was actually exceedingly modest.

Mercantilist ideas influenced foreign trade policies. The system of discriminatory import duties which varied according to the nationality of the importers and which were in effect in Russia in the seventeenth century remained in force throughout Peter's reign. Under this arrangement goods consigned to Russian merchants were taxed at much lower rates than similar articles imported by foreigners. There was widespread evasion of these regulations by making use of Russian agents who posed as independent importers but were actually representatives of foreign firms. In 1724 the above discriminatory laws were repealed and were replaced by a stiff tariff which was applied irrespective of the nationality of the consignees. The change ended one form of evasion but invited another: the very high rates of the tariff fostered contraband, which thrived on the corruption of customs officials and assumed huge proportions. From time to time the government prohibited the importation of certain commodities (for instance, silks, brocades, and velvets in 1717) to maintain the monopolistic privileges granted to Russian manufacturers.

Paradoxically, the desire to prevent evasion encouraged liberal domestic trade policies. The Code of 1649 intended to make domestic retail trade the

---

[6] Production of pig iron increased from 15,000 poods in 1700 to 1,000,000 poods, or 16,500 long tons, in 1725. Throughout the nineteenth century and until quite recently Russian production of pig iron in 1718 was invariably given as 6.6 million poods, or 109,000 long tons, an incongruously high figure. S. G. Strumilin, a Soviet economic historian of note, has definitely established that the use of this figure for 1718 was due to a typographical error in the original source: *1718* should read *1778;* S. G. Strumilin, *Istoriia chernoi metallurgii v SSSR* (*History of Ferrous Metallurgy in the USSR*) (Moscow: Academy of Science, 1954), vol. I, pp. 180–185, 205–206). It is amazing and lamentable that a figure which overstates the production of pig iron more than six times should have been used by historians of Russia for 150 years before the error was detected.

preserve of the burghers, but these provisions were never fully enforced and members of other social groups, especially the peasants, kept shops in contravention of the law. A decree of 1711 permitted everyone, irrespective of legal and social status, to engage freely in trade, provided they paid the appropriate tax. The abolition in 1719 of a number of state monopolies broadened the field of private commerce, but the principle of state trading was retained and was again used extensively in the middle of the eighteenth century.

Peter's ambition to make Russia an industrial nation exporting manufactured goods under her own flag was not realized. He succeeded, however, in diverting, by stringent measures, to St. Petersburg much of the trade that formerly went to Archangel. The advantages of a Baltic port over the one on the White Sea would have undoubtedly lead to an eventual shift of trade to St. Petersburg, but the change was greatly accelerated by government intervention.

Social and Cultural Policies

The Western Look. While the effects of Peter's administrative and economic reforms are debatable and inconclusive, there is no question that he succeeded in eradicating, in a surprisingly short time, some of the more striking external differences between Russia and the West. In the seventeenth century the dress of the Russian upper class was of an Oriental pattern, comprising long vestments with flowing sleeves and high bonnets. Men wore beards, as prescribed by the Church. Peter did not follow these customs, was clean-shaven, and dressed like his friends from the German Settlement. The country was soon forced to emulate his example. At a court function on his return from Europe in 1698, the tsar proceeded, with the assistance of the court jester, to cut off the beards of the assembled dignitaries, as well as the sleeves and skirts of their garments. Decrees issued in 1700 and repeated thereafter directed the entire population, male and female, except for the clergy and the peasants, to wear Western clothes which were variously described as Hungarian, German, Saxon, and French. As severe punishments were provided for disobedience, by 1705 Western fashion in dress was generally followed, at least by the upper class. The use of tobacco, on which the Church frowned, was fostered by the state tobacco monopoly and by the example of the tsar, who was an inveterate pipe smoker. Another departure from custom was the termination of the seclusion of women: they were to participate in officially sponsored social gatherings where the tsar, officialdom, and the nobility mingled with merchants, artisans, and foreign craftsmen. A breach of tradition of some importance was the adoption by Russia of the Julian calendar in 1699.[7]

Schools. The Petrine innovations—the navy, the modernized army and civil service, and the manufactories—needed trained people to make them function. The sending of young Russians to study abroad and the employment of foreigners continued, but the shortage of naval and army officers and civil servants persisted. The obvious solution was the opening of schools which would provide adequate instruction. The task, however, was a formidable one: seventeenth-century Russia had no schools except a few theological academies, and Peter and his government were confronted with the lack of teachers and textbooks as well as with the hostility of the community. Nevertheless, several schools were established. Their main objective was to train personnel for government service, especially the army and the navy. The best-known institution was the "school of mathematics and navigation" which was founded in Moscow in 1701, was transferred to St. Petersburg in 1715, and became the Naval Academy, a Russian Annapolis which exists to this day. The student body of the Naval Academy and that of the school for army engineers established about the same time were exceedingly small. A secondary school organized in 1705 by the German Pastor Ernst Glück, the first institution designed to offer non-professional instruction, closed its doors 10 years later for lack of students. There were major difficulties about the curricula. Peter imagined that geometry and trigonometry, about which he knew little, were the key to all knowledge. These subjects, therefore, were prominent in the programs of all lay schools established during his reign. A decree of 1714 ordered the opening of two "mathematical" schools in each province. Their student body was recruited among the children of local residents, and failure to complete the course brought upon the unsuccessful students severe penalties, including the prohibition to marry. These stringent rules failed to achieve their objective. Of the 1,400 students enrolled during the first 10 years of the "mathematical" schools, fewer than 100 completed the course.

The Church schools which were organized during this period and catered chiefly to the sons of the clergy proved more viable. The more important were the parochial schools established under the provisions of the Church Statute of 1721; some of them grew into theological seminaries which offered a 9-year course and were an important addition to the school system.

---

[7] Prior to this reform, time in Russia was reckoned from creation, and the calendar year began on September 1. A difference between the Russian and the Western calendar persisted, however, because the West used the Gregorian calendar. See Preface.

Beard-clipping during Peter's reign, a contemporary cartoon

Undaunted by the meager success of his educational endeavor, Peter made plans for an Academy of Science. The fellows of this institution of higher learning were imported from abroad, since no Russians were qualified for the position. The Academy was not inaugurated until the end of 1725, after Peter's death. He also organized the first Russian museum, which was a collection of strange and unusual objects rather than of works of art; it was eventually incorporated in the Academy of Science.

Literature. With the appearance of schools the importance of the printed word increased. In 1703 the first Russian newspaper was published. The Old-Slavonic alphabet was simplified, and from 1708 on, the modernized version was used in all lay publications, the ancient form being retained in Church books.

Most of the books printed in Russia under Peter were translations. The tsar took keen interest in deciding what should be made available to the reading public, still a tiny and highly selective minority, and the literary output bears the mark of his preferences. The titles published were chiefly dictionaries and textbooks on arithmetic, geometry, trigonometry, fortification, architecture, geography, engineering, navigation, shipbuilding, and so on, as well as manuals on how to behave in polite society. The translations were often very poor, and the few treatises on history and other subjects written by Russian authors showed no originality or literary merit. Uninspiring as was this output, it was a departure from the stale Byzantinism and medievalism of the seventeenth century and the first timid step towards the integration of Russia in the intellectual currents of the West.

The Church. Important changes occurred in the position of the Church. Peter attended regularly divine services which he knew by heart, but he took little interest in religious matters, displayed an outrageous lack of respect for Church institutions (as evidenced by the character and ways of the All Drunken *Sobor* of Fools and Jesters), and viewed the Church primarily as an agency for the implementation of official policies. He was intolerant of criticism and, perhaps, remembered the conflict between his father, Tsar Alexis, and Patriarch Nikon, while the higher clergy looked askance at Peter's domestic disorders, unorthodox behavior, association with foreigners, and contempt for custom. We know that subservience to the secular power was in the tradition of the Russian Church. Nevertheless, the possibility of conflict between the two existed and appeared the more likely so long as the Church was headed by a patriarch. After the death in 1700 of the last incumbent of that office, Peter did not fill the vacancy but appointed the metropolitan of Riazan, Stephen Yavorsky, as "keeper and administrator of the patriarchal see." It is noteworthy that the two leading clerics of the Petrine era, Yavorsky and Theophan Prokopovich, had once come under the sway of Catholicism and had studied in Catholic schools abroad but eventually returned to the fold of Greek Orthodoxy. Yavorsky nevertheless retained the Catholic belief in the supremacy of the spiritual power, a notion that Prokopovich vehemently denied. He was the author of the Church Statute of 1721, which abolished the Russian patriarchate and substituted for it the Holy Synod, a collegial body whose members were drawn from the ranks of the clergy but did not enjoy permanency of tenure. A decree of 1722 put the Holy Synod under the control of a lay chief procurator who was to be selected among "good and courageous" army officers. The abolition of the patriarchate and the establishment of the Holy Synod completed the process of subjugation of the Church by the state.

The Church suffered other diminutions of authority. In 1701 it was deprived of the right to administer its vast landed estates, which, although not secularized, were transferred to the control of a lay department that used part of the revenue to defray state expenditure, such as the cost of the war. With the creation of the Senate, the consecration of the bishops was made subject to its preliminary approval.

There were shifts in government policies towards the dissenters. After the fall of Sophie (1689) persecution subsided but was resumed when the old-believers showed opposition to the reforms. The rate of the tax levied on the dissenters was doubled in 1716, and six years later they were compelled to wear a special dress. There was a resurgence of mass flight to the wilderness of eastern Russia and of the epidemics of self-burning. Unlike his predecessors, however, Peter was concerned with the suppression of a subversive political movement rather than with the eradication of a heresy.

The Service Class. Peter made no major changes in the legal status of the service class, but his rule had a great effect on the position of its members. At the beginning of the eighteenth century, as in the seventeenth, the chief duty of the *dvoriane* was government service and their chief privilege the ownership of landed estates populated by serfs. The protracted character of the Northern War and the prolification of administrative agencies strained the available reserves of manpower and increased the burdens of the service class. Stringent rules provided for the registration of the young *dvoriane* still in their teens or even younger, assigned them to schools, regiments, and offices, and mapped out their official careers. Evasion of service, although severely punishable, was common. As the capacity of the existing schools was inadequate to accommodate all the candidates, many of the *dvoriane* were

Church in Akhimovo (Vologda Province), 1708

enrolled as privates in the regiments of the guards but were eventually awarded commissions in the armed forces or were transferred to the civil service. Peter frequently used guardsmen as his personal emissaries who superseded regular officials even of the highest rank. This complexion of the regiments of the guards explains the political role which they were to play throughout the eighteenth century.

Since government service was the hereditary duty of every *dvorianin,* it was logical that members of the other social groups who entered government service should be raised to the dignity of the highest estate of the realm. Provisions to this effect were made in the Table of Ranks (January 1722), which arranged all offices in both the armed forces and the civil service, in a hierarchical order, into 14 classes. A soldier who had reached the lowest officers' rank and a civil servant who had attained Rank Eight were entitled to the dignity of hereditary *dvorianstvo.* Government service thus became the method of acquiring a title of nobility. The Table of Ranks remained in force until the end of the empire.

The enforced absence of the *dvoriane* from their estates tended to weaken local ties. The very appearance of the members of the upper class—clean-shaven faces, powdered wigs, and Western dress—set them apart from the common people of the countryside.

The power of the *dvoriane* over their servile population, already comprehensive in the seventeenth century, was further broadened. The estate owners were made responsible for the payment of the poll tax assessed on their serfs, and in 1731 they became government agents for the collection of this tax.

Unrest and the Security Police. Peter's wars were onerous and his rule exacting and harsh. Forced labor was extensively used in fortifying the Azov region, in constructing internal waterways, and above all in building St. Petersburg in the Finnish marshes. An untold number of people employed on these huge public works died of hunger, cold, and disease. These conditions generated social unrest, and the peasant revolts common in the seventeenth century continued with undiminished force throughout Peter's reign. Notable was the uprising in 1707 led by Konrad Bulavin. The Ukraine and the Volga region, where many dissenters had sought refuge, were seething with discontent, and there were many people throughout the land, including Moscow and St. Petersburg, even in court circles, who were perturbed by the tsar's policies and conduct, particularly by the execution of Tsarevich Alexis. What they said about their master was, of necessity, not always flattering.

In these talks Peter showed the greatest interest. He built up a vast network of security police and made liberal use of private informers. Incidentally, this organization proved to be one of his lasting contributions to the practice of the Russian government.

The Law of Succession. Peter was concerned with the question of succession to the throne. His infant son Peter, born in 1715, had died in 1719. The tsar's only surviving male descendant was his grandson Peter, son of Tsarevich Alexis. The emperor was determined, however, that the boy should not reign and in February 1722 issued a decree empowering the tsar to appoint his successor so as to eliminate the unworthy members of the dynasty. Peter might have intended to nominate his wife Catherine, who was crowned in May 1724, but at the end of that year he discovered that she had a lover. The tsar's sudden death in January 1725 presumably saved Catherine from sharing the fate of her paramour, who was executed, but Peter died without appointing a successor. The absence of a law of succession introduced into the political situation an element of uncertainty the consequences of which were felt throughout the eighteenth century.

11

The Doldrums, 1725-1761

The Rulers

Palace Revolutions. The period from 1725 to the opening year of the nine-teenth century was the age of palace revolutions. In the absence of a definite law of succession the decision as to who was to occupy the throne came to rest upon casual gatherings of high state and palace officials supported by the regiments of the guards. The political role played by the guards needs a few words of explanation. Since schools were few, service with the guards came to be looked upon as a substitute for scholastic training, with the result that not only the officers but also the majority of the privates belonged to the nobility; they were destined eventually to fill the more important posts in the armed forces and in the civil administration. Peter I had leaned heavily on guardsmen as his special emissaries, who had been entrusted with various missions at home and abroad. The guards were conscious of their importance, and their regiments—stationed as they were in the capital—were the only organized group capable of concerted action in an emergency. They were largely responsible for the bewildering pattern of succession to the throne depicted in the diagram on page 192.

Empress Catherine I. Although Peter I died somewhat unexpectedly, it was long known among his intimates that his health was failing, and the

ORDER OF SUCCESSION TO THE THRONE, 1645–1762 *

*Order of succession after the death of Peter I is indicated by
Roman numerals*

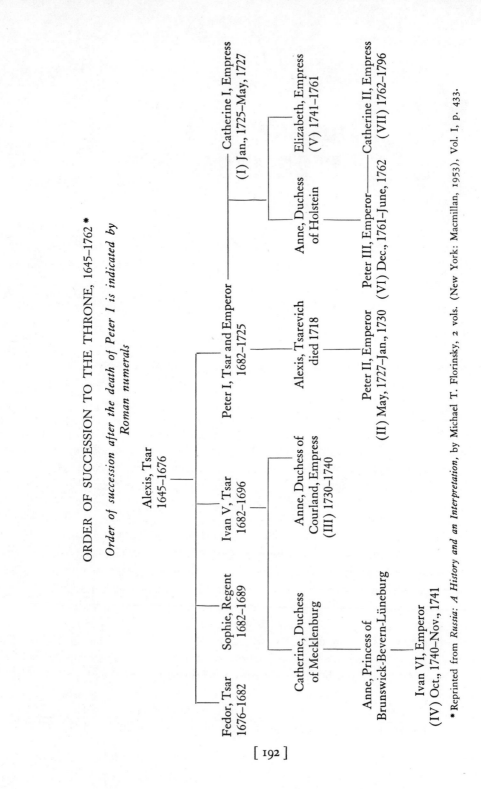

* Reprinted from *Russia: A History and an Interpretation*, by Michael T. Florinsky, 2 vols. (New York: Macmillan, 1953), Vol. I, p. 433.

question of his successor was a cause of anxiety in palace circles. A too drastic change of the political regime, especially the accession of the boy Peter—son of Tsarevich Alexis and the only surviving male member of the dynasty—was dreaded by Peter I's councillors, especially by those who were directly involved in the tragic death of Alexis. Empress Catherine, an ignorant and licentious woman devoid of political ambition, appeared to many as a suitable figurehead whose assumption of the crown would leave things much as they were. She was popular with the guardsmen, particularly with the lower ranks, whose loyalty was stimulated by propaganda and the distribution of bounties organized by Menshikov and her other supporters. With the soldiers assembled in front of the palace clamoring for Catherine, a gathering of high officials decided that she should succeed her husband. Her accession was announced in a manifesto issued in the name of the Holy Synod, the Senate, and the higher functionaries. The official explanation for this unprecedented step was the coronation of Catherine which had taken place the year before.

Catherine lived up to the expectations of those who had engineered her accession: she took no part in government and left the conduct of public affairs in the hands of a newly-established Supreme Privy Council of six members dominated by Menshikov. She was in poor health, however, and her political mentors were almost immediately confronted with the vexing question of succession. Sensing that the claims of young Peter could not be kept indefinitely in abeyance, Menshikov contrived the ingenious plan of marrying his daughter Maria to the emperor-to-be; Catherine, shortly before she died in May 1727, gave her consent to the proposed marriage. A meeting of the Supreme Privy Council, the Holy Synod, the Senate, and the higher officials confirmed a last testament allegedly written by Catherine (but presumably a forgery) which nominated Peter as her successor; the announcement of this decision was received with cheers by the guardsmen who filled the approaches to the palace.

Emperor Peter II. Peter's bethrothal to Maria Menshikov was celebrated soon after his accession, when he was 11 years of age. Menshikov, in whose mansion the youthful emperor came to reside, appeared to be at the height of his power, but actually his lucky star was about to suffer an eclipse. He had numerous enemies and fell victim of an intrigue plotted by the Dolgorukys, an aristocratic family of ancient lineage. In September 1727 he was arrested and deprived of his offices, titles, and dignities; his properties were confiscated; and he was exiled to Siberia, where he and his daughter Maria—the former imperial fiancée—died two years later.

The place left vacant by Menshikov was filled by the Dolgorukys, a large and ambitious family. In 1728 the court and the government were moved to Moscow; soon thereafter Peter became betrothed to Princess Catherine, a member of the Dolgoruky clan and some six years his senior. This marriage, however, like that to Maria Menshikov, was fated never to take place: Peter died of smallpox in January 1730, the very day set for the wedding ceremony.

Empress Anne. The unexpected death of Peter II threw the Supreme Privy Council, which actually ruled the country, into a state of confusion. In 1730 the council had eight members, of whom six (four Dolgoruky princes and two Golitsyn princes) belonged to the old Muscovite aristocracy. At an all-night session following the demise of the young emperor, the council decided to offer the crown to Anne, duchess of Kurland (daughter of Ivan V, Peter I's half-brother and at one time co-ruler). The offer, however, was subject to "Conditions" which were set out in a separate highly secret document and vested all real powers in the existing Supreme Privy Council, which was "to continue indefinitely" and retain direct control over the regiments of the guards. In selecting Anne the council was motivated by the desire to eliminate Petrine innovations and to revert to the old Muscovite tradition, although the form of government which they actually proposed was an oligarchy of a few noble families and was presumably inspired by the aristocratic political regimes of Poland, Sweden, and probably England. The chief argument in favor of Anne (as with Catherine I five years earlier) was her utter insignificance, which appeared to ensure the unchallengeable rule of the Supreme Privy Council. The invitation to the duchess of Kurland was confirmed at a meeting of the higher officials and members of the Holy Synod and the Senate, who were not, however, informed of the "Conditions," although some of the participants knew of their existence.

The proposed constitutional changes provoked much hostility among the nobility and the officeholders, especially those who were identified with the policies of Peter I: they had little to hope for from the supporters of the Muscovite tradition. Moreover, there were many to whom the oligarchical rule of the Dolgorukys and the Golitsyns appeared even less attractive than the familiar evil of autocracy. Although Anne was forewarned that the "Conditions" did not command general support, she signed (at the end of January 1730) in Mittau, Kurland, the document which was submitted to her on behalf of the Supreme Privy Council and which deprived her of all real power. Two weeks later, however, on her arrival in Moscow, she assumed command of the regiments of the guards (one of the things which she had undertaken not to do), and a few days later (February 25), prompted by the opponents of the Supreme Privy Council and with the noisy approval of the soldiery, she dramatically tore up the "Conditions," thus restoring the autocratic powers of the Crown. The Supreme Privy Council was abolished, and its members (except for the Chancellor Golovkin and the Vice Chancellor Ostermann, who had switched over to the side of the supporters of autocracy) were deprived of their offices and suffered various penalties. The events of January–February 1730 are noteworthy as the only instance prior to the twentieth century of an attempt to impose by non-revolutionary means constitutional limitations on the Russian autocracy; but the form of government contemplated by the conspirators was an oligarchy, not a democracy.

Anne was an unprepossessing woman and a sinister political figure. Married at an early age to the duke of Kurland, who died soon thereafter, she had lingered in Mittau—a minor and poverty-stricken court—for nearly 20 years and was 37 at the time of her election to the Russian throne. Dependence on the generosity of her Russian relatives had taught her humility, which was a factor in the decision of the Supreme Privy Council to offer her the Russian crown. She had neither the inclination nor the ability to govern and spent her time in elaborate public festivities which were held chiefly in St. Petersburg, where the court had returned in 1731. A small executive committee known as the Cabinet and created in November 1731 became the successor of the Supreme Privy Council. Its rule was arbitrary and harsh and rested on a police regime of great severity. The conduct of the affairs of state was in the hands of a small clique of favorites and high officials, of whom many happened to be Germans: Ernst Johann Biron (or Bühren), Anne's paramour, who was created a count in 1730 and duke of Kurland in 1737 but who had no standing in the Russian government and spoke no Russian; Andrew Ostermann, a native of Westphalia, who entered the Russian service in 1704, a baron and, later, a count, vice chancellor since 1725, and "first cabinet minister" in the reign of Empress Anne; and Field Marshal Count Burkhard Cristoph von Münnich, a native of Oldenburg, a member of the Russian service since 1721 and commander of the Russian armies under Anne. Other Germans ranked high in the councils of the empress, and there was organized the Izmailovsky regiment of the guards, whose officers were drawn from among the Baltic nobility. Nevertheless no recognizable "German party" appeared, and the personalities just mentioned worked most of the time at cross purposes and intrigued one against the other. They greatly contributed to the unpopularity of the regime.

Anne had no children. She appointed as her successor Ivan, the infant son of her niece, Princess Anne of Mecklenburg, who was married to Prince Anthony Ulric of Brunswick-Bevern-Lüneburg. Princess Anne, known in

Russia as Anna Leopoldovna, was the daughter of the empress's sister Catherine and the duke of Mecklenburg. The successsion to the throne was thus
to remain in the senior branch of the Romanov dynasty, that is, the descendants of Peter I's half-brother and co-ruler, Ivan V. The boy Ivan was born
in August 1740; Empress Anne died in October of that year. She directed
that Biron was to exercise the regency until Ivan VI, as the boy-emperor was
known, had reached the age of seventeen.

Ivan VI and the Regency. This arrangement, however, proved unworkable. Biron was on the worst possible terms with Ostermann, Münnich,
Princess Anne, and her husband, and he incautiously toyed with the notion
of a reform of the guards. Three weeks after his taking office he was arrested by a handful of the military led by Münnich and was exiled to Siberia
(he received partial amnesty from Empress Elizabeth and was restored to
the throne of Kurland by Catherine II). Princess Anne, a strange and neurotic
woman, became regent, but her rule, too, was brief. Dissension among the
members of the governing German clique weakened the position of the regency and created discontent which was aggravated, especially among the
guardsmen, by the outbreak of war with Sweden. A new palace revolution
was hastily engineered, and the bloodless *coup d'état* of November 25, 1741,
resulted in the overthrow of Ivan VI and the regency and the accession of
Empress Elizabeth. The deposed boy-emperor was kept in confinement and
was killed in 1764 when an attempt to liberate him was made.

Empress Elizabeth. Elizabeth, daughter of Peter I and Catherine, was
born in 1709, that is, before her parents were lawfully married. Pleasure-
loving and a woman of great charm, she had many love affairs but never
married and, like her mother, was popular with the guardsmen. Although
Elizabeth avoided political entanglements during the reign of Empress Anne,
she nevertheless came to be looked upon with hope by those who were hostile
to the regime in power. In spite of her reserve and aloofness from politics, the
palace revolution of November 1741 had a political tinge. The policy of
Ostermann, which was based on an alliance with Austria, was strongly disliked in France, while Sweden, not yet reconciled to the territorial losses
suffered in 1721, was seeking an opportunity to recover the provinces ceded
to Russia. The St. Petersburg representatives of the two countries intrigued
against Ostermann and the other advisers of Empress Anne and, after her
death, of the regent, and they worked assiduously for the accession of Elizabeth, with whom they entertained secret relations and from whose rule they
expected the gratification of their national ambitions. Sweden went so far as

to declare war on Russia in July 1741, ostensibly to liberate that country from the unholy rule of "the Germans." Forewarned of the plot, the regent on November 24, 1741, ordered the guards to prepare to leave for the Swedish front. There was no time to lose. In the early hours of November 25 Elizabeth, wearing a cuirass and carrying a cross, appeared at the barracks of the guards and was given an enthusiastic reception. At the head of a small band of conspirators and mutinous soldiers she invaded the Winter Palace and arrested the child-emperor, the regent, and the higher officials of the fallen regime, including Ostermann and Münnich. There was no resistance. Since the events leading to the accession of Elizabeth are often represented as a "national revolution," it may be well to emphasize that the leading participants in the movement were foreigners, including the mastermind of the conspiracy, the Frenchman Armand Lestocq, Elizabeth's physician and factotum.

On her accession Elizabeth announced her intention to rule in the tradition of Peter the Great and to revive the constitutional arrangements and administrative institutions of 1725, but few changes were actually made. The Cabinet of Empress Anne was abolished, and the Senate was to resume its place as the central governmental organ. There was formed, however, Her Majesty's private chancery, headed by the empress's private secretary and known as the "cabinet," which actually became the chief executive agency. In 1756, with the outbreak of the Seven Years' War, there was established a Conference of ten members, all of them high officers of state, which exercised powers as comprehensive and ill-defined as those of the Supreme Privy Council of Catherine I and Peter II or the Cabinet under Empress Anne. The supremacy of the Senate, which was to function under the personal leadership of the empress, remained a fiction.

Elizabeth had no time for affairs of state. Her days were fully occupied by court and Church functions of great splendor and by visits to Moscow and pilgrimages to religious shrines. Moreover, intervention by the empress's favorites (especially her lovers, Alexis Razumovsky, a powerfully-built Cossack lad who once had sung in the palace choir, and, later, the youthful and handsome Ivan Shuvalov) carried far more weight with the sovereign than the opinions of her official advisers. Under these conditions the institutional setup mattered little, and Russia continued to be ruled, as she had been in the seventeenth and much of the earlier part of the eighteenth century, by the whims of the ruler's favorites.

Elizabeth was childless, and she appointed as her heir and successor her nephew Charles Peter Ulric, duke of Holstein, who on his admission to the

Greek Orthodox Church assumed the name of Grand Duke Peter and later became Emperor Peter III. In 1745 he married a German princess, the future Empress Catherine II.

War and Diplomacy

Russia and Europe. During the three and one-half decades which elapsed between the death of Peter I and the accession of Catherine II, Russia engaged in several European wars. They differed from those of the seventeenth century in being largely motivated by considerations of a "European" character, among which the ambitions and "interests" of the German ruling houses which were related to the Russian court played an important and, at times, decisive part. In a sense, the wars waged during this period were a continuation of Petrine policies, whereas the conduct of Russian foreign relations was largely determined by the predilections of, and the theories held by, the titular heads of the Russian department of foreign affairs: Count Andrew Ostermann (1725–1740), who in 1734 became "first cabinet minister," and the chancellor, Count Alexis Bestuzhev-Riumin (1741–1758); from 1755 on, however, the vice chancellor Michael Vorontsov exercised considerable influence, as did at various times Menshikov, Biron, Razumovsky, Shuvalov, and other favorites of the rulers. The general lines of the policy followed by Ostermann and by his successor and personal enemy Bestuzhev were derived from the belief in the necessity for an alliance with Austria and hostility towards France: it was held in St. Petersburg that Russia's vital interests in the key states of Sweden, Poland, and Turkey were jeopardized by the French. Russian intervention in the affairs of Kurland, a fief of Poland, and those of the duchies of Holstein and Schleswig was a frequent source of friction and international conflict.

The War of Polish Succession. Poland's political disorders, forerunners of her impending elimination as an independent state, offered opportunities for foreign intervention which the Russians did not overlook. The death of King Augustus II of Poland early in 1733 raised the issue of his successor, which assumed a European significance because the Polish throne was filled by election. There were two principal candidates: the former King Stanislas Leszczynski, father-in-law of King Louis XV of France, and Frederick Augustus, elector of Saxony and son of Augustus II. The governments of France and Sweden supported Leszczynski, while Russia and Austria were determined to secure the accession of Frederick Augustus. After much manoeuvering by the opposing groups, the Polish diet elected Leszczynski

(September 1733). St. Petersburg retaliated by sending Russian troops into Poland, while a "confederation" of noblemen subservient to Russian wishes elected to the throne Frederick Augustus, who took the name of Augustus III. Meanwhile Leszczynski fled to Danzig and eventually escaped abroad when that city was captured by the Russians after a protracted siege (June 1734). Resistance to Augustus in Poland continued for a time, but early in 1736 Leszczynski, abandoned by France and Sweden, abdicated the Polish throne. His Polish supporters lost heart, and in June of that year Augustus was installed as king of Poland. France and Sweden had suffered a political defeat, and Ostermann had achieved his objective.

The Russo-Turkish War, 1735–1739. Conflicts with Turkey were a perennial feature of Russian foreign relations in the eighteenth century. In the 1730's both countries were in a belligerent mood. There was a dispute of long standing over some ill-defined territories in the region of the Caucasus. Constantinople resented Russian interference in Poland, while St. Petersburg was vexed by Tatar raids on Russian southern provinces. The two antagonists, moreover, held low opinions of each other's military capacity, and both believed that a war would be short and victorious. In St. Petersburg a military party headed by Münnich favored an aggressive policy towards the Ottoman Porte on the assumption that a Russian invasion would be welcomed by Turkey's large Christian and Slavic population and would bring early laurels to Russian army leaders. Ostermann appeared to have shared this aberration; in the late summer of 1735 Russian troops crossed into Turkish territory on the pretext of repulsing Tatar raiders, but war on Turkey was not formally declared until a year later. Contrary to expectations the campaign, in spite of some notable Russian victories, proved long-drawn and arduous. The indecisive nature of the fighting, ravages caused by the epidemics, the aloofness of Turkish Christians, and the slowness of Austria in fulfilling her obligations as Russia's ally forced Empress Anne and Ostermann to seek a peace settlement in the autumn of 1736. These efforts failed and the war continued for another three years. Austria finally declared war on Turkey in the summer of 1737 but concluded a separate peace two years later, at the very time when the Russian army under Münnich won distinguished victories in Moldavia. The Russo-Turkish war was terminated by the treaty of Belgrade (September 1739), which was negotiated through the mediation of France. Under its provisions Russia retained the city of Azov and the adjoining territory, but all Russian fortifications in that region (including Azov and Taganrog) were dismantled. Russia was not to maintain any vessels in the Black Sea, and her trade in these waters was to be carried in Turkish bottoms.

This was hardly peace with victory, although it was represented as such in St. Petersburg.

War with Sweden, 1741–1743. Conflicts with Sweden, like those with Turkey, were quasi-permanent features of Russia's eighteenth-century foreign policy. It took some time for Sweden to become reconciled to the loss of her continental possessions resulting from the Northern War. Russia's internal disorders during the brief reign of the infant Emperor Ivan VI appeared to present the opportunity for which the rulers of Sweden had been waiting. In July 1741 the Swedish government declared war on Russia, ostensibly (and surprisingly) to free that country from the inequitable and oppressive rule of German usurpers. In the only major battle of the war (at Vilmanstrand, August 1741) the Swedish army was overwhelmingly defeated by a much larger Russian force.

The accession of Elizabeth (November 1741), whose cause the Swedish government championed, led to the removal, trial, and banishment of Ostermann, but his successor as director of Russian foreign policy, Count Alexis Bestuzhev-Riumin, shared his predecessor's dislike for France and her ally Sweden and was a supporter of the Austrian alliance. Peace negotiations initiated after the accession of Elizabeth dragged on for several months; meanwhile the Russians conquered a large portion of Finland, including the cities of Helsingfors and Abo, which was then the Finnish capital. Fighting stopped by the end of 1742, and the war was formally terminated by the treaty of Abo (October 1743), by virtue of which Russia annexed a strip of Finland with the fortified cities of Vilmanstrand and Frederikshamn but restored to Sweden the other and much larger portion of the Finnish territory which was held by the Russian troops. As a part of the peace settlement—which may well explain its relative leniency—Sweden accepted as her king (the Swedish throne had become vacant in November 1741) the Russian candidate, Adolphus Frederick of Holstein. The new Swedish ruler, however, did not live up to the expectations of his Russian sponsors and continued Sweden's traditional pro-French and anti-Russian policy.

The War of Austrian Succession. The death of Empress Anne of Russia (October 1740) coincided with other important changes among the occupants of European thrones. In May of that year Frederick II became king of Prussia, and in October the death of Emperor Charles VI of the Holy Empire opened the thorny question of the so-called pragmatic sanction by his settling on his daughter Maria Theresa of the succession of the territories of the house of Hapsburg. In December 1740, however, Frederick invaded Silesia; there followed the War of Austrian Succession in which Frederick, in alliance with France and Bavaria, fought Maria Theresa, then queen of Hungary and Bohemia, and which kept Europe busy for the next eight years. Although both Ostermann and Bestuzhev, who was soon to succeed him, were protagonists of Austria, the Russian government eluded at first the obligation to lend military support to Austria, as required by the terms of the Russo-Austrian alliance. Moreover, early in 1741, during the brief interlude of the reign of Ivan VI, the government of the regent had concluded, under the influence of Münnich, a defensive alliance with Prussia. The two alliances—with Austria and with Prussia—were mutually incompatible. The outbreak of the Russo-Swedish war in July 1741 provided a more decorous reason for Russia's failure to fulfill the obligations of either alliance.

Contrary to what might have been expected, the accession of Elizabeth (November 1741), followed by the disgrace of Ostermann and the advent of Bestuzhev, did not basically alter Russian policy. In her struggle for power Elizabeth had leaned heavily on the support of the French, especially that of her factotum Armand Lestocq and the French ambassador, Marquis de la Chétardie. Bestuzhev, however, succeeded in counteracting the pro-French influences in Elizabeth's immediate circle as well as the pro-Prussian leanings of the heir-apparent, the Grand Duke Peter, and his wife Catherine, both of them admirers of Frederick II. There was also a *rapprochement* with England: the London government wished to protect England's Russian trade and disliked the political consequences of the Franco-Prussian cooperation. An Anglo-Russian agreement, signed in 1747 after laborious negotiations, provided for Russian participation in the war, subject to the payment of a substantial subsidy by England. Accordingly, a Russian expeditionary corps was sent to the Rhine in January 1748, but the War of Austrian Succession was brought to an end by the peace of Aix-la-Chapelle (to which Russia was not a party) before the Russian troops saw any fighting. The dispatch of the Russian corps, even though it did not constitute a formal declaration of war, led to a breach of diplomatic relations between St. Petersburg and Paris.

The Seven Years' War. During the seven years following the peace of Aix-la-Chapelle Russia remained at peace. Bestuzhev took advantage of the relaxation of political tension to build up what came to be known as his "diplomatic system," that is, a new alignment of powers aimed at the isolation of Prussia and closer relations with England, while preserving the framework of the Russo-Austrian alliance. Anglo-Russian cooperation, which Bestuzhev regarded as essential, appeared to be assured with the signature in the autumn of 1755 of an agreement with London: in return for a large annual subsidy Russia undertook to maintain on her western border an army of a specified size that could be used for the defense of the possessions of the king of England and his allies.

The Anglo-Russian convention, which was the consummation of Bestuzhev's patient efforts, was never applied in practice. In January 1756, much to his distress, England and Prussia concluded a military alliance. Its immediate consequence was a defensive Franco-Austrian alliance (May 1756) to which Russia acceded in December of the same year. Meanwhile Frederick II, who did not expect Russia to side with his enemies, had invaded Saxony (August 1756). The Seven Years' War had begun. It was fought by Austria, France, and Russia against Frederick II of Prussia, who was assisted by Hanoverian troops and subsidies from England.

Russia's participation in the Seven Years' War was rather a mixed affair. The Russians won some remarkable military victories and particularly distinguished themselves in routing the Prussians at Kunersdorf, near Frankfort (August 1759). East Prussia was occupied by the Russians early in 1758, and they held Berlin for a short time in the autumn of 1760. In other encounters with the Prussians, however, the Muscovites fared far less well, and even their victories were oddly inconclusive. From 1757 to the end of 1761, when Russia withdrew from the war, she had four commanders-in-chief, all of whom were removed in disgrace. Bestuzhev, suspected of pro-British and anti-French sentiments and slackness in the prosecution of the war, was removed from office early in 1758, tried, and exiled to his estates. He was succeeded as chancellor by the pro-French vice chancellor, Michael Vorontsov.

The setbacks of Russia and her allies notwithstanding, Prussia, devastated by successive waves of invading armies, appeared more than once on the verge of total defeat. She was saved by the disintegration of the enemy coalition. France became involved in a separate war with England in an unsuccessful attempt to defend her overseas empire. Austria and the other allies— Sweden, Saxony, and various other German states—showed little inclination to continue the war. The death of Empress Elizabeth (December 1761, O.S.–January 1762, N.S.) dealt the death blow to the tottering coalition. Her successor, Emperor Peter III, concluded with Frederick an immediate armistice followed by a peace treaty, which Frederick wrote himself, and by a Russo-Prussian alliance against Austria. Although Peter III was deposed soon thereafter, the agreement with Prussia held good, and under the terms of a treaty with the other allies (1763) Frederick retained all his dominions.

Economic and Social Developments

Finance, Industry, and Trade. The trend of financial and economic affairs, unlike that of foreign relations, was uneventful. The poll tax, important as it was as a source of revenue, failed to meet the rapidly mounting needs of the treasury and proved difficult to administer. Arrears under this heading accumulated and as early as 1725 reached the staggering figure of 1,000,000 rubles. This situation and the prevalence of evasion led to the repeated reduction in the rate of the poll tax and an increase in indirect taxation: the prices of salt and alcohol, which were sold by government monopolies, were substantially raised. Desperate attempts were made to cut down the cost of the military establishment and of the civil service, as well as to discourage corruption among tax officials by providing Draconian penalties for malfeasance. These measures achieved little, however. Both Anne and Elizabeth sporadically preached economy and issued decrees prohibiting costly dress, yet extravagance among the upper class was encouraged by lavish entertainments held at the imperial court. The heavy outlays necessitated by the outbreak of the Seven Years' War led to the depreciation of the currency through the debasement of the copper coins: they were withdrawn from circulation and were reissued at twice their face value (1757). This measure, which had numerous precedents in Russian monetary history, was proposed —like many other economic reforms—by Count Peter Shuvalov, Elizabeth's principal economic adviser.

There was no progress in industry and, indeed, quite a few of the larger industrial enterprises which were established in the reign of Peter I—perhaps one-quarter of their total number—closed their doors. The quality of the goods produced by the manufactories which survived remained exceedingly low. Domestic trade derived some benefit from the organization in St. Petersburg of the Commercial Bank (1754) and especially from the removal of internal customs barriers (1753) with the resulting freedom of the circulation of goods throughout the empire. Other trade policies were less liberal, however. The reign of Elizabeth witnessed the massive return of trade monopolies, which were usually controlled by men with powerful court connections and led to much abuse. A high external tariff was enacted in 1757, marking a return to the exorbitant protectionism of the beginning of the century.

The Nobility and the Peasants. While the economy continued to stagnate, changes of some importance were taking place in the social structure. They followed two principal lines: improvement in the legal and social status of the nobility and extension of its authority over the servile population, which of course meant the deterioration of the position of the serfs. The part played by the nobility in the palace revolutions of this period suggested that the time might be ripe for seeking relief from the burden of service. This objective was not fully achieved until the second half of the century, but progress was registered during the earlier period. The wishes of the upper class were made known to the Crown in the petitions presented by the *dvoriane* to Empress Anne on the occasion of her accession. Some of them were met by subsequent legislation. A state-sponsored academy (*kadet-skii korpus*) for boys of noble descent was established in 1731; its graduates received army commissions and joined the forces as officers, not as privates. The student body remained small, however, and the academy could accommodate but a fraction of the young men subject to the draft. In 1732 native Russian army officers were granted an increase in pay that brought it up to the level of that of foreigners of the same rank in the Russian service. The State Nobility Bank was formed in 1754; it provided credit for the *dvoriane* at a moderate rate of interest.

Of greater import, and designed to meet a basic grievance of the nobility, was a manifesto of December 1736 which cut down the term of service to 25 years and exempted from service one member of each family comprising two or more males. The official reason for this legislation was the need to improve the management of agricultural estates and to increase their tax-paying capacity, both of which were believed to have suffered because of absentee ownership. Simultaneously the rules governing the drafting of young noblemen into service were made more explicit and stringent. When the manifesto was put into effect in 1739, at the end of the Turkish war, the demand for retirement was so great that the government was forced to restrict the field of its application. It is notable that many applicants for retirement were men in their early thirties: their names had been inscribed on regimental lists when they were boys, and they reckoned their term of service from that date. The manifesto of 1736 wrought no immediate important changes, but it was significant as the forerunner of the impending abolition of obligatory service.

The comprehensive power wielded by the *dvoriane* over the servile population of their estates was further extended. Much of it was derived from custom and administrative practice rather than from legislative enactments. The standing of the estate owners was enhanced by making them responsible for the assessment and, since 1731, the collection of the poll tax. The few loopholes which permitted the serfs to escape the all-pervasive authority of their masters were being closed. A decree of Peter I which authorized a serf to enlist in the armed forces without his lord's consent was repealed in 1727. In 1754 it became an offense for a female serf to marry, without her master's written permission, a man who was not her master's serf. Serfs could not engage in trade without their lord's written authorization, and under a law of 1737 they could acquire land and industrial and commercial establishments only in the name of their owner and with his approval. The practically unlimited police powers of the *dvoriane* were provided with a statutory basis. A decree of 1736 empowered the landowner to determine what punishment should be meted out to a fugitive serf, including the knout, the application of which at times resulted in death. By virtue of a decree of December 1760 the estate owners could deport their delinquent serfs to Siberia, the deportees being credited towards the owners' quota of army recruits.

The Code of 1649 laid down the rule that the ownership of estates populated by serfs was a prerogative of the *dvoriane* which, however, they shared with the Church, the Crown, and the ruling dynasty. In practice this stipulation was not always observed, and in the first half of the eighteenth century such estates were owned by members of groups other than those mentioned above. Legislation enacted in the 1730's, 1740's, and 1750's ordered their dispossession, and by the end of Elizabeth's reign the nobility consolidated its position as the sole owner of serfs to the exclusion of all other private owners.

The onward march of serfdom met with the resistance of the peasantry, which took the familiar form of mass desertion and rebellion. Servile labor was valuable property, and landowners spent much time and energy in litigation for the recovery of runaway serfs. Legislation providing heavy penalties for both the fugitives and those who harbored them piled up, and the courts were swamped by innumerable lawsuits for the recovery of fugitive serfs. In an attempt to keep litigation within bounds, a law of 1754 made the census of 1719 the limit beyond which the serf-owners could not go in proving their claims.

Fugitive bondsmen sought a haven in the sparsely populated eastern provinces, in the no-man's land of the southern steppes, and—which is more surprising—in Catholic Poland and on the estates of the Baltic nobility. Repeated promises of amnesty and land grants made by the Russian government proved of no avail.

Schools, Literature, and Art

Schools. The untidy and haphazard school system created by Peter I did not fare well under his successors. Shortages of teachers, textbooks, and students persisted. The low level of instruction and the harshness of school discipline fostered the unwillingness of the parents to send their children to school. The attempt to impart a class character to the school system, that is, to make admission to various types of schools dependent on the social status of the prospective student's parent, even though it was never fully enforced, proved destructive of some of the schools. The "mathematical" schools,[1] which were established in 1714, found themselves competing for students with the parochial schools (organized under the provisions of the Church Statute of 1721) and were gradually closed. In 1744 the eight surviving "mathematical" schools were absorbed by the so-called "garrison" schools, which trained their students for the army and were maintained with regimental funds. Narrow professionalism was the dominating feature of teaching. Parochial schools, which drew their student body chiefly from the children of the clergy, were the only ones which registered progress. Some of them became theological seminaries with a 9-year course. They were reorganized under a law of 1737 and in 1738 numbered 17, with about 2,600 students. Many of their graduates, although trained primarily for the priesthood, actually joined the civil service.

The closing years of Elizabeth's reign brought forth comprehensive schemes for the advancement of education. Characteristically, and following the predecent established by Peter I, they emphasized the development of schools of the higher grades. The originator of these proposals was Ivan Shuvalov, Elizabeth's youthful favorite, who had traveled abroad and had intellectual ambitions. On his initiative the University of Moscow was founded in 1755; simultaneously two secondary schools for boys were opened in Moscow and, three years later, one in Kazan. The university had three faculties—law, medicine, and philosophy; instruction was conducted in Latin and in Russian. The university encountered mountainous difficulties, had few students, and did not reach the status of a true institution of learning until decades later. The plan advanced by Shuvalov in 1760 for secondary schools in the principal cities and for elementary schools in the major towns never passed the discussion stage.

Literature and History. The birth of Russian lay literature may be traced

---

[1] See above, p. 184.

to the second quarter of the eighteenth century, when appeared the first Russian fiction writers, playwrights, and poets. The better-known members of this group were Vasili Trediakovsky (1703–1769), Alexander Sumarokov (1718–1777), and Michael Lomonosov (1711–1765). All three had studied in western Europe and were under the influence of the Western classical or pseudo-classical school. Trediakovsky and Sumarokov, admired as they were by their contemporaries, were not distinguished authors, but they contributed to the evolution of the Russian literary language and prosody. Lomonosov, son of a Kholmogory fisherman, was a professor of chemistry at the Academy of Science, as well as a grammarian, a poet, and an artist. He is credited with numerous discoveries in the various fields of knowledge and, although his admirers tend to exaggerate his achievements, he was unquestionably an arresting intellectual figure. Another important author was Prince Antiokh Kantemir (1708–1744), who, however, was not a professional man of letters but a member of the Russian foreign service. His talented satires, moreover, were not published until nearly 20 years after his death.

The first Russian literary journals—*Monthly Essays,* issued by the Academy of Science, and *Busy Bee,* edited by Sumarokov and published privately —appeared respectively in 1755 and 1759. Russian historical science made a modest beginning with the writings of Vasili Tatishchev and the German expatriate, Gerhard Frederick Miller. Tatishchev's *Russian History,* like Kantemir's satire, did not appear in print until many years after its author's death.

Art. Painting and sculpture, for which the Russians have shown a marked lack of aptitude (perhaps because of the narrow and exclusive traditionalism of the Russian Church), received some encouragement from the founding in 1757 of the Academy of Arts, another creation of Ivan Shuvalov and something of an exotic growth in Russian conditions. Its influence was hardly felt until the nineteenth century. There was a great improvement in the appearance of St. Petersburg, which, however, owed its most distinguished buildings of this period to foreign—chiefly Italian—architects, especially Count Bartholomew Rastrelli. Russian music was untouched by Western influences, although an Italian operatic company made its appearance at the court of Empress Anne.

To sum up: by the middle of the eighteenth century Russian cultural advancement along Western lines was still in its initial stage.

12

The Age of Enlightenment, 1762-1800

Peter III

The Grandson of Peter I. The long reign of Empress Catherine II (1762–1796) is traditionally known as the era of enlightened absolutism. It was preceded by the brief and tragic reign of her husband, Emperor Peter III, and was followed by the slightly longer but equally tragic reign of her son, Emperor Paul I.

The future Emperor Peter III, son of Peter I's daughter Anne and Charles Frederick, duke of Holstein, was born in Kiel in 1728. He was brought to Russia after the accession of his aunt, Empress Elizabeth, was received in the Russian Orthodox Church (he was a Lutheran), and proclaimed heir to the Russian throne. In 1745 he married Sophia Augusta Frederica, princess of Anhalt-Zerbst, the future Empress Catherine II. Peter succeeded Elizabeth, after her death in December 1761, in a decorous and legitimate manner, without the support of the guards or of a palace clique—which was a poor augury in eighteenth-century Russia.

Peter III is usually represented as a cretin and his overthrow as an act of historical necessity. These strictures are based largely on evidence emanating from Catherine and members of her entourage which are both biased and highly colored. It is clear, however, that Peter was an ardent Holstein patriot and a man of limited gifts and that his conduct was often odd and offensive to Russian national and religious sentiments. The principal domestic measure of his reign, which lasted for six months, was the manifesto of February 18, 1762, freeing the *dvoriane* from the obligation of compulsory service, an act that should have endeared him to the landed nobility. Yet he fell victim to a conspiracy engineered by the guards.

It would be an error to ascribe his unpopularity with the upper class to his reversal of Elizabeth's foreign policy by withdrawing from the Seven Years' War and concluding an alliance with Frederick II of Prussia. War with Prussia never commanded popular support; it had dragged on for years, and the resources of Russia were nearly exhausted. Most unwisely, however, Peter embarked at once on a war with Denmark in order to re-store Schleswig, which was held by that country, to Holstein. This was hardly a war to arouse enthusiasm among the Russians. Even more detri-mental to Peter's position were his hostility towards the Russian guards, drastic revision of the conditions of service, which were made much more exacting, and threats to revoke the guards' privileges. The disaffection of the guardsmen was the mainspring of the palace revolution which toppled Peter from his throne.

The Revolution of June 1762. Unlike her husband, Catherine, an am-bitious and scheming woman, worked assiduously to build up a following in the very circles which in eighteenth-century Russia decided the fate of the Crown. She claimed later in her *Memoirs* that at the time of her en-gagement to Peter she was already convinced that she would eventually be-come empress of Russia in her own right. To achieve this object she solicited and obtained, while still a grand duchess, subsidies from England. Peter's liaison with Elizabeth Vorontsov and the uncivil manner in which he treated his wife led to probably unwarranted rumors that he contemplated divorcing or even imprisoning Catherine. His eccentricities and discourtesies alarmed and alienated some of the higher military and civil officials, who were taken into Catherine's confidence and were planning for a palace revolution that would make her empress. Her essential support, however, came from the guards.

About 1760 Catherine became the mistress of Gregory Orlov, one of five brothers—all of them officers in the guards. Their efforts on behalf of Catherine fell on fertile ground: Peter's order to the guards to get ready for the Danish campaign had greatly increased his unpopularity. The arrest of an officer involved in the conspiracy and the resulting danger of exposure necessitated immediate action. In the early hours of June 28, 1762, Catherine was aroused from her sleep by Alexis Orlov at the imperial residence of Peterhof, near the capital, and was taken to the barracks of the guards where, like Elizabeth some 20 years earlier, she was given an enthusiastic reception. The Senate, the Holy Synod, and the higher officials rallied to her support. There was a solemn mass, and a manifesto proclaimed the dethronement of Peter and the accession of Catherine. Peter, caught unawares at the nearby residence of Oranienbaum, offered no resistance and meekly abdicated. He was put under arrest and a few days later was assassinated by his guards, commanded by Alexis Orlov. The details of the murder and the part played in it by Catherine are not known, but Orlov and other men involved suffered no punishment.

Catherine II: Diplomacy and War

Empress Catherine II. At the time of her accession Catherine was in her thirty-third year. Born in Stettin, Germany, she received no formal education but acquired a good knowledge of French and, later, a fluent command of spoken Russian. She read a great deal, was familiar with contemporary Western literature, and corresponded regularly with outstanding European political and intellectual figures, including Voltaire, Diderot, D'Alembert, and the other leaders of the Enlightenment. This correspondence had for its object not only to satisfy Catherine's intellectual curiosity and snobbery but also to build up her reputation abroad. She was inordinately sensitive to adulation and longed to hold the center of the stage. French philosophers, recipients of Russian bounties and flattered by marks of imperial favor, were most of the time only too willing to extol the glories of the Semiramis of the North.

The feeling of insecurity experienced by every Russian ruler since the days of Peter I was aggravated, in the case of Catherine, by the circumstances of her accession. The uncertainties of the law of succession notwithstanding, many influential Russians, including participants in the overthrow of Peter III, believed that he should be succeeded by his son, the future Emperor Paul I (born in 1754), and that Catherine was at best entitled to the office of regent during the boy's infancy. Catherine, however, did not wish to step down, and although Paul did nothing to enforce his claim, the threat of a palace revolution remained a possibility.

Sensuous and uninhibited by moral restraints, Catherine had many lovers and elevated favoritism to the dignity of a state institution. Three of her favorites—Gregory Orlov, from 1762 to 1772, Gregory Potemkin, from 1774

Catherine II, portrait by Giovanni Battista Lampi

to his death in 1791, and Platon Zubov, from 1789 to the end of the reign—exercised great political influence, especially in international affairs. Unlike her predecessors (Catherine I, Anne, and Elizabeth) Catherine took personal interest in government and in the conduct of foreign relations. She had literary ambitions and wrote plays, fables, and political and historical tracts, as well as memoirs which presented a highly selective account of the events which led to her accession. In politics she displayed at times liberal and even radical tendencies, although these were seldom reflected in practical measures, but after the outbreak of the French Revolution she espoused the cause of legitimism and reaction.

Rapprochement with Prussia. Catherine's first move in international affairs was to end the unpopular war with Denmark. An imperial manifesto condemned Peter III for withdrawing from the Seven Years' War, yet the empress confirmed the peace treaty with Prussia and was soon engaged in an animated and friendly correspondence with Frederick, who had joined the ranks of her admirers. A Russo-Prussian treaty of alliance was concluded in April 1764 and proved to be the beginning of an intimate and durable collaboration between the two governments.

The international policy of Catherine was primarily concerned with Poland, Turkey, Sweden, and, in the closing years of her reign, resistance to the inroads of the French Revolution.

First Partition of Poland and the Turkish War of 1768–1774. Russian domination of Poland was an article of Catherine's political faith. The earliest instance of her intervention in Polish affairs occurred in 1763, when Russian troops restored Biron to the throne of Kurland, a principality which was a fief of Poland but which St. Petersburg treated as if it were under Russian rule. Other and more significant infringements of Polish sovereignty were to follow soon.

In the middle of the eighteenth century Poland was a major European state, drifting nevertheless to its doom because of an archaic and anarchic constitution. The basic weakness of Poland's political system was the *liberum veto,* that is, the right of any member of the diet to enter a veto which had the effect of dissolving the diet and of annulling all its previous decisions. The upper class, *szlachta,* was empowered to form "confederations," or military associations, which were entitled to impose their programs by force of arms. Participation in government, including the diet, was limited to *szlachta,* which accounted for less than 10 per cent of the population; the rank and file of *szlachta* were as a rule clients of a few powerful magnates who controlled through their retainers the decisions of the diet and the mechanics of government. The nominal head of this peculiar and restricted democracy was an elective king exercising no real authority. The 1764 Russo-Prussian treaty of alliance bound the contracting parties to uphold, if necessary by military force, the Polish constitution.

The immediate reason for the Russo-Prussian alliance was the death, in October 1763, of King Augustus III of Poland, which raised the question of his successor. The immediate issue was easily solved: a Polish diet dominated by pro-Russian elements and supported by Russian troops elected to the Polish throne the Russian candidate, Count Stanislas Poniatowski, member of the powerful Czartoryski clan and a former lover of Empress Catherine. Russian influence appeared to be firmly entrenched. Nevertheless difficulties between Poland, on the one hand, and Russia and Prussia, on the other, arose at once. They centered on two problems: the legal position of the so-called "dissidents" and the reform of the Polish constitution.

The "dissidents," or dissenters, were members of the Greek Orthodox and the Protestant Churches living in Poland; they were deprived of political rights and suffered social disabilities, although non-discriminatory treatment of the non-Catholics was stipulated in several Russo-Polish treaties. The 1764 Russo-Prussian treaty of alliance provided for concerted action of the two powers to secure the emancipation of the "dissidents," a policy that militant Catholic opinion in Poland stubbornly opposed.

The constitutional issue was raised by Poniatowski and his supporters, who, their reliance on Russia notwithstanding, favored a drastic revision of the constitution that would establish a hereditary kingship and place a limitation on the *liberum veto*. A conflict became inevitable. Russian intervention in Poland was undertaken on the pretext of defending Polish liberties (the existing constitution) and religious tolerance (emancipation of the "dissidents"). Actually neither Catherine nor Frederick cared about principles of constitutional law or Christian ethics. What they wanted was a weak and divided Poland incapable of concerted action, and they counted on the emancipated "dissidents" as a dependable tool for the implementation of their predatory designs.

Russian resistance to the king's program of constitutional reform was supported by a section of *szlachta*. Poland found herself in the throes of acute political turmoil. On the instigation of Russian agents "confederations" were organized throughout the land and in June 1867 were merged at Radom in a "general confederation" that in September occupied Warsaw and summoned a diet. Russian troops overran Poland, and under the ruthless pressure of Catherine's special envoys, Prince Nicholas Repnin and the

Holstein diplomat Caspar von Saldern, the diet accepted the Russian demands with some minor face-saving reservations in the matter of the *liberum veto*. The disabilities of the "dissidents" were removed, the constitution was upheld, and the Russo-Polish treaty of February 1768 put it under Russian protection "for all time to come."

The 1768 settlement brought no peace. Russia's neighbors—Austria, Turkey, and Sweden—as well as France, were alarmed and incensed by the political ambitions and methods of St. Petersburg. So were some of the Poles. A "Confederation of Liberty and Faith" was organized at Bar, in the Ukraine, in March 1768; it was directed against Poniatowski and the Warsaw diet and was supported by France and Austria, while the Polish government leaned heavily on Russian troops. The state of civil war lasted for four years.

Russian intervention in Poland led to a war with Turkey. Constantinople would not recognize the election of Poniatowski because it was imposed by the Russians, and when in the summer of 1768 Turkish border provinces were invaded by Cossack raiding parties, the Sublime Porte demanded the withdrawal of Russian troops from Poland and, receiving no satisfaction, arrested the Russian ambassador to Turkey. There followed a war which was to last, with interruptions, for six years. Although Russia was poorly prepared for the struggle, Catherine's imaginative advisers, notably Gregory Orlov, devised fanciful schemes for the dismemberment—with the assistance of the Christian populations under the Turkish rule—of the Ottoman empire, the creation of the independent states of Moldavia, Wallachia, and the Crimea, and finally the eviction of the Turks from Europe. These "projects" appealed strongly to the empress, and she retained interest in them until the end of her reign.

The four opening years of the Turkish war were fought by the Russians simultaneously with their military action against the Polish confederates. The Turkish campaign began inauspiciously for Russia with the invasion of her southern provinces by the Crimean Tatars, but from the second half of 1769 to the suspension of the fighting early in 1772 the Russian armies won a number of important victories in the Danubian principalities, re-occupied Azov and Taganrog, and established themselves in the Crimea. At the beginning of 1772 military operations were brought to a standstill, and in July Russo-Turkish armistice negotiations began in Foshany; they were later transferred to Bucharest.

An unprecedented feature of Russian strategy was the dispatch of the Russian fleet from the Baltic ports to the Turkish Archipelago by way of the

Mediterranean. The two Russian squadrons which left for their voyage round Europe in July and in the autumn of 1769 were commanded by Alexis Orlov, a novice in maritime warfare, assisted by two English and several Russian admirals. The Russian squadrons reached Turkish waters in the spring of 1770 and in June of that year practically destroyed the Turkish fleet at Chesme (Tchesme). This unexpected victory produced a strong impression in Russia and Europe—especially because many observers had inclined to take a dim view of Russian ships and naval personnel—but it had little practical effect on the course of the war. The anticipated revolt of the Balkan Christians did not materialize, and the subsequent operations of the Russian fleet in the Archipelago, in spite of the reinforcement sent from the Baltic in 1770, were coastal raids of minor significance.

The armistice negotiations provided a breathing space that was used to deal drastically with the Polish question. Russian policies in both Poland and Turkey, especially rumors of the impending dismemberment of the Ottoman empire, alarmed Austria, Sweden, France, England, and even Prussia, although Frederick had concluded with Russia in April 1767 a new alliance whose object it was to prevent armed Austrian intervention in Poland. The eastern powers—Russia, Austria, and Prussia—found a temporary solution of their divergent national policies in the partition of Poland. The possibility of partitioning Poland had been discussed for many years. It was taken up in earnest in 1770–1771 when agreement was made possible by Russia's formal renunciation of all claims to the Turkish provinces of Wallachia and Moldavia, which Austria would not concede. The three powers signed the partition treaty in August 1772. In spite of the desperate protests of King Stanislas Poniatowski, the Polish diet was bribed and coerced into ratifying the partition treaty, which deprived Poland of about one-third of her territory and more than one-third of her population. Russia's share was an area of 36,000 square miles (including Byelo-Russia and a portion of Livonia) with a population of 1.8 million, predominantly Greek Orthodox and of Russian stock.

The partition of Poland did not facilitate the Russo-Turkish peace negotiations, for the Turks rightly sensed that what happened to Poland might well be in store for the Ottoman empire. As Russian demands for the independence of the Crimea and for ports on that peninsula were deemed inadmissible, negotiations broke down and hostilities were resumed in the spring of 1773. Disregarding the counsel of moderation and prudence pressed upon her by foreign governments and her own generals, and in spite of the alarming success of the Pugachev peasant rebellion, Catherine continued

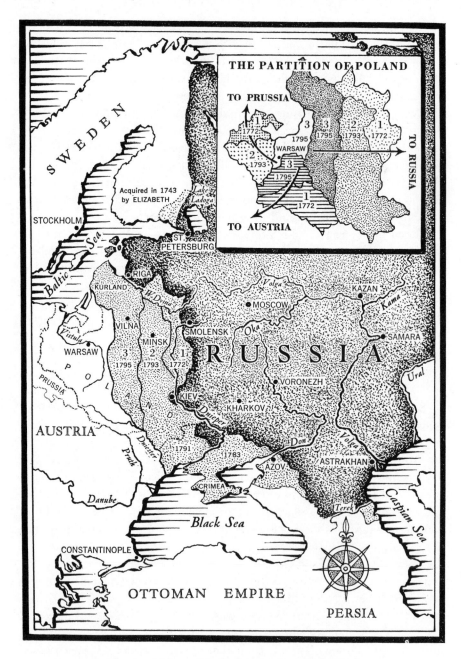

THE PARTITION OF POLAND

TO PRUSSIA

1 1772

3 1795

3 1795

2 1793

1 1772

WARSAW

3 1795

2 1793

1 1772

TO RUSSIA

TO AUSTRIA

SWEDEN

STOCKHOLM

Acquired in 1743 by ELIZABETH

Lake Ladoga

Baltic Sea

ST. PETERSBURG

RIGA

KURLAND

W. Dvina

VILNA

WARSAW

PRUSSIA

P O L A N D

3 1795

2 1793

1 1772

SMOLENSK

MINSK

KIEV

Dnieper

AUSTRIA

Dniester

Prut

1791

1783

CRIMEA

AZOV

Danube

Black Sea

CONSTANTINOPLE

OTTOMAN EMPIRE

Volga

KAZAN

Kama

MOSCOW

Oka

R U S S I A

SAMARA

VORONEZH

KHARKOV

Don

Volga

ASTRAKHAN

Terek

Ural

Caspian Sea

PERSIA

The acquisitions of Catherine the Great, 1762–1796

the war with great determination. Russian armies led by Rumiantsev and Suvorov, who during the earlier part of the Turkish war was engaged in Poland, won some notable victories. Peace negotiations were resumed and led to the conclusion of the treaty of Kuchuk-Kainardzhi (July 1774), which signified the Porte's acceptance of Russian terms, even though the Ottoman empire survived and the Turks were not ejected from Europe. The treaty provided for the independence of the Crimea, transferred to Russia the Crimean ports of Kerch and Enikale as well as important territories between the Dnieper and the Bug and in the Caucasus, and permitted the fortification of Azov and Taganrog and the navigation of Russian merchant vessels in the Black Sea (both had been forbidden by the Belgrade treaty of 1739). Russian merchant ships were given free passage through the Bosphorus and the Dardanelles, and St. Petersburg secured ill-defined rights to protect the Christian population of Turkey. Moldavia and Wallachia, however, remained under the suzerainty of the sultan. The treaty of Kuchuk-Kainardzhi was not the complete fulfillment of Catherine's program, but it was an important step in that direction.

New Alliances and the "Greek Project." The Russo-Prussian alliance of 1764 was concluded for eight years. Renewed twice, it was permitted to lapse in 1788, but relations between the two governments became less intimate before that date. Frederick II died in 1787 and was succeeded by Frederick William II, who aligned Prussia with England and Holland and favored anti-Russian policies in Sweden, Turkey, and Poland.

In 1774 Potemkin became the official favorite; he was responsible for the revised version of Gregory Orlov's plan for the dismemberment of Turkey. The "Greek Project," as Potemkin's proposal was known, envisaged the restoration of the Byzantine empire under Catherine's grandson Constantine (born in 1779), the creation of the kingdom of Dacia (which was to comprise the Danubian territories of Moldavia, Wallachia, and Bessarabia, and which Potemkin was to rule), and the expulsion of the Turks from Europe. The Russo-Austrian alliance, concluded in 1780, was designed to facilitate the fulfillment of this plan. The alliance was directed against Turkey, but it also guaranteed the existing Polish constitution.

The first step in the execution of Catherine's grand design was the annexation of the Crimea. As was to be expected, the independent state of the Crimean Tatars did not prove viable and under relentless Russian pressure was drifting towards its doom. The annexation of the Crimea was proclaimed by St. Petersburg in April 1783 after the puppet Tatar ruler abdicated and surrendered his powers to the Russian Crown. In the same year the kingdom of Georgia, in the Caucasus, became a Russian protectorate.

Early in 1787 Catherine undertook a spectacular journey through the southern territories recently annexed from Turkey. Potemkin, governor of these provinces, organized a remarkable display of the alleged achievements of his brief administration. Some of them were mere stage settings—the famous "Potemkin villages"—but others were real. In the bay of Sevastopol Catherine reviewed Russia's newly-built Black Sea fleet. This and other manifestations of naval and military might, as well as the presence among Catherine's guests of Emperor Joseph II of the Holy Roman Empire and, for a short time, of King Stanislas Poniatowski, suggested that the imperial journey was more than a pleasure excursion. The Porte was properly alarmed and, not without prodding from England and Prussia, demanded (August 1787) the restoration of the independence of the Crimea and the strict observance by Russia of the treaty of Kuchuk-Kainardzhi.

Wars with Turkey and Sweden, 1787–1792. War between Russia and Turkey followed. Austria, recognizing the obligations which she had assumed under her treaty of alliance with Russia, declared war on Turkey. As in 1768–1774, Russia was poorly prepared for the struggle. There were grievous shortages of army stores and munitions and bitter feuds among the Russian generals themselves—Suvorov, Potemkin, and Rumiantsev—and between the Russian army leaders and their Austrian opposite numbers. The Russian army and the Black Sea navy won some notable victories; yet, in spite of the unpreparedness of the Turks, which was as patent as that of the Russians, the war dragged on for four years. Plans were made for sending the Russian Baltic fleet to Turkish waters; it was expected, as in 1768, that the Russians would be enthusiastically welcomed by the Christian populations in revolt against the Porte. England, however, would not grant the necessary facilities, and her opposition to the Russian expedition was backed by Prussia, Holland, Spain, and France. The plan was dropped in the summer of 1788 when Sweden declared war on Russia.

Throughout the eighteenth century Sweden, like Poland and Turkey, lived under the threat of dismemberment by Russia and other neighboring states. Since 1720 Sweden had had a constitution that deprived the Crown of most of its traditional powers; the resulting weakness of the executive was regarded by many as favoring the predatory policies of Sweden's enemies. The first partition of Poland served as a salutory warning and was the immediate cause of a successful *coup d'état* that was executed by the young King Gustavus III in August 1772 and strengthened the central government by restoring to the Crown its traditional authority. Russia and Prussia were alarmed, especially because their alliance of 1764 bound them to maintain the 1720 Swedish constitution. Nevertheless no action was taken at the time by the guarantors. Gustavus met Catherine in 1778 and in 1783, but relations between the two countries remained strained, and it was a fact of common knowledge that the Russian embassy in Stockholm was a center of intrigues directed against the Crown.

Sweden's ambition to eliminate Russian interference in her domestic affairs and to recover some of the territories lost to Russia was encouraged by England and Prussia. The Russo-Turkish war of 1787 offered the desired opportunity, and the Swedish-Turkish alliance of 1739, long dormant, furnished a thin pretext for Swedish intervention. Gustavus denounced Russian policies in Turkey and Poland and demanded the restoration of Karelia and Finland. These demands, of course, could not be accepted. The Russo-Swedish war began in June 1788 and continued until the summer of 1790. Since Russia had few troops in the north and because of the proximity of Sweden to St. Petersburg, the Russian capital appeared to be in immediate danger. These widely-held apprehensions proved unwarranted. The Russian Baltic fleet fought gallantly, both countries had defeats and victories, both suffered heavy losses, and the war ended in August 1790 on the basis of the *status quo ante bellum*. Russia, however, had to give up her position as a guarantor of the Swedish constitution.

Meanwhile the Russo-Turkish war continued. The military campaign of 1788 and 1789 was on the whole favorable to Russia and Austria, but the international situation was not. The loss of the Danubian principalities by Turkey led Frederick William to conclude with the Porte an alliance that bound Prussia to fight for the liberation of the Turkish territory from Russian and Austrian troops (January 1790); Frederick William also entered into an alliance with Poland. Revolt against the Hapsburg rule in Belgium, Hungary, and Galicia made it difficult for Vienna to continue the Turkish war. Emperor Joseph II died in February 1790 and was succeeded by his brother Leopold II, who in the summer of that year agreed to an armistice with the Porte and entered into peace negotiations on the basis of the *status quo ante bellum*. Proposals for negotiations on a similar basis made to Russia by England and Prussia were rejected by Catherine. The mediating powers would not go beyond admonitions and threats, and to these Russia would not yield. Military operations continued their course, Russian armies won a few more victories, the Turks became more amenable, and the war ended by the treaty of Jassy (January 1792), by which Russia annexed the fortress of Ochakov and territories between the Dniester and the Bug and obtained the confirmation of the treaty of Kuchuk-Kainardzhi and of the annexation of the Crimea. During the second as well as during the first Turkish war, important decisions were made by the empress herself. She displayed fortitude and determination and would not listen to those who, like Potemkin, urged moderation. The treaty of Jassy is regarded as a major advance in the Russian policy of territorial expansion and as a great personal triumph for Catherine, even though the Turks remained in Constantinople.

Second and Third Partition of Poland, 1793–1797. Russian involvement in Turkey and Sweden had grave repercussions in Poland. Following the first partition, Poland, notwithstanding the presence of Russian troops and the high-handed methods of the Russian ambassador, enjoyed a period of relative domestic peace. Economic and social reforms removed or mitigated some of the worst abuses of the existing order; but while there was no overt opposition to the political regime imposed by Russia, agitation for constitu-

New York Public Library, Slavonic Division

Catherine's Dream, English cartoon, 1791

tional reform continued. It was given powerful stimulus by Russia's simultaneous engagement in wars with Turkey and Sweden. The Polish so-called Four Years' Diet, which met in the autumn of 1788, assumed the leadership in an exciting program of change that would liberate Poland from Russian shackles. King Stanislas' warnings and the threats of the Russian ambassador were ignored. Austria and Prussia for a time lent their support to the reform movement. In the spring of 1789 Russian troops were withdrawn, as requested by the Polish government, and in March 1790 Frederick William signed a treaty of alliance with Poland that promised Prussian military assistance if Russia or Austria were to attempt to impose their will on Poland. The culminating point of the anti-Russian revolt was the adoption by the diet of the constitution of May 3, 1791, N.S., which did away with elective kingship, made the throne hereditary in the house of Saxony, abolished the *liberum veto* and the "confederations," and made various other changes. This constitution, which remained in force for only a brief time, is rated as a major event in Polish history. It was approved by Austria and Prussia, but Russia would have none of it.

The termination of the Swedish and Turkish wars freed the hands of the Russian government. Meanwhile Frederick William and Emperor Francis II, who had succeeded Leopold II, concluded in April 1792 a military alliance and became involved in an onerous war with France that made it difficult for them to intervene effectively in Poland even if they had wished to do so. In that unhappy country events moved swiftly. In May 1792 a small group of disaffected Poles organized, on the instigation of St. Petersburg, the "confederation" of Targowica, which denounced the constitution of May 3 as revolutionary and appealed to the Russian empress for help. Once more a large Russian army invaded Poland. In July King Stanislas subscribed to the demands of the confederates. Prussia, which had suffered heavy defeats in the war with France, did not fulfill the obligations of her 1790 Polish alliance. Instead, Berlin and St. Petersburg negotiated the second partition treaty (January 1793), which deprived Poland of over one-half of her territory and population. Russia annexed an area of some 89,000 square miles with over 3 million inhabitants. Under strong Russian pressure the second dismemberment of Poland was ratified in September 1793 by a Polish diet which met in Grodno. Austria did not participate directly in the second partition but was promised assistance in her annexationist designs on Bavaria. The Russo-Polish treaty of "perpetual alliance" (October 1793) made Poland virtually a Russian protectorate. The constitution of May 3 and the legislation enacted by the Four Years' Diet were repealed.

Western Europe was shocked, but nothing was done to help Poland. The

Poles themselves made a desperate eleventh-hour attempt to save their country from its doom. An uprising against the partitioning powers led by Thaddeus Kosciuszko, of American War of Independence fame, broke out in the spring of 1794. The insurgents gained some surprising victories, occupied Warsaw and Vilna, and forced Frederick William (who in August 1792 had concluded a new alliance with Russia) to lift the siege of Warsaw and retreat behind his border. Yet the outcome of the struggle was a foregone conclusion. In November, Kosciuszko was made prisoner by the Russians, and Polish resistance collapsed. Meanwhile Russia, Austria, and Prussia were carrying on negotiations for the final liquidation of Poland. The third partition treaty was made by Russia and Austria in January 1795; it was acceded to by Prussia in October of that year; and the final convention for the partition of Poland was signed in January 1797, that is, shortly after Catherine's death. Among the Polish territories formally annexed by Russia by the third partition were Kurland (held by the Russians since 1795) and Lithuania; the city and region of Cracow went to Austria and those of Warsaw to Prussia. Poland was erased from the map of Europe.

Armed Neutrality and the "Oriental Project." Mention must be made of the Armed Neutrality Declaration, which lies outside the main stream of Russian foreign policy. This famous document, issued in 1780, enunciated the principle that a neutral flag protects enemy cargoes on the seas. Directed against England and promulgated during the American War of Independence, the Declaration became the cornerstone of the doctrine of the freedom of the seas, but it had little direct effect on Russian foreign relations.

The "Oriental project," associated with Platon Zubov, was an elaboration of Potemkin's "Greek project." The revised version aimed not only at the conquest of Constantinople and the restoration of Byzantium, but also at the invasion of the Caucasus, Persia, Tibet, and India. The empress in person was to lead the Black Sea fleet, while the 24-year-old Valerian Zubov, brother of the favorite, was appointed leader of the Asia Minor expeditionary force. He actually took over the command of the Caucasian army and had occupied Baku and Derbent when the death of Catherine in November 1796 and the accession of Paul terminated this reckless adventure that could bring nothing but disaster.

Government

The Legislative Commission, 1767–1768. Catherine's grandiose "projects" of conquest had their counterpart in far-reaching plans of domestic reforms.

In both cases the results achieved were vastly different from what was intended.

A much-advertised enterprise was the proposed enactment of a new code of laws which would provide Russia with the most advanced legislation in the world. The code was to be prepared by the Legislative Commission, for which the empress wrote an elaborate *Instruction*. This celebrated document, which was issued in the summer of 1767, was built around the proposition that Russia was a European state and should be governed in accordance with "European principles." The latter may be summarized as those of an absolute monarchy, resting, however, on the foundation of the rule of law. Catherine admitted that her own contribution to the contents of the *Instruction* was slight: in drafting the text she and her associates leaned heavily on Montesquieu's *L'Esprit des lois* and Beccaria's treatise on crime and punishment. The *Instruction* dealt in generalities and provided no concrete program of legislative action. The Commission, an unwieldy body of over 560 members elected by various social groups and roughly patterned on the seventeenth-century *zemskii sobor,* convened in Moscow in July 1767 but transferred to St. Petersburg early in 1768. It adjourned, never to meet again, in December of that year, officially because of the outbreak of the Turkish war. Some of the committees continued their work for a few years longer, but not a single section of the code was completed or even drafted. Criticism, guarded as it was, by the delegates of the existing order, particularly serfdom, was presumably one of the real reasons for the speedy closing down of the Commission.

Local Government Reform. The institutions of local government established by Peter I did not prove viable, and under his successors the administration of provincial Russia reverted to the crude bureaucratic methods of the seventeenth century. The freeing of the nobility from the obligation of compulsory service in 1762 created a new situation. The *dvoriane,* formerly rare visitors to their estates, returned to the countryside in large numbers, eager to participate in local affairs. Their wishes were partly gratified by the Law on the Administration of the Provinces of November 1775 and the Charter of the Nobility of April 1785. The number of provinces was increased from 15 in 1762 to 40 in 1781 and to 50 in 1796. Government was decentralized by granting comprehensive powers to the new provincial agencies; these agencies were subordinated directly to the Senate and no longer to central departments ("colleges") as was the case before. Each new provincial agency was put in charge of a specified branch of public administration—schools, public health, finance, justice, relief, the police. The segregation of functions was designed to eliminate confusion and inefficiency. Finally, whereas some of the provincial officials were appointed by the Crown, others were elected by social groups—the nobility, the merchants, the burghers, and the peasants living on state-owned land.

The reform of 1775 provided a durable territorial-administrative framework that was retained, with modifications, until the end of the empire. The segregation of functions contributed (although more in theory than in practice) to efficient government, but the application of the principal of electivity in filling provincial offices brought no significant change. Each province was ruled, as in the past, by an appointed governor vested with comprehensive powers. With the exception of the provincial and county marshals of the nobility,[1] the elected officials held subordinate positions and enjoyed none of the real autonomy that is the essence of self-government.

The municipal government was remodeled by the Charter of the Towns (1785), which endeavored to organize the urban population into six corporations on the basis of property qualifications, occupation, social origin, and educational standards. The six corporations were reminiscent of medieval guilds; they elected a town council that, in turn, chose a 6-member executive board. Police powers, however, were vested in an appointed Crown official. The corporate organization attempted by the Charter was foreign to Russia's tradition and proved stillborn. Until the reform of the second half of the nineteenth century, Russian towns continued to be governed by appointed officials headed by the chief of the police.

The reform of 1775–1785 added greatly to the cost of administration by multiplying the number of officials, but it accomplished little in improving the standards of government.

Disintegration of Central Government. Although no systematic reform of the central government was undertaken in the reign of Catherine, there were important changes in the structure of central institutions. An early proposal by a Moscow professor who had lived in England for the reorganization of the Senate as a parliament was not acted upon. More in line with Russian realities was the modest plan for the appointment of a small council advisory to the sovereign. Its chief object was to eliminate the irresponsible influence of favorites. Catherine agreed; pertinent legislation was drawn and signed in 1762, but the empress changed her mind and the act establishing the council was not promulgated. An advisory council of nine members, however, was appointed early in 1769, shortly after the outbreak of the Turkish war. Originally a wartime measure, the council nevertheless

_____
[1] See below, p. 226.

continued to meet until the end of the reign. It had no statutory or executive powers and did nothing to check the rule of the favorites.

The law on the administration of the provinces of 1775, by delegating comprehensive authority to local agencies and by subordinating them directly to the Senate, made seemingly superfluous most of the central government departments ("colleges"), which indeed were abolished one by one between 1780 and 1786. The department of foreign affairs and that of the army and the admiralty were the only ones retained. The Senate, although theoretically the highest organ of judicial and administrative control, was actually dominated by its procurator general, an office held by Prince Alexander Viazemsky from 1764 to 1792. The resulting situation, especially in view of the influence exercised by Catherine's favorites, was the reverse of the rule of law.

A notable feature of domestic policies was administrative integration, that is, the elimination of local institutions and the substitution for them of governmental agencies patterned on those of Russia proper. An early victim of this sinister procedure was the Ukraine. Her last hetman, Cyril Razumovsky, was forced to resign in 1764; in 1781 her territory was divided into three provinces which were given the institutions provided by the act of 1775; and in 1783 her population (except for the privileged classes) was made subject to the poll tax. In the 1780's a similar fate befell the Baltic provinces and the districts of Finland held by Russia. The territory annexed from Poland under the three partitions was governed like any other Russian province.

Social Structure

The Nobility. There is justification for describing the second half of the eighteenth century as the golden age of the Russian nobility. The basic gain of the *dvorianstvo* was the abolition by Peter III of compulsory service (manifesto of February 18, 1762). This legislation was retained by Catherine and was amended and expanded in the Charter of the Nobility of April 1785. Under its provisions the status of nobility, with the exception noted below, was hereditary; it could not be revoked without a trial. The estate of a nobleman convicted of a serious crime was not confiscated but went to his heirs. The *dvoriane* were free to resign from government service and to travel abroad. They were exempt from the poll tax, the billet, and corporal punishment and were entitled to own land populated by serfs, as well as industrial enterprises, and to sell wholesale the produce of their estates,

Some of the provisions of the Charter were recapitulations of rights and privileges which the nobility had long enjoyed.

The Charter broke new ground, however, by laying down the rules for the organization of corporations of the nobility. These were established on two levels: provincial (*guberniia*) and county (*uezd*). The organs of the corporations were the general assembly of the hereditary nobles of the province or county, which met every three years, and the marshals of the nobility, provincial or county, elected by the respective assemblies. The powers of the assemblies were narrowly circumscribed and were limited to the local and professional needs of the *dvorianstvo*. There was no organization of the nobility above the provincial level, which may explain why the corporative organs played but a minor part in Russian political history. They were established in the provinces which had a sufficient number of noble land-owners and towards the end of the empire existed in 39 provinces. None were formed in the northern regions of European Russia and in Siberia.

The Charter retained the provisions of the Table of Ranks (1722), which conferred the title of hereditary nobility on army officers and on civil servants who had reached the prescribed rank in the official hierarchy. Government servants of lower rank received the status of "personal nobility" (*lichnoe dvorianstvo*), which was not hereditary and did not entitle them to participation in corporate activities. Government service remained the normal source of gaining admission into the ranks of the *dvorianstvo*.

The power of the nobility over the servile population, comprehensive as it was, was further broadened. The judicial authority of estate owners extended to all crimes except robbery and murder. Amending earlier legislation, a decree of 1765 empowered the owner not only to sentence his serfs to penal servitude in Siberia but also to claim them back at will. There were vague stipulations in the law designed to prevent "immorality, extravagance, tyranny, and cruelty" among the serf-owners, as well as provisions imposing upon them the obligation to provide for their indigent serfs in time of famine, but these rules were seldom invoked and were unenforceable.

In spite of the formidable power conferred upon the *dvoriane* by law and custom, their status, with some exceptions, was unimpressive. Under serfdom the economic standing of a nobleman was reckoned in terms of "registered souls," that is, the male serfs whom he owned. While statistics of serf ownership inspire little confidence, it is believed that in the second half of the eighteenth century about 60 per cent of the landed proprietors owned fewer than 21 serfs each; some 25 per cent, from 21 to 100; and 15 per cent, over 100; in other words, the vast majority of estate owners were small holders of modest means and humble social status. At the opposite end of the scale were a few hundred noble families, perhaps one per cent of the total number, who owned among them one-third of the entire servile population.

The Peasantry. In the eighteenth and nineteenth centuries the term "peasants" (*krestiane*) was used to describe the rural population subject to the poll tax. There were two principal groups of peasants: serfs (*krepostnye krestiane*), or peasants living on the estates of the nobility, and state peasants (*gosudarstvennye krestiane*), or peasants living on state-owned land. In 1764 the Church estates were secularized and their servile population was merged with the state peasants. There were two numerically less important groups of the peasantry: peasants living on the land owned by the Crown and the imperial family, and the so-called "possessionary" peasants, who were permanently attached to industrial enterprises.[2] There were important similarities as well as significant differences in the status of state peasants and that of the serfs. Members of both groups paid the poll tax, provided recruits for the armed forces, and performed other obligations for the state—the billet, repair of roads, supply of lodgings and means of transportation for government officials, and the like. The essential difference in the position of the two groups was that the state peasants were permanently attached to their allotments and could not be sold without the land; the serfs, on the other hand, could be removed from the land by their owners and could be sold or otherwise disposed of as any other movable property.

The financial obligations of the state peasants consisted, in addition to the poll tax, of the *obrok,* an annual payment that was in the nature of rent for their allotments. Serfs on private estates lived under the regime of either *barshchina* or *obrok*. Under *barshchina* the land of an estate was divided into two parts: one was farmed for the benefit of the estate owner by servile labor, and the other part was farmed by the serfs on their own account. Under the *obrok* system serfs paid to their masters an annual tribute (*obrok*) but were not called upon to perform services. It is believed that in the reign of Catherine somewhat more than one-half of the servile population lived under the *barshchina* regime. The *obrok* of the state peasants was determined by a government agency and was relatively moderate and stable, although it tended to rise. The *obrok* of the serfs and the other exactions imposed upon them by their masters were not regulated by law; actually the amount of such tributes varied within a surprisingly wide range, from one ruble or less to several hundred rubles, according to the financial stand-

[2] See above, pp. 181–182.

ing of the serf. Although legally serfs could purchase industrial enterprises and land only in the name of their masters, some of them were allowed considerable freedom in the management of their business affairs and were well-to-do, a situation from which their masters profited. Both state peasants and serfs enjoyed a modicum of crude self-government under the watchful eye either of petty police officials or of the estate owners.

Throughout the eighteenth century the burden of the peasants, especially that of the serfs, tended to increase. By and large, state peasants were in a better position than serfs, but their status was precarious. Russian eighteenth-century rulers made lavish gifts of state land to their favorites, generals, and distinguished foreigners; peasants living on such estates ceased to be state peasants and became serfs. Moreover, in the closing years of the century, serfdom was introduced in the Ukraine and in other southern territories.

The Peasant War, 1773–1774. The emancipation of the nobility from the obligation of compulsory service generated persistent rumors that the serfs, too, were soon to be set free. Instead came increased rigors and exactions. The mass flight of bondsmen that we have noted during the earlier period went on unchecked. There were frequent scattered peasant uprisings, which culminated in the great revolt led by Emilian Pugachev. His movement originated in the Volga region, which harbored masses of destitute and desperate humanity—runaway serfs, old-believers escaping religious persecution, Cossacks nursing grudges against Russian authorities, and native tribes (Bashkir, Tatar, Kirghiz) displaced by Russian settlers. Pugachev, an illiterate Cossack who pretended to be Emperor Peter III, raised the banner of rebellion in September 1773. For a time he was remarkably successful, and the very fate of Catherine's rule appeared to hang in the balance. His victories, however, proved ephemeral; he was captured in September 1774 and, after a trial by a special court, was executed in Moscow in January 1775. The ferocity, short-lived success, and ultimate failure of the rebellion were typical of the Russian peasant movement in the eighteenth and nineteenth centuries.

Industry, Trade, and Finance

Industry. The economic policies of Catherine appear singularly unimpressive when viewed against the background of territorial expansion and broad, albeit abortive, plans for administrative and social reforms. Actually the state of economic stagnation that set in under Peter I's immediate successors continued throughout the later part of the century.

There are no reliable statistics of industrial development during this period, but it is believed that the number of industrial enterprises increased from fewer than 1,000 in 1760 to over 3,000 in the 1790's. It seems likely, however, that some of the establishments listed as industrial enterprises were actually small shops employing a few men. The total labor force in industry towards the end of the century is variously estimated at from 100,000 to 500,000. The higher figure presumably includes many small producers, some of them part-time, engaged in domestic (cottage) industry. It would seem also that an increasing portion of the workers employed in large-scale industrial enterprises were hired and were not serfs of the entrepreneurs. They were recruited among the urban population, state peasants, and serfs on *obrok*.

The policy of fostering monopolistic trading companies that the government had followed since the days of Peter I gradually lost its popularity and was finally abandoned in 1775 when the establishment of industrial enterprises was made free for all and no longer required authorization. Although one of the reasons for this change of policy was the contention that monopolistic companies stifled technical advancement, the reform of 1775 had no appreciable effect on industrial techniques, which remained at the low level of the early eighteenth century.

Foreign Trade. The picture of the evolution of foreign trade under Catherine is unclear. Its average annual value, according to rather unreliable figures which are the only ones available, rose from less than 30 million rubles in the 1770's to over 80 million in the 1790's, but during that period the ruble lost approximately one-third of its value. The bulk of foreign trade—well over 90 per cent—was seaborne and went through the ports of the Baltic Sea; the share of the White Sea and the Black Sea was small. St. Petersburg was by far the principal commercial port. Russian expansion in the Black Sea region, the annexation of the Crimea (1783), and the founding of Odessa (1792), eventually the principal grain exporting port, were too recent to affect markedly the direction of foreign trade, in spite of the greatly privileged treatment granted to imports and exports based on southern ports. Turkey still guarded jealously the exit from the Black Sea, and although Russian merchant vessels enjoyed, after 1774 (treaty of Kuchuk-Kainardzhi), the right of passage through the Turkish straits and of navigation in Turkish waters, this was denied to merchantmen of other nations. The Russian merchant marine was numerically weak, and Russian foreign trade was carried predominantly in foreign bottoms. Exports consisted chiefly of flax, hemp, flat iron, rough linen cloth (for re-export to the colonies), naval stores (sail cloth, timber, tar, cordage), bristle, furs, and hides. Exports of grain were small and were effected chiefly through the Baltic port of Riga. The principal articles of import were woollen and cotton textiles, colonial products (sugar, dyestuffs, tea, coffee, fruit), and luxury items such as silk, wines, and spirits. England was Russia's leading trading partner. Commercial relations with that country were regulated by the treaty of 1734, which was renewed in 1766 and again in 1797 after a lapse of 11 years: the treaty of 1766 had expired in 1786 and was not immediately renewed because of the estrangement between Russia and England caused by the Russian-sponsored Declaration of Armed Neutrality (1780). In the 1780's Russia concluded several other commercial treaties.

The general trend of Catherine's policy from mild liberalism to reaction was reflected in tariff legislation. The tariff act of 1766 was relatively moderate; tariff rates were substantially increased by the act of 1782, and in 1793–1796 there were enacted highly restrictive and prohibitive measures directed primarily against revolutionary France and culminating in the suspension of all trade with that country. Concern with the rapid depreciation of the paper ruble (to be discussed in the next section) was another consideration behind the growth of aggressive protectionism.

Taxation, Money, and the Public Debt. The disorder of public accounts in the eighteenth century was such as to preclude any well-founded generalization concerning the condition of the treasury. Nevertheless, the financial consequences of frequent and protracted war, costly government reforms, extravagance of the imperial court, and economic stagnation were inexorably reflected in the state of public finance. According to the more reliable estimates, public revenue increased from 14 million rubles in 1763 to 55 million in 1796. The rise in revenue was not, however, due to economic advancement, and its sources were the same as at the end of Peter I's reign: the poll tax, which provided more than one-third of the total yield in 1763–1796, and revenue from spirits, salt, and customs. The massive increase in tax receipts was the consequence of the natural growth of the population and of higher tax rates (particularly the latter), that is, the taxpayers carried a heavier burden at the end of Catherine's reign than they had 30 years earlier.

Expenditure grew even more rapidly than revenue. To fill the gap between the two the government used expedients novel in Russian financial history: paper currency and borrowing. Substitution of paper money for metallic tokens had been considered in Russia since the beginning of the eighteenth century. A decree of Peter III ordered the establishment of a bank of issue, but it was rescinded after his overthrow. At the end of 1768, following the outbreak of the Turkish war, two banks for the issue of assignats (bank notes) were established, in St. Petersburg and Moscow. The total volume of paper currency was at first limited to one million rubles, and the notes were freely convertible into silver coins. These restrictions were soon dropped. In 1796 the volume of notes in circulation reached 156 million rubles, convertibility was suspended in 1777, and the paper ruble depreciated and by 1796 had lost about one-third of its face value. Inconvertibility and depreciated paper currency remained features of the Russian monetary system until the introduction of the gold standard in 1897.

Borrowing, as a method of raising revenue, was adopted simultaneously with the introduction of paper currency. By the end of Catherine's reign the aggregate public debt, foreign and domestic, was about 60 million rubles, of which 35.5 million represented foreign borrowing. The service of foreign loans (interest and amortization) amounted to 11 per cent of the public revenue. The chief lending country was Holland.

Schools, Letters, and Arts

Schools. The intellectual resources of eighteenth-century Russia were too limited and the drain of war on her finances too severe to allow much room for cultural advancement. Nevertheless the need for schools received some recognition. A subcommittee of the Legislative Committee produced in 1770 a project for the opening of one village school for each 100 to 250 peasant households; the cost was to be defrayed from local funds. No action was taken on this proposal. A law of 1786 provided for schools on two levels— elementary and secondary—with a course of instruction, respectively, of two and four years. Textbooks, chiefly translations of Austrian school manuals (the leader of the reform was a Serb educated in Austria), were published and a teachers' college was founded, but progress was slow and the results disappointing, partly because of the absence of adequate financial provisions. Towards the end of the century Russia had a handful of lay schools located predominantly in urban centers with an aggregate student body of less than 20,000, or one student per 1,600 of the population. A similar number of students was enrolled in Church schools.

The lack of schools and their low scholastic standards had an unforeseen result: it became customary to send children of the upper class to study abroad or to have them educated by foreign tutors, usually French or Swiss, many of them men of liberal or radical leanings. The example was set by the empress, who entrusted the education of her favorite grandson, the future Emperor Alexander I, to César La Harpe, the well-known Swiss statesman. The result was that many young Russians were brought up on ideas which were not easily reconcilable with the conditions in their homeland. This situation explains much in the intellectual history of the nineteenth century.

Letters. Catherine took great personal interest in the advancement of literature and left a number of written works. She had, however, but a hesitant command of both written French and written Russian, and her compositions underwent extensive editing before they were released. The literary manner of the later eighteenth century was the continuation of the pseudo-classicism of the previous era. The writings of even the outstanding contemporary authors—Kheraskov, Kniazhnin, Bogdanovich, Khemnitser—have not withstood the test of time and today are, at best, curious period pieces. There was, nevertheless, an important improvement in style and language which cleared the way for later poets and novelists. Moreover, two of the authors of this period, Denis Fonvizin (1745–1792) and Gabriel Derzhavin (1743–1818), wrote works which have achieved the status of near-classics: Fonvizin with his still-popular play *The Minor,* and Derzhavin —"the bard of Catherine"—with his high-sounding odes glorifying the empress and her favorites and generals. Numerous translations of ancient and modern classics familiarized the Russian reading public with foreign literary masterpieces.

The fate of Radishchev and Novikov revealed Catherine's real attitude towards enlightenment and also the true measure of her liberalism. Alexander Radishchev (1749–1802), who had studied in Germany and travelled abroad, published in 1790, with the approval of the censor, a notable volume, *Journey from St. Petersburg to Moscow,* which was inspired by *A Sentimental Journey* of Laurence Sterne and presented a moving but unflattering picture of Russian conditions, including serfdom and monarchical absolutism. The author was arrested, tried, and sentenced to death but was actually exiled to Siberia. Nicholas Novikov (1744–1818) was a freemason, a public-minded journalist, and head of the largest publishing house in Russia, as well as leader of a society that provided scholarships for Russian students in Russian and foreign schools. His principal concern was the advancement of education and public welfare. Catherine, who had the wrong notion about freemasonry, ordered the closing of Novikov's many business enterprises and in 1792 sentenced him, by imperial decree and without a trial, to incarceration in the fortress of Schlüsselburg for 15 years. Both Radishchev and Novikov were released on the accession of Emperor Paul.

Art. While Russian national art made little progress in the second half of the eighteenth century, the appearance of St. Petersburg was much improved and the national endowment in art treasures was greatly extended. Catherine and the wealthy noblemen imported noted foreign artists and architects—chiefly French and Italian—whose work lent distinction to the Russian capital and the residences of the empress and the nobility. The purchase of three large European collections of paintings and other works of art laid the foundation of the Ermitage museum, an annex of the Winter Palace, built by the Frenchman Vallin de Lamothe. There appeared, for the first time, Russian architects—V. I. Bazhenov, M. F. Kazakov, I. E. Starov —and portrait painters—F. S. Rokotov, D. G. Levitsky, V. L. Borovikov. Their work, however, stemmed not from the Russian but from the Western tradition. Starov was the architect of the magnificent Taurida Palace, built by Catherine for her favorite, Prince Potemkin of Taurida, and, in the twentieth century, the seat of the Russian parliament (State Duma). It was during this period that the classical style of architecture known as the Russian *empire* and reminiscent of the colonial style in the United States gained popularity.

The year 1779 was a landmark in Russian cultural history: in that year Catherine established in St. Petersburg a ballet school patterned after that of Paris. It became the cradle of the Russian ballet.

Emperor Paul I

Paul and the Historians. Catherine died in November 1796 and was succeeded by her son, Emperor Paul I. Like his father, Peter III, Paul has been treated with great harshness by historians, probably more so than he deserves. The reason for this ungenerous attitude is seemingly the same in the two cases: both father and son fell victims of palace conspiracies involving their immediate successors: Catherine II, wife of Peter III; and Alexander I, son of Paul I. Catherine II and Alexander I are outstanding historical figures; it became quasi-mandatory therefore to represent their predecessors—and victims—as fools and villains. Actually Emperor Paul, his eccentricities, inconsistencies, and failings notwithstanding, was not markedly below the level of the rulers who preceded and followed him.

Domestic Policies. Paul was disliked by his mother, and he knew that

Catherine intended to disinherit him and to appoint his eldest son, Alexander, her successor. Although Paul was denied any part in the administration of the affairs of state, he nevertheless prepared himself carefully for the duties of kingship and secured the advice and guidance of some of the leading contemporary statesmen, particularly his tutor and life-long friend Nikita Panin, titular head of the department of foreign affairs from 1763 to 1780. Paul's principal constitutional innovation was the repeal of the Petrine law of 1722 empowering the emperor to appoint his successor. An act promulgated on the day of the coronation of Paul (April 5, 1797) made the Crown hereditary in the house of Romanov and instituted a firm order of succession. The disorders characteristic of the succession to the throne in the eighteenth century were thus brought to an end. Of some significance were other government reforms. The agencies of the central administration which were abolished under Catherine[3] were restored, while the cumbersome and costly machinery of local government created by the law of 1775 and the Charter of the Nobility was drastically streamlined; the latter measure involved the abolition of numerous elective offices and was interpreted by the nobility as a violation of its privileges.

Foreign Relations. Paul, like Catherine, left a strong personal imprint on the conduct of foreign affairs. One of his first measures was to proclaim his devotion to peace and to cancel the expedition to the Near East planned by Catherine. He shared, however, his mother's detestation of the French Revolution. Late in 1797 and early in 1798 the French *émigré* corps of Prince Condé, formerly in the Austrian service, and of the Comte de Provence (the future Louis XVIII) found in Russia generous hospitality and financial support. There was formed in 1798–1799 an anti-French coalition consisting of Russia, England, Austria, Turkey, and the kingdom of Naples. Meanwhile Russian foreign policy became entangled with the affairs of the Maltese order of the knights of St. John of Jerusalem. Napoleon on his way to Egypt occupied Malta in June 1798. Paul took the order under his protection and in October was elected grand master by the knights of the Russian priory.

Russian participation in the anti-French coalition produced some of the most spectacular, albeit futile, exploits in Russian war annals. Alliance with Turkey permitted the Russian Black Sea fleet to sail through the Dardanelles and to occupy, first, the French-held Ionian Islands and then Corfu. Early in 1799 Suvorov was appointed commander-in-chief of the allied armies. He won remarkable victories over the French in Italy and in the autumn of that year led his soldiers over the Saint Gotthard pass in Switzerland, a campaign

[3] See above, p. 225.

rated as an outstanding feat in military history. Other allied armies, however, were far less successful; there were bitter disagreements with the Austrian and British command; and in January 1800 Suvorov and his troops were recalled to Russia. Simultaneously the orientation of Russian foreign policy was reversed. The overthrow of the Directorate and the establishment of the Consulate in France (November 1799) convinced Paul that Napoleon was moving towards the restoration of the monarchy, while the tsar's hostility towards England mounted. The British had prevented Russia from taking Malta, which they occupied themselves in September 1800 at the very time when Napoleon agreed to cede that island to Russia. The St. Petersburg government retaliated: it imposed an embargo on English shipping, arrested English seamen, and in December 1800 organized—jointly with Sweden, Prussia, and Denmark—the Second Neutrality League (based on the amended 1780 Declaration of Armed Neutrality), which had for its object to defend the freedom of the seas and was directed against England. Diplomatic relations between St. Petersburg and London were severed.

Meanwhile a Franco-Russian *rapprochement* was in progress. The French released with military honors the Russian prisoners of war, while the French *émigré* corps was dismissed from the Russian service and the Comte de Provence was asked to leave Mittau, where he resided on Paul's invitation in the palace of the dukes of Kurland. Negotiations took place for a Franco-Russian alliance that would lead to the partition of the Ottoman Porte and the dismemberment of the British colonial empire. In January 1801 Russia formally annexed Georgia, in the Caucasus, which had been a Russian protectorate since 1783, and proceeded to organize an expedition for the conquest of India by way of the Asiatic khanates of Khiva and Bukhara. The murder of Paul put an end to this foolish and reckless venture.

The Murder of Paul. Paul, like his father, antagonized the very elements on which in the eighteenth century rested the power of the Crown: the bureaucracy, the nobility, and the guards. He did not repeal the Charter of the Nobility, but he curtailed effectively the exercise of some of the privileges which it guaranteed—exemption from direct taxation, corporal punishment, and compulsory service. He was an exacting and ruthless disciplinarian, with the result that service in the guards, which under Elizabeth and Catherine had been a sinecure leading safely to a comfortable career, became a full-time perilous occupation because any infringement, however trivial, of army regulations was likely to bring upon the culprit severe penalties. Paul, moreover, instituted a vexatious police regime that endeavored to regulate in minute detail the dress, way of life, and intellectual fare (books, journals, and even music) of the upper class. These unreasonable and offensive measures were made even less palatable by the emperor's eccentric and perverse sense of humor, of which those within his reach were the defenseless victims. Disaffection in court and army circles mounted. There came into existence a conspiracy organized by a handful of guardsmen and high officials, among them an intimate of the tsar, Count Peter Pahlen, military governor of St. Petersburg. Paul's eldest son, Alexander, approved of the plot. In the night of March 11, 1801, the conspirators invaded the bedchamber of the tsar and murdered him. According to the official announcement, he had died from an attack of apoplexy. This was the last palace revolution in Russian history.

PART FOUR

1801-1917

CHRONOLOGY OF PRINCIPAL EVENTS

1809–1812, March	Strong influence of Speransky
1810	Founding of the Council of State
1810–1811	Reorganization of the ministries
1812, May	Treaty of Bucharest; Russia annexes Bessarabia
1812, June–December	Napoleon in Russia
1812, August 26	Battle of Borodino
1812, September–October	Napoleon in Moscow
1813, October	Treaty of Gulistan; Russia annexes oil lands in the Caucasus
1813–1814	Russian troops in Europe
1814, March	Alexander I enters Paris
1814, September–1815, June	Congress of Vienna
1815, June	Treaty of Vienna; Russia annexes large portion of Poland
1815, September	Treaty of Holy Alliance announced
1815, November	Alexander I grants constitution to Russian Poland
1815–1825	Russia in the European alliance
1816–1820	Early works of Pushkin published
1816	Military colonies organized
1816	University of Warsaw founded
1816–1819	Emancipation of serfs in Baltic provinces, second round
1816–1824	First secret revolutionary societies
1819	University of St. Petersburg founded
1820	Mutiny in the guards
1822, August	Secret societies prohibited
1825, December 14	Decembrist uprising
1825–1855	Emperor Nicholas I
1826–1828	War with Persia
1828	Treaty of Turkmanchai; Russia annexes provinces of Nakhichevan and Erivan
1828–1829	War with Turkey
1829, September	Treaty of Adrianople; Russia annexes Danubian and Caucasian territories
1830–1831	Polish insurrection
1832	Polish constitution abrogated; Universities of Vilna and Warsaw closed
1830's–1850's	Beginning of "The age of the Russian novel" (Gogol, Turgenev, Dostoevsky, Leo Tolstoy)
1833	Full Collection of Laws and Code of Laws published

1833　Treaty of Unkiar Skelessi; Russia acquires important rights in Turkey

1833–1840　Russo-Turkish alliance

1834–1841　Reorganization of state peasants

1834　University of Kiev founded

1836　First Russian opera: Glinka's *Life for the Tsar*

1844　"Inventories" introduced in western provinces

1849　Russian intervention in Hungary

1850's　Expansion in the Far East

1851　St. Petersburg-Moscow railway line open for service

1853　Naval battle of Sinope; Russians defeat Turkish fleet

1854–1856　Crimean War

1854, September–
1855, August　Siege of Sevastopol

1855–1881　Emperor Alexander II

1856　Treaty of Paris; demilitarization of Black Sea; Russia loses portion of Bessarabia

1859　Russian Music Society founded

1860　Vladivostok founded

1860　State Bank founded

1860's　Rise of revolutionary movement

1860, November　Treaty of Peking; China recognizes Russian annexations

1861　Emancipation of the serfs

1863　University charter amended

1863　Polish insurrection

1864　Reform of elementary and secondary schools

1864　*Zemstvo* (local government) reform

1864　Reform of the judiciary

1864–1885　Expansion in central Asia

1867　Sale of Alaska

1869　Finnish constitution

1870　Reform of municipal government

1871　Abrogation of the Black Sea clause of the Treaty of Paris (1856)

1871–1872　Reform of secondary schools

1873　Alliance of the three emperors

1873–1874　Movement "to the people"

1874　Army reform

1875　Russia acquires Sakhalin

1877–1878	War with Turkey
1878, March	Treaty of San Stefano, triumph of Russian Pan-Slavism
1878, June–July	Congress of Berlin
1878, July	Treaty of Berlin; Treaty of San Stefano set aside
1878	The revolutionary organization "Land and Freedom" established
1879	The revolutionary organization "People's Will" established
1881	Loris-Melikov's proposal for reform of legislative procedure
1881, March 1	Murder of Alexander II
1881–1894	Emperor Alexander III
1882	State Peasant Bank founded
1882	Beginnings of factory legislation
1883	"Liberation of Labor," first Russian Marxist organization, founded in Geneva
1884	University charter amended
1885	State Nobility Bank founded
1887	Quotas for Jewish students in secondary schools introduced
1887	Russo-German "reinsurance" treaty
1890	*Zemstvo* act (1864) amended
1890's	Early works of Chekhov and Gorky published
1891–1905	Trans-Siberian railway built
1892	Municipal government act (1870) amended
1893, December–1894, January	Treaty of the Franco-Russian alliance
1894–1917, March	Emperor Nicholas II
1897	Gold standard introduced
1898	Moscow Art Theatre founded
1898, March	Russian Social Democratic Labor Party founded
1898	Russia obtains a lease for Liaotung Peninsula
1899	Russian disarmament proposals
1900–1906	Socialist Revolutionary Party organized
1903	Social Democrats split into Bolsheviks and Mensheviks
1904	Union of Liberation founded
1904, November	University charter amended
1904–1905	Russo-Japanese War
1904, December	Capitulation of Port Arthur
1905, January	"Bloody Sunday"

1905, February	Battle of Mukden
1905, May	Russian fleet destroyed in Straits of Tsushima
1905, August–September	Russo-Japanese peace negotiations at Portsmouth, New Hampshire
1905, September	Portsmouth Treaty; Russia loses to Japan Liaotung Peninsula and half of Sakhalin
1905, October	General strike
1905, October–December	Soviet of Workers' Deputies in St. Petersburg established
1905	Manifesto of October 17: Russia becomes a constitutional monarchy
1905, October	Witte appointed president of the council of ministers
1906, March	Trade unions legalized
1906, April	Fundamental Laws (April 23) enacted
1906, April	Witte resigns
1906, April–July	First State Duma
1906–1911	Stolypin land reform
1907, February–June	Second State Duma
1907, June	Election law amended (June 3)
1907, November–1912, June	Third State Duma
1907, August	Anglo-Russian convention dealing with the Near East
1908, May	Reform of primary education
1908–1909	The Bosnia-Herzegovina crisis
1909	Russian ballet in Paris
1911	Murder of Stolypin
1912, November–1917, February	Fourth State Duma
1914, June	Archduke Francis Ferdinand murdered in Sarajevo (June 28, N.S.)
1914, July	Russian mobilization (July 24–July 30, N.S.)
1914, August	World War I begins
1914, August	Unions of *Zemstvos* and of Towns for the relief of war sufferers formed
1914, August–September	Russian advance and defeat in East Prussia
1914, August–September	Russian advance in Galicia
1914, August–December	German advance in Russian Poland
1914, December	Members of the Bolshevik faction of the Duma arrested
1915, March–April	Russia resumes advance in Galicia

1915, March	Russia is promised by the allies Constantinople and the Straits
1915, May–October	Austro-German offensive on the Russian front
1915, August	Emperor Nicholas assumes command of the army; ascendancy of the empress and Rasputin
1915, August	Special council for supplying the army and war industries committees established
1915, August	Progressive Bloc formed
1915, August–September	Germans take Warsaw, Vilna, and several fortresses
1916, June–October	Successful Russian offensive in Galicia
1916, November	Miliukov denounces the empress and Stürmer, the prime minister, in the State Duma
1916, December	Rasputin murdered
1917, February 23	Street riots begin in Petrograd
1917, February 27	Defection of troops of Petrograd garrison
1917, February 27	State Duma prorogued (February 26) but forms provisional committee
1917, February 27	Petrograd Soviet of Workers' and Soldiers' Deputies formed
1917, March 1	Army Order No. 1
1917, March 2	Nicholas II abdicates in favor of his brother Michael
1917, March 2	Provisional Government formed
1917, March 3	Grand Duke Michael refuses crown; future of Russia to be decided by Constituent Assembly
1917, March	Factory committees established
1917, March–April	Peasant Soviets established
1917, April 3	Lenin returns to Petrograd
1917, April 4	Lenin's *April Theses*
1917, April	Decrees establishing land committees and committees to prepare elections for the Constituent Assembly
1917, April	Demonstrations against foreign policy of the Provisional Government
1917, May 1 and 2	Guchkov and Miliukov resign
1917, May	First All-Russian Congress of Soviets of Peasants' Deputies
1917, May–June	First coalition government
1917, June 3–24	First All-Russian Congress of the Soviets of Workers' and Soldiers' Deputies
1917, June	Ukrainian Central Rada organized
1917, June–July	Russian offensive in Galicia and its failure
1917, July 3 and 4	Unsuccessful Bolshevik uprising in Petrograd

1917, July 7	Prince Lvov resigns as prime minister and is succeeded by Kerensky
1917, July–October	Lenin in hiding in Finland
1917, July	Trotsky and other Bolshevik leaders arrested
1917, July 18	Kornilov appointed commander-in-chief
1917, July–August	Second coalition government
1917, August 13–15	State Conference in Moscow
1917, August 21	Germans take Riga
1917, August 26–31	The Kornilov "mutiny"
1917, August 27	Kerensky appeals for help to the Bolsheviks
1917, August 31	Bolsheviks gain control of Petrograd Soviet
1917, September 1	Kornilov surrenders
1917, September 4	Trotsky released on bail
1917, September 6	Bolsheviks gain control of Moscow Soviet
1917, September	Congress of national minorities in Kiev
1917, September 23	Trotsky elected chairman of Petrograd Soviet
1917, September 14–22	Democratic Conference in Petrograd
1917, September–October	Third coalition government
1917, October 6–25	Provisional Council of the Republic, Petrograd
1917, October 10	Central Committee of the Bolshevik Party accepts Lenin's resolution demanding armed insurrection
1917, October 20	Military revolutionary committee appointed by Petrograd Soviet
1917, October 25	Kerensky leaves Petrograd
1917, October 26	At 2:10 A.M. Provisional Government arrested at the Winter Palace

13

The New Era: Alexander I, 1801-1825

The New Era

Nature of the Change. The accession of Alexander I was in more than one respect the beginning of a new era in Russian history, even though the economic and social conditions inherited from the eighteenth century remained practically unchanged. The law of succession enacted by Emperor Paul was instrumental in terminating the arbitrary selection of the rulers which we have observed in the eighteenth century and in ending the interference of the guards. The Napoleonic wars, followed by Russia's participation in the European Alliance and her leadership in the Holy Alliance, created for Alexander a position unique among the crowned heads of Europe. Close and protracted contact with the West had a profound effect on an important segment of Russian opinion and led to the emergence of Russia's first revolutionary movement, which thrived on the progress of education. Pushkin and several of his contemporaries were the first distinguished Russian authors.

Alexander the Blessed. Alexander I (1801–1825), son of Emperor Paul, was born in 1777. He was brought up at the court of his grandmother, Empress Catherine II, who entrusted his education to César La Harpe, later a well-known Swiss political leader. It was to La Harpe that Alexander owed his familiarity with, and his superficial attachment to, liberal thought. The position of the young grand duke between his grandmother, on the one hand, and his father, on the other, was delicate. He knew and approved of Catherine's intention to disinherit Paul and to appoint himself her successor. Nevertheless he was a frequent visitor, especially in the 1790's, to Gatchina, his father's estate near St. Petersburg, where liberalism was taboo and where he was introduced, under the watchful eye of Paul, to the art of drilling soldiers according to Prussian army regulations. Continuous and perilous manoeuvering between the warring worlds of the Winter Palace and Gatchina may account for Alexander's consummate mastery in concealing his true feelings and for his uncanny ability to pursue simultaneously seemingly irreconcilable policies. Alexander knew and approved of the conspiracy to overthrow his father, although he might have deluded himself into believing that Paul would be only deposed but not murdered. There is evidence that Alexander never fully freed himself from the memory of that gruesome event. At the early age of seventeen he married a German princess, had by her two daughters who died in their infancy, and became estranged from his wife, but a reconciliation between them took place towards the end of his reign.

Alexander was endowed with great personal charm and was a good linguist, although he received little formal education. He began in life as a freethinker and a tepid liberal but about 1810 became converted to morbid religiosity and later embraced extreme conservatism. His religious and political views had important repercussions on Russian domestic and foreign policy. The air of mystery that shrouds much of Alexander's life and work persisted after his death, which occurred in Taganrog, on the Sea of Azov, in November 1825. According to a legend that is not yet entirely discarded, Alexander escaped and lived in Siberia until 1864 as the holy hermit Fedor Kuzmich. This theory is not supported by evidence and should be rejected as a flight of fancy.

Early Policies. The new reign began in a manner that seemed to encourage the hopes of the nobility and of a small group of liberals who formed Alexander's immediate circle. The more objectionable restrictive police measures of Paul were repealed. The Charter of the Nobility and the law of 1775 on provincial government were again made fully effective. The security police, on which the government had leaned so heavily since the days of Peter I, was abolished. Alexander, moreover, gave evidence of his desire for fundamental reforms. In the summer of 1801 there was established the "non-official committee," which consisted of the tsar's personal friends (Count Paul

Alexander I, portrait by François Gérard, Paris, 1815

Stroganov, Nicholas Novosiltsev, Prince Adam Czartoryski, Count Victor Kochubey), young progressive aristocrats educated abroad. The object of the committee was to prepare a constitution for Russia. Nothing constructive came from its efforts except an inconsequential law of September 1802 that renamed the central government agencies "ministries" but otherwise left things as they were before. The "non-official committee" ceased meeting presumably late in 1803, and the proposed constitution remained unwritten. Even more ominous and indicative of the prevailing trend was the revival, in the autumn of 1805, of the security police.

The opening years of Alexander's reign witnessed a shifting of international alignments and a measure of political *détente*. The invasion of India planned by Emperor Paul and Napoleon was put aside. Diplomatic relations with London were resumed. Russia was the first power to withdraw from the anti-British Second Neutrality League (June 1801) and was soon followed by the other two members, Denmark and Sweden. Reconciliation with England inevitably made Franco-Russian relations less close, especially since England and France were engaged in a war. Nevertheless a Franco-Russian treaty of friendship was signed in October 1801. About the same time the state of war between England and France ended and was formally terminated by the peace of Amiens (March 1802).

The Napoleonic Epic

The Anti-French Coalition. The resulting improvement in the international situation proved of short duration, and in May 1803 England was again at war with France. Franco-Russian relations, too, took a turn for the worse. Alexander, his liberal proclivities notwithstanding, shared his grandmother's and his father's detestation of the French Revolution, upheld the principle of legitimacy, which was violated by Napoleon's unceremonious re-drafting of the political map of Europe, and watched with dislike and suspicion the rapid stages by which the "usurper" was consolidating his power: in August 1802 Napoleon became consul for life and in November 1804 he was proclaimed emperor. The execution (March 1804) by the French of the Duke d'Enghien, a Bourbon prince accused of conspiring against the consular regime, brought a sharp protest from Russia and was followed by an equally sharp rebuttal from the French and a severance of diplomatic relations between the two countries.

Russian policy, however, was not entirely determined by current events. Alexander and his minister of foreign affairs, Prince Adam Czartoryski, elaborated—in the tradition of the eighteenth century—a vast plan designed to "liberate" Europe, eliminate war, gratify the national ambitions of Poland, and bring about the fulfillment of Russia's "historic mission." Prince Adam, a wealthy and ardently nationalistic Pole, dreamed of the restoration of a unified autonomous Poland under the Russian Crown. A personal friend of Alexander, he was Russian foreign minister from 1804 to 1806. In the autumn of 1804 Novosiltsev, another friend of Alexander, was sent to London bearing secret proposals for an Anglo-Russian league that would free Europe, including France, from Napoleon. Under the Russian plan the principle of national self-determination was to receive general application, the German and the Italian states were to be organized into separate federations, and arbitration of international disputes was to be mandatory prior to the use of armed force. The Russian Crown was to exercise sovereignty over a reunified Poland (Prussia and Austria were to receive compensation elsewhere), and Russia was to annex Malta, Corfu, Cattaro, and large slices of the Ottoman empire, including the Danubian principalities, Constantinople, and the Dardanelles. Not all of these demands were pressed by Novosiltsev, and some, for instance the cession of Malta, were rejected by William Pitt, prime minister since early in 1804, who was more concerned with the struggle against Napoleon than with the new European order. In spite of these divergencies of approach, the Anglo-Russian treaty of alliance was signed in April 1805. Sweden was already aligned with England, and Austria joined the anti-French coalition. The Anglo-Russian treaty stipulated, among other things, a large subsidy to be paid by England to her continental allies; the actual amount was to be determined by the number of troops contributed by each government, provided the total force was not less than 400,000 men. In the war that followed, the German states sided with France, but Prussia in 1805 remained neutral.

In the meantime Napoleon, who was toying with the notion of an invasion of England and was massing men and ships in the channel ports, abruptly revised his plans and marched his troops across Europe to the Danube. There followed a brief and, to the allies, disastrous campaign. The Austrians were defeated at Ulm (October 1805), Vienna was occupied by the French (November), and early in December a joint Austro-Russian force commanded by the Russian Field Marshal Kutuzov was routed at Austerlitz. Emperor Francis of Austria hastened to make peace, while the shattered remnants of the Russian army withdrew into Russian territory. Frederick William III of Prussia, with whom Alexander was bound by close personal ties, had agreed to side with the allies if peace was not restored on terms satisfactory to them, but Ulm and Austerlitz made him change his mind. A treaty of February 1806 aligned Prussia with France; she closed her ports to English commerce and was rewarded with the annexation of Hanover. St. Petersburg was genuinely alarmed, the Franco-Prussian alliance being interpreted as a direct menace to Russian Poland and to Russia's position in Turkey. Meanwhile the anti-French coalition was falling apart. Pitt, its chief architect, died in January 1806. His successor Fox (who was to die in September of that year) was in favor of peace negotiations with France, and a similar tendency manifested itself among Russian leaders.

This change in the political climate and the ruinous economic consequences of the Franco-Prussian alliance greatly distressed Frederick William. Prussia's participation in the Continental System led to war with England and Sweden and to the seizure of her ships by these maritime powers. There were, moreover, persistent reports that Napoleon was about to make a settlement with his enemies at Prussia's expense: it was rumored that Hanover would be restored to King George III of England and that Prussia's Polish provinces would be given to Russia and Pomerania to Sweden. Frederick William changed his mind once more. He concluded a treaty of alliance with Russia (July 1806) and at the end of September sent an ultimatum to Napoleon demanding the withdrawal of French troops behind the Rhine. This was a declaration of war. What had happened to Austria and Russia a year earlier happened now to Prussia, except that events moved even faster. The Prussians suffered two major defeats (Jena and Auerstädt) in the middle of October, and Berlin was occupied by the French before the end of the month.

The Russian army again took the field against the French, as provided by the Russo-Prussian alliance. There was much heavy fighting, of which perhaps the most important instance was the battle of Preussisch Eylau (February 1807), claimed by both sides as a victory. Although, following the débâcle of October, the Prussian army was greatly reduced in size and Frederick William was engaged in sterile peace negotiations with the French, Alexander did his best to keep Prussia in the war. A convention signed by the two governments in April 1807 confirmed the Russo-Prussian alliance and invited other states to join it. England, which had remained aloof and indeed found it difficult to deal with Prussia because both countries had conflicting claims on Hanover, acceded to the convention in June 1807. It was too late, however. In the middle of June the Russian army under Count Bennigsen was routed by the French at Friedland. An armistice was arranged at once; simultaneously Alexander offered Napoleon an alliance with

Russia that, the tsar wrote, "alone could guarantee the happiness and peace of the world." This was a surprising move.

The Franco-Russian Alliance. Alexander's offer was welcomed and, indeed, encouraged by Napoleon. His primary objective was the defeat of England, which he believed would lead to European peace; alliance with Russia would serve this purpose well. The two emperors met alone on a raft in the middle of the Niemen River (June 25, N.S.). Subsequent negotiations, in which Frederick William participated, took place at nearby Tilsit. The gist of the Tilsit agreements (there were several documents, public and private, signed in July) was the Franco-Russian alliance, which made Alexander a full-fledged partner of Napoleon in the struggle with England and in the implementation of expansionist policies. The agreements contained provisions for important territorial changes. Prussia was saved from total dismemberment by Alexander's gallant intervention but nevertheless was deprived of much of her territory and population. Her Polish provinces, except for the district of Belostok, which was annexed by Russia, were reorganized as the duchy of Warsaw. Russia ceded to France the islands in the Ionian Sea which she had held since the reign of Paul but was promised French assistance against Turkey and the eventual annexation of Turkish territories, which, however, did not include Constantinople. There was much talk about Franco-Russian collaboration in Europe and elsewhere and the division of the world into French and Russian spheres of inflence. Alexander was treated with much courtesy, appeared pleased with the results of the negotiations, and believed that Russia had emerged from the débâcle of Friedland "with a kind of luster." This aberration did not last long.

The immediate consequence of Tilsit was the involvement of Russia in several wars. As Russia's mediation in bringing about an Anglo-French settlement, as provided at Tilsit, failed, St. Petersburg declared war on England (November 1807). However, there was no actual fighting, hostilities being limited to the enforcement by Russia of the Continental Blockade, while England seized a few Russian vessels. War with Sweden came next. The Swedish government was irreconcilably opposed to Napoleon and would not be a party to the Continental Blockade, while Russia had long coveted Finland, then a province of Sweden, partly because of its uncomfortable proximity to St. Petersburg. Napoleon fostered these ambitions. In February 1808 Russian troops invaded Finland and won an easy victory over the Swedes; the annexation of Finland was announced in March, but Finnish guerrillas offered a spirited resistance that was not overcome until the spring of 1809. By the peace treaty of September 1809 Russia acquired Finland

and the Aland Islands. Meanwhile a change of government took place in Stockholm, and the new king, Charles XIII, aligned his country with France and imposed embargoes on British commerce. Since 1806 Russia had also been engaged in a war with Turkey; it was to last for six years and was prolonged by Russian territorial demands, which Napoleon encouraged, although he gave his ally no real assistance.

In February 1808 Napoleon offered Alexander a breath-taking plan of Franco-Russian cooperation that provided for the partition of Scandinavia and of Turkey and for the invasion of India. Arrangements for the proposed campaigns were to be made at a meeting of the two emperors at Erfurt. Alexander seemed satisfied and, although the Russian ambassador to Paris warned him that Napoleon was not in earnest and was merely gaining time, both countries made preparations for the execution of the plan. The outbreak of a powerful anti-French movement in Spain following the election under French pressure of Joseph Bonaparte to the Spanish throne (March 1808) necessitated the indefinite postponement of the execution of Napoleon's proposal. It was in this situation, which was quite different from that in the spring, that the Erfurt meeting was held in September–October 1808. It confirmed the alliance, renewed offers of peace to England subject to her acquiescence in the territorial changes which had taken place in Europe, and approved the annexation by Russia of Finland and, at a future date, of Moldavia and Wallachia. Of greater practical importance than these somewhat academic official agreements were the private negotiations held at Erfurt by Alexander and Talleyrand, until recently French foreign minister, who had secretly turned against Napoleon and urged the tsar to make common cause with Austria in resisting French ambitions. Alexander indeed showed marked friendliness towards the Austrian representative. Erfurt was an important turning point in Franco-Russian relations. Formally the alliance was preserved, but its spell was broken, and evidence of impending conflicts was rapidly multiplying.

Meanwhile Austria, exasperated by Napoleon's arrogance and prodded by Alexander and Talleyrand, made a desperate attempt to free herself from French domination. The Franco-Austrian war, begun in April 1809, proved short and disastrous: early in July the Austrians were wiped out at Wagram and fighting came to an end. Alexander formally fulfilled the obligations of the French alliance and declared war on Austria, but his troops were marking time and had but a minor part in military operations. The tsar was not represented at the Schönbrunn peace conference that deprived Austria of much of her territory. Russia was allocated a portion of eastern

Galicia but, much to the annoyance of St. Petersburg, the much larger western Galicia was annexed to the duchy of Warsaw. Napoleon, however, was not really concerned with Polish independence and shortly after the Schönbrunn conference gave the Russian government assurances to this effect. Negotiations concerning the future of Poland became entangled with Napoleon's plans for a dynastic alliance. He decided to divorce Josephine and sought to marry the Grand Duchess Anne, Alexander's 15-year-old sister (November 1809). When it became clear that the tsar would not agree, Napoleon withdrew his demand of marriage and announced his engagement to Archduchess Marie Louise of Austria (February 1810). Simultaneously negotiations for a Franco-Russian convention guaranteeing the non-restoration of a unified independent Poland were dropped.

In 1810 and 1811 friction between France and Russia increased. In Russia the alliance was never popular. Prior to Tilsit, Napoleon was denounced in a manifesto read in every church as a dangerous revolutionary and a vessel of iniquities. To the conservative Russian nobility he was the usurper and the enemy of legitimacy, and the unhappy affair of the Duke d'Enghien was not forgotten. Adherence to the Continental System inflicted serious losses on Russian commerce, because England was Russia's chief trading partner. The strengthening of the duchy of Warsaw by the annexation of western Galicia was made all the more disturbing by persistent rumors that Prussia was to be finally partitioned and Silesia added to the Polish state. These rumors seemed the more plausible because of the continuation of the French occupation of Prussia in violation of the Tilsit agreement. Pursuing relentlessly the enforcement of the Continental System, Napoleon annexed the littoral of the Northern and the Baltic Seas, including Holland and the Hanseatic cities of Hamburg, Bremen, and Lübeck, as well as the duchy of Oldenburg, whose ruling house was closely related to the Romanovs, although the integrity of Oldenburg was safeguarded by the Tilsit agreement. The Russian tariff act of December 1810 was clearly an evasion of the obligations imposed by the Continental Blockade.

Tension between Russia and France reached a stage where the likelihood of an open conflict was recognized in responsible circles, and preparations were made for war. Both antagonists massed troops on the Russian border. Early in 1812 Napoleon concluded military alliances with Prussia and Austria, but Alexander was assured by the leaders of these countries that they did not wish to fight Russia. The tsar made an unsuccessful attempt to win the Poles to his side by promising them broad autonomy under the Russian Crown. In April Russia made an agreement with Sweden that removed the danger of an attack by that country, and in May the long-drawn war with Turkey was terminated by a treaty that transferred Bessarabia to Russia. War with Persia, which had been in progress since 1804, ended in 1813 with the treaty of Gulistan. Under its provisions Russia acquired a large territory between the Black and the Caspian Seas, which comprises most of the oil wealth of the Caucasus.

Napoleon in Russia. On June 24, 1812, N.S., Napoleon, without a declaration of war, crossed the Niemen River and invaded Russia. Alexander, who happened to be in nearby Vilna, made a desperate attempt to stave off the war by an appeal to the French emperor, but Napoleon would not be swayed from his course. The invading Grand Army numbered some 400,000 men; about half again as many were drafted later as reinforcements. In this large force the French were in a minority, the bulk of the troops being recruited in Poland, Germany, Switzerland, Holland, Portugal, and other lands. The Russian army under the supreme command of Barclay de Tolly was much smaller, actually less than 200,000. This being the case, there was little choice for the Russians but to retreat. Vilna fell to the enemy four days after the beginning of the invasion, Smolensk in the middle of August. There was some sharp fighting but no major attempt at resistance. This strategy, which was dictated by necessity and which probably won the war, was regarded by many as treason, and the tsar and his generals were subject to unsparing criticism. Barclay de Tolly was dismissed after the fall of Smolensk; he was succeeded by the elderly Field Marshal Prince Golenishchev-Kutuzov, whom Alexander disliked but who enjoyed great popularity—yet the retreat of the army continued. Finally, under the pressure of an excited militant opinion Kutuzov gave major battle to the enemy at Borodino, on September 7, N.S. In all some 250,000 men participated in the fighting, and total casualties in dead and wounded exceeded 100,000. A week later Kutuzov ordered his troops to evacuate the capital, and on September 14, N.S., less than three months after crossing the Russian border, Napoleon entered Moscow.

This seemingly decisive victory actually accomplished nothing. Much of Moscow's population had fled, about three-fourths of the city was destroyed by a fire of unknown origin that Napoleon ascribed to arson, and—worst of all—the Russians would not talk peace. The crisp and dramatic victory that Napoleon had anticipated was not there. Alarming news from western Europe, particularly from Spain, combined with mounting difficulties in obtaining supplies and the uncertainty of the general outlook, forced him to make the inevitable decision: on October 19 began the retreat of the Grand Army. The autumn and early winter were particularly severe, and the retreating troops were harassed by Russian "partisans" (guerrillas), while the army of Kutuzov exercised relentless pressure, although it avoided large-scale contact with the enemy. Cold, unspeakable living conditions, disease, and desertion reduced both armies to a mere shadow of their former selves. By the middle of December, when the last French detachment re-crossed the Niemen, the Grand Army had dwindled to some 30,000 men, while Kutuzov had even fewer soldiers, having lost nearly three-fourths of the troops under his command at the beginning of the French retreat. Early in December, Napoleon appointed Marshal Murat commander-in-chief and left for Paris. The invasion was over. The course of events confirmed Alexander's conviction that distances, absence of roads, and the climate would defeat any invading army.

Alexander in Western Europe. The war, however, was not yet ended. The tsar and his government had to decide what to do next: should they be

The Bettmann Archive

Napoleon in Moscow, 1812

satisfied with the defeat of the invasion, or was the "patriotic" war to be transformed into a war for the "liberation" of Europe? Many of Alexander's advisers, including Kutuzov, favored the former course, but the tsar decided otherwise. Spurred by the traditional urge for territorial aggrandizement and his newly-born religious and messianic zeal, Alexander decreed that Russia should continue the war. He had two main objectives: restoration of a unified Poland under his own rule, and the freeing of Europe from the ungodly domination of the French.

In January 1813 the Russian army crossed the Niemen and proceeded to invade Prussia and the duchy of Warsaw. Napoleon's erstwhile allies— Prussia and Austria—turned against him and formed with Russia an anti-French coalition that was joined by Sweden and, in June, by England. The French emperor, however, was not yet at the end of his resources. He raised a huge army of 700,000 men, which was faced by a combined allied force of 500,000, of whom somewhat fewer than 200,000 were Russians. The French won their last major victory in the battle of Dresden (end of August 1813) but suffered a shattering defeat at Leipzig (middle of October). French resistance and will to fight faltered. German kings and princes and some of the French marshals deserted Napoleon and went over to the side of his enemies. Alexander, who carried on a secret correspondence with Talleyrand, pressed for speedy advance; Paris capitulated, and on March 31, 1814, N.S., the tsar, accompanied by Frederick William, entered the French capital.

Alexander was at the pinnacle of his power. He was the true architect of the treaty of Fontainebleau (April 1814), which made Napoleon sovereign of Elba, and of the first treaty of Paris (May 1814), which ended the war with France on relatively generous terms. The tsar was a dominating figure at the Congress of Vienna (September 1814 to June 1815), which was to lay the foundation of the new European order. Although the monarchs or representatives of practically every European state assembled in Vienna, the decisions of the congress were actually made by what came to be known as "the concert of the great powers"—Austria, Great Britain, Prussia, and Russia, as well as France.

The allied powers were by no means of one mind. Their sharp disagreements came to the fore at the end of 1813, were patched up in the spring of 1814, and reached a near breaking point at Vienna. The heart of the matter was the question of Poland, which Alexander wished to reunify under his own rule. Frederick William agreed, provided Prussia were restored to the position she held before the Tilsit agreement of 1807, which would involve the annexation of Saxony. To this program the representatives of Britain,

Austria, and, in a lesser degree, France strenuously objected; indeed they appeared to be prepared to resist it by force of arms. Early in January 1815 Great Britain, Austria, and France signed a secret treaty of military alliance directed against Russia and Prussia; other powers were invited to join. The storm blew over, however, and in February (that is, before Napoleon returned from Elba early in March 1815) a compromise settlement was reached. By the final act of the Congress of Vienna Russia was awarded the bulk of the former duchy of Warsaw, which was to be reorganized as a constitutional kingdom under the Russian Crown, Prussia was assigned the Polish territories known as the grand duchy of Posen, and Austria received Galicia, while Cracow became a free city under the control of the three eastern powers.

The dispute over Poland and the escape of Napoleon from Elba, which was attributed to the unwarranted meekness of the first treaty of Paris, greatly weakened the position of Alexander in the council of the allies. In the spring of 1815 there were no Russian troops in western Europe to fight a resurgent Napoleon. The Russians did not participate in the battle of Waterloo (June 1815) and the occupation of Paris in July, which was carried out by the English and the Prussians. Louis XVIII was restored to the French throne against the wishes of Alexander, and it was the British and the Prussians who were primarily responsible for the second treaty of Paris (November 1815), which reduced French territory (as compared with that provided by the first treaty of Paris), imposed an indemnity, and decreed the occupation of France by the allies for five years. Of the 150,000-man occupation force, 30,000 were Russians. Napoleon was sent to the island of St. Helena, where he died in 1821.

After Napoleon, 1815–1825

The Holy Alliance. Russian foreign policy was given an unexpected turn by Alexander's conversion to mysticism and religiosity, which occurred about 1810. The tsar came to believe, as he himself put it in 1821, that he was "the depository of a sacred, holy mission." This took the form of the Holy Alliance, which Alexander dramatically announced to the world in 1815. The object of the alliance, in his own words, was "to apply more efficaciously to civil and political relations between states the principles of peace, concord, and love which are the fruit of religion and Christian morality." How this exalted religious concept was to be translated into terms of practical policies was never explained, and although the heads of all European states (with

the exception of the pope, the sultan, and the prince regent of England—
the last for technical constitutional reasons) adhered to the Holy Alliance,
it became the object of derision in diplomatic chancelleries and was of small
consequence except eventually as a symbol of extreme reaction.

The European Alliance. The intra-European organization that actually
came into existence was the Quadruple Alliance of Austria, Great Britain,
Prussia, and Russia based on the treaty of November 1815. Directed originally
against France, it was extended to include that power in 1818 and became
known as the Grand or European Alliance. It rested on the principle that
the great powers have special rights and duties in maintaining international
order and domestic stability. The Alliance was to operate through conferences at fixed intervals of the heads of states or their representatives.
Actually the organs of the European Alliance were at first the meetings of
the ambassadors of the great powers in Paris, London, and Frankfort. Full-
fledged conferences attended by the monarchs and the leading statesmen
were held at Aix-la-Chapelle (1818), Troppau (1820), Laibach (1821), and
Verona (1822). At Aix-la-Chapelle French war indemnities and the occupation of France were terminated, and that country was formally admitted to
the Alliance. The three conferences in 1820, 1821, and 1822 were concerned
with the revolutions which had occurred in Spain, Naples, Portugal, Piedmont, and Greece. In each instance the congress decreed the suppression of
the revolution and the restoration of the legitimate ruler, although this policy
was eventually revised in the case of Greece. The speedy victory of Austria
in Piedmont and Naples, and of France in Spain, prevented Alexander from
sending Russian troops to fight for the cause of the deposed rulers of these
distant lands. Great Britain, however, developed a strong dislike for intervention and after 1822 took no further part in the European Alliance, which
became inactive. Nevertheless the Alliance was not dissolved, and the principal of legitimacy and intervention continued to be upheld by Austria,
Prussia, and Russia. It was invoked in 1830 against France and again in 1848
during the Hungarian revolution.

Government

The Reforms of Speransky. In the reign of Alexander, as in that of
Catherine, the spectacular course of Russia's foreign affairs had no counterpart in domestic policies. Ambitious proposals of constitutional change, which
were discussed immediately after Alexander's accession, died in an embryonic
stage.[1] Plans for reform were revived, however, after Tilsit, perhaps because

---

[1] See above, pp. 247-248.

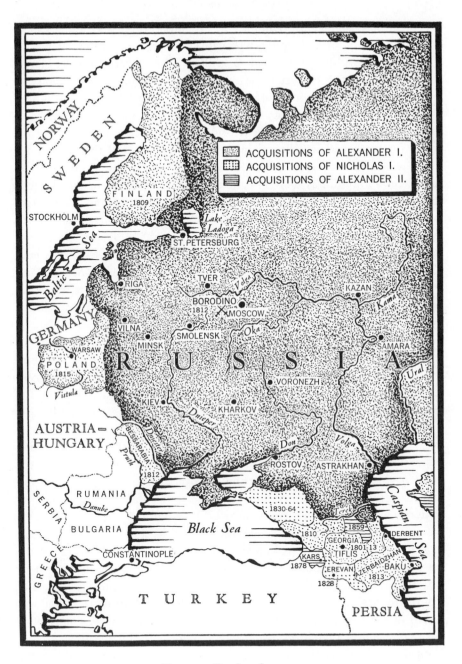

European Russia, 1801–1914

of Napoleon's contagious example. Their author this time was Michael Speransky, son of a village priest, who gained the patronage of the emperor's friend Victor Kochubey and made a brilliant administrative career. He accompanied the tsar to Erfurt (1808) and in 1810 was appointed secretary of state. From 1809 to the spring of 1812 his influence with Alexander was very great. In 1809 he prepared, at the tsar's request, a comprehensive plan of constitutional and administrative reform. Speransky had a remarkable capacity for work and was versed in contemporary political theory, and his draft, which embodied the principle of separation of powers, is rated by competent authorities as more enlightened and advanced than the Western constitutions of that period. Alexander appeared interested and impressed, but his inborn conservatism and the pressure of ultrareactionary circles led by Arakcheev and the historian Karamzin made him reject Speransky's proposal. Only two elements of the Speransky draft were enacted into law: a manifesto of 1810 created the State Council (*Gosudarstvennyi Soviet*), and legislation issued in 1810 and 1811 gave a new organization to the ministries (central executive departments). The State Council, an assembly appointed by the tsar and advisory to the Crown, examined legislative bills, but its decisions were not binding on the emperor, nor did it enjoy the right of legislative initiative. The creation of the Council, therefore, imposed no limitation on the autocratic powers of the Crown. The State Council, reorganized as the upper house of the Russian parliament in 1906, survived until the revolution of 1917.

Legislation dealing with the ministries did away with the remnants of the "collegial" principle introduced by Peter I. The minister was made fully responsible for the department over which he presided; the functions of the ministries were clearly defined to eliminate overlapping with legislative and judicial agencies; and in their inner administration they were governed by comprehensive and precise rules. Two earlier decrees (1809) drew a sharp line between court appointments and the civil service and made advancement in the civil service conditional on the holding of a university degree or the passing of a stiff examination. These measures were exceedingly unpopular with the service, especially the older officeholders, but they proved viable and fruitful in raising the level of the civil service. The bureaucracy that was rooted in the legislation of 1809–1811 remained to the end the mainstay of the empire and in a modified form survived under the Soviet regime.

Speransky's proposals for dealing with the acute economic crisis experienced by Russia in the early 1800's contributed to his unpopularity in influential circles. His program for halting the depreciation of the paper ruble was what would be called today deflationary: cutting down of expenditure, discontinuation of the issue of paper currency, increased taxation, a large state loan. He was responsible for the enactment in 1812 of a progressive tax on revenue from landed estates, which was a revolutionary innovation and seemingly a violation of the privileges granted to the *dvoriane* by the Charter of the Nobility. Meanwhile Alexander, perhaps under the pressure of groups hostile to Speransky but more likely swayed by one of those inexplicable changes of mind to which he was susceptible, turned against his erstwhile trusted adviser. In March 1812 the all-powerful minister had a protracted private audience with the tsar and was sent into exile directly from the Winter Palace. What took place between Alexander and Speransky was never disclosed. Later Speransky won forgiveness, was appointed governor general of Siberia, and in 1821 was allowed to return to St. Petersburg. By that time both his influence and his liberalism had worn thin. With the Napoleonic invasion, Russian involvement in European affairs, and Alexander's conversion to morbid religiosity, no further reform of the autocracy was attempted, although the tsar retained to the end an academic interest in, and an emotional attachment to, the notion of constitutional change.

The Grand Duchy of Finland. Foreigners—Poles, Corsicans, Greeks, Germans, Swiss, French, and English—were numerous in Alexander's intimate circle. Characteristically, representative government, which was denied to Russia proper, was experimented with in Finland and Poland.

The Finnish territory annexed in 1809 was merged with the Finnish provinces held by Russia since 1721 and 1743 and became known as the grand duchy of Finland. Its constitutional position within the framework of the Russian empire had been the source of much legal controversy and confusion resulting largely from the fact that, while at the time of the annexation both the Russians and the Finns spoke of the preservation of the Finnish "constitution" (or "constitutions"), no such constitution actually existed. Prior to 1809 Finland was not an autonomous state but a province of Sweden and governed by Swedish laws. The Finns stubbornly resisted the early attempts of the Russians to interfere with their customs, liberties, rights, and indemnities. Alexander, in his capacity of grand duke of Finland, summoned in Börgo, in March 1809, a Finnish diet (parliament) which was elected in conformity with local laws and customs. The diet, however, was a consultative assembly (not a legislative one, as was its prototype, the Swedish parliament), and legislative power in Finland was vested exclusively in, and exercised by, its grand duke, who was also emperor of Russia. Finland nevertheless retained its language, Sweden's criminal and civil law, and her customary and legal arrangements bearing on taxation, the budget, the judiciary, the church, local government, and social structure. The Börgo diet was soon dissolved and did not meet again until 1863. It would seem, therefore, that prior to 1869, when the diet was endowed with legislative powers, Finland was not an autonomous state but a province of Russia governed by Finnish laws and institutions. During this period relations between Russia and Finland were uneventful and on the whole friendly.

The Kingdom of Poland. A situation quite different from that in Finland obtained in Poland. The Congress of Vienna established Russian Poland as a constitutional state under the Russian Crown. The tsar was enjoined to give his new domain institutions which "he shall judge proper." A Polish constitution, prepared in consultation with Prince Adam Czartoryski and other Polish leaders and based on that of the duchy of Warsaw, was enacted in November 1815. According to its provisions, Russian Poland, a hereditary monarchy under the rule of the tsar, became practically a sovereign state, except that the control of foreign relations was reserved for St. Petersburg. There was a bicameral parliament elected on the basis of a restricted franchise, as was customary in the early nineteenth century. Poland had her own army and civil service, and the Polish language was used in the administration and in the courts.

In spite of the enlightened and liberal character of the constitution, relations between Russia and Poland were strained and became increasingly hostile with the passing of the years. The principal reasons for the mounting discord were the tactless conduct of high Russian officials in Poland and the ardent Polish nationalism that called for complete independence and the recovery of the eastern borderlands which the Russians regarded as Russian and the Poles as Polish. Alexander had at first enjoyed the part of a constitutional ruler and in his address to the Polish diet in 1818 had spoken enthusiastically of the advantages of "free institutions"—while Russian policy grew increasingly reactionary. Polish discontent and disaffection took the form of secret societies and nationalistic agitation directed against the Russian-controlled regime. The Russians both provoked and retaliated against the manifestations of Polish nationalism by arrests, trials, deportations, and suspension of Polish constitutional liberties. Things went from bad to worse and culminated in the Polish insurrection of 1830.

Industry, Commerce, and Finance

Industry. The economic development of Russia in the first quarter of the nineteenth century was hesitant and slow. According to incomplete and not-too-reliable data (the only ones available) the number of manufacturing enterprises more than doubled, from 2,000 at the beginning of the century to over 5,000 in 1825; the number of their workers during the same period increased from fewer than 100,000 to over 200,000. Most of the enterprises were small, employing but a few workers, although it is believed that the importance of establishments with more than 100 workers each was rising. The leading industries were the manufacture of cotton, woollen, and linen textiles. Cotton manufactories benefited by the exclusion of British cotton goods during Russia's participation in the Continental Blockade. Between the beginning of the century and 1825 the number of cotton manufactories rose from fewer than 200 to nearly 500, and the number of workers employed leaped from about 8,000 to nearly 50,000. Many cotton manufacturers were serfs (their properties were registered in the name of their masters), especially the serfs of Count Sheremetev, who favored and facilitated their endeavors but seldom granted them emancipation. The manufacturing industries were concentrated around Moscow.

Industrial labor continued to be drawn, as in the eighteenth century, from among the state peasants, the urban population, and the serfs paying their masters a fixed annual tribute (*obrok*) instead of performing services. Some of the manufacturing industries, especially cotton textiles, depended predominantly on hired labor, that is, workers in these enterprises were not the serfs of their employer, while other industries—those owned by the nobility, such as woollens and crystals—employed a high percentage of servile labor.

The situation was different in the mining and metallurgical industries, which were located chiefly in the Ural mountains. Here individual enterprises were much larger than in the manufacturing industries, employing on the average over 400 workers each. An important percentage of labor in these industries were possessionary workers,[2] and the enterprises were subject to stifling government control. At the beginning of the nineteenth century some 100,000 workers were employed full-time in metallurgy and mining, and there were perhaps four times as many attached in an auxiliary capacity to smelting works, foundries, and mines. With the progress of the industrial revolution in England, Russian export of iron dwindled and then came to a stop, contributing to the depressed condition of Russian heavy industries, which were also plagued with recurrent labor unrest.

Foreign Trade. There was little change in Russian foreign trade as compared with the second half of the eighteenth century. Exports increased but slightly from an annual average of 75 million gold rubles in 1801–1805 to 81 million in 1821–1825, and imports from 53 million to 72 million. Exports

---

[2] See above, pp. 181–182, 227.

of grain, eventually Russia's principal export commodity, remained low. Most of the foreign trade continued to be seaborne and moved through the ports of the Baltic Sea, chiefly in foreign bottoms. The Russian merchant marine was still very small. Tariff policy, except for a brief period at the beginning of Alexander's reign and a short-lived attempt at liberalization in 1819, remained aggressively protective.

Money and the Public Debt. As is frequently the case, the economic cost of war and imperial expansion was mirrored in the state of public finance —budget deficits, increase in the volume of paper currency and its depreciation, and the growth of the public debt. Although a ministry of finance was established in 1802 and reorganized in 1811, no unified budget existed until the reform of 1863. Nevertheless official reports, incomplete as they were, disclosed that revenue and expenditure never balanced and that deficits of as much as 50 per cent were not unusual. The principal method of bridging the gap was the issue of paper currency (assignats) the volume of which rose from 213 million rubles in 1800 to 836 million in 1817. By 1800 the value of the paper ruble in terms of precious metal had declined by half, to 50 silver copecks, and in 1810 it reached the all-time low of 20 silver copecks. There were attempts at stabilizing the paper ruble beginning in 1810; it was made the sole legal tender for the payment of taxes and other government obligations, and proceeds of several domestic loans were used to retire the assignats, whose volume by 1823 was reduced to 596 million rubles. These measures were only partly successful. Although the printing press was not used during the next twenty years, the value of the assignat ruble remained substantially below par.

The second method of meeting budget deficits was borrowing. By 1823 the interest-bearing public debt rose to about 214 million silver rubles; approximately half of this amount was foreign borrowing. The service of the public debt—interest and amortization—absorbed some 15 per cent of the total revenue.

Social Policies

The Peasantry. Whereas the inequities of serfdom under Catherine II and Paul were felt by but a few individuals (Radishchev, Novikov), this awareness became much more common in the first quarter of the nineteenth century. This change of attitude was fostered by Alexander himself, who made no secret of his detestation of bondage and showed interest in proposals for emancipation, of which some were prepared at his request, for instance the project written by Arakcheev in 1818. It would seem that the emperor's espousal of extreme reaction and his abandonment of all thoughts of liberating the serfs occurred in 1820 as a consequence of a mutiny in the Semenovsky regiment of the guards, interpreted by him, quite wrongly, as the work of the international revolutionary movement, which the Holy Alliance endeavored to destroy. Characteristically the tsar's concern with the position of the peasantry led to no positive action except perhaps in the Baltic provinces. A law of February 1803, enacted on the initiative of a wealthy landowner, provided for a new class of "free farmers"; these were former serfs who owned land allotments and had gained freedom by voluntary agreement with their masters. This measure, which was regarded by some as the first decisive step towards general emancipation, proved of small practical import. It was seldom invoked and led to the emancipation of but a few thousands of serfs. Other legislation dealing with the peasantry was equally perfunctory. A decree of 1808 prohibiting the sale of serfs at markets was not enforced and was generally ignored. A law of 1765 empowering the landowners to sentence their serfs to penal servitude was repealed (1809), but the right to deport them to Siberia was specifically confirmed in 1822.

Curiously, emancipation was tried first in the Baltic provinces, where the landowners were German and the peasant population Estonian, Latvian, and Lithuanian. The reform was carried out in two stages: the laws enacted in 1804 proved unsatisfactory and were revised in 1816–1819. Under this legislation the peasant farmers were freed from personal dependence on the estate owners but were deprived of their land allotments. It is believed that the reform, which was accompanied by waves of agrarian unrest, was unfavorable to the peasantry. It created an important precedent of emancipation without the land that commended itself to some of the Russian landowners but was rejected by the framers of the Russian emancipation acts some 40 years later.

Military Colonies. Another experiment in peasant administration was the organization of military colonies. The idea of setting up military colonies was derived from the practice of Muscovy, from communal agricultural settlements of the Cossacks and of military groups in frontier regions of Austria, as well as from the writings of French military authors. First tried in Russia in 1810, the military colonies were taken up in earnest in 1816, at the end of the Napoleonic wars. Under this scheme the entire male population of designated regions was enrolled in military units while continuing to engage in farming. The resulting combination of agricultural pursuits and family life with army discipline was supposed to confer important benefits

on the colonists while relieving the treasury of a heavy outlay for the maintenance of the armed forces. These expectations were not fulfilled. The
colonies, which at their peak numbered nearly 400,000 men, actually combined the worst features of serfdom and army barracks and proved very
costly. The government lost interest in them after the death of Alexander,
but a few of the colonies survived until the 1850's.

The administration of the military colonies was in the hands of Count
A. A. Arakcheev, one of the emperor's most trusted friends, whose influence
with the tsar lasted from the beginning to the end of his reign. A curious
aspect of this relationship was Arakcheev's ostentatious devotion to the
memory of the murdered Emperor Paul. Arakcheev was minister of war in
1808–1810 and Alexander's constant companion during the Napoleonic
campaign and after 1812, although no longer a member of the government,
exercised nearly dictatorial powers. He was a ruthless but efficient administrator and an extreme reactionary; his rule has gone down in history under
the sinister name of *Arakcheevshchina*.

Schools

The School Reform. In spite of the establishment of the Academy of
Science in 1725 and of the University of Moscow in 1755, Russian schools
made hardly any progress in the eighteenth century. The few educated Russians who formed the intellectual élite of the country had studied abroad
or under foreign tutors. The statute of schools enacted in 1803 endeavored
to remedy this situation. It divided Russia into six school regions, each endowed with a closely integrated system of schools arranged on four levels
and ranging from parish (elementary) schools to the universities. Integration
found its expression in both the hierarchical administrative subordination of
the lower schools to the higher and in the character of the scholastic programs
designed to facilitate the progress of the students from schools of the lower
to those of the higher grade.

The implementation of this program, which was never made fully effective, met with difficulties similar to those encountered by Russian would-be
school reformers in the eighteenth century: shortage of funds, lack of trained
personnel, and the mistrust of schools, especially government-sponsored
schools, by the community. Military expenditure inexorably absorbed most
of Russia's meager and uncertain revenue. Nevertheless three new universities were established—in Kazan and Kharkov in 1804 and in St. Petersburg
in 1819. The number of universities (excluding Finland) was thus brought

to six: at the beginning of the century Russia had, in addition to the University of Moscow, a Polish university in Vilna and a German university (founded by Emperor Paul) in Dorpat, in the Baltic provinces. Russian university statutes were based on those of Germany, and academic corporations, in theory, enjoyed broad autonomy; in practice, however, the higher schools were administered by Crown officials. The situation, which was never satisfactory, deteriorated with Alexander's conversion to religiosity, militant conservatism, and struggle against the revolution. The appointment of Prince Alexander Golitsyn, a religious maniac and a fanatical reactionary, as minister of education (1816) was followed by ruthless purges of the higher schools and the elimination of the last vestiges of liberalism and autonomy.

Consequences of the Reform. The expansion of the school system and the paucity of Russians qualified for academic positions led to the recruitment of a large number of foreign scholars, chiefly German and Austrian. This policy raised novel problems: there developed serious friction between native and foreign faculty members and many of the non-Russian teachers were eventually dismissed, and since Russian students could not understand the language of their foreign teachers, courses came to be given in Latin. This, in turn, necessitated the introduction of Latin into the curricula of the secondary schools, providing the foundation for the future Russian classicism. Another consequence of the shortage of teachers was the renewal, on a larger scale, of the eighteenth-century practice of sending Russians to study abroad. Thus was formed a nucleus of trained Russian scholars who were soon to transform the face of Russian universities.

Mention must be made of the state-controlled *lycée* for boys of aristocratic families established at Tsarskoe Selo, near St. Petersburg, in 1811. Somewhat similar schools, although privately endowed and less exclusive, were founded in Yaroslavl and Nezhin. Among the early graduates of the Tsarskoe Selo *lycée* was the poet Alexander Pushkin.

The immediate results of the 1803 school reform were niggardly. In 1825 the university student body (exclusive of the Polish university in Vilna and the Finnish university in Helsingfors) was about 1,700; half of these were enrolled in the University of Moscow. The number of secondary school students was less than 8,000. These were not impressive figures for a population of probably over 50 million. No data on the number of students in the elementary schools are available, but it is known that the number of such schools was small—some 400 in 1825, located chiefly in urban areas.

Modest as were these achievements, their impact on Russian intellectual development and the awakening of political thought was great. They were a determining element in the emergence of Russia's nineteenth-century literature and science and in the appearance of the liberal and revolutionary movement.

The Revolutionary Movement

Its Origins. While peasant uprisings were a familiar feature of Russian history throughout the ages and palace revolutions occurred frequently in the eighteenth century, it was not until after the Napoleonic wars that there appeared in Russia a revolutionary movement, that is, a body of men who deliberately sought to change by violent methods the country's political, economic, and social structure. These early revolutionaries came from the upper class and were chiefly officers of the guards, many of them titled and with court connections. The basic reason that made young aristocrats brought up in comfort and luxury and standing on the threshold of life sacrifice the advantages of an easy career to the perils of an open struggle against autocracy was their profound dissatisfaction with Russian conditions. The liberal ideas, sponsored but imperfectly practiced by Catherine II, left a profound imprint on many Russian minds. Alexander, during the earlier part of his reign and, sporadically, to the very end, encouraged liberal aspirations. In Finland and in Poland he appeared to enjoy the part of a constitutional monarch. The war of 1813–1815, followed by three years of occupation of France, brought a great many young Russians into intimate contact with western Europe at the very time when extreme reaction permeated Russian policies at home and abroad. What the liberal-minded Russians longed for were far-reaching domestic reforms and not the restoration of the "legitimate" monarchs in Spain and Naples.

Secret Societies. The revolutionary movement took the form of secret societies which derived their organization from that of the Masonic lodges. The first of these societies—the Union of Salvation—was founded in St. Petersburg in 1816 by a small group of officers of the guards. It was soon dissolved and was succeeded in 1818 by the Union of the Public Good, whose official program was concerned with social work but whose secret and principal objectives were the establishment of a representative government and the emancipation of the serfs. Although the membership of the society was small, probably fewer than 200, there was a sharp cleavage between the more conservative elements, led by Prince Serge Trubetskoy and Nikita Muravev, who favored a constitutional monarchy, and the radical wing led by Colonel Paul Pestel, advocate of a republic and, if necessary, of the extermination of the imperial family. Partly because of these disagreements, the Union of the Public Good was declared dissolved in January 1821, although whether it was actually dissolved remains uncertain. Meanwhile Pestel, who held a command in southern Russia, organized a secret Southern Society. In August 1822 all secret societies were prohibited by imperial decree. Nevertheless the Southern Society continued to function, and its counterpart, the Northern Society—successor of the Union of the Public Good—was organized in St. Petersburg at the end of the year. Leaders of both societies drafted for the Russia of the future programs or constitutions which, however, remained unfinished. The plan of the Northern Society, written by Nikita Muravev, called for a federal constitutional monarchy. Pestel's project—*Russian Truth* —visualized Russia as a unified, centralized, egalitarian, and democratic republic. The political and economic program of Pestel was much more radical than Muravev's and, surprisingly, was imbued with the spirit of militant Russian nationalism: national minorities, including the Jews, were to be assimilated or expelled. Although the two societies were at odds on many essential issues, they finally agreed on common action to achieve their main objective—the overthrow of the absolute monarchy—in the spring of 1826. The death of Alexander made them revise their plans.

The Uprising of December 14, 1825. Emperor Alexander died in Taganrog, on the Sea of Azov, on November 19, 1825, but the news of his death did not reach the capital until eight days later. It became the source of great confusion because of the odd arrangements concerning the succession to the throne. Having died childless, Alexander was to be succeeded by his brother Constantine, who, under the law of 1797, was next in line to the throne. Constantine, however, had secured in 1820 imperial consent to a divorce from his first wife, a German princess, and to his marriage to a commoner. This dispensation was granted on the condition that he would renounce his right to the throne in favor of the next heir, his younger brother Nicholas. Whether Constantine or Nicholas would succeed Alexander was hardly a matter of real consequence, but for reasons which were never disclosed the above arrangement was kept secret. Pertinent documents, including a manifesto appointing Nicholas heir apparent and signed by Alexander in 1823, were deposited in a sealed envelope in the Moscow Uspensky Cathedral, and copies thereof, also in sealed envelopes, were entrusted to the State Council, the Senate, and the Holy Synod. These institutions were directed to open the envelopes immediately upon Alexander's death. Nicholas knew that he was to succeed Alexander, but neither he nor Constantine was informed of the actual arrangements.

On the receipt of the news of Alexander's death, authorities in St. Petersburg and Moscow deemed it prudent to ignore the instructions contained in the sealed packages. Nicholas was very unpopular with the troops, and he was forewarned by the security police of the unrest and disaffection among the guards. It was believed that unless Constantine, who as commander-in-chief of the Polish army resided in Warsaw, issued an emphatic statement renouncing his right to the throne—and such a statement was not forthcoming—an attempt to administer to the troops an oath to Nicholas might well meet with overt resistance. This consideration proved decisive and, on the order of Nicholas, officials, members of the armed forces, and the population were administered the oath to Constantine except in Warsaw, where the administration of the oath was delayed until December 21, that is, after Nicholas' formal accession.

The resulting state of confusion, uncertainty, and excitement was deemed propitious to the plans of the secret societies and spurred them to action. On December 12 Nicholas received a detailed report from Taganrog giving particulars of the proposed mutiny that was to take place both in St. Petersburg and in the south. On the same day Jacob Rostovtsev, a young guards officer, confirmed in a report submitted to Nicholas the existence of the conspiracy. Simultaneously he sent a copy of his report to Prince Eugene Obolensky, one of the leaders of the Northern Society, who had attempted to enroll him as a member. Neither side had time to waste. The government decided that a new oath—this time to Nicholas—should be administered in the morning of December 14. This was the moment chosen by the leaders of the Northern Society to strike. Their immediate objective was to prevent the troops of the St. Petersburg garrison and the higher governmental bodies—the State Council and the Senate—from taking the oath. In this endeavor they failed. Most of the troops meekly took the oath to Nicholas, but 3,000 men with 30 officers drawn from various units refused to comply and marched to the Senate Square shouting that they wanted Constantine. Meanwhile the State Council and the Senate had taken the oath. The mutineers, their original plans frustrated, were at a loss as to what to do next. Their leaders, including those most outspoken and uncompromising, proved remarkably ineffectual, and some of them made but passing appearances in the Senate Square, while troops loyal to the government and directed by Nicholas himself proceeded to encircle the insurgents. There was some shouting and a few men on both sides were killed or wounded. Cold, hungry, and leaderless the mutineers nevertheless refused to surrender. They found support among the populace, which attacked the government troops, and the possibility was not excluded that the military uprising might become a popular revolt. As darkness set in, the government brought into action the four field guns which were posted in the square. After a couple of volleys the mutinuous soldiers fled, pursued by the loyal troops. About 80 people, including civilians, were killed. The uprising was over. A mutiny in the south was attempted at the end of December but proved as futile as that in the capital.

The immediate effects and the long-range repercussions of the events of December 14 were grave and out of proportion to the number of victims and of the men involved. A specially constituted court of high officials investigated the outbreak and its ramifications. Over 600 people, the flower of Russia's intellectual and social élite, were examined, and more than 120 were put on trial and received severe penalties. Five of the leaders, including Pestel, were hanged, and over 100 were sentenced to penal servitude or deportation to Siberia. Many of the Decembrists, as the participants in the uprising of December 14 are known, were accompanied into exile by their wives and families. Mitigation of the sentences was granted from time to time, but the last surviving Decembrists were not amnestied until the 1850's.

The Decembrist uprising and its aftermath formed a somber anticlimax to the sanguine expectations raised by Alexander's accession. Its immediate consequence was the intensification of the estrangement between the Crown and the liberal faction of the nobility, and of the rigors of Nicholas' police regime. Yet the ideas of liberty, equality, and representative government, reflected however imperfectly in the thinking of the Decembrists, were not forgotten, and the sacrifices of the guardsmen who perished on the gallows or went to Siberia became an inspiration to the generations to come and the foundation of Russia's nineteenth-century liberal and revolutionary movement.

14

The Reaction: Nicholas I, 1825-1855

The Background

Nicholas I and the Ideology of the Regime. Nicholas I (1825–1855), the third son of Emperor Paul, was born in 1796. Unimaginative and dull, he received a fairly good education, spoke foreign languages well, and showed some aptitude for engineering, especially army engineering. Although destined to succeed Alexander, he had no part in the conduct of the affairs of state in his brother's lifetime and merely commanded—with considerable enthusiasm —a brigade of the guards, which may in part account for his unpopularity with the troops of the St. Petersburg garrison. In politics Nicholas was an extreme conservative; he believed unwaveringly in autocracy "by the grace of God" and regarded it as his primary duty to uphold the principle of legitimacy. Notwithstanding the freeing of the nobility from the obligation of compulsory service (manifesto of 1762 and the Charter of the Nobility, 1785), Nicholas held—in the Petrine tradition—that every nobleman should serve his country. Like his three brothers he was a devotee of the parade ground, and he pictured the state as a well-drilled army unit—he liked to refer to Russia as his "command"—over which the Crown in its God-inspired wisdom exercised a benevolent but unchallengeable authority.

The ideology of the regime was well summed up in 1832 by Count S. S. Uvarov, minister of education from 1833 to 1849. A former liberal turned reactionary, Uvarov reduced the essential elements of the Russian state to three: "Orthodoxy, autocracy, and nationality." The English term "nationality" does not convey the true meaning of the Russian "narodnost" that was used by Uvarov; it is believed, moreover, that in the original version he referred to "serfdom" rather than to "nationality." A better translation of the revised formula—if revised it was—would be "the Church, the Crown, and the common people." In its practical application, "nationality" became synonymous with crude, militant, and aggressive Russian nationalism. Trite and foolish as it may sound today, Uvarov's *dictum* enjoyed remarkable popularity with the Russian conservatives for nearly a century.

The Decembrist uprising came as a severe blow to Nicholas, especially because of the confidence that he had placed in the guards. He was shocked, frightened, and profoundly disturbed: the revolution that the Holy Alliance was fighting in distant lands was raising its ugly head in the streets of St. Petersburg. The tsar's reactionary proclivities were further strengthened by events in Poland.

The Polish Insurrection, 1830–1831. Friction with Poland, which developed in the closing years of Alexander's reign, increased after the accession of Nicholas. Although Polish secret societies were not directly involved in the Decembrist uprising, they had maintained relations with the Russian revolutionary movement. This led to the arrest and trial of prominent Poles. Nevertheless, Nicholas visited Warsaw in the spring of 1828, took the oath of the Polish constitution, and was crowned king of Poland. He was again in Warsaw for the meeting of the Polish diet in May–June, 1830. The French and the Belgian revolutions, which occurred respectively in July and September 1830, and Nicholas' reaction to these events greatly excited Polish opinion. The tsar was planning military intervention on behalf of the "legitimate" rulers of these countries and intended to include Polish regiments in the Russian expeditionary force. This policy was repugnant to the Poles; moreover, as the arrest of the Polish revolutionary leaders was seemingly imminent, they decided to take action. The uprising began at the end of November 1830 when the insurgents, many of them young officers and cadets, invaded the residence of the Grand Duke Constantine and attacked Russian troops stationed in Warsaw. Constantine and the army units under his command withdrew from the Polish capital and, eventually, into Russian territory. The leadership of the insurgent movement was first in the hands of the aristocratic and conservative elements but passed rapidly into those of radicals. In January 1831 the Polish diet deposed Nicholas and the house of Romanov. There followed bitter fighting that lasted from February to October 1831. Although, because of the disparity in the resources of the two belligerents, the issue of the struggle was a foregone conclusion, the spirited resistance of the Poles inflicted heavy losses on the Russian invading army, which was commanded by Field Marshal Dibich and, after his death from cholera in June, by Field Marshal Paskevich. The insurgents appealed to the European powers for aid. Austria and Prussia, apprehensive of the possible repercussions of the uprising in their own Polish provinces, remained aloof. England and France were sympathetic and lyrical but unhelpful.

With the collapse of the insurrection Poland had to face the consequences of defeat. There were mass trials *in absentia* of insurgent leaders, including Prince Adam Czartoryski, who had sought refuge abroad, and confiscation of the estates of the Polish nobility. The 1815 constitution was set aside, although seemingly not formally abrogated, and was superseded by the Organic Statute of February 1832. Poland, proclaimed an "indivisible part" of Russia, retained the appellation of kingdom, but the tsar was no longer crowned separately as king of Poland. The statute provided for administrative Polish institutions, in part elected by the population, and the retention by Poland of her civil liberties, civil and criminal codes, and the use of the Polish language in the schools, the administration, and the courts. Some of these provisions were never made effective, and others were gradually withdrawn. Paskevich, created prince of Warsaw, was Russian viceroy in Poland from 1832 to 1856. He believed firmly in the virtue of the total assimilation of Polish administrative and cultural institutions with those of the empire, a policy he relentlessly and ruthlessly enforced, with the result that towards the end of his stewardship administrative unification was practically complete. The universities of Vilna and Warsaw, the latter founded in 1816, were closed. They were replaced by the Russian university in Kiev. Russian was the language used in the administration and in the schools. The Roman Catholic Church was the target of particularly vexatious and restrictive measures. Its properties were sequestrated (1834), some of the Catholic monasteries were taken over by the Orthodox and the Uniats, and in 1839 the Uniats formally returned to the fold of Greek Orthodoxy. Censorship would not tolerate even references to some of Poland's most revered authors. The hostile reaction of Europe to these policies was an element in the making of the Crimean war.

Government and Social Policies

The Dilemma. The experience of the Decembrist uprising and of the Polish insurrection, superimposed upon the solid foundation of Nicholas's inborn conservatism, produced two main conflicting currents of thought which heavily colored his attitude towards questions of policy: a keen, albeit reluctant, realization of the necessity for fundamental change, and the fear that any attempt at reform would lead to a new and perhaps major revolutionary upheaval. The two tendencies successfully counteracted each other, with the result that throughout the 30 years of Nicholas' reign the notion of reform was seldom entirely absent, while the apprehension of disastrous consequences prevented any constructive move. Profound mistrust of both public opinion and the bureaucracy (indispensable as it was) caused the government to depend on secret committees appointed by and responsible to the tsar as agencies for framing policies of which the Crown was nominally the fountainhead. The mainspring of the regime was the security police, who exercised wide powers and upon whom the tsar entirely relied.

The Committee of December 6, 1826. The political and social program of the reign was formulated by the secret "Committee of December 6, 1826," which consisted of five high officials, including Speransky, under the chairmanship of the erstwhile liberal Victor Kochubey. The committee examined the grievances of the Decembrists, which were collected in a separate volume, agreed that many of them were justified, and made cautious proposals for the betterment of administrative agencies and the re-defining of the rights and duties of the social groups. The completion of the committee's report in 1830 corresponded with the outbreak of the July revolution in France and the Polish insurrection, and its recommendations, jejune and timid as they were, were not fully acted upon but provided a foundation for subsequent discussion. Some minor changes were made in the organization of the ministries, in the statute of the State Council, and in the structure of local government.

His Majesty's Own Chancery. A characteristic by-product of the tsar's mistrust of both the community and the bureaucracy was the expansion of the jurisdiction of His Majesty's Own Chancery. Originally an agency concerned with questions which demanded the personal attention of the emperor, the chancery gradually extended its authority over a wide range of issues. By 1843 the number of its sections, or departments, reached six. The more important and better-known among them were Section II, on codification, Section III, in charge of the security police, and Section V, dealing with the state peasants. Nominally the sections of the chancery were under the direct control of the tsar, but actually they differed little from conventional bureaucratic agencies, except when Nicholas took real personal interest in the work of a section, as was the case with Section III. The impression of a dictatorship exercised by the emperor that was created by the expansion of His Majesty's Own Chancery was strengthened by his reliance on the members of his military establishment whom he appointed to the more important state offices or who, in their capacity as his personal representatives, superseded duly appointed officials. Nicholas never admitted that the authority of the Crown could be limited by the delegation of power to institutions or officeholders.

Codification. Codification was the one branch of government where real progress was made. At the time of Nicholas' accession the legal situation was chaotic: the only comprehensive law collection available was the archaic code of 1649. In 1826 Section II of His Majesty's Own Chancery undertook, under the direction of Speransky, the work of codification. In 1833 there was issued the *Full Collection of Laws* in 51 volumes, and the *Code of Laws,* a systematic collection of enactments still in operation, in 15 volumes. Simultaneously provisions were made for the revision and implementation of these collections. Although the work of codification was not above criticism—the *Full Collection,* for instance, deliberately omitted certain enactments—it was a major event in the history of Russian jurisprudence and a vast improvement on the conditions which previously had prevailed. In 1840 the *Code of Laws* was applied in the western provinces, where the Lithuanian Statute of 1588 was formerly in force. This measure was another step towards the integration by Russia of the borderlands which the Polish nationalists regarded as Polish.

The Nobility. The position of the nobility under Nicholas I was, in a sense, anomalous. The Decembrist uprising, which involved the flower of the Russian aristocracy, left an indelible imprint upon the relations between the Crown and the *dvorianstvo:* both were suspicious and resentful, and yet they were united into an indissoluble partnership by the common fear of the masses. Nicholas was in sympathy with the more conservative elements among the nobility and took steps to gratify their wishes to raise their social and economic status, but these modest concessions were purchased at the price of the further bureaucratization of the corporate institutions of the nobility provided by the Charter of 1785. Legislation enacted in 1831, 1836, and 1845 re-defined the functions of the provincial and county assemblies of the nobility as well as those of the officials whom they elected and whose number was increased. They were given the same status—promotions, decorations, and so on—as the members of the civil service, while the control exercised by the appointed provincial governor over the corporate institutions was tightened.

The kinship between the nobility and government service (civil or in the armed forces) was emphasized by the qualifications for voting in the assemblies of the nobility. As under the Charter of 1785, attainment of the lowest rank in government service under the 1722 Table of Ranks was retained as a prerequisite for the right to vote. There were introduced high property qualifications (100 male serfs or 3,000 dessiatines of land), which limited the right of direct vote to the relatively small group of wealthy landowners. This requirement was drastically reduced (to five male serfs or 150 dessiatines) in the case of *dvoriane* who had reached Rank Five under the Table of Ranks. The noblemen whose holdings were below the norms indicated above but had no fewer than five serfs or 150 dessiatines voted through representatives whose number was determined by the aggregate number of serfs, or aggregate acreage, owned by the voters (one representative per 100 serfs or 3,000 dessiatines). Noblemen who owned fewer serfs or less land than the prescribed minimum were denied participation in corporate activities.

The purpose of these regulations was to enhance the standing, in the assemblies of the nobility, of the large landowners and the upper level of the bureaucracy. The government, however, rejected the recommendation of the Committee of December 6, 1826, that elevation to the status of hereditary nobleman should become a distinct act of imperial favor instead of a matter of routine resulting from advancement in the official hierarchy, an arrangement which the aristocratically-minded *dvoriane* greatly disliked. A manifesto of 1845 merely decreed that henceforth Rank Five, instead of Rank Eight as provided by the Table of Ranks, would carry the right to hereditary nobility, that is, government service was retained as the road to *anoblissement,* but the achievement of this distinction was made somewhat more difficult. These measures were of minor practical consequence. The *dvoriane* displayed notable indifference towards their corporate institutions, and in spite of high fines for unjustified absence, attendance of the assemblies was poor. Similarly ineffectual was a law of 1845 that endeavored to put a check on the parcellation of landed properties, about which the *dvoriane* complained. This law permitted the creation of entailed estates, but since it applied exclusively to very large holdings (of not less than 400 peasant households, 10,000 dessiatines of improved land, and an annual revenue of 12,000 rubles), it was seldom used. An unsuccessful attempt was made to impart to the school system a class character, that is, to ensure that each social group, especially the *dvoriane,* would receive scholastic training appropriate to their expected station in life. Less ambitious but of greater immediate usefulness were measures facilitating the advancement of the *dvoriane* from non-commissioned to commissioned rank in the armed forces. On the other hand, in violation of the 1785 Charter, the right of noblemen to travel and reside abroad was curtailed, especially during the period following the revolutions of 1830 and 1848.

The Peasant Question. Hesitation and uncertainty were the characteristics of official policy in the peasant question. Some of the tsar's advisers, including his brothers Constantine and Michael and his son, the future Emperor Alexander II, were opposed to emancipation. Count Uvarov extolled serfdom as a pillar of autocracy. Nicholas did not share these extreme views. He was aware of the inequities and dangers of serfdom, which he characterized (in 1842) as "a flagrant evil," but he added that "to attempt to remedy it now would be an evil even more disastrous." Recurrent peasant unrest was a constant reminder that something would have to be done. The matter was indeed under constant review. No fewer than nine secret committees busied themselves with the discussion of measures for the betterment of the conditions of the peasants but accomplished next to nothing.

A law of April 1842 provided for the emancipation of the serfs by voluntary agreement with their masters; the former bondsmen were to receive the use of land allotments which, however, remained the property of the estate owners. The original bill was drafted by General (later Count) P. D. Kiselev, who favored emancipation, and contained provisions concerning the size of the allotments and the compensation to which the owners were entitled, but these stipulations were dropped in the course of the examination of the draft by a secret committee that sat for three years. The law of April 1842 was akin to that of February 1803;[1] its publication created a stir as a forerunner of the emancipation, but it was actually hardly used and proved inconsequential, as did a law of 1844 permitting the emancipation by voluntary agreement of household serfs. Except for these and a few other minor changes, the position of the serfs remained unaltered.

The above generalization did not apply to the western provinces, where the nobility was largely Polish and the peasantry Russian and Ukrainian. The policy of Russification, enforced in Poland after the insurrection of 1830–

---

[1] See above, p. 265.

1831, extended to the relationship between masters and serfs and took the form of "inventories" which set forth their respective rights and obligations. The introduction of the inventories began in the early 1840's, but the methods used varied from region to region and were frequently revised, with the result that the inventories were not fully in operation at the time of the emancipation of 1861. In the hands of nationalistic Russian administrators, they proved a convenient weapon to curb the power of the Polish land-owners and submit them to vexatious supervision. They invited abuse and graft, but it is less certain that the peasantry derived any real benefit from the change.

A reorganization of some importance took place in the administration of the state peasants, a group comprising about half of the total peasant popu-lation. The originator of the reform was General Kiselev, whose object it was to create a class of well-to-do farmers organized into self-governing communities; the emancipated serfs were eventually to merge with this group. His proposals, formulated in 1834, were taken over by the newly-established Section V of His Majesty's Own Chancery, which in 1837 was reorganized as the ministry of state domain. Kiselev was appointed its head, a post he held until 1855. The reform endeavored to equalize the size of peasant allotments and tax burdens as well as to provide medical assistance and to promote temperance and literacy. During Kiselev's administration the number of schools attended by state peasants increased from 60 to over 2,500, and the number of students from fewer than 2,000 to over 110,000. This was a substantial improvement but still no more than a beginning—the number of state peasants of both sexes in the 1850's was about 25 million. Changes in peasant government introduced by Kiselev had little to commend themselves; the administrative agencies which he established were dominated by appointed officials and the police and instituted an arbitrary and authori-tarian regime that was no better than the one that preceded it.

The Economic Development

Industry. Russia's political climate and social structure being what they were, it would have been unreasonable to expect important changes in eco-nomic conditions. The first half of the nineteenth century, however, was in Europe a period of rapid population growth accompanied by revolutionary changes in seaborne and overland transportation, mechanical inventions, im-provements in chemical processes, and—towards the end of the period—a more liberal attitude towards foreign trade. These novel developments had but a slight effect upon the Russian situation. The number of enterprises engaged in manufacturing increased from 5,200 in 1825 to nearly 11,000 in 1855 and to over 15,000 in 1860. It will be remembered, however, that Russian industrial statistics were notoriously unreliable and that while the average number of workers per enterprise in 1860 was about 50, many of the industrial establishments were smaller, employing but a few workers and no motor power. The total number of workers engaged in manufacturing industries rose from 200,000 in 1825 to 480,000 in 1855 and to probably 565,000 in 1860, of whom 430,000, or 75 per cent, were hired workers and the balance were the serfs of their employers. The more progressive industries were cotton and woollen textiles, sugar, and, on a smaller scale, the manufacture of metal goods.

The situation was different in mining and metallurgy, which experienced considerable difficulties. The industrial revolution in England and its repercussions on the continent of Europe eliminated the slim margin of leadership in the production of iron that Russia had enjoyed in the eighteenth century. In the opening years of the nineteenth century the production of Russian pig iron actually declined. It was exceeded by England not later than in 1805, by France and the United States about 1825, and by Germany and Austria in the middle of the 1850's. At the end of the eighteenth century England was still a large importer of Russian iron. After 1825, English exports of iron rose rapidly, while Russia ceased to be an iron-exporting country. Her heavy industry did not benefit by the technical advances which revolutionized output in western Europe, partly because the export of machinery from England, except by license, was prohibited until 1843, but the chief reason for the lack of progress was the shortage of capital and the cumbersome and backward legal and economic structure of Russia's heavy industry. Most of the mining and metallurgical enterprises were located in the Urals and belonged to the possessionary type, that is, they employed servile labor that could not be used for any other purpose, and they were subject to minute and vexatious government control bearing on the volume of production, quality of the goods, technical progress, wage rates, prices, and so on.

With the changing conditions in the nineteenth century these restrictive regulations became increasingly oppressive. Low productivity, high costs, and recurrent labor unrest forced the owners of possessionary works to agitate for the removal of the special status attached to their enterprises. Government control was gradually eased. In 1840 the owners were empowered to emancipate their possessionary workers. The industrialists who availed themselves of this law received no indemnity if the workers had been originally acquired through a public grant but were entitled to compensation of 36 silver rubles per male serf if the serfs had been originally acquired by purchase. The law obligated the owners to make cash allowances to the emancipated workers to defray the cost of transportation and resettlement (70 assignat rubles to a male and 40 rubles to a female), that is, in the case of possessionary workers acquired through public grant, the owners actually paid to be relieved of servile workers and of the restrictive conditions attached to their employment. The 1840 law received little publicity but is known to have been applied in 20 or 30 instances. The number of workers employed in heavy industry in 1860 was estimated at 245,000; approximately 70 per cent of this total were the serfs of their employers and 30 per cent were hired workers.

In 1860, on the eve of the emancipation, the aggregate labor force in all branches of industry—manufacturing, metallurgy, and mining—was roughly 800,000, or slightly more than one per cent of the total population; servile labor accounted for about one-third of this figure. These estimates are tentative.

Foreign Trade. Foreign trade, like industry, made some progress in the second quarter of the nineteenth century. The average annual value of exports rose from 86 million gold rubles in 1826–1830 to 152 million in 1846–1850; it declined to 135 million rubles in 1851–1855, chiefly because of the Crimean War, and reached 226 million rubles in 1856–1860. The respective figures for imports were 80 million, 132 million, 130 million, and 206 million rubles. The composition of exports was roughly similar to that at the beginning of the century and comprised chiefly agricultural and other natural produce. Exports of iron declined to a vanishing point, while those of timber and grain increased. A notable change in the trend of grain export occurred in the 1840's. In 1826–1830 Russia shipped abroad an annual average of 24 million poods [2] and in 1841–1845 still only 27 million, but in 1846–1850 grain exports rose to 51 million poods and in 1856–1860 to 69 million. This upward trend, which was to continue at an accelerated pace until the outbreak of World War I, was due to improved transportation, to lower freight, and, initially, to the repeal of the English corn laws in the late 1840's. Russian imports consisted of manufactures, especially textiles, colonial goods, and luxury articles. Towards the end of the period imports of machinery and machine tools increased substantially. Foreign trade was largely seaborne and moved through the ports of the Baltic Sea, but in the middle of the

[2] One pood = 36 lbs. = 0.616 long ton.

century the share of both the Black Sea route (because of the growth of grain exports) and of the overland trade became more important. England retained her position as Russia's chief trading partner.

Russian tariff policy remained highly protective and, although some of the formal prohibitions of imports were dropped in 1836, 1838, and 1841, they were replaced by prohibitive protective duties. A more liberal tendency manifested itself in the tariff act of 1850 and particularly in that of 1857, which removed almost all prohibitions on imports and somewhat lowered the rates of duty.

Public Finance. The government was much concerned with the conditions of the currency, which consisted largely of depreciated paper rubles (assignats) of uncertain exchange value and purchasing power. Under the ultraconservative administration of Count E. Kankrin, minister of finance from 1825 to 1844, the printing press was not used to meet extraordinary expenditures, and the volume of the assignats in circulation was maintained unchanged. Simultaneously measures were taken to increase the treasury reserves of precious metal. Reversing regulations enacted early in the century, silver and gold (1827–1833) were made legal tender for all payments to the government. In 1839 the silver ruble was given the status of the basic monetary unit, and the official rate of the assignats to the silver ruble was 3.5:1. A new paper currency, treasury notes redeemable on call, was issued in 1841, and in 1843 the assignats were compulsorily exchanged for treasury notes at the above rate. As a consequence the volume of paper currency in circulation fell from 596 million rubles to 170 million. The treasury notes were backed by "all the resources of the state" as well as by a reserve fund of precious metals of not less than one-sixth of the value of the notes in circulation. This ratio was deemed adequate to ensure convertibility. The management of the treasury notes and of the reserve fund, however, was left in the hands of the treasury rather than in those of an independent agency that could have resisted official pressure. This arrangement proved fatal to the stability of the currency. The reserve fund was used for purposes other than those for which it was intended, and the printing press was soon put to work again: the volume of treasury notes in circulation rose to over 300 million rubles in 1848, to 360 million in 1855, and to over 730 million in 1858. Convertibility into metallic rubles was at first restricted and then discontinued in 1854. The rate of the treasury notes fell below par. The final results of the reform were disappointing: the assignats were gone, but depreciated and fluctuating paper currency remained and survived for about half a century.

Kankrin disliked public borrowing. Nevertheless the national debt increased, although chiefly after his resignation. In 1843 it was 586 million silver rubles, or nearly treble its amount at the beginning of the reign. It rose to 1,760 million rubles in 1858, when the service of the debt consumed about two-fifths of the total national revenue. The principal causes of the mounting indebtedness were military campaigns, including the suppression of the Polish uprising and of the Hungarian revolution and above all the Crimean War, as well as the cost of railway construction.

Railways. The building of railways began in Russia, as in most other countries, in the 1830's. There was at first considerable doubt in high bureaucratic circles concerning the usefulness of this innovation. Nevertheless the first Russian line, a stretch of some 17 miles between St. Petersburg and the imperial residence of Tsarskoe Selo, was open to traffic in 1837. Warsaw was linked with the Austrian railway leading from the Polish border to Vienna. The St. Petersburg–Moscow line, the major railway enterprise of this period, was begun in 1842 and completed in 1851. In 1855 Russia had some 650 miles of railways, a modest network if compared with those of the major European countries. The first Russian railways were built by the state, and the cost per mile was very high. There was no railway south of Moscow, a situation that made the Crimean War the more difficult.

Crisis in Farming. It is believed that in the middle of the nineteenth century Russian agriculture was going through a critical phase caused by the impact of the expanding market relationship upon an economy based on serfdom. We have noted the increase in grain exports. There also gradually developed in the less fertile areas a demand for agricultural produce of the better-endowed farming regions. Demand for grain for both export and the domestic market, however, developed slowly. Exports remained at a low level, and according to official estimates, no more than one-quarter of the harvest reached the market in 1850. Expansion of the grain trade was hindered by the instability of grain prices, the moderate growth of the urban population, and the transportation difficulties due to the remoteness of the producing areas from the centers of consumption and the seaports. The transition from a closed economy to a market economy proceeded at a deliberate pace and led to an excess of supply over demand and the stagnation of agriculture.

A change from primitive methods of farming to a more diversified form of husbandry required capital, agricultural machinery, fertilizers, and technical skill which were seldom available. Rationalization was discouraged by the sharp fluctuations of agricultural prices and the instability of demand.

Sugar refining was the only agricultural industry that was both progressive and financially rewarding. The alternative to rationalization was the more intensive exploitation of servile labor. During the second quarter of the nineteenth century the average amount of the *obrok* (annual payment by the serf to his master) increased by perhaps as much as 50 per cent. There developed a tendency to expand the portion of the estate under the direct management of the owner by reducing peasant allotments and bringing under cultivation meadows and waste land. The percentage of household serfs—those employed in their master's household and not engaged in farming—increased, and there developed a new group of landless laborers known as "monthly workers" (*mesiachniki*), who were former farmers deprived of their allotments. These policies were motivated by the expectation, which proved well founded, that when emancipation came, the fact of occupancy (of land) would prove an element in determining the size of the allotments to which the serfs were entitled. The deterioration of the position of the bondsmen led to fresh waves of peasant unrest.

The economic status of the landed nobility, too, was precarious. Although by the middle of the nineteenth century some 100,000 noble families owned nearly one-third of the Russian territory, the vast majority of the members of this group were people of modest means, and few were really wealthy. Most of the landed estates were hopelessly mortgaged. The unsatisfactory state of farming and the impoverishment of both landowners and serfs have been interpreted as evidence that serfdom had outlived whatever usefulness it might have had. There are, however, Russian historians and economists who disagree with this view and believe that the serf economy was sound and that the emancipation was not an economic necessity.

Cultural Policies

Schools. The reactionary character of the regime was reflected in educational policies. Under the law of 1803 the schools were organized, at least in theory, on the principle of integration, which was designed to facilitate the progress of the students from the elementary school to the university and provided for the hierarchical administrative subordination of the schools of the lower grade to those of the higher grade. Under Nicholas I the school policy, which owed much to the inspiration of Uvarov, even though it was inaugurated before he became minister of education in 1833, operated on the opposite principle: each type of school was to minister to the social groups from which it was deemed to draw its students and to provide them with an education appropriate to their expected station in life. The hierarchical administrative subordination of the schools was terminated, and all educational institutions, irrespective of grade, were brought under the control of appointed officials, curators of the school regions. These policies were made effective by laws passed in 1828 and 1835. Among the changes introduced by the earlier law was the extension of the course in the gymnasium (secondary school) from four to seven years. Beginning with the fourth year two parallel courses of instruction were offered: one omitted classical languages, emphasized the sciences (the German *Realschule*), and was intended for students who did not wish to continue their studies; the other division taught classical languages and prepared its students for the university.

In spite of the official effort to reserve secondary schools of the gymnasium type for children of the upper classes and to discourage—by measures such as burdensome administrative regulations and higher tuition fees—the enrollment of students from the other social groups, this object was not achieved. A few educational institutions, among which the boarding schools for boys of noble descent were the more important (they numbered about 60 in 1860), catered exclusively to the offspring of the nobility, but segregation of students on the class principle through the entire school system could not be attained because of the looseness of Russia's social structure. In the 1850's children of the non-privileged groups constituted a substantial percentage of the student body of the gymnasiums and the universities, while children of noble parents were well represented in the parochial schools which were intended for children of the lower orders. Moreover, the community, especially the wealthier strata, showed a marked predilection for private schools, which the government wished to eradicate.

The new university charter, issued in 1835, did not abrogate the autonomy of the academic corporations (which actually led a shadowy existence) but limited its scope and invited intervention by Crown officials. The universities were brought under the control of the curators of the school regions, and the minister of education was given discretionary powers in appointing professors, although election by the faculty was retained as the normal procedure. The university curricula were revised, introducing courses in theology, Church history, and Church law compulsory for all students. A crude and aggressive nationalism was strongly encouraged. Unrest among Russian students that followed the French revolution of 1848 led the government to reduce the size of the student body to 300 per university (not counting holders of government fellowships and medical students). Uvarov's cautious defense of the universities, whose impending closure was rumored, led to his dismissal and to the appointment of the ultrareactionary Prince P. A. Shirinsky-Shikhmatov as minister of education (September 1848). An amendment of the university charter (October 1849) provided for the appointment by the government of the rectors (presidents) of the universities— they were formerly elected by the faculty—and gave the minister of education the power to replace elected deans by men of his own choice. The university administration was to ensure the conformity of classroom teaching with the official nationalistic and reactionary doctrines.

In spite of this austere regime there was a notable improvement in the level of instruction. The practice of sending promising Russian students to foreign universities, prevalent during the earlier part of the nineteenth century and continued under Nicholas I with interruptions caused by the European revolutions, brought a rich reward. The young Russian scholars who were trained abroad returned home armed with the methods of Western science; some of them proved gifted teachers and made important contributions in their respective fields. They met with the ready response of attentive audiences eager to learn. It is from the collaboration of these two elements—teachers and the student body—that was born the cultural tradition of the Russian universities. It is ironical that this revolutionary departure in Russian intellectual history should occur in the reactionary era of Nicholas I.

The quantitative growth of education, measured by statistics which inspire little confidence, was modest and, in the upper levels, uneven. The number of university students in institutions controlled by the ministry of education rose from 1,700 in 1825 to 4,600 in 1848 but declined to 3,600 in 1854, and that in the gymnasiums increased from 7,700 in 1825 to 18,900 in 1848 and declined to 17,800 in 1854. The reduction in the size of the student body during the later period is explained in both cases by the restrictive policies of the government which followed the European revolution of 1848. In the middle of the 1850's the number of schools below the level of secondary schools (they were maintained by the ministry of education, the Church, the ministry of state domain, and the ministry of appanages) was about 1,400 and their aggregate student body probably 350,000. The majority of these schools were located in urban areas, and it seems likely that a substantial proportion of the schools reported by the Church (their number is said to have increased from 100 in 1837 to 4,800 in 1853) did not actually exist but were the product of the imagination and enthusiasm of ecclesiastical statisticians. The level of instruction in all these schools was exceedingly low. Finally, the figures quoted above should be viewed against a population that in the 1850's probably exceeded 70 million.

Censorship. There was of course no room for freedom of the press in the Russia of Nicholas I. The censorship law of June 1826, issued on the morrow of the Decembrist uprising, vested the censors with practically unlimited powers and actually made it their duty to direct public opinion "according to the existing conditions and the views of the government." The law was somewhat liberalized in April 1828 but was amended and tightened again after the French revolution of 1830, especially with Uvarov's appointment as minister of education in 1833. There was an extraordinary prolifigacy of agencies exercising censorship functions, the tsar himself acting occasionally as censor. Censorship became even more stringent and capricious when, following the outbreak of the French revolution, the committee on censorship headed by Count D. P. Buturlin was appointed in April 1848; it continued to function until the end of 1855, when it was disbanded.

Slavophiles and Westerners. Sobered by the experience of the Decembrists, the educated Russians of the 1820's and 1830's shunned political issues and withdrew into the safer realm of abstract philosophical speculations. There was much interest in German philosophy—Schelling, Kant, Fichte, and Hegel—and later in the doctrines of French social thinkers—Saint-Simon, Fourier, Proudhon, and others. In the early 1840's there emerged two opposing schools of thought which were to exercise an influence on political and intellectual movements—the Westerners and the Slavophiles. Contrary to what their name might suggest, the Westerners did not advocate the acceptance of Western institutions. Their basic belief was in the uniformity of European culture, which in the nature of things should lead Russia along the path of Western countries. Broadly speaking, the Westerners were liberals, favoring representative government, intellectual freedom, and the abolition of serfdom. Some of the Westerners, however, were extreme radicals.

Slavophilism was a highly romantic nationalism glorifying the virtues of Russian national ways and those of the Orthodox Church as highly superior to the decadent West and Catholicism. The Slavophiles believed that the harmonious course of Russian history had been disrupted by the reforms of Peter I. The national institutions which they particularly admired were the seventeenth-century *zemskii sobor* (about which little is known) and the village commune. The outstanding representatives of Slavophilism were Alexis Khomiakov (1804-1860), the brothers Ivan (1806-1856) and Peter (1808-1856) Kireevsky, the brothers Constantine (1817-1860) and Ivan (1823-1886) Aksakov, and Yuri Samarin (1819-1876). The Slavophiles exercised no immediate political influence and their following was small, but their views affected the thinking of later movements—both reactionary (Pan-Slavism) and radical (populism)—and survived in the twentieth century in the doctrines of the Socialist Revolutionary party.

A tragic consequence of the intellectual revival of the 1840's and of its conflict with autocracy was the case of M. V. Butashevich-Petrashevsky, a nobleman and an official of the ministry of foreign affairs. Petrashevsky was an admirer of Saint-Simon and Fourier, author of a small philosophical encyclopedia (*Dictionary of Foreign Words*), and leader of an informal group interested in social and political problems. After the European revolution of 1848 the Petrashevsky circle discussed the desirability of forming a society for revolutionary propaganda but took no action. In 1849 the members of the group were arrested, tried by a military court, and sentenced to death or deportation to Siberia. At the place of execution death sentences were dramatically commuted to imprisonment. Among those who went through the ordeal and served a sentence of penal servitude in Siberia was Fedor Dostoevsky.

The Eastern Question

Nicholas I, England, and the Eastern Question. Nicholas exercised considerable personal influence on the course of Russian foreign relations. Count Charles Nesselrode, foreign minister for 40 years (1814–1856), was not a statesman but a self-effacing and pliant instrument of the imperial will. The moving forces behind the tsar's policies were his rigid conservatism, fear of revolution, and determination to maintain legitimacy—largely through the instrumentality of the Holy Alliance. The inability of Nicholas to grasp the limitations imposed upon the Crown by a representative form of government led to curious and fatal misunderstandings in his relations with England. The impetuous and aggressive policies pursued by St. Petersburg in the Near East antagonized many of Great Britain's statesmen, who came to look upon the tsarist empire as England's implacable enemy. The leading personalities of this group were Lord Palmerston and the two successive British ambassadors in the key post of Constantinople—Lord Ponsonby (1832–1841) and Sir Stratford Canning (later Viscount Stratford de Redcliffe, 1841–1858). Their influence in determining the policies of London was great. The focal point of the Anglo-Russian conflict was the so-called "eastern question," that is, the survival or dissolution of the Ottoman empire, the control of the Bosphorus and the Dardanelles, and the fate of the Christian populations in Turkey.

Greek Independence and the Turkish War, 1828-1829. The eastern question entered an acute phase with the outbreak of the Greek revolt against Turkey in 1821, that is, prior to the accession of Nicholas. Emperor Alexander I at first looked upon the Greeks as rebels against their legitimate sovereign and followed a policy of non-intervention, but he gradually reversed himself and accepted the notion of Greek independence, which came to be sponsored also by England and France. Although Nicholas shared his brother's doubts concerning the legitimacy of the Greek national aspirations, he associated himself with Great Britain and France in advancing a policy designed to establish Greece as an independent state. Prussia and Austria, Russia's partners in the Holy Alliance, were not parties to the agreements which, after much delay, resulted in the founding of the kingdom of Greece under Prince Otto, second son of King Louis of Bavaria (January 1833).

Meanwhile Russia was involved in wars with her Near Eastern neighbors. From 1804 to 1813 she had fought a war with Persia which was terminated by the treaty of Gulistan (October 1813); under this treaty Russia acquired a vast territory stretching from the Black Sea to the Caspian Sea. In 1826 the Persian government, seemingly at the instigation of English agents, denounced the treaty of Gulistan. There followed a war in which the Russian troops under Paskevich did uncommonly well: the fortress of Erivan was taken by assault (October 1827), Russian detachments appeared within easy reach of Teheran, and the government of the shah hastened to conclude the treaty of Turkmanchai (February 1828), which transferred to Russia the provinces of Nakhichevan and Erivan and acknowledged her right to maintain a navy in the Caspian Sea. The end of the Persian war permitted Russia to concentrate her forces against Turkey.

While the war with Persia was in progress, relations with Turkey followed an eventful course. Both Great Britain and Russia were engaged in negotiations concerning joint action to establish an independent Greece and simultaneously endeavored to strengthen their own influence in Constantinople. A virtual ultimatum sent by St. Petersburg to the Porte led to the Russo-Turkish Akkerman convention (October 1826), which restored to the Danubian principalities (Moldavia and Wallachia) the autonomous institutions abolished by the sultan in 1821, promised to maintain in Serbia the privileges granted by earlier agreements, recognized Russian sovereignty over the disputed territories on the Caucasian littoral, and granted Russian merchantmen free passage through the Black Sea straits and access to Turkish waters. Although the provisions of the Akkerman convention greatly disturbed London, negotiations and measures to ensure the creation of an independent Greek state were continued. In October 1827, without a declaration of war and seemingly by accident, an Anglo-Franco-Russian naval force under a British admiral became involved in the Bay of Navarino, in the Ionian Sea, in a major battle with the Turks in which the Turkish fleet was annihilated. Constantinople protested vigorously, denounced the Akkerman convention, demanded compensation and apologies, and, when these were not forthcoming, proclaimed a holy war against the Christian powers. In the meantime there was a change of administration in London. The new government headed by the Duke of Wellington displayed a conciliatory attitude towards Turkey and deplored the Navarino battle as an "untoward event."

St. Petersburg took a very different view of the situation and in June 1828, after the termination of the Persian war, invaded Turkey's Danubian principalities. The war that followed was brief and disastrous to the Turks. The Russian troops under Paskevich, in the Caucasus, and under Dibich, on the Danube, won some notable victories and by the end of August 1829 were approaching Constantinople. The treaty of Adrianople (September 1829) that ended the war was a triumph for Russian imperialism. Russia annexed the mouth of the Danube and territories in the Caucasus, including the Black Sea littoral with Anapa and Poti. Her recent territorial acquisitions from Persia and the right of passage for Russian merchant vessels through the Straits and navigation and trade in the Black Sea were confirmed. Moldavia and Wallachia were to receive "independent national governments" and were placed under Russian protection, although nominally they remained under Turkish suzerainty.

It was believed in both St. Petersburg and London that the treaty of Adrianople was an important step in the subjugation of the Ottoman empire by Russia.

The Russo-Turkish Alliance, 1833. The French revolution of July 1830, followed by the Belgian revolution and the Polish insurrection, led to the revival of the spirit of the Holy Alliance and to the renewal of the alliance of Russia, Austria, and Prussia, which was formalized in 1833. Nicholas's plea for armed intervention in western Europe, however, met with no response, and the outbreak of the Polish uprising forced the tsar to abandon his war plans.

Meanwhile Russia appeared to be making good progress in consolidating her control over Turkey. A constitutional government in Moldavia and Wallachia that actually made these territories a Russian protectorate was established under the forceful leadership of General Kiselev, and in 1834 the

Russian troops were withdrawn from the Danubian principalities seemingly without weakening Russia's hold over Turkey. The novel and portentous factor in the situation was the secret treaty of alliance concluded by Russia with the Porte in 1833.

This startling development was the by-product of a rebellion against Turkey by her powerful vassal Mehemet Ali, pasha of Egypt (November 1831). The Egyptian army commanded by Ibrahim Pasha overran Syria and in the middle of 1832 advanced towards Constantinople. The Porte appealed for aid to the Western powers and, when they failed to respond, turned in despair to its old antagonist, Russia. St. Petersburg welcomed this opportunity to uphold legitimacy and to strengthen its control over the Ottoman empire. On the invitation of the Turkish government, Russian war vessels entered the Straits in February and April 1833 and landed some 10,000 troops on the Asiatic shore. The occupation of Constantinople by the Russians appeared all but inevitable, and the Western powers, as well as—belatedly— the sultan himself, were profoundly alarmed. Under the pressure of Great Britain, France, Austria, and Prussia, a Turko-Egyptian peace treaty on terms exceedingly onerous to the Porte was hastily arranged in May. The crucial issue, however, was—what would Russia do next? To the general surprise the Russian expeditionary force was withdrawn in July, the day after Ibrahim and his soldiers had re-crossed the Taurus mountains and, what was more important, Count A. F. Orlov, the tsar's special envoy to Constantinople, had signed with Turkey the secret treaty of Unkiar Skelessi (July 1833). Concluded for eight years, the treaty provided for "eternal" peace, alliance, and friendship between the two empires. Existing Russo-Turkish agreements were confirmed, and Russia undertook to maintain the independence of Turkey, while the obligations of the Porte as an ally were limited to the closing of the Dardanelles to "any foreign vessel of war." The advantage of the treaty from the Russian standpoint, as Nesselrode put it, was that her "intervention in the affairs of Turkey acquired a basis of legality." Western statesmen of the Palmerstonian school, however, were convinced, in spite of Russia's official denials, that a secret article of the Unkiar Skelessi treaty granted Russia the right to send her warships through the Straits.[3] International tension was greatly increased. France and Great

---

[3] Conclusive evidence that Russia's contentions were genuine and that she did not claim the right of egress from the Black Sea for her war vessels was provided by Philip Mosely, who discovered in Russian archives a confidential report from Nesselrode to the tsar (1838) that stated explicitly that no stipulation in the Unkiar Skelessi treaty or elsewhere "authorizes us to request the admission to the Bosphorus of our warships." Philip E. Mosely, *Russian Diplomacy and the Opening of the Eastern Question in 1838 and 1839* (Cambridge, Mass.: Harvard University Press, 1934), pp. 141–147. The aberration of the Western statesmen of the

Britain refused to recognize the validity of the treaty of Unkiar Skelessi, which became one of the important reasons for England's bolstering of Turkey.

The Ebb and Flow, 1833–1848. The 15 years following the signature of the treaty of Unkiar Skelessi witnessed some odd twists in Anglo-Russian relations. The Russophobia of some influential Englishmen was strengthened by the conviction that Russia harbored sinister designs on India. This belief made a section of British opinion particularly sensitive to Russian advances in central Asia and in the Near East, which were regarded as the likely roads of an expected invasion. Anglo-Russian clashes in these remote and little-known lands were inconclusive, except that they suggested that any attempt to reach India through the valley of the Euphrates or the central Asian khanate of Khiva would encounter formidable, indeed insurmountable, geographical obstacles. Nevertheless many in Great Britain followed with sympathetic interest the insurgent movement against the Russian rule that broke out in 1830 under the leadership of Shamil in the recently-conquered Caucasus, assumed the character of a holy war of Islam, and was not suppressed until the 1860's. It was one of Palmerston's favorite theories that Russia had no legal title to the Caucasus and that the severance of these provinces from the tsarist empire was in England's best interests. Elsewhere Russian and British agents clashed in Herat and Kabul, but Russian penetration in those regions was notoriously ineffectual, the British usually having things their own way, and a major conflict was avoided.

The eastern question remained the central problem of European politics. Peace between Turkey and Egypt was of brief duration, and the struggle was resumed in April 1839. The Porte was again decisively defeated, the sultan died, the entire Turkish fleet went over to the Egyptians, and hostilities were terminated in the summer of 1839.

In the meantime there were important modifications in the European diplomatic situation. Alliance with France was the cornerstone of English policy, yet the British government was determined to prevent Mehemet Ali, who was backed by the French, from establishing himself in Syria, partly because it was believed that a powerful Egypt might conclude an alliance with Russia and become a threat to India. This line of reasoning tended to weaken the Anglo-French ties. London was also anxious to annul the treaty of Unkiar Skelessi by merging it into a general European agreement.

Russia's political orientation, too, underwent a change. The alliance with

1840's is still shared by historians. See, for instance, Herbert C. F. Bell, *Lord Palmerston* (London: Longmans, Green and Company, Ltd., 1936), I, 183, and Jesse D. Clarkson, *A History of Russia* (New York: Random House, 1961), p. 288.

Austria and Prussia did not live up to expectations. The treaty of Unkiar Skelessi notwithstanding, Turkey did not become a Russian dependency, and British influence in Constantinople remained as strong as ever; moreover, the treaty which was concluded for eight years was due to expire in 1841. To Nicholas, France was the hotbed of revolutions, and he welcomed signs of estrangement between Paris and London. Like so many European statesmen of that period, the tsar admired England even when he hated her policies.

The military defeat of the Porte by the Egyptian army under Ibrahim Pasha should be viewed against this political background. The European powers feared Russia's military intervention in Turkey as provided by the treaty of Unkiar Skelessi. These apprehensions proved unwarranted. St. Petersburg joined London, Paris, Vienna, and Berlin in a common policy for the settlement of the Turko-Egyptian conflict (July 1839). After protracted negotiations four of the five great powers agreed on the terms of a convention to restore peace between the Porte and Mehemet Ali (July 1840). France, whose attitude was considered as too favorable to Egypt, was not informed of the convention until it was signed. The French government was indignant, and its relations with the signatory powers, especially Great Britain, were greatly strained. Mehemet Ali, however, rejected the proposed settlement, but the Syrian revolt against Ibrahim and the successful naval action against Egypt by a joint British, Austrian, and Turkish squadron under Sir Charles Napier reversed the situation and forced the capitulation of Mehemet Ali and his unconditional acceptance of the European terms. The feud with France was patched up. In July 1841 Great Britain, France, Russia, Austria, and Prussia signed the Straits convention, which confirmed the "ancient rule" closing the Straits in time of peace to war vessels as well as the rights conferred upon Russia by the earlier treaties with Turkey, except for the treaty of Unkiar Skelessi, which was permitted to lapse; the regime of the Straits could not be changed without the consent of the signatory powers, which jointly assumed the responsibility for the maintenance of the integrity of Turkey. Both Russian and British statesmen claimed the convention of 1841 as a victory for their national policies. It was held as an important step towards the consolidation of European peace, but these optimistic expectations proved to be not in agreement with the facts.

Nicholas was encouraged by the measure of collaboration achieved in Anglo-Russian relations and endeavored to secure an agreement, if necessary an informal one, for London's participation in the struggle against revolution—in the spirit of the Holy Alliance. Such an understanding would be directed primarily against France, with which Russia maintained no regular diplomatic relations between 1842 and 1848. In 1844 the tsar visited England, where he engaged in direct negotiations with the Earl of Aberdeen, the foreign secretary. These conversations disclosed the identity of views of the two governments on the following points: it was desirable to maintain the *status quo* in Turkey, and, in the event of the dissolution of the Ottoman empire, Great Britain and Russia were to reach a preliminary agreement concerning the new order. There was a basic difference in the significance attached to these conversations by the two parties. To Nicholas and his advisers, they had produced a binding agreement, a "new political system." To Aberdeen and to Palmerston, who succeeded him as foreign secretary in 1846, what took place in 1844 was "a mutual expression of opinion," creating no binding obligation. This curious misunderstanding became the source of grievous complications.

The Revolution of 1848 and Intervention in Hungary. The French revolution of February 1848, which led to the overthrow of Louis Philippe and the Orléans dynasty, was accompanied by waves of social and political unrest throughout continental Europe and a revival of national agitation among Italians, Hungarians, Poles, Czechs, and Rumanians. Nicholas was greatly alarmed, massed Russian troops along his western border, and contemplated military intervention, but the rapid success of the revolution and the establishment of representative governments in Austria and Prussia necessitated the abandonment of these plans. Russia nevertheless tried to salvage whatever possible of the old order.

A strong national movement in Moldavia and Wallachia directed against Russia and Turkey led to a military intervention by these two powers (1848) and the revision (Russo-Turkish agreement of Balta-Liman, May 1849), in a restrictive sense, of the "organic statute" that had been granted to the Danubian principalities by the treaty of Adrianople (1829) and which contained elements of a representative government. As nationalistic agitation subsided, Russian and Turkish troops were withdrawn from the Danubian principalities early in 1851.

Distressed as they were by the inroads made by the revolutionary and radical elements in Vienna, Nicholas and Nesselrode believed that the downfall of the Austrian monarchy should be prevented at all costs. Moreover, it was apparent by the autumn of 1848 that Austrian conservative forces were rapidly recovering from their temporary defeat. The Russian government, therefore, lent financial and diplomatic assistance to Austria in her struggle with the insurgent Italian provinces and assumed the unrewarding task of suppressing the Hungarian revolution. The revolt in Hungary, which broke out in March 1848, was ably led by Louis Kossuth, who was supported by an important contingent of Polish *émigrés*. The Hungarians held their ground well against an Austria weakened by political strife and the struggle with the Italian insurgents. From October 1848 a state of war existed between Austria and Hungary. In March 1849 Vienna appealed to St. Petersburg for help. Nicholas responded eagerly, partly because he was apprehensive of the repercussions of a successful Hungarian insurrection on Russia's Polish provinces. In June 1849 some 180,000 Russian troops led by Paskevich crossed the frontier into Hungary, where they fought jointly with an Austrian army of approximately the same number. The Russo-Austrian forces suffered heavy losses owing to epidemics and the spirited resistance of the Magyars, who were vastly outnumbered; the ultimate issue of the struggle was a foregone conclusion. In August 1849 Kossuth fled to Turkey and the Hungarian troops capitulated, throwing themselves on the mercy of the tsar. Paskevich, however, turned over his prisoners to the Austrians, who treated them with extreme and purposeless harshness. Western Europe and the United States showed much sympathy for the case of Hungary but gave her no direct assistance.

Another reason for Russia's bolstering of the Hapsburg monarchy was the desire of St. Petersburg to maintain the framework of the German confederation created in 1815 and to check the growth of aggressive German nationalism, which was associated with Prussia and which, moreover, was tinged with political liberalism. In spite of close dynastic ties between the ruling houses of Russia and Prussia (Nicholas I had married a sister of Frederick William IV of Prussia) and the traditional pro-Prussian bias of the Russian court, St. Petersburg successfully blocked Prussian attempts at leadership in the Germanic world. Both policies—the bolstering of Austria and the resistance to the fulfillment of Prussian ambitions—tended to weaken the effectiveness of the alliance of the three eastern powers: Vienna was uneasy about her growing dependence on the tsarist empire, while Prussia resented the obstacles put in the road of her political progress by Russia.

The Crimean War, 1854–1856. The ebbing of the revolutionary tide in France, which led to the election of Prince Louis Napoleon Bonaparte as president (December 1848), brought a *détente* in Franco-Russian relations. Relations with England, too, markedly improved after the resignation of Palmerston as prime minister (December 1851) and especially with the formation of a government under Aberdeen (December 1852), who since his meeting with the tsar eight years earlier enjoyed Nicholas's special favor.

Nothing appeared to foretell the imminence of a European conflict. In January and February 1851 Nicholas outlined to Sir Hamilton Seymour, British ambassador to St. Petersburg, a comprehensive program of measures to be taken jointly by Russia and Great Britain in the event of the anticipated demise of the "dying bear," that is, the dissolution of the Ottoman empire. The tsar proposed the eventual extension of Russian, British, and Austrian control over portions of the Turkish territory. The British government was alarmed and shocked and gave an elusive answer, but Nicholas, as in 1844, persisted in the belief that London and St. Petersburg were agreed to take joint action to ensure Turkey's succession.

The immediate cause of the Crimean war was the Franco-Russian dispute over the Holy Land. Over centuries the Roman Catholics and the Greek Orthodox Church had accumulated conflicting rights bearing on the protection of Christian shrines and Christian populations in the Ottoman empire. The Catholic countries had, for decades, showed little interest in the Holy Land, a situation of which the Greek Orthodox took full advantage. In the middle of 1850, however, France requested the restoration to the Catholics of the rights to which they were entitled under the existing treaties and which were allegedly usurped by the Orthodox. The immediate issues were trivial: possession of the key to the great door of the Church of Bethlehem and the right to replace the silver star marking the birthplace of Christ. The Porte found an ingenious temporary solution: it conceded the French claims and simultaneously assured the Russians that the existing situation remained unchanged (February 1852). Strong pressure from Paris, however, resulted in the formal granting of the French demands (December 1852).

Nicholas would not accept this diplomatic defeat, which, moreover, coincided with the worsening of Franco-Russian relations because of the refusal by St. Petersburg to recognize fully the imperial title assumed by Louis Napoleon contrary to Russian advice. Prince Alexander Menshikov, the tsar's special envoy, was sent to Constantinople (February 1853) to negotiate with the Porte a secret alliance that would place under Russian protection not only the Orthodox Church but also the Orthodox laymen residing in Turkey, who numbered some 12 million. The Porte, prodded by Stratford de Redcliffe, refused. A Russian ultimatum requesting immediate compliance with Menshikov's demands was ignored, the Russian legation was withdrawn from Constantinople, and Russian troops occupied the Danubian principalities without, however, declaring war (May–July 1853). The disclosure of the Menshikov terms and the Russian ultimatum forced the British government of Aberdeen, who did not wish to intervene in the Holy Land dispute, to revise its position: in the middle of June an Anglo-French naval force weighed anchor at the entrance to the Dardanelles and in September it entered the Straits. In October, Turkey declared war on Russia and in December—following the battle of Sinope, in which the Russians destroyed a portion of the Turkish fleet—the British and French squadrons sailed into the Black Sea. War between Great Britain and France, on the one hand, and Russia, on the other, was declared in April 1854.

To Napoleon III and Palmerston war with Russia was "the battle of civilization against barbarism," in which the other Western powers were invited to participate. Fortunately for St. Petersburg the kingdom of Sardinia alone joined the anti-Russian coalition and sent 15,000 Piedmontese soldiers to the Crimea. Russia received no assistance, however, from her traditional allies—Prussia and Austria; the attitude of the latter country was indeed inimical to Russia and brought her twice to the brink of war. Naval action on the high seas took place at such remote geographical points as the Baltic, the White Sea, and the Pacific, but the Black Sea remained the principal theatre of war. Hostilities unfolded on three separate fronts: those of the Danubian principalities, the Crimea, and the Caucasus. The localization of the hostilities to southern Russia was less of an advantage from the Russian standpoint than might appear at first glance: there were no railways south of Moscow, and roads were in poor condition; thus the supplying of the armies in the field was one of Russia's chief problems, while the allies had total control of the Black Sea and had at their disposal the world's greatest navies and merchant marines.

The Danubian campaign, which was to lead to the occupation of the Balkans, was brief and inglorious. Moldavia and Wallachia were taken by the Russians in July 1853, that is, before the formal declaration of war, and the Danube was crossed in March 1854; but the menacing attitude of Austria, military reverses, and epidemics among the troops forced the Russian withdrawal to the east of the Pruth River in September 1854. Thus ended the Danubian campaign.

The central area of war was the Crimea. In September 1854 a huge armada of 300 transports protected by 90 war vessels and carrying over 60,000 allied troops sailed from Varna, on the Black Sea, and landed in Eupatoria, in the Crimea. There followed the siege of the naval base of Sevastopol, an epic in Russian military history, which lasted for 11 months. The three admirals who commanded the Sevastopol garrison—Kornilov, Istomin, and Nakhimov—were all killed in action, while General Totleben, who in record time built a line of fortifications around the besieged fortress that for months withstood the assault of the enemy, was seriously wounded. In September 1855 the shattered remnants of the Russian naval base were finally taken by the enemy.

The Russians were more fortunate in the Caucasus, where they were faced with the Turks and where military operations were conducted on a smaller scale than in the Crimea. The taking by assault of the fortress of Kars proved helpful in negotiating the peace settlement.

Both the Russians and the Allies had fought gallantly under adverse conditions. The ending of the war was due to Russia's military defeats and to a diplomatic situation highly unfavorable to the tsarist empire. From a maze of international negotiations and agreements there emerged concrete policies which profoundly affected the course of events. The concentration of Austrian troops in Transylvania in the summer of 1854 forced the Russian government to yield to the Austrian demand, supported by Prussia, for the abandonment of the Danubian campaign. A conference attended by Austria, France, and Great Britain and held in Vienna in August 1854 formulated a 4-point program. This provided for a European (instead of a Russian) protectorate over Moldavia, Wallachia, and Serbia; freedom of navigation on the Danube; revision of the 1841 Straits convention; and protection of the Christian populations of Turkey by the five powers and no longer by Russia alone. This program, which eventually became the basis of peace negotiations, was not accepted by Russia until January 1856, after Austria had issued an ultimatum threatening military measures unless Russia agreed to immediate peace negotiations on the terms laid down in the Vienna note. The peace conference met in Paris in February 1856, and the peace treaty was signed a month later, at the end of March. It embodied the program laid down in the Vienna 1854 conference, with some modifications which made its terms less palatable to the Russians: Russia recovered Sevastopol, which was "exchanged" for Kars, but she had to cede to Moldavia the portion of Bessarabia controlling the mouth of the Danube and was prohibited from maintaining naval and military establishments on the Aland Islands, off the shores of Finland, which the British had occupied early in the war. The Black Sea was neutralized, that is, it was thrown open to world commerce, but Russia and Turkey were denied the right to maintain navies in these waters. The congress of Paris also issued a declaration dealing with maritime law.

Nicholas I had died a year earlier, in February 1855, at a time when evidence of Russia's military defeat was mounting. The Crimean War was to him a severe blow, for it exposed the failure of his diplomacy and exploded the myth of the invincible strength of the Russian military forces. The cost of the war was exceedingly high; losses in human lives on both sides, including the men who had died from epidemics, were reckoned at about 600,000. Russian disappointments were shared by the victors. The British and the French governments were savagely criticized for the inept manner in which the war was conducted. The outcome of the struggle was not what Palmerston had wished. He had urged the severance from Russia of Finland, the Crimea, and the Caucasus, but this program met with no support among his allies and went by default.

15

Reforms and Counter-Reforms: Alexander II and Alexander III, 1855-1894

Two Tsars: A Characterization

Alexander II. Alexander II (1855–1881), who at the age of 37 succeeded his father in the midst of the Crimean War, received a fairly good education and spoke foreign languages well; a man of conservative disposition, he admired his predecessor's unimaginative methods of government. Conservatism, of course, is essentially a dislike for change; this attitude colored heavily Alexander II's policies and explains much in the character of his reforms. One should not underestimate, however, the momentous difficulties which the rulers of Russia had to face in the second half of the century. The emancipation of the serfs—the most important of Alexander II's reforms—would have taxed the ingenuity of the most resourceful and enlightened statesmen. Yet the fact remains that the solutions devised in Russia did not withstand the test of time but inexorably led the monarchy to its doom. The situation was greatly complicated by the emergence, for the first time in Russian history, of an organized revolutionary movement, to which Alexander II eventually fell victim.

Alexander III. Alexander III (1881–1894), born in 1845, was the second son of Alexander II and became heir apparent in 1865 after his elder brother had died of consumption. The new tsar was an extreme reactionary, instinctively and unfalteringly attached to the notion of absolutism. His short reign was dedicated to the undoing of what he and his advisers regarded as the unduly liberal reforms of Alexander II.

Russian policies in the second half of the nineteenth century bear the imprint of the ultrareactionary and nationalistic views of a small group of men whose influence in the ruling circles was great. The more prominent among them were C. P. Pobedonostsev (1827–1907), tutor of Alexander III and Nicholas II and chief procurator of the Holy Synod from 1880 to 1905; Count D. A. Tolstoy (1823–1889), chief procurator of the Holy Synod (1864–1880), minister of education (1866–1880; he held the two offices simultaneously), and minister of the interior (1882–1889); and M. N. Katkov (1818–1887), an erstwhile liberal and editor of the conservative newspaper *Moskovskiia Vedomosti*.

The Great Reforms

Emancipation of the Serfs. Alexander II, like his father, was aware of the inequities and dangers of the Russian situation, and his belief in the necessity of what came to be known as the great reforms was strengthened by Russia's defeat in the Crimean War. Incessant peasant unrest and the need for modernizing the economy called for the abolition of serfdom. Addressing the nobility of Moscow in March 1856, Alexander stated that "it is better to abolish bondage from above than to wait until it will begin to abolish itself spontaneously from below." In September 1859, when preparations for the emancipation were well advanced, Alexander told the nobility that the liberation of the serfs "cannot be accomplished without sacrifices" but that he would do his best so that these should be "as light as possible." These statements sum up well the spirit in which the government approached the reform.

The March address quoted above, which came as a surprise even to Alexander's closest advisers, ended with an appeal to the nobility to make proposals as to how the emancipation should be brought about. When the nobility did not respond, the government, at the end of 1856, fell back on the familiar and trusted device of appointing a secret committee, which became engrossed in sterile discussions. In November 1857, however, under the pretext of replying to a petition of the nobility of the western (Lithuanian) provinces for the permission to emancipate their serfs without the land,[1] the emperor issued a general directive concerning the "voluntary"

---

[1] The petition was exacted from the nobility by the threats of the governor-general of that region, V. I. Nazimov, to impose "inventories" (see above, p. 279) of great severity.

establishment of provincial committees of the nobility to make proposals for the emancipation of the serfs. Not without prodding from the authorities, such committees, consisting exclusively of noble landowners, were organized in every province between January 1858 and April 1859. Their reports, which reflected the aspirations of the local landed proprietors, were completed by the end of 1859 and were studied by the editorial committee that drafted the actual legislation. The editorial committee, again, consisted exclusively of noblemen, many of them large landowners and high officials. The chairman of the committee was General J. I. Rostovtsev, who in 1825 had informed Emperor Alexander I of the Decembrist conspiracy. Some of the members of the committee, including Rostovtsev, favored the reform; others opposed it. Rostovtsev died in February 1860 and was succeeded as chairman of the committee by the minister of justice, Count V. N. Panin, an opponent of emancipation. The editorial committee completed the draft legislation in October 1860. It was revised, in a sense unfavorable to the peasants, by several agencies, including the State Council—another body consisting of noblemen and large landowners—and was promulgated into law on February 19, 1861.

The emancipation statutes comprised 22 enactments and were frequently amended in later years. The complexity of this legislation was due in part to the fact that there were different regulations for the several categories of bondsmen. The two largest groups were the serfs, that is, peasants living on privately owned estates (10.7 million males in 1859), and the state peasants [2] (12.8 million males in 1859), who lived on land owned by the state.

The process of the emancipation of the serfs, with which this section is primarily concerned, was divided into three stages. During the introductory stage lasting for two years (until February 1863) the former serfs received personal freedom (they could marry, acquire property, engage in trades, bring actions in courts), and preliminary arrangements were made for the settlement of property relations between the landowners and the erstwhile bondsmen. During the second stage, beginning in February 1863 and known as the period of "temporary obligation," the former serfs and the landowners were to reach final settlements concerning the land allotments which were transferred to the peasants and the actual amount of the latter's financial obligations—the "redemption payments." The terms of the settlements were to be kept within the provisions of the emancipation statutes (size of the allotments, amount of the redemption payments), but they were voluntary and no time limit was set for the duration of stage two. Actually the period of

[2] See above, p. 146.

"temporary obligation" was brought to an end on January 1, 1883, when redemption of all allotments was made compulsory. The third stage began with the conclusion of the agreements between the peasants and their former lords. The government issued to the estate owners interest-bearing securities which represented the indemnity to which they were entitled. The amount of the indemnity was calculated by capitalizing at 6 per cent the annual charge that the peasants were assessed in return for the land that they received. The payments made to the owners were to be reimbursed, with interest, to the government by the peasants by annual installments extending over 49 years. It was only on the fulfillment of this obligation that stage three was closed and the former serfs received a clear title to their allotment land.

In practice the above arrangements proved unworkable. The land allotments of the liberated bondsmen were as a rule smaller than those they had farmed on their own account under serfdom, when they were required to work half of the time for their lord. Under the existing conditions of farming, the allotments were inadequate to occupy fully the members of the household or to provide proper maintenance for the owner's family. The inevitable consequence was that the village was both idle and hungry. The redemption payments, which were determined by rather involved rules, were much too high and did not reflect either the renting capacity of the land or its market value. Characteristically, the higher charge was attached to the first unit (acre) of a peasant's holding, that is, the larger the allotment the smaller the payment per acre. The higher charge for the first unit contained an element of indemnification for the loss of servile labor which, theoretically, was denied to the estate owners; they were to receive compensation only for the land that was ceded to the former serfs.

The emancipation statutes retained the traditional organization of the peasantry into village communes. Under this system the right to land was vested, not in the individual households or farmers, but in the commune as a whole, which allocated the land, after dividing it into strips, among its members. The inevitable consequence of communal tenure and its concomitant, the intermixture of strips, was the compulsory rotation of crops, the 3-field system under which one-third of the land lay fallow; and the very possibility of more progressive farming was precluded. Membership in a village commune was compulsory for all peasants, who were jointly responsible for taxes and redemption payments. The peasants, moreover, continued to be organized into households, which were the basic administrative unit: members of a household enjoyed no individual property right. The emancipation statutes created a new administrative subdivision, the township (*volost*), which comprised several village communes and whose authority extended exclusively to the peasants. Both the township and the village commune were, within narrow bounds, self-governing communities, electing elders, police-men, and other officials, and wielding comprehensive judicial and police powers over their members. Peasant officials, however, were closely super-vised by officers appointed by the Crown. It is noteworthy that the quasi-unanimous recommendations of the provincial committees that the nobility should retain after the emancipation its police, judicial, and supervisory powers, were ignored. No peasant could obtain a passport, which was nec-essary in order to absent himself from the village, without the approval of the township and communal authorities and, if a junior member of a house-hold, the permission of the household elder. The slow growth of industry and restrictions on internal migration which were not lifted until the end of the century contributed to the immobilization of the peasantry and created a situation that has been aptly described as "rural overpopulation," even though the density of the population in Russia was considerably below that of other European countries.

The administrative and legal provisions of the emancipation acts applied, broadly speaking, to the peasantry as a whole, but other provisions varied for the different categories of the peasant population. The household serfs (*dvorovye*), that is, those employed in their master's household but not en-gaged in farming, received no land and were not required to make payments. They either continued to work in their former capacity or drifted to the cities in search of employment. Serfs in the western provinces, where the nobility was largely Polish, benefited by the Polish uprising of 1863: their allotments were larger and financial burdens lighter than those of the former serfs in Russia proper. The large group of state peasants, too, received larger allotments and made smaller payments than the serfs.

The general results of the emancipation were technical stagnation of agri-culture, impoverishment of the peasants and the nobility, and recurrent peasant unrest.

Local Self-Government. The emancipation of the serfs was the necessary preliminary to other reforms. Local government based on the legislation of the late eighteenth century had never worked well and gradually degenerated into petty tyranny on the part of appointed officials. The statute of 1864 introduced into Russian local self-government the *zemstvos,* which were organized on two levels, provincial (*guberniia*) and county (*uezd*). Each provincial and county *zemstvo* consisted of an assembly and an executive board. The members of the county assemblies were elected for a term of three years by the local population voting in three separate colleges: individual landed proprietors, irrespective of their belonging to the nobility or to other social groups; urban population; and the peasant village communes. The county assemblies elected the provincial assemblies, and the *zemstvo* assemblies on both levels—provincial and county—chose their respective executive boards. The right to vote in *zemstvo* elections, as well as the number of delegates sent by each of the three electoral colleges to the county assemblies, were determined by property qualifications: ownership of a specified area of land or, in urban settlements, of property of equivalent value. The *zemstvos* were introduced gradually; in 1865 they were established in 19 provinces, by 1914 in 43. They were to concern themselves with "local economic needs," which included such important branches of public administration as schools, public health, and the promotion of industry and agriculture. The path of the *zemstvos* was beset with difficulties; their revenue, which was derived from local rates, was narrowly circumscribed and, having no executive agencies of their own, they had to depend for the implementation of their decisions on the often unwilling cooperation of the police and Crown officials.

The municipal government, which was in a pitiful condition, was reorganized by the city government act of 1870. It was the outcome of a discussion extending over a period of eight years, which, in its initial stage, called for proposals from over 500 specially appointed committees of representative citizens. The draft legislation was amended several times and in its final version provided for a city government consisting of a municipal council (*duma*), an executive board, and a mayor (*golova*). The council was elected for a term of four years by the urban taxpayers voting in three separate colleges, participation in which was determined by the size of the taxpayer's tax assessment. Under this system taxpayers in the higher brackets were represented in the municipal councils, proportionately, by more councillors than those with lower assessments. Each council elected an executive board and a mayor, who was confirmed in office by the minister of the interior or by the appointed provincial governor. The new municipal institutions, like the *zemstvos,* were concerned primarily with local economic needs and depended on Crown agencies for the implementation of their decisions.

The local government reforms of 1864 and 1870, for all its limitations and imperfections, were an important step forward. They introduced in Russia the principle, generally accepted in nineteenth-century Europe, of property qualification as the basis for participation in government. Moreover, the institutions of local self-government proved viable, gradually building extensive welfare and economic services and eventually assuming a major part in the liberal and revolutionary movement.

The wave of extreme reaction that swept over Russia with the accession of Alexander III, after the assassination of his father, led to the revision of the statutes of local self-government. The architects of the administrative counter-reforms were: Count Dimitry Tolstoy, minister of the interior from 1882 to his death in 1889; his colleague and then successor (1889–1895) Ivan Durnovo; and A. D. Pazukhin, director of the chancery of the ministry of the interior under both ministers. As Pazukhin wrote in an article published in 1885, "our objective today should be to restore what was destroyed" by the reforms of Alexander II. Both he and Tolstoy were particularly interested in strengthening the position of the nobility.

The chief—and surprising—criticism leveled by the reactionaries against the institutions of local self-government was that they were too independent and enjoyed a measure of autonomy incompatible with autocracy and Russia's historical tradition. To correct this situation the *zemstvo* act of 1890, while retaining the framework of the existing *zemstvo* institutions, reorganized the franchise on a class ("estate") basis and strengthened bureaucratic controls. Under the new dispensation only members of the nobility voted in the first electoral college, which provided more than half of the members of the *zemstvo* assemblies. Since, as under the 1864 act, the county and the provincial marshals of the nobility were retained as chairmen of, respectively, the county and the provincial *zemstvo* assemblies, the predominance of the nobility in the *zemstvo* institutions was assured. The 1890 act greatly extended the control exercised by the minister of the interior, the provincial governors, and other Crown officials and agencies over every phase of *zemstvo* endeavor. Under certain conditions the minister or provincial governor could set aside the decisions of the *zemstvo* organs and substitute for them their own directives.

The city government act of 1892 followed similar lines. It retained the administrative framework established in 1870 but further restricted the franchise by raising property qualifications and altering their basis. Bureaucratic controls were generally tightened. Under the new *zemstvo* and city government acts the Jews were disfranchised, but within the Jewish pale (area of Jewish settlements) a small number of Jews could be appointed by the authorities to city councils.

The Judiciary. In the middle of the nineteenth century Russian law courts presented a picture of unspeakable disorder. Judges were ignorant and venal, rules of procedure were hopelessly complex and confused, and litigation tended to drag on indefinitely and frequently resulted in the financial ruin of the parties to a case. The necessity for a reform of the courts was acknowledged and discussed for decades, especially in the 1850's, but little real progress was made until 10 years later. In 1862, the "basic principles" of the proposed legislation were circulated to, examined by, and commented on by the universities and the legal profession, and in November 1864 the statutes of the judiciary were enacted. Much credit for the completion of this task is due to the eminent jurists S. I. Zarudny and D. N. Zamiatnin. The latter was appointed minister of justice in the autumn of 1862.

The 1864 statutes marked a breach with the pre-reform courts. They strove to introduce in Russia the accepted principles of western European jurisprudence: equality of all before the law, uniformity of judicial procedure, independence of the courts and irremovability of the judges, and trial by jury. The remodeled court system was simple. Petty cases were tried by justices of the peace, who were elected by the county *zemstvo* assemblies or, in the provinces which had no *zemstvos,* were appointed by the Crown. The more important cases were tried by courts on two levels. The judges of these courts were appointed by the Crown from lists of candidates submitted by the judiciary. The Senate was reorganized and continued to function as the supreme court.

The reformed courts were a vast improvement on their predecessors, yet some of the features of the pre-1864 regime survived. The principle of the uniformity of judicial procedure was not consistently applied. There were retained military courts, ecclesiastical courts, which dealt with matters such as divorces, and township courts, which tried minor cases involving peasants alone. Extrajudicial authority comprising the power of arrest and deportation was exercised by administrative officials; it was extensively used in dealing with persons regarded as undesirable. Whole blocks of cases were denied trial by jury. In 1868 Zamiatnin was dismissed and was succeeded as minister of justice by Count C. J. Pahlen, who did not believe in the independence of the courts. He remained in office for 10 years. The independence of the judges was vitiated by the fact that they were government officials and that their professional career depended on the minister of justice. A law of 1889, a characteristic enactment of the era of counter-reforms, abolished the justice of the peace, except in the cities. Minor cases involving peasants alone were transferred to the jurisdiction of newly-created officials, the land captains (*zemskii nachalnik*), who were appointed by the minister of the interior from among local noble landowners. Land captains held practically unlimited authority over the peasants, their institutions, and their officials, and vesting them with judicial functions was a violation of the principle of the separation of powers (executive and judicial), which was a cornerstone of the reform of the courts. In the 1880's and 1890's irremovability of the judges, publicity of proceedings, and trial by jury suffered further curtailments. The 1864 statutes had provided for the establishment of a bar, which was soon to provide the liberal and radical movements with some of their outstanding leaders. There was no discrimination against the Jews. However, a decree of 1889 made admission to the bar of persons of "non-Christian persuasion" subject to the approval of the minister of justice, with the result that to the end of the century nearly all Jewish candidates were rejected.

The Army. The condition of the Russian army in the middle of the nineteenth century was as pitiful as those of local government and the courts. The burden of service, which lasted for 25 years, was borne exclusively by the lower classes, with the nobility and the merchants (the latter on the payment of a special tax) exempt. Army service was a collective rather than a personal obligation: the number of the recruits needed every year was apportioned among urban and rural communities which designated the men liable for service. "Volunteers," whose services were paid for, could be substituted for the original draftees. Discipline was exceedingly severe, the army being regarded and used as a penal institution. In the 1850's the novelist Fedor Dostoevsky served a sentence of several years in the armed forces.

The author of the army reform was General Dimitry Miliutin, minister of war from 1861 to 1881. He shortened the term of service to 15 years, humanized discipline, improved the living conditions of the troops, and modernized their equipment, but the reform that basically altered the conditions of service was the conscription law of 1874. By virtue of this enactment military service became a personal obligation of every male, irrespective of social status, on reaching the age of 20. Not all men of that age were drafted. Some were deferred or exempt for family reasons, such as breadwinners and only sons. The order of drafting (within the non-exempt category) was determined by lot. The term of active service was, as a rule, six years, followed by nine years in the reserve and five more years in the militia. Shorter terms of active service were provided for holders of academic diplomas. Moreover, graduates of secondary and higher schools could join the forces as "volunteers," that is, without drawing lots, and thus secure further reduction of their terms of service: university graduates who had "volunteered" served merely three months. The broadening of the basis of the draft was accompanied (1875) by the introduction of a comprehensive educational program that endeavored to teach the soldiers at least the rudiments of reading and writing. Although the shortening of the term of service for the holders of academic diplomas constituted a bias in favor of the proprietary groups, and although some of the brutality characteristic of the pre-reform army was tolerated and survived until the end of the empire, the conscription law of 1874 was a striking move in the direction of social equality.

Central Government. No comparable trend could be detected in the attitude of the tsar and his advisors towards central government. The second half of the nineteenth century was in Russia a period of intellectual ferment, and there were many who felt that some form of popular participation in government could not be much longer postponed. Alexander II, like his uncle Alexander I, had at times encouraged such expectations. In 1863, addressing the Finnish diet, which was reconvened for the first time since 1809, the emperor stated that "in the hands of a wise nation . . . liberal institutions are not only not dangerous, but are guarantees of order and well-being," and in 1879 he confirmed a liberal constitution for liberated Bulgaria. In the Russian empire however, with the exception of Finland (to be noted presently), the autocratic powers of the Crown were fully maintained. The only mild and ineffectual attempt at constitutional reform was made towards the very end of Alexander II's reign, under the pressure of mounting political terror. In the spring of 1880 there was established the Supreme Executive Commission, headed by Count M. T. Loris-Melikov, formerly governor-general of Kharkov. His brief administration, known as "the dictatorship of the heart," endeavored to combine firmness in dealing with the revolutionaries with minor concessions to liberal opinion: easing of censorship, dismissal of particularly reactionary ministers, reform of the security policy. There was some relaxation of tension, and the Supreme Executive Commission was dissolved in August, with Loris-Melikov continuing in office as minister of the interior. He proposed a change in the legislative procedure: the creation of a commission that was to comprise representatives of *zemstvos* and municipalities to advise the State Council (an advisory body to the Crown) on pending legislation. This jejune and innocuous proposal, which historians have sometimes dignified with the appellation of "the Loris-Melikov constitution," was approved by Alexander II on the morning of March 1, 1881, a few hours before his assassination. Alexander III, on his accession, dismissed Loris-Melikov, and the proposed commission was never called into being.

Poland and Finland

The Polish Insurrection, 1863. Although Alexander II, like his father, was no friend of Poland, his accession appeared to usher in an era of better Russo-Polish relations. Paskevich, Russia's unbending proconsul in Poland, died in February 1856. Of the five Russian viceroys who followed him in rapid succession during the next seven years, three (Prince Michael Gorchakov, Count Lambert, and the tsar's brother, the Grand Duke Constantine) believed in making concessions to Polish opinion, while two (General Sukhozanet and Count Liders—their joint tenure of office lasted but a few months) opposed it.[3] On the Polish side Marquis Alexander Wielopolski, a wealthy landowner and a leader of the 1831 insurrection, now advocated the necessity and feasibility of a reconciliation with Russia. His immediate objective was a return to the Organic Statute of 1832 (see above, p. 274). This program was approved in St. Petersburg, although not without hesitation. Appropriate legislation was enacted in 1861 and 1862, and a Polish government enjoying a measure of autonomy was organized under Wielopolski. These policies did not achieve their purpose, however. Polish national opinion was inflamed, and while the Polish left- and right-wing groups were bitterly at odds among themselves, they were united in their hatred of Russia and opposition to Wielopolski. What the Polish national leaders were dreaming of was an independent Poland in her 1772 frontiers. Clashes between the Polish patriotic groups and the authorities multiplied and culminated in the uprising that broke out in January 1863.

Insurgent Poland, the brave talk of her leaders notwithstanding, was totally unprepared for the struggle against Russia's military might. Some 10,000 badly equipped and poorly disciplined Polish troops were pitted against 80,000 Russian regulars; hence the partisan character of the campaign, which was fought by small bands of men in woods and marshes and which made it possible for the insurgents to carry on for a year and a half. The central authority of the rebellion was unstable and went through several transformations, the leaders putting their faith in the patriotism and devotion of the community, including the peasantry, to the national cause; in the sympathy of the Russian liberal and revolutionary movement; and in the support of Western governments and opinion. None of these hopes were

---

[3] The actual order of viceroys, which indicates the fluctuation of Russian policies, was Gorchakov, Sukhozanet, Lambert, Liders, and Constantine.

realized. The insurgents drew their support predominantly from the middle class, while the peasantry remained largely neutral or, in the Ukrainian and Lithuanian provinces, was even hostile. The bulk of Russian liberals and revolutionaries succumbed to pan-Russian nationalistic emotions, and while Western governments and Western opinion were prolific in the expression of their admiration for Poland's struggle for independence, they did nothing, except to protest, to help it.

The crushing of the rebellion brought its retribution: first, a dictatorial regime under General Count Michael Muravev, an implacable enemy of Polish nationalism and Roman Catholicism, and then, between 1867 and 1869, the repeal of Polish autonomous institutions and the integration of Poland into the administrative framework of the empire. Administrative assimilation went hand in hand with aggressive Russification. There were mass deportations of Polish landowners, whose estates were sold to Orthodox Russians. The Russian language was introduced in the administration, the courts, and the schools.

The University of Warsaw, revived in 1857, was reorganized in 1869 as a Russian university. The Roman Church, which had encouraged the insurrection, bore the brunt of Russian persecution. The only beneficiaries of the rebellion were the Polish peasants, whose emancipation settlements were revised to their advantage (1864), but the subsequent history of Russo-Polish relations suggests that the peasants did not become reconciled to Russian rule.

The Finnish Autonomy. Russian relations with Finland, unlike those with Poland, were uneventful and peaceful. The Finnish self-government established in 1809 functioned reasonably well, and no important conflict arose between the Finnish institutions and the Russian Crown. The imperial government would seem to have accepted the view that Finnish laws could not be changed without the approval of the Finnish diet, which, however, had not been convened since 1809. The awakening nationalism that swept over Europe in the middle of the nineteenth century had repercussions in Finland. St. Petersburg showed uneasiness but after some delays convoked the Finnish diet in 1863. It continued to meet regularly and adopted a constitution, based on Swedish law and confirmed by Alexander in 1869, which provided that Finnish "fundamental laws" could not be changed without the consent of the diet. As grand duke of Finland, the tsar was a constitutional monarch, but he remained an autocrat in Russia proper and in his other dominions.

Cultural Policies

Censorship. The accession of Alexander II and the end of the Crimean War brought some relaxation of the regime of rigorous censorship that had been in effect in Russia since the outbreak of the European revolution of 1848. More newspapers and journals were permitted to appear and were allowed to comment on current domestic and foreign affairs, while previously periodicals, with few exceptions, were nonpolitical. The censorship law of 1865 removed, partly, the preliminary censorship formerly in force and substituted, also partly, the judicial procedure for the administrative in dealing with the offenses committed by editors and publishers. It was left to the authorities, however, to decide which of the two procedures was to be used and, since the former course was almost invariably followed, except in cases of libel, the situation was not vastly changed. Enacted as a temporary measure, the law of 1865 was amended, tightened, and made more arbitrary by the "provisional rules" of 1882 and remained in force until the revolution of 1905.

Schools. Throughout the second half of the nineteenth century the school policy pursued an uneven course. There were important reforms of higher and secondary education, as well as the broadening of the base of the school system; for the first time a genuine attempt was made to lay the foundation of elementary education, yet the forces of reaction hostile to a liberalization of school policies and to the advancement of literacy were aggressive and firmly entrenched. Prince Shirinsky-Shikhmatov, the ultrareactionary minister of education, was dismissed in 1854, and his immediate successors, A. S. Norov and E. P. Kovalevsky, repealed or eased the more oppressive measures in force at the universities since 1848. Significant reforms were enacted during the administration of A. V. Golovnin, a man of liberal views and minister of education from 1861 to 1866: the university charter of June 1863, the law on secondary schools of November 1864, and the law on primary schools of July 1864. The university charter of 1863 was an attempt to prevent the recurrence of student disorders, which since 1861 had assumed the character of a mass movement. The charter restored university autonomy, but it did not authorize student organizations or corporate activities. The 1864 law on secondary schools retained the existing gymnasiums (secondary schools), which offered a 7-year course and were of either the classical or "science" (*Realschule*) type. The former taught Latin and Greek, and their graduates were admitted to the universities without entrance examinations.

Gymnasiums of the *Realschule* type omitted classical languages but emphasized sciences (mathematics, chemistry, physics, natural history) and modern languages. Their graduates could continue their studies at the higher technical schools but were not qualified for admission to the universities. Secondary schools were open to all boys, "irrespective of faith or social status." The amount of tuition fees was determined by the school boards.

The law on primary schools of July 1864 was intended to promote "true religious and moral principles" and to impart "useful elementary knowledge." Primary schools were to be established by the "free cooperation of the government, the clergy, village communes, and private persons." The cost of primary education was to be borne by the urban and village communities, with only minor subsidies from the government. The administration of the schools was entrusted to provincial and county school boards which consisted of Crown officials, the clergy, and representatives of the *zemstvos.* The local bishop was, *ex officio,* chairman of the provincial school board. Tuition fees were permitted. Instruction was given exclusively in the Russian language. The drafts of the university charter of 1863 and of the 1864 laws on secondary and elementary schools were translated into foreign languages and circulated for comments to educational institutions and qualified persons at home and abroad.

This relatively liberal era in Russian education was of short duration. In April 1866 D. V. Karakozov, a former university student, made an unsuccessful attempt to murder Alexander II. The reactionary forces laid the responsibility for the would-be assassination at the door of the universities. Golovnin was dismissed and was succeeded as minister of education by the vicious reactionary Count Dimitry Tolstoy, who remained in office until 1880; two years later he returned to the government as minister of the interior. Tolstoy worked assiduously to undo the work of his predecessor. Student unrest was dealt with by police measures. A new university charter abolishing university autonomy was drafted but was not enacted into law until 1884, in the administration of Count Ivan Delianov, minister of education from 1882 to 1897 and a co-author of the reform. Under the 1884 charter rectors (presidents), deans, and professors were no longer to be elected by the university councils but were appointed by the minister of education. The powers of the curator of the school region—a Crown official—over the university administration and the student body were greatly extended.

The reform of the secondary schools initiated by Tolstoy was inspired by the desire to eliminate the "destructive notions" (as an official contemporary document put it) which were held responsible for Karakozov's attempt on the life of the tsar. To achieve this objective the students were to be shielded from the disciplines which might have political or social implications and also to obtain an education appropriate to their expected station in life. The secondary schools law of June 1871 endeavored to attain the former objective by making both classical languages mandatory in every gymnasium and by reducing the number of hours formerly allocated to Russian, literature, history, and geography. In classical studies the emphasis was on vocabulary, grammar, and syntax, and a high degree of proficiency in these subjects was expected from the students. The law also abolished the gymnasiums of the *Realschule* type, but such schools, no longer called gymnasiums, continued to function by virtue of a law of March 1872. They were expected to draw their students from lower middle-class families, and their graduates were denied admission to the universities.

The sharp differentiation between gymnasiums and the *Realschulen* introduced by the legislation of 1871 and 1872 was a part of Tolstoy's grand design, enthusiastically endorsed by Katkov and Pobedonostsev, to provide members of every social class with an education befitting their station—a revival of the theories popular in the 1830's. Although the principle was never formally enacted into law, the minister of education Delianov, in June 1887, issued a notorious circular that directed gymnasium authorities to scrutinize applicants for admission from the standpoint of the financial and social standing of the prospective students' families in order to keep out the children of "coachmen, footmen, cooks . . . and other similar people . . . who should not be led to break away from the milieu to which they belong." Neither policy—elimination of "destructive notions" or segregation of students on the class principle—proved feasible. Russian schoolboys showed notable resistance to the acquisition of the required mastery of classical languages, and whatever familiarity with Homer and Virgil they succeeded in acquiring did not make them immune to revolutionary ideas. Segregation of students on a class basis was incompatible with the looseness of Russia's class structure and was no more successful in the second half of the century than it had been in the first, when it was originally attempted.

Considerable progress was made with education for women. Day schools for girls were authorized in 1858, and the law of May 1870, which remained in force until the end of the empire, provided for girls' gymnasiums with a 7-year course. These schools were financed chiefly from local sources, the state treasury's appropriations being small. The girls' gymnasiums were open to all girls irrespective of their social status, but the tuition fees which were charged introduced an element of discrimination. The university charter of 1863, like its predecessors, denied admission to female students. As a consequence the first Russian university for women was established by private initiative and with private financial support in Moscow in 1869. Similar schools were organized in the 1870's in St. Petersburg, Kiev, and Kazan. Their academic standards were not inferior to those of corresponding institutions for men.

Russian nineteenth-century school statistics are incomplete, erratic, and difficult to summarize. According to the more reliable estimates, Russia, in the middle 1890's, had 63 higher schools, including 10 universities, with an aggregate student body of 29,000, of whom 1,200 were women; 900 secondary schools of various types with 224,000 students, of whom 75,000 were girls; and 65,000 primary schools, including 35,000 Church schools, with an aggregate enrollment of 3.5 million. These figures indicated marked progress as compared with those of the earlier period, but they were humble indeed for a population of 126 million (according to the 1897 census). Towards the end of the century the *zemstvos* began to take a leading part in the promotion of primary education, but there was still a long way to go before one could speak in earnest of compulsory school attendance for all children. The 1897 census disclosed that only 21 per cent of the total population were literate; the percentage of literacy was higher for men (29 per cent) than for women (13 per cent), and for the urban (45 per cent) than for the rural (17 per cent) population.

Anti-Semitism and National Minorities

The Jews. Discrimination against the Jews was introduced in Russian school policies for the first time in the 1880's. Prior to the partition of Poland in the second half of the eighteenth century, Jews in Russia were few and there was no Jewish problem, although some of the earlier rulers, for instance Peter I, at times gave vent to crude emotional anti-Semitism. Legislation under Catherine II in 1783 and 1791 established the Jewish "pale," that is, made it legal for the Jews to reside exclusively within designated provinces of western and southern Russia. In 1794 the Jews were made subject to discriminatory taxation at twice the rate assessed on other groups, while the area of the pale was extended. In the first half of the nineteenth century the imperial government pursued a policy of assimilation of the Jewry, which was still deeply attached to its traditional racial and religious exclusiveness. A law of December 1804 provided that Jews should be admitted to Russian schools without restriction and that they were eligible for university degrees. Army draft was extended to the Jews in 1827. Jewish schools were brought under the control of Russian authorities (1842, 1844) as a preliminary measure towards their eventual elimination. In 1844, the *kahals,* the Jewish autonomous communities, were ordered dissolved, and six years later (1850) the wearing of traditional Jewish dress was prohibited. The policies of assimilation were stubbornly resisted by the orthodox Jews.

The attitudes of both the Jewish communities and the imperial government were reversed in the second half of the nineteenth century. Reformed Judaism, shunning traditional taboos, was making rapid progress, while during Alexander II's reign there was a bettering of the condition of the Jews. In 1859 well-to-do Jewish merchants were permitted to reside outside the pale; this dispensation was extended to the holders of higher academic degrees in 1861, to skilled artisans and craftsmen in 1865, and to all university graduates in 1879. The shortening of the term of army service for holders of academic diplomas (1874) was a factor in changing the attitude of the Jewry towards Russian schools, which was all the more notable because the earlier legislation aiming at the abolition of Jewish schools was repealed or was not enforced. The number, and ratio, of Jewish students in Russian schools of every grade, including the universities, increased rapidly, while many Jews achieved prominence in finance, business, and the professions as well as in the revolutionary movement.

The highly-placed anti-Semites—Pobedonostsev, Dimitry Tolstoy, Katkov, Delianov, Alexander III—became alarmed by this unwanted success of assimilation. The participation of a Jewish woman, Jessie Helfman, in the assassination of Alexander II (1881) tended to dramatize the "Jewish peril." There followed a number of discriminatory measures: Jews were forbidden to settle in rural areas even within the pale (1882); they were excluded *de facto* from the legal profession (1889); and they were disfranchised by the *zemstvo* and city government acts of 1890 and 1892. In 1891 some 20,000 Jewish artisans were expelled from Moscow. Perhaps the most striking reversal occurred in school policies. In 1887 there were instituted quotas for Jewish students in the secondary and the higher schools: 3 per cent in St. Petersburg and Moscow, and 5 per cent elsewhere except within the Jewish pale, where it was 10 per cent. The even worse manifestations of anti-Semitism were the Jewish pogroms tolerated and sometimes instigated by the police; the first major pogrom occurred in Odessa in 1871. Revolting and medieval was a "ritual murder" trial staged in 1878. The Jewish defendant charged with murdering a Christian girl for ritual purposes was acquitted, but similar trials were to follow. These policies were responsible for the mass migration of Russian Jewry to the United States and fostered the Zionist movement.

Religious and National Minorities. Anti-Semitism was but the extreme expression of aggressive Russian nationalism characteristic of the closing decades of the nineteenth century. It was manifest in the attitude of the imperial government towards the Poles, Ukrainians, and other national minorities. Nationalism was identified with Greek Orthodoxy and led to discrimination against, and persecution of, dissenters (that is, the old-believers and other religious groups which became separated from the official Church), Roman Catholics, Protestants, Moslems, and so on. Russian was to be the only language officially accepted throughout the empire. The apostles of anti-Semitism—Pobedonostsev, Dimitry Tolstoy, Katkov, and their peers—were also the instigators of militant nationalism. They did not, however, speak for the nobility as a whole or even for the upper level of the bureaucracy. It is significant that the more reactionary bills sponsored by Tolstoy were enacted into law over the opposition of the majority of the State Council, an assembly consisting of high officials and large landowners appointed by the Crown.

Economic Conditions

Stagnation of Agriculture. Conditions in rural Russia after the emancipation were not conducive to the advancement of agriculture. Accumulation of arrears on account of the redemption payments (that is, payments for the land that the former serfs received under the emancipation settlements) provided melancholy evidence that the financial burden imposed upon the farmers was far too heavy. Arrears were written off, accumulated again, and were reassessed over long periods of years, well into the 1950's (law of May 1896). The plight of the peasantry attracted much attention and called for remedial action. The poll tax was abolished in 1885, but since it was one of the principal sources of state revenue, the resulting loss to the treasury was made good by increasing the excises on spirits and the charges borne by the former state peasants (law of June 1886). Other measures enacted in the 1880's and the 1890's tended to perpetuate the conditions which were responsible for the stagnation of peasant farming. The objectives of these policies were to strengthen the control of the peasant commune over its members and to make allotment land a distinct and restrictive form of tenure. A characteristic enactment was a law of December 1893 that prohibited the sale of communal land by the village communes without the consent of the administrative officials, forbade the mortgage of allotment land, and decreed that such land could be sold only to peasant purchasers. The land bought by village communes and individual peasant households (as distinct from the land that they received by virtue of the emancipation settlements) was not subject to these restrictions. Such purchases were facilitated by the State Peasant Bank, which was founded in 1882.

The landed nobility, too, derived no benefit from the emancipation. Much of the large sums paid to the estate owners by the government for the land that they had ceded to the former serfs reverted to the treasury in settlement of outstanding mortgage loans. Little was invested in agricultural improvements; the methods of husbandry—with rare exceptions—remained as before the emancipation, and productivity per acre was low. In the 1880's the nobility's mortgage debt exceeded its pre-emancipation level. Foreclosures were frequent, and the aggregate acreage owned by the nobility was inexorably shrinking.

Industry. The slow growth of industry, which offered but limited opportunities for employment, was an element in the Russian agrarian problem. Since the greater proportion of industrial enterprises before the emancipation were manned by hired rather than by servile labor, the liberation of the serfs had an immediate adverse and disorganizing effect only on those branches (woollens, heavy industry in the Urals regions) which had a large proportion of serfs in their labor force. Reckoning as a "factory" any industrial enterprise employing at least 16 workers, the number of factories increased from 2,500 in the middle of the 1860's to some 9,000 at the end of the century. The annual average number of workers engaged in manufacturing, mining, and metallurgy rose from 800,000 in 1861–1870 to 1,640,000 in 1891–1900, that is, more than doubled. Russian nineteenth-century labor statistics, however, have no claim to mathematical exactness and contain a wide margin of error. There was a tendency towards the concentration of production, that is, a larger proportion of the labor force was engaged in enterprises employing 1,000 and more workers each, a development usually interpreted as evidence of advancing capitalism.

As in other countries in the early stages of industrialization, conditions of labor in Russia, judged by the standards of a more enlightened age, were appalling: working hours were long, wages were low and were paid infrequently and at irregular intervals, living conditions were exceedingly poor, female and child labor was extensively used, and there were no labor organizations, the workers being entirely at the mercy of the employers. The first

Russian factory law, enacted in 1882, prohibited employment of children under 12 years of age and limited to eight hours the working day of those 12 to 15 years old. The enforcement of these regulations was entrusted to a new body of public officials, the factory inspectors. A law of 1885 forbade night work in textile mills for women and persons under 17, while a law of 1886 directed that wages must be paid at least once a month and outlawed other practices detrimental to the financial interests of the workers. Simultaneously penalties for strikes were increased, while the powers of factory inspectors were broadened to include both the enforcement of factory legislation and the supervision of the entire field of worker-employer relations. It is noteworthy that the factory legislation of the 1880's was sponsored by Dimitry Tolstoy, then minister of the interior, who for all his reactionary proclivities believed that a modicum of security for labor was a precondition of industrial peace. Although the factory acts were but loosely enforced and the number of factory inspectors remained too small to make their intervention uniformly effective, the above laws were a landmark in the history of Russian industrial relations: for the first time public authority stepped in as a regulatory factor between employers and workers.

Railways. The expansion of the railway network in the second half of the nineteenth century in Russia, as in most countries, was a factor in the growth of Russian industry. The extent of the railway lines increased from 650 miles in 1855 to 22,000 miles in 1895. The Trans-Siberian line, Russia's greatest railway enterprise, begun in 1891, was not completed until 1905. The early Russian railways were built by the state, a method that proved unsatisfactory and costly. In the 1850's a shift was made to enlist private capital—first foreign and then Russian—in railway construction. A protagonist of this policy was Count Michael Reutern, minister of finance from 1862 to 1878. Railway concessions which were granted to private interests usually carried a government guarantee of 5 per cent interest on the capital invested. In practice this method of financing led to gross abuses and heavy losses to the treasury. After an extensive investigation of the railway companies the government decided in 1880 to resume an active part in both the construction and the administration of the railways. A number of privately owned lines were purchased by the state. This policy was continued until the end of the empire.

Foreign Trade. Growth of productivity, improvement of international transportation by land and sea, and the liberalization of European commercial policies in the second half of the nineteenth century resulted in the expansion of the volume of international trade, in which Russia had a share.

Her exports rose from an annual average of 226 million gold rubles in 1861–1865 to 698 million in 1896–1900; the corresponding figures for imports were 207 million and 607 million. Nevertheless, Russia's share in world trade remained approximately the same as at the beginning of the century, that is, somewhat less than 4 per cent. The principal changes in the pattern of Russian trade were the increase in the percentage of overland trade (due to the construction of railways), the substitution of Germany for England as Russia's chief trading partner, and the rapid growth of grain exports. In 1856–1860 the average yearly export of grain was 69 million poods; in 1896–1897 it was 434 million. From 1870 to the end of the century exports of grain represented about 15 per cent of the total yield of grain and accounted for about half of the value of Russian exports. In the 1890's nearly 80 per cent of the grain exports were shipped from the ports of the Black Sea and the Sea of Azov.

The liberalization of Russian commercial policy by the tariff acts of 1857 and 1868 proved short-lived; tariff rates were revised upwards in the 1870's, especially in connection with the Turkish war of 1877–1878, and protection reached a new high level in the tariff act of 1891.

Banking and Public Finance. The closing years of the nineteenth century brought about a measure of modernization of Russia's financial structure. There came into existence a diversified network of private banks, which previously had not existed. In 1860, the State Bank was founded and eventually became the central financial institution of the empire, and in 1885 the State Nobility Land Bank, whose primary object—which was never attained—was to check the liquidation of large estates. A technical improvement of vast importance was a law of 1862 that unified the budget, creating a single treasury (formerly various branches of revenue were administered by different departments) and raised the standard of auditing. The ministers of finance of this period—Reutern, Bunge, Vyshnegradsky, Witte—were men of conservative views who believed in the virtues of a balanced budget and sound currency. Their efforts to stabilize the ruble were defeated (until the middle 1890's) by events largely beyond their control: the aftermath of the Crimean War, the Polish insurrection, expansion in Central Asia, the Turkish war of 1877–1878, as well as the costly involvement of the government in railway construction. Except for the repeal of the poll tax in 1885 the sources of state revenue were unchanged. The value of the paper ruble continued to fluctuate, but the ministry of finance succeeded in accumulating a sizable reserve of precious metal and in keeping within bounds the volume of the paper money in circulation. These developments were essential preliminaries to the adoption of the gold standard in the late 1890's. Meanwhile the public debt continued to grow, and by 1892, when Witte became minister of finance, it exceeded 4.9 billion rubles. In that year the service of the debt accounted for more than one-quarter of the total state expenditure. In the 1880's and the 1890's there was a considerable influx of foreign investment, which was used to finance industry, banking, and public utilities. Foreign capital was largely responsible after 1890 for the development of the coal and metallurgical region of the Donets valley in the south of Russia.

An Industrial Revolution? The above observations indicate that in the decades between the emancipation and the turn of the century the Russian economy had undergone a significant transformation and had acquired some of the characteristics of a modern industrial state. There were, however, many survivals of the past, the change was slow and gradual, and there is no justification for speaking of a Russian industrial revolution, as some historians do.

Foreign Relations

Continuity and Change. Seen as a whole, Russian foreign policy in the second half of the nineteenth century presents curious elements of continuity and change. During that period Russia had but two foreign ministers: Prince Alexander Gorchakov, from 1856 to 1882 (he became vice chancellor in 1862 and chancellor in 1867), and Nicholas Giers, from 1882 to 1895. Long tenure of office, however, did not ensure continuity of policy. Neither Gorchakov nor Giers was a statesman of deep conviction and vision, the views and policies of both being subject to brisk reversals under the pressure of events. Moreover, there were influences other than that of the titular head of the foreign ministry which at times determined Russia's foreign policies.

The Crimean War had shattered the traditional alignment of European powers. Post-war St. Petersburg was profoundly anti-English and anti-Austrian and, to a lesser degree, anti-French and anti-Prussian. Nevertheless the notion of the Holy Alliance survived and continued to influence the decisions of Alexander II and Alexander III and their advisors. It found itself in conflict with the desire, which had influential advocates in both St. Petersburg and Paris, for a *rapprochement* with France. Extreme hostility characterized Anglo-Russian relations throughout this period, while the Russian attitude towards Austria fluctuated from collaboration and alliance to almost open conflict. These trends form the background against which unfolded the policies of Russia as a member of the concert of European powers, her expansion in the Far East and in central Asia, her withdrawal from the American continent, the Balkan policies, and the fateful shift from the alliance with the Germanic powers to one with France.

Russia and the European National Movements. As a major European power Russia had a part in shaping the course of the movements for national unification and independence which swept over Europe. Gorchakov and Napoleon cooperated in establishing a unified Danubian state by the merger of the Turkish provinces of Moldavia and Wallachia (1858–1866), a policy opposed by England and Austria. In 1866 Russia made an unsuccessful attempt to block the election of Prince Charles of Hohenzollern to the throne of the principality of Rumania (as the new state was known after 1866). On this occasion France and Prussia, as well as England, opposed Russia, who withheld recognition of Rumania until 1868. Rumania became a kingdom in 1881.

St. Petersburg looked askance at the unification of Italy, whom it had indirectly assisted by maintaining an attitude of friendly neutrality towards Paris during the Franco-Austrian war that resulted in the speedy defeat of Austria (1859). To Alexander II and Gorchakov, Victor Emmanuel and Garibaldi were dangerous revolutionaries; moreover, St. Petersburg was much concerned—in the tradition of the Holy Alliance—with the fate of the legitimate rulers of the petty states swept away in the process of Italian unification.

The reaction of western Europe to the Polish insurrection of 1863 brought a new factor into the international situation. Great Britain, France, and Austria made sharply worded, albeit ineffectual, representations to Russia, in which several other states (but not the United States) concurred, while Prussia offered St. Petersburg her full support. This diplomatic episode, which did not help Poland, resulted in the further estrangement of Russia from France, England, and Austria, and in a *rapprochement* between Russia and Prussia.

In spite of their divergent views in other fields, Russia, Great Britain, and France succeeded in coordinating their policies in Greece, which, since her inception as an independent state, had been placed under their joint protection. The forced abdication and flight of King Otto (October 1862) raised the question of his successor. The protecting powers agreed without too great difficulty on Prince William of Denmark, who assumed the name of George I and was installed as king in 1863. A new crisis arose in Greece in 1867 when the people of Crete, instigated by Russian and Greek agents, demanded the incorporation of their island, which was a Turkish possession, in the Hellenic kingdom. Russia at first supported this claim; it was opposed by Britain. Turkey threatened naval action, and a hastily summoned international conference decided the issue in favor of Turkey. Gorchakov, abandoning his former position, acquiesced (January 1869).

The friendly attitude of Prussia during the Polish insurrection revitalized the tradition of monarchical solidarity uniting the courts of St. Petersburg and Berlin; the Russians, in turn, lent support to Bismarck in his struggle for Prussian supremacy in the Germanic world. They countenanced the annexation by Prussia in 1866 of the duchies of Schleswig and Holstein (formerly held by Denmark) that was an element in Bismarck's ultimate success. Assurance was given that Russia would never side with the enemies of Prussia and would neutralize any Austrian attempt to help France. This attitude of St. Petersburg was of great usefulness to Prussia in the war with France that led to the formation of the German empire (January 1871). Towards the end of the Franco-Prussian War (October 1870) Gorchakov dramatically announced the abrogation of the neutralization of the Black Sea clause of the Treaty of Paris (1856). This declaration, because of its unilateral nature, provoked a major diplomatic crisis for which there was no real ground: the signatories of the Treaty of Paris were in general agreement that the offending provision should be dropped. Its abrogation was confirmed, with some face-saving devices, by an international conference (March 1871). Another consequence of the Russo-Prussian *rapprochement* was a perfunctory reconciliation, sponsored by Bismarck, between St. Petersburg and Vienna that culminated in the conclusion in 1873 of the secret Alliance of the Three Emperors—of Russia, Germany, and Austria-Hungary (the Austrian empire became the Austro-Hungarian empire in 1867).

Expansion in the Far East. Russian expansion in the Far East and in central Asia, which was of greater importance to Russia and to the world than Gorchakov's much-advertised schemes, took place more or less spontaneously and by accident. The basic elements responsible for the Russian acquisition of vast territories in those remote regions were the weakness of China and of the lesser states in that area and the venturesome spirit and drive of a small group of Russian military leaders. Their policies were often at variance with those of the government and thrived on the inability of the central authority to control its own agents because of their remoteness from the capital and the absence of rapid communications.

Russia's initial thrust towards the Pacific was largely the work of Nicholas Muravev (later Count Muravev-Amursky), governor-general of eastern Siberia from 1847 to 1861. Beginning in 1850 he proceeded to invade the

Chinese-held territories along the Amur River and in 1852 crossed to Sakhalin Island. The city of Khabarovsk was founded in 1854 and the port of Vladivostok ("Ruler of the East") in 1860. The Russian conquest, which comprised an enormous area, was accomplished by a surprisingly small armed force that met practically no resistance. This was a period when the Celestial empire, torn by domestic strife and foreign wars, was compelled to make important concessions to the West. By the Treaty of Peking (1860) China recognized Russia's annexations and granted to her trading privileges in Mongolia and Chinese Turkestan.

After 1855 Sakhalin was under the joint administration of Russia and Japan, but in 1875 the Japanese ceded to Russia their rights to this island in exchange for the recognition of their own sovereignty over the Kurile Islands, which St. Petersburg had claimed as Russian territory. In the 1880's the rivalries of the Western powers and of Japan were extended to Manchuria and Korea, which for geographical reasons were of particular interest to Russia and Japan. Russian concern with this area was intensified by the building of the Trans-Siberian railway and the operations of the Russo-Chinese Bank, founded in 1895. In the spring of 1895 Russia, in concert with Germany and France, blocked the annexation by Japan of the Liaotung Peninsula; three years later (March 1898), in the general scramble of the European powers for territorial concessions in China that followed the seizure of Kiaochow by Germany (November 1897), St. Petersburg wangled from the Chinese a 25-year lease for the Liaotung Peninsula, with Port Arthur and Talienwan (Dalny). Therein lay the seeds of the Russo-Japanese War of 1904–1905.

Expansion in Central Asia. Expansion in central Asia followed a pattern somewhat similar to that in the Far East. In the middle of the nineteenth century there was no definite boundary between Siberia and the territory of central Asia inhabited by nomadic tribes (Kirghiz, Kalmyk, Turkoman, and others). Gradually, Russian military outposts and settlers advanced south and east and in the 1850's reached the borders of the settled Moslem khanates of Kokand, Khiva, and Bokhara. The conquest of these and adjacent regions began in the 1860's and was due largely to the endeavor (and insubordination) of three generals—M. G. Cherniaev, C. P. von Kaufmann, and M. D. Skobelev. In 1866 some of the territories held by Russia were formally annexed and became the governorship-general of Turkestan; in 1868 the khanates of Kokand and Bokhara, and the khanate of Khiva in 1873, were coerced into accepting the status of Russian protectorates. A revolt in Kokand brought upon that country a Russian punitive expedition, its autonomous government was abolished in 1876, and its territory was annexed by Russia and became the Ferghana region. Khiva and Bokhara retained the status of protectorates until the end of the empire.

In the 1870's and the 1880's Russia proceeded to conquer the vast regions inhabited by the Tekke Turkoman tribes east of the Caspian Sea. In 1881 Skobelev took the Turkoman stronghold Gheok Teppe; in 1884 the Russians seized Merv and in 1885 the Penjdeh district. These Russian advances in the Afghan region were watched with great nervousness in London as a threat to Herat, the "key" to India. In 1885 Great Britain and Russia appeared to be on the verge of war, but common sense prevailed and the Anglo-Russian dispute over the Afghan border was settled by negotiation in 1886 and 1887.

Somewhat earlier the long-drawn struggle in the Caucasus came to an end. The expansion and consolidation, under the treaties of Turkmanchai (1828) and Adrianople (1829), of Russian conquests in this difficult region were met with fierce resistance on the part of the freedom-loving mountaineers. The holy war of Islam broke out in 1830 and from 1834 was led by Shamil, who for a quarter of a century successfully defied the Russians until captured in 1859. The subjugation of the Caucasus was officially completed in 1864.

Sale of Alaska. The expansion in the Far East and in central Asia coincided with Russia's withdrawal from the American continent. In the second half of the eighteenth century Russian trappers, hunters, and adventurers began to settle on the Aleutian Islands, in Alaska, and along the northwestern coast of America. They were attracted by the prospects of a lucrative fur trade. In 1799 there was established the Russian-American Company, the agency of the imperial government in North America. A treaty between Russia and the United States (1824) regularized the position of the Russian colonies; their record, however, was unsatisfactory, and by the middle of the nineteenth century it became clear that they were economically unrewarding and politically dangerous. According to an official report (1863) the Russian colonies "present a picture of complete stagnation in all matters of colonization, industry, commerce and citizenship; in general the Company did not justify the confidence placed in it by the Government." It was believed that the colonies could not be defended and sooner or later would be taken over by Great Britain or the United States. Negotiations for the sale of the colonies to the United States began in 1854 and were completed in 1867. The purchase price was $7.2 million, that is, 2.2 million more than the minimum price the Russian negotiators were permitted to accept. The

Imperial Russia's expansion in Asia

O C E A N

Novosibirsk Ilds.

Lena

B   E   R   I   A

Indigirka   *Kolyma*

E   M   P   I   R   E

YAKUTSK

OKHOTSK

KAMCHATKA

Bering Sea

Sea of —
Okhotsk

1697
PETROPAVLOVSK

ALEUTIANS

1858-60

SAKHALIN   1875

MANCHURIA

Amur

1905 TO
JAPAN

KURILES

MUKDEN

VLADIVOSTOK

PEKING

PORT
ARTHUR   KOREA

TOKYO

J   A   P   A   N

	ACQUISITIONS OF PETER I.
	ACQUISITIONS OF ALEXANDER I.
	ACQUISITIONS OF NICHOLAS I.
	ACQUISITIONS OF ALEXANDER II.
	ACQUISITIONS OF ALEXANDER III.

transaction was criticized at the time in both countries, especially in the United States.

Pan-Slavism and the Turkish War, 1877–1878. Prior to the middle of the nineteenth century the Russian government took but sporadic and casual interest in the Balkans. After the Crimean War, however, a small but vocal and influential group of publicists and high officials (among them Pobedonostsev and Katkov) espoused Pan-Slavism, a doctrine that proclaimed the superiority of Slavic civilization and Eastern Christianity over those of the decadent West. For practical purposes the theories of the Pan-Slavs may be reduced to aggressive Russian nationalism and the imposition of Russian leadership on Slavic nations. The Pan-Slav movement experienced a remarkable but short-lived effervescence in 1876–1879.

In the summer of 1875 a revolt broke out among the Slavic population of the Turkish provinces of Bosnia and Herzegovina and in 1876 spread to Bulgaria, Serbia, and Montenegro, territories under Turkish rule. The Bulgarian revolt was suppressed by the Turks with a harshness that shocked the Western world. In the summer of 1876 Serbia and Montenegro declared war on Turkey; a wave of boundless enthusiasm for the Slavic brethren swept over Russian intellectuals and the clergy; some 5,000 Russian volunteers went to Serbia; and General Cherniaev, hero of conquests in central Asia, assumed the command of the Serbian army. The results of the Pan-Slav crusade were unrewarding. Within a few weeks the Serbs and the Montenegrins were defeated, Cherniaev and the volunteers ingloriously withdrew, the war was over, and Russian diplomatic intervention brought about the restoration of peace on the basis of the pre-war *status quo.* Serbia lost its popularity with the Russian Pan-Slavs, its place being taken by Bulgaria.

Russian Pan-Slavism never was a broad popular movement, and its sudden ascendancy was all the more puzzling because neither the emperor nor Gorchakov shared its doctrines. By the end of 1876, however, Russia was too committed to the cause of Slavdom to allow a retreat. The most influential advocate of intransigence was Count Nicholas P. Ignatev, an ardent Pan-Slav and Russian ambassador to Constantinople (1864–1877). Measures preparatory for war were taken by the St. Petersburg government in 1876. Troops and military supplies were massed on the Turkish borders, while Gorchakov negotiated an agreement with Austria that provided for the occupation by that country of Bosnia and Herzegovina in return for maintaining a benevolent neutrality (Reichstadt agreement, July 1876; confirmed in January 1877). Simultaneously the Russian government continued to press for a solution of the Balkan issue through international action. A conference of great powers held in Constantinople (December 1876–January 1877) drafted a program of reform to be enacted by Turkey that the Porte, counting on the support of England, refused to accept. Further negotiation having failed, Russia declared war on Turkey (April 1877).

The war, which was fought in the Danubian-Balkan area and in Transcaucasia, began with successes for the Russians, followed in the summer of 1877 by severe reverses. The tide of war turned again in Russia's favor towards the end of the year; in the Caucasus the Russians took the fortress of Kars (November), and in the Danubian theatre Plevna, an important Turkish road junction that had repulsed attacks in July and September, surrendered to the besieging Russians (December). The Turks were disorganized and staggering. In blinding snow the Russian troops surged over the Balkan passes, occupied Adrianople, and rapidly advanced towards Constantinople. In January 1878, the Porte, at its rope's end, accepted an armistice on Russian terms.

Victory, particularly a costly one, is not conducive to moderation. Early in 1878 Gorchakov's ingenious and carefully balanced diplomatic schemes were cast aside, and for a brief spell the control of Russian policy in the Balkans passed into the hands of Ignatev, who during the war had been attached to the tsar's army headquarters. By threatening the immediate occupation of Constantinople he coerced the Turks into accepting early in March 1878 the Treaty of San Stefano (the town where the negotiations were held, some six miles from Constantinople). The essence of this treaty was the creation of a large autonomous Bulgaria and an enlarged Montenegro, both dominated by Russia. It was believed by the Russian Pan-Slavs, as well as in London and Vienna, that this situation would eventually lead to the annexation by Russia of Constantinople and the Straits, a contingency that Great Britain and Austria-Hungary were determined to prevent. The English and Austrian governments made it clear that they would not countenance territorial changes which they regarded as contrary to their interests and violations of existing international agreements. Meanwhile Russian leaders came to realize that in spite of recent victories the position of the Russian army in Turkey was precarious. The nationalist and Pan-Slav fever subsided; Ignatev was dismissed in May; and, after discreet negotiations had brought about a measure of agreement between St. Petersburg and London, the Treaty of San Stefano came up for revision at a congress of the great powers held in Berlin in June–July 1878. Under the Treaty of Berlin, which superseded that of San Stefano, Bulgaria lost more than half of the territory assigned to her at San Stefano and was divided into the *politically* autonomous principality of Bulgaria, tributary to the sultan, and the *administratively* autonomous province of Eastern Rumelia "under the direct political and military auhority" of the Porte. Montenegro, too, was deprived of much of her San Stefano gains. Bosnia and Herzegovina were occupied and administered by Austria-Hungary. The independence of Montenegro, Serbia, and Rumania received official recognition. Russia's annexations were roughly similar to those she had made at San Stefano and comprised the districts of Bessarabia which she had lost in 1856 and territories in Asia Minor, including Kars and Batum. Rumania was compensated for the loss of Bessarabia, which she vainly tried to resist, by the annexation of Dobrudja. The Russian agencies for the administration of the Balkans instituted at San Stefano were replaced by European commissions.

Viewed by itself the Treaty of Berlin was a victory for Russia, but the manner in which it was brought about and comparison with San Stefano made it appear as a crushing defeat; it was interpreted as such by Russian nationalist and Pan-Slav opinion. There was much resentment in official Russian circles of the attitude of Austria-Hungary and Germany, and particularly that of Bismarck, who had presided at the Berlin congress. These sentiments, however, proved to be but a passing mood, and the alliance of the three emperors was revived for three years in 1881.

Russia and Bulgaria. The enforcement of the Treaty of Berlin, which called for a reshuffling of national territories and an extensive revision of frontiers, met with determined resistance in some cases (Albania, Bosnia and Herzegovina, Rumania). The fact that Russia occupied much of the Balkans was a source of great uneasiness. Contrary to the expectations prevalent in European capitals, Russian troops were withdrawn from Turkey without delay (March 1879) and from Bulgaria in the summer of 1879, as provided by the treaty. In the spring of that year Emperor Alexander II approved a constitution for Bulgaria, which, though prepared by Russian officials, was extensively revised in the direction of parliamentary democracy by a Bulgarian national assembly at Tyrnovo. With the consent of the great powers Alexander of Battenberg, a kin of both the Russian empress and the queen of England, was elected prince of Bulgaria (April 1879). He was at first on excellent terms with St. Petersburg, and numerous Russian officers were employed in the Bulgarian army and administration. The Russo-Bulgar cooperation, however, was of brief duration; the stormy rule of Prince Alexander was filled with sharp clashes with the St. Petersburg government and with his Russian advisers and ended with his forced abdication in September 1886. Ironically, one cause of disagreement was the unification of the principality of Bulgaria with Eastern Rumelia, which Russia had at first vigorously sponsored but which she opposed in 1886 when it was accomplished under the leadership of Prince Alexander, who in the meantime had fallen from Russian favor. In spite of Russia's strenuous opposition, Battenberg was succeeded by Ferdinand of Saxe-Coburg-Gotha (1887). In protest Russia withheld her recognition of the new prince (he was to assume royal status in 1908) until 1895, a sad epilogue to the Pan-Slav crusade. Nevertheless, the war of 1877–1878 lives in the Russian and Slavic tradition as "the war of liberation," and its effects continue to be felt in the twentieth century.

The French Alliance. There had been a major change in Russia's international alignment. The secret alliance of Russia, Germany, and Austria-Hungary, concluded in 1881, was renewed for three years at the expiration of its term in 1884. Meanwhile Alexander III's dislike for Vienna was intensified by the conflict of Russian and Austrian policies in the Balkans, and when the treaty came up for extension in 1887, the tsar refused his consent. Instead, Russia and Germany concluded a treaty of alliance, the so-called "re-insurance treaty," which was to remain in force for three years. In 1890, when the renewal of the treaty was regarded as virtually assured, Bismarck, whose fixed policy it was to prevent a Franco-Russian alliance, was forced out of office. His successor, Chancellor Count Caprivi, decided against the renewal of the Russian treaty on the ground that it was incompatible with the Triple Alliance (Germany, Austria-Hungary, and Italy) concluded in 1882. The Russian foreign minister Giers, a supporter of the alliance with Germany (and Austria-Hungary), was distressed and tried to persuade Berlin to change its position. Meeting with no response, Giers turned to France. The idea of a Franco-Russian alliance was not novel and had influential friends in both countries. The floating of large Russian loans on the French market facilitated the *rapprochement.* Formal negotiations for a Franco-Russian alliance, begun in 1891, were consummated in December 1893–January 1894. Its terms remained secret until revealed by the Soviets in 1918. The severance of political ties between Russia and Germany was soon to prove fatal to both imperial regimes.

The Revolutionary Movement

The Background. It is clear, with the benefit of hindsight, that the rise of the revolutionary movement was the most portentous Russian develop-

ment in the second half of the nineteenth century. Peasant uprisings had occurred frequently in the past, but the Decembrist rebellion (1825) was the
first attempt at overthrowing autocracy by an organized group. Its suppression and the fate of its leaders had a lasting deterrent effect. During most
of the stern reign of Nicholas I, radical-minded intellectuals shunned political and social issues and dwelt in the ivory tower of philosophical speculations. The European revolution of 1848, Russia's defeat in the Crimean War,
and, later, the reforms of Alexander II caused a revival of revolutionary
fermentation, which differed from its predecessor: the Decembrists were
aristocrats and army officers, while the revolutionaries of the 1860's came
from every class of society.

An outstanding figure of the revolutionary movement of this period was
Alexander Herzen (1812–1870). A man of culture, he spent most of his adult
life abroad and from 1858 to 1867 published in London a journal *Kolokol*
(The Bell) that was widely read in Russia and for a time exercised great
influence. Herzen was primarily concerned with social and economic issues
and, especially during the earlier part of his career, relied on the Crown
for the introduction of essential reforms. He at first welcomed the emancipation acts of 1861 but almost immediately became one of their most unsparing critics. In 1863 he espoused the cause of Poland, an unpopular attitude that cost him much of his following. Herzen coined (in 1861) two
slogans which profoundly affected revolutionary thinking and the course of
the revolutionary movement: "land and freedom" (*zemlia i volia*) and "to
the people" (*v narod*), the latter an admonition to young people to carry
on revolutionary propaganda among the peasants.

Populism. Herzen was one of the several authors whose doctrines came
to be known as populism (*narodnichestvo*). Other prominent members of
this movement were Chernyshevsky, Dobroliubov, Lavrov, Mikhailovsky,
Bakunin, Tkachev, and Nechaev. The essence of their teaching was that
Russia's political and economic order was doomed and must be overthrown
by a socialist revolution. The peasant land commune (*obshchina*) and cooperative associations of working men (*artel*), allegedly purely national institutions containing the elements of socialist society, set Russia apart from
western Europe and made it unnecessary for her to pass through the stage
of capitalism before reaching the socialist stage. According to the populists,
the peasantry was the moving force of a revolution; later, they emphasized
the importance of political terror as a revolutionary weapon. The doctrines
of populism have been well described as "peasant socialism" (Lenin).

Populism commanded a sizable following and succeeded in establishing

Michael Bakunin, photograph by Nadar

Alexander Herzen, photograph by Nadar

a number of underground organizations. Its leaders, while in general agreement on questions of doctrine, were divided on strategy and tactics. In the 1860's and early 1870's the prevalent view was that the peasantry was ready —or nearly ready—for an uprising; the revolutionaries had merely to carry on propaganda in the countryside. This naive belief was responsible for the movement "to the people" in the summers of 1873 and 1874, when thousands of young propagandists of both sexes, disguised as peasants, invaded rural Russia to preach the revolutionary gospel. Their efforts brought no response, however. The peasants were bewildered, sometimes interested, but more often suspicious. The police were on the tracks of the revolutionaries; there were mass arrests followed by mass trials, but no revolt by the peasants. The attempt at "going to the people" was repeated, in a slightly different form, in 1877 and 1878 but proved equally unsuccessful.

The failure of the crusade "to the people" led to a change of heart and a revision of revolutionary tactics. Under the new dispensation the struggle against autocracy and for socialism was to be conducted primarily by the intellectuals, the leaders of the masses, rather than by the masses themselves. Land and Freedom, an underground populist organization established in 1876–1878 (an earlier organization bearing the same name existed from 1862 to 1864), adopted political terror as a legitimate weapon. The campaign of political assassinations that followed was fostered by the case of Vera Zasulich, a young revolutionary who attempted to murder, and severely wounded, the military governor of St. Petersburg, General F. F. Trepov. Her action was a reprisal for Trepov's mistreating a political prisoner. Zasulich did not personally know either Trepov or his victim. She was acquitted by the jury amidst scenes of wild enthusiasm (March 1878).

The revolutionaries took heart. In June 1879 Land and Freedom decided that the assassination of Alexander II was to be its chief and immediate objective. The execution of this bloody assignment became the task of People's Will, a populist organization that evolved from Land and Freedom in October 1879. Its leaders were Sophie Perovsky, the daughter of a former governor-general of St. Petersburg, and Andrew Zheliabov, who came from a peasant family. People's Will organized with great resourcefulness and daring at least seven attempts against the life of the tsar. On one occasion the revolutionaries blew up a railway track over which the imperial train was traveling and on another exploded a bomb under the banquet hall of the Winter Palace shortly before an official dinner. Alexander II was finally killed by a bomb on March 1, 1881.

Beginnings of Russian Marxism. The murder of the tsar so ardently desired by the People's Will accomplished nothing of significance: Alexander II was succeeded by Alexander III and one reactionary government by another even more reactionary. Members of People's Will were arrested or fled abroad, but the organization continued for several years. One of the last major endeavors of the populists was the attempt against the life of Alexander III (March 1887) for which Alexander Ulianov, Lenin's older brother, was executed. Towards the end of the century the populists became known as socialist revolutionaries.

Disillusionment with populism led some of the Russian radicals towards Marxism. Although a Russian section of Marx's First International was formed by émigrés in Geneva in 1870 and a Russian translation of Volume I of Marx's *Capital* (published in 1867) appeared in 1872, prior to any other foreign translation, Marxism was slow in making converts in Russia. An early outstanding Russian Marxist was George Plekhanov (1857–1918), a former populist who broke with Land and Freedom in 1879 and in 1883 founded in Geneva the first Russian social-democratic organization, Liberation of Labor. According to its program Russian historical development was not different from that of other European countries; the peasant land commune was not a precursor of socialism, and Russia, like other countries, would have to go through the capitalist stage before establishing a socialist society; the socialist revolution could be accomplished only by the industrial proletariat, not by the peasantry; a closely-knit revolutionary party rather than political terror was necessary for the success of the revolution. Meanwhile Marxist groups began to appear in Russia and engaged in vehement polemics with the populists. As events were to show, the most important convert to Marxism was Lenin. In 1895, under his and Julius Martov's leadership, some 20 Marxist groups in St. Petersburg merged into the Fighting Union for the Liberation of the Working Class, which carried on intensive revolutionary propaganda among the workers. In March 1898 nine delegates of Marxist organizations—none of them outstanding leaders—assembled in Minsk and founded the Russian Social Democratic Labor Party, precursor of the Communist Party of the Soviet Union. This modest beginning passed practically unnoticed.

16

Closing Years of the Empire, 1894-1914

The Last Tsar

Nicholas II. Emperor Nicholas II, who succeeded his father Alexander III in 1894, was born in 1868. He received a good education, spoke foreign languages well, and had traveled extensively in Russia and abroad. A man of limited abilities, both weak and obstinate, Nicholas was retiring, affable, and deeply religious. He shared the reactionary views of his tutor Pobedonostsev, including a strong aversion towards representative government, which he eventually found himself compelled to grant in Russia. Prior to his accession Nicholas took but a perfunctory part in the conduct of the affairs of state.

The Empress and Rasputin. The tsar was married to Princess Alice of Hesse-Darmstadt, a granddaughter of Queen Victoria of England. Alexandra Fedorovna, as the empress was known in Russia, was a highly-strung neurotic woman and, after her conversion to Greek Orthodoxy, a devout member of the Russian Church. Her union with Nicholas was an exceptionally happy one and led to the birth of four daughters and finally (1904) of a son, Alexis, heir to the Russian throne. It soon appeared, however, that the infant was suffering from an incurable ailment, hemophilia, which was hereditary in the male line of the house of Hesse and was transmitted to

Tsar Nicholas II and Alix, 1904

Alexis by his mother. This intimate family tragedy had important political repercussions. Science had no remedy for hemophilia, which manifests itself in severe bleedings, and the empress, in her distress, sought the guidance and assistance of charlatans and impostors. The most notable among them was Gregory Rasputin, a depraved illiterate peasant and unordained religious teacher (*starets*) from Siberia. Introduced to the imperial couple in 1905,

The Bettmann Archive

Rasputin

he is reliably reported to have succeeded on several occasions in stopping the bleedings of Alexis. This inexplicable success—according to some reports Rasputin was endowed with hypnotic power and was trained by a professional medium—made him appear to the tsarina and her consort as the God-sent protector of the heir to the throne. Rasputin's loose living and association with adventurers, which were ignored by his imperial patrons, created a scandal, and his presence at court attracted much attention, especially in 1911 and 1912, but it was not until the outbreak of World War I and the departure of the tsar for the army that his influence became all-powerful.

The Opposition: Liberal and Revolutionary

The Liberals. The closing decade of the nineteenth century witnessed a development novel in Russian history: the appearance of an organized opposition, that is, a coherent body of opinion critical of official policies and agitating for reform; its more extreme elements merged with the revolutionary movement whose origins went back to the earlier nineteenth century. The emergence of the liberal opposition may be traced to the famine and epidemic of cholera of 1891-1892, when the government found itself compelled to allow considerable leeway to non-bureaucratic agencies, especially the *zemstvos,* in organizing relief work. Common endeavor unfettered by official controls whetted the desire of the liberal-minded Russians for a broader field of public activity. The *zemstvos'* original program centered on two issues: popular representation in central government and the creation of a national organization of the *zemstvos.* Beginning in 1896 conferences of *zemstvo* leaders, although not authorized by the government, met at irregular intervals and from 1901 to 1906 functioned as a quasi-permanent institution, their resolutions acquiring an increasingly political and aggressive character. The government retaliated by curtailing the already limited powers of the *zemstvos,* and there were persistent rumors that they might be abolished.

The political campaign of the liberal *zemstvo* leaders met with the wholehearted support of like-minded men in every walk of life. In 1902 there was founded in Stuttgart a radical Russian newspaper *Osvobozhdenie* (Liberation), which advocated the introduction of a constitutional regime in Russia. The Union of Liberation, a *zemstvo*-sponsored underground organization, was formed early in 1904. Its object was to agitate for a representative government on a broad democratic basis. A similar program was pressed by 14 professional unions (those of university professors, teachers, doctors, pharmacists, journalists, and so on) which came into existence and in May 1905 established the Union of Unions.

The Bolsheviks and the Mensheviks. The rise of the liberal opposition coincided with the consolidation and growth of the revolutionary movement. Although the Russian Social Democratic Labor Party, founded in Minsk in 1898, had an inauspicious beginning—its central committee as well as those of the organizations represented at the Minsk congress were arrested—it proved an important rallying point of Marxist opinion. At the Second Party Congress, which was held in London in June 1903 and adopted the party program and charter, there occurred the fateful cleavage of the party into the Bolshevik (majority) and Menshevik (minority) factions. The immediate causes of the cleavage were trivial: the struggle for control, which proved ephemeral, by conflicting groups of delegates of the party central committee and of the editorial board of *Iskra* (The Spark), the party newspaper. It soon became clear, however, that the division had a deeper significance.

While the Bolshevik-Menshevik differences elude precise definition, it is broadly correct to say that most of the time the Bolsheviks, led by Lenin, upheld a more extreme and uncompromising position than did the Mensheviks. Both factions agreed on the necessity and imminence of the revolution. The Bolsheviks, however, held, although not consistently, that the overthrow of the monarchy would be followed immediately by the establishment of the dictatorship of the proletariat and that no lasting cooperation with the bourgeois liberal groups was necessary or permissible. The Mensheviks took the view that a successful revolution would usher in a protracted period of democracy during which the social democrats should collaborate with the liberal *bourgeoisie:* the socialist commonwealth of the future was to be born of this collaboration. The other basic issue was one of party organization. Both factions shared the belief in the leading role of the party in the revolution and in the building of socialism; but the Bolsheviks advocated rigid authoritarian centralism in party organization, while the Mensheviks favored a more flexible "democratic" approach. Much of the time and energy of the Marxist leaders was spent in mutual recriminations and in quarrels with other revolutionary groups. The Bolshevik-Menshevik cleavage was formalized in 1905, but a perfunctory reconciliation took place in 1906. At the Sixth Party Congress, however, held in Stockholm in 1912, the Bolsheviks succeeded in expelling the Mensheviks from the party. The two factions, their disagreements notwithstanding, carried on intense revolutionary propaganda among the industrial workers.

The Socialist Revolutionaries. The socialist revolutionaries, heirs to the populists, formed the second main stream of the revolutionary movement. An underground Socialist Revolutionary Party loosely uniting the scattered populist groups was organized in 1900 but did not acquire a program and a charter until 1906. The socialist revolutionaries, like the social democrats, believed in the imminence and inevitability of the revolution, but unlike the Marxists, they put their faith in the revolutionary proclivities of the peasantry and the efficacy of political terror. Political assassinations were carefully planned and executed by the Fighting (Terroristic) Organization of the party. The leader and the principal theorist of the party was Victor Chernov, and the most notable terrorist Evno Azef, who was simultaneously an agent of the security police. His treachery was exposed in 1908. The socialist revolutionaries, in the populist tradition, centered their propaganda on the peasantry.

Popular Unrest. The agitation of the opposition, both liberal and revolutionary, fell on fertile ground. The universities, which were relatively quiet in the 1880's, became again the scene of violent political outbreaks and in 1899 were closed for several months. Strikes of unprecedented violence took place in the industrial centers, especially in St. Petersburg and Moscow, while the countryside was ablaze with agrarian disturbances. These were the unmistakable signs of the approaching crisis.

The opposition took advantage of this situation to press its demands. There was an intensification in the pace of the agitation for reforms, especially after a conference in Paris in September 1904 of the representatives of the radical and revolutionary organizations. The Bolsheviks and the Mensheviks did not take part in the conference, but the national minority groups (Finnish, Polish, Georgian, Armenian, Latvian) sent delegates. The conference directed its members to carry on, by methods left to their discretion, the struggle for the overthrow of autocracy and for social reform. Meanwhile the socialist revolutionaries embarked on a campaign of political assassinations. Their first notable victim was the minister of education, N. P. Bogolepov (1901), followed by many others, among them the two successive highly reactionary ministers of the interior, D. S. Sipiagin (1902) and V. K. von Plehve (1904). The unexpectedly disastrous course of the Russo-Japanese War, which began in February 1904, fostered public unrest and disaffection.

The Revolution of 1905. Unnerved and shaken the government attempted to stem the tide of discontent by making minor concessions to the opposition. In August 1904 Plehve was succeeded as minister of the interior by Prince P. D. Sviatopolk-Mirsky, a man of conciliatory disposition who endeavored to win the support of moderate liberal opinion by repealing the more unpopular restrictive measures then in force. The "political spring," as his administration was known, was brief. In St. Petersburg on January 9, 1905, a monster demonstration of workers bearing a petition to the tsar and led by the priest George Gapon (who was both a socialist revolutionary and an agent of the security police) was fired upon by the troops. A large number of demonstrators were killed or wounded. Sviatopolk-Mirsky resigned, while the "bloody Sunday" spurred revolutionary agitation: in February the socialist revolutionaries murdered the Grand Duke Serge Alexandrovich, military governor of Moscow and the tsar's uncle and brother-in-law.

A few days later (February 18) the government announced its decision to summon an *advisory* (that is, not a *legislative*) representative assembly. This tardy and pusillanimous move satisfied no one, the *zemstvos* and other liberal groups clamoring for the convocation of a *constituent* assembly. Disaffection spread to the armed forces: in June a mutiny broke out on the battleship *Potemkin* of the Black Sea fleet. Waves of Jewish pogroms, of which few occurred in the 1880's and the 1890's, swept over southern and western Russia. They were organized by the ultra-nationalist Russian elements and thrived on the inaction and connivance of the authorities. The publication in August of a law for the elections to the proposed consultative assembly that gave a large representation to the peasantry but, by requiring high property qualifications from urban voters, practically disfranchised industrial workers and intellectuals caused another explosion of anti-governmental feelings. A general strike begun in October brought the life of the country to a standstill. On October 13 the St. Petersburg Soviet of Workers' Deputies—a purely revolutionary assembly and precursor of the present Soviet government—met for the first time; the first issue of its official newspaper *Izvestiia* (News) appeared on October 17.

On the same day Emperor Nicholas signed a manifesto written by Serge Witte that guaranteed fundamental civil liberties (freedom from arrest, freedom of opinion, of the press, of assembly, and of association), promised to extend the franchise provided by the law of August, and proclaimed that no law would be promulgated without the approval of the State Duma—Russia's new parliament—which was also to exercise control over the executive. By a stroke of the emperor's pen Russia became a constitutional monarchy.

The publication of the October manifesto was greeted by a wild outburst of enthusiasm and led to a gradual ebbing of the revolutionary tide. Yet it took time before a semblance of order was restored. The general strike petered out. Peasant revolts were suppressed by punitive expeditions. The entire bureau of the Peasants' Union, an underground revolutionary organization formed in August 1905, was arrested in November. The St. Petersburg Soviet of Workers' Deputies, in which Trotsky played a leading part, was dispersed early in December, and its members found themselves behind bars. An armed uprising attempted in Moscow was easily defeated by government troops. Order in Finland was restored by abrogating legislation, enacted in 1899, that the Finns regarded as unconstitutional. Polish demands for independence or autonomy were silenced by punitive expeditions. Mutinies in the armed forces, especially along the Trans-Siberian line, were gradually brought under control. By the end of 1905 the revolution had spent itself.

It is noteworthy that although the Soviet was the acknowledged and militant central organ of the revolution, only 52 of the 300 deputies arrested were brought to trial; of those tried, 16 were found guilty and the balance acquitted. Trotsky received a life sentence in Siberia but escaped before reaching his destination, and after spending some time in St. Petersburg and Finland he went abroad.

The Constitutional Monarchy

The Fundamental Laws, 1906. Serge Witte, father of the manifesto of October 17, is a controversial figure in Russian historiography. He was minister of finance from 1892 to 1903, when, because of his disagreement with Russia's Far Eastern policy, he was relegated to the honorary position of president of the committee of ministers. In 1905 Witte headed the Russian delegation to the peace conference at Portsmouth, New Hampshire, that terminated the Russo-Japanese War and was rewarded with the title of count. In politics he claimed to be an admirer of Alexander III, but at times —as in October 1905—he favored the liberal solution. Emperor Nicholas and Empress Alexandra came to look upon Witte, especially after the October manifesto, as a dangerous revolutionary. Nevertheless, in 1905 he appeared to be the only man capable of dealing with the situation, and he was appointed president of the newly-created council of ministers (October 19). His attempts to include in his administration representatives of the opposition were unsuccessful, and the ministry he formed consisted exclusively of seasoned bureaucrats. The refusal of the opposition leaders to participate in the government was unfortunate, because it deprived the liberals of any part in framing the legislation that transformed Russia into a constitutional monarchy; this was published on April 23, 1906, as the Fundamental Laws.

These statutes failed to live up to the promises of the October manifesto. Under the amended laws, freedom of the press, speech, and assembly continued to be narrowly circumscribed. The new parliament consisted of two chambers (instead of one, as stated in the October manifesto): the State Duma and the State Council. The State Duma was elected on the basis of a restricted franchise. One-half of the members of the State Council, which was the upper house, were appointed by the Crown; the other half were elected by designated groups (clergy, nobility, commerce and industry) and institutions (*zemstvos,* the academy of science, the universities, the Finnish diet). No law could be passed without the affirmative vote of the two houses and the assent of the Crown. Nevertheless the powers of the chambers were limited: about one-third of the budget was exempt from parliamentary supervision, and parliament exercised no effective control over the executive —the ministers continued to be responsible to the emperor alone. The Fundamental Laws could not be amended except on the initiative of the Crown.

The publication of the Fundamental Laws was greeted by a storm of protest from the liberal groups. Meanwhile Witte, exasperated by the hostility of the tsar and the criticism heaped upon him from right and left, tendered his resignation, which was accepted (April 22, 1906) five days before the convocation of the first State Duma. He was succeeded by I. L. Goremykin, an elderly colorless bureaucrat of unimpeachable conservatism.

The Constitutional Regime in Action. The introduction of a democratic representative regime in a backward, largely illiterate country having little experience in self-government presented immense difficulties. Prior to 1905 Russia had no political parties in the Western meaning of the term: the Social Democratic and the Socialist Revolutionary parties were underground political organizations. A number of political parties were organized in the closing months of 1905. On the extreme right was the disreputable Union of the Russian People, led by the notorious Jew-baiter and instigator of pogroms, Dr. A. I. Dubrovin. In spite of its criminal record the Union was under the patronage of the tsar and counted among its members many high officials, among the Pobedonostsev and Goremykin. Bourgeois and conservative but sedate and respectable was the Union of October 17, which took its stand on the October manifesto. Its leader was Alexander Guchkov, a member of a well-known Moscow merchant family. Further to the left was the Constitutional Democratic (or Cadet) Party, which was launched by the *zemstvo* leaders and the Union of Unions, represented the flower of Russian liberalism, and was led by the distinguished historian, Professor P. N. Miliukov. Its program, approved in January 1906, demanded a parliamentary regime under a constitutional monarchy (although many liberals favored a republic), full powers for the State Duma in framing a new constitution, and comprehensive social and economic reforms, including the expropriation of large estates, subject to compensation, and the allocation of land among the peasants. Immediately to the left of the Constitutional Democratic Party was the Labor Group (*Trudoviki*), a merger of ten splinter factions more radical than the Cadets but less so than the social democrats and the socialist revolutionaries. The number of parties was large: at least 26 parties and 16 national groups, chiefly of radical affiliation, were represented in the first Duma. With the appearance of the political parties and, later, of the Duma the conference of the *zemstvos* was discontinued, and the Union of Unions and the professional unions which formed it went out of existence.

The first State Duma was elected under the law of August 1905, which, even as amended in December of that year, gave a large representation to the peasantry: it was believed in palace and bureaucratic circles that peasant deputies would form a solid conservative bloc in parliament. About 200 of the 524 members of the first Duma were peasants, but they failed to live up to the expectations of the legislators, joined left-wing parties, and voted solidly for a radical land reform. The parties of the right did not elect a single deputy. The socialist revolutionaries and the social democrats boycotted the election, Lenin having opposed participation on the mistaken assumption that the country was on the verge of an armed uprising. The Duma was actually dominated by the Constitutional Democratic Party (some 180 deputies) and the Labor Group (100 deputies). It was inaugurated on April 27, 1906.

The "address to the throne" adopted by the quasi-unanimous vote of the Duma and embodying the demands of the program of the Constitutional Democratic Party, which included the expropriation of large estates, was peremptorily rejected by the government, while the parliamentary vote of non-confidence was ignored. As highly secret negotiations for the formation of a liberal ministry, which, curiously, were inspired by reactionary palace circles, failed, the Duma was dissolved early in July 1906. Simultaneously Goremykin was dismissed and was succeeded as president of the council of ministers by P. A. Stolypin, a provincial administrator of strongly nationalistic leanings who had held the office of minister of the interior in the Goremykin cabinet.

Realizing the value of the Duma as a sounding board for revolutionary propaganda, the Social Democratic and the Socialist Revolutionary parties abandoned the policy of boycott and participated in the elections to the second Duma, which was to meet in February 1907. The new assembly proved even less manageable than its predecessor. The number of deputies of the Constitutional Democratic Party, which was attacked from the left and discriminated against by the government, was reduced by one-half, to slightly over 90. The socialist parties and the Labor Group had over 100 deputies each. The moderate conservatives were represented by some 30 deputies, and there was a small faction (20 members) of the extreme right, led by V. M. Purishkevich, a notorious reactionary and anti-Semite. The balance of the deputies belonged predominantly to national groups. The supporters of the government being hopelessly outnumbered and party feelings running high, cooperation between parliament and the executive was precluded. The conflict centered on the Stolypin land reform (to be discussed in the next section), which was enacted in November 1906 as a temporary measure without the approval of parliament. However, the official pretext for the dissolution that was ordered on June 3, 1907, was the unwillingness of the Duma to waive the parliamentary immunity of the Social Democratic deputies who were accused of sedition. These charges were presumably a frame-up staged by the security police.

Simultaneously with the dissolution decree came the new election law, which, through an intricate system of indirect voting and the segregation of the voters into electoral colleges, drastically reduced the representation of the peasantry and of the national minorities and increased that of the proprietary groups. This statute, promulgated without the approval of parliament and a violation of the Fundamental Laws, achieved its immediate objective. The third Duma (November 1907 to June 1912) was dominated by the conservatives. The opposition was in a hopeless minority: the Constitutional Democratic Party was represented by some 50 deputies and the Social Democrats and the Labor Group by 14 each. The fourth and last Duma (November 1912 to February 1917) was even more to the right than its predecessor. The socialist revolutionaries boycotted the elections to the third and the fourth Dumas. As was intended, parliaments elected under the law of June 3, 1907, proved docile and cooperative, even though the fourth Duma, aroused by the military reverses during World War I and the Rasputin scandal, displayed in 1915 and 1916 an unexpected spirit of independence.

Political Stabilization. The defeat of the 1905 revolution notwithstanding, the two years immediately following were stormy. There were many who shared Lenin's view that mass insurrection was imminent. After the dissolution of the first Duma (July 1906) some 200 deputies, among them over 100 members of the Constitutional Democratic Party, signed in Viborg, Finland, an appeal urging the population to refuse, until the convocation of the next Duma, to pay taxes or comply with army drafts. The appeal had no practical results except that the trial and conviction of the signatories made them ineligible for service in the Duma, thus depriving the opposition of many of its leaders. Mutinies flared up in the armed forces, including the garrison of Kronstadt near St. Petersburg, and there was a massive resurgence of political terror. In 1906 and 1907 over 4,000 people, chiefly government officials of various ranks, were murdered by the socialist revolutionaries. In 1908, however, partly because of the exposure of the employment of Azef (a leading terrorist) by the security police, terror declined markedly. The ruthless policies of the government in suppressing the revolution appeared to be successful: the revolutionary organizations were in disarray and their leaders either in exile abroad (Lenin, Trotsky) or in Siberia (Stalin).

Yet Stolypin's methods, effective as they were, were not conducive to the establishment of the rule of law (*pravovoi poriadok*) that he claimed to be his aim. The election law of June 3, 1907, responsible for the conservative third and fourth Dumas, was passed in violation of the Fundamental Laws. Stolypin made extensive and unwarranted use of a constitutional provision (Article 87) that allowed the government to promulgate emergency legislation when parliament was not in session, subject to subsequent ratification by the chambers. His flamboyant nationalism manifested itself chiefly in the persecution of national minorities—Poles, Finns, Ukrainians, and of course the Jews. A Russian law of June 1910, promulgated in violation of the Finnish constitution without the consent of the Finnish diet, curtailed the powers of the Finnish parliament. Stolypin, moreover, leaned heavily on the security police and in his capacity as minister of the interior condoned and encouraged the use of *agents provocateurs*. He was himself a victim of this vicious system. In August 1906 his summer residence on the Aptekarsky Island was blown up with the loss of 32 lives; the minister's son and daughter were injured, but he was unharmed. The attempt was organized by a socialist revolutionary who was also an agent of the security police. Another *agent provocateur* shot and fatally wounded Stolypin at a gala performance held in the imperial presence at the Kiev opera house in September 1911. By that time his political career was practically over, and his dismissal was generally expected.

Stolypin was succeeded as president of the council of ministers by V. N. Kokovtsov, a bureaucrat of the traditional school and minister of finance, an office that he continued to hold after he became president of the council. Kokovtsov claimed in his memoirs that he had enjoyed his relationship with the third and fourth Dumas. He had, however, little liking or respect for representative institutions and condoned the election of R. V. Malinovsky, an undercover security police agent, to the fourth Duma, where he led the small Bolshevik faction. Malinovksy resigned in 1914, went abroad, returned to Russia after the revolution, and was executed by the Soviets.

Kokovtsov, created a count, was dismissed in January 1914. Goremykin, aged 75 and suffering from senility but a believer in autocracy and a friend of Rasputin, was appointed president of the council of ministers. He remained at the head of the imperial government during the first year and a half of the World War.

Economic Conditions and Policies

The Wind of Change. Russia's economy, like her constitutional structure, underwent important changes in the two decades preceding the war. In both cases much of the traditional arrangement was retained, yet the elements of novelty were significant and held the possibility of further evolution and advance.

The Gold Standard. The financial and economic policies of this period were largely shaped by Witte, minister of finance from 1892 to 1903, and by Kokovtsov, who held that office (with but a brief interruption in 1905–1906) from 1904 to 1914. Witte was a protagonist of an economic development that was to be achieved by attracting foreign investments. One obstacle to the implementation of this program was the state of the Russian monetary system. Since the introduction by Catherine II of the paper ruble, which soon came to fluctuate widely in terms of precious metals and foreign exchanges, Russia had lived under a regime of inconvertible paper currency. Several attempts in the nineteenth century to link the ruble to gold or silver failed because of heavy war outlays and the temptation to meet current expenditure by the use of the printing press. The fact that in the 1880's and 1890's Russia was not engaged in any major war and that Witte's predecessors at the ministry of finance adhered to conservative monetary policies permitted the accumulation by the treasury of a sizable reserve of precious metals and foreign currencies, and the maintenance of the volume of paper rubles in circulation at a stable level.

Witte took advantage of this situation. His monetary reform, which is usually dated 1897 although it actually extended over a period of six years, introduced a new paper ruble freely convertible into gold coins; it also stipulated a limit between the size of the monetary reserve and the volume of paper currency in circulation. A currency based on gold and a stable rate of exchange have obvious advantages and favored the flow of foreign capital into Russia. These benefits, however, were purchased at a price. In view of the state of Russia's international accounts, the only long-range method of preventing the outflow of gold that would force the eventual suspension of convertibility was to maintain a favorable balance of trade, that is, an excess of exports over imports. By far the more important article of Russian exports was grain, which had to be shipped abroad irrespective of prices and conditions of domestic supplies, even in years of famine. According to a Russian minister of finance, "we may starve but we have to export grain"—hardly an attractive program. The gold standard came under a severe strain at the end of the Japanese war but was saved from disaster by a timely French loan. Convertibility was suspended, however, with the outbreak of World War I and has never been fully restored since.

Public Debt, Budget, and Taxation. The state of Russia's national accounts during the two decades prior to World War I suggests steady economic advance. While the public debt increased from 4.9 billion rubles in 1892 to 8.8 billion at the end of 1913, the service of the debt in the latter year accounted for less than 14 per cent of the total expenditure. Much of the increase was due to outlays on railway construction. Total expenditure rose from 1.06 billion rubles in 1890 to 3.38 billion in 1913. There was invariably a budget surplus, except during the war and revolutionary years of 1904–1906. The methods of financing, however, were those of a backward country. On the eve of World War I four-fifths of the revenue was derived from indirect taxation. The chief single source of revenue was the state monopoly of the sale of liquor, which was introduced in 1893 and in 1913 provided 28 per cent of the total budget revenue, operated some 26,000 retail stores, and sold annually 290 million gallons of vodka. The almost exclusive use of strong intoxicants explains the prevalence of drunkenness, although the per head consumption of alcohol in Russia was lower than in the western European countries. After the dismissal of Kokovtsov the government, while retaining the monopoly, embarked on a jejune program for the promotion of temperance. A few months later, with the outbreak of World War I, the monopoly was unexpectedly abolished.

Railways. Railway construction continued on a large scale along the lines adopted by the government in 1880, that is, with the active participation of the state. The length of the network increased from 22,000 miles in 1895 to 41,000 miles in 1912. The greatest railway enterprise was the Trans-Siberian line, 3,800 miles long. Construction began in 1891 and was completed in 1904 during the Russo-Japanese war. The difficulties encountered were formidable. About two-thirds of the railway mileage was owned by the state. Prior to 1910 the state-owned railways were unprofitable. The subsequent improvement in their financial status was accomplished by a policy of drastic economies which affected adversely their efficiency and paved the way for the breakdown of the transportation system during World War I.

Growth of Industry. The economic growth experienced by Russia at the turn of the century is indicated by the progress of industry. According to tentative estimates the number of workers employed in all branches of industry increased from 1.4 million in 1890 to 3.1 million in 1914. The value of the production of the larger industrial enterprises (those subject to the control of the factory inspectors) was 1.5 billion rubles in 1890 and nearly four times that amount (over 5.7 billion rubles) in 1913. The more progressive industries were cotton textiles, coal, and iron and steel. The oil industry in the Caucasus made a good start in the 1890's and for a brief spell led the world output, only to be immediately outstripped by the United States. Between 1890 and the outbreak of the war the rich coal and iron-ore region of the Donets, in the south of Russia, increased its output many times. Changes in the organization of industry were revealed by the higher ratio of workers employed in the larger establishments. In 1914 over 50 per cent of the workers engaged in the manufacturing industries were employed in establishments with 500 and more workers each, a development in which Russian Marxists jubilantly detected the harbinger of the socialist revolution.

Industrial expansion was fostered by the influx of foreign capital, which Witte did his best to encourage. On the eve of the revolution of 1917 foreign investments in Russian industry, banking, and commerce were estimated at some 2.2 billion rubles. The development of the Donets region was largely the work of foreign capital. The principal lending countries were France, Great Britain, and Germany. The share of the United States was small, about 5 per cent of the total. Foreign capital was attracted by the exceptionally high rates of return and the apparent security provided by the guarantees of the imperial government.

Industrial Labor. Industrial labor both increased numerically and gained a measure of recognition of its professional interests. The mass strikes of the 1890's led to the promulgation of a law of 1897 that introduced the 11½-hour day, limited overtime, and made other concessions to labor. Although loosely enforced it was a landmark in the history of factory legislation. A law of 1903, amended and extended in 1912, provided for the financial responsibility of the employer in case of injury or death resulting from industrial accident. Another law of 1903 authorized the election by the workers of "factory elders," who were spokesmen of labor, but the administration of this enactment was hedged with so many reservations and restrictions as to render it ineffectual. In fact, it was seldom invoked. The "provisional rules" of March 1906, which ostensibly implemented the promises of the October manifesto, legalized trade unions and organizations of employers. The powers of the trade unions, however, were both indefinite and restricted, while strikes continued to be prohibited as "disturbances of social peace." Nevertheless several hundred trade unions (the exact number is not known), with a membership comprising perhaps 10 per cent of the total labor force, were organized in 1907. Most of them were closed or ceased operating during the stern rule of Stolypin, a few of the smaller unions alone continuing in existence on the eve of the war. The only labor organizations which proved viable were the sick benefit funds established under a law of 1912. They were financed by contributions of workers and employers, and labor participated in their management. In 1914 there were some 2,800 funds with a membership of over 2 million.

Strikes, although violations of the law, occurred but gradually receded from their high point in 1905 and in 1910 reached the low level of 200 involving fewer than 50,000 workers. The trend was then reversed, and on the eve of the war, in January–June 1914, there were 4,000 strikes with 1.5 million participants. The strikes of this period were predominantly political.

Wages remained low. In 1913 the average monthly industrial earnings were 22 rubles ($11); the lowest rate was 16 rubles (textiles), and the highest 34 rubles (metallurgy). The vast reserve of unemployed labor in the countryside and the relatively slow growth of industry explain the modest level of industrial earnings. The fact that industrial workers were peasants and that their families usually lived in the villages made it possible for them to survive on a lower wage than would have been the case if they had to provide for their families at their place of employment.

Foreign Trade. Foreign trade reflected the economic advance of the turn of the century. Exports increased from the annual average of 698 million gold rubles in 1896–1900 to 1.54 billion in 1911–1913; the corresponding figures for imports were 607 million and 1.24 billion. The chief article of export was grain, which, while subject to sharp fluctuations from year to year, accounted in the first decade of the twentieth century for nearly half of the aggregate receipts from exports. Nine-tenths of the grain trade was carried through the ports of the Black Sea and the Sea of Azov. There were shifts in the direction of trade. England lost to Germany her traditional position as Russia's principal trading partner. In 1913 about one-third of Russia's exports went to Germany, and nearly half of her imports came from that country. This change was all the more notable because in 1893 Russia and Germany became involved in a tariff war, which, however, was ended a year later. Meanwhile the Russian tariff was repeatedly revised upwards and reached a very high level with the act of 1903, which became effective in 1906.

The Land Reform, 1906–1911. The deterioration of farming and peasant unrest bore evidence that the emancipation of 1861 had failed to establish agriculture on a sound foundation. Gradually and reluctantly the government came to the conclusion that communal land tenure, which it had bolstered, especially in the 1880's and the 1890's, was incompatible with agricultural progress and the betterment of the conditions of the peasantry. Some of the disabilities attached to the status of peasant were removed: joint responsibility of the commune for the state obligations of its members in 1903; corporal punishment in 1904; passport restrictions in 1906. A manifesto of November 1905 wrote off redemption payments (that is, payments for the land received by the peasants under the emancipation settlements) which amounted to 1.1 billion rubles, and the ukase of November 9, 1906, initiated a revolutionary reorganization of peasant landholdings. The ukase was promulgated under Article 87, without the approval of parliament, but after a long delay it was confirmed and its provisions extended by a law of June 1910 and a land settlement act of May 1911.

The reform, which was conceived and carried through with great determination by Stolypin, whose name it bears, endeavored to achieve three main objectives: dissolution of the land commune, which was to be superseded by individual peasant farming; consolidation of scattered strips into compact holdings (enclosures); and the abolition of the archaic institution of joint family ownership. The reform was applied ruthlessly, paying little attention to the wishes of the farmers. By the end of 1915 over 7 million households,

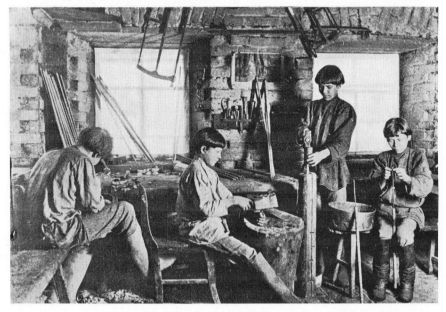

The Bettmann Archive

A Russian workshop, c. 1905

or more than half of the total number in the 50 provinces of European Russia for which information is available, had passed to a regime of individual
tenure. The consolidation of strips, a cumbersome land-surveying operation,
proceeded at a slower pace and by the end of 1915 was completed on the land
of fewer than half of the households which had applied for it. The lack of
coordination between the two elements of the reform—dissolution of the
commune and enclosures—tended to detract from its efficacy, because transition to individual ownership unaccompanied by consolidation was of small
practical consequence, except that the land so transferred could be sold. The
forms of consolidation favored by the government were of the *khutor* and

The Bettmann Archive

A peasant village, late nineteenth century

the *otrub* type. *Khutor* was a compact holding with the homestead adjoining arable land. Under the *otrub* system cultivable land was consolidated into one or two plots, but the farmhouse remained in the village. The less ambitious forms of consolidation dealt with the reduction of the number of strips, delimitation of boundaries, building of roads, and the like. The ukase of November 1906 abolished joint family ownership and made the household elder the sole owner of the allotment land of the household. This measure cut through the complexities of family ownership, but it dispossessed the "junior" members, who were frequently full-grown men with large families. After the reform of 1906–1911 most of the disabilities formerly attached to the status of peasant (and that of allotment land) disappeared, but some survived until the end of the empire.

The Stolypin land reform, which was slowed down with the outbreak of World War I and then came to a standstill, was in effect for too brief a time to allow a definite appraisal, which, moreover, is precluded by the chaotic state of Russian land statistics. It would seem, nevertheless, that the abolition of the land commune was a move in the right direction; were it accompanied by the partition of large estates among the peasants, as demanded by the first and the second Dumas, the subsequent course of Russian history might have been radically changed.

Other agricultural policies should be mentioned. Reversing its traditional attitude the government encouraged, especially from 1906 on, peasant migration to Siberia. Colonization was poorly organized, however, and many of the would-be settlers trailed back. The total number of colonists absorbed by Siberia in 1894–1914 was 3.5 million. The natural growth of the population during that period was estimated at 30 million, which suggests that internal migration brought little relief to European Russia's condition of "rural overpopulation." Encouragement was given to the peasants to buy land. The State Peasant Bank (founded in 1882) was reorganized and its policies liberalized in 1895 and again in 1905 and 1906. Meanwhile the landholdings of the nobility (in 47 provinces of European Russia) declined from 87 million dessiatines in 1862 to 43 million in 1911, that is, by more than half. Most of the land sold by the nobility was purchased by individual peasants, peasant associations, and village communes. In 1913 as much as half of the area privately owned by the peasants [1] was mortgaged in the State Peasant

---

[1] Land privately owned by the peasants should be distinguished from allotment land, which remained a restricted form of tenure even after its transfer to individual ownership by virtue of the legislation of 1906–1911. Allotment land still could not be mortgaged, it could be owned exclusively by *bona fide* peasants, and the size of a holding could not exceed statutory provisions.

Bank, and the accumulation of arrears on account of amortization and interest suggested that the financial burden assumed by the purchasers was excessive. On the other hand, the cooperative movement in rural areas, which began in the 1860's, made rapid progress after 1905. From 1905 to 1914 the number of cooperative societies increased from 5,000 to 32,000, and their membership from less than one million to over 10 million. This was an encouraging development.

A Retrospect. The economic changes noted in this section were not unimportant, but, like those of the second half of the nineteenth century, they did not constitute an industrial revolution. They were rather the elements of the nascent Russian capitalism grafted on the body of a backward agricultural country.

The Schools

Higher and Secondary Schools. The process of modernization extended to the school system. The stifling regime imposed upon the universities by the charter of 1884 came to an end. The "provisional rules" of August 1905 enacted in the midst of the revolutionary upheaval restored the autonomy of the academic corporations, but these liberal provisions were frequently violated and the course of academic life was stormy, particularly in 1904-1906 and again in 1910-1911. Students' strikes became a quasi-permanent feature of the university routine. In spite of these adverse conditions higher education registered a substantial advance. In 1914 Russia had 67 higher schools with 90,000 students, three times as many as in the middle 1890's. Of this number 36,000 were enrolled in the universities, and over 20,000 were women.

The principal development in secondary schools was the abandonment of the aggressive classicism of Dimitry Tolstoy's era. The revision of the programs of the classical gymnasiums began in 1902, and by 1914 Latin was, as a rule, the only ancient language taught in these schools. The student body of the secondary schools in 1914-1915 is variously estimated at from 680,000 to 770,000, or about three times the number in the 1890's.

Primary Education. There was an increase of interest in primary education as well as a growing recognition of its importance. The *zemstvos* took a leading part in the promotion of elementary schools, while the role of the Church schools declined. This was a welcome shift, because the Church schools had earned an unenviable reputation; the *zemstvo* schools, on the contrary, were as a rule well-equipped, well-organized, and strove to maintain high scholastic standards. A law of May 1908 provided for the gradual enforcement of compulsory school attendance for all children aged 8 to 11; instruction was free and extended over four years. Although it was unlikely that compulsory attendance could be fully in effect by 1922, as provided by the law, the act of 1908 was indicative of a novel attitude towards primary education. Some of the difficulties encountered, all of them long familiar, were the rapid growth of the school population and shortages of funds, teachers, school buildings, and books. Nevertheless the basis of elementary education was broadened. In 1915 Russia had 122,000 primary schools with 8.1 million pupils, more than twice their number 20 years earlier.

Foreign Relations

Russia Faces East and West. The principal developments in Russian foreign policy during the period under review were expansion in the Far East, which led to the war with Japan; subsequent reconciliation with that country; estrangement from Austria and Germany; and its concomitant, closer ties with France, then with Great Britain, and the emergence of the Triple Entente. The five Russian ministers of foreign affairs who from 1895 to 1916 succeeded one another were not men of ability or strong character and had but an imperfect control of the situation. Under the Fundamental Laws of 1906 the Crown retained its traditional prerogatives of directing foreign relations, but the personal interventions of Nicholas were sporadic, were usually due to the pressure of a court clique, and were invariably disastrous. The international situation was highly fluid, and there were many moments when, in spite of Russia's alliance with France, her alignment with that country, England, and Japan against the central empires, a situation that actually obtained in 1914, would have seemed highly improbable.

Disarmament. It was customary for Russian monarchs to begin their reign by proclaiming their devotion to peace. Nicholas' somewhat belated declaration along these lines went further than those of his predecessors. In 1898 he issued an appeal to the governments of the world for "the maintenance of peace and a possible reduction of excessive armaments." Russia's real motive for making this startling proposal remains unclear. Witte claimed that the true reason was the modernization of Austrian artillery, which, for financial reasons, Russia was unable to match, an explanation that is not entirely convincing. Although the Russian proposal was given a chilly reception, two international conferences were held at The Hague, on Russia's initiative, in 1899 and 1907. The first conference established an international court of arbitration, and the second busied itself with various problems of international law. These conferences, precursors of the international organizations of a later age, exercised no influence on the foreign policy of Russia or other countries.

The Japanese War, 1904–1905. The Russian 1898 peace proposals were difficult to reconcile with her aggressive policy in the Far East, where Russian and the Japanese penetration in Korea and Manchuria inexorably prepared the clash of imperial ambitions. Russia's participation in blocking the Japanese annexation of the Liaotung Peninsula in 1895, followed by the securing of a Russian lease for that territory, was a setback to Japanese expansion and an affront to Japanese nationalist opinion. In 1903 the Russian province of Kwantung (with Port Arthur), on the Liaotung Peninsula, and the province of Amur were reorganized as a vice-royalty under Admiral E. I. Alekseev. This move was generally interpreted as evidence of Russia's intention to annex the stretch of Manchuria that separated the Kwantung and the Amur provinces. Alekseev, moreover, was associated with a small band of men influential in palace circles who agitated for Russia's expansion in Korea and Manchuria. The Japanese could count on powerful foreign support. England displayed a strong dislike for Russian Far Eastern policy and in 1902 concluded an alliance with Japan. The United States government and opinion were avowedly pro-Japanese. These were probably the decisive factors in spurring Japan to action. The Japanese attempt at reaching agreement with Russia concerning their respective spheres of influence in Korea and Manchuria having failed, Tokyo broke diplomatic relations with St. Petersburg and on February 8, 1904. N.S., without a declaration of war, attacked the Russian fleet at Port Arthur and Chemulpo.

The war that followed and that Russia had done so much to provoke was fought in a distant, arid, and little-known country linked with the center of the Russian empire by the single-track Trans-Siberian railway still partly under construction. In the early stage of the campaign the Japanese army was numerically superior to the Russian, but this relationship was eventually reversed. The Russian navy, although larger than the Japanese, had but one ice-free port, Port Arthur; Vladivostok, Russia's other Pacific port, was some 800 miles north of Liaotung and was ice-bound part of the year, while the Japanese navy had easy access to numerous home ports.

The St. Petersburg government and the bulk of Russian opinion anticipated a victorious and, probably, a short war. These expectations were belied by events. The Russian campaign by both land and sea presents a practically unrelieved record of disaster. The naval squadron based on Port Arthur suffered a major reverse in April 1904 when its flagship *Petropavlovsk* was torpedoed and sunk and several other vessels were severely damaged. Admiral Makarov, the commanding officer, went down with his ship. Meanwhile the Japanese invested Port Arthur, and, as the ring of the blockade narrowed, the inner harbor came within the range of enemy artillery. To avoid destruction the Port Arthur squadron put out to sea in August but was intercepted by the Japanese and annihilated. In December 1904, after a siege of five months, Port Arthur capitulated to the enemy.

In Manchuria, which was the principal theater of land warfare, the Russian armies commanded by General Kuropatkin avoided massive contacts with the enemy and were slowly retreating while fighting a delaying action. A large-scale encounter on the Sha-ho River in September 1904 failed to check the advance of the Japanese, who in February 1905 occupied Mukden after another exceptionally fierce and bloody battle in which over 600,000 men were engaged. The front was then stabilized north of that city and remained practically unchanged until the end of the war.

The decisive blow to Russia was dealt on the high seas. After the destruction of the Port Arthur squadron the Baltic fleet was hastily refitted and in October 1904 sailed for the Far East. The coaling service for which Russia had no facilities was assured by the Hamburg-American Line. The voyage began inauspiciously with the sinking by the Russians in the North Sea, near the Dogger Bank, of two British fishing smacks which they mistook for Japanese torpedo boats. This untoward incident provoked an acute outburst of Russophobia in England, which was already strongly anti-Russian, but the matter was peacefully settled by an *ad hoc* international court. The Russian fleet resumed its course and reached Madagascar in December, at the very time when Port Arthur capitulated to the enemy. There followed a delay, with Admiral Rozhdestvensky, who was in command of the Russian expeditionary force, awaiting the arrival of reinforcements. The few ships, slow and obsolete, remaining in Russia's naval Baltic establishment were hastily reconditioned and in February sailed for the Far East. Rozhdestvensky's reinforced squadron, consisting of eight battleships, twelve cruisers, nine destroyers, and a number of auxiliary craft, attempted to break through to Vladivostok. On May 27, N.S., in the straits of Tsushima, it was attacked and annihilated by the far more modern and efficient fleet of Admiral Togo. Rozhdestvensky, severely wounded, was made prisoner; Japanese losses were slight.

This naval disaster, the stalemate in Manchuria, and revolutionary disturbances at home forced St. Petersburg to accept President Theodore Roosevelt's good offices in arranging peace negotiations. A Russo-Japanese conference met in Portsmouth, New Hampshire, in August 1905, and early in September the peace treaty was signed. The Russian delegation was headed by Serge Witte and the Japanese by the foreign minister, Baron Komura. By the Portsmouth Treaty Russia ceded to Japan the lease to the Liaotung Peninsula with Port Arthur and Talienwan (Dalny), the southern portion of Sakhalin Island that the Japanese had occupied, and the section of the Southern Manchurian Railway leading to Port Arthur. Russia recognized Japan's special interest in Korea, but both imperial governments renounced any claims to special rights in Manchuria, which was to be evacuated by their troops and restored to China. The terms of the treaty were relatively mild in spite of Russia's undistinguished war record; this was presumably due to the fact that the impact of the war effort on the human and economic resources of Japan was greater than on those of Russia, a much larger country. The treaty was more unpopular in victorious Japan than in defeated Russia. In the turmoil of the 1905 revolution the loss of Port Arthur and half of Sakhalin, places which meant little to the majority of the Russians, passed nearly unnoticed.

Russia and Japan, 1906–1914. The decade following the Portsmouth Treaty brought about a remarkable reversal in Russo-Japanese relations. Agreements, both public and secret, concluded by the two countries in 1907, 1910, and 1912 delimited, in violation of the Portsmouth Treaty, their respective spheres of influence in Manchuria and Mongolia. In 1910 Japan, with the preliminary consent of Russia, annexed Korea, and in 1911 Russia established a *de facto* protectorate over Outer Mongolia. The attempt of the United States government to enforce in Manchuria the policy of the Open Door—that is, equality of trading and investment opportunities for all nations—and the ambitious plans for the domination of that country by a powerful American financial group (E. H. Harriman, Jacob Schiff, and J. P. Morgan) were resented by Tokyo and St. Petersburg as infringements of their "special interests." Resistance to these policies and recognition by the Russians of Japan's growing power were the causes of the Russo-Japanese reconciliation, which was favored by Great Britain and France.

European Policies, 1894–1914. Russia's European policies in 1894–1914 were less dramatic than in the Far East, but their consequences were even graver. The official disclosure in 1897 of the existence of the alliance with France did not preclude friendly relations with Austria-Hungary and Germany. The fate of Constantinople continued to hold the attention of St. Petersburg. The occupation of the upper Bosphorus was decided in principle by the Russian government in 1896 in connection with Turkish domestic disorders, but a year later an agreement with Austria, which was renewed in 1903, provided for the preservation of the *status quo* in the Balkans. Close relations were maintained with Germany. Emperor William II had encouraged Russia's Far Eastern ambitions, and agreement with Germany for the coaling of the Russian fleet made possible Rozhdestvensky's ill-fated expedition. In July 1905, in the seclusion of the imperial yachts cruising in Finnish waters, Nicholas and William signed a secret treaty of military alliance (Treaty of Björkö). The tsar's advisers, however, belatedly informed of this new military commitment, insisted on its abrogation as incompatible with the Franco-Russian alliance (November 1905). The impassioned protests of Emperor William went unheeded. The improvement in Anglo-Russian relations was formalized in a convention signed by the two countries in August 1907. A. P. Izvolsky, Russian foreign minister from 1906 to 1910, was a protagonist of close cooperation with Great Britain and Japan. The convention endeavored to reconcile conflicting Russian and British policies in Iran, Tibet, and Afghanistan. Although it failed to achieve this objective, the convention played an important part in the establishment of the Triple Entente.

Distrust of Germany was the real cause of the Franco-Anglo-Russian *rapprochement*. The nationalistic groups in France were thinking in terms of *revanche* for the defeat of 1870, and in 1905 and 1911 there were serious clashes between France and Germany in North Africa. Germany's drive for a place in the colonial sun and her "big navy" policy, which was intensified in 1908, alarmed and antagonized England, while St. Petersburg found itself at odds with Berlin on numerous issues. One source of friction was the building of the Bagdad railway, for which Germany secured a concession from Turkey in 1902. The entente powers, which had extensive treaty rights in Asia Minor, raised objections. Nevertheless in August 1911 Russia gave her consent, provided Germany refrained from seeking economic concessions in northern Iran, which was a Russian sphere of influence. England and France, although they criticized Russian action as a breach of entente solidarity, decided to follow suit. An agreement allowing the completion of the building of the railway was initialled in June 1914 but was not ratified because of the outbreak of the war.

Complications of greater import arose in connection with Izvolsky's attempt to open the Dardanelles to Russian warships. The gist of this episode, famous in the annals of diplomacy, was the agreement reached in private conversations at the castle of Buchlau, in Moravia, between Izvolsky and the Austrian foreign minister, Count von Aehrenthal (September 1908). The two ministers agreed not to oppose each other's demands: Izvolsky's, for the opening of the Dardanelles to the Russian warships; and Aehrenthal's, for the annexation of Bosnia and Herzegovina, the two provinces—largely Serbian —occupied by Austria-Hungary in permanence (*sine die*) under the Berlin treaty of 1878. Izvolsky was motivated by the desire for a spectacular diplomatic success that could be interpreted as leading to the fulfillment of Russia's "historic mission" in the Balkans; Aehrenthal wished, by annexing Bosnia and Herzegovina, to check the expansionist policies of Serbia which he regarded as a menace to the Dual Monarchy. The Buchlau conversations produced no written agreement, but Izvolsky appeared to believe that the implementation of the two parts of the bargain—annexation of Bosnia and Herzegovina and the opening of the Straits—was to take place more or less simultaneously. This did not happen. The annexation of the Serbian provinces was proclaimed early in October, earlier than Izvolsky had expected, while the proposed opening of the Straits foundered on the opposition of England. Izvolsky's attempt to block or at least delay the ratification of the annexation by the signatories of the Treaty of Berlin was frustrated by the request of the German government for a "precise Yes or No" answer (to the demand for ratification), a communication which he described as a "diplomatic ultimatum of the most violent character." His back to the wall, the Russian minister capitulated and formally approved the annexation (March 1909).

The political consequences of the Bosnia-Herzegovina crisis were out of proportion to its immediate cause, the substitution of "annexation" for "permanent occupation" being largely a matter of semantics. For a time Serbia and Turkey threatened to make war on Austria and boycotted Austrian goods. The budding Anglo-Russian entente was nearly wrecked. Anti-Austrian and anti-German feelings in Russia ran high, while Izvolsky personally was the target of vitriolic attacks in the nationalistic press. In September 1910 he left the foreign office and was appointed ambassador to Paris, where he threw his influence against Berlin and Vienna. As foreign minister he was succeeded by S. D. Sazonov, who held that office until 1916.

The Austrian annexation of Bosnia and Herzegovina and the proclamation of Bulgarian independence that occurred simultaneously were followed by a round of wars for the dismemberment of the Ottoman empire. In October 1912 Italy, after a short war, annexed Tripoli and Cyrenaica. In March 1912 Serbia and Bulgaria concluded a treaty that in its public part upheld the *status quo,* ostensibly to prevent further Austrian annexations, but in a secret annex provided for the partition of Turkey. Sazonov favored the maintenance of the *status quo,* while some of the Russian agents in the Balkans did their best to stir Slav nationalism. They were the architects of the Balkan League, which waged a successful war against Turkey in 1912–1913; its members, however, hopelessly quarrelled over the division of the spoils and attacked one another. At the London conference of ambassadors that dealt with the Balkan situation, Russian and Austrian policies were in sharp conflict, Austria endeavoring to win the support of the other Balkan countries at the expense of Serbia, whose interests Russia defended. The Balkan wars thus contributed to the estrangement between St. Petersburg and Vienna.

Serious friction between Russia and Germany developed in connection with the Liman von Sanders mission to Turkey. Sanders was one of the European military experts engaged by the Young Turk government to supervise the modernization of the armed forces. Unlike his predecessor, who was also a German officer, Liman von Sanders was appointed commander of a Turkish corps stationed in Constantinople; this arrangement, it was argued in St. Petersburg, made the foreign ambassadors in the Turkish capital dependent on a German general. The incident lasted for but a few weeks (November 1913–January 1914) and was amiably settled by Sanders' transfer to another command. Nevertheless Sazonov detected in the Liman von Sanders affair additional evidence of Germany's sinister designs in the Near East and was increasingly suspicious of the policies of Berlin.

The future of the Anglo-Russian entente, too, appeared uncertain. A British squadron visited Kronstadt in June 1914, there was an exchange of official delegations, and negotiations for a naval convention were in progress. Yet the Anglo-Russian convention of 1907 failed to improve the situation in Iran, and as late as June 1914 the British ambassador told the tsar that developments in that country "might prove fatal to the Anglo-Russian understanding."

Such, in the briefest outline, was the devious course of Russia's policies on the eve of World War I.

17

Letters, Arts, and Science, 1800-1914

Turn of the Century

Lack of Progress. The eighteenth century witnessed a remarkable ascendancy of Russia as a political power. During the reign of Catherine II some 200,000 square miles were added to the national territory, and the population increased from 19 million to 36 million. Russia was firmly established on the shores of the Black Sea and extended her control over the littoral of the Baltic. By the end of the eighteenth century she was a full-fledged and, at times, the leading member of the quarrelsome community of European states.

There was no corresponding transformation in the field of cultural endeavor, partly because the energies and resources of the nation were diverted to war. The cultural heritage of the eighteenth century was meager and uninspiring: a few pretentious institutions with high-sounding names, such as the Academy of Science and the Academy of Arts; the University of Moscow, which had few students and bore little resemblance to a higher school; hardly any schools at lower levels; a few literary journals; a handful of professional men of letters and historians. Music, painting, and architecture were dominated by western European influences, and the exponents of these arts were predominantly foreigners. The ballet and the ballet school, which was transplanted to St. Petersburg from Paris, remained a French institution for over a hundred years. But the nineteenth century wrought a revolutionary change in these conditions.

Literature

Pseudo-Classicism and Sentimentalism. Pseudo-classicism and sentimentalism dominated Russian literature at the end of the eighteenth century. The leading representative of the former was Gabriel Derzhavin, who achieved eminence by extolling in his odes the virtues and greatness of Catherine. The founder of Russia's short-lived sentimentalism was Nicholas Karamzin (1766–1826). The publication of his *Letters of a Russian Traveler* (1791–1792) brought him recognition. Sentimentalism, a reaction against the formalism and artificiality of pseudo-classicism, strove for simplicity in both the subject matter and the form of a literary work. Karamzin, his success with his contemporaries notwithstanding, failed to achieve these objectives: his fictional writings were as remote from the Russian realities which they ostensibly endeavored to portray, and his style was as artificial and labored, as those of the pseudo-classicists. Karamzin was also a noted historian. In 1803 he was appointed official "historiographer," and in 1816 the first eight volumes of his massive *History of the Russian State* were published; four more volumes were issued later. Karamzin's history, like his literary work, did not withstand the test of time and, although acclaimed by contemporary opinion, is largely forgotten. He made, however, a lasting worthwhile contribution to the evolution of the literary language, chiefly by adopting constructions and terms translated from the French. In politics Karamzin was a militant reactionary. His *Memorandum on Ancient and Modern Russia,* glorifying autocracy and imbued with aggressive nationalism, was submitted to the tsar in 1811 and was presumably one of the causes of the disgrace of Speransky. Contrary to contemporary opinion, which saw in Karamzin the prophet of a new era, his work belongs to the eighteenth rather than to the nineteenth century.

The popularity of poetry continued undiminished and, indeed, with the appearance of Pushkin, reached an all-time high. A number of gifted poets benefited by the simplification of the literary language and the elucidation of the rules of prosody achieved in the eighteenth century and did creditable work, especially in translating ancient and Western classics. The more prominent members of this group were Nicholas Gnedich (1784–1833), Constantine Batiushkov (1787–1855; his literary career was terminated in

1820 by a mental ailment), and especially Vasili Zhukovsky (1783–1852), who produced a Russian version of the *Odyssey*. In the poetry of these authors sentimentalism acquired a sincerity and dignity which were lacking in the work of Karamzin. Zhukovsky became the leading representative of the Russian romantic school.

Beginnings of Modern Literature. The fountainhead of modern Russian literature may be traced to several authors of the early nineteenth century. They differed widely among themselves in their gifts and the nature of their work, but each left a lasting mark on Russian letters. Ivan Krylov (1786–1844), Russia's only fabulist of note, published in 1809 the first volume of his fables, which revealed his genius for drawing concise word-pictures and his mastery of the popular tongue. Krylov's fables are an integral part of the education of every Russian child, and his picturesque and witty dicta are continuously quoted by his countrymen. Alexander Griboedov (1795–1829), a diplomat and a man of the world, wrote but one major work, *The Misfortune of Being Wise,* a comedy in verse dealing with contemporary Moscow society. It is rightly rated as one of the greatest plays in the Russian language, and its significance and popularity have not been impaired by the passing of years. Griboedov was killed in a popular uprising in Teheran, where he was Russian minister, before his comedy appeared in print or on the stage.

Unlike Krylov and Griboedov, Alexander Pushkin (1799–1837) excelled in every form of literary endeavor. He came from an aristocratic but impoverished family and had a strain of African blood, of which he was proud. Pushkin began to write poetry as a child, his early poems appearing in print when he was fifteen. He was the author of numerous lyrics, poems, plays, novels, and stories, all of them among the best which Russian literature has to offer. From the large number of his publications, the novel in verse *Eugene Onegin,* the play *Boris Godunov,* and the prose novel *The Captain's Daughter* may be mentioned more or less at random. Pushkin felt the influence of pseudo-classicism, sentimentalism, and romanticism, but he emancipated himself from the sway of these movements and became one of the founders of Russian realism. His private life was an unhappy one. He was close to the Decembrists but escaped persecution chiefly because from 1820 to 1827 he was exiled from the capital. Later he made his peace with Nicholas I and accepted the tsar's patronage, which, however, he soon came to resent. Rumors involving his wife led to a duel, in which he was killed.

Michael Lermontov (1814–1841), like Pushkin, belonged to the aristocracy and was master of both poetry and prose writing. Influenced by Byron,

Alexander Pushkin

Nicholas Gogol

he liked romantic subjects. Romanticism is much in evidence in his major poem *The Demon* and, in a smaller degree, in his novel *The Hero of Our Time,* but he also wrote numerous lyrics reflecting the feelings of the ordinary man which are models of simplicity and restraint. His promising literary career was cut short by a duel, in which he was killed. Another notable author was Alexis Koltsov (1809–1842). He was the son of a small cattle dealer, had hardly any schooling, and learned to write poetry from a manual of versification that he picked up at a country fair. His poems, inspired by the sentiments of the lower classes, disclose a sincerity and depth of feeling and a unique command of the popular tongue which assure him of a permanent place in Russian letters. They began to appear in print in the 1830's and were first published in a separate volume in 1835. Koltsov introduced into Russian literature a novel strain that was successfully developed by later writers—Nekrasov, Turgenev (in *A Sportsman's Sketches*), and Gorky.

The Age of the Novel. The authors of the earlier nineteenth century, especially Pushkin, Griboedov, and Lermontov, paved the way for the advent of realism and the great novels of Gogol, Turgenev, Dostoevsky, and Tolstoy. Nicholas Gogol (1809–1852) was born in the Ukraine into a family of the lesser nobility. He began his literary career with the publication of stories and short novels on Ukrainian themes, written in the romantic vein. These were followed by the so-called St. Petersburg stories and plays, which established Gogol as the leading author of the realistic school. In 1836 came his celebrated comedy *The Inspector General* and in 1842 the novel *Dead Souls,* the most thoroughly national masterpiece of Russian literature. *Dead Souls* has no plot; it presents a devastating picture of provincial Russia and is written in an often ungrammatical but inimitable and irresistible Russian that eludes adequate interpretation in foreign languages. *Dead Souls* was acclaimed as the first truly great work of the Russian realistic school and as an indictment of the existing social order. This was not the author's opinion, however. In 1836 Gogol went to live in Rome and came increasingly under the influence of Catholicism. The publication in 1847 of his *Correspondence with Friends* revealed him as an extreme reactionary and a religious mystic intent on saving the world through a process of moral betterment. Social reform meant nothing to him. Gogol endeavored to undo his work by writing a second volume of *Dead Souls* that was to present the positive aspects of Russian life; he failed lamentably and burned the completed manuscript. In spite of his efforts, and contrary to his will, his influence as the leading writer of the realistic school proved powerful and lasting.

Sovfoto

Ivan Turgenev

Sovfoto

Fedor Dostoevsky

Ivan Turgenev (1818–1883) was born into a family of landed nobility and received a good education. His poems and stories began to appear in periodicals in the 1840's; important among them were the unadorned pen-pictures of peasant conditions under serfdom, which were re-issued in 1852 in book form as *A Sportsman's Sketches*. This was followed by several novels depicting the contemporary Russian upper class. The best-known among them were *The Nest of Gentlefolk* (1858), and *Fathers and Sons* (1861). His last novel, *Virgin Soil,* was published in 1876. Turgenev had a long liaison with the French singer Pauline Garcia-Viardot and spent much of his time abroad. Unlike Gogol or Dostoevsky, he was a "European" in both spirit and literary manner and the first Russian novelist to gain recognition in the West. His influence on Russian and world literature was great, and his books continue to be widely read 100 years after they were written.

Fedor Dostoevsky (1821–1881), son of an army doctor and graduate of a school for military engineers, is probably the most influential and disturbing of the Russian novelists. He came from an unhealthy and tortured background and lived through many harrowing experiences. His father and two of his brothers were alcoholics. Dostoevsky suffered from epilepsy, was an inveterate gambler, was most of the time hopelessly in debt, and for years was the unhappy lover of a cruel and heartless woman. He was tried on a fantastic charge of subversion and received the death penalty, which was commuted, however, to penal servitude, followed by a term as a private in a Siberian regiment. He spent the years 1849 to 1859 serving his sentence in Siberia. Dostoevsky's first novel, *Poor People* (1846), brought him immediate recognition. He related his prison experiences in *Memoirs from the House of Death* (1861–1862). His famous novels are: *Crime and Punishment* (1866); *The Idiot* (1868); *The Possessed* (1871); and *The Brothers Karamazov* (1880). During the closing years of his life Dostoevsky published *A Writer's Diary,* a running commentary on literary, political, social, and philosophical issues. He began as a liberal with moderate socialist leanings but during his incarceration in Siberia became converted to militant religiosity and mystical nationalism. His novels disclose the obscure working of the human mind. According to Dostoevsky he was "a realist in the higher meaning of the term" because he depicted "all the depth of the human soul." It is this quality that gives his writings their universal appeal and value. They were not intended to be, and are not, a representation of Russian conditions.

Count Leo Tolstoy (1828–1910) was a novelist and a playwright as well as a philosopher and a religious thinker. He studied for two years in the University of Kazan, which he left without taking a degree, served in the army but resigned after the Crimean War, and spent practically his entire life on the family estate of Yasnaia Poliana. His writings began to appear in print in the early 1850's. His *The Tales of Sevastopol,* an eyewitness account of the ordeal of the defenders of the besieged naval base, made his literary reputation. Tolstoy is a towering figure in world literature. His greatest novels are *War and Peace* (1869) and *Anna Karenina* (1877). In the 1870's he experienced an acute moral crisis that led to his "conversion" to a rationalized form of Christianity, stripped of ritual and dogma and built around the notion of non-resistance to evil. He repudiated the state as an instrument of oppression, the Church, and private property, as well as his own literary work as morally and artistically wrong. In his famous tract

The Bettmann Archive

Leo Tolstoy

What Is Art? he deprecated world classics, among them Shakespeare and Pushkin, and denigrated realism on the ground that it was overburdened with superfluous details: true art should follow the austere pattern of the Scriptures. Nevertheless, while much of Tolstoy's later work was proselyting and didactic, he continued to write stories, short novels, and plays in his pre-conversion "sinful" manner. Some of them were published in his lifetime and others posthumously. Tolstoy's conversion brought him no peace of mind. His attacks on the dogma and institutions of the established Church led to his excommunication by the Synod in 1901. His communist views were in conflict with the comfortable life he was leading on the family estate. A deep cleavage developed between Tolstoy and his wife, with whom he had been very happy but who shared none of his political and religious views. Restless and distraught, Tolstoy, at the age of 82, secretly left Yasnaia Poliana in search of a new life. He was accompanied by his daughter Alexandra and his doctor, became ill a few days later, and died in the quarters of the station master of the Astapovo railway junction.

Some Lesser Writers. There were numerous other writers of the realistic school, distinguished but less well known—especially abroad—than those discussed in the previous section. Serge Aksakov (1791–1859) was a government official and country squire who turned to writing late in life. His two major books, *A Family Chronicle* (1856) and *Years of Childhood of Bagrov-Grandson* (1858), are partly autobiographical and present an attractive picture of life on the estates of the lesser nobility. Ivan Goncharov (1812–1891), author of three novels, owes his great reputation to the novel *Oblomov*. Its hero, Oblomov, has become the symbol of atrophy of the will and moral debility characteristic of a section of the nobility, and the term "oblomovism" (*oblomovshchina*) has gained wide acceptance. Alexis Pisemsky (1820–1881), a forceful and profoundly pessimistic writer, was the author of plays and novels, of which the most important, perhaps, was *A Thousand Souls* (1858). Paul Melnikov (1819–1883) published under the name of Andrew Pechersky two bulky volumes, *In the Woods* (1868–1874) and *On the Hills* (1875–1878), a fictional account of the life of the old-believers (dissenters), a subject on which he was a recognized authority. Michael Saltykov-Shchedrin (1826–1889), a member of the nobility and a civil servant, was the satirist of official, especially provincial, Russia and a review editor. He wrote numerous short pieces as well as the novel *The Golovlev Family,* which was widely read, and exercised considerable influence on contemporary and later writers.

While poetry in the middle of the nineteenth century lost some of its former popularity, several poets of talent and skill carried on the tradition of Pushkin and Lermontov. The more notable among them were Fedor Tiutchev (1803–1873), Athansius Fet (1820–1892), Jacob Polonsky (1819–1898), Alexis Pleshcheev (1825–1893), Count Alexis Tolstoy (1817–1875), and Nicholas Nekrasov (1821–1877). Alexis Tolstoy was also a playwright and a novelist, and Nekrasov, whose poetry was uneven and at times tendentious, was a leading magazine editor.

Literary Criticism. A significant development in the middle of the nineteenth century was the emergence of literary criticism of a novel type. It came to be used not so much as a vehicle for comments on books but as a medium for the dissemination of the writer's political and social views and radical doctrines. The founding of this type of criticism is associated with Vissarion Belinsky (1810–1848), who is widely regarded as Russia's greatest and most influential literary critic. Another member of this group was Nicholas Chernyshevsky (1828–1889), son of a priest and a contributor to the review *Sovremennik* (The Contemporary), who, although not formally a Marxist, was an advocate of socialism and held that literature must serve a social purpose. He was arrested in 1862 and wrote in prison the novel *What Is to Be Done?*, which had no literary merit but was highly successful with the radical youth. Chernyshevsky was eventually deported to Siberia, where he remained until 1882. Lenin revered him as his teacher. Nicholas Dobroliubov (1836–1861) was, like Chernyshevsky, the son of a priest and a contributor to *Sovremennik* and shared Chernyshevsky's belief that literature should serve a socially useful purpose. In spite of the brevity of his career— he died at the age of 25—Dobroliubov was very influential. Dimitry Pisarev (1840–1868), who came from the nobility, won a large devout following as the standard-bearer of "nihilism," that is, the rejection of all traditional values. He was arrested in 1862, wrote most of his essays in prison, and was accidentally drowned soon after his release. Nicholas Mikhailovsky (1842–1904) came from the nobility and was an outstanding radical journalist, sociologist, philosopher, and literary critic. Although one of the pillars of populism, which extolled the virtues of the specifically Russian national ways, particularly the peasant commune, Mikhailovsky was responsible for introducing to the Russian reading public some of the Western thinkers, among them Darwin and Marx. His prudence and good luck saved him from persecution and allowed him to contribute for years to the leading journals: first, *Otechestvennyia Zapiski* (Notes of the Fatherland) and, from 1892 on, *Russkoe Bogatstvo* (Russian Wealth). This long uninterrupted record of journalistic work, rare among radical writers, accounts in part for the very great influence enjoyed by Mikhailovsky.

Journalism in the Belinsky-Dobroliubov manner left a profound mark on the thinking of two or three generations of Russian intellectuals. It performed a double function: enlightened literary criticism stimulated interest in and paved the way for the recognition and acceptance of new talented authors, while insidious political comments proved an effective medium for the dissemination of radical and revolutionary ideas.

Literature on the Eve. The nineteenth-century tradition of realism was maintained in the closing decades of the empire; simultaneously vanguard literary movements—symbolism and futurism—made their appearance. The principal authors of the realistic school, in addition to Leo Tolstoy, were Chekhov, Gorky, and Bunin. Anton Chekhov (1860–1904), son of a former serf who became a merchant, graduated from the medical school of the University of Moscow but did not practice medicine and turned instead to literature. His earlier writings were humorous sketches, rather crude albeit financially rewarding, which appeared in cheap popular magazines. Chekhov's association with the conservative newspaper *Novoe Vremia* (New Times), which lasted from 1886 to 1897, freed him from dependence on popular magazines and made it possible for him to write in a different vein. His world-wide reputation rests on the psychological insight and literary artistry of a highly personal nature of his stories and plays. At least two of his plays —*The Cherry Orchard* and *The Three Sisters*—rate among the masterpieces of the stage and are being continually revived.

Maxim Gorky (Alexis Peshkov, 1868–1936), short-story writer, novelist, and playwright, was a self-made man. Born into a working-class family he was orphaned at an early age and spent his early years wandering along the Volga and in southern Russia. He never attended school and was taught to read and write by a friendly cook on a Volga steamer. This was not a promising beginning, yet Gorky had a great talent and the urge for self-expression. His first story, *Makar Chudra,* appeared in a Tiflis journal in 1892; he then wrote for the St. Petersburg magazine *Russkoe Bogatstvo;* two volumes of his stories were published in 1898 and were acclaimed as a major literary event. Disregarding precedent, the Academy of Science elected Gorky as a member in 1902, but the election was cancelled by the government on political grounds: Gorky was close to the social democrats and later to the Bolsheviks; after the advent of the Soviets to power he became the leading "proletarian" writer. Gorky's earlier writings showed the influence of romanticism, but in the late 1890's he espoused realism. His principal novels of the pre-revolutionary era are: *Foma Gordeev* (1899); *The Mother* (1907); *Okurov City* (1910); and *Matvei Kozhemiakin* (1911). Two volumes of his

3-volume autobiography, *Childhood* and *Among Strangers,* appeared respectively in 1913 and 1915 and are among his more important books. Gorky's play *The Lower Depths* (1902), set in a night refuge for vagabonds, has lost none of its popularity, especially outside Russia. Excessive moralizing was one criticism raised against his fictional writings.

Ivan Bunin (1870–1953), poet, novelist, short-story writer, and translator, came from a family of the landed nobility. His poems began to appear in print in 1887. The outstanding traits of his art are a notable economy of means, a masterful use of the language, and pessimism of the darkest hue. *The Village* (1910) and *The Dry Valley* (1912) are memorable evocations of the decadence of rural Russia. *The Gentleman from San Francisco* (1916), perhaps Bunin's greatest story, deals with the helplessness of man and the futility of human endeavor. After the revolution of 1917 Bunin went to France, where he continued his literary work. In 1933 he became the first Russian author to receive the Nobel Prize for literature.

Among the other writers of the realistic school were V. G. Korolenko

Sovfoto

Anton Chekhov and Maxim Gorky in Yalta, 1900

(1853–1921), A. I. Kuprin (1870–1938), M. P. Artsybashev (1878–1927), and Leonid Andreev (1871–1919), whose later stories, novels, and plays, however, belonged to the symbolist school.

The ascendancy of symbolism was fostered by the publication in 1893 of a pamphlet *On the Causes of the Decline of Contemporary Russian Literature* by the poet and novelist D. S. Merezhkovsky (1865–1941). Symbolism was a protest against the positivism and materialism prevalent in Russian literature. The essence of symbolism was the rejection of realism, extreme individualism, "art for art's sake," and, later, emphasis on Russia's past and on religion. The movement centered on a group of writers and artists known as *Mir Iskusstva* (The Art World), which published (1898–1904) a review under that name and was led by Serge Diaghilev, the well-known director of the Russian ballet. The principal authors of the symbolist school were Merezhkovsky, his wife the poetess Zinaida Hippius (1867–1945), Valery Briusov (1873–1924), Constantine Balmont (1867–1943), Fedor Sologub (F. K. Teternikov, 1863–1927), Andrew Bely (B. N. Bugaev, 1880–1934), and Alexander Blok (1880–1921), this latter probably the most talented of them all. The achievements of the symbolist school, particularly of its poets, were the notable improvement in prosody, great ingenuity in the use of words, and the freeing of literary criticism from the political and sociological trappings with which it was burdened since the days of Belinsky. Symbolist writings, however, were often loaded with metaphors and verbal obscurities which, among other things, made practically impossible their rendition into foreign languages.

Futurism, another vanguard movement, was related to symbolism and stemmed, although indirectly, from its Italian namesake founded by Marinetti. It appeared in Russia about 1910 and, full of exuberance and youthful daring, aimed at nothing less than the creation of the "dynamic art of the future." The founder of the movement was Victor Khlebnikov (1885–1922) and its outstanding representative the poet Vladimir Maiakovsky (1894–1930). The first volume of his verse appeared in 1912. After the advent of the Soviets, Maiakovsky became the leading revolutionary poet.

The above outline suggests that while literary levels of the closing years of the empire (especially since the death of Chekhov) were lower than during the great periods of the nineteenth century, literature nevertheless showed robust vitality and produced many works of lasting value.

The Press. A few words may be added about the press. Complete freedom of the press did not exist in imperial Russia, and the "provisional rules" on censorship of November 1905, which remained in force until the end of the empire, presented considerable perils for authors, editors, and publishers. Nevertheless the political range of the press was exceedingly broad, extending from the ultra-reactionary *Russkoe Znamia* (Russian Flag) to the Bolshevik *Pravda* (The Truth), which began to appear in St. Petersburg in April 1912. The ill-advised policy of Russification was imperfectly reflected in the status of the press. The 2,200 periodicals published in Russia (exclusive of Finland) in 1912 were issued in 33 languages—a surprisingly high figure.

Drama, Ballet, and Cinematography

The Theater. The evolution of the theater paralleled that of literature but was slower and was influenced by conditions peculiar to that art. Theatrical companies, private and sponsored by the state, began to appear in Russia in the middle of the eighteenth century, but for nearly 150 years the stage was dominated by the state theater. The leading dramatic theaters of this group were the Maly in Moscow (founded in 1806, named Maly in 1823) and the Alexandrinsky, established in St. Petersburg in 1832. In 1826 the state theaters were given the appellation of "imperial" and were brought under the control of the ministry of the imperial court. Thirty years later (1856) the government, fearing the influence of the stage as an instrument of revolutionary propaganda, prohibited private theatrical companies in St. Petersburg and Moscow, where the imperial theaters were situated. Although this decision was an informal directive of the emperor and not a law or decree, it effectively stifled private theatrical enterprise. Such companies continued to operate in the provinces, but their repertories were trivial and their artistic standards exceedingly low. It was only after the abolition in 1882 of the monopoly of the imperial theaters that private theatrical enterprise asserted itself and, indeed, made striking progress.

By the beginning of the nineteenth century the theater had gained a measure of acceptance as legitimate recreation, but its intrinsic achievements were modest. Pseudo-classicism and sentimentalism were supreme, and acting was rhetorical and declamatory. The successful dramatists were Vladislav Ozerov (1770–1816), Prince Alexander Shakhovskoy (1777–1846), Michael Zagoskin (1789–1852), N. A. Polevoy (1796–1846), and N. V. Kukolnik (1809–1868). The prevalent genres were crude ultra-patriotic tragedies in the classical manner and sentimental melodramas. Representative of plays of the first group were Ozerov's *Dimitry Donskoy* and Kukolnik's national epic characteristically entitled *The Hand of the Almighty Protects the Father-*

land. The alternative to aggressive patriotism was the adaptation of Western classics (Shakespeare, Molière, Schiller) and of light French comedies. Beginning in the 1830's the dominance of pseudo-classicism was undermined by the plays of Pushkin, Griboedov, Gogol, Turgenev, and Tolstoy. The ascendancy of realism was promoted by the work of Alexander Ostrovsky (1823–1886), a minor employee of a Moscow commercial court and author of some 50 plays (of which the first was produced in 1853) portraying the unadorned conditions of the lower middle class. The immediate and resounding success of Ostrovky's comedies dealt a final blow to pseudo-classicism. Good plays called for good actors. One of the first distinguished Russian actors was Michael Shchepkin (1788–1863), a former serf who created at the Moscow Maly Theater memorable interpretations of the leading characters in the plays of Griboedov and Gogol.

Although the monopoly of the imperial theaters was never fully enforced, its abrogation was followed by a remarkable effervescence of private theatrical enterprises. Among the new theatrical companies was the Moscow Art Theater, founded in 1898 by the novelist V. I. Nemirovich-Danchenko (1859–1943) and the actor-producer K. S. Stanislavsky (1863–1938). The Moscow Art Theater had a carefully selected repertory consisting of plays by eminent Russian and foreign authors and a company of talented and skillful actors and stage designers. It was at the Moscow Art Theater that Chekhov's plays were first produced. The evolution of the theories of the Moscow Art Theater went through several phases. It felt the influence of naturalism (that is, adherence to nature, avoidance of conventions), impressionism, symbolism, and "psychological realism," or the "Stanislavsky method," which required the psychological identification of the actor with the character whom he portrayed. The Moscow Art Theater was an unqualified success and already prior to World War I was rated, in spite of its youth, with the *Comédie Française* as one of the illustrious theatrical enterprises in the world. Other famed producers who broke fresh ground were: Vsevolov Meyerhold (1874–1942), for a time director of the imperial Alexandrinsky Theater in St. Petersburg; Vera Kommissarzhevskaya (1864–1910), an actress and founder of the Theater of the Drama in St. Petersburg; Eugene Vakhtangov (1883–1922), the inventor of "fantastic realism," an attempt to present the "inner truth of acted emotion" against the background of an unreal stage setting; Nicholas Evreinov (1879–1953), a master of brilliant stylized productions, proponent of the theory of "the theater for the theater's sake," and founder of the St. Petersburg satirical theater *Krivoe Zerkalo* (Twisted Mirror); and Alexander Tairov (Knoblit, 1885–1950), an actor and director of the

Kamerny Theater in Moscow, where he staged spectacles of great beauty ranging from Racine to Schnitzler and, later, Eugene O'Neill.

The example of St. Petersburg and Moscow revitalized the provincial stage. In the two or three decades preceding World War I the repertory and acting of the provincial companies were vastly improved. The larger provincial cities had their own permanent repertory theaters where good plays were competently produced and acted, while numerous road companies toured the smaller towns. The work of Russian directors was followed with close interest abroad and had repercussions in western Europe and throughout the world.

The Ballet. The ballet company that had been transplanted from Paris to St. Petersburg at the end of the eighteenth century proved an unbending and conservative institution. For over a century it adhered closely to the tradition of its founders and shunned all innovations. The dance technique, choreography, and inspiration remained French. The famed St. Petersburg ballet masters of the nineteenth century—Didlo, Saint Leon, Marius Petipa —were Frenchmen. Petipa joined the St. Petersburg ballet in 1847, and in 1903 he was still the leading ballet master. He staged some 50 ballets, which followed an immutable pattern even though some of them—*Sleeping Beauty, Swan Lake*—are classics. The ballerinas, too, were as a rule French and, later, Italian. The technical perfection of the St. Petersburg ballet, and of its Moscow counterpart, was due to the steady flow of highly skilled dancers supplied by the ballet school, a state-sponsored institution that subjected its students to a long and rigorous training.

The revolt against the conventional beliefs that swept Russian artistic circles at the turn of the century was instrumental in the transformation of the ballet. The change, which was revolutionary, was largely due to the novel concept of choreography held by a young St. Petersburg choreographer Michael Fokin (1880–1942); while retaining the traditional dance technique, he abandoned or modified some of the previously sacrosanct conventions. The scores used by Fokin were those of the greatest Russian and foreign composers, and the stage settings were designed by noted avant-garde artists. The appearance of several exceptionally talented Russian dancers—Anna Pavlova, Tamara Karsavina, Vaslav Nijinsky—lent luster to the "new" Russian ballet. It was dramatically revealed to Europe and the world in 1909 during Diaghilev's first season of the Russian ballet in Paris. The impact on the world of the dance was tremendous. This position of pre-eminence the Russian ballet has retained since then.

Cinematography. At the beginning of this century cinematography was

Nijinsky in *Scheherezade*, 1911

still in its infancy. Motion-picture equipment was introduced in Russia in 1896 by a French firm. The first studio was opened in Moscow in 1908, and by 1917 there were seven studios and slightly over 1,000 motion-picture theaters. The technique of the early films was poor and their subject matter uninspiring: supra-patriotic tales, sentimental melodramas, and detective yarns. On a higher level, although technically unsatisfactory, were the dramatizations of Russian classics—Pushkin's *The Queen of Spades,* Turgenev's *The Nest of Gentlefolk,* and others. Russian pre-revolutionary cinematography was, at best, a humble beginning.

Music

Russia Discovers Music. Non-specialists familiar with current concert programs may be surprised to hear that until relatively recently Russia had no operas or musical compositions suitable for platform performance. There were, of course, folksongs which were transmitted orally from generation to generation, as well as religious chants. The Greek Orthodox services, however, do not allow instrumental music, and the Church did not contribute to its development and, indeed, hindered it. The presentation by foreign companies of Italian operas at the St. Petersburg court in the seventeenth and eighteenth centuries stimulated interest in lay music. Several foreigners living in Russia and a few natives tried their hand at musical scores patterned after those of Germany and Italy. These efforts were unrewarding and are of no interest today, except to the antiquarians. The better-known among the early undistinguished composers were the Italian Caterino Cavos (1776–1840), a resident of St. Petersburg after 1789 and author of some 50 compositions, including the supra-patriotic opera *Ivan Susanin* (named after an epic hero who allegedly saved Michael Romanov from assassination by the Poles in 1613), which, its subject notwithstanding, sounded distressingly Neapolitan; and Alexis Verstovsky (1799–1862), a Russian who wrote the once-popular opera *The Tomb of Askold,* another highly patriotic subject, and many less ambitious pieces. These compositions, and others on a similar level, were devoid of merit, and their popularity with contemporaneous audiences must be ascribed to the ignorance of music on the part of the public.

The first Russian composer worthy of the name was Michael Glinka (1804–1857). He studied in Germany, Italy, and France and acquired a good knowledge of the theory and technique of music which he was the first to apply to Russian themes. His more important compositions were the operas *Life for the Tsar* (1836, re-named *Ivan Susanin* under the Soviets) and *Ruslan and Liudmila* (1842), based on a fairy tale by Pushkin. He also wrote a symphony, pieces for piano and strings, and numerous romances. Not all of his music was at first well received, but he is regarded as the founder of the Russian national school of music and his influence with generations of composers was great.

A major development in making the Russian public music-conscious was the founding in 1859 of the Russian Music Society. It was organized largely through the efforts of Anton Rubinstein (1829–1894), son of a Jewish manufacturer converted to Christianity. Rubinstein, once a boy prodigy, was a world-famous pianist and a prolific composer in the Western classical and romantic tradition. His opera *The Demon* (he wrote 19 operas) has often been heard in Russia, but as a composer, he received little recognition abroad. The Russian Music Society maintained branches in St. Petersburg, Moscow, and some 30 provincial cities. It established conservatories in St. Petersburg (1862) and in Moscow (1866) and music schools in several of the provincial centers. The level of instruction in these institutions, especially in the two conservatories, was high. Another major activity of the society was to maintain symphony orchestras and to arrange concerts and recitals by Russian and foreign artists. Anton Rubinstein was the director of the St. Petersburg conservatory, and his brother Nicholas, like Anton a composer and a pianist, was director of the Moscow conservatory. The work of the society gave a powerful stimulus to the promotion, understanding, and appreciation of music. The situation in this respect was indeed revolutionized in a surprisingly short time.

The Later Age: Composers and Performers. Of great consequence was the appearance of an array of composers, conductors, and performing artists of real eminence. The ground broken by Glinka proved fertile. Alexander Dargomyzhsky (1813–1869) and Alexander Serov (1820–1871) continued Glinka's work, although with less distinction. Serov is chiefly remembered as a music critic and a popularizer of the ideas and music of Richard Wagner. A major event was the emergence of "The Five," a group of composers who became the founders of the neo-Russian school. They were M. A. Balakirev (1837–1910), Alexander Borodin (1834–1887), Modest Mussorgsky (1839–1881), Cesar Cui (1835–1918), and Nicholas Rimsky-Korsakov (1844–1908). The neo-Russian school opposed the classical tradition represented by Anton Rubinstein and the conservatory, admired—at times, excessively—Glinka, and insisted on the importance of national motives in music. As a counterpoise to the conservatory, The Five founded in St. Petersburg in 1862 the Free School of Music, which through its teaching and concerts exercised considerable influence. The only fully-trained professional musician among The Five was Borodin, yet their contribution to the world of art was great. Their better-known operas are *Boris Godunov,* by Mussorgsky, *Prince Igor,* by Borodin, and *Le Coq d'Or,* by Rimsky-Korsakov. Peter Tchaikovsky (1840–1893), Alexander Glazunov (1865–1936), Serge Rachmaninoff (1873–1943), and Igor Stravinsky (1882–   ) belong at the top of the list of composers that could be extended many-fold. Serge Prokofiev (1891–1953), who graduated from the St. Petersburg conservatory in 1914, spent much of his adult life in Soviet Russia and presumably should be regarded as a Soviet composer. The work of these and other Russian masters received world-wide recognition and became a standard part of the operatic, ballet, and concert repertory of every country.

Sovfoto

Modest Mussorgsky, portrait by Ilya Repin

The Russian music schools produced an imposing roster of performing artists whose names are familiar in the concert halls of the world. Among the conductors were E. F. Napravnik, V. I. Safonov, Alexander Ziloti, Glazunov, Rachmaninoff, and Serge Koussevitzky, and among the pianists and violinists, Joseph Hofmann, Safonov, Alexander Scriabin, Efrem Zimbalist, Mischa Elman, and Jascha Heifetz. The diversity and intensity of musical life are suggested by the large number of opera houses. St. Petersburg had four, each with an excellent permanent company and an eight- or nine-month season. It was customary to see the same familiar operas performed by different companies at short intervals. Many of the larger provincial cities had their own opera houses with a full season. Symphony orchestra concerts and recitals by individual artists were numerous and varied. Music lovers would have found the Russia of the closing years of the empire a rather congenial place.

The Bettmann Archive

Igor Stravinsky rehearsing *The Rite of Spring,* 1913, drawing by Jean Cocteau

Painting, Sculpture, and Architecture

Painting, Earlier Nineteenth Century. The record of Russian painting was undistinguished and its evolution in the nineteenth century was not as rewarding as that of literature and music. The Academy of Arts (1757) still wielded a powerful stifling influence over the entire field. Art students, both those trained in Russia and studying abroad, were taught to copy slavishly the work of the classic masters. The range of subject deemed appropriate for pictures was limited. Portraits were encouraged, as were paintings on biblical, mythological, and historical themes; Italian landscapes were permitted, but nothing as vulgar and low as Russian scenes. Academic classicism heavily tinged with romanticism reached its zenith with the work of Karl Brüllov (1799-1852) and Fedor Bruni (1799-1875). Brüllov's huge pretentious canvas *The Last Day of Pompeii* (1836) was acclaimed as a masterpiece and is said to have inspired Bulwer-Lytton's novel; it was actually a tasteless, artificial, and labored composition.

Realism and genre painting, that is, unadorned portrayal of everyday life, was a reaction against the artificiality of academic classicism; an early representative of this school was Alexis Venetsianov (1780-1847). Compared with the canvases of Brüllov and Bruni the pictures of Venetsianov were models of restraint and simplicity, but, although the subjects and their treatment were different, the manner of painting remained strictly academic. Paul Fedotov (1815-1852) was another noted painter of the realistic school. Alexander Ivanov (1806-1858), sometimes considered Russia's greatest painter, studied in St. Petersburg and in Italy and spent some 30 years working on a vast canvas *The Appearance of Christ to the People,* which, however, was given a mixed reception when finally exhibited in Russia in 1858. Ivanov's ambition to create a work of outstanding spirituality failed, but the restrained manner of his painting had a lasting and beneficial effect upon Russian art.

Painting, 1860-1917. The intellectual ferment and desire for change which prevailed among Russian intellectuals in the 1860's extended into the realm of art. In a rebellious mood the graduating students of the Academy of Arts in 1863 refused to participate in the contest on the prescribed mythological subject and were expelled. This trivial episode led to the formation of the Society of Circulating Exhibitions (*peredvizhniki*), an association with which most of the artists were affiliated and which, as indicated by its name, organized shows which toured the country. The society, an important art center until the end of the empire, adhered to a definite ideological program. It rejected both classicism and (later) the notion of "art for art's sake" and held that what really mattered was the social content of the picture. This theory was endorsed by an influential literary and art critics—Dobroliubov, Pisarev, Nekrasov, Chernyshevsky. Theory did not agree with practice, however. The work of the members of the society demonstrated conclusively that heartfelt protest against social injustice does not necessarily produce great or even tolerable art. The more prominent members of the society were its founder Ivan Kramskoy (1837–1887) and Vasily Perov (1834–1882); also Vasily Vereshchagin (1842–1904), a battle painter, and Vasily Surikov (1848–1916) who painted historical subjects. Their oversized canvases had a short-lived popularity, only to slip into deserved oblivion. On a somewhat higher level were the seascapes by Ivan Aivazovsky (1817–1900) and the landscapes by Ivan Shishkin (1832–1898). By far the most renowned "social" painter was Ilya Repin (1844–1930). Although enshrined in the official tradition as a great master, his work in restrospect seems singularly pallid, unimaginative, and stale.

The *peredvizhniki* movement was born as a protest against academic classicism; the sterility of social realism brought forth, in turn, a host of vanguard movements which made their appearance in the 1890's and the 1900's. The original impetus might have come from young Russian artists who had studied abroad, especially in Paris. In the middle of the 1890's opposition to social painting centered on *Mir Iskusstva* (The Art World), which was mentioned earlier in this chapter in connection with avant-garde literary movements. Led by Diaghilev and the painter and art critic Alexander Benois (1870–1960), *Mir Iskusstva* advocated "art for art's sake" and extreme individualism. Its annual exhibitions presented the work of distinguished artists, among them Isaak Levitan (1861–1900), perhaps Russia's first impressionist; Constantine Korovin (1861–1939); Valentin Serov (1865–1911), a noted portrait painter; Boris Kustodiev (1878–1927); Igor Grabar (1871–1960), an eminent art historian; Constantine Somov (1869–1909); Nicholas Roerich (1874–1947), a remarkably prolific artist; and Leon Bakst (1868–1924). The members of *Mir Iskusstva* were not painters in the grand manner, but they were sensitive artists, expert draftsmen and illustrators, and imaginative stage designers. Their cooperation with Diaghilev was a vital element in the success of the Russian ballet.

In the twentieth century the traditional seclusion of Russian art came to an end. From 1900 on Russian painters exhibited abroad. A special Russian section was presented by Diaghilev at the Paris Autumn Salon in 1906, while exhibitions of advanced foreign masters—Cézanne, Gaugin, Picasso—were held in Russia. Vanguard movements flourished. Impressionism made its appearance about 1905; it was followed by post-impressionism, expressionism, futurism and cubism (about 1912), and various ill-defined brands of abstract painting (imagists, rayonists, suprematists, constructivists). Not all these movements were sound or viable, but there was certainly no lack of diversity.

Sculpture. Sculpture was the Cinderella among Russian arts, partly because the Orthodox Church does not allow the use of statues in the decoration of places of worship. Nevertheless, following the establishment of the Academy of Arts (1757) sculptors of merit began to appear—F. I. Shubin (1740–1805), F. F. Shchedrin (1751–1825), Ivan Martos (1752–1835), Count Fedor Tolstoy (1783–1873), and Baron P. K. Clodt (1805–1867). These artists were rooted in the academic and classical tradition. Some of the work of Clodt, however, especially his moldings of animals, showed the influence of the realism that was to characterize the work of Mark Anotokolsky (1843–1902) and of Prince Paolo Trubetskoy (1866–1938), the only Russian sculptor to gain wide recognition in western Europe and in the United States. Sculpture proved less responsive to vanguard movements than literature and painting, perhaps because the number of artists engaged in that branch of art was relatively small and technical conditions made experimentation with novel methods of expression difficult.

Architecture. The nineteenth century added little of value to the record of Russian architecture, even though imposing public and private structures were built in St. Petersburg and elsewhere. In the reign of Alexander I some of the leading architects were still foreigners: the Frenchman Thomas de Thomon (1754–1813) designed the monumental stock exchange building in St. Petersburg (1805), and August Montferrant (1786–1858), another Frenchman, the Saint Isaac Cathedral, which took 40 years to build (1817–1858). But native talents came increasingly to the fore. Andrew Voronikhin (1760–1814) was the architect of the Kazan Cathedral in St. Petersburg (1801) and of the Institute of Mines (1806), and Adrien Zakharov (1761–1811) was the creator of the admiralty building (1806), one of St. Petersburg's famous landmarks. The gracious "Russian *empire,*" or neoclassical style evolved in the later part of the eighteenth century was widely used for town and country residences of the nobility, but in the second half of the century it was superseded by an unimaginative eclecticism, that is, a mixture of styles borrowed from western Europe. Moreover, under Nicholas I a pseudo-Russo-Byzantine style became quasi-obligatory for all types of buildings, from cathedrals to peasant cottages. The Grand Palace in the Kremlin, designed by K. A. Ton (1794–1881), is a notable example of this ornate and unattractive style of architecture. The better-known architects of this period, which produced no masters, were V. I. Hartmann (1834–1873), D. I. Grimm (1823–1898), and I. P. Ropet-Petrov (1845–1908). The two tendencies just mentioned—eclecticism and pseudo-national style—dominated Russian architecture until the end of the monarchy. The trend towards modernism that manifested itself in western Europe at that time was slow in making itself felt in Russia.

Science

A Late Start. The Academy of Science organized by Peter I (1724)—an exotic growth in the desert of Russia's ignorance and illiteracy—achieved little in promoting the advancement of knowledge. A small group of foreign scholars—Leonard Euler, John and Daniel Bernoulli—came to reside for a while in St. Petersburg. In the middle of the eighteenth century Michael Lomonosov, a versatile native scientific genius, carried on important investigations in chemistry, physics, and other disciplines, but the significance of his discoveries and achievements has been greatly exaggerated by a nationalistic historiography. The founding of the University of Moscow (1755) did not improve the situation, because of the absence of primary and secondary schools. It was not until the middle of the nineteenth century, after large contingents of Russian students trained abroad returned to their homeland and became teachers in the Russian higher schools, that one can speak of Russian science. Among the small group of early Russian scholars who gained recognition in western Europe were the astronomer Vasily Struve (1793–1864), founder of the Pulkovo observatory near St. Petersburg (1833), and the mathematician Nicholas Lobachevsky (1792–1856). Struve, however, was German by birth and education and taught in the German-language University of Dorpat (Russia). In later years Russian science progressed rapidly. The chemist D. I. Mendeleev (1843–1907), the biologist I. I. Mechnikov (1845–1916), and the physiologist I. P. Pavlov (1849–1936) were among the acknowledged leaders in their respective fields. The social sciences, too, marked an important advance and did creditable, solid work, but Russia produced no philosophers or social thinkers comparable to the great intellectual figures of the West, except perhaps for the revolutionary leaders (Lenin, Trotsky), who prior to 1917 were hardly known outside narrow revolutionary circles.

Ilya Mechnikov in his laboratory

Ivan Pavlov demonstrating the conditioned reflex

Conclusion

Characteristics of Russian Culture. A bird's-eye view of Russian cultural development suggests certain general observations, which will be limited to three. Although historically Russia is an ancient country, her literature, art, and science were recent and seldom went further back than the first half of the nineteenth century. In spite of the narrowness of Russia's cultural tradition, her achievements in the various fields of endeavor, while uneven, were great. Finally, Russian culture was the treasured possession of a small minority of the educated class. The socially and politically unfortunate consequences of this situation were to accentuate the cleavage between the privileged few and the disinherited masses. Lack of social unity, a by-product of the lack of cultural unity, was a major factor in shaping the character of the revolution of 1917.

18

Imperial Russia and the First World War, 1914-February 1917

The Outbreak of the War

Changing Views on Responsibility for the War. The question of responsibility for the First World War has attracted much attention and has created a vast literature, some of it valuable. Unfortunately, historians who dealt with this subject, which came to be known as that of war guilt, tended at times to ascribe to individual statesmen or groups of statesmen the deliberate intention to bring about the armed conflict. Distance helps to give a right perspective. Now that over half a century has elapsed since the events of 1914 and much historical evidence has been brought to light and analyzed, it can be plausibly argued that the great conflagration that devastated Europe and had far-reaching repercussions throughout the world was not actually desired or planned by the leaders of any country but was rather the consequence of their inability to foresee the results of policies which appeared to them as essential to national security and welfare. The misconceptions of European statesmen bore on two main points: the notion of national interest, a treacherous and elusive concept, and the evaluation of what foreign governments were likely to do. Viewed from this angle the outbreak of World War I appears as the culminating act of a tragedy of errors and not as the implementation of someone's grand design.

[390]

June–August, 1914. On June 28, 1914, N.S., Archduke Francis Ferdinand, heir apparent to the Austrian throne, and his morganatic wife, the Duchess of Hohenberg, were murdered during a state visit to Sarajevo, capital of the predominantly Serbian province of Bosnia, which had been annexed by Austria-Hungary in 1908–1909. The assassin was a Bosnian student affiliated with Serbian nationalist and terroristic organizations. The Serbian government was not implicated in the plot, but it had tolerated and encouraged anti-Austrian agitation.

Political murders in the Balkans were not unusual, and the archduke was not a major political figure. His assassination, therefore, was at first taken as a matter of course, and no serious complications were expected. The basic decision rested with the Viennese government. Count Berchtold, the Austrian minister of foreign affairs, and Baron Conrad von Hötzendorf, Austrian chief of staff, firmly believed that Pan-Serbian agitation was a deadly menace to the Dual Monarchy—because of the large Slavic population within its borders—and that Serbia should be taught an exemplary lesson. Emperor William II of Germany and the German chancellor Bethmann Hollweg—the Berlin government was the only one consulted by Vienna (July 5, N.S.)—signified their unconditional approval and promised to support the strong measures to be taken against Serbia, although their exact nature had not yet been determined. The reason for this imprudent commitment was the belief that a show of firmness would bolster the prestige of Austria, Germany's principal ally. Neither the Austrian nor the German government anticipated that retribution on Serbia, however ruthless, would lead to a European war. Berchtold, his resolve strengthened by Germany's unconditional endorsement, proceeded to prepare a note to Serbia that embodied conditions of extreme severity. The tenor of the note was at first resisted as a "fatal mistake" by Count Tisza, the Hungarian minister-president, but he was prevailed upon to withdraw his objections (July 14, N.S.) in return for the promise that war with Serbia would not lead to the annexation by the Dual Monarchy of Slavic territories, which Tisza regarded as inimical to Hungarian interests. The secret of the impending diplomatic step was well guarded, but there was some uneasiness in European capitals as to the reasons for Austria's long delay in announcing her demands. The Austrian note, actually completed on July 19, N.S., was not delivered until July 23, N.S., to make sure that Raymond Poincaré, the French president, who was paying a state visit to St. Petersburg, had left the Russian capital. Meanwhile Russian opinion as reflected in the press and public pronouncements was anti-Austrian and pro-Serbian but remained within the bounds of moderation and propriety. Public interest centered on the French presidential visit (July 20–23, N.S.) and the accompanying waves of strikes.

The violence of the Austrian note, which took the form of an ultimatum demanding a reply within 48 hours (by July 25, N.S.), suddenly revealed the seriousness of the situation. Partly under the pressure of Sazonov, the Russian minister of foreign affairs, the Serbian government accepted all Austrian demands except that for the participation of Austrian officials in the proposed investigation of the Sarajevo murder. As this was not deemed sufficient, the Austrian ambassador immediately left the Serbian capital (July 25, N.S.), and Austria declared war on Serbia on July 28, N.S., and the next day bombarded Belgrade. Meanwhile there was a plethora of proposals emanating from European capitals for the solution of the crisis, in which the Berlin government, reversing itself, participated beginning July 27, N.S.

While Berchtold held fast to the theory that a chastisement of Serbia was essential to the preservation of the Dual Monarchy, Sazonov and the Russian military leaders were convinced that Russia's national interest demanded the protection of Serbia. A dilemma that confronted every government in the great emergency was the conflict between policies aimed at the preservation of peace and the needs of national defense. In the case of Russia the central issue was one of mobilization. Sazonov and other Russian leaders hesitated between partial and general mobilization. The imminence of a mobilization was agreed upon as early as July 24 and 25, N.S., partial mobilization was announced on July 28, N.S., but after several changes it was replaced by a general mobilization on July 30, N.S. It is often held that it was the Russian mobilization that, by forcing Germany to take similar measures, actually precipitated the war; yet this argument is not convincing, and it is difficult to see what other course St. Petersburg could have followed. Germany and France mobilized their armed forces, and declarations of war between the various states came early in August. Italy, after abortive negotiations for territorial "compensation" from Austria, took officially the view that war was due to Austrian aggression and that therefore she was under no obligation to come to the assistance of her partners in the Triple Alliance. The German ultimatum to Belgium (August 2, N.S.) was the final argument in making a reluctant England enter the struggle on the side of France and Russia. The transformation of a local war with Serbia into a European war was something that no one had wished and Vienna and Berlin had not foreseen, while the outcome of the war provided conclusive evidence that the notions of national interest held by the leaders of the three eastern empires —Austria-Hungary, Germany, and Russia—were hopelessly at variance with the exigencies of history.

Military Campaigns

East Prussia. The fortunes of war did not favor the armies of the tsar. The strategic plan of the Russian general staff called for an advance into Austria and defensive policies on the German front. The Austrian offensive was to relieve pressure on Serbia and to prevent invasion from the south of Russian Poland, which, protruding dangerously into enemy territory, was in an exposed position. It was also believed in St. Petersburg that the Austro-Hungarian army, which comprised a large Slav element (over 50 per cent, according to an official estimate), was a lesser menace than the German war machine. Russian strategic arrangements were frustrated by the rapid German advance through Belgium and France and the desperate appeals of the Western allies for a diversion on the eastern front. This took the form of a massive Russian invasion of East Prussia which began on August 17, N.S., under the command of Generals P. K. Rennenkampf and A. V. Samsonov. Generals Hindenburg and Ludendorff were in charge of the East Prussian defenses. After some initial successes the Russian army, which was numerically superior to the German but was short of artillery and technical equipment, was entrapped by the enemy in the Tannenberg-Soldau region (August 30, N.S.). Samsonov committed suicide, two of his army corps surrendered, and Rennenkampf, reputedly a gallant cavalry officer, abandoned his troops and fled into Russian territory. The Russians lost 300,000 men and 650 guns. By the middle of September the invasion was over; except for operations of a purely local character the Russians made no further attempts at entering East Prussia.

Galicia, 1914–Spring 1915. The Russian offensive in the Austrian province of Galicia began on a front 300 miles long on August 18, N.S., simultaneously with the advance in East Prussia, and during the opening weeks scored important victories. The Russians captured Lemberg (Lvov, the capital of Galicia), Czernovitz (the capital of Bukovina), besieged the fortress of Przemysl, reached the southern slopes of the Carpathian Mountains, and took some 350,000 prisoners. Large groups of Ukrainians, Slovaks, and Czechs serving with the Austrian army surrendered; many of the Poles, however, were ardently anti-Russian, and a Polish legion organized by Pilsudski fought with the Austrian army. The Dual Monarchy was in a serious predicament, and Germany came hastily to its rescue. At the end of September, Hindenburg mounted a powerful offensive in the southwestern provinces of Russian Poland and advanced to the outskirts of Warsaw (middle of October) but was forced to withdraw some 100 miles west. A second German thrust towards Warsaw (middle of November) was again successfully resisted by the Russians, and in December the front was stabilized for the winter some 35 miles west of that city. The Russian campaigns in East Prussia and Galicia relieved German pressure on the Western allies during the crucial battles of the Marne and Ypres (October and November) and foiled Austrian attempts at crushing Serbia (August, November, and December). But they also disclosed grave inadequacies in the organization of the Russian army and revealed disturbing signs of the demoralization of the troops and lack of confidence in victory.

The offensive in Galicia was resumed in the spring of 1915. Przemysl capitulated after a siege of six months, the Russians capturing 2,500 officers, 120,000 men, and over 900 guns. There was a renewal of activity on the Carpathian front, and the invasion of Hungary loomed as a distinct possibility. Meanwhile Petrograd (the name of the capital was changed from St. Petersburg to Petrograd at the beginning of the war) viewed Galicia as a permanent conquest. Swarms of Russian lay and ecclesiastical officials descended on that province and proceeded to remodel its cultural, administrative, and religious institutions according to the Russian pattern. The Ukrainian national movement was treated as reprehensible "separatism," and its leaders, including the historian Michael Hrushevski and the Uniat metropolitan Count Szepticki, were deported to Russia. At the end of April, Emperor Nicholas paid a state visit to Galicia and at a function in Lemberg spoke of an "indivisible" Russia stretching to the Carpathian Mountains. His train had barely time to recross the Russian border before the Central Powers launched a formidable offensive in that section of the front.

The Austro-German Offensive. The operation was carefully prepared. During April eight German divisions were moved secretly from France to the Cracow region and on May 1, N.S., began the joint Austro-German offensive that took the Russians by surprise. The attackers, supported by artillery fire of an intensity the Russians had not experienced before and by a strong air force, advanced on a wide front. The Russian lines faltered and then broke down, and soon the troops were in full retreat. The allied attacks in Flanders and at Artois, undertaken at the request of the Russian command, and the entry of Italy in the war on the side of the *entente* (May 23, N.S.) failed to improve the situation. Przemysl and Lemberg were evacuated in June, and by the end of that month Galicia was practically cleared of the Russian troops. The Germans then turned to Russian Poland and the Baltic provinces. They captured Warsaw early in August and Vilna in the middle of September; a string of Russian fortresses (Novogeorgievsk, Kovno, Brest-

Litovsk) fell to the enemy, some without offering any resistance. On the Baltic littoral the Germans occupied the ice-free port of Libau, but their advance stopped short of Riga. By the autumn of 1915 the front ran two to three hundred miles east of the Russian border, which meant the loss of some of the more industrialized provinces. A small stretch of Galicia east of the Sereth River was all that was left of the Russian conquests.

The bitterness of military reverses was made even less palatable by the scorched-earth policy devised by army headquarters—the advancing enemy was to encounter a desert. This was presumed to be the re-enactment of the "retreat of 1812" that had led Napoleon to Moscow and perdition. The difference between 1812, when the French advanced along a few roads, and 1915, when the front stretched from the Baltic to the Rumanian border, was strangely overlooked. The scorched-earth policy meant in practice that the civilian population of the invaded provinces was evicted, while farms, villages, and crops were laid waste. No adequate arrangements were made for the reception of the evacuees, who died by the thousands from hunger, exposure, and disease. In the spring of 1916 the number of registered refugees was well over 3 million, but many, no doubt, went unregistered. The council of ministers protested vainly against the policy of forced evacuation, which it regarded as criminal folly.

In spite of Russian military reverses and the other disappointments suffered by the allies in 1915—stalemate on the Western front, Bulgaria's entry in the war on the side of the Central Powers (September), conquest of Serbia and Montenegro by the Austro-Germans (October–November), and the withdrawal of the allied Dardanelles expedition (December)—Russia was not prepared to accept defeat. The army had retained its cohesion, the will to resist appeared to be strengthened by adversity, and in the later part of 1915 a real effort was made to organize the country for the war. The spurring of domestic production and massive shipments of war materials and equipment from the allies succeeded in overcoming the worst military shortages, and by the end of 1916 the army supply service was vastly improved.

Galicia, 1916. From October 1915 to March 1916 the eastern front remained quiescent. At an allied conference at Chantilly, in December 1915, the Russian command assumed the obligation to resume the offensive not later than June 1916. Plans were made for a thrust in the direction of Vilna, but they were not carried out. Instead, responding to an urgent appeal of the allies for a diversion to relieve pressure on Verdun, the Russians improvised an attack on the German positions in the area of Lake Naroch that was repulsed with heavy losses. Then came an even more urgent clamor for help from the Italians, who experienced severe reverses at the hands of the Austrians in the Trentino. To meet this situation the Russian high command accepted, after much hesitation, the plan of General Brusilov for a major assault in Galicia. The Russian offensive began early in June and proved remarkably successful. By October, when the military operations came to a standstill, Brusilov had occupied some 10,000 square miles of Austrian territory and taken 400,000 prisoners. Meanwhile the proposed operation in the region of Vilna was abandoned, and little action took place on the German sector of the Russian front.

The strategic gains of the Brusilov offensive were substantial. Austria's military power suffered a blow from which it never entirely recovered. The transfer of 18 German divisions from the west to the Russian front staved off the collapse of the Italian army and eased the pressure on the allies at Verdun, on the Somme, and at Salonika. Russia's military successes were instrumental in bringing about the long-deferred decision of Rumania to join the allies (August). But from the narrow Russian point of view the results of the offensive were inconclusive and disappointing and did not justify the losses, which in 1916 amounted to 2 million killed or wounded and 350,000 prisoners. There was much criticism of Brusilov and the high command as well as mounting evidence of the fatigue and disaffection of the troops and of their unwillingness to fight. The accession of Rumania to the allied cause proved a questionable military asset. The record of the Rumanian army during World War I was undistinguished. Most of that country was speedily overrun by the enemy, and the eastern front was lengthened by 250 miles, which were to be defended chiefly by the Russians.

The Caucasian Front and Naval Warfare. The Black Sea and the Caucasian front were of secondary importance. Naval warfare in the Black Sea began at the end of October 1914 with the bombardment of Russian ports by the German battle cruisers *Göben* and *Breslau,* which were transferred to Turkish ownership. Russia and her allies retaliated by declaring war on Turkey early in November. A menacing Turkish advance in the Caucasus led to the Russian request (December 1914) for an allied diversion, which became the starting point of the Dardanelles expedition. The Turkish offensive petered out, however, and the subsequent course of the Caucasian campaign was, as a whole, favorable to Russia and resulted in the occupation of Armenia.

The part taken by the Russian navy in the hostilities was insignificant and was limited to coastal action.

Imperial Diplomacy

Japan, Turkey, Italy, and the Balkans. The Anglo-Franco-Russian alliance was formalized in the treaty of September 5, 1914, N.S., and bound the contracting parties not to conclude a separate peace and to consort about future peace terms; this agreement did not preclude serious friction among the allies. There were several countries which for political and geographical reasons were of great importance and which both belligerents endeavored to win to their respective sides. The case of Japan presented no difficulty. The Tokyo government joined the allies (August 1914), seized German-controlled territories and naval bases on the Chinese mainland and in the Pacific islands, and supplied Russia with much-needed war material, although chiefly obsolete. The Japanese entry into the war eased the Russian situation in the Pacific area by removing the danger of attack on Russian installations in those regions by either Japan or Germany.

Turkey presented a different problem. The allied governments were anxious to prevent her from joining the Central Powers. Surprisingly Sazonov was prepared to go further than his British and French colleagues in offering concessions to Constantinople. Thus he proposed the transfer to Turkey of the Greek island of Lemnos and of German holdings in Asia Minor, but these offers were vetoed by London and Paris, mindful of Greek susceptibilities. In Constantinople, however, the pro-German faction of the Young Turk government had the upper hand, and the attacks by the *Göben* and *Breslau* on Russian Black Sea ports led to the declaration of war on the Ottoman Porte by the *entente* powers (early November 1914). From the Russian standpoint Turkish belligerency had two major consequences: it meant definitely the closure of the Dardanelles to Russian and allied shipping, and it allowed Russia to claim Constantinople as her principal war aim.

Italy's entry into the war on the side of the allies was preceded by protracted bargaining with both belligerent groups, not a very dignified procedure. In the course of these laborious negotiations Sazonov was often at odds with his Western colleagues, who, he held, were all-too-willing to sacrifice the legitimate interests of the Balkan Slavs (particularly those of Serbia and Montenegro in the Adriatic) to the territorial ambitions of Italy. The 4-power treaty of London (April 26, 1915, N.S.) that defined Italian territorial acquisitions in case of allied victory was characterized by Sazonov as a "capitulation" before Italian demands; he had agreed to sign it reluctantly "under strong pressure from the allies."

Relations with the Balkan countries—Bulgaria, Greece, and Rumania—were complicated by the mutual jealousies and conflicting territorial claims of these states and by Russia's designs on Constantinople, which made Petrograd exceedingly suspicious of Sofia and Athens, which allegedly were harboring similar plans. Bulgaria, Rumania, and Greece had German dynasties and powerful pro-German parties, but the principal issue was territorial. While the chief territorial demands of Rumania and Greece could be satisfied at the expense of the Dual Monarchy, this was not true of Bulgaria, whose government clamored for Macedonia, a province held by Serbia and Greece. Serbia was reluctant to make to Bulgaria the concessions which alone might have prevented that country from entering the war on the side of the Central Powers. This she did in September 1915.

At the outbreak of the war Rumania, in spite of the recent improvement in her relations with Russia and the other *entente* powers, was definitely in the German-Austro-Hungarian orbit. She was linked to the Triple Alliance (Germany, Austria-Hungary, and Italy) by a treaty of defensive alliance that went back to 1883 and had been renewed as recently as 1913. King Charles, who had headed the Rumanian government since 1881, was a Hohenzollern and leader of the pro-German party. Moreover, Rumanian national aspirations included both provinces held by the Dual Monarchy and Bessarabia, which was under Russian rule. King Charles favored immediate intervention on the side of Berlin and Vienna, but he was overruled by his government and Rumania remained neutral until August 1916, when, after practically all her territorial demands were conceded by the allies, she joined the *entente* powers. Sazonov, who ceased to be minister of foreign affairs in July 1916, doubted the military value of Rumania's military intervention and favored her benevolent neutrality, but Britain and France insisted that Rumania should declare war. Subsequent events on the Rumanian front indicated that Sazonov's apprehensions were justified.

Greece adhered traditionally to the Western orientation, and Russian influence in Athens was less pronounced than in the Slavic Balkan states. Russian and Greek policies clashed over Greek participation in the Dardanelles expedition, a favorite project of Winston Churchill (then first lord of the admiralty) that, however, was not implemented until early in 1915, after reverses in the Caucasus made the Russian high command appeal to the allies for a diversion in the Near East. The British and the French favored Greek participation in the Dardanelles operation, but Sazonov, who in the meantime had espoused the view that Constantinople should belong to Russia, would have none of it. There followed a sharp disagreement among the allies that was probably gratuitous, because it is unlikely that Greek intervention would have made much difference. However, eminent authorities, among them Churchill, believed that Russian obstructions were fatal to the Dardanelles expedition, which ended miserably: after suffering heavy losses the allied forces based on Gallipoli were withdrawn in December 1915. In the subsequent events in Greece, from the allied landing in Salonika in October 1915 to the deposition of King Constantine and the entry of Greece into the war on the side of the *entente* in the summer of 1917, Russia played but a subordinate part.

War Aims. In the modern age belligerents must have concrete war aims, that is, it is not enough to denounce the wickedness and brutality of the enemy or to extol the alleged virtues of its victim—Serbia in the case of World War I. In the middle of September 1914 Sazonov dutifully outlined to the British and French ambassadors Russia's positive war aims. Under his proposal, the tsarist empire was to acquire eastern Galicia and a stretch of territory on the Niemen River; Posen, Silesia, and western Galicia were to be incorporated into an autonomous Poland under the Russian Crown. The other and more numerous items listed by Sazonov dealt with the "historical grievances" of the European states, including such uninspiring bits of political archaeology as the restoration of Schleswig-Holstein to Denmark. At the end of September Sazonov amended his program by demanding the opening of the Turkish Straits to Russian warships. Constantinople, often cited as one of the main causes of the war, was not mentioned, but Turkey was not yet a belligerent.

With the outbreak of war with Turkey the situation changed. A Russian imperial manifesto spoke of the imminent solution of "the historic task bequeathed to us by our forefathers on the shores of the Black Sea." Parliamentary opinion and the press took up this theme with much flourish and an appearance of unanimity that looked impressive. There were many doubters, but their voices were not heard. The British thought it imprudent to oppose Russia's quasi-unanimous wish and, reversing their nineteenth-century policy, signified their willingness to settle the issue of Constantinople and the Straits in accordance with Russian interests. An Anglo-Russian agreement providing for the annexation by Russia of Constantinople and of the littoral of the Bosphorus, the Dardanelles, and the Sea of Marmora was signed in March 1915; it was adhered to by France in April of that year and by Italy in December 1916. Russia, in turn, approved the proposed partition of enemy territories among the Western allies. The Constantinople agreement became the foundation of a complex structure of secret treaties dealing with the division of the spoils that, when eventually disclosed, did much harm to the cause of the allies.

Ironically Sazonov, whose Pan-Slavism was jejune and tepid, became one of the principal advocates of the annexation of Constantinople. He had little faith, however, in the efficacy of international agreements unsupported by force and urged military and naval action that would assure Russia the physical possession of the Straits. His plea brought no response: the high command was unable to provide the ships and men needed. In the meantime Russia became party to other inter-allied agreements dealing with the distribution of territories in the Near East (April 1916) and in eastern Europe (Franco-Russian agreement, February 1917). Constantinople, however, remained the highest prize, and, to bolster the sagging morale of the nation, allied acceptance of the proposed Russian annexation was announced in the Duma in December 1916. Coming in the midst of an acute political and military crisis (the murder of Rasputin and the collapse of the Rumanian army) the announcement, to quote the British ambassador, "fell perfectly flat." It is clear that the issue of Russia's historical mission on the shores of the Bosphorus was an artificial one and commanded no real popular support. This conclusion is corroborated by public reaction to the revival of the question of Constantinople by the Provisional Government, after the revolution of February–March 1917.

War and the Economy

Labor, Industry, Agriculture, and Railways. Among the illusions shattered by the war was the widely-held belief that a backward economy, such as Russia's, was relatively immune from the ill effects of belligerency. Actually, alarming signs of the approaching collapse became evident months before the revolution of 1917 dealt the Russian economy the final blow.

The principal factors responsible for the deterioration of the economic situation were: the shortage of labor resulting from the mobilization of a very large number of men; shrinkage of the supplies of manufactured goods and foodstuffs; reduction of productive capacity owing to the loss of territory; appearance of a huge new demand represented by the armed forces; breakdown of the transportation system; disruption of foreign trade and the isolation of Russia from the outside world; decline in revenue, rise in prices, and depreciation of the ruble; and, last but not least, tardiness in realizing the nature of the war economic problems and the ineffectualness of the official policies to meet them.

The total number of men drafted into the army during the war was over 15 million; 12 million were mobilized by the end of 1915. It was estimated that, in 1917, 37 per cent of the male population of working age served in the armed forces. In industry the consequence of the draft was not the shrinkage of the labor force but its structural changes. It is believed that while industry lost many of its workers, including skilled workers, the aggregate number of those employed increased during the war by some 400,000. This increment and the replacement consisted of women, young persons, Oriental labor (Chinese, Persian), and refugees, that is, people largely lacking in skill and experience. Influx of labor of this type resulted in less efficient production. Eventually skilled workers needed by industry were released from the armed forces (where they often lingered in idleness in recruitment depots), but this measure accomplished little in easing the situation.

In agriculture the labor shortage was a greater problem on large estates than on peasant farms, which, because of their small size and backward methods of husbandry, had in peacetime more hands than they actually needed. Growing demand and rising prices spurred peasant farming, which actually extended its area under crops during the war, while the cultivated acreage of large estates shrank substantially. This development was one of the causes of the shortage of food supplies, because large estates produced chiefly for the market. The other major causes of food shortages were the growth of the demand, the unwillingness of the peasants to sell their grain, and the breakdown of transportation.

The emergence of a new large and inelastic demand was due to the fact that the government had to provide for millions of soldiers whose army fare was far more substantial than what they used to have at home (where, moreover, supplies came chiefly from the peasants' own farms), as well as for the refugees. The diversion of the entire industrial capacity for production for the army after the adoption in 1915 of the policy of "mobilization of industry" led to the curtailment, and disappearance, of the stock of commodities needed by the peasants, such as fertilizers, agricultural machinery, tools, and various consumers' goods. This situation tended to deprive the farmers of the incentive to market their grain and other produce.

The strain and stress of the war disclosed the vulnerability of the railways, which held the key position in the economic system. Their network was of low efficiency, their rolling stock was too small and run-down, and their technical services proved incapable of meeting the greatly increased demands resulting from the war. Transport disorders became a major factor in the breakdown of the service of supply, and the situation in this respect deteriorated progressively as the war went on.

Foreign Trade, Finance, and Economic Policies. With the outbreak of hostilities Russia was practically cut off from the outside world. The European land frontier, except for the unimportant section with Rumania, was closed. The Baltic Sea was controlled by the German navy, while the Turks blocked the entrance to the Black Sea. The only direct sea routes available to Russia were those of the Pacific and of the White Sea, both distant and difficult of access. Archangel, Russia's principal port on the White Sea, is icebound part of the year. A railway hastily built from Petrograd to Murmansk, an ice-free port in the extreme north, was not completed until the end of 1916. Transit through neutral Sweden was entangled in the legalistic intricacies of the allied blockade of Germany, which impeded the usefulness of this route.

Wartime conditions played havoc with international trade. The value of Russian exports declined to a fraction of their pre-war figure, while that of imports, which consisted of war supplies and materials, increased. Foreign trade expressed in terms of a rapidly depreciating currency does not, however, give a fair picture of the situation, because the volume (weight) of both exports and imports declined, although the rate of decline of the former was greater than of the latter. Grain exports, that foundation of Russia's international solvency, practically disappeared. The favorable balance of trade (excess of exports over imports), which was the immutable rule of Russian pre-1914 finance, was dramatically reversed: during the first three years of the war the cumulative deficit in Russian international accounts reached 2.5 billion rubles.

The treasury found itself in a dire predicament: revenue declined, partly because of the loss of territory, while expenditure mounted. To make things worse the government, presumably on the initiative of the tsar, prohibited the sale of liquor (August 1914) for the duration of the war, thus depriving the state of its principal single source of revenue. Prohibition accomplished nothing in advancing temperance. Bootlegging and home distilling flourished, much of the home-made liquor was not fit for human consumption, and drunkenness showed no sign of decline. The cumulative cost of the war was unofficially estimated, as of August 1917, at 38.6 billion rubles. New taxes, including the income tax introduced in 1916, merely covered the loss of revenue, and the cost of the war was defrayed by borrowing and by the issuance of paper currency. During the first three years of the war the public debt increased by 24 billion rubles, while the volume of paper currency in circulation, which was 1.6 billion rubles in July 1914, rose to 9 billion by the end of 1916 and to 19 billion by October 1917. In terms of foreign currencies the ruble lost 39 per cent of its pre-war value by the end of 1916 and 63 per cent by October 1917.

In 1914 there was little understanding in Russia of the problems of war economy, and the safest policy appeared to be to do nothing, that is, no government intervention was contemplated and the official policy was "business as usual." The calamitous shortage of army supplies during the retreat of 1915, the breakdown of the railways, and mounting economic disorders, among which the inadequacy of food supplies to the urban centers was particularly grave, called for remedial action. In the middle of 1915 "business as usual" was discarded in favor of "mobilization of industry" for the needs of defense. The new policy was directed by specially-created agencies of a semi-official, semi-public character. A measure of success was achieved in improving army procurement services, but the diversion of productive capacity into war channels meant a further shrinkage of supplies for the civilian population. No comprehensive attempt at fixing prices of foodstuffs and rationing consumption was made until the end of 1916; and in 1917, a period when the disorganization of the market had reached an advanced stage, the authority of the government was practically nil, and prices were irresistibly moving upwards, reaching levels several times those of the pre-war years.

War and the Government

Evolution of the Government. A casual glance at the Russian government during the war may suggest that no significant change occurred between 1914 and the outbreak of the revolution. This impression would be unjustified. Actually the government evolved simultaneously in two opposite directions: on the one hand, the personal rule of the emperor, guided by his wife and Rasputin, was strengthened; on the other hand, the State Duma, the *zemstvos,* and the community at large came to exercise a bigger part in public affairs than ever before.

The Emperor, the Empress, and Rasputin. The ascendancy of Rasputin was a factor that came to dominate Russia's domestic policies. The tsar, traditionally the head of the government, retained that status after the constitutional changes of 1906, but prior to the war he rarely participated directly in the conduct of the government except through the appointment of ministers, who, however, were usually drawn from a small circle of high officials. Rasputin was introduced to the imperial family in November 1905. His presence at the palace and the influence that he appeared to exercise at times over ministerial and other appointments and other matters of public interest attracted much unfavorable attention but had not yet reached the dimensions of a major political issue. A novel situation arose in and after

August 1915, when Emperor Nicholas, partly at the instigation of his wife, took over from the Grand Duke Nicholas Nikolaevich the supreme command of the army. In his capacity as supreme commander the tsar resided at the army headquarters at Mogilev, while his place in Petrograd was filled by the empress, eager, in her own words, "to wake people up, to put order into all, and unite all forces." The emperor approved: "I am so glad . . . that you have found at last a worthy occupation," he wrote to his wife.

What followed would be entirely incredible were it not established beyond a shadow of doubt by the voluminous correspondence (conducted in English, often unidiomatic and ungrammatical) between the empress and the tsar; fortunately for posterity these letters have been preserved and published. The picture that emerges from this remarkable candid and detailed correspondence is one of total domination of the tsar by his wife, who relied entirely on Rasputin's "wonderful God-sent wisdom." Every appointment to a higher office and some strategic decisions required the "blessing" of "Our Friend." Rasputin was not, as it was occasionally alleged, a German agent, but he was venal, debauched, and surrounded by a host of shoddy clients. He and his *entourage* were the instigators of the numerous ministerial changes which were made in the later part of 1915 and in 1916.

The Rasputin situation became a blatant scandal that, in Russia, overshadowed the war and world events. In November 1916 Miliukov, leader of the Constitutional Democratic Party, spoke in the Duma of the empress and Stürmer, then president of the council of ministers, as leaders of the pro-German clique, and he and the right-wing deputy Vladimir Purishkevich denounced Rasputin. Various aristocratic and conservative groups brought great pressure to bear on the tsar to put an end to the influence of the "dark forces," but Nicholas, as obstinate as he was weak, would not give in. There was much talk of a palace revolution in the eighteenth-century manner. Finally, a small group of men, including the nephew of the tsar, the Grand Duke Dimitry Pavlovich, and Purishkevich, murdered Rasputin (December 17, 1916) in the palace of Prince Felix Yusupov, who was related by marriage to the imperial family. The body of the murdered man was recovered from under the ice of a canal where it was hidden by the conspirators and was buried in the grounds of the imperial residence in the presence of the tsar and his family. There was no formal prosecution of the culprits.

The Bureaucracy. The bureaucracy, that mainstay of the imperial government, underwent, like the Crown, important modifications which extended all the way from the council of ministers to humble provincial offices.

There were two main reasons for this process of decadence of a venerable and firmly-rooted institution: wartime legislation that curtailed the powers of the civilian administration and the kaleidoscopic changes of the incumbents of higher offices resulting from the rule of Rasputin. Under the law on the administration of the army in wartime (June 16, 1914) army commanders in the "military zone" superseded the civilian administration and were given quasi-dictatorial authority. In 1915, with the retreat of the Russian army, the "military zone" came to embrace a large portion of European Russia, including the city of Petrograd. The military proconsuls took their duties seriously and were not easy people to deal with. In July 1915 the minister of the interior complained in the council of ministers that he "was deluged" with telegrams from provincial governors "depicting the intolerable situation created by the military authorities." The interference of the military, he stated, resulted "in total confusion and disorganization." The civilian officials were buffeted about most unceremoniously and, if they attempted to object, were threatened with arrest.

The formal disintegration of the bureaucratic system stemmed from the emperor's capricious moves. During the war Russia had four presidents of the council of ministers: Ivan Goremykin (January 1914 to January 1916), Boris Stürmer (January 1916 to November 1916), and A. F. Trepov and Prince N. D. Golitsyn, who filled that office consecutively during the remaining weeks of the empire (November 1916 to February 1917). Goremykin was 75 and Stürmer 68; both were cynical, senile, and reactionary bureaucrats and appointees of Rasputin. Among the most unpopular members of the Goremykin administration was General V. A. Sukhomlinov, minister of war since 1909. One of his close associates was convicted of treason and hanged. Sukhomlinov, a favorite of the tsar, was dismissed in June 1915 and charged with crimes ranging from corruption to treason. He was arrested in October 1916, was tried and sentenced to life imprisonment after the revolution, but escaped to Germany. He was a worthless minister of war, but he was probably innocent of the crimes for which he was convicted. Three other ministers unpopular with the Duma were dismissed simultaneously with Sukhomlinov. They were replaced by men of relatively liberal views, anxious to cooperate with the chambers, but Goremykin was retained as president of the council of ministers.

The decision of the tsar to assume the high command provoked a ministerial crisis. Fearing the repercussions of military reverses on the position of the Crown if the emperor was to bear the immediate responsibility for the conduct of the war, and apprehensive of the political consequences of his departure from the capital, 10 of the 12 ministers sent to Nicholas, over the protest of Goremykin, a collective letter begging him to rescind his decision. To the empress the request was near-treason, the ministers were ordered to continue in office—the letter implied collective resignation—and the tsar went, as planned, to headquarters. The reconstruction of the cabinet nevertheless took place: in the course of the following 18 months the offending ministers were replaced one by one by men who had the endorsement of the empress and Rasputin. The newcomers often had no qualification for office and remained in power for a few weeks or a few months. Purishkevich aptly described the resulting situation as the "ministerial leap-frog." Nicholas, in one of his rare moments of lucidity, wrote in September 1916: "All these changes make my head go round; in my opinion they are too frequent. In any case they are no good for the internal situation . . . as each new man brings with him alterations in the administration." This, of course, was true, but the shifting of ministers continued.

The New Agencies. The inability of the bureaucracy to cope with wartime problems led to an expansion of the basis of government. Immediately after the outbreak of the war the government approved the formation of the Union of *Zemstvos* and the Union of Towns for the relief of sick and wounded soldiers. The president of the Union of *Zemstvos* was Prince George E. Lvov, a well-known *zemstvo* leader of moderately liberal views and later the first president of the Provisional Government that succeeded the empire. The two unions concerned themselves at first with the relief of the victims of the war, establishing an extensive network of hospitals, canteens, and medical stores and operating hospital trains. With the adoption in 1915 of the policy of "mobilization of industry" the two unions formed a joint agency, Zemgor, which participated in the work of providing supplies for the army. The unions operated chiefly with funds coming from the public treasury, and they built up a creditable record of achievement, which was not, however, above criticism. They were disliked by the more conservative bureaucrats as intruders into areas formerly closed to public endeavor and by the empress as subversive and revolutionary. Through the wide-flung network of their institutions, staffed largely by young men and women of radical leanings, the unions were in close touch with both the civilian population and the army and were an element in fostering discontent and disaffection.

The reaction to the defeat of 1915 and the acceptance of the policy of mobilization of industry brought forth two sets of institutions: the war industries committees and the special councils. The war industries committees were established on the initiative of business and had for their purpose the self-mobilization of industry for national defense. They were largely independent of the government. The network of local war industries committees, which in the spring of 1916 numbered about 240, was headed by the central war industries committee presided over by Alexander Guchkov, a member of a prominent Moscow merchant family, a founder and leader of the Octobrist (moderate liberal) Party, and a former president of the State Duma. Each of the committees was to consist of representatives of government departments, the Unions of *Zemstvos* and of Towns, management, and labor. The participation of labor was, in Russia, a novel departure, and its implementation led to a split in the ranks of social democracy. The Mensheviks, who supported the war effort, favored participation, while the Bolsheviks opposed it and succeeded at first (September 1915) in blocking the election of representatives of labor to the central war industries committee, but this decision was soon reversed (November 1915) and in the spring of 1916 labor was represented on over 100 local committees as well. Most foolishly, the labor group of the central war industries committee was arrested by the imperial government in January 1917. Its members were released after the revolution.

The five special councils—for national defense, transportation, fuel, food supply, and refugees—were established by the State Duma in August 1915. Each council consisted of representatives of government departments, the legislative chambers, the Unions of *Zemstvos* and of Towns, and the central war industries committee, and were endowed with comprehensive powers to coordinate policies in their respective fields. Inevitably there was overlapping and confusion in the haphazard structure of industrial controls erected during the war, and not all the policies devised by these agencies were wise and fruitful. Nevertheless they largely achieved their objective of organizing the supply of the army and opened new inviting avenues for public endeavor.

The State Duma and the Progressive Bloc. The war unexpectedly revitalized the unprepossessing conservative fourth State Duma. The appeal for national unity in face of danger was met by the Duma with a decorous display of patriotic feelings. At the one-day sessions convened at the outbreak of the war, the Bolsheviks, the Mensheviks, and the Labor Group (*Trudoviki*) led by Kerensky—a mere handful of deputies—abstained from voting for war credits, but the Mensheviks and the Labor Group agreed to support the government in a defensive war. The intransigeant Bolshevik faction was soon arrested (November 1914), tried on charges of sedition (February 1915), found guilty, and deported to Siberia. The arrest and trial caused no labor unrest, and with the elimination of the Bolsheviks from the Duma cooperation between that body and the government appeared likely.

These expectations were not fulfilled. During the recess that followed the first wartime session the Duma continued to function as a provisional committee for the relief of the victims of the war. It grew into a center for the exchange of views and the framing of policies. The trend of events at the front and at home created much anxiety, and although the fiction of national unity was studiously maintained at the short session of the Duma in January 1915, it became clear that a deep cleavage was developing between liberal opinion, as represented by the lower chamber and by the non-bureaucratic agencies, on the one hand, and the ultra-conservative elements at the court and in the government, on the other. Parliamentary opinion agitated for the active participation of the Duma in the conduct of public affairs, the reorganization of the army supply service on a more democratic basis, the removal of the more unpopular ministers, and the formation of a government "enjoying the confidence of the nation," an ambiguous formula that did not mean a government responsible to parliament but merely one consisting of men acceptable to liberal circles.

Under the impact of the adverse situation at the front, some—but only some—of these demands were met in the summer of 1915. New non-bureaucratic agencies, described in the preceding section, were created to direct defense work, four of the more odious ministers were dismissed, but Goremykin remained at the head of the council of ministers, and a government "enjoying the confidence of the nation" was as distant as ever. Moreover, with the assumption of the high command by the tsar in August, the political ascendancy of the empress and Rasputin became a major national issue.

Another consequence of the 1915 defeat was the formation in August of the Progressive Bloc, a parliamentary combination comprising six of the larger parties of the Duma (ranging from the Constitutional Democrats, on the left, to the Progressive Nationalists, led by V. V. Shulgin, on the right) as well as several factions of the State Council (the upper house). The program of the Progressive Bloc called for national unity, which was to be achieved through the mitigation of the traditional hostility between the bureaucracy and the community, the removal of the more vexatious measures discriminating against the national and religious minorities and the trade unions, and the formation of a government "consisting of persons enjoying the confidence of the country" and willing to cooperate with the legislative chambers. Several of the ministers lent their support to this program, but

Goremykin regarded it as revolutionary and the formation of the Bloc as unconstitutional. The empress shared this view. The Duma, which had been in session since July, was abruptly prorogued in September.

The Unions of *Zemstvos* and Towns, institutions of local self-government, war industries committees, and other agencies and public bodies endorsed the program of the Bloc, but some of them went further and called for a government responsible to parliament. Agitation along these lines continued at an accelerated pace throughout 1916. In that year the State Duma met twice: from February to June and again in November, when Miliukov delivered the attack on the empress and Stürmer, the prime minister, that led to his resignation.

The Coming Breakdown

The Reason Why. The Rasputin episode—for in the context of Russian history it was no more than an episode—did much harm to the prestige of the monarchy with the educated classes, as did the hostility of the government towards any manifestation of liberalism, however modest, including the program of the Progressive Bloc. Nevertheless these developments cannot be regarded as the true or a major cause of the revolution. The empress was unpopular with the masses, not because of Rasputin or of her meddling in the affairs of state, but because she was of German birth (she was, indeed, frequently referred to as "the German") and was suspected of pro-German sympathies, which is contrary to all available evidence. Nor is it reasonable to ascribe the revolution to the skillful propaganda of subversive groups, to say nothing of a carefully-thought-out master plan devised by Lenin or someone else. During the war the organized revolutionary movement was at low ebb. The strikes of July 1914, staged on the occasion of the visit of the French president to St. Petersburg, were followed by massive police retaliation that all but wiped out the revolutionary organizations. Their leaders, who were soon to acquire world-wide fame were scattered, and many of them behind bars. Lenin was in Switzerland, Trotsky in New York, Stalin in Siberia. The revolution took many of them by surprise. Revolutionary policies had numerous adherents in wartime organizations and in the armed forces, but if their preachments proved successful it was because they fell on fertile ground. The true and basic causes of the revolution were military defeats, staggering losses, demoralization of the army, plight of the refugees, economic hardships, lack of understanding of the objects of the war, and general longing for peace at any price.

An unsuccessful war is never popular, and the war of 1914–1917 on the Russian front was unsuccessful. Russian casualties were officially estimated at over 7 million, half of them missing and prisoners-of-war. According to confidential official reports, refusals to fight and mass surrender to the enemy began in 1914 and became widespread during the retreat in 1915. The Russian steamroller, in which the Western allies put their hope in the dark hours of the war, did not come up to expectation. Food shortages, the patent inability of the government to cope with mounting emergencies, frustration, and near chaos bred weariness, disaffection, and disillusionment. It is the sum total of these conditions that spelled the end of the monarchy and made the revolution inevitable.

19

The Revolution,
February-October, 1917

The Abdication, the Provisional Government,
and the Soviets

Fall of the Monarchy. The revolution actually began in Petrograd on February 23, 1917, in a manner that no one had foreseen, with disorders in the long lines of householders waiting for supplies in front of foodshops. At first the police had the situation well in hand, but the disturbances persisted and troops were called out. As the temper of the crowds grew more violent, police stations, prisons, and other public buildings were attacked and set afire. There were ominous instances of defection among the troops, which assumed a mass character on February 27. With the soldiers going over to the insurgents the defense of the regime disintegrated rapidly.

On the eve of the outbreak the emperor left the capital for the army headquarters in Mogilev, and on the 26th he ordered the prorogation of the Duma which, however, remained informally in session; on the 27th it formed a provisional committee, which consisted of leaders of the Progressive Bloc with the addition of two left-wing deputies—Kerensky and N. S. Chkheidze, a Menshevik. On the same day the Soviet (Council) of Workers' Deputies met for the first time at the Taurida Palace, the seat of the Duma; three days later it changed its name to that of Soviet of

Workers' and Soldiers' Deputies. Meanwhile, with the defection of the troops, the imperial administration collapsed. On February 28 most of the ministers and other high officials were arrested and brought to the Taurida Palace, where the provisional committee of the Duma and the Petrograd Soviet found themselves at the center of events and the depository of state authority.

With the worsening of the political situation the tsar was urged, first, to make concessions to liberal opinion and, then, to abdicate. He decided instead to return to the capital on the 28th, but his train was detained at Pskov, headquarters of the northern front. The president of the State Duma, Michael Rodzianko (a wealthy nobleman of moderately liberal views), the higher commanding officers, including the Grand Duke Nicholas Nikolaevich, and the emissaries of the Duma, Guchkov and Shulgin, who succeeded in making their way to Pskov (but not until after the final decision was made), begged Nicholas to renounce the throne in favor of his 10-year-old son Alexis, with the tsar's brother, the Grand Duke Michael, as regent. The emperor at first agreed but later changed his mind and on March 2 (March 15, N.S.) abdicated in favor of Michael. This final act of the imperial will could not be made effective. On the same day (March 2) the provisional committee of the Duma, after long-drawn arduous negotiations with the Executive Committee of the Soviet, appointed a Provisional Government. On March 3, when the emissaries of the Duma returned to Petrograd, the preservation of the monarchy was no longer feasible. The Grand Duke Michael declined to accept the Crown unless it was offered to him by the Constituent Assembly to be convened at a future date. In the meantime the supreme authority was to be exercised by the Provisional Government. This was a situation that the liberals had not wished or foreseen.

The monarchy collapsed like a house of cards. There was hardly any organized attempt at defending it, although the number of people killed or injured in Petrograd was officially estimated at 1,500. The revolutionary thrust that overthrew the empire was a local development, that is, it was limited to the capital. The provinces and the army had no direct part in the events of February, but they acquiesced in the momentous change, some with enthusiasm, others without audible protest.

The Provisional Government. The Provisional Government appointed by the provisional committee of the Duma and the Executive Committee of the Soviet had no foundation in constitutional law and was a revolutionary improvisation; as to its membership, it was the belated realization of that "government enjoying the confidence of the nation" that liberal opinion had so long and so persistently demanded. With few exceptions, the new ministers were men well known and popular in Duma and *zemstvo* circles. The president of the Provisional Government and minister of the interior was Prince George E. Lvov, a distinguished *zemstvo* leader and president of the Union of *Zemstvos*. Courteous and well-meaning, Lvov had Slavophile leanings and never tired of extolling the "Russian soul," which, to him, was "a fountain of truth, verity, and freedom." His enthusiasm was indeed boundless and carried him to such extremes as the assertion (April 27, 1917) that "we can consider ourselves as the happiest of men; our generation is fated to live in the happiest period of Russian history," a statement that he would not have cared to repeat six months later. Belief in the goodness and wisdom of one's fellow men may be an enviable quality, but it is not necessarily an asset for a political leader in the midst of a revolution.

The other outstanding personalities in the first Provisional Government were the foreign minister Miliukov and the war and navy minister Guchkov. Miliukov, leader of the Constitutional Democratic Party and an eminent historian, was the Duma's principal spokesman on foreign relations. Guchkov, leader of the Octobrist Party, chairman of the central war industries committee, and an authority on military affairs, was a man of strong convictions and impetuous disposition. He had fought with the Armenians and the Greeks against Turkey and with the Boers against the British, headed the Russian Red Cross during the Russo-Japanese War, and was made prisoner by the Japanese. Other members of the Provisional Government came chiefly from the lists of cabinets "enjoying public confidence" which were circulated privately before the revolution. Oddly, the name of Kerensky, who was fated to become the symbol of the Provisional Government, did not appear in these lists.

Alexander Kerensky (born in 1881), a lawyer who had achieved some prominence as a defense counsel in political trials, was the leader of the small Labor Group in the fourth State Duma and was close to the Socialist Revolutionary Party, which he joined in 1917. His mercurial ascendancy must be ascribed to his unwavering faith in the greatness of the revolution with which he identified himself and to an emotional oratory that, for a time, proved remarkably successful. Moreover, Kerensky was simultaneously minister of justice in the Provisional Government and vice-chairman of the Executive Committee of the Petrograd Soviet and, in this double capacity, the only direct link between the two bodies. Stemming from the populist tradition Kerensky, like Lvov, believed in the "Russian soul." Although definitely a left-wing politician, he was not a flamboyant revolutionary. He was carried to prominence by the revolutionary tide and rode its crest until the Bolsheviks' advent to power.

With the formation of a Provisional Government that was both bourgeois and liberal, the revolution appeared to be channeled in the direction of moderation. The authority of Lvov and his colleagues, however, proved tenuous and was immediately challenged by the Soviet of Workers' and Soldiers' Deputies.

The Soviets. The Petrograd Soviet, like the Provisional Government, was a product of the revolution, but its ideological and historical antecedents may be traced to its namesake of 1905. The founding of the 1917 Soviet was due to the simultaneous uncoordinated decisions of several persons and groups, ranging from the left-wing deputies of the Duma to the recently-arrested labor representatives on the central war industries committee released from prison by the insurgents. In the afternoon of February 27 a gathering of uncertain complexion set up at the Taurida Palace the Executive Committee of the Petrograd Soviet, and in the evening of the same day there was convened, also at the Taurida Palace, the first plenary session of the Soviet. There was no question of regular elections; the actual founders of the Soviet system were the intellectuals, workers, and soldiers who happened to be drifting through the halls of the Taurida Palace in the afternoon and evening of that fateful day.

The membership of the Soviet was fluid and tended to grow; at the beginning of March it was about 1,500, and twice that number a week later. The representatives of the soldiers were more numerous than those of the workers, although the latter accounted for a considerably larger portion of the Petrograd population. On March 18 the Petrograd Soviet directed that there should be one deputy for each 2,000 workers or soldiers, but this rule was loosely enforced. The plenary sessions, because of their unwieldy size, were transferred from the Taurida Palace, first to the Mikhailovsky Theater and then to the Naval Academy. The Soviet had no definite jurisdiction or rules of procedure, and its very size prevented it from functioning as an orderly representative assembly. Its influence was exercised chiefly through its Executive Committee. The one elected on February 27 had 14 members. Chkheidze, a Menshevik, was its president; M. I. Skobelev, a Menshevik, and Kerensky were the two vice-chairmen. At the end of March the membership of the Executive Committee was increased to 90 to include representatives from local and army Soviets; simultaneously there was established a bureau of 24 members. A further reorganization took place at the First Congress of the Soviets (June 1917), which elected an All-Russian Executive Committee of 250 members, but the Petrograd Soviet retained its position as the true spokesman of "revolutionary democracy."

Soviets of various types were rapidly organized throughout the country and by August numbered about 600. Their membership and functions followed no definite pattern, but by superseding the organs of the former administration they exercised considerable influence in local affairs. Prince Lvov, speaking in his capacity of minister of the interior, characterized this haphazard and disorderly process as creating "the very core of the future democratic self-government." However, there was little he could do to check the disintegration of local administration, even had he tried.

The kernel of the political problem was the relationship between the Provisional Government and the Soviets. In the parlance of 1917 the Provisional Government represented the *bourgeoisie* and the Soviets the "revolutionary democracy." In the early stage of the revolution it was believed that a measure of cooperation between the two was necessary, and the Executive Committee approved the participation in the Provisional Government of two of its members—Kerensky and Chkheidze, the latter as minister of labor. The plenary session of the Soviet repudiated this agreement and prohibited its members from serving in a bourgeois cabinet. Accordingly, Chkheidze declined the proffered ministerial post, but Kerensky was authorized by the Soviet to retain both the ministry of justice and the vice-chairmanship of the Executive Committee. As if to emphasize the cleavage, Kerensky used to refer to himself as "the hostage of democracy" in the camp of the *bourgeoisie*.

The slogan "All power to the Soviets" was put into circulation at the beginning of March but was not pressed immediately, nor indeed for some time to come, as a program for the overthrow of the Provisional Government. A resolution approved by the Petrograd Soviet on March 3 stated that the assembly would support the policies of the Provisional Government "in so far as they correspond to the interests of the proletariat and of the broad democratic masses of the people." A contact committee and, later, the bureau of the Executive Committee were to maintain a close liaison between the Soviet and Provisional Government and "to bring pressure on the Provisional Government in order to exercise ceaseless control" over its policies (resolution of March 8). The resulting uneasy coexistence or, rather, tug-of-war between the organ of the *"bourgeoisie"* and that of the "revolutionary democracy" became known as "dual power."

"Dual Power." As was to be expected, and as was presumably intended

by the Soviet leaders, the kind of coexistence provided by the March agreement did not prove viable. No serious friction arose in connection with the implementation of the program announced in a manifesto of March 6: convocation of a Constituent Assembly, removal of discriminatory legislation, democratization of local government, political amnesty. Capital punishment was abolished, Jews were given full civic rights, and committees were set up to draft legislation bearing on land reform, the reform of local government, and the convocation of the Constituent Assembly.

Serious disagreements between the Provisional Government and the Soviet arose in connection with two basic issues: democratization of the army and foreign policy. As a reward for their part in the overthrow of the monarchy, the units of the Petrograd garrison were promised by the Soviet and the provisional committee of the Duma that they would remain in the capital and that soldiers would be granted full civic rights. Immunity from combat duties, and proper indoctrination, made these units the obedient instrument of the Soviet, which used them to exercise pressure on a helpless Provisional Government. The implementation of the second provision of the agreement was Order No. 1 issued by the Soviet on March 1. It provided for the establishment of elective committees in every army unit; the sending of delegates to the Soviet by each unit; the control of all political activities in the army by the Soviets and the army committees; the prohibition of complying with orders conflicting with those of the Soviet; the control by the lower (company, battalion) committees of all arms, to which officers should have no access; the use of simplified formulas in addressing officers; and the abolition of the compulsory salute.

At the beginning of 1917 the Russian army was battered, disillusioned, and tired, and instances of defection and refusal to obey combat orders were on the increase. Mutinies and massacres of officers occurred at the end of February, especially at the naval bases. Order No. 1, by shattering the traditional notion of subordination and discipline, greatly contributed to this process of disintegration of the armed forces. A belated attempt to explain that Order No. 1 applied exclusively to the troops stationed in Petrograd went unnoticed. Committees were organized in army units at the front and in the rear, and the minister of war Guchkov, a stern disciplinarian who disapproved of the committees, found himself compelled to legalize them belatedly (April 16). He resigned two weeks later. Army regulations were revised, without adding anything of importance to Order No. 1, in "The Declaration of Rights of Soldiers," which was not promulgated until May, after Kerensky became minister of war.

An even sharper conflict between the Soviet and the Provisional Government developed over questions of foreign policy. Miliukov, the foreign minister, was doctrinaire, stubborn, and unbending. He devised the theory, which was shared by his colleagues, that the revolution was a protest against the ineffectual conduct of the war by the imperial regime; this interpretation was pure fancy in a country that had no wish to fight. The revolution, according to Miliukov, had changed nothing in Russian foreign policy; war was to be pursued to a victorious end, and Russian war aims remained the same as before: first and foremost among them was the annexation of Constantinople and the Straits, as well as of the Ukrainian provinces of Austria-Hungary. The Soviet took a different view. In the "Manifesto to the Peoples of the World" it voiced its faith in the impending revolution in the Western countries, especially in the central empires, and demanded peace "without annexations and indemnities" and the revision of war aims. To these demands was soon added that for the publication of secret treaties. There were violent street demonstrations directed against Miliukov and his program. The position of the foreign minister was particularly difficult because some of the ministers, among them Lvov and Kerensky, favored peace "without annexations and indemnities." It was axiomatic in March that the Provisional Government that emerged from the revolution was to lead the country to the Constituent Assembly and that its composition could not be altered. This was no longer true in April. Mass demonstrations against the continuation of imperial foreign policy led to the resignation of Guchkov and Miliukov (May 1 and 2, respectively). The Provisional Government was reconstituted on May 5 with the participation of members of parties represented in the Soviet and responsible to that assembly. This was formally the end of the regime of "dual power."

The Bolsheviks

Enter Lenin. The course of the revolution was profoundly influenced and probably given a new turn by a seemingly trifling event that occurred early in April: the return of Lenin to Russia. Vladimir Ilich Lenin (Ulianov, 1870–1923), son of a high-school official, was a professional revolutionary, one of Russia's early Marxists, and the leader—since its inception in 1903—of the Bolshevik faction of the Russian Social Democratic Labor Party. His elder brother, Alexander Ulianov, was executed in 1887 for an attempt on the life of Emperor Alexander III. Lenin spent his early years on the Volga, in Simbirsk, Kazan, and Samara, took a law degree at the University of

St. Petersburg (1891), was affiliated with various revolutionary groups, and had a long record of arrests and deportations. From 1906 to March 1917 he lived abroad. Lenin was well known in underground revolutionary circles as an uncompromising revolutionary and an advocate of extreme policies. During the war he was in Switzerland and was one of the organizers of the socialist Zimmerwald (September 1915) and Kienthal (April 1916) conferences which endeavored to revive the Socialist International and to transform the European war into a civil war. He was a prolific writer.

No one familiar with Lenin's biography and teaching and the facts of Russian history could reasonably deny that he played a decisive part in determining the course and character of the revolution. Nevertheless there is no justification for the aura of infallibility created around Lenin by the very magnitude of the events with which he was associated and by the relentless pressure of Communist propaganda in which Western non-Communist historians occasionally join. His judgment, far from being unerring, was often seriously at fault, although he had the uncanny gift of drawing

Lenin

correct (from the revolutionary standpoint) conclusions from wrong prem-
ises. In January 1917, when the imminence of the fall of the monarchy was
freely discussed in Petrograd, Lenin told a Zurich audience that his generation was not likely "to see the decisive battles of the approaching revolution,"
but when the news of Russian events reached him, he went to the opposite
extreme and became convinced that the socialist revolution *"is beginning
in Europe."* This assumption, which of course was unwarranted, underlay
all his subsequent policies; nevertheless the end result—the victory of Bolshevism—was exactly what he desired.

The April Theses. At the end of March Lenin and a group of Russian
émigrés left Switzerland; they traveled in a "sealed" railway carriage through
Germany and then Sweden and in the evening of April 3 reached Petrograd, where a huge and enthusiastic crowd awaited Lenin. He was driven
atop an armored car to the palace of the well-known dancer, Madame Kshesinsky, which had been taken over by the Bolsheviks. The next day, April 4,
Lenin presented to the All-Russian Conference of the Soviets at the Taurida
Palace his program, which was embodied in the so-called *April Theses.* It
demanded: the non-support of the bourgeois and imperialist Provisional
Government; rejection of the notion of defensive war; transfer of political
power to the proletariat and the poor peasantry; the Soviet form of government; elimination of the police, the army, and the bureaucracy; nationalization of land; merger of all banks into one bank controlled by the Soviets;
institution of immediate Soviet control over social production and distribution; revision of the party program and adoption of the name of Communist party; formation of the Communist International. These were baffling
demands which ran contrary to the policies of the Bolshevik leaders (Stalin,
Kamenev) who had returned to Petrograd before Lenin: they expected a
protracted period of a bourgeois republic and advocated a measure of cooperation with the Provisional Government. Lenin's *Theses* were overwhelmingly rejected by the Petrograd committee of the Bolshevik Party
(13 votes to 2, with 1 abstention) and were given a hostile reception by the
left-wing press. It was argued that Lenin had lived too long abroad and was
out of touch with the Russian situation.

Peace and Land. Lenin was certain, however, that he knew better than
his critics, and he would not be discouraged. From the balcony of the
Kshesinsky palace he carried on a one-man propaganda campaign in which
the subtleties of the Marxian analysis underlying the *April Theses* were reduced to simple straightforward slogans: "Immediate end of the war" and
"All land to the peasants." This was exactly what the land-hungry peasantry

and the soldiers longing to go home wanted to hear. Lenin's tireless harangues were immediately and immensely successful. The All-Russian Conference of the Bolsheviks held at the end of April reversed the recent decision of the Petrograd committee and endorsed Lenin's program by a large majority. The conference also approved the slogan "All power to the Soviets" as a long-term objective; meanwhile the Soviet system was to be strengthened and brought under Bolshevik control.

The Army and the Revolution

The Role of the Army. The attitude of the army was an important and often determining element in the revolution. The defection of the Petrograd garrison and the acquiescence of the armed forces at the front and in the rear were the immediate causes of the fall of the monarchy. The allegiance of the Petrograd garrison to the Soviet undermined the authority of the Provisional Government, while the army as a whole exercised an even more decisive influence on the course of events. The revolution took place when Russia was engaged in a major war that the Provisional Government wished to pursue to a victorious end. This objective could not be achieved unless the army was prepared to fight for it, and its lack of support for official policies on this vital issue could only lead to the destruction of the Provisional Government.

Immediate Effects of the Revolution. Even before the revolution the army, as we know, was in no mood for fighting. The introduction of the committee system, with its overt and implied mistrust of officers, weakened and then destroyed traditional relationships based on discipline, respect for rank, and hierarchical subordination. In 1917 Russia was seized with a passion for talk; army committees at every level were no exception and spent endless hours in desultory and often purposeless debate. Combat orders, like all other orders, required the committees' approval, and no motion was too preposterous or foolish not to be carried by unanimous vote. How could war, a grim and exacting business, be carried on under these conditions? The formula peace "without annexations and indemnities," which gained quasi-general acceptance, kept the army committees busy. "Without annexations and indemnities" is rendered in Russian by terms of foreign origin— *bez anneksii i kontributsii*—which, it is safe to say, meant nothing to the average Russian soldier and was actually given innumerable divergent interpretations. The formula was generally understood to authorize only defensive war, but how this notion could be translated into practical measures under front-line conditions was anybody's guess. The view was prevalent that the right policy was to fraternize and talk things over with the enemy, just as one did in the committees. Even more insidious and destructive of discipline was the impending land reform. The promised redistribution of land was paramount in the mind of the peasant soldier, but the only way to make sure that he would get his full share would be to return at once to his native village; hence the increase in the number of desertions, which soon assumed the character of a mass movement.

Professional soldiers, with a few exceptions (General Brusilov was one of them), had little illusion about the state of the army and the chances of improving the situation; yet something had to be done. Political civilian commissars were appointed to army units; they joined lustily in the talking but achieved nothing in easing the tension between officers and men. After Kerensky had succeeded Guchkov as minister of war in May, there were organized "shock" or "death" battalions of "revolutionary volunteers" pledged to maintain strict discipline, fight valorously, and if needed "die gladly" for the revolution. The "death" battalions did nothing of the kind, notwithstanding their awe-inspiring insignia—skull and crossbones against a red and black background—and the futility of the experiment became apparent even before the final breakdown of the army. Equally unsuccessful as a method of reviving the fighting capacity of the armed forces was the formation of national units—Polish, Ukrainian, Lettish, and so on. Finally, a women's battalion was organized in June; it is claimed that it fought gallantly during the June offensive, but these reports inspire no confidence.

The June Offensive and Its Aftermath. Kerensky, however, put his trust in persuasion and particularly in the effectiveness of his own speeches. An important decision was to be made. At an allied conference held in Petrograd on the eve of the revolution, in January–February 1917, the imperial government agreed to participate in a joint allied offensive at an early date. In the spring of 1917 most of the Russian military leaders took a dim view of the possibility of honoring this pledge, but Kerensky, after an extensive speech-making tour of the front that brought forth the customary manifestations of enthusiasm, persuaded himself, the government, and the majority of the Petrograd Soviet that the army was ready for the offensive and, indeed, eager to fight.

The Russian advance began on June 18 on a wide front, but the chief thrust was in Galicia, in the direction of Lemberg (Lvov). The Russians had a marked superiority in both men and artillery and scored some initial successes on parts of the front. In other sectors, however, army units which had only recently pledged themselves to die for the revolution would not leave their trenches. Front-line committees became bogged down in the discussion of the all-too-familiar issue: is advance compatible with a defensive war? Operations in Galicia came to a standstill by July 1. On July 6 Austria launched, with strong German support, a massive counter-offensive that met with practically no resistance. The Russian retreat rapidly became a rout, "death" battalions fleeing as fast as the others. By the end of July Galicia was cleared of Russian troops, and the enemy might have penetrated deep into Russia had they so wished. Actually the front was stabilized somewhat east of the pre-war border.

From the débâcle of the June offensive the armies of the Provisional Government never recovered. The impact of the defeat was great, both at home and abroad. An official Russian statement referred to the situation at the front as an "immeasurable calamity that threatens the ruin of revolutionary Russia." Kerensky, sobered by the experience, went through the motions of restoring order and discipline. General L. G. Kornilov, who having dramatically escaped from Austrian captivity was something of a national hero and had a reputation for common sense and firmness, was appointed commander of the southwestern front (July 7) and then commander-in-chief (July 18), a post held previously by General M. V. Alekseev (former chief of staff of the tsar) from March to May and by General Brusilov from May to July. The death penalty was reintroduced at the front, and special military courts were created to deal with desertion and breach of discipline. With the state of the army as it was, it is unlikely that these or similar measures would have succeeded even if a determined effort had been made to enforce them. Kerensky, however, with whom the Provisional Government became identified in July, while extolling "iron will" and "unbending determination," was temperamentally and emotionally unfit for strong action. Moreover, he became involved almost immediately in a hopeless feud with Kornilov, and the program for the restoration of discipline went by default. Meanwhile the soldiers had but one thought—to go home—and this they did by the thousands in the late summer of 1917. The armies of the revolution were melting away.

The Russian Expeditionary Force. The Western allies had romantic and unreasonable ideas of Russian manpower and the irresistible strength of the Russian steamroller. Caught unprepared and frightened by the rapid advance of the Germans, the English (August 1914) and later the French pressed Petrograd for the dispatch of large contingents of Russian troops to the Western front. Russian authorities were not enthusiastic; nevertheless four Russian brigades totalling 43,500 men with 750 officers were shipped to France in 1916; two of the brigades went to Salonika, in Macedonia, and the other two remained in France. The Russian troops did some creditable fighting, but after the revolution their morale declined rapidly and they were moved to the rear, in France in June 1917, and in Macedonia some six months later. Shortage of shipping prevented their repatriation, and in December 1917 the 19,000 Russian soldiers in France were given the opportunity of choosing among labor battalions, internment in Africa, and active service with the French army in the Russian legion. Few availed themselves of this last opportunity. At the time of the armistice of November 1918 the Russian legion numbered fewer than 600 men—the humble remnant of the steamroller. A similar procedure was followed in Macedonia and produced like results.

The Economic and Social Impact of the Revolution

Economic Decline. A revolution superimposed upon an economic and social structure already undermined by two and a half years of war is bound to have dire and far-reaching consequences. The process of economic deterioration noted in Chapter 18 continued and gained momentum. Its familiar manifestations—financial disorders, inflation, depreciation of the ruble, mounting public debt, spiralling prices, breakdown of the transportation system, shortages of various kinds, lowering of the standards of living—were aggravated by the uncertainties and excesses of the revolution that, although born in the breadlines, far from remedying the supply situation, made it considerably worse. But while economic hardships were borne by all, there were two social groups on which the revolution conferred, at least in theory, important benefits: industrial labor and the peasantry.

Industrial Labor. The Petrograd workers shared with the soldiers of the capital the honor of having brought about the fall of the monarchy. The establishment of the Soviets of Workers' and Soldiers' Deputies and their political ascendancy were striking recognition of the new role of labor. The Petrograd Soviet, although it dealt at times with questions concerning the workers, was a quasi-parliament rather than an institution for the protection of their professional interests. These were the immediate concern of the trade unions and the factory committees.

The trade unions, legalized in 1906 but long persecuted and few in number, expanded rapidly in 1917. Some 160 trade unions with a membership of 2.3 million were registered by the first congress of trade unions in January 1918. The growth of the movement, however, was too rapid to make it an effective instrument of the working class. Union leaders of experience were rare and often thought in terms of conditions which no longer existed.

Unlike the trade unions, the factory committees were a product of the revolution. Some were organized spontaneously, others in conformity with a directive issued by the Petrograd Soviet on March 5. The Petrograd Association of Manufacturers negotiated with the Petrograd Soviet an agreement that regularized the position of the factory committees. Its provisions were recapitulated in a national law of April 23 that provided that factory committees were to be elected by secret ballot in any shop or enterprise at the request of at least one-tenth of the workers concerned or at that of the management. The committees were to represent the workers in all matters bearing on the conditions of work (wages, hours, and so on) as well as to provide for their economic and cultural needs. Committee members could not be dismissed except under highly restrictive conditions which actually assured them permanence of employment. In practice, factory committees exceeded by far the powers conferred upon them by the law and tended to take over the management of enterprises. Their ultimate objective was the establishment of "workers' control," a policy advocated by the Bolsheviks and eventually enacted by them into law. In extreme but not infrequent cases the factory committees, in contravention of the law and over the protests of the Provisional Government, crowded out the owners and established themselves as managers of enterprises.

Meanwhile the economic conditions of labor went from bad to worse. There were large sporadic increases in wages, but they did not keep up with the rise in the cost of living. Faced with political uncertainty, exorbitant costs, shortages of raw materials and fuel, and ruinous labor demands, many owners closed their establishments or surrendered them to the government. Militant labor interpreted these desperate moves as sabotage and assumed control of such factories and shops. The elimination of private enterprise was welcomed by the socialists, but production kept on declining drastically and hardships increased. There was much friction between trade unions and factory committees: the leadership of the former was largely Menshevik, of the latter, Bolshevik. This conflict was not resolved until after the establishment of the Soviet state, when, in February 1918, factory committees were absorbed by the trade unions, by then Bolshevik-controlled.

The Agrarian Revolution. In 1917 Russia was an overwhelmingly peasant country. The peasantry, unlike the industrial workers, had no direct part in the overthrow of the monarchy, except that soldiers in Petrograd and elsewhere were chiefly peasants. The countryside remained aloof from the revolution, and information about events in the capital was incomplete and slow in coming; it was received at first with bewilderment and reserve. When the immensity and finality of what had happened were finally grasped and sank into the consciousness of the villagers, the secular longing for land that forms the background of Russian history came irresistibly to the fore. The ambition of the peasants was simple and clear-cut: division among themselves of the land of the large estates in their neighborhood. This they were determined to achieve at any cost. The legal trappings—nationalization, socialization, municipalization—and the economic problems of modernization and efficient management were not even considered.

The necessity and inevitability of a comprehensive land reform were generally conceded, and an extensive network of land committees was set up under a law of April 23 to collect information and make recommendations. The Provisional Government held that the transfer of land to the peasants must be orderly and equitable and that to achieve this objective a great deal of preparatory work was needed. The final decision, that is, the issuance of the land law, was reserved for the Constituent Assembly. All this was fair and reasonable, perhaps too much so, for an agrarian revolution is not likely to wait for the collection of land statistics and other pertinent data. Lenin's approach was less pragmatic. While formally deprecating violence, he urged the peasants "to generate revolutionary energy." His slogans, "Immediate end of the war" and "All land to the peasants," welded neatly into a single understandable program of action. Since the war was about to end, the obvious thing for "the peasant in uniform" (Lenin's phrase) to do was to hurry to his village so as not to miss his share of the neighboring estate. This is exactly what the soldiers were doing in ever-increasing numbers.

The revolution produced an extensive network of peasant Soviets patterned after those of Workers' and Soldiers' Deputies. The initiative of setting up peasant Soviets originated with a group of peasant delegates in the middle of March, and the first congress of the Soviets of Peasants' Delegates was held in Petrograd in May and elected an Executive Committee. The functions of the peasant Soviets were, broadly, similar to those of the workers' Soviets, with perhaps a greater emphasis on the land question. Delegates to the peasant Soviets were elected by the peasants, but they did not need to be peasants themselves. This explains why the All-Russian Congress of the Soviets of Peasants' Deputies and its Executive Committee were dominated by intellectuals, members of the Socialist Revolutionary Party, which traditionally claimed to speak for the farmers. The Bolsheviks were represented at the congress by a mere handful of delegates.

The non-peasant complexion of the higher peasant agencies accounts for the fact that some of their resolutions, which as a rule paralleled those of the workers' Soviets, were contrary to the wishes of the rank and file of the peasantry, for instance, the endorsement of the Kerensky offensive or of the government's policy that the land reform must await the decision of the Constituent Assembly. Peasant Soviets and land committees at the lower levels, especially that of the township (*volost*), were in closer touch with the village and reflected more accurately its aspirations. Moreover the Socialist Revolutionary Party, which dominated peasant organizations, was itself hopelessly split: the right-wing faction, which controlled the Executive Committee, supported the Provisional Government, while the left wing, which was prominent in the township Soviets, favored the Bolsheviks.

Actually, the leading role in the agrarian revolution belonged to the village assemblies and the township Soviets. Trespassing, seizure of stock, cattle, and agricultural machinery and implements, and eviction of owners began soon after the outbreak of the revolution but grew in volume and importance; most of the looting and burning of manor houses was done in the late summer and autumn of 1917. Deserters from the armed forces, often carrying arms, took a leading part in the agrarian movement. Destruction was systematic and thorough: buildings were razed to the ground, trees were felled, and gardens and orchards were plowed into fields—to make sure that the owners would never come back. The movement was directed not only against the estates of the nobility but also against the holdings of the peasant farmers who had become individual owners under the provisions of the land reform of 1906–1911. By the autumn of 1917 the agrarian revolution was in full swing. Lenin's recognition of the role of the peasantry in a Russian revolution—even though this was a violation of Marxian orthodoxy —was one of his major contributions to the victory of Bolshevism.

The Provisional Government in Flux

The First Coalition Government. The conflict over foreign policy in April that led to the resignation of Guchkov and Miliukov ushered in the era of the so-called coalition governments. The cabinet that took office on May 5 consisted of six socialist and nine non-socialist ministers who, unlike their predecessors, were responsible to the political parties or organizations which they represented; in the case of the socialists, this was the Soviet. The creation of the coalition formally ended the regime of "dual power," but since there was no reconciliation between the two factions, the first reconstruction of the cabinet was followed by others. Prince Lvov retained the office of president in the new government, Kerensky succeeded Guchkov as minister of war and navy, and M. I. Tereshchenko, formerly minister of finance, succeeded Miliukov as foreign minister. Tereshchenko, then in his early thirties, came from a family of wealthy sugar manufacturers and was reputedly one of the richest men in Russia. He was the former chairman of the Kiev war industries committee; after the revolution he became an ardent partisan of Kerensky, which explains why he remained at the foreign ministry until the fall of the Provisional Government. Victor Chernov, leader of the Socialist Revolutionary Party and a member of extreme international left-wing movements, was appointed to the highly sensitive post of minister of agriculture. The first coalition government, seen as a whole, was an ill-assorted group of men whom it would have been unreasonable to expect to work together harmoniously even under conditions less trying than those with which they were actually faced. It succeeded nevertheless in agreeing on a program that accepted the Soviet formula of peace "without annexations and indemnities" but otherwise dealt in noncommittal generalities.

During the next six months the successive coalition governments lived under the relentless pressure of the Bolsheviks from the left and in fear of the largely imaginary danger of counter-revolution from the right. The outward gains of the Bolsheviks were not striking. Their representation in the Soviets and other agencies of the "revolutionary democracy," such as the municipal councils elected under the amended liberal law of April 15, remained small. Yet the same bodies which voted for Menshevik and Socialist Revolutionary deputies passed Bolshevik resolutions unanimously. The All-Russian Congress of Peasants' Deputies and its Executive Committee were solidly behind the Provisional Government in asserting that Constituent Assembly alone was competent to settle the land question, but this did not prevent the peasants, aided and abetted by the lower level committees, from taking over the landed estates and dividing them among themselves, as urged by Lenin.

Bolshevism in Petrograd was reinforced in May by the arrival of Trotsky from New York, even though he did not formally join the Bolshevik Party until July. Leon Trotsky (Bronstein, 1879–1940), organizer of the 1905 Soviet, was, like Lenin, a professional revolutionary with a long record of arrests, deportation, and exile. His boundless enthusiasm, devotion to the cause, resourcefulness, and great literary gift placed him high among the revolutionary leaders. He was eager for the struggle, which was entering a new phase. The unexpected display of Bolshevik strength during the April demonstrations was a warning that the Provisional Government could not ignore.

Danger from the right was in a different class and supposedly resided in anti-socialist organizations such as the Military League, the Union of Officers, the Association of Manufacturers, the bourgeois political parties, and so on, as well as in the upper level of the army command. The patent weakness of these organizations and groups was their lack of popular following, especially among the soldiers. Kerensky, the socialist ministers, and the leaders of the Soviet, however, were left-wing politicians who instinctively looked for enemies to the right rather than to the left. The Bolsheviks, including Lenin, were former comrades in arms with whom many links survived, while the liberals and especially the generals were traditional adversaries. This attitude proved decisive at a crucial turn of events.

Encouraged by the success of the April demonstration, the Bolsheviks were planning another on June 10, but it was called off. Incautiously the anti-Bolshevik leaders of the Soviet on June 18 staged a demonstration of their own that was to rally the "democratic forces" behind the Provisional Government. This plan hopelessly miscarried: the posters carried by huge crowds evidenced overwhelming pro-Bolshevik sympathies. Still another street demonstration in Petrograd, which was to have grave consequences, took place on July 3 and 4. It will be remembered that this was the time when the Russian offensive in Galicia came to a standstill and the Austro-German counter-offensive was about to begin (July 6). The manifestation of July 3 originated with the First Machine-Gun Regiment, which was joined by other army units, Kronstadt sailors, and the populace of the capital. It was estimated that on July 4 nearly half a million people marched in the columns which converged upon the Taurida Palace. The Bolsheviks at first opposed the outbreak on the ground that it was premature, but when they proved unable to stop the insurgents, they assumed the leadership.

The object of the insurrection was to prevail upon the Executive Committee of the Soviets, which they besieged in the Taurida Palace, to supersede the Provisional Government. The Executive Committee refused to comply, and long-drawn negotiations led nowhere. The demonstrators did not, however, attempt to impose their demands by force. The number of casualties was small, public buildings were not occupied, and although Kerensky had a narrow escape from arrest as his train was leaving for the

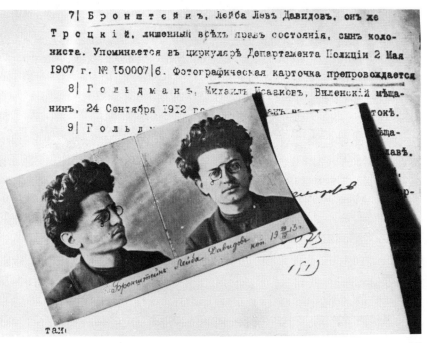

Trotsky, age 25, police photograph

July Days in Petrograd, 1917

front and the minister of agriculture Chernov was assaulted by the crowd, the other ministers were not interfered with. The inconclusive nature of the negotiations and the absence of a program of action dampened the enthusiasm of the crowds, which gradually dispersed. Some of the troops of the Petrograd garrison took no part in the demonstration and remained "neutral." To win their allegiance the minister of justice, P. N. Pereverzev, communicated to them, and then to the press, secret documents which purportedly established that Lenin and his confederates were paid German agents. The documents were inconclusive, Pereverzev was dismissed from office by Kerensky on the ground that the premature disclosure of incomplete evidence weakened the case against Lenin, but the "neutral" regiments were impressed and went over to the side of the Provisional Government. Public opinion swung, at least temporarily, against the Bolsheviks. The plant and offices of *Pravda* were raided and wrecked, and the Bolsheviks were ejected from the Kshesinsky palace. In a leaflet issued on July 6 they announced that "the demonstration was over." Orders were issued for the arrest of Bolshevik leaders. Lenin and G. E. Zinovev went into hiding, but several others were taken into custody, among them Trotsky and A. V. Lunacharsky. Penal legislation dealing with subversion was enacted but not enforced. Mutinous regiments were disbanded and the men distributed among front units, a measure not likely to contribute to the morale of the combat troops.

Charges that the Bolsheviks received funds from the German government were substantiated by official German documents which came into the possession of the allies during World War II. However, as Leonard Schapiro rightly notes, "there is no evidence that the Bolsheviks at any time received instructions from the Germans on their policy or tactics. If the Germans did indeed pay them, as seems very probable, it is because Bolshevik aims coincided with their own—to 'knock Russia out of the war.'" Receiving funds from the enemy in wartime may be legitimately regarded as treason; on the other hand, it should be remembered that Lenin was convinced—wrongly, as we know—that a Communist revolution in Germany was imminent. The German funds which he might have received were to serve, even though indirectly, the attainment of this supreme aim.

The Second Coalition Government. The Provisional Government, which had to deal with the Bolshevik insurrection and the disastrous retreat in Galicia, was itself in a state of lamentable disorder. Disagreement within the cabinet brought its disruption. The minister of commerce and industry, A. I. Konovalov, a liberal, resigned on June 18; six ministers, members of the Constitutional Democratic Party, on July 2 tendered their resignations, which were accepted on July 7. On the same day Prince Lvov resigned as minister-president because of disagreement with his socialist colleagues, especially the minister of agriculture, Chernov. Lvov was succeeded by Kerensky. There followed a fortnight of complex negotiations and subtle manoeuvers (including Kerensky's resignation of July 21) out of which emerged, on July 24, the second coalition government. It was headed by Kerensky. Of the 18 ministers, 11 were socialists. Tereshchenko remained at the foreign office and Chernov at the ministry of agriculture. The authority of the government —in so far as it had authority—rested with Kerensky alone.

Paradoxically, the near collapse and disintegration of central authority generated a quasi-irresistible longing for real leadership. Kerensky, the Soviet leaders, the leaders of the liberal parties, and the commanding officers of an army that would not fight or obey orders all talked incessantly about strong government, iron will, and unflinching discipline. All agreed that the salvation of the nation, the defense of the newly-gained freedom, the honor of Russia, and the happiness of all depended on the establishment of a government that could and would govern. It was the quest for a strong government that was at the bottom of the tragic "Kornilov affair." Kerensky was convinced that a cabinet of which he was the head was directed by an "iron will," but those outside the narrow circle of his admirers may be forgiven for feeling differently. With the apparent ebbing of the Bolshevik tide after the July uprising, the more conservative elements turned with hope to General Kornilov as an alternative to Kerensky. In the desperate plight of the Galician retreat Kerensky appointed Kornilov commander-in-chief (July 18). Kornilov's stern program of measures for the restoration of discipline, which re-introduced the death penalty at the front, was formally approved by the Provisional Government but never effectively enforced. Kornilov, born into a poor Cossack family, was a professional soldier, believed in the virtues of the traditional military organization, and detested the army committee system and the revolutionary ebullience and trappings which were the very kernel of Kerensky's creed. It soon became clear that cooperation between the two men would not last long.

On August 18 the Germans resumed the offensive in the northern sector of the Russian front and on the 21st took Riga. The road to Petrograd appeared to lie open, and the necessity of the evacuation of the capital was freely discussed. The left-wing elements objected strenuously to this proposal, because to them Petrograd was the center and the symbol of the revolution. There were persistent rumors that the Bolsheviks were planning a new demonstration in Petrograd on August 28 or 29 that might well prove fatal to the Provisional Government. Boris Savinkov, war minister and a friend of Kerensky, requested Kornilov to send a cavalry corps to Petrograd to protect the Provisional Government. Meanwhile Kornilov had reached, independently of Savinkov, the decision to dispatch reliable troops to the capital to ensure the formation of a "strong government" of which Kornilov would be the head and Kerensky, probably—this was not sure—a member. At this stage the unsolicited intervention of a conservative politician, V. N. Lvov (not to be confused with Prince G. E. Lvov), who became possessed with the idea of a Kornilov-Kerensky reconciliation, produced a spurious "agreement" for the transfer of all power to Kornilov; Kerensky was to hold office in a reconstructed cabinet. To Kerensky, however, the "agreement" was a conspiracy. Lvov was arrested; Kornilov, relieved of his command (August 27), denied the official allegations and refused to comply with the dismissal order. The Provisional Government was frantic. On August 27 Kerensky appealed to the Bolshevik Party for assistance. Red guards (workers) were issued arms, "committees for the salvation of the republic" were formed, and the Bolshevik leaders who had been arrested after the July uprising—among them Trotsky —were set free. The left-wing movement dominated by the Bolsheviks was greatly strengthened.

There was little justification for the alarm that swept government circles. The "counter-revolutionary" corps, detained by railway men, made little progress. Its commanding officer, General Krymov, was arrested and committed suicide, while the cavalrymen pledged allegiance to Kerensky (August 31). Kornilov, who had remained at his headquarters in Mogilev, surrendered without offering any resistance and was taken into custody. A swarm of right-wing and liberal personalities, among them the former war minister of the Provisional Government, Guchkov, were arrested. Kerensky believed and proclaimed that he had saved the country and the revolution from a mortal danger. This claim was a gross exaggeration. Actually the Kornilov "mutiny" confirmed what was long known: "counter-revolution," that is, a movement calling for the continuation of the war and respect for traditional institutions, including property rights, commanded no popular support and had no chance of success.

The Third Coalition Government. On August 26 all the ministers tendered their resignations but continued in office on a day-by-day basis. Four days later (August 30) Kerensky became commander-in-chief. The so-called "directory," an inner cabinet of five members, was created on September 1, and on September 25 the third and last coalition government was formed. It was headed by Kerensky, who had continued to act as minister-president during the interregnum, and had six non-socialist and 10 socialist members. To placate the Soviets, which were passing under Bolshevik control, the Provisional Government proclaimed Russia a republic (September 1) and dissolved the State Council and the State Duma (October 6). These paltry gestures could not stave off the progress of Bolshevism that spelled the end of the Provisional Government.

Substitutes for Parliament. It was believed in liberal circles that the absence of a representative popular assembly was a source of weakness for the Provisional Government. The Constituent Assembly was a thing of the future; the statute regulating elections to that body was not issued until September, and elections were set for the middle of November 1917. The earliest attempt at providing a substitute for parliament was the one-day session of the members of the four State Dumas held on April 27. A more representative body, the State Conference, was convened in Moscow from August 13 to 15. It had nearly 2,500 members delegated by various institutions, organizations, associations, and groups, but the Bolsheviks were excluded. The rift between Kerensky and Kornilov became manifest at the sessions of the State Conference: the minister-president was acclaimed by the left, while the commander-in-chief was enthusiastically applauded by the right. After the Kornilov "mutiny" the Executive Committee of the Soviets summoned in Petrograd and Democratic Conference (September 14 to 22), whose membership was drawn from among the left-wing factions of the State Conference. The Provisional Government at first denied recognition to the Democratic Conference, which was then reorganized as the Provisional Council of the Republic, or pre-parliament, with a membership of 550, including 150 non-socialists. The opening session of the Provisional Council was held on October 7; on the same day the Bolsheviks withdrew their delegates. The Council nevertheless functioned until October 25, when it was swept away by the Bolshevik revolution.

These assemblies generated a great deal of talk but accomplished nothing useful.

Self-Determination and Independence. The revolution gave a powerful impetus to the long-suppressed national aspirations of Poland, Finland, the Ukraine, and other minority groups. From every borderland and ethnic entity came passionate appeals for cultural and political autonomy or independence. The Provisional Government approved self-determination in principle but held that the final decision must rest with the Constituent Assembly. At the end of March it issued a manifesto that spoke of establishing—subject to approval by the Constituent Assembly—"an independent Polish state comprising all territories inhabited predominantly by the Poles" and "united with

Russia by a free military alliance." Since the whole of Poland was in enemy hands, the thorny question of determining what these territories were did not arise.

The position of Finland was different and called for positive action. The Provisional Government hastened to repeal the restrictive and discriminatory measures enacted in Finland by the imperial regime. The Finns, however, wanted independence, and their aspirations were encouraged by eminent international jurists who held that allegiance to the Crown was the only valid link between Finland and Russia and that this link had been severed by the abdication of the tsar. The Provisional Government did not accept this view and looked upon itself as a trustee whose duty it was to preserve for the Constituent Assembly the heritage it received from the empire. The involved argument between Petrograd and Helsinki dragged on throughout 1917 and was finally resolved by the proclamation of Finnish independence in December, that is, after the fall of the Provisional Government.

The case of the Ukraine, which in recent times had had no experience of statehood, was complicated by the fact that to many Russians the Ukraine was not a foreign province but an integral part of Russia. The Ukrainian national movement had its roots in the Austrian province of Galicia and was led by intellectuals—M. Hrushevski, M. Vinnichenko, and S. Petlyura. In the Russian Ukraine, where the movement was weak, it found support in 1917 among the Russians, who believed that Ukrainian nationalism might prove a barrier against the inroads of Bolshevism.

The Ukrainian Central Rada, a quasi-parliament of uncertain origin, foregathered in Kiev in the early summer and elected a general secretariat that acted as a cabinet. A Ukrainian army was created (chiefly Russian regiments which declared themselves "Ukrainian"), and the Ukrainian language was introduced in the administration, the courts, and the schools. These changes were effected partly with the consent of the Provisional Government and partly over its objections. The inconclusive and acrimonious negotiations with the Provisional Government were brought to an end by the Bolshevik revolution. Subsequently the Ukraine proclaimed its independence, only to be almost immediately absorbed in the Soviet state.

Other national minorities, too, were restless and vocal. A congress of national minorities attended by representatives of some 20 national ethnic and religious groups was held in Kiev in September and passed resolutions favoring self-determination and the reorganization of Russia as a federal state.

Fate of the Imperial Family. A few words must be added concerning the fate of the tsar and his family. After the abdication of Nicholas, the former tsar, his wife, and children were held under arrest in the palace of Tsarskoe Selo, near Petrograd. It was originally intended to send them to England, via Murmansk, but the British government eventually withdrew its offer of asylum, nor would the Soviets let Nicholas go. The German threat to Petrograd and the menacing attitude of extreme revolutionary groups led to the removal of the prisoners to Tobolsk, in Siberia (August 1917), where they were confined in the residence of the governor. In the spring of 1918 they were moved again, this time to Ekaterinburg (now Sverdlovsk), in the Urals, and were kept under arrest at the Ipatiev house; they were assassinated in the cellar of that building in July 1918, presumably by order of the local Soviet.

The October Revolution

Lenin and the Fateful Decision. The failure of the July insurrection led to the temporary recession of Bolshevism. The circulation of Bolshevik newspapers in the armed forces was prohibited, the more forceful Bolshevik speakers—Lenin, Trotsky—were no longer heard, and the charges that the Bolshevik leaders were in the pay of Germany were given wide publicity. Nevertheless elections to trade unions and municipal councils in August and September showed an increase in the Bolshevik vote. The membership of the party was small, perhaps 200,000, but this was a great deal more than the pre-revolutionary figure of 20,000. A seemingly important tactical move was the temporary abandonment by Lenin of the slogan "All power to the Soviets" on the ground that they were dominated by counter-revolutionary elements (Mensheviks and Socialist Revolutionaries) and were cooperating with the *bourgeoisie.* This interpretation was endorsed, although not without hesitation, by the Sixth Congress of the Bolshevik Party (July 26 to August 3), which held that factory committees and trade unions, rather than the Soviets, were the truly revolutionary agencies.

The Kornilov "mutiny" brought a new reversal of strategy. The arrested Soviet leaders were released (although Lenin remained in hiding in Finland), and Bolshevik propaganda was given leeway. On August 31 the Bolshevik Party won a majority in the Petrograd Soviet and on September 6 in the Moscow Soviet. Lenin therefore revived the slogan "All power to the Soviets," which was given a different twist, "All power to the *Bolshevik* Soviets." It was no longer, as in the early phase of the revolution, the question of a "peaceful assumption of power by the Soviets"; the road to victory was that of "a successful insurrection." Beginning in September, Lenin relentlessly pressed this policy upon a rather reluctant party. He was particularly insistent that the armed insurrection should be launched before the opening of the Second Congress of the Soviets, which was scheduled for October 20 but actually met on October 25. A session of the central committee of the Bolshevik Party held in Petrograd on October 10 and attended by Lenin approved by a vote of 10 to 2 his resolution stating that "armed insurrection is inevitable and the time for it fully ripe." Lenin rightly held, in support of his resolution, that the Bolsheviks had gained control in the leading Soviets, that the agrarian revolution was in full swing, and that Bolshevik slogans enjoyed great popularity with the masses. He was wrong, however, in asserting that "the world socialist revolution in the whole of Europe" was making rapid progress, that "the Russian *bourgeoisie* and Kerensky" were determined to surrender Petrograd to the Germans, and that "a second Kornilov movement" was in the offing. Lenin's long-time associates, Kamenev and Zinovev, voted against the resolution. In spite of their opposition to a cardinal decision of the party, Kamenev and Zinovev were elected to the 7-member political bureau, which included also Lenin, Trotsky, and Stalin.

Fall of the Provisional Government. Trotsky, released from prison by Kerensky to combat counter-revolution, was elected chairman of the Bolshevik-controlled Petrograd Soviet at the end of September and was the chief organizer of the insurrection. The Petrograd Soviet decided on October 9 to set up a military revolutionary committee to defend the capital "against the openly prepared attack by . . . the supporters of Kornilov." The military revolutionary committee was actually organized on October 20 under the chairmanship of Trotsky. As the general staff of the insurrection, it distributed arms to the Red guards, made arrangements for the seizure of public buildings, and decreed that it alone had the authority to issue military orders. The troops of the Petrograd garrison, whom the Provisional Government had threatened to send to the front, pledged their allegiance to the military revolutionary committee, which promised to keep them in the capital. Some of the army units remained "neutral," and only a small number of troops— cadets of the military schools, the women's battalion, and detachments of Cossacks—were loyal to the Provisional Government. This was the decisive factor. As Trotsky put it, "the weakness of the government exceeded all expectations."

The imminence of the insurrection was generally known but not the exact date, which was not decided by the leaders until the last moment. On October 23 and 24 the Provisional Government attempted a final show of force. A call was sent for loyal troops, orders were issued for the arrest of the members of the military revolutionary committee and of the Bolshevik leaders free on bail, and the offices of two Bolshevik papers were raided by the cadets. The pro-Bolshevik cruiser *Aurora,* which came to anchor in the Neva, opposite the Winter Palace, was ordered to put out to sea, which, however, it refused to do. Both sides issued dramatic appeals proclaiming that the revolution was in danger. Kerensky, in a highly emotional speech—his swan song—at the Council of the Republic pledged himself to crush the revolt of "the rabble," and when the Council expressed its disapproval of the policy of the Provisional Government, he threatened to use the supreme weapon—to resign (October 24). Throughout these eventful days he was haunted by the specter of a counter-revolution from the right. In the morning of October 25 Kerensky left the Winter Palace, where the Provisional Government was in session, and drove to Gatchina in search for loyal troops.

Lenin arrived at the Smolny, headquarters of the Petrograd Soviet and of the Bolshevik central committee, in the evening of the 24th. During that night and on the 25th, troops under the orders of the military revolutionary committee occupied telephone exchanges, the post office, and other public buildings. They met with no resistance. About 6 o'clock in the afternoon of October 25 there began the siege of the Winter Palace, where the Provisional Government (minus Kerensky) was huddled behind a frail rampart of detachments of cadets, the women's battalion, and a small number of Cossacks. As an ultimatum demanding surrender was left unanswered, the guns of the *Aurora* and, later, those of the fortress of Peter and Paul across the river fired a few volleys, but only two shells hit the palace, causing minor damage. Meanwhile the defenders of the palace drifted away, and about 2 o'clock in the morning of October 26 the ministers of the Provisional Government who were present were arrested amidst scenes of great confusion.

A new chapter in the history of Russia and the world had begun.

PART FIVE

October 25, 1917-1939

CHRONOLOGY OF PRINCIPAL EVENTS

1917

October 25–26		Second All-Russian Congress of Soviets: decree on peace; decree on land; Council of People's Commissars formed
"	November 1	Kerensky flees abroad
"	November 2	"Declaration of the Rights of Peoples of Russia"
"	November 7	Ukrainian people's republic proclaimed
"	November 10	Class distinctions abolished
"	November 14	Decree on workers' control
"	November 14	Private banks nationalized
"	November 15	Soviets of Workers' and Peasants' Deputies merged
"	November	Elections to the Constituent Assembly
"	November	Left Socialist Revolutionaries enter Council of People's Commissars
"	November	Patriarchate restored
" November–1918, March		Brest-Litovsk peace negotiations
"	December 6	Finland proclaims independence

	(December 19, N.S.)	
	December 7	CHEKA (security police) established
1918	1918–1921	Civil war and War Communism
"	January–May	Civil war in Finland
"	January 5	Constituent Assembly meets and is dispersed
"	January 9	Rada proclaims Ukrainian independence
"	January 21	State loans annulled
"	February 5	Separation of the Church from state and schools
"	February 9	Ukrainian Rada concludes peace treaty with the Central Powers
	February 10	Trotsky announces "no war, no peace" policy
"	February 14	Russia introduces Gregorian calendar; old-style (Julian) calendar disappears. All subsequent dates are given according to the Western calendar
"	February 18	Germans begin advance
"	March 3	Peace Treaty of Brest-Litovsk
"	March–1919, October	Allied intervention
"	March 10–11	Capital transferred to Moscow
"	March	Left Socialist Revolutionaries withdraw from the government
"	March	Agreement with the Czecho-Slovak legion
"	April 22	Monopoly of foreign trade introduced
"	May	Breach with the Czecho-Slovak legion
"	June 28	Nationalization of large industrial enterprises
"	July	Constitution of RSFSR adopted
"	July 6	Count Mirbach murdered
"	August 30	Dora Kaplan's attempt to murder Lenin
"	October	"Unified labor schools" established
"	November	Admiral Kolchak proclaimed supreme ruler of anti-Soviet forces
"	November 11	Treaty of Brest-Litovsk annulled by allied armistice
"	November 13	Treaty of Brest-Litovsk annulled by the Soviets
1919	March	Third (Communist) International formed
"	March	Program of Communist Party adopted
	July	Soviets renounce special rights in China
	1920–1932	Period of relative freedom and experimentation in literature and the arts
1920	January	Allied blockade lifted

"	February	Independence of Estonia recognized
"	February	Kolchak executed
"	March	Committee of electrification (Goelro) established
"	April–1921, March	War with Poland
"	July	Independence of Lithuania recognized
"	August	Independence of Latvia recognized
"	September	First (Baku) congress of eastern peoples
"	November	Evacuation of Volunteer Army to Turkey
"	December	*De facto* incorporation of the Ukraine
	1921–1927	Soviets cooperate with Chiang Kai-shek
1921	February	*De facto* incorporation of White Russia
"	February	State Planning Commission (Gosplan) established
"	March 21	New Economic Policy introduced
"	March 21	Peace treaty (Riga) with Poland
"	April	Communist University of the Toilers of the East founded in Moscow
"	August	First industrial trusts formed
"	August	Introduction of economic (cost) accounting (*khozraschet*)
"	October	State Bank established
	1922–1923	"Scissors crisis"
1922	February	CHEKA reorganized as GPU
"	April–May	Genoa conference
"	April	Rapallo treaty with Germany
"	May–1923, June	Patriarch Tikhon held under arrest
"	October	Japanese evacuate Vladivostok
"	October	*Chervonets* (new monetary unit) introduced
"	December 28	Union of Soviet Socialist Republics (USSR) formed
1923		*Chapaev,* novel by Furmanov
"	July	Lausanne convention dealing with the Turkish straits
	November–1924, October	GPU reorganized as OGPU
1924		Soviets recognized by Great Britain, France, Italy, and other European countries
"	January 21	Lenin dies
"	January 31	Constitution of the USSR adopted
"	February–March	Stabilization of the ruble
1925		First control figures published
"		*Battleship Potemkin,* film produced by Eisenstein
"		Academy of Science of the USSR reorganized

1925		Japanese evacuate Sakhalin
"	January	Trotsky dismissed as commissar for war
	1926–1940	*The Quiet Don*, by Sholokhov
1926		*Days of the Turbins*, play by M. Bulgakov
"	July	Exports of rubles prohibited
	1927–1932	Diplomatic relations with China suspended
	1927–1936	*The Life of Klim Samgin*, by Gorky
1927		*The Red Poppy*, ballet by R. Gliere
"	December	Trotsky expelled from party and deported to Alma Ata, Kazakhstan
1928		First Machine Tractor Stations organized
"	March	Imports of rubles prohibited
"	March	First "show trial" (Donets engineers)
" October–1932, December		First Five-Year Plan
	1929–1930	Collectivization drive
	1929–1936	Rationing of foodstuffs and consumer goods
1929		Liquidation of the *kulaks* as a class
"		*Peter the First*, by A. N. Tolstoy
"	January	Socialist emulation inaugurated
"	February	Trotsky banished to Turkey
	1930's–1940's	Controversy over Marr views on linguistics
	" "	The Lysenko-Vavilov controversy over genetics; Vavilov dismissed and deported
1930		Unemployment insurance abolished
"	September	Turnover tax introduced
	1931–1937	Soviets conclude numerous non-aggression pacts, including pacts with border countries
	1932–1959	*The Virgin Soil Upturned*, by Sholokhov
1932	April 13	Decree on "Reconstruction of Literary and Art Organizations"—triumph for socialist realism
1933	January–1937, December	Second Five-Year Plan
"		People's commissariat for labor abolished; administration of social insurance transferred to All-Russian Central Council of Trade Unions
"	November 16	USSR recognized by the United States
1934		School reform
	July	OGPU put under the NKVD (People's Commissariat of the Interior)
"	September 18	The Soviet Union admitted to the League of Nations
"	December	Kirov murdered

1935		*How Steel Is Tempered,* by N. Ostrovsky
"		Model Charter of the Agricultural Artel
"	March	Sale of Chinese Eastern Railway to Japanese interests
"	May	Mutual assistance pacts with France and Czecho-slovakia
"	July	The Lausanne Straits convention revised at Montreux
"	August	Stakhanov movement inaugurated
"	August	First political show trial (Zinovev, Kamenev, and others)
	1936–1938	Mass purges
1936	December 5	"Stalin" constitution adopted
1938	January–1942	Third Five-Year Plan
"		Meyerhold Theatre closed

20

The Soviets Take Over, 1917-1923

Foreword

The Soviets and the Historians. The historian who values the integrity of his craft may well approach the Soviet period of Russian history with trepidation. Books on the Soviet Union are numerous and come in an endless stream. This may seem encouraging. Yet the truth of the matter is that as far as history is concerned, the Iron Curtain is no mere figure of speech or figment of one's imagination but a stark reality: conformity in ideas and even modes of expression, censorship that amounts to the obliteration of all but official views, and non-intercourse with foreigners that borders on exclusion have erected around the Soviet Union a nearly impregnable barrier, a kind of Chinese or Berlin wall. The Berlin wall—a sinister evocation of medievalism in an age of jet and nuclear power—is symbolic of the attitude of the Kremlin towards the West. In the closing years of Stalin's rule the release of commonplace information bearing on Soviet affairs or an unauthorized talk with a foreign visitor was an actionable offense. Since 1953 this is no longer the case, but although Soviet leaders talk incessantly and at cruel length, they succeed in leaving many vital questions unanswered. Bulky collections of opaque statistics are released, visa regulations have been greatly simplified, foreign tourists are welcome, and an exchange of students—on a very modest scale

—is in progress. Nevertheless, the basic shortage of information and historical data persists, and, while the broad lines of Soviet development are reasonably clear, the more detailed study of essential points remains exceedingly difficult and in many cases impossible. These melancholy observations may be kept in mind while reading the chapters which follow.

The First Steps

Peace, Land, and Soviet Government. The foundation of the future Soviet state was formally laid at the Second All-Russian Congress of Soviets, which opened after several delays in the late evening of October 25, 1917, some three hours before the arrest of the Provisional Government. No detailed information on the party allegiance of the delegates and the methods by which they were elected is available, but it is known that the Bolsheviks were the largest single party and had a majority that was reinforced by the support of the left-wing Socialist Revolutionaries and of the representatives of smaller political groups. The total number of deputies was about 650; the Bolsheviks and their allies controlled probably more than two-thirds of the votes. At its first session the congress proclaimed the transfer of all power to the Soviets. The anti-Bolshevik opposition withdrew after protesting against the insurrection and the overthrow of the Provisional Government. This unwise action facilitated the task of the majority. At the second and last session of the congress, in the evening of October 26, the Bolsheviks and their supporters passed, by unanimous or quasi-unanimous vote, the decrees on peace, land, and the formation of the Council of People's Commissars. The decree on peace, which, as E. H. Carr observed, had a Wilsonian flavor, invited "all belligerent peoples and their governments to begin immediate negotiations for an honest democratic peace . . . a peace without annexations and indemnities" There should be an immediate armistice. Secret diplomacy was to be abolished, and the Russian government was to publish immediately all secret treaties and abrogate those directed "to securing advantages or privileges for Russian landlords and capitalists."

The decree on land abolished, without compensation but subject to approval by the Constituent Assembly, private ownership of large estates. All such land, as well as that held by appanages and ecclesiastical institutions, was to be brought under the control of land committees and peasant Soviets. An instruction attached to the decree stated that, subject again to the approval of the Constituent Assembly, private ownership of land, including that of peasants and village communes, was abolished; land could not be sold, bought, mortgaged, leased, or transferred in any way. The former owners were entitled to a maintenance allowance from public funds. The entire land of the country was to constitute a national land reserve, and every citizen willing to work on land was entitled to an allotment the size of which was to be determined by his family status (number of people able to work or of dependents receiving maintenance). The use of hired labor was prohibited. Periodical re-apportionments of land were to take place to safeguard the equalitarian principle on which the whole scheme was based. The implementation of this program, which Lenin had borrowed from the Socialist Revolutionaries, would require a massive resettlement of millions of farmers. This plan, known as socialization of land, was clearly utopian and was never enforced. Nevertheless it served the purpose of sanctioning by implication that partition of large estates among the peasants which was already an accomplished fact.

The same night session of the congress provided the new regime with its chief political institution, the 15-member Council of People's Commissars— or Sovnarkom (an abbreviation of its Russian name)—and elected a new All-Russian Central Executive Committee of Soviets. The Council of People's Commissars was headed by Lenin and had Trotsky as commissar for foreign affairs and Stalin as commissar for nationalities. The Central Executive Committee had slightly more than 100 members, including 62 Bolsheviks and 29 Left Socialist Revolutionaries; the balance of the committee members belonged to splinter pro-Bolshevik parties.

Opposition from the Left. Although the victory of the Bolsheviks in Petrograd was seemingly effortless, the consolidation of Soviet rule was a protracted and difficult business. In this respect the situation in October–November was strikingly different from that in February–March, when the fall of the monarchy was accepted throughout the country with almost fatalistic resignation if not indifference.

Unexpectedly, the earlier challenges to the authority of the Bolshevik government came not from the generals and the *bourgeoisie* but from the ranks of "revolutionary democracy." Kerensky's effort to raise loyal troops was short-lived and a failure. On October 25 he drove from Petrograd to Gatchina and then to Pskov, where he prevailed upon General P. N. Krasnov, commanding a cavalry corps, to come to the assistance of the Provisional Government. A proclamation issued by Kerensky as he and Krasnov advanced hesitantly towards the capital at the head of a small detachment of Cossacks declared that "Bolshevism has ceased to exist in Petrograd." Encouraged, the cadets of Petrograd military schools rose against the Bolsheviks October 29.

Their sacrifices were in vain. The Krasnov detachment was defeated; Kerensky retreated to Gatchina, on November 1 escaped in disguise as he was about to be arrested, and went abroad. His stormy and meteoric career was over.

The army headquarters at Mogilev offered but perfunctory resistance to the Bolsheviks. General Dukhonin, who became chief of staff after the Kornilov "mutiny" and commander-in-chief after Kerensky's flight, refused to carry out the orders of the Council of People's Commissars to open peace negotiations with the enemy (November 8 and 9). He was dismissed and was succeeded by N. V. Krylenko, an ensign. Dukhonin refused to comply with the order of dismissal but submitted to arrest; he was murdered by mutinous soldiers. While still commander-in-chief he ordered the release of General Kornilov and other officers under arrest at Bykhov; they fled to the Don region, where they joined General Alekseev in organizing the anti-Bolshevik Volunteer Army.

The counter-revolution of the generals, however, did not take shape for another six months. Meanwhile the authority of the Bolshevik government was flouted from the left, chiefly by agencies controlled by the socialist parties which had withdrawn from the Second Congress of Soviets. The lead was taken by the Petrograd city council, which in the night of October 25 made a half-hearted attempt at relieving the Provisional Government besieged in the Winter Palace. Having failed in this endeavor, the councillors returned to the City Hall and formed a Committee for the Salvation of the Country and of the Revolution, on which were represented, in addition to the city council, the Central Executive Committee of Soviets of Workers' and Soldiers' Deputies (elected in June), the Executive Committee of the Congress of Peasants' Deputies, the Council of the Republic, the Mensheviks, the Socialist Revolutionaries, the trade unions, and various "democratic" organizations at the front and in the rear. The committee issued an appeal denouncing the Bolsheviks as usurpers and urging the population not to comply with their orders.

Similar appeals were made by other left-wing bodies. The Central Executive Committee elected in June refused to recognize the legality of its successor appointed by the Second Congress in October; it continued to function openly for two more months and published a newspaper. The members of the Provisional Government, released from the fortress of Peter and Paul, constituted themselves as a cabinet, issued orders, and attempted to rule side by side with the Council of People's Commissars. On November 17 they published an appeal stating that they were "the sole legitimate organ of power" and inviting the population to rally to the support of the Constituent Assembly. This gesture of defiance proved their undoing. The papers which printed the appeal were closed, and the signatories were ordered deported to Kronstadt, a maritime fortress noted for its intransigeant revolutionary spirit. The Senate, Russia's supreme court, was not interfered with until it made a ruling (November 24) annulling the decree that established the Council of People's Commissars on the ground that it was unconstitutional. Three days later the Senate was dissolved.

There was discord and strife within the institutions of "revolutionary democracy"—the Soviets, trade unions, factory committees, and municipal councils. A significant development was the formal recognition of the split, which existed for some time, of the Socialist Revolutionary Party into two parties, of which one—the Left Socialist Revolutionaries—cooperated with the Bolsheviks. On November 15, 1917, the Central Executive Committee of Soviets and the Peasant Executive Committee reached an agreement merging these two institutions into the All-Russian Central Executive Committee of Soviets of Workers', Soldiers', and Peasants' Deputies. Its delegates numbered over 350, including 100 each from the workers, the peasants, and the armed forces, and 50 from the trade unions. The formal integration of the two types of Soviets took place in January 1918, when the Third All-Russian Congress of Peasants' Deputies was fused with the Third All-Russian Congress of Soviets of Workers' and Soldiers' Deputies. Similar unification was carried out through the entire structure of the Soviet system—a tangible expression of the "alliance" between workers and peasants.

The opposition encountered by the Bolshevik regime in Petrograd was duplicated in Moscow and in the provinces. The Second All-Russian Congress of the Soviets directed the local Soviets to assume full power. The implementation of this order led in many cases to the formation of local military revolutionary committees, but not everything went smoothly. Committees for the Salvation of the Country and of the Revolution, patterned after that of Petrograd, were organized in many localities. Moscow, where Lenin expected no resistance, put up a stiff struggle that involved the bombardment of the Kremlin, lasted a week, and cost hundreds of lives. Fighting took place in a number of cities; some were still under a non-Bolshevik government as late as April 1918.

Early Legislation. The inaugural phase of Bolshevik rule was one of insecurity and confusion. The dream of power had come true, but no one knew how long it would last. The early Soviet legislation, therefore, comprised two elements: legislative improvisations dictated by the exigencies of the situation and measures inspired by ideological considerations and addressed to the future rather than to the present—what Trotsky called "the enunciation of a party program in the language of power"—a heritage that would inspire generations to come if the revolution should fail. The scope and character of this legislation are suggested by the listing of the principal measures. On October 29 the Sovnarkom proclaimed its right to close hostile newspapers. Class distinctions sanctioned by law were abolished and replaced by a uniform citizenship status (November 10). Women were given equal rights, and civil marriages were introduced (December 18). The Church was "separated from the state and from the schools" (February 5, 1918). All army commanders (no longer called officers) were to be elected by appropriate army committees (December 16), and all ranks, titles, decorations, and insignias were abolished (December 23). The principle of electing the commanding personnel, however, did not apply to the Red Army and the Red Navy, the organization of which, at first on a voluntary basis, was announced respectively on January 15 and February 1 (14), 1918.[1] The 1864 system of law courts, which was retained by the Provisional Government, was replaced by "people's courts" and elective judges; as a provisional measure judges could be appointed by local Soviets (November 22).

The existing laws were to be applied "only in so far as they . . . were not in conflict with revolutionary conscience." Offenses against the new order were tried by revolutionary tribunals (December 19). Early in December the Petrograd military revolutionary committee was dissolved, and its police functions were taken over by the Special Committee for the Struggle Against Counter-Revolution, Sabotage, and Speculation, or CHEKA, which was headed by F. E. Dzerzhinsky (December 7). This sinister institution was the fountainhead of the security police, which, in its various transformations, has remained one of the pillars of the regime. Agencies of local government, including the township (*volost*) *zemstvos* formed under a law of May 21, 1917, were set aside and replaced by a hierarchy of Soviets (December 24). The Seventh Congress of the Bolshevik Party, held in March 1918, changed the name of the party to Russian Communist Party of the Bolsheviks.

There was a steady flow of economic legislation. The State Bank was taken over by the Bolsheviks on October 25, all private banks were nationalized on November 14, and safe deposit boxes were opened and the valuables which they contained confiscated. Payments of interest and dividends, as well

---

[1] On February 1, 1918, the Gregorian, or New Style, calendar replaced the Julian calendar formerly used in Russia. February 1 became February 14, and the difference between the Russian and the Western calendar disappeared. All dates beginning with February 14, 1918, are given in accordance with the Gregorian (N.S.) calendar.

as dealing in securities, were prohibited (December 29). State foreign and domestic loans were annulled (January 21, 1918). The 8-hour day was introduced in industrial enterprises (October 29). "Workers' control," long a favorite idea of the Bolsheviks, became law on November 14. Socialization of land, announced in the night of October 26, was elaborated in a decree of February 19, 1918, and foreign trade was nationalized on April 22, 1918.

Much of the above legislation, haphazard as it was, was aimed at smashing the existing order before rebuilding the administrative machinery from the ground. There were three issues, however, which called for immediate positive action: the Constituent Assembly, war or peace, and the complexion of the government.

The Constituent Assembly. Support of the Constituent Assembly was one policy shared by all revolutionary parties in 1917. Defense of the Constituent Assembly against the allegedly sinister designs of the Provisional Government was a much-publicized justification of the October insurrection. Elections to the Constituent Assembly were held, as scheduled, in the middle of November, that is, under Bolshevik rule. From the returns available early in 1918 (they have remained incomplete) Lenin computed that the Bolsheviks received 25 per cent of the total vote cast and the Socialist Revolutionaries 58 per cent. Of the 703 delegates accounted for, 168 belonged to the Bolshevik Party, and 419 to the Socialist Revolutionary Party, of which 39 were members of the left faction and 380 of the right. These figures indicate that the Bolsheviks and their Left Socialist Revolutionary allies were a minority in the Constituent Assembly, a situation the Council of Peoples' Commissars would not countenance. One way out of the difficulty would have been to have some of the elections declared invalid and then hold by-elections. Authority to initiate such action was conferred upon the Soviets by a decree of November 21, 1917. It was argued by the Bolsheviks that the poor showing of the Left Socialist Revolutionaries was due to the fact that the electoral lists required by the system of proportional representation (used in the November election) were drawn before the split of the Socialist Revolutionary Party was formally recognized. The argument was ingenuous, but for technical reasons the decree of November 21 was never used. A more dependable weapon was needed. This was provided by Lenin's *Theses on the Constituent Assembly* published on December 13. Lenin claimed that the Soviet government was "a higher form of democratic organization" than a bourgeois republic with a constituent assembly. The Constituent Assembly, if it was to survive, was to accept unconditionally "Soviet power, Soviet revolution, and its policies of peace, land, and workers' control." The alternative was "a solution by revolutionary means." What this meant was soon made clear.

The Constituent Assembly held its first and only session on January 5, 1918, at a Taurida Palace bristling with armed Bolshevik sailors and soldiers. It elected Chernov to the chair and rejected the Bolshevik motion restating Lenin's demands. The Bolshevik delegates and their political friends withdrew; the non-Bolshevik members kept on making discourses into the early hours of the morning until they were told by the guards (acting on orders from the central committee of the Bolshevik Party) that it was time to go home. The assembly adjourned, ostensibly for 12 hours, but actually never to meet again: it was dissolved the same day by the Central Executive Committee. The lamentable and grotesque end of what was to be a landmark in Russian history grieved the few politically-minded but had no broad repercussions of any kind.

National Self-Determination: Finland and the Ukraine. The question of war and peace, or, more precisely, of Russia's withdrawal from the European war, became entangled with the independence movement in Russia's western borderlands—Finland and, especially, the Ukraine. The "Declaration of the Rights of the Peoples of Russia" issued by the Council of People's Commissars under the signature of Stalin, commissar for nationalities, spoke of the equality of the peoples of Russia and their right of "secession and the formation of an independent state" (November 2, 1917). Finland therefore appeared to be on safe ground when on December 19, N.S., she proclaimed her independence, which was speedily recognized by the Soviet government. However, the Bolshevik doctrine of self-determination as formulated by Lenin, Stalin, and the first program of the Communist Party (March 1919) held that the exercise of this right depended, as Stalin put it, "on the concrete factors of the international situation, on the interests of the revolution." The histories of Finland and the Ukraine offer an illustration of how the two elements of the doctrine operated in practice.

Finland, after the proclamation of her independence, was under the non-socialist government of Svinhufud, which in January 1918 was overthrown by a left-wing Finnish movement acting in close collaboration with, and probably instigated by, the Russians. The Finns, however, do not give in easily—this is a remarkable national characteristic which may help to explain their survival as a nation. The country became involved in a civil war of great bitterness: the Whites held the north, while a Finnish Workers' Republic was formed in the south and on March 1 concluded a treaty of friendship with the Soviets. However, six days later, on March 7 (that is, four days after the signature of the Soviet-German Treaty of Brest-Litovsk), Svinhufud, who had retained the leadership of the Whites, made an agreement with Germany. A German expeditionary force landed in Finland, the Workers' Republic disintegrated, its leaders took refuge in Russia, the Finnish civil war was over early in May 1918, and Finland retained her independence.

Events in the Ukraine prior to the German defeat followed a similar pattern, except that the Russians intervened openly. A plausible pretext was provided by the geographical location of the Ukraine, whose territory separated Soviet Russia from the southern regions where the former Russian generals—Alekseev, Kornilov, Denikin—were organizing the anti-Bolshevik Volunteer Army. The Soviets accused the Ukrainian national government of aiding and abetting the rebellious generals and the Cossacks. The Ukrainian Central Rada (parliament) and the secretariat (cabinet) that it appointed had been negotiating with the Provisional Government since the spring of 1917. On November 7, that is, after the October revolution, the Rada proclaimed the formation of the Ukrainian People's Republic, which was pledged, however, "not to separate from the Russian republic" pictured as a federation of "equal and free peoples."

These conciliatory pronouncements failed to ease the Russo-Ukrainian tension. In the Russian Ukraine, Ukrainian nationalism was a frail and precarious growth. Soviets began to appear in the Ukraine in the summer of 1917; they commanded a sizable following and were a convenient tool in the hands of the Petrograd government. On December 4 the Sovnarkom accused the Rada of assisting the White generals, made drastic demands, and threatened, in case of non-compliance within 48 hours, to consider the Rada "in a state of open war against the Soviet power in Russia and in the Ukraine." The Ukrainian Soviet in Kiev was mobilized in support of the Russian program, but although the reply of the Rada was unsatisfactory, the breach with Petrograd was delayed. Instead, the Ukrainian Bolsheviks reassembled in Kharkov where, with the connivance of the Russians, an all-Ukrainian congress of Soviets elected an All-Ukrainian Executive Committee, which proclaimed itself the legitimate government and deposed the Rada (December 14). Civil war followed. Early in January the Russian Soviet troops invaded the Ukraine. On January 9 (January 22, N.S.) the Rada, at its rope's end and not to be outdone by the Kharkov Communists, proclaimed the Ukraine "an independent and sovereign state . . . subject to no other authority." Meanwhile the Russian troops from the north overran the country, occupied Kiev (February 9, N.S.), and overflowed into the southern Cossack territories. The Rada fled to Zhitomir, then to Sarny. The successes of the Reds notwithstanding, the Soviet rule in Kiev in 1918 lasted merely three weeks. The sovereign Ukrainian republic proclaimed by the Rada was recognized by the Central Powers (February 1, N.S.) and on February 9, N.S., these governments concluded with the representatives of the Rada at Brest-Litovsk a treaty that invited the Austro-German occupation of the Ukraine and the south of Russia. On March 2 the Bolsheviks withdrew from Kiev. The Soviet regime in the Ukraine was at its end—until the final breakdown of the German power eight months later.

Brest-Litovsk. The peace decree of October 26 startled both allies and foes but brought no immediate response. A note stating that the decree was "a formal offer of an immediate armistice . . . and immediate peace negotiations" was circulated by Trotsky to the allies and to the ambassadors of neutral states for transmission to the Central Powers. The allied governments protested the armistice proposals as a violation of the treaty of September 1914, binding the signatories not to conclude separate peace. Krylenko, who succeeded Dukhonin as commander-in-chief, directed the army units to make their own armistice arrangements on sectors of the front. An over-all armistice agreement was concluded at Brest-Litovsk (December 5, N.S.) and remained in force until denounced by the Germans on February 10, 1918, N.S.

As the Brest-Litovsk conference opened on December 9 (December 22, N.S.), the mood of the Soviet press and the Soviet delegation was one of extreme optimism. *Pravda* held the acceptance of the Russian armistice proposals as evidence of the strength of the Russian revolution and of the weakness of its enemies. There was a widely-held belief that an attempt to send German troops against Russia would lead to a German revolution, and Trotsky thought that the final stage of the negotiations would be with the German Communist Party.

Actually two worlds which had little in common were facing each other across the conference table at Brest-Litovsk. The Central Powers were represented by a royal prince (Leopold of Bavaria, commander of the German eastern front), high-ranking statesmen and diplomats (von Kühlmann, German foreign minister; Count Ottokar Czernin, Austrian foreign minister; Talaat Pasha, the Turkish grand vizier; V. Radoslavov, prime minister of Bulgaria), and generals (Max von Hoffmann, of the German high command); the Russians by a group of seasoned professional revolutionaries headed at first by Adolf Ioffe, then by Trotsky, and finally by G. Sokolnikov. The allied governments were repeatedly invited by the Russians to attend but did not reply. A conventional agreement between delegations so far apart in their upbringing and outlook was out of the question, nor was one intended by the Bolsheviks. The Russians, particularly Trotsky, were convinced of the propaganda value of the negotiations and used various subterfuges to make them drag. But time did not necessarily work in their favor. When the conference resumed on December 22 (January 9, N.S.) after a 10-day recess requested by the Russians, Trotsky (who had succeeded Ioffe) was unpleasantly surprised by the presence at Brest-Litovsk of the delegation from the Ukrainian Rada, which was recognized by the Central Powers. Trotsky went on talking about self-determination and "democratic" peace, but on January 5 (January 18, N.S.) General Hoffmann made it clear that Germany intended to retain the eastern territories which she held, that is, Russian Poland, the Baltic provinces, and White Russia (Byelo-Russia). There was another adjournment for 10 days, and Trotsky went to Petrograd.

Hoffmann's statement shattered Russian illusions. Lenin understood its implications at once and tackled them boldly in *Theses on the Question of a Separate and Annexationist Peace,* written on January 7 (January 20, N.S.) but not published until after the German terms were accepted. He argued that the success of socialism in Russia required a breathing space. "There is no doubt that the socialist revolution in Europe must and will come," wrote Lenin. "All our hopes for the *final* victory of socialism are based on this conviction, on this scientific foresight." But it would be a great mistake to assume that "the European, and particularly the German socialist revolution will come in the next half year (or similar short period)." The immediate task was the preservation of the socialist revolution in Russia until the revolution materialized in other countries. Furthermore, the Russian army was no longer capable of fighting. The peasants would welcome peace on any terms, and if they were compelled to carry on the war, they would overthrow the Soviet government, probably within a week. Immediate peace at whatever price was indispensable to save the revolution.

As in April, Lenin's trenchant analysis ran contrary to party opinion. At a conference in Petrograd on January 8 (January 21, N.S.) attended by 63 Bolshevik leaders, 15 voted for immediate peace; 32 supported the policy of "revolutionary war"; and 16 favored Trotsky's imaginative proposal to stop war, not to conclude peace, and to demobilize the army. The Trotsky formula was again approved by the central committee of the party on January 11 (January 24, N.S.). This was the mandate he took with him to Brest-Litovsk when the conference resumed on January 17 (January 30, N.S.). A novel development was the appearance at Brest-Litovsk of a second Ukrainian delegation—one representing the Ukrainian Soviet government and recognized by the Russians. The familiar debate on self-government and "democratic" peace seemed once more to monopolize the attention of the delegates, but the Germans had enough of it and meant business. On January 26 (February 8, N.S.) they signed a peace treaty with the delegation of the Ukrainian Rada. Two days later (February 10, N.S.) Trotsky exploded a bombshell: he announced that Russia would not sign an annexationist peace but declared war with the Central Powers at an end. The same evening the Soviet delegation left Brest-Litovsk.

There was some hesitation among the delegates of the Central Powers as to the next step, but General Hoffmann would have no more revolutionary nonsense. He interpreted the breach of the negotiations as the end of the armistice and advised the Russians on February 17 that military operations would be resumed next day (the armistice agreement stipulated a 7-day notice before the resumption of hostilities). A massive German offensive along the entire front, from the Baltic to the Black Sea, was launched on February 18 and encountered no resistance.

While the German troops relentlessly pressed on, the Bolshevik leaders continued to argue. Lenin's motion demanding immediate acceptance of the German terms was voted down twice by slim margins but was finally adopted in the evening of February 18 by a vote of 7 to 6 of the central committee of the Bolshevik Party. The Sovnarkom approved, and a telegram of acceptance was sent to Brest-Litovsk. There was no reply until February 23, while the German army continued to advance. The Sovnarkom lost its nerve and on February 21 issued, with Lenin's concurrence, a highly emotional appeal for the "mobilization of all forces" to defend the revolution. The German terms received on February 23 were even more exacting than the earlier version. Lenin called for immediate acceptance, which was granted by the central committee of the party by a 7 to 4 vote, with 4 abstentions. Acceptance was confirmed by the Central Executive Committee of Soviets by 116 to 85 votes, with 26 abstentions. The treaty was signed at Brest-Litovsk on March 3, 1918, by G. Sokolnikov, who headed the Soviet delegation. It was ratified by the Fourth Congress of Soviets on March 16, 1918, after a 2-day debate, by a vote of 784 to 261.

The peace of Brest-Litovsk deprived Russia of her Polish, Ukrainian, Baltic, and White Russian provinces and of the territories of Kars, Batum, and Ardakhan in the Caucasus, an aggregate territory of 1.3 million square miles with a population of 62 million. The Russians were not at first required to make financial reparations, but a supplementary treaty of August 27, 1918, obligated the Soviets to pay Germany, in installments, 6 billion marks for "losses caused to the Germans by Russian measures."

Russia after Brest-Litovsk, March 1918

Brest-Litovsk throws interesting light on the dialectics of the revolution. Trotsky's policy of "no war, no peace" was based on the mistaken assumption that the Germans and their allies would not resume the offensive against a revolutionary Russia. Had this proposal been adopted, it would probably have led the Soviet regime to disaster. Lenin's policy of peace at any price was predicated on the equally erroneous belief in the imminence of the proletarian revolution in western Europe, especially in the central empires. This "scientific foresight" did not come true; yet the Treaty of Brest-Litovsk, as Lenin had anticipated, was set aside, although not by the socialist revolution in central Europe: it was annulled by Article 15 of the armistice of November 11, 1918, imposed upon a defeated Germany by the victorious allies; the abrogation was confirmed by Article 116 of the bourgeois and "annexationist" Treaty of Versailles. The All-Russian Central Executive Committee, too, annulled the Brest-Litovsk treaty, on November 13, two days after the German-allied armistice. Lenin—and this is the peculiarity of his revolutionary genius—was wrong as to the basic assumption and method (socialist revolution in the West), but he was right as to the results: the Soviet regime survived and fulfills the part assigned to it by its founders, that of leading the world along the path of socialist revolution.

A by-product of the Brest-Litovsk negotiations, or, rather, of the German offensive that they unleashed, was the transfer of the capital from Petrograd to Moscow (officially, March 10 and 11, 1918).

The Early Governments and the Constitution
of the RSFSR

Towards the One-Party State. On the morrow of the October revolution the political complexion of the government was heatedly discussed in socialist circles. The Council of People's Commissars appointed on October 26, 1917, was exclusively Bolshevik, but this arrangement was not deemed final and there were numerous proposals for the formation of a government that would comprise various shades of socialist opinion, even to the exclusion of the Bolsheviks. The split of the Socialist Revolutionary Party into two factions, the left and the right, the former supporting the Bolsheviks, became manifest at the first All-Russian Congress of Soviets in June 1917. It was formally recognized in November 1917, when the Bolsheviks and the Left Socialist Revolutionaries, led by Maria Spiridonova, entered into a coalition and three Left Socialist Revolutionaries joined the Council of People's Commissars. The coalition did not work well, however. The Left Socialist Revolutionaries were inexorably opposed to the Brest-Litovsk treaty, and after its acceptance their representatives resigned from the Council of People's Commissars (March 1918). The one-party government was thus restored. The socialist opposition—chiefly the Mensheviks and the Socialist Revolutionaries—were still tolerated in the Soviets, but with the outbreak of the civil war and intervention in the spring of 1918 they came under a cloud.

There were several focal points of disagreement between the Bolsheviks and the opposition. The Socialist Revolutionaries were particularly critical of the committees of poor peasants organized in the villages and of the revival and extensive use of capital punishment, which had been abolished by the Second Congress of Soviets on October 25. The newborn cordiality in Soviet-German relations was heartily disliked. On July 6, 1918, the German ambassador to Moscow, Count Mirbach, was assassinated by a Left Socialist Revolutionary who was a member of CHEKA. The motive for the crime was political—to disrupt Soviet-German relations. There followed an abortive attempt by the Socialist Revolutionaries to seize power in Moscow and in several provincial cities. The government retaliated. The Left Socialist Revolutionary members of the Fifth All-Russian Congress of Soviets, then in session, were arrested, and at least 13 of them were executed. Among those arrested was Spiridonova; released after several months she was later banished to Siberia. The Fifth Congress passed a resolution expelling the Socialist Revolutionaries from the Soviets. A similar ban was imposed upon the Mensheviks in June 1918. This was another step in the direction of the one-party state. Meanwhile the Socialist Revolutionaries stuck to their traditional weapon of political murders. In July they assassinated General Eichhorn, commander of the German troops in the Ukraine, and on August 30, 1918, M. S. Uritsky, head of the Petrograd CHEKA. On the same day Lenin was fired on and seriously wounded by Dora Kaplan, a Socialist Revolutionary. The Sixth Congress of Soviets, held in November 1918, was the first almost-exclusively Bolshevik congress.

The civil war, which was the starting point of the persecution, brought eventually a measure of reconciliation. Both the Mensheviks and the Socialist Revolutionaries did penance and repudiated any intention of overthrowing the Soviet power. The interdict on Menshevik participation in the Soviets was lifted by the Central Executive Committee in November 1918 and that on the Socialist Revolutionaries in February 1919. Throughout 1919 and 1920 both parties were tolerated, but with the end of the civil war and mounting evidence of widespread discontent the Bolshevik attitude stiffened. The Eighth All-Russian Congress of Soviets (December 1920) was the last one to admit

Menshevik and Socialist Revolutionary delegates, and then without voting rights.

The New Economic Policy (March 1921), which removed some of the rigors of War Communism, had no counterpart in political relations. The trend in government was towards greater intransigence. The reorganization in February 1922 of the CHEKA as the state police administration, or GPU, under the commissariat of the interior, was greeted with a general sigh of relief, which, however, was unwarranted. In its new incarnation the security police proved an even more ruthless and arbitrary instrument of persecution than its predecessor. The still surviving political parties were doomed. Pressure brought to bear upon the Mensheviks in 1921 forced them either to recant their "errors" or to face banishment into the wilderness of the north or Siberia; the more fortunate succeeded in emigrating to the West. The demise of the Socialist Revolutionary Party was more dramatic. Some 50 of its leaders were arrested by the newly-founded GPU in February 1922. Thirty-four were tried on a variety of charges in the summer of 1922; 14 of them received death sentences, which were commuted, however. This was the end of the Socialist Revolutionary Party in Russia.

Dissenting opinions are incompatible with the Leninist concept of government. Bourgeois political parties were disbanded immediately after October; non-Bolshevik left-wing parties were grudgingly tolerated until July 1918; they were allowed to linger until 1921 or 1922, when they were finally obliterated.

Constitution of the RSFSR. During the opening months of the Bolshevik regime a harassed and insecure government and party, faithful to Lenin's dictum that a revolutionary government must be built up from the ground, were chiefly concerned with the destruction of the existing administrative machinery and gave no thought to constitutional issues. As we know, the agencies of local government were superseded by various Soviets, and the Council of People's Commissars exercised dictatorial powers. According to E. H. Carr, Lenin's voluminous writings during this period contain no reference to constitutional changes. Nevertheless in April 1918 the drafting of a constitution was entrusted to a committee of which Stalin was the ranking member. The draft was approved by the Fifth All-Russian Congress of Soviets (which had just ordered the exclusion of the Socialist Revolutionaries) in July 1918.

The constitution created the Russian Soviet Federated Socialist Republic, or RSFSR, the territory of which was not defined but was actually much smaller than that of imperial Russia because of territorial losses resulting from the Treaty of Brest-Litovsk and the independence movements in the borderlands. The constitution included, as its introductory section, the "Declaration of the Rights of the Toiling and Exploited People" which had been adopted by the Third Congress of Soviets in January 1918. It proclaimed Russia "a federation of Soviet national republics" and stated that "all authority, central and local," was vested in the Soviets. The constitution then recited the principal measures already adopted: socialization of land, workers' control, repudiation of state loans, nationalization of banking, and so on. The institutional structure consisted of a pyramid of Soviets of workers', soldiers', and peasants' deputies and their congresses, arranged in a hierarchical order. At the bottom of the pyramid were the village and town Soviets, then came the Soviets of the larger territorial subdivisions, with the All-Russian Congress of Soviets at the apex. The members of the village and town Soviets were elected directly by open ballot; delegates to all other Soviets were elected by the Soviets next below. The franchise was discriminatory and favored the urban population, that is, the city proletariat: there was one delegate for each 25,000 town electors, and one delegate for each 125,000 rural inhabitants. The disfranchised were: persons employing hired labor or living on unearned income, private traders, ministers of religion, former police officers and members of the former dynasty, people of unsound mind, and convicted criminals. Congresses at each level elected executive committees. The All-Russian Congress of Soviets elected the All-Russian Central Executive Committee, which formed the Council of People's Commissars.

The constitution made no reference to the judiciary and ignored the principle of separation of powers. It was basically a propaganda document rather than a constitutional charter. The functions of the Soviets, especially those at the lower level, were not defined, and the supreme authority—executive and legislative—remained, as prior to the issuance of the constitution, with the Council of People's Commissars, which derived its authority from its members' leadership of the Communist Party.

Civil War, Intervention, and Independence Movements

Civil War. Civil war and intervention, which form the somber background of Soviet history from 1918 to 1921, unfolded in four main areas on the periphery of the Russian state: in the south, in the Ukraine and the Cossack lands on the littoral of the Black Sea and in the Caucasus; in the east, on the shores of the Pacific and in Siberia; in the north, in the Murmansk and

Archangel regions; and in the west, in Estonia, in the tantalizing proximity of Petrograd. The involved and shifting pattern of the civil war, which was fought simultaneously on four fronts, was complicated by three external factors: the Czech legion, the defeat of Germany, and allied intervention. The years 1918 to 1921 in Soviet Russia present, indeed, a confused and crowded picture.

The nucleus of resistance in the south was the Volunteer Army organized by Alekseev, Kornilov, Denikin, and other officers who had made their way to the territory of the Don Cossacks beginning in November–December 1917. It was at first commanded by Kornilov and after his death in action (April 1918) by Denikin, who in March 1920 was succeeded by General Wrangel. Its objectives, as defined by its founders, were to protect southern Russia from the Bolsheviks and the Germans, to uphold civic liberties, and to ensure the convocation of the Constituent Assembly. Broadly, the Volunteer Army was pro-ally and anti-German, as well as bourgeois and traditionalist in its outlook. Originally a small force of a few thousand men, the Volunteer Army fought in alliance with the various Cossack hosts; disagreements among the participants in these joint campaigns were sharp and frequent.

The Czech legion evolved from a Czecho-Slovak brigade recruited at the beginning of World War I by the Russian government among the Czechs and Slovaks residing in Russia. It was extended by drafting Czech and Slovak prisoners-of-war and deserters and in 1917 was given the status of an independent corps numbering—the estimates vary—from 30,000 to 50,000 men. Thomas Masaryk and Eduard Benes, who were in Russia, refused to allow the Czech legion, which had retained its discipline and fighting capacity, to participate in the Russian civil strife. Arrangements were made to ship the legion from Vladivostok to America and then to France, and in March 1918 the Soviets signed an agreement for its transportation by rail across Siberia. Friction developed immediately, and clashes in May between the Czechs and the Soviets at Cheliabinsk, Siberia, resulted in a state of open warfare. The legion established control over a large section of the Trans-Siberian railway, sealed off Siberia, and expanded along the Volga, taking Samara in June. Under its protective shield several anti-Bolshevik governments sprang up in the east. There was the Samara government, which consisted of members of the Constituent Assembly, almost exclusively Socialist Revolutionaries. A government of bouregois complexion was· organized in July at Omsk and for four months claimed authority over western Siberia. Ataman Semenov, chieftain of the Siberian Cossacks, established himself in Chita and controlled a section of the vast Trans-Baikal region. A "provisional all-Russian government" uniting several shadowy anti-Soviet political agglomerations was formed in Ufa in September 1918 under the presidency of N. Avksentev, a prominent Socialist Revolutionary. In the meantime the Czechs withdrew from the Volga area to Siberia, and the new government settled in Omsk. In November it was overthrown by Admiral Alexander Kolchak, formerly commanding officer of the Black Sea fleet and a man of conservative views. He assumed the status of "Supreme Ruler" and was recognized as such by the leaders of other White armies. Kolchak lasted until the beginning of 1920, when the demoralized and disgruntled Czechs turned him over to the Bolsheviks. He was tried and executed in February 1920.

The northern center of resistance, based on Murmansk and Archangel, was relatively unimportant. It was established on the initiative of the allies, who were anxious, after Brest-Litovsk, to prevent the vast army stores assembled in these ports from falling into enemy hands. In the summer of 1918 there was formed in Archangel an anti-Bolshevik government headed, at first, by the veteran Socialist Revolutionary N. V. Chaikovsky and, after his withdrawal in January 1919, by General E. Miller. The venture proved totally unrewarding. Allied troops, chiefly British, stationed in this area were withdrawn in the autumn of 1919, and in February 1920 Miller fled from Archangel, which two days later (February 21) was taken over by the Reds.

The northwestern front of General N. N. Yudenich in Estonia was created in 1919 with the assistance—as was the northern front—of the allies, especially Great Britain. Yudenich made two attempts at taking Petrograd, one in the spring and the other in October 1919. Both failed, the latter after a promising beginning. The northwestern army lost its foothold in Russia and was forced to withdraw into Estonia, where it was disarmed in November 1919. Yudenich went to Paris and then to the French Riviera.

Viewed as a whole the White movement was a tragic failure, but there were moments when the outlook for the anti-Bolshevik forces seemed bright. Indeed, in the spring and again in the summer and autumn of 1919 the enemies of Bolshevism appeared to be converging upon Moscow. In March 1919 Kolchak launched an offensive that made good progress. His troops took Perm and Ufa and were approaching Viatka and Kazan, that is, they were within easy reach of the Volga. By the end of April, however, the advance was checked, and the invaders were soon in full retreat. Early in 1919 the forces based on Archangel made a southward thrust that might have led to a junction with the Kolchak armies advancing from the east. Nothing came of this effort, which collapsed in the initial stage, as also nothing came of Yudenich's two assaults on Petrograd, yet combined with other military developments, these campaigns appeared at the time to present a real menace to Soviet power.

The Denikin offensive, which began in the spring of 1919, was at first promising. The Volunteer Army pushed ahead steadily and took Kursk (September 21) and Orel (October 13). The road lay open to the important munition center of Tula and from there to Moscow; but at this juncture came the Bolshevik counter-offensive, which the Volunteer Army proved unable to resist. Under the relentless pressure of the enemy—including the Budenny cavalry corps—the White troops rolled back until they reached the Crimea, where Denikin, who in November succeeded Kolchak as "Supreme Ruler," transferred his command to General Baron Peter Wrangel (March 1920). The new commander attempted some reforms and scored local military successes in connection with the Soviet-Polish war, but by 1920 the anti-Bolshevik movement outside the Crimea had collapsed and the troops went home. The position of the remnants of the Volunteer Army confined to the Crimean peninsula was truly desperate. In November 1920 some 130,000 soldiers and civilians were evacuated by the allies from the Crimean ports to Constantinople. Most of them were eventually settled in Yugoslavia.

This was the pitiful end of the anti-Bolshevik crusade, the cost of which in human lives, wealth, and mental sufferings was great. The reasons for its failure have been frequently analyzed. Some of the credit for Soviet victories should go to Trotsky, commissar for war and organizer of the Red Army, as well as to other Soviet leaders. The revolutionary fantasies of 1917 were discarded. Drafts replaced voluntary army service (May 29, 1918), and strict discipline of the conventional type was introduced (March 1919). One should not overrate, however, the importance of purely technical changes. Throughout the civil war the professional military standards of both the Red Army and its opponents were exceedingly low. The Bolsheviks had the advantage of unity of command and purpose, while the anti-Soviet forces were plagued with geographical dispersal and lack of a unified program. Former tsarist generals were at a loss to find a common language with partisan chieftains, such as the Ukrainian peasant leader Makhno, who made embarrassing and indeed perplexing cómrades-in-arms. There was shocking cruelty on both sides, and not much to choose from between White and Red terror. An army on the move and having no permanent base inevitably lives off the land, and this, as well as dependence on foreigners, does not make it any more popular. The anti-Bolshevik forces were unskillfully led and commanded no popular support. This statement should not be interpreted to mean that the

Bolsheviks were liked. But they *were* the government, and what most Russians wanted desperately was to be left alone, that is, the end of the civil war.

Allied Intervention. The reasons for allied intervention, which was an element in the civil war, changed with the international situation. As long as the Treaty of Brest-Litovsk was in force, the allied powers were largely motivated by the desire to save whatever was possible of the eastern front and to prevent the seizure by the enemy of army stores at the Russian seaports of Murmansk, Archangel, and Vladivostok. Following the defeat of Germany (November 1918) the chief grounds for intervention were the fear of the spreading of Bolshevism, assistance to the Czechs stranded in Russia, and the pursuit of "national interests" in the narrow meaning of the term. As already noted, a small British force was landed in Murmansk in March 1918; British, French, and American troops came to Archangel beginning in August 1918. The Japanese landed at Vladivostok in April 1918 and were followed by contingents of British, French, and American soldiers. The Japanese had annexationist ambitions, occupied Sakhalin, and coveted eastern Siberia to Lake Baikal. Shortly after the Bolshevik revolution the British and the French concluded a convention (December 23, 1917, N.S.) delimiting their respective spheres of occupation in southern Russia: the French zone included the Ukraine, Bessarabia, and the Crimea; the British, the Caucasus and the Cossack territories. As W. H. Chamberlin notes, these arrangements corresponded to the economic interests of the two countries—the French had large investments in Ukrainian coal and iron, and the British in Caucasian oil. After the armistice of November 1918 had unsealed the Black Sea, British and French men-of-war entered these waters and carried on the occupation of the regions assigned to them by the agreement of December 1917.

Except for the Japanese (and, of course, the Czechs) allied forces in Russia avoided fighting but lent much material and financial support to the anti-Bolshevik armies. The resulting cooperation proved extremely uneasy and created much ill-will on both sides. Embittered and disillusioned, Western statesmen reached the conclusion that Bolshevism could not be defeated by civil war. Russian disorders, indeed, proved contagious: there were serious mutinies in the French fleet in the Black Sea. The year 1919 brought the withdrawal of foreign troops: the French left Odessa in April, the British the Caucasus in the summer (except for Batum, where a small force remained until July 1920); Archangel was evacuated in September and Murmansk in October. The British, American, and other European troops withdrew from Siberia in the autumn of 1919. The Japanese, clinging to their dream of empire, were the last to go: they remained at Vladivostok until October 1922 and in Sakhalin even longer, until 1925. Before leaving they secured long-term concessions for the exploitation of Sakhalin coal and oil.

The allied blockade of Russia, which, after the Bolshevik revolution, was an informal extension to that country of the blockade of Germany, came under severe criticism in 1919. An attempt in October of that year to induce neutrals and Germany to participate in the economic boycott of the Soviets met with no response, and the blockade was formally lifted in January 1920.

Independence Movements. Independence movements among Russia's national minorities thrived on the confusion of the civil war and the state of turmoil created by the defeat of Germany. The weakness of Russia and the powerful surge of national sentiments rather than Bolshevism's ostensible acceptance of the principle of self-determination resulted in the separation from Russia of several territories formerly ruled by the empire. Bessarabia was occupied by Rumanian troops soon after the advent of the Soviets; the Council of People's Commissars protested, but the annexation was recognized by the Central Powers in March 1918 and by the allies in October 1920. Finland, as related in an earlier section of this chapter, succeeded in defeating Soviet subversion and in maintaining the status of a sovereign state.

The sovereignty of Poland was not contested by the Bolsheviks, but they wished ardently to have that country converted to Communism. As long as Poland was occupied by the Germans, Soviet revolutionary ambitions were in abeyance, and, after Germany's defeat, Moscow was too weak and engrossed in civil war and domestic disorders to take advantage of the interregnum produced in Poland by the collapse of German power. It was Poland that took the initiative. The appearance on her eastern border of the small and helpless states of White Russia (Byelo-Russia) and Lithuania, and the patent inability of Moscow to protect them, provided Poland with the tempting opportunity to gain control of the lands which had been a bone of contention between her and Russia since the fourteenth century. J. Pilsudski, head of the Polish state, took advantage of this situation. His troops occupied Vilna, in Lithuania, in April and Minsk, in White Russia, in August 1919. At the end of April 1920 the Poles invaded the Russian Ukraine, and war with Russia followed. At first the fortunes of war favored Pilsudski; his armies advanced without meeting much resistance and on May 6 occupied Kiev. The Soviets, however, reorganized their forces and mounted a successful counter-offensive. In June the Poles were forced to evacuate Kiev and, pursued by the Red Army under the famed cavalry commanders Tukhachevsky and Budenny, retreated as rapidly as they had advanced. On August 1 the

Russians entered Brest-Litovsk and a few days later were at the gates of Warsaw.

The decision to invade Poland was Lenin's, who counted on the revolt of the Warsaw proletariat and overruled the counsel of prudence tendered, surprisingly, by Trotsky. To Lenin, as E. H. Carr notes, war against Poland was a true war for world revolution. As usual, he was certain of the infallibility of his judgment. But the Warsaw workers did not respond. On August 16 Pilsudski, with the advice of General Maxime Weygand, head of a small French military mission, launched a massive counter-offensive that cut through the Russian lines. The Red Army retreated at an even faster pace than it had advanced, the withdrawal becoming a catastrophe and a rout. In September the front was a considerable distance east of the positions held by the Poles in April, when the war began. The armistice signed in October and confirmed by the Treaty of Riga (March 8, 1921) gave Poland most of the territories which she had coveted. Her new boundary passed further east than the so-called "Curzon line" drawn by allied experts in 1920.

Conditions in, and the evolution of, Estonia, Latvia, and Lithuania, the three former Russian Baltic provinces, which achieved independence after World War I, have many elements in common. Estonia and Latvia were never before sovereign states, and Lithuania had not been for several centuries. In each case the population and territory were small, but each ethnic community had its own language and a measure of national consciousness. Their proximity to the Baltic, where the British navy re-asserted its supremacy after the collapse of Germany, and the interest in their fate taken by the London government were essential in preventing their absorption by the Soviets after World War I. The pattern of events in these territories was similar. Following the Bolshevik revolution Soviet regimes were proclaimed in each country but were immediately swept away in the advance of the German army and were replaced by national non-Bolshevik governments. Soviets were restored in Estonia, Latvia, and Lithuania after the defeat of Germany but were again superseded by non-Communist administrations in 1919: in Estonia, in January; in Lithuania, in April (in connection with the Polish occupation of Vilna); and in Latvia, in June. The Soviets, weakened by the civil war and economically exhausted, accepted the *fait accompli* and in 1920 signed treaties of peace with the bourgeois governments of Russia's former provinces, recognizing their independence: with Estonia, in February; with Lithuania, in July; and with Latvia, in August. These countries survived as sovereign states until World War II.

Except for Poland, Finland, and the three Baltic states, the Russian lands aspiring to statehood failed to achieve their objective, although some of them eventually secured a measure of national autonomy within the framework of the Communist state. This failure may be explained in some cases by the geographical factor—the remoteness of Asian and Caucasian territories from potential friends and allies and their total dependence on Russia. These considerations do not apply to the Ukraine and White Russia (Byelo-Russia), and an explanation of their inability to attain independence must be sought in the complex crosscurrents of national and territorial ambitions rife in that tormented part of Europe and, perhaps, in the weakness of the national movement in the two countries.

After the Treaty of Brest-Litovsk, the Ukraine was occupied by the Germans. In the three years following the Bolshevik revolution Kiev, the capital of the Ukraine, had 10 successive regimes, including the brief rule (May–November 1918) of Hetman Paul Skoropadsky, an appointee of Germany and a former officer in the Russian guards. With the collapse of Germany, the withdrawal of the allies, and the defeat of Denikin and Wrangel, the Ukraine was left at the mercy of Moscow. A Ukrainian Soviet government was installed in January 1919, and the Ukrainian SSR (Soviet socialist republic) concluded with the RSFSR a treaty (December 28, 1920) that, while scrupulously observing the outward forms of independence, was actually a major step towards a *de facto* unification under Moscow. White Russia (Byelo-Russia), whose constitutional history in 1917–1918 conformed to the pattern of the Baltic provinces, became a Soviet socialist republic in February 1919 and made with the RSFSR a treaty (February 21, 1921) identical with that of the Ukrainian SSR.

During the civil war a large number of quasi-independent or autonomous states made their appearance in the territory of the former empire, some of them—for instance, those in the Caucasus and in central Asia—with the connivance of the foreign occupation authorities. Originally these ephemeral political formations were often ruled by anti-Bolshevik elements, but with the withdrawal of the allies and the defeat of the White movements, they came under Communist domination. At the end of 1920 nine nominally independent states existed in the Soviet-controlled territory of the former empire: the RSFSR, the Ukrainian SSR, the White Russian SSR, the three Caucasian SSR (Azerbaidzhan, Armenia, and Georgia), the Far Eastern Republic (created in 1920 as a buffer state against the Japanese), and two central Asian Soviet republics (Khorezm and Bokhara). The RSFSR, by far the largest political unit, comprised about 20 (the actual number varied) nominally autonomous subdivisions. A complex system of treaties broadly similar to those of the Ukraine and White Russia bound the smaller states to the RSFSR, while the ubiquitous Communist Party ensured the unfaltering coordination of policies. Consolidation took place in 1922. The Far Eastern Republic—the Japanese having gone—was incorporated in the RSFSR. The three Caucasian republics were merged into the Transcaucasian SFSR (socialist federal Soviet republic).

In December 1922 the Ukrainian SSR, the White Russian SSR, and the Transcaucasian SFSR passed resolutions proposing the formation of a union of Soviet socialist republics. A similar resolution was adopted by the Tenth All-Russian Congress of Soviets (December 28, 1922). The Union of Soviet Socialist Republics—the USSR—was born. The two Asian republics, not being "socialist," did not qualify for full membership in the union but remained unreservedly in the Soviet orbit. As a part of the administrative reorganization resulting from the establishment of the union, the GPU (security police) was taken out of the Commissariat of the Interior of the RSFSR and became the unified state political administration, or OGPU, a federal department under the Council of Ministers of the USSR (November 1923; statute confirmed October 1924). Its authority and powers were enhanced.

Economic Policies

War Communism. The economic policies of the years 1918 to 1924 were experimental and something of an improvisation. As E. H. Carr observes, none of the opening measures of the Soviet regime (listed in an earlier section of this chapter) "bore the authentic stamp of socialism—or, still less, of communism—in the Marxian sense of the term." The period of War Communism that followed lasted from the summer of 1918 to the spring of 1921 and coincided with the civil war. Its policies were partly a response to war emergencies and partly a translation into administrative and legislative terms of a doctrinaire approach that discerns in extreme regimentation the blueprint of the future communist society. War Communism was a comprehensive system that affected every aspect of economic life. The farmer was requested to surrender, at fixed prices, his "surplus" stock, that is, everything in excess of his own and his family's needs, and not infrequently everything he had was taken away. Requisitions were enforced by special detachments of workers "of unimpeachable honesty and devotion to the revolution" (August 1918) assisted by the committees of poor peasants (Kombedy) organized in June 1918. In 1918 and 1919 some 45,000 men are said to have been employed in these tasks. In April 1920 the workers' detachments were disbanded and their functions taken over by the security police. The requisitions were to apply primarily to the *kulaks,* or well-to-do peasants, but it was left to squads and the village Soviets to decide who the *kulaks* were. Collectivization, that is, transition from individual to collective forms of husbandry, was prompted by a decree of February 14, 1919, which stated that all individual farming was "transitory and obsolete" and provided for the establishment of collective farms of three types: communes, *artels,* and associations for the joint cultivation of land.[2] Unlike the earlier legislation, the decree of February 14 proclaimed the principle of nationalization, which reserves for the state the authority to decide how land should be used.

Nationalization and administrative centralization were the policies applied to industry. A decree of June 28, 1918, nationalized large industrial enterprises—their number was officially given as about 3,700—and in December 1920 nationalization was extended, at least in theory, to enterprises employing more than five workers with mechanical power or ten workers without mechanical power. Workers' control, institutionalized by a decree of November 14, 1917, was incompatible with administrative centralization and ceased to function. Nationalized enterprises were managed by *glavki* and *centers,* bureaucratic administrations under the Supreme Economic Council, which was established in December 1917 originally as a central coordinating and planning body. Labor in skilled categories was made subject to the draft early in 1918, and labor conscription was applied to all workers in January 1920. Labor armies were organized and controlled by special Soviets. As Baykov puts it, by the end of 1920, workers were "conscripted, militarized and attached to their place of work." To quote E. H. Carr again, "the ultimate result of War Communism in the field of labor was to leave no other incentives in operation except revolutionary enthusiasm and naked compulsion." Distribution, too, was drastically reorganized. Separate trades were nationalized during the early months of 1918; on November 21, 1918, all commerce was nationalized. Private commercial establishments were replaced by state and cooperative stores. Foreign trade became a state monopoly by virtue of a decree of April 22, 1918, but since practically no goods moved across the frontier, the effects of this measure at the time was negligible.

The financial picture was bleak. Banks were nationalized and in a state of disorder. Since the cancellation of state obligations prevented the raising of funds by floating loans and only a fraction of expenditures was covered

[2] See below, p. 511.

by the tax revenue, the budget was hopelessly unbalanced, and the only means of meeting the deficit was the use of the printing press. In 1920 10,000 people were busy in four establishments turning out paper monetary tokens. Supra-hyperbolic inflation brought its inevitable consequences: spiraling prices and the total depreciation of the ruble. The doctrinaire Communists viewed this result with satisfaction: Russia was moving in the direction of a moneyless economy. Indeed, two principal theoretical objectives of War Communism were nearly achieved: concentration of economic authority and substitution of requisitions (including labor), price fixing, and rationing for monetary and commercial forms of distribution.

From the practical point of view the results of War Communism were disastrous. Russian economic statistics, at their best, inspire but moderate confidence; those for the period under consideration are largely worthless. There is no question, however, that industrial production declined drastically, industrial employment shrank by a large percentage, and the urban population, too, decreased. Prices climbed to fantastic levels, and distribution was carried, not through the state and cooperative stores, but through the black market and the so-called bagmen, desperate or venturesome souls who, in contravention of the law, carried food supplies in bags from the country and, at a considerable risk to themselves, saved city dwellers from starvation. The end of the civil war made exactions from the farmers appear particularly intolerable, and resistance to requisition squads was strengthened by demobilized Red Army men who, as in 1917, brought home rifles and hand grenades. In 1920 waves of peasant risings swept rural Russia, reaching particular violence along the Volga in the provinces of Saratov and Tambov. In March 1921 the sailors of the naval base of Kronstadt—"the pride and glory of the revolution"—mutinied and clamored for "Soviets without communists and commissars." Lenin saw the writing on the wall, and, civil war being over, War Communism was brought to an abrupt end. Its termination came too late to prevent the great famine of 1921, when the American Relief Administration, under Herbert Hoover, came to Russia and saved countless lives.

The New Economic Policy. The New Economic Policy, or NEP, was a series of measures designed to eliminate the excesses of War Communism, to foster the alliance (*smychka*) between the workers and the peasants, and to create conditions which would favor greater production. The first measure of NEP was the tax in kind on the farmers, which replaced requisitions. It was proposed by Lenin and was enacted by the Central Executive Committee on March 21, 1921. The object of the NEP was the restoration of a degree of economic freedom within the framework of a socialist economy. The farmers were permitted to dispose of their product as they pleased and were no longer pressed to join collective farms. Industry was liberated from excessive centralized bureaucratic controls, and industrial enterprises were re-arranged under "trusts" which were independent of the central authority. Labor conscription was abolished, and the trade unions recovered some of their independence as agencies representing the interests of the workers rather than of the state. Distribution reverted largely into private hands (although state and cooperative trading was kept), and some of the lesser industrial enterprises were leased to private individuals. The state retained control of the "commanding heights"—banking, foreign trade, and the larger industrial enterprises. Lenin called the resulting system "state capitalism." It proved viable and favored economic recovery. But it was not, as many in the West imagined, an abandonment of socialism. It was, said Lenin, "a retreat—for a new attack."

End of an Era

Soviets, 1924. The years 1921–1924 form a distinct landmark in Soviet history. For the first time since the revolution the authority of the government extended effectively over the entire territory within its borders. The Union of Socialist Soviet Republics, formed in December 1922, was provided with a legal framework in the constitution ratified by the Second All-Russian Congress of Soviets on January 31, 1924 (the numbering of congresses was started anew with the formation of the USSR). Under the new constitution the congress of Soviets remained, in theory, the supreme authority. It elected a Central Executive Committee, which was a bicameral body consisting of the Council of the Union elected on the basis of population, and the Council of Nationalities, made up of five representatives from each constituent and autonomous republic and one representative from each autonomous region. The four constituent republics were the RSFSR, the Ukrainian SSR, the White Russian (Byelo-Russian) SSR, and the Transcaucasian SFSR. The autonomous republics and the autonomous regions ranked next to the constituent republics in the hierarchy of territorial-administrative subdivisions. The discriminatory franchise and indirect elections of the 1918 RSFSR constitution were retained. The Central Executive Committee appointed the Council of People's Commissars. Authority in questions of war and peace, foreign relations, foreign trade, fiscal policy, armed forces, national economic planning and control over the economy, and certain other matters were reserved for the federal government. The constitution, its verbal federal trappings notwithstanding, provided for a unitarian form of government. The Communist Party, that mainstay of the regime, was not mentioned in the constitution of 1924, as it was not in that of 1918.

The situation in 1924 was very different from that five years earlier. In spite of the severe trials of the revolutionary years, the Soviets had survived both politically and economically. The economy was definitely on the up-grade. Contrary to widely-held expectations, capitalism and socialism (or Communism) were fated to live side by side, although it was not realized at first that this coexistence would extend over decades. The isolation of the Bolshevik regime was over. The Soviets were not represented at the Versailles peace conference in 1919 but made their first appearance at an important international conference at Genoa in April–May 1922. They were officially recognized by Germany in 1922, and in 1924 by Great Britain, Italy, and France.

The Death of Lenin. There was a major change in leadership. Lenin suffered a stroke in May 1922. He largely recovered but in December had a second stroke that left him half-paralyzed and in March 1923 a third that deprived him of the power of speech. He died on January 21, 1924, at the age of 53. His embalmed body was placed in a specially-built mausoleum in the Red Square, where it is viewed by multitudes of people coming from every part of the world. Petrograd became Leningrad, the first city since the revolution to have its name changed for honorific reasons (January 26, 1924). In 1963 the fifth edition of Lenin's works, in 50 volumes, was in preparation.

Lenin has left an indelible imprint on the history of Russia and of the world. He was not the unerring prophet of legend, but he was an unfaltering and ardent revolutionary, and Leninism—his views analyzed, interpreted, re-interpreted, and often distorted—is a mighty and disturbing force in the world.

21

The Stalin Era, 1924-1939: Government

The Rise of Stalin

Stalin. The illness and then death of Lenin created a vacuum in Soviet leadership that was not easy to fill. In 1922, when Lenin had his first stroke, Trotsky was the only revolutionary leader of comparable stature. It was the recognition of the strength of his potential claim to succeed Lenin that arrayed against him his strategically-placed competitors and led to his elimination and the triumph of Stalin.

Joseph Vissarionovich Stalin (1879–1953), whose real name was Dzhugashvili, was born in Gori, Georgia, son of a poor and drunken cobbler. He studied at the theological seminary of Tiflis but was expelled for revolutionary activities in 1899, before graduation. In 1898 he joined the newly-formed Russian Social Democratic Labor Party and became a professional revolutionary. Beginning in 1902 he was arrested, banished, and escaped several times. Much of his revolutionary work was in the Caucasus. In December 1905 he met Lenin for the first time at a Bolshevik conference in Tammerfors. In 1912 he was co-opted as a member of the central committee of the Bolshevik Party, edited *Pravda* in St. Petersburg, and spent some time with Lenin in Cracow. On his return to Russia early in 1913, Stalin was arrested and banished to Siberia. Released after the 1917 revolution and back in Petrograd, he favored at first qualified support of the Provisional Government but then rallied to Lenin's *April Theses*. From that time on he was close to Lenin, was a member of the Politburo—the leading party body created on the eve of the 1917 insurrection but abolished soon thereafter—and of the Politburo reconstituted by the Eighth Party Congress in March 1919. In April 1922 Stalin was appointed secretary general of the party central committee, an office that, prior to Lenin's incapacitation, did not carry the implications of unlimited power it has acquired since.

At that time Stalin was practically unknown outside narrow party circles. Probably the least intellectual among Soviet leaders, he was crude, tenacious, and ruthless. In December 1922 Lenin, shortly after his second stroke, dictated in the seclusion of his sick room a memorandum, known as his "testament," in which he expressed a candid opinion of the leading Bolsheviks. A few days later he added a postscript (January 4, 1923) stating that Stalin's rudeness "becomes insupportable in the office of secretary general" and suggesting that a way be found to remove him. The testament and the postscript were read to a meeting of party leaders in 1924; the full text was published by Max Eastman in the United States in 1926 but was not released in the Soviet Union until 1956. The significance of Lenin's outburst has been greatly exaggerated by the historians. The record of the Bolshevik Party is full of denunciations and excommunications. One more, coming from a very sick man—even though he was Lenin—would not seem to make much difference, especially since Stalin's crudities were no secret. Although the contents of the testament were known in party circles, they had no adverse effect on the career of Stalin.

The Road to Power. The ascendancy of Stalin was the result of complex manoeuvers, moves, and counter-moves on the upper levels of the Communist Party, a twilight zone that has never been, and probably will never be, fully explored. The Communist Party has ruled Russia since the October revolution, but the relationship between state and party organs was often loose. The mechanics of party control were tightened by the Eighth Party Congress in March 1919. The death of Lenin altered the formal relationship between party and state. Lenin was both the unchallengeable leader of the party and, as chairman of the Council of People's Commissars, the head of the government. This personal union came to an end with his death. Alexis Rykov, a minor political figure, succeeded Lenin as chairman of the Sovnarkom. As a result, since all important decisions emanated from party organs, the role of the party—as well as of its secretary—was enhanced.

The struggle for power was a clash of personalities rather than of doctrines. No attempt will be made here to probe the mysteries of what has been well called "the doctrinal niceties of the Russian party strife." The major conflict was between Trotsky and Stalin. In 1922 and 1923 Trotsky appeared at the height of his power. He was commissar for war since 1918,

Lenin and Stalin at Gorky (near Moscow), 1922

member of the Politburo, and organizer and leader of the Red Army, and was widely held as the architect of Soviet victories over the White movement. Many of the policies which he advocated—rapid industrialization, centralized planning, government control of trade unions—were eventually enforced by Stalin. It was not Trotsky's views but his eminence, aloofness, and intellectual acumen which precipitated his downfall. He was feared as a potential dictator, a Soviet Bonaparte, and this danger, it was argued, was to be counteracted by the dictatorship of the party, by "collective will, collective thought, collective energy, and collective determination."

Opposition to Trotsky crystallized around the triumvirate—*troika*—of Stalin, Zinovev, and Kamenev. There is no information as to how the triumvirate was formed, but early in 1923 it was spoken of in party circles as the ruling group. Both Gregory Zinovev (Radomyslsky) and Lev Kamenev (Rosenfeld) were professional revolutionaries and old associates of Lenin, with whom, however, they had at times sharp disagreements, particularly in October 1917, when they opposed insurrection. Both were members

Wide World

Stalin, Rykov, Kamenev, and Zinovev, 1925

of the Politburo. The strength of the triumvirate resided in the fact that Zinovev headed the party organization in Petrograd, Kamenev held a similar post in Moscow, and Stalin, as secretary general, controlled the machinery of the party. By packing party agencies, including the Politburo and the central committee, with his supporters, he succeeded in eradicating democratic procedure, which was replaced by "disciplined unanimity organized through the power of the secretariat" (E. H. Carr). Trotsky, with whom at the end of 1924 Stalin became involved in a protracted controversy over the theory of "socialism in one country" (discussed in the next section), was the first victim of this sinister procedure. He was dismissed as commissar for war in January 1925, expelled from the party and deported to Alma-Ata (Kazakhstan) in 1927, banished to Turkey in 1929, and finally murdered in Mexico City in August 1940 by a "Jacques Mornard," believed to be an agent of the Soviet security police.

The triumvirate, having achieved its objective, did not last long. In 1925 Zinovev and Kamenev aligned themselves against Stalin with the Right Opposition and then with Trotsky; they were both expelled from the party twice, in 1927 and in 1932, but were reinstated each time, only to perish in the great purge of 1936. There were several opposition groups within the party during this period, of which the more important was the Right Opposition led by the Communist theorist N. Bukharin, Rykov, and Michael Tomsky. It had at one time supported Stalin against Trotsky but became critical of the policy of rapid industrialization and collectivization provided by the first Five-Year Plan, which was put into operation in 1928. By that time Stalin was firmly in control of the party and the government, and in 1929 the members of the Right Opposition were censured and dismissed from the party and government positions they held.

No criticism of Stalin's rule was tolerated in the 1930's. The murder of Serge Kirov, head of the Leningrad party organization (December 1934), was the starting point of mass purges in which untold thousands of Communists lost their lives or suffered degradation. E. H. Carr speaks of the "peculiar and exceptional quality" of Stalin's "political genius" and ends with the enigmatic statement that "few great men have been so conspicuously as Stalin the product of the time and place in which they lived." This is a surprising assertion coming from a historian of Carr's eminence. Nikita Khrushchev was nearer to the truth when he said (March 8, 1963) that "Stalin was seriously sick . . . suffering from suspiciousness and persecution mania" in his last years. This is the only rational explanation of the purges of the 1930's.

The Communist Doctrine and the State

Marxism-Leninism. The Soviet government differs from the governments of the non-Communist countries in that it claims to possess an unerring guide that determines its policies: the doctrine of Marxism-Leninism, founded in the writings of Karl Marx (1818–1883) and Friedrich Engels (1820–1895) and elaborated by Lenin. A basic element in Marxism is the economic interpretation of history, which states that the economic factors, "the mode of production," determine the character of the political, social, and cultural institutions of an age. Operating with the dialectic method (which no attempt will be made here to describe) Marx and Engels analyzed the capitalist society and reached the conclusion that human history must be interpreted in terms of class struggle. The two classes which confront each other under capitalism are the capitalists, or exploiters, and the workers, or exploited. Although the capitalist society presents the outward appearance of invincible strength, it is rent by irreconcilable inner contradictions which prepare its downfall—it is "digging its own grave." The might of the working class is inexorably growing, and the exploiters will be swept away in the proletarian revolution that will lead through the dictatorship of the proletariat to communism.

Lenin applied the Marxian analysis to what he called the era of imperialism and monopoly capitalism; his findings were analogous to those of Marx and Engels: contradictions within the imperialistic system of states (struggle for markets, sources of raw materials, and opportunities for investments) inexorably lead to international wars for the redivision of a world that has been already divided. Out of imperialistic wars will come colonial uprisings and national revolutions, which will merge into the world revolution. Marxism-Leninism claims to have discovered the immutable laws of historical development; according to its doctrine, the downfall of capitalism and imperialism is not a mere hope or expectation—it is a certainty. These are the notions which control Soviet policies.

Withering Away of the State. The doom of the capitalist society having been established to the satisfaction of communist theorists, the next thing was to decide what would take its place. The fullest answer to this vital question was given by Lenin in his short book *The State and the Revolution,* written while he was in hiding in Finland in September 1917. The essence of Lenin's argument, which was an elaboration of the views of Marx and Engels, was that the state, a by-product of the class struggle, was always the dictatorship of the ruling class, whatever its constitutional trappings. The communist society will be classless and therefore, by definition, cannot be a state. The state will survive for a time after a successful revolution in order to suppress the resistance of the dispossessed classes, but it will be so organized that "it will at once begin to wither away and cannot fail to wither away." A practical revolutionary by temperament, Lenin in *The State and the Revolution* allowed himself an unusual flight of fancy. He held that the withering away of the state will manifest itself in the abolition of the standing army, which will be replaced by a militia, and in the elimination of the bureaucracy. He imagined that the functions of government would be so simplified that they could be performed by anyone for "the wage of a working man"; the draft should be applied immediately to the civil service, and by making everyone a "bureaucrat" for a time, no one would become a "bureaucrat." Such proposals coming from any one else but Lenin would have been brushed aside as nonsense; they are, instead, a revered, albeit embarrassing, element of the doctrine. Lenin did not say how long it would take the state to wither away but merely that this would be a natural and gradual process. Social evils which call for corrective or punitive measures will vanish with the capitalist system that generated them. Human nature will be changed. Classes will disappear with the elimination of private ownership of the means of production, and in a classless society the state will be both "unnecessary and impossible."

Before reaching the communist phase, society will go through the period of socialism that Marx called "the first stage of communism." Means of production will be nationalized; every one will work ("He who does not work shall not eat") and will be rewarded according to the work performed; the state will survive and carry on the function of enforcing private property rights in goods which are not means of production. The features of communism in its final stage were outlined by Marx and Lenin only in most general terms: hostility between physical and mental work will disappear, and labor will become "a primary necessity of life"; the great increase in social wealth will allow the application of the principal of communism: "From each according to his ability, to each according to his needs"; and the state will finally disappear. Neither Marx nor Lenin indicated how long this transformation would take.

Socialism in One Country. The doctrine of the withering away of the state became linked with that of socialism in one country, which gained prominence in 1924. Prior to that year it was generally accepted by the socialists that a revolution to be successful should occur simultaneously in several advanced industrial countries. The fact that the socialist revolution was victorious in imperial Russia, a backward agricultural state, was disturbing, but the Communists took heart in the belief that revolution in western Europe was imminent. A flare-up of Soviet rule in Bavaria and Bela Kun's brief Communist dictatorship in Hungary in 1919 seemed to justify these expectations. But the Communist movement in western Europe collapsed in its initial stage, and a protracted period of coexistence with capitalism appeared likely. The issue—what Soviet Russia should do to meet this un-expected situation—was complicated by a personal feud between Trotsky and Stalin. Trotsky's fertile mind devised the doctrine of "permanent revo-lution," of which an important facet was the contention that a socialist revo-lution in a country such as Russia could not win unless it was helped by revolutions in advanced countries. Had this view prevailed, Russia's policy would have been directed exclusively towards the promotion of revolutions abroad, since any attempt at building up socialism in an isolated country was doomed to failure. Stalin, who had a mediocre capacity for theoretical thinking, had shared the prevalent view but changed his mind at the end of 1924. He took the position that a socialist system could be built in one country if that country had a large territory, large population, and abundant natural resources. This was not, however, a final victory, because the capitalist environment contained the constant threat of intervention.

Socialism in one country, its humble theoretical contents notwithstand-ing, played a major role in shaping the course of events. For years it was under perennial discussion by Communist bodies, was used as the chief weapon against Trotsky, and—what is more important—became the theoreti-cal basis of Soviet planned economy. Stalin held that the assurance that a socialist society could be built in the Soviet Union was the essential pre-requisite for the vast program of industrialization and collectivization em-barked upon under the successive Five-Year Plans. In a sense, the acceptance of socialism in one country was the victory of nationalism over interna-tionalism. Trotsky was a Westerner among Russian revolutionaries and thought in terms of European revolutions. To Stalin, who had little foreign experience, the Russian revolution came first, and its progress was not to depend on what might happen abroad.

The Doctrine Revised. The 1920's and 1930's witnessed notable economic recovery and the consolidation of Soviet power, but constitutional develop-ments did not conform to the pattern prescribed by Lenin. In the 1930's the Soviet Union had officially reached the socialist stage and had no more classes, yet there was no evidence that the state had become "unnecessary and impossible." The standing army was large and more conspicuous than ever, and the bureaucracy permeated and directed every aspect of the nation's life. There was uneasiness among party members concerning the discrepancy between theory and practice and, although Soviet citizens ask no indiscreet questions, Stalin in his report to the Eighteenth Party Congress in March 1939 deemed it wise to address himself to the uncomfortable issue of the survival of the state in a classless society. He explained that the failure of the state to wither away was due to the persistence of the capitalist environment and activities of foreign spies in Russia. Since there are no more classes, there are no class enemies, and the Russians who fail to appreciate the advantages of Soviet rule are agents of foreign intelligence services. The survival or disappearance of the state will depend on the fate of the capitalist environment: the state will continue to exist as long as the capitalist environment exists; it will wither away when the capitalist environment is gone. This interpretation was held to be in agreement with Lenin's views: *The State and the Revolution* having remained unfinished, Stalin had written the final chapter that Lenin had intended but had no time to write. Stalin's report, coming on top of the great purge, was accepted as the final verity. According to one commentator (1949), "Stalin has conclusively proved that the withering away of the state will be accomplished not through the weakening of the state power but through the maximum increase in its strength," which is a far cry from Lenin's assertion that the proletarian state "is so organized that it must begin at once to wither away and cannot fail to wither away."

The Stalin doctrine, whatever its validity as a piece of Marxian analysis, had important political implications. Combined with the theory of socialism in one country, it marked a step towards the integration of Communist objectives: the final victory of socialism (elimination of the danger of capitalist aggression) and the establishment of communism (withering away of the state) were made dependent on the achievement of one objective—the elimination of the capitalist environment. The Russian term *okruzhenie*, rendered here as "environment," is frequently translated as "encirclement," which might be misleading. Encirclement suggests anti-Soviet arrangements such as NATO or American military and naval bases, which, of course, did not exist in the 1930's. Environment connotes the sum total of the institutions of the Western world—political, social, economic, and cultural. It is the elimination of the capitalist *okruzhenie* in this sense that Stalin singled out in 1939; it has remained to this day the avowed objective of Soviet policy.

The Communist Party

The Party and the State. The Communist Party is the cornerstone and the mainspring of the Soviet regime. Originally a conspiratorial organization stemming from the Russian Social Democratic Labor Party founded in 1898, of which it became the Bolshevik faction in 1903, it assumed the name of the Russian Communist Party of the Bolsheviks in March 1918. Following the formation of the USSR the party name was changed to All-Union Communist Party of the Bolsheviks (December 1925); it was changed again to Communist Party of the Soviet Union (CPSU, dropping "of the Bolsheviks") by the Nineteenth Party Congress in October 1952. Prior to 1936 there was no constitutional link between the party and the state, the influence of the party being derived from its all-pervasive *de facto* control of every aspect of national life. With the adoption of the 1936 constitution the party divested itself of its former status of anonymity. According to the party statutes adopted by the Twenty-second Party Congress in October 1961, the party is "the militant, tried vanguard of the Soviet people, uniting on a voluntary basis the advanced, most socially conscious part of the working class, collective farm peasantry, and intelligentsia of the USSR. . . . It is the highest form of socio-political organization, the leading and guiding force of Soviet society. The party directs the great creative activity of the Soviet people and imparts an organized, planned and scientific character to their struggle to achieve the ultimate goal, the victory of communism." This statement summarized well the part the party has endeavored to play in Soviet affairs since its inception.

Organization and Membership. The organization of the Communist Party has been altered several times, the more important changes being those of 1922, 1925, 1934, 1939, 1952, and 1961. The earlier charters characterized the party in terms similar to, although not identical with, those of the 1961 statutes quoted above. The party organization embodies the principle of "democratic centralism" and consists of an extensive network of territorial agencies. The basic units are the primary party organs, formerly known as cells. They are set at the places of work of the party members— at plants, factories, collective and state farms, offices, army units, and so on, where there are three or more members. On the foundation of the primary party organs is built a pyramid of higher party organs with a steadily expanding territorial jurisdiction; the party organization parallels the administrative structure of the Soviet Union. The all-Russian congress of the party and its central committee form the apex of the pyramid. The congress, in theory the supreme party body, elects the central committee, which, again in theory, carries on the work of the party when the congress is not in session. Prior to 1952 the central committee appointed three agencies which actually ran the party: the Politburo (political bureau), the Orgburo (organization bureau), and the secretariat. The Politburo and the Orgburo were abolished by the Nineteenth Party Congress in October 1952 and their functions transferred to the enlarged presidium of the central committee, but the secretariat was retained. The membership of both the congresses and the central commitee tended to increase. The Seventh Party Congress, in March 1918, had slightly over 100 members; those held in the 1930's had about 2,000. The central committee elected in March 1918 had 23 members; in 1939, over 100; and in 1952, over 200. Moreover, meetings of the congresses became less frequent. Nine party congresses were held between 1918 and 1927; the Sixteenth convened in 1930, the Seventeenth in 1934, the Eighteenth in 1939, and the Nineteenth not until 1952. Sessions were brief, lasting but a few days. The membership of the Politburo and Orgburo (as long as they lasted) and of the secretariat was held low, to about a dozen men and at times fewer. The basic principle of the organization is the unconditionally binding nature of the decisions of the higher bodies upon the lower ones.

Admission to full membership is preceded by a period of probation, when the prospective member is known as a candidate. Conditions for admission were originally hedged with cumbersome requirements, which varied with the standing of the applicant (industrial worker, collective farmer, employee, and so on), but these have been greatly simplified since 1939. The principal obligation of members and candidates is to carry out party decisions "firmly and undeviatingly." The delinquent members may be subject to a variety of penalties, of which the most severe is expulsion. Mass purges, which reached a high point in 1936 to 1938, will be examined in the closing section of this chapter. Party membership grew substantially in the 1930's, although it remained a small percentage of the population. It increased from perhaps 80,000 in April 1917 to 730,000 in March 1921, declined to 380,000 by April 1923 (because of numerous expulsions in 1921 and 1922), only to rise again to 860,000 (including candidates) in May 1924 and to nearly 2.5 million in March 1939. During and after World War II the growth of party membership was greatly accelerated.

In its internal organization the party, in theory, is governed by the principle of "intra-party democracy," which stipulates the right to discuss freely questions of policy and to criticize any leader, regardless of his position.

Available records of meetings of party congresses and conferences do not support these claims. Some freedom of opinion appears to have existed in the early 1920's, but it vanished with the consolidation of Stalin's dictatorship. Unanimity unrelieved by the slightest disagreement is the unwritten, unwavering rule in the deliberations of Communist bodies.

Komsomol and Pioneers. The Komsomol, or Young Communist League, founded in 1918, is in fact, if not in law, a subsidiary of the Communist Party and is primarily concerned with the indoctrination of young people; it also performs concrete tasks, such as participation in the development of eastern and northern territories. The Pioneers, founded in 1922, is the children's (aged 9 to 15) subdivision of Komsomol. The administrative structure of both parallel, roughly, that of the Communist Party; their membership has increased markedly in recent years and in 1960 was about 19 million in each organization.

The Stalin Constitution

The Background. During the 12 years in which the constitution of 1924 remained in force, it underwent but minor changes. The number of constituent republics was originally four (the RSFSR, the Ukraine, White Russia, and Transcaucasia) but was increased to seven by the addition of the Turkmen SSR and the Uzbek SSR in October 1924 and the Tadzhik SSR in 1929. The addition to the number of constituent republics was due to administrative re-arrangements, not to an extension of territory. The record of Soviet democracy under the 1924 constitution was unimpressive. The All-Union Congress of Soviets, an assembly of over 2,000 members, met eight times between 1924 and 1936; its sessions were brief and perfunctory. The meetings of the Central Executive Committee elected by the congress also became "progressively rare" and during the entire lifetime of the committee totaled 139 days (Towster). The work of the Central Executive Committee was actually carried on by its 27-member presidium, which was described in the constitution as "the highest legislative, executive, and administrative organ of the USSR," and by the Council of People's Commissars. Each constituent republic had its own constitution conforming to the federal model.

The decision to adopt a new constitution was announced at the Seventh Congress of Soviets in February 1935. The motives behind it were not disclosed, but it is possible that, in view of the advent of Hitler to power, it was thought desirable to bring the structure of the Soviet government more in line—at least in theory—with the accepted western European practice.

The draft of the constitution was released in June 1936 and became the center of a vast publicity campaign under the slogan "The people make a constitution." According to official figures, the draft was discussed at 527,000 meetings attended by 36.5 million people. Although 154,000 amendments were offered, only 43 changes were made, practically all in wording. The final text was approved by the Eighth Congress of Soviets on December 5, 1936, which became a national holiday.

Main Provisions. Under the new constitution the Soviet Union remained "a socialist state of workers and peasants" resting on the foundation of Soviets of working people's deputies, a federation "formed on the basis of the voluntary association" of Soviet socialist (constituent) republics (SSR). Their number was increased to 11 by adding to the seven mentioned above the newly-formed republics of Kazakh and Kirghiz and by splitting the Transcaucasian republic, which ceased to exist, into three republics: Armenia, Georgia, and Azerbaidzhan. As will appear later, the number of constituent republics was increased to 16 in 1940 and reduced to 15 in 1956.

The constitution lists the following territorial-administrative subdivisions within the union: constituent republics, autonomous Soviet socialist republics, territories (*krai*), provinces (*oblast*), autonomous provinces, regions (*okrug*), counties (*rayon*), cities and towns, and rural localities (villages). In December 1936 the RSFSR comprised 17 autonomous republics, five territories, 19 provinces, and six autonomous provinces; six other constituent republics had a substantially smaller number of administrative subdivisions, and four (Armenia, White Russia, Turkmen, and Kirghiz) had none. The territorial-administrative structure is continually revised. In June 1949 the RSFSR embraced 12 autonomous republics, five territories, 48 provinces, and six autonomous provinces.

The constitution retained much of the existing institutional framework but was subject to extensive revisions. The highest organ of the union is, in theory, the Supreme Soviet, which consists of two chambers: the Council of the Union, elected on the basis of one deputy for each 300,000 of the population, and the Council of Nationalities, elected by the administrative subdivisions, which are represented by a specified number of deputies (25 from each constituent republic, 11 from each autonomous republic, five from each autonomous province, and one from each national region). The Supreme Soviet chooses a presidium (the number of its members was changed several times) and appoints the Council of People's Commissars (its name was altered to Council of Ministers in March 1946), the chief executive agency. The people's commissars (ministers) are heads of the people's commissariats (ministries). The Council of People's Commissars that was appointed in 1917 had 13 members; the 1936 constitution raised the number to 18. It continued to grow and in the 1940's was well over 60 but was drastically cut down in the reorganization of 1957.

The governments of the constituent republics, autonomous republics, and smaller subdivisions duplicate, with suitable modifications, that of the union. The lower administrative units are ruled by Soviets which elect their executive committees. The constituent and autonomous republics have their own constitutions (adopted in 1937 and again in 1940, when five new constituent republics were created by annexation of territory), which are drawn "in full conformity with the constitution of the USSR." The powers reserved for the federal government (Article 14) are broad, comprehensive, and widely used, with the result that Soviet federalism means little in practice, except for a cultural autonomy which is held strictly within the bounds of Communist orthodoxy.

The 1936 constitution contained several novel features. The discriminatory franchise and indirect voting of the 1918 and 1924 charters were replaced by universal, equal, and direct suffrage and the secret ballot, which applied to elections at every level, from the village Soviet to the Supreme Soviet of the USSR. The Communist Party was for the first time given official recognition. Article 126 referred to the party as "the leading core of all organizations . . . both social and state," and Article 141 entitled it to nominate candidates for elective assemblies. These provisions added nothing to the party's unchallengeable authority. Charter X listed the protection offered to the right of the citizens to work, rest and leisure, social security, and education. The implementation of these provisions, as it will appear later, had a checkered record. The 7-hour day in industry provided by the constitution was abandoned in 1940 and restored in the late 1950's. Similarly free education stipulated by the constitution was restricted in 1940 and revived in 1956. Freedom of speech, press, and assembly were ensured, in theory, by placing at the disposal of the workers the necessary facilities (printing plants, paper, assembly halls, and so on), but these freedoms must be exercised "in conformity with the interests of the working people, and in order to strengthen the socialist system"; that is, no opinions of which the Communist Party did not approve could be heard.

It is notable that the much-publicized constitutional charter, which contained novel and seemingly important provisions, left things as they were. This should not be a surprise. "I must admit," said Stalin at the Eighth Congress of Soviets on November 25, 1936, "that the draft of the new constitution actually leaves in force the regime of the dictatorship of the working class as well as preserves unchanged the present leading position of the Communist Party."

The Regime in Action

Elections and Unanimity. Elections to the Supreme Soviet of the USSR were held in December 1937 and to the republican supreme Soviets in June 1938. They set a pattern that has been followed ever since. In every electoral district there was but one candidate, nominated by a show of hands, the secret ballot being used in the final voting. The nomination was arranged by a bloc of Communists and "non-party people." No attempt at opposing the bloc has ever been made. Lists of voters are kept by local Soviets, no registration is needed, and everyone is urged to go to the polls. The actual voting is secret, but many voters prefer to indicate their approval of the sole candidate in full view of the election officials. Election day is a national holiday, with bands, loudspeakers, and side shows. Election managers can look at the results with confidence: nearly 100 per cent of the voters go to the polls, and nearly 100 per cent of those who vote cast their ballots for the sole candidate.

Except during the war years the Supreme Soviet has met at frequent, albeit somewhat irregular, intervals. As with the congresses of the Communist Party, the sessions are brief, perfunctory, and dreary. There are long speeches by the leaders, blanket approval of the budget and of decrees issued by the presidium between the sessions, and endless ovations for those in power—Stalin, Malenkov, Khrushchev. Votes are always unanimous. Harold Denny, Moscow correspondent of the *New York Times,* related that at the opening session of the Supreme Soviet in January 1938, a visiting group of Kazakhs from Central Asia, attired in colorful native robes, enthusiastically threw up their hands every time a vote was taken. No one stopped them: a few more hands made no difference to the monotonous unanimity of the vote. This is Soviet democracy in action.

The Security Police. Since its inception the Soviet regime has relied on political terror. The reorganization in November 1923 of the security police as the unified state political administration, or OGPU, added greatly to its already vast powers. As the CHEKA, the security police was a revolutionary improvisation; as the GPU, it was nominally under the people's commissariat of the interior of the RSFSR; but since its re-organization as the OGPU, it acquired the status of a federal department, was directly represented in the

Council of People's Commissars, and exercised practically unlimited control over a ramified network of subordinate agencies throughout the land. It had its "special army," well paid and enjoying a privileged status, numbering—according to some estimates—hundreds of thousands of men, and its own courts, where cases were tried sometimes in the absence of the accused; it administered numerous prison camps and penal institutions, some of them beyond or near the Arctic Circle. For all practical purposes the OGPU was above and outside the law. In the early 1930's it was extensively used in enforcing collectivization and in stamping out opposition to Stalin in the party. In July 1934 the OGPU was brought under the NKVD (people's commissariat of the interior of the USSR), within which the main administration of state security (GUGB) was formed. There was some reorganization of the judicial and penal powers of the security police, but they remained comprehensive and played a major part in the purges of the later 1930's. Ironically, the three successive heads of the security police—G. Yagoda (1934–1936), N. Yezhov (1936–1938), and L. Beria (1938–1953)—all perished at the hands of the executioners: Yagoda and Yezhov during the 1930 purges in the organization of which they had so important a role, and Beria in 1953, after Stalin's death.

The security police was a pillar of the rule of Stalin. It remains an important arm of the government.

Purges. Purges are an accepted method of maintaining the purity of the party. They are rooted in the notion that Communists are an élite that by definition must be small, especially during the earlier phase of socialist construction. At the beginning of 1917 the Bolshevik Party counted but a few thousand members. It expanded rapidly after the October revolution, and inevitably many of the new converts fell short of the required standards of orthodoxy. In March 1919 the Eighth Party Congress decreed the re-registration of the entire membership to eliminate unworthy elements. Some 100,000 members were expelled. Other purges followed in 1921, 1926, 1927, and 1929. With the elimination of Trotsky and other opposition movements, and the outlawing of Trotskyism as a mortal sin, persecution became more violent. It will be noted that purges were directed not against external enemies but against party members who had strayed from the party line. Oddly, the consolidation of Stalin's dictatorship intensified the purge movement. In 1933 the central committee of the party appointed a purge commission, which, with the assistance of local committees, undertook the revision of the entire membership. Public examinations held throughout the country led to the expulsion of reportedly 800,000 members; 340,000 more were said to have been expelled in 1934. Simultaneously the character of the purges was changed. It was no longer a question of cleansing the party of undesirable members but of eliminating them from public life and, indeed, destroying them physically.

A notable feature of the persecution was the so-called "show trials," of which the first was held in the early summer of 1928. The defendants were 47 engineers from the Donets basin charged with sabotage; 11 received death sentences, of which six were commuted. There followed several trials of technical employees accused of "wrecking" activities. The murder of Kirov, head of the Leningrad party organization, in December 1934 ushered in a new phase of the purge. The first trial involving major political figures was held in August 1936, with Zinovev and Kamenev among the 16 defendants. They were charged with plotting the assassination of Soviet personalities and connivance with the enemy. Other trials at which sensational accusations were made against the leading Bolsheviks took place in 1937 and 1938. The roster of the defendants read like the *Who's Who* of the Russian revolution and included high government and party officials, ambassadors, trade union leaders, the head of the Communist International, two former chiefs of the security police, and many others. Most of them were charged with spying for foreign powers and conspiring with Trotsky, who vainly protested and denied the accusations from his place of exile abroad.

An unprecedented aspect of the trials was the confessions which followed one another with monotonous regularity: the defendants admitted their guilt and insisted on ascribing to their actions vile and base motives. Much ingenuity has been spent by foreign observers in attempting to explain this inexplicable behavior, but with little success. One thing is certain: the conduct of the accused should not be ascribed, as has often been done, to some unfathomable peculiarities of the Russian character derived by the more imaginative commentators from their misinterpretation of the novels of Dostoevsky. At several political trials held behind the Iron Curtain since World War II, the defendants, who were non-Russians (among them a few western Europeans and Americans), behaved in a manner reminiscent of that of their opposite numbers in Moscow. A closer look at the methods of the Communist security police should prove a surer guide than Freudian excursions into the mysteries of the human mind. The above generalization is supported by evidence from an authoritative source.

In February 1956, at the Twentieth Congress of the Communist Party, Khrushchev launched his by-now-famous attack on Stalin's rule, including purges. The Kremlin acknowledged that the speech was delivered, but its official text was never released. A version believed to be authentic was secured and published by the United States State Department. Khrushchev has returned frequently to this theme and has supplied some revealing information. He told the Twenty-second Party Congress (October 27, 1961) that "many outstanding government and public figures" were the innocent victims of the purge. "Many splendid commanders and political officials of the Red Army were executed," said Khrushchev. "Here among the delegates there are comrades . . . who spent many years in prison. They were being 'persuaded'—persuaded by quite definite techniques—that they were either German or British or some other kind of spies. And several of them 'confessed.' Even in cases when such people were told that accusations of espionage had been withdrawn, they themselves insisted on their previous testimony, because they believed that it was better to stand on their false testimony in order to put an end as quickly as possible to the torment and to die as quickly as possible." This evidence should not be taken lightly. Khrushchev, a high Moscow party official during the purges and a member of the Politburo since 1938, was in the thick of it. He speaks with an intimate knowledge of the subject.

The bulk of the victims of the purges did not get a public trial. Some, like Marshal Tukhachevsky and his co-defendants, all high army officers accused of spying for a foreign power, were tried *in camera* and were sentenced to death (June 1937). The majority simply disappeared, and no one seems to know what actually happened to them. The number of victims was large but cannot be ascertained with any degree of precision. When the Nineteenth Party Congress convened in March 1939, most of the familiar faces were missing. This did not prevent the newcomers and the few survivors—among them presumably Khrushchev and Mikoyan—from acclaiming the wisdom and greatness of "eternal" (as one delegate put it) Stalin. Times have changed. Since 1956 the rehabilitation of many of the purge victims has been in progress, and at the Twenty-second Party Congress Khrushchev spoke approvingly of a monument to be erected in Moscow "to the memory of the comrades who fell victim to arbitrary rule." This proposal was greeted with "prolonged stormy applause"—just as Stalin was at the Nineteenth Congress. The 1939 amendment of the party statutes abolished mass purges, but the right of the party to cleanse its ranks of undeserving members "as a matter of routine" was confirmed.

If it is difficult to find an entirely plausible explanation for the behavior of the accused, it is even more difficult to suggest a reason for Stalin's decision—for it was *his* decision—to institute the purges. There was nothing in the situation to justify them. The history of the Bolshevik Party is full of factional dissensions, Stalin had his disagreements with Lenin, and he had adopted eventually many of the policies of the outlawed Trotskyism. There was no evidence that his rule was endangered. As stated earlier in this chapter, Khrushchev said that Stalin was a very sick man suffering from the mania of persecution. This may well be the true explanation of the purges which wiped out so many of his close associates as well as the élite of the Communist Party.

But what are we to think of the "science" of Marxism-Leninism and Soviet democracy?

A New Constitution? At the April 1962 session of the Supreme Soviet, Khrushchev proposed the drafting of a new constitution. He stated that the existing constitution was "obsolete" and that the one to come "should prepare conditions for the transition to communist and public self-government." The Supreme Soviet appointed a drafting commission headed by Khrushchev.

22

The Stalin Era, 1924-1939:
Economics

NEP and Recovery

A Checkered Record. The growth of the Soviet economy is the most striking
and significant feature of the history of the USSR. Many aspects of this
process are unclear and the results achieved, in part, debatable. It is uncontroversial, however, that although the main objectives of the Kremlin—
collectivization and industrialization, with particular emphasis on heavy industry producing means of production—have consistently been maintained,
progress before and after the institution of a planned economy was accompanied by sharp fluctuations and reversals of policy. This generalization
holds good for both the shorter and the longer periods of Soviet history.

The Peasantry. The New Economic Policy, which succeeded War Communism in the spring of 1921, remained in effect until the introduction of
the first Five-Year Plan in 1928. During these few years the Soviet economy
underwent several major changes and lived through a severe crisis. The
NEP, which brought a welcome relief from the rigidities and rigors of War
Communism, aspired at effecting a reconciliation between the Communist
government and an exasperated and embittered peasantry. In this endeavor
it succeeded for a time almost too well.

The agrarian revolution that broke out in 1917 was practically completed by the end of 1918, and the land of the former large estates, with the exception of a small area retained as model farms by the government, was parceled out among the peasants. The agrarian revolution also engulfed the enclosed peasant holdings established before the war under the Stolypin land reform. With the termination of the requisitions of the period of War Communism, the farmers were encouraged to extend their sown area and to sell their surpluses. Beginning in 1923 they were permitted to pay in cash a part of the tax in kind imposed upon them in March 1921.

The land code of December 1922 was "neutral" in the sense that the peasants were left free to decide what form of land management they preferred, individual or collective. The collective farms organized during the early years of the revolution lacked agricultural machinery, they proved unproductive, and their number dwindled. The land code authorized, with reservations, the leasing of land and employment of hired labor, which were prohibited by earlier revolutionary legislation. Nationalization of land was retained but was of minor immediate importance. Most of the land reverted to the traditional pre-revolutionary communal tenure, there was a leveling in the size of peasant holdings, and by 1920, as a Soviet economist put it, the whole of rural Russia became "the petty bourgeois realm of small peasants." The elimination of the larger agricultural enterprises and the prevalence of subsistence farming reduced the supply of marketable grain.

While the peasant uprisings of the period of War Communism subsided, much discontent and resentment remained. The exactions of War Communism left deep scars, as did the famine of 1921, when entire regions were depopulated and peasants died by the million. The insidious classification, introduced by the Communist government, of the farmers into poor, medium, and *kulaks* fostered, as it was intended to do, social discord in the village. Yet things looked brighter under NEP, and the bumper crop of 1922, combined with the more liberal policy of the government, started the peasantry on the road to recovery. The trend of prices until September or October 1922 favored the farmers, that is, the rise of agricultural prices was greater than that of industrial commodities. This trend was reversed in the autumn of 1922 and led to the "scissors crisis," a pronounced disparity between agricultural and industrial prices, this time to the disadvantage of the peasantry, a situation that endangered the "alliance" between peasants and industrial workers that was regarded as politically essential.

Industry. The desire to benefit the farmers, which was the basic idea of NEP, was reflected in industrial policies. Measures were taken to encourage artisans and small producers engaged in domestic (cottage) industries whose wares went chiefly to the village market. Numerous small industrial establishments were leased to private individuals and cooperatives, but the state continued to operate the larger ones. In 1923 over 84 per cent of the industrial workers were employed in government-managed enterprises, which accounted for 92 per cent of all production by value. The consumer goods sector was strengthened. The administration of large nationalized enterprises was reorganized in a manner designed to promote independence and initiative. This was to be achieved by the separation of large-scale industry from state management. Industrial enterprises were brought together into trusts to which, according to a decree of April 10, 1923, "the state accorded independence . . . , and which operate on the principle of commercial accounting with the object of earning a profit." *Khozraschet,* or economic or business accounting, at this stage of NEP meant business for profit and led the trusts and enterprises to compete with one another. "The struggle between communist and individualistic economies is now being transferred to the economic ground, to the market," stated a resolution of the Eleventh Party Congress in March 1922; "here the nationalized industry controlled by the proletarian state must, following the competitive methods of the market, assert its unchallengeable superiority." The first trusts were organized in August 1921; a year later they numbered over 400, and the trustification of industry was completed.

The trusts were independent of direct administration by government agencies and were responsible for their profit and loss accounts. They ceased to receive appropriations from the budget (as was the case under War Communism) and depended for the financing of their operations on earnings and bank credit based on profitability. Welcome as was the emancipation from the controls of War Communism, the trusts found themselves in great difficulties. Industrial productivity was very low: it is believed that in 1920 it was less than 20 per cent of the 1913 level. Buildings, machinery, and equipment received by the trusts were run down, stocks of raw material and fuel were inadequate or non-existent, and the enterprises—cut off from state financing—were desperately in need of working capital. One way of raising the funds required was to dispose of the available stocks of goods at whatever price they would fetch. This is what many trusts proceeded to do, with the result that industrial prices practically collapsed.

The "Scissors Crisis." Early in 1922 the price situation was favorable to the farmers. The difficulties experienced by industrial enterprises affected adversely the earning of labor and contributed to the widely-held belief that the industrial proletariat had been sacrificed to the peasants. Several steps were taken to remedy this situation, of which the more important were the formation by trusts and enterprises, beginning in March 1922, of syndicates to prevent excessive competition, and the elimination of the less efficient industrial establishments, partly by merger. These policies brought results, and by August 1922 industrial and agricultural prices had reverted to their 1913 relationship. During the next 12 months the price situation became increasingly unfavorable to the farmers and created an acute "scissors crisis," a term put into circulation by Trotsky. The principal reasons for the shift were the better organization of industry and the abundant harvest of 1922.

Much of the blame for price vagaries was attributed, probably wrongly, to the private traders—nepmen—who were responsible for over 80 per cent of the retail commerce in the early years of NEP. The legalization of private traders under NEP was the recognition of a situation that has long been in existence. The nepmen were small dealers, lineal descendants of the War Communism bagmen. Their prominence proved equally effervescent. The "scissors" of October 1922–October 1923 endangered the "alliance" between town and village. The government decided on intervention, which took the form of the drastic rationing of credit to industry and the imposition of price control (October 1923). In some cases "goods' intervention" was used, that is, cheaper foreign goods were imported by the government and sold on the Russian market in order to force the syndicates to lower their prices. Spectacular rather than effective measures were taken against nepmen: in December 1923 several hundred private traders were arrested in Moscow and deported. The "anti-scissors" policies achieved their objective. Beginning in October 1923 the gap between agricultural and industrial prices was narrowed and was rapidly reduced to a manageable size. Indeed, until the end of NEP the price situation tended to favor the peasants.

Budget, Banking, and Money. The greatest service rendered by NEP to the economy was the restoration of order in public finance and the stabilization of the ruble. War Communism left behind it a state of unspeakable financial disorder, which took a few years to be straightened out. The financial reform comprised three main elements: balancing of the budget, rebuilding of the bank system, and stabilization of the currency.

The catastrophic progressive depreciation of the ruble imparted total unreality to all economic and financial computations during this period. According to a Soviet financial authority (K. N. Plotnikov), budget expenditure in 1920, expressed in terms of "commodity ruble," amounted to merely 4.4 per cent of the corresponding figure in 1913. The budget deficit in 1920 exceeded one trillion rubles. Measures directed at balancing the budget included reduction of expenditure, creation of new sources of revenue, and rebuilding of a reasonably efficient machinery for tax collection. Multiple taxes were imposed. The first state loan—a "grain" loan—was floated in May 1922; bonds were sold for cash but could be redeemed in cash or in kind and could be used for payment of taxes. This financial extravaganza fell flat and was abandoned. The first "gold" loan, issued in October 1922, met with little success, and subscription was made compulsory for state, cooperative, and private enterprises. The restoration of the bank system began with the establishment in October 1921 of the State Bank, which eventually became the central credit institution of the Soviet Union. Several state and cooperative banks, including an extensive network of agricultural credit societies, were formed in 1922.

These and other economic measures were of minor usefulness as long as the depreciation of the ruble went unchecked. The introduction by the State Bank in October 1922 of a new monetary unit, the chervonets, equal to 10 pre-revolutionary gold rubles, was a major move towards the elimination of inflation. The new currency was issued at first in small quantities, and safeguards were used to ensure its stability. The chervonets bills circulated side by side with the depreciated paper currency of various types, exchangeable into one another at shifting and fanciful rates. Stabilization was achieved in February–March 1924, when new state treasury notes were substituted for those in circulation at a rate that varied according to the vintage of the notes: one new ruble was equal to 50,000 rubles of the 1923 pattern and to 50 billion rubles of the pre–1921 pattern. Conversion was completed by May 10, 1924.

The monetary reform was acclaimed as a great success and removed the chief source of disorders. It was not, however, the gold standard in any meaning of the term. Convertibility of the ruble was suspended in March 1926. In July 1926 the export, and in March 1928 the import, of Soviet monetary tokens were prohibited, making the ruble a purely internal currency. Its international value was fixed by Soviet authorities in relation to the dollar from 1926 to 1936, to the French franc in 1936–1937, and again to the dollar after 1937. The 1924 injunction against the use of the printing press for meeting budget deficits was not observed. The volume of currency in circulation was 322 million rubles at the beginning of 1924, 1.263 billion in 1926, 2.773 billion in 1930, and 11.256 billion in 1937, when the publication of circulation figures was discontinued. Yet the currency situation after the reform was a great improvement on what it was prior to 1924.

NEP—A Retrospect. To sum up, NEP brought a measure of economic recovery. By the end of 1927 Russia had returned to the economic levels of 1913. Life was easier than at any time since the beginning of the revolution. Nevertheless NEP was under severe attack. Allegedly, it favored the peasants at the expense of the industrial proletariat, strengthened the *kulak* element in the village, and fostered consumer goods industries to the detriment of those producing means of production. Worst of all, NEP was rooted in the *laissez-faire* mentality of the free market that inevitably bred bourgeois attitudes incompatible with economic planning, which alone, it was held, could ensure transition to socialism.

Economic Planning

Why Have a Plan? In the era after World War II, when planning was taken for granted, it is difficult to realize that until the late 1920's it attracted hardly any attention. Even among the socialists there was little understanding of the problems of planning, although its necessity in a socialist society was admitted. Under a system of private enterprise the economic life of a country is governed, although not without considerable friction, by the interplay of economic forces; the interaction of supply and demand regulates, in the last analysis, the level of prices and the flow of capital and labor from one branch of the economy to another. In other words, the determining influence is that of the market. In a socialist economy there is no market, no private enterprise, no private investments. Something, however, must take the place of the non-existent market mechanism, and there seems to be no alternative to an all-inclusive plan prepared by statesmen and economists. This was understood by the Bolshevists before they began to learn the technique of planning. The program of the Russian Communist Party, which was adopted in March 1919, called for "the maximum unification of all economic activities of the country in a comprehensive state plan." It was easier, however, to enunciate a principle than to apply it in practice, especially in a backward agricultural country in the midst of a revolution. Some of the left-wing leaders believed that the controls of War Communism were the harbingers of the future communist society, but this view was not officially accepted. The results of War Communism were hardly encouraging; moreover, the measures of this period were concerned primarily with pressing emergencies, not with long-range objectives characteristic of state planning. There was no comprehensive planning under NEP, and it was not tried in earnest until the introduction of the first Five-Year Plan in 1928.

The necessary prerequisites of planning, according to Soviet doctrine, are the nationalization of the means of production and unified leadership. The broad objectives of the plan were stated in Article 11 of the 1936 constitution: increase in public wealth, steady improvement in the material and cultural standards of the working people, and the strengthening of the independence of the USSR and its capacity for defense.

Planning Agencies and Procedure. The central planning agency is the Gosplan, or State Planning Commission, which was established in February 1921 and was subordinated, at first indirectly, to the Council of People's Commissars. The Gosplan, like other administrative agencies, went through several transformations and in 1948 was reorganized as the State Planning Committee of the Council of Ministers of the USSR. Although vested with broad powers, Gosplan is an executive rather than a policy-making body. The general directives concerning the contents of the plan come from the Communist Party and the Soviet government.

The Gosplan of the USSR heads an extensive network of planning institutions arranged according to the horizontal, or territorial, and vertical, or functional, principle. The horizontal network comprises the planning bodies of the constituent republics and those of the smaller territorial subdivisions; the function structure embraces the planning organs of separate branches of economic activity—agriculture, banking, commerce, industry (steel, machine building, textiles), and so on. Universities, museums, theaters, schools—all have their planning commissions. Planning agencies reach down to the smallest units: collective and state farms, shops, factories, and offices. The Gosplan and its subordinate organs perform a double function: they collect information, which is integrated into a comprehensive plan and then broken into segments which are apportioned among the territorial subdivisions, enterprises, and institutions, and they check on the performance. Before the plan is adopted, its component elements are examined and discussed by planning agencies at every level. This is a complex and umbersome system, and there is inevitably much duplication in the work of territorial and functional organs.

The Five-Year Plans. The first comprehensive attempt at planning—on a theoretical level—was made in March 1920, when a committee on electrification (Goelro) was appointed at the suggestion of Lenin. Its purpose was to translate into concrete terms the policy summarized later (November 1920) by Lenin in the much-quoted dictum: "Communism is Soviet power plus electrification of the whole country." In February 1921 Goelro was merged in Gosplan. Nothing came of this early move; Russia's economic plight and the philosophy of NEP were inimical to planning. But planning there was to be. In 1925 came the so-called "control figures," which were a program of economic development for the year 1925–1926. The first Five-Year Plan was put into operation on October 1, 1928, and was completed in four years and three months, on December 31, 1932. Henceforth the planned year coincided with the calendar year. The second Five-Year Plan extended from the beginning of 1933 to the end of 1937; the third was inaugurated in January 1938, but its completion was interrupted by the German invasion. Planning was resumed after the war. The fourth Five-Year Plan came in 1946, the fifth in 1951, and the sixth in 1956, but it was not permitted to run its full course and was superseded in 1958 by the Seven-Year Plan, which is to expire in 1965.

Each "Plan for the Development of National Economy," to use the full name of the gigantic enterprise, is a huge program of expansion that embraces not only the economy but social, cultural, and educational activities as well. Under each heading the plan sets targets and also outlines, not always clearly, by what methods the results desired are to be achieved. It provides the amount of capital to be invested in each field, establishes the percentage by which the production of each branch of industry is to rise, and sets targets for higher labor productivity, lower prices, increased monetary and real wages, reduced illiteracy, and so on. The broader objectives of the first three Five-Year Plans were rapid industrialization with special emphasis on the expansion of heavy industry, collectivization of farming, and a sustained effort to reduce prices and increase the productivity of labor. The fourth Five-Year Plan was primarily concerned with the recovery from the frightful damages suffered by the Soviet Union during the war, and the subsequent plans deal with conditions conducive to the creation of a socialist society and transition to communism. This program includes reaching, and then exceeding, the per capita production of the capitalist countries, particularly the United States.

The Plan Is Not a Blueprint. Information on the plans is incomplete, contradictory, and difficult to interpret. It is often imagined that the plan, as suggested by its name, is a closely coordinated program all parts of which are carefully integrated. This is not a correct picture of Soviet planning. "To us, Bolsheviks, the Five-Year Plan is not something complete and ordained once and for all," Stalin told the Sixteenth Party Congress in the summer of 1930. "To us the Five-Year Plan, like any other plan, is but a plan, adopted as a first approximation, one that must be refined, amended, and improved in the light of local experience in carrying out the plan." This statement describes well the Soviet planning procedure. The Five-Year Plans are subdivided into yearly plans, six- and three-month plans, and plans for shorter periods, all of which amend the original targets. If examined in detail, the performance at the end of the five-year period differs widely from the assignments. Soviet authorities deprecate and chastise under-fulfillment and encourage and reward over-fulfillment of the planned quotas. Were the plans properly integrated, over-fulfillment would be as disturbing as failure to meet the assignments.

Disparity between targets and performance may be traced to three principal reasons: changes in the policy of the government, conditions outside the Soviet Union over which the Kremlin has no control, and the inability of Soviet enterprises to meet their quotas. A notable example of a change in Soviet policy that affected planning was the acceleration of collectivization under the first Five-Year Plan. The unforeseen rapid expansion of the collective sector necessitated a fundamental revision of the plan for machine-building, because collectivization depended on large supplies of tractors and combines; this, in turn, demanded a revision of the plan for steel, fuel, skilled labor, financing, and so on. An instance of failure to meet assignments because of conditions in the outside world is provided by foreign trade. Under the first Five-Year Plan the value of Soviet exports was to increase two and one-half times, but because of the depression of 1929 it actually declined by nearly one-third. One consequence of this experience was that foreign trade was not included in the subsequent Five-Year Plans.

Failures to reach targets by domestic enterprises were frequent and openly acknowledged. Productivity of labor proved particularly resistant to the efforts of the planners. The first Five-Year Plan called for an increase of labor productivity by 110 per cent; it actually rose—if official figures are to be trusted—by 41 per cent. The result was that the number of wage earners (workers and employees), which was to increase from 11.3 million in 1926–1927 to 15.8 million in 1932, was actually 22.8 million in the latter year. The unplanned absorption by industry of 7 million workers (most of them came probably from the farms) necessitated far-reaching revisions of other parts of the plan—finance, housing, and others. Statements by Soviet leaders (particularly the annual budget reports of the minister of finance) and the press provide numerous instances of failure by enterprises and whole branches of industry to fulfill their assignments; nevertheless, it is invariably claimed that the plan, as a whole, is fulfilled nearly 100 per cent. The deceptive nature of these summary figures, arrived at by averaging those of over- and under-fulfillment, has been frequently denounced by high Soviet officials, but they continue to be widely used.

Flexibility is a notable feature of Soviet planning, which is more in the nature of a drive than of a blueprint.

Industry

Industry and Planned Economy. Expansion of industry, state-owned and state-controlled, was and remains one of the main objectives of Soviet planning. According to the official interpretation, the period of restoration, that is, of expanding production on the basis of existing technical methods and equipment, came to an end in 1925–1926, and the Soviet Union was ready to enter the phase of socialist reconstruction, which required large new investments and construction. Concessions made to private enterprise during the earlier stage of NEP were temporary——to meet an emergency—and private business was squeezed out with the progress of recovery. Privately-owned enterprises were small, employing on the average two workers. Their share in aggregate industrial production fell from 19.9 per cent in 1925–1926 to 12.7 per cent in 1927–1928, and in the production of small-scale industry, where private enterprise predominated, from 82.9 per cent in 1925–1926 to 67.6 per cent in 1927–1928. This decline, which continued during the years of reconstruction, explains in part the acute shortage of certain consumer goods which were manufactured by the small producers.

An attempt at reviving the sagging economy by injecting foreign capital was considered in 1918 and tried under NEP. Over 2,200 demands for concessions were received between 1920 and 1927, and 163 agreements were concluded, but in 1927 only 40 concessions using foreign capital were in operation in industry and mining. Their share in over-all production was small, a fraction of one per cent, and they did not survive long.

The organization of industry under socialism was a novel and challenging, but also elusive, task of paramount importance to the future of the Soviet Union. Nearly 50 years after the establishment of Soviet rule, administration of business enterprise is still in flux. Its history has made clear that Lenin's notion of the simplicity of state functions under socialism has no relation to reality. Industrial trusts created during NEP as a method of business management under market conditions were retained after the adoption of the planned economy, but the principles on which they operated were changed. The independence formerly enjoyed by the trusts was narrowed down, and they came increasingly under the control of government agencies —the Supreme Economic Council, the Gosplan, the Council of People's Commissars. The "model charter" of June 1927 redefined the position of the trusts. Their administration was to be regulated, as in the past, by *khozraschet,* but the meaning of this term was altered. Originally *khozraschet* signified the "commercial principle," or business for profit. Under the new dispensation it became the "economic, or cost accounting, principle" and required fulfillment of, and compliance with, the provisions of the plan. The efficiency of the enterprise was to be measured by this yardstick. Both trusts and *khozraschet* have been retained and are part of the Soviet picture today.

The adaptation of the trusts to new conditions did not solve the riddle of business management under socialism. Other troublesome and recurrent issues were: the exact chain of command, particularly the relationship between the enterprise and the trust; the position and powers of the manager; and the ultimate authority in deciding industrial issues. There were several reorganizations of industry, of which the more important occurred in 1929, 1934, and also 1957, when the functions of the control of industry were transferred from the numerous ministeries of the USSR and of the constituent republics to the councils of the newly-created administrative-economic regions, which numbered about 100. It would not be surprising if other major changes were to follow before long.

Prices and Productivity. The all-important question of prices is one of the unsolved problems of the Soviet economy. In the absence of a market mechanism, all prices are determined by government agencies. The methods by which they are arrived at are not disclosed. Until the 1950's they were supposed to stem from the "unchangeable prices of 1926-1927," the last year of NEP, an obscure and baffling notion. Prices nevertheless are extremely important in the economy of an enterprise. Its standing depends on its ability to balance its costs (wages, fuel, raw material) and receipts (sales of goods of prescribed grades in prescribed quantities and at prescribed prices). If the assignments on both sides of the ledger are properly fulfilled, the enterprise gets a "planned profit." Greater efficiency and productivity are promoted through the operation of the "director's fund," which was introduced in 1936 and was revived after the war. The fund consists of contributions from planned profits and "surplus profits," that is, profits in excess of those planned. Surplus profits originate chiefly from greater efficiency: the expenditure of smaller amounts of labor, fuel, and raw material per unit of production. The proceeds of the fund are spent on the expansion of production, construction, and housing, as well as amenities for the workers and bonuses for individual employees. It is the application to the enterprise of the principle that governs Soviet wages: "From each according to his ability, to each according to his work." Director's funds are in operation, wherever feasible, throughout the economy.

Some Results. The cost of industrialization, which is high, is examined in the closing section of this chapter. Quantitatively the results achieved under the first and second Five-Year Plans are impressive:

OUTPUT OF SELECTED COMMODITIES, 1913, 1928, AND 1938

	1913	1928	1938
Pig iron, million tons	4.2	3.3	14.6
Steel, " "	4.2	4.3	18.0
Coal, " "	29.1	35.5	133.0
Oil, " "	9.2	11.7	30.2
Paper, thousand tons	262.0	284.0	832.0
Leather footwear, million pairs	60.0	58.0	192.9

The volume of production resumed its upward course after the war. This was no mean achievement, even though costs were exorbitant, the percentage of defective production very high, and the quality often inferior.

Labor

Incentives and Efficiency. "Productivity of labor is, in the last resort, the most important, the most essential condition for the victory of the new social order." This often-quoted pronouncement of Lenin sums up well the attitude of the Soviet government towards the labor problem. The path of labor in the country of workers and peasants has not been an easy one. After demobilization from the "labor armies" of War Communism, workers had to face low wages, a mounting cost of living, appalling housing conditions, and a hard core of unemployment that was not wiped out until the unplanned absorption of 7 million workers in industry during the first Five-Year Plan.

Incentive wages have consistently been maintained. The Communist Party program of 1919 stated that leveling of wages was not an immediate objective of the regime. A unified schedule of wages and salaries prepared by the government and the trade unions in 1920–1921 provided for 17 grades of pay; the higher brackets applied to technicians and white-collar workers. Earnings in grade seventeen were eight times as high as in grade one. In spite of this differentiation there was a tendency—to which Stalin took strong exception—towards the equalization of wages. With the appearance of a labor shortage after the introduction of the first Five-Year Plan, the wage schedule was revised (1931) in a way to make employment in key industries attractive—coal, oil, electric power, metallurgy, machine building. A nation-wide campaign exorcised *obezlichka* (facelessness), or work that cannot be traced to its performer, and *uravnilovka* (leveling), or equalization of earnings—two picturesque terms coined by Stalin—as enemies of labor productivity and socialism. Piecework was introduced wherever possible throughout the economy, and the principle of socialism "to each according to his work" was enshrined in Article 12 of the 1936 constitution.

A serious obstacle to higher productivity was the fluidity, or high turnover, of labor, the incessant wandering of workingmen from one place of employment to another. This phenomenon is explained by the situation prevailing since the introduction of the planned economy: the disappearance of unemployment, which made it easy to find jobs, and the extraordinary variety in wage rates and housing and supply conditions from industry to industry and from enterprise to enterprise. Rationing of foodstuffs and consumer goods began in 1929 and lasted through 1935. Under this system consumers received ration cards which entitled them to make purchases in small amounts at low fixed prices in "closed" shops. In the case of industrial workers "closed" shops were attached to plants and factories; the assortment and quality of the goods they carried differed widely, and the desire to secure access to reputedly better shops was one reason for changing employment.

Different measures were tried to increase labor productivity and to make workers stay on their jobs. The 7-hour working day was adopted in 1927. The "continuous" 6- or 5-day week (five or four workdays followed by a day of rest), designed to intensify the use of industrial equipment by employing three consecutive 7-hour shifts, was instituted in the early 1930's. There was an elaborate system of bonuses for workers who exceeded their "norm," or standard performance set for every type of work. "Shock brigades," consisting of exemplary workers, were formed in 1928, and in 1932 began the "excellence" movement (*otlichnichestvo*), which took the form of pledges by workers to improve their technical qualifications and train fellow workers. Special benefits were provided in recognition of the continuity of employment. Vacations, opportunities for staying at rest homes, bonuses, and the entire system of social insurance were linked to the length of uninterrupted service in one enterprise. There were also deterrent measures. A decree of March 1933 directed that reasons for every change of employment should be entered on the worker's labor card. Workingmen dismissed for breach of discipline or convicted of a crime were summarily evicted and were not entitled to "living space" elsewhere. Unemployment insurance was abolished in 1933. Punishments were imposed on those guilty of truancy, tardiness, laxity, and negligence. On the other hand, the government conferred upon diligent workers medals and honorary titles, of which the highest is Hero of Socialist Labor, entitling the recipient to tangible privileges.

The two better-known and characteristic devices for promoting efficiency are socialist "emulation" (*sorevnovanie*) and the Stakhanov movement. Socialist emulation stems from an article written by Lenin in 1919 but not published until January 1929. Stalin stated that socialist emulation was different from "competition" (*konkurentsiia*). "Emulation," he told the Sixteenth Party Congress in June 1930, ". . . . transforms labor from a shameful and heavy burden . . . into a deed of honor, a deed of glory, a deed of valor and heroism." In less ornate language, emulation consists of contracts entered into by individual workers, groups of workers, factories, plants, collective farms, and whole provinces with similar persons, groups, or institutions elsewhere to exceed planned quotas, cut down costs, maintain high levels of discipline, reduce absenteeism, improve technical qualifications, and rehabilitate and train inefficient workers. Socialist emulation, a curious device especially in a planned economy, is still widely used in the post-Stalin era.

The Stakhanov movement originated in the achievement of the Ukrainian miner Alexis Stakhanov, who on August 31, 1935, knocked down in a 6-hour shift 102 tons of coal, 14 times the standard norm. Stakhanov was immediately acclaimed as an innovator, and his performance, which was presumably contrived with the assistance of the authorities, was the starting point of the upward revision of norms and of a huge publicity campaign for more efficient methods of work devised by the workers themselves. Stakhanovism mushroomed, and notable records were established in various fields. It was soon observed, however, that striving for records is not conducive to the smooth working of enterprises. In the 1950's the Stakhanov movement lost its popularity, which was presumably synthetic, and is no longer mentioned in the Soviet press.

Legislation of 1940. The legislation of 1940 opened a new chapter in the history of Soviet labor. A decree of June 26, 1940, substituted the 8- for the 7-hour day guaranteed by the constitution. The "continuous" 6- or 5-day week was replaced by the conventional 7-day week, with Sunday as the day of rest. Far more important, the decree of June 26 prohibited workers from relinquishing their jobs without release from the director of the enterprise.

Violations of these provisions, as well as truancy, were dealt with by people's courts and were punishable by "corrective labor." The decree applied to "all state, cooperative, and public enterprises and institutions," that is, to practically every enterprise and institution in the land. Another decree of June 26 provided for the retention of existing monthly earnings in spite of the longer hours. On October 2, 1940, came the decree for the drafting of 800,000 to 1,000,000 boys to be trained in trade and factory schools. The graduates of these schools constituted the State Labor Reserves and were under the obligation to work for four years wherever they were assigned. On the same day (October 2, 1940) tuition fees were introduced in the three upper grades of the secondary schools and in all higher schools. This, again, called for an amendment of the constitution, which guaranteed free education at every level. Tuition fees, especially in the higher schools, were high as compared with the monthly earnings of workers and tended to make higher education the preserve of those in the upper income brackets.

The above legislation has often been described as war measures, but this is probably not a correct interpretation. The drafting of young people was extended to girls and retained after the war; the fourth Five-Year Plan provided for the training of 4.5 million workers under the State Labor Reserves scheme. Attachment of workers to jobs was the logical consequence of the failure of other measures to achieve efficiency, high productivity, and stability of employment. It was fully consonant with the authoritarian philosophy of Soviet planning, and it was not until 1956, eleven years after the termination of the war, that workers regained the right to change employment; in the same year tuition fees in schools were abolished.

Wages. The wage picture is obscure, especially in the pre-war period. The average annual monetary earnings of workers and employees rose from 700 rubles in 1928 to 4,100 rubles in 1940. The lumping together of workers and employees is confusing. In the absence of an index of prices, which was discontinued in 1929 and was not resumed until after the war, and under a system of multiple prices (rationed, commercial stores, open market, black market), it is impossible to determine the trend of real wages. Walter Duranty, the Moscow correspondent of the *New York Times,* wrote in February 1934 that the average monthly wage of a Russian industrial worker would buy in Moscow "on the open market no more than $3 will buy in America." During the period of rationing, changes in monetary wages meant little.

Trade Unions. The position of trade unions in the USSR is different from that in the capitalist countries. During the 1920's, when a measure of free discussion was still tolerated by the Communist Party, there were several passionate debates concerning the role of the trade unions in a so-cialist state. The real issue was between the advocates of the independence of the trade unions and their active participation in the administration of industry, and those who held with Trotsky that they should be absorbed by the state. Trotsky was defeated, but his trade union policies prevailed. In 1929 Michael Tomsky, a trade union leader since 1918 and a champion of their autonomy, was removed from office and in 1936 committed suicide. He was succeeded as president of the Central Council of Trade Unions by N. M. Shvernik, who brought the unions in line with Stalinist policies.

The principal functions of the trade unions are to represent labor in government agencies; to administer social insurance (formerly under the commissariat of labor, which was abolished in 1933); to negotiate collective agreements—a mere formality, because hours, wages, and so on are regulated by law and government agencies; to minister to the cultural and physical needs of the members—clubs, housing, recreation, and sports facilities; and above all, to strive for higher labor productivity and the fulfillment and over-fulfillment of the plan. The promotion of Stakhanovism (as long as it lasted) and socialist emulation are among the unions' principal functions.

Soviet unions are industrial unions, which include all persons employed in the same industry. Their number varied greatly. There were 23 unions in 1930; 168, in 1939; and 22 in 1961. Membership, which is voluntary (but pressure to join is strong), is large and growing: 2 million in October 1917; 10 million in 1929; 25 million in 1939; and 53 million in 1957. Frequent complaints by Soviet leaders and in the Soviet press about the indifference of the membership toward unionism is explainable by the uninspiring nature of its functions. Of the three agencies concerned with the management of an enterprise—the appointed director, the primary organ of the Communist Party, and the factory committee (*fabkom*) elected by the union members —the last is by far the least active. Strikes are not prohibited by law, and some occurred in the early 1920's, but they are no longer tolerated; any attempt to strike would be regarded as a counter-revolutionary activity insti-gated by foreign agents.

Farming

Advent of Collectivization. The reprieve granted to individual farming under NEP was of brief duration. The system of landholding resulting from the revolution of 1917–1918, which was characterized by the disappearance of large estates and the multiplicity of subsistence farms, confronted the Soviet government with grave problems of both a practical and a theoretical nature. The supply of marketable grain declined from 26 per cent of the gross output in 1913 to 11 per cent in 1928, and of grain for exports from 12 per cent to a fraction of one per cent. The shrinkage occurred at the very time when a vast increase in the volume of marketable agricultural produce was regarded as essential to the success of the industrialization program. On the theoretical level, the "contradiction" between town and country was a familiar tenet of Marxism. It was held that large-scale socialist agricultural enterprises equipped with advanced technique and using modern machinery would greatly raise productivity and simultaneously contribute to the elimination of the psychological differences between workers and peasants and of the latter's "petty bourgeois" attitude, especially among the *kulaks*. The failure of earlier attempts at collectivization was explained by the lack of necessary prerequisites—managerial experience and, above all, large agricultural machinery. A lively debate concerning the "correct" policy towards the peasants kept the Communist bodies busy in 1924–1928 and ended in the defeat of the groups opposing Stalin's program of all-out collectivization, which was applied in the winter of 1929.

The collectivization drive had to begin from scratch. Few of the collective farms organized immediately after the revolution survived under NEP. Their number declined from 22,000 in 1925 to 14,000 in 1927, when they comprised less than one per cent of peasant households. The first Five-Year Plan stipulated a modest advance of collectivization: the area under crops in the socialized sector (state farms and collective farms) was to increase from 2.7 per cent of the total sown area to 17.5 per cent, and the number of households in the collective farms was to rise by 10 per cent of their total number. A marked decline in grain collection in 1928, for which the *kulaks* were held responsible, brought about a drastic upward revision of planned agricultural assignments. In 1932 the socialized sector comprised 78 per cent of the sown area. The proportion of peasant households in the collective farms rose to 8 per cent in October 1929 and jumped to 58 per cent in March 1930.

The state of chaos in the countryside resulting from these breath-taking changes frightened Soviet leaders. An article by Stalin, "Dizziness with Success," published on March 2, 1930, denounced the excesses of collectivization. The movement went immediately into reverse gear, and the proportion of collectivized households declined to 20 per cent in September 1930, only to rise again—after new pressures were applied—to 62 per cent in 1932 and to

93 per cent in 1937, when the sown area of the collective farms amounted to 99 per cent of the area of peasant cultivation. The *kulaks,* an elastic term embracing all farmers who did not approve of collectivization, were blamed for food shortages in 1929 and were "liquidated as a class," that is, they were deported to the labor camps of the OGPU. The number of deportees was not disclosed, but it is believed to have been between 4 and 5 million. Many of them never came back.

Forced collectivization took a heavy toll of livestock. Between 1928 and 1933 the number of horses declined from 33.5 million to 16.6 million; of long-horned cattle, from 70.5 million to 38.4 million; of sheep and goats, from 146.7 million to 50.2 million; and of pigs, from 26.0 million to 12.1 million. Severe droughts in 1930 and 1931, especially in the Ukraine, aggravated the plight of farming and created near-famine conditions.

State Farms. Soviet socialized agriculture comprises two kinds of enterprises: the *sovkhoz* (plural *sovkhozy*), or state farm, and the *kolkhoz* (plural *kolkhozy*), or collective farm. The *sovkhoz* is a large state-owned and state-managed agricultural enterprise operated by hired labor. It had originally a double purpose: to raise agricultural production by using advanced methods of husbandry and the scientific utilization of land, and to create model institutions which would provide object lessons of the advantages of large-scale farming. A few *sovkhozy* were organized on large estates on the morrow of the revolution, but they made little progress until 1928. Highly specialized enterprises, they were spoken of as "grain factories," "meat factories," and so on. There was at first a firm belief in the virtue of bigness. In 1930 an average grain *sovkhoz* covered an area of over 100,000 hectares.[1]

A state farm is managed by an appointed director; labor is paid on a piecework basis, and there is a director's fund. There were 1,400 *sovkhozy* in 1928 and over 4,000 in 1940, although by that time their significance had declined. The management of *sovkhozy* proved difficult and the results obtained unsatisfactory. In 1934 they came in for severe criticism by the Communist Party for waste and inefficiency. As a consequence, *sovkhozy* were broken into smaller units, and some were reorganized as collective farms. They employed 300,000 people in 1928, 1.9 million in 1932, and 1.3 million in 1938. They continued to play a minor part until the 1950's, when they became the principal form of agricultural enterprise in the newly-developed virgin lands.

[1] One hectare = 2.47 acres.

Collective Farms. A *kolkhoz,* or collective farm, is, in law and in theory, a voluntary association for the cultivation of land. The land code of December 1922, and earlier legislation, recognized three types of collective farms: the commune, the artel, and the association for the joint cultivation of land. The difference among them is in the degree of collective ownership, which is strongest in the commune and weakest in the association. The artel was pronounced the only suitable form under the conditions prevailing in the 1930's and practically all Soviet collective farms belong to this type. It is the only one dealt with in this discussion.

There were fewer than 15,000 *kolkhozy* in 1927, uniting less than one per cent of the peasant population; in 1938 collective farms numbered 242,000 and comprised 18.5 million, or 95.5 per cent, of peasant households. The number of collective farms remained practically stationary until the 1950's, when it was drastically reduced through amalgamations.

The organization of the *kolkhozy* is regulated by "The Model Charter of the Agricultural *Artel"* of February 1935, which in fact, if not in law, is obligatory for every collective farm. The *kolkhoz* is granted in perpetuity the enjoyment of the land assigned to it. In an artel—and this is its distinctive characteristic—the bulk of the land is under collective management and is cultivated collectively, but each member—*kolkhoznik*—retains control of his homestead and the adjoining plot (household allotment) the size of which varies from one-quarter to one hectare. The farm is managed, in theory, by the general assembly of the members and by the president and executive board which it elects. In practice, however, the president, with whom rests true authority, is an appointed official. Collective farmers are organized into brigades (as are industrial workers and practically every one else in the USSR) under a brigadier and are assigned to specific work, such as plowing, taking care of the animals, and the like. Every kind of work is evalued in terms of "labor days" to which the farmer is entitled if he performs satisfactorily the prescribed norm. The share of the member in the proceeds of the farm, which are distributed in kind and in cash, is determined by the number of labor days that he has to his credit. There is an elaborate system of bonuses for the fulfillment and over-fulfillment of the assignments and an equally elaborate schedule of deductions from the base earnings for those who fail to meet the target, a highly complex arrangement that invites evasion, malfeasance, and abuse of power. The principal financial burden of the *kolkhozy* was compulsory deliveries: the obligation to surrender to the government at very low prices a substantial part of the produce calculated on the basis of fixed quotas per hectare of the planned sown area. This method of taxation, onerous from the farmers' point of view, was maintained practically unchanged until the mid-1950's.

A high degree of mechanization is regarded as essential to the success of collectivized agriculture. In the 1920's the Soviet Union had hardly any agricultural machinery, but a great effort was made to remedy this situation. The number of tractors rose from 25,000 in 1927 to 483,000 in 1938, and of combines from 25,000 in 1933 to 153,000 in 1938. The earlier tractors were of foreign, chiefly American make, but after 1932 practically all of them were manufactured in the Soviet Union. At first large agricultural machinery was owned by state and collective farms, but in the later 1930's ownership was concentrated in the hands of the state-owned Machine Tractor Stations, or MTS. There were 6 MTS in 1928, 158 in 1930, and 6,350 in 1938. The MTS performed a double role: they carried on, with the assistance of collective farmers, plowing, sowing, reaping, and other work on the farm; they were also expected to ensure the fulfillment by the *kolkhoz* of the plan and watched over the Communist orthodoxy of its members. The political function was of particular importance, because in the 1930's and 1940's very few *kolkhozy* had primary party organs. It was mandatory for the collective farms to enter into agreements with the MTS the terms of which were regulated by law. The MTS were paid by the farms in kind and in cash, according to prescribed schedules. Both economically and politically the MTS were the chief agents of the government in the countryside. They were abolished in 1958, and their equipment was sold to collective farms as a part of a major reorganization of agriculture.

The produce retained by the *kolkhozy* after meeting their statutory obligations (compulsory deliveries and other obligatory sales to the state, and allocations to various funds: seed, feed, reserve, and others), as well as that distributed to the members on the basis of labor days, is sold on the *kolkhoz* market, which had long existed as a black market but was legalized in May 1932. This is the only market in the USSR where prices are not directly regulated by the state. They are kept in line with official prices as long as state and cooperative stores have adequate supplies of similar goods, but in times of shortages (for instance, during the periods of rationing) *kolkhoz* market prices rise substantially, much to the benefit of the farmers.

The involved arrangements merely touched upon above did not work satisfactorily and have generated friction and discontent. It was expected when collectivization was instituted that the communal sector of the farm would be the chief source of income of the members and that household allotments would play a subordinate part. This did not happen. On the contrary, *kolkhozniki* shunned and neglected the communal fields and concentrated on their household allotments, which were often enlarged in contravention of the law, and on their private livestock. The government and the party took strong measures against such "fictitious collective farmers"; a decree of May 1939 ordered the expulsion from the farm of able-bodied members who had failed to earn the prescribed minimum of labor days during the year. The original quota was 60 to 100, according to the locality; it was amended and refined (a specified number of labor days during the harvest season, and so on) by subsequent legislation. The institution of compulsory labor days changed the theory of the organization of labor on a collective farm. The fiction of voluntary participation was dropped, and work in the communal sector became a legal obligation enforceable by severe penalties: expulsion from the farm actually means the farmer's total ruin. It may be significant that the imposition of compulsory labor days was soon followed by the attachment of industrial workers to their jobs. The elimination of household plots is one of the government's objectives in revising farm policies.

Distribution

Domestic Trade. Planned economy brought about the destruction of private trade. The liquidation of nepmen was decided in principle in 1924, and in 1930 retail trade was formally taken over by state shops, which operated chiefly in urban areas, and by cooperative shops catering primarily to the rural population. The third element in the distribution system was the *kolkhoz* market discussed in the previous section. Soviet cooperatives are akin to state trading rather than to the cooperative movement as it is known in the West. Prices in state and cooperative shops are officially determined; those on the *kolkhoz* market are free. During the period of rationing (1929–1935) there were also state-owned "commercial shops," where commodities were sold without ration cards but at higher prices. The *Insnab* shops provided rationed goods for foreigners, and *Torgsin* shops catered to those who were in a position to pay in foreign currencies or precious metals. The resulting multiple-price system presented great inconveniences and was discarded after the abolition of rationing.

Foreign Trade. The monopoly of foreign trade instituted in April 1918 has been maintained since, although its organization was altered several times. The volume of foreign trade remained low. During the period before

World War II both Soviet exports and imports reached their highest point in 1930 but were still considerably below Russia's pre-war level. In the following years they declined sharply and in 1938 were, roughly, one-third of the unimpressive 1913 figures.

Cost of Planning

Investments. Industrial expansion and the re-equipment of agriculture with modern machinery require large capital investments. They amounted to 52.5 billion rubles under the first Five-Year Plan and 137.5 billion under the second; the third Five-Year Plan, which was interrupted by the war, called for a capital outlay of 181 billion rubles. The volume of investments continued to grow in the post-war era.

The Budget and the Turnover Tax. A striking feature of Soviet finance is the rate of growth of the budget. State revenue was estimated at 2 billion rubles in 1923–1924, at 8.8 billion in 1928–1929, at 25 billion in 1931, and at 156 billion in 1939. The Soviet budget comprises practically every economic activity of the nation and is not comparable with the budgets of the capitalist countries.

The chief single source of Soviet revenue is the turnover, or sales, tax, which was instituted in September 1930, simultaneously with the revised "withholding from profits" of state enterprises. No fewer than 61 separate taxes were consolidated in these two levies: 54 in the turnover tax and seven in withholding from profits. The rates of the turnover tax are set, in most cases, as a percentage of the planned transfer (or sales) price, the tax is paid by the first purchasing agency, and the proceeds are immediately turned over to the state treasury. The rates of the tax, which is levied primarily on foodstuffs and articles of general consumption, were, and still are, very high. In the 1930's, for instance, rates on bread and flour varied from 70 to 80 per cent; on meat, from 61 to 82 per cent; on salt, from 66 to 83 per cent; on cigarettes, from 75 to 90 per cent; on cottons, from 44 to 65 per cent; and so on. Withholding from profits, as its name implies, is the appropriation by the treasury of a portion of the profits of the state-owned enterprises.

Receipts from the turnover tax increased from 11.7 billion rubles in 1931 to 96.9 billion in 1939. In 1935, 1936, and 1937 they accounted for nearly 70 per cent of the total revenue; their share declined during the war but rose to about 60 per cent in the late 1940's. It was about 45 per cent in the 1950's and remained at that level in the early 1960's. The share of withholding from profits in the total revenue is much smaller: it was 6.3 per cent under the second Five-Year Plan (1932–1937) but increased to about 20 per cent in the late 1950's.

The government relies on the turnover tax rather than on the profits of nationalized enterprises, because the former offers a more flexible and dependable source of revenue. The yield of the turnover tax is determined by three factors: the volume of production, the price of the goods, and the rate of the tax. Under the Soviet planned economy all three are controlled by the state, while withholding from profits is conditioned by the fulfillment by the enterprise of the planned quotas for higher productivity and lower costs, which are often not met. A high proportion of the yield of the turnover tax comes from the sales of agricultural commodities obtained by compulsory deliveries from the collective farms, which means that industrialization and collectivization are financed largely by the peasants.

Except for the devaluation of the ruble in 1936 and post-war monetary and credit reforms, the Soviet financial system has undergone no important changes since the middle 1920's.

A Retrospect. The course of the development of the Soviet planned economy during its formative decade suggests that Soviet socialism had no easy and ready solution for the economic riddles of the modern world. To measure the economic advancement of a country merely in terms of economic growth is a common but fatal error. As it will appear from subsequent chapters, after half a century of Soviet rule, the path ahead is by no means clear.

23

The Stalin Era, 1924-1939: Foreign Relations

World Revolution and Imperial Tradition

Early Hopes. The remarkable growth of the Soviet economy noted at the beginning of the previous chapter was fully matched by and an integral element of the even more remarkable change in the position of the Soviet Union in the community of nations. The transformation did not take place at once, and the attainment by the USSR of the status of a leading world power belongs to the post-1945 era and was due largely to the disintegration, under the impact of two world wars, of the international political system inherited by the twentieth century from the nineteenth; but the foundation of the great change was laid in the 1930's.

Judged by the accepted standards of international behavior as they were understood prior to 1917, the position of Soviet Russia among the states was anomalous. The Soviets were the leaders of the international proletariat in the struggle for world revolution and, simultaneously, heirs to a great empire with far-flung interests and commitments. Conflicts inherent in this duality were not apparent at first because of the international situation and the belief that coexistence between socialism and capitalism was bound to be short-lived. As long as world war and then civil war, intervention, and the Russo-Polish war were in progress, coexistence was largely an academic issue.

In Moscow the speedy victory of Communism was taken for granted. The prevalent Bolshevik view was forcibly stated by Zinovev, president of the Communist International, in May 1919: "Old Europe is dashing at mad speed towards the proletarian revolution. . . . Separate defeats will still occur in the near future. Black will perhaps still win a victory here and there over red. But the final victory will, nevertheless, go to the red; and this in the course of the next months, perhaps even weeks. The movement is proceeding at such terrific speed that we may say with full confidence, within a year we shall already begin to forget that there was a struggle for communism in Europe, because in a year the whole of Europe will be communist. And the struggle for communism will be transferred to America, perhaps to Asia, and to other parts of the world. . . . Perhaps for a few years—and side by side with communist Europe—we shall see American capitalism continue to exist. Perhaps even in England capitalism will continue to exist for a year or two, side by side with communism, victorious in the whole of continental Europe. But such coexistence cannot last long."

These expectations were not realized. The Treaty of Brest-Litovsk was set aside by the victorious allies, the civil war was ended, foreign troops were withdrawn, and Lenin was still in the Kremlin. From the Soviet standpoint this was eminently satisfactory, but the course of events in Europe was not. The communist rule of Bela Kun in Hungary proved ephemeral, and communist outbreaks in Munich and elsewhere in Germany were inconsequential. Political revolutions in central Europe stopped short of socialist revolutions, and none came about in western European countries, to say nothing of the United States. A situation that was not foreseen arose: socialism and capitalism had to live side by side for an indefinite period. "We have learned in the course of the last three years," a chastened Lenin told the Tenth Party Congress in March 1921, "that our stake in international revolution does not mean that we expect it to materialize within a definite period of time, that the pace of development, which is growing more and more rapid, may or may not bring revolution in the spring, and that therefore we must coordinate our activities . . . in order to maintain for a protracted period the dictatorship of the proletariat. . . ." At home, this meant the New Economic Policy and, later, acceptance of Stalin's doctrine of socialism in one country. Foreign policies were adjusted to the new situation, and the "imperial" element inherent in Russia's tradition re-asserted itself in a perhaps somewhat roundabout way.

Coexistence: First Phase. The earliest moves towards the normalization of Soviet international relations were the peace treaties with the border states, formerly parts of the Russian empire—Finland, Estonia, Lithuania, Latvia, and Poland. As related in an earlier chapter, this was accomplished in a rather devious way in 1920 and 1921. Treaties establishing friendly relations with Iran, Afghanistan, and Turkey were signed in 1921. In March 1921 Great Britain concluded a trade agreement with the Soviets, the first great power to indicate an intention to resume normal relations. In April-May 1922 the Soviets participated in their first important international conference, the Genoa conference on the financial and economic restoration of Europe. The results were negative, except that Germany and Soviet Russia negotiated in April 1922 at nearby Rapallo a treaty that stipulated close political and economic relations between the two countries. At the end of 1922 the Soviets were represented at the Lausanne conference, which prepared the convention of July 1923 regulating the regime of the Turkish Straits. In 1924 the Soviet Union was recognized *de jure* by Great Britain, Italy, Greece, Sweden, Norway, France, and several other countries.

The principles of Soviet foreign economic policy resulting from the institution of planned economy were formulated in a resolution of the Fifteenth Party Congress in December 1927: "We must base our policy on the idea of the maximum development of our economic relations with foreign countries, in so far as such relations (expansion of foreign trade, foreign credits, concessions, employment of foreign technical advisers, and so on) contribute to the economic strength of the nation. We must make it more independent of the capitalist world, and broaden the socialist foundation for further industrial expansion of the union." The implementation of these directives led to a great outburst of diplomatic activity. According to one estimate, Soviet Russia between 1920 and 1937 concluded 237 bilateral agreements and became party to 57 international conventions. Soviet foreign ministers took an increasingly prominent part in world affairs. From October 1917 to the outbreak of World War II Soviet Russia had four people's commissars for foreign affairs: Trotsky, October 1917 to March 1918; George Chicherin, 1918 to 1930; Maxim Litvinov, 1930 to May 1939; Viacheslav Molotov, 1939 to 1949. Chicherin came from an aristocratic family and had served briefly in the imperial foreign office before emigrating to England in 1907. His successor, Litvinov, was Jewish, an old Bolshevik like Chicherin, and one of the most loquacious protagonists of collective security at the League of Nations in the 1930's. His resignation was rightly interpreted abroad as a sign of Soviet-German *rapprochement*. Litvinov was an active and influential Soviet diplomat in the 1920's, that is, before he became head of the foreign office.

A serious setback to Soviet relations with the West was the British police raid on Arcos, the Soviet trade agency in London, which led to the severance of Anglo-Soviet diplomatic relations from May 1927 to October 1929.

The Comintern. In spite of the reappearance of Russia, in a new guise, as a full member of the circle of great powers, and the plethora of non-aggression pacts, friendship treaties, and commercial agreements to which she became party, world revolution remained the immutable ultimate objective of her policy. The direction of the world-wide revolutionary movement was nominally in the hands of the Third (Communist) International, or Comintern, which, in theory, was independent of the Moscow government. The First International, a revolutionary workingmen's association, was founded by Marx and Engels in 1864 and dissolved in 1872; the Second International, established in 1889, was controlled by moderate socialists and was repudiated by the Communists. Lenin demanded the creation of a communist international in his *April Theses,* and the announcement of the convocation of its inaugural congress was issued under his and Trotsky's signatures in January 1919. The congress, which met in Moscow in March, was attended by 35 voting and 19 non-voting delegates. Only five of the members came specially from abroad: the international communist movement was still in an embryonic stage, and the obstacles in the path of those who wished to travel to Russia were great. The congress formally constituted the Comintern (March 4, 1919) and elected Zinovev its president. The Second Congress, attended by over 200 delegates from 41 countries, convened in Moscow in the summer of 1920. It adopted the statutes of the Comintern which stipulated a high degree of integration of the communist movement. There was to be "a single communist party of the entire world," the national parties were to be sections of the International, and their object was "to struggle by all available means, including armed force, for the overthrow of the international *bourgeoisie* and the creation of an international Soviet republic as a transition stage to the complete abolition of the state." A manifesto issued by the Second Congress proclaimed that "the international proletariat will not lay down its sword until Soviet Russia has become a link in the federation of Soviet republics of the world."

The policies of the Third International, its pretenses at independence notwithstanding, reflected closely the view of the Soviet government. While the notion of world revolution dominated Soviet thought, congresses of the International met annually, from 1919 to 1922. The Fifth Congress convened in 1924, the Sixth in 1928, and the Seventh and last in 1935. In the meantime Zinovev, having fallen from grace, was removed from the leadership of the

Comintern in 1926, and the post of president was abolished. Trotskyism became the chief heresy. The Sixth Congress of the International, held in 1928, approved as its program one which was prepared by Stalin and Bukharin, who 10 years later was to be executed during the great purge. In conformity with the Soviet policy of coexistence, the program emphasized the duty of the international proletariat to defend the USSR against "capitalist aggression," a surprising shift for an institution dedicated to the advancement of world revolution. On the question of united front policies, as on other matters, the attitude of the International duplicated the devious course of the Kremlin. Throughout the 1930's international communism made little progress, and "the general staff of the world revolution," as the Comintern was occasionally called, led the obscure existence of a minor government department, toeing the line of the Soviet Communist Party. When during World War II it became clear that the very presence in Moscow of an institution whose avowed object was the overthrow of the capitalist system was a source of friction with the Western allies, the International was summarily dissolved. This purely institutional change was in no way a repudiation of world revolution, even though public opinion in the West inclined at the time (1943) to take the view that it was.

Colonial Countries and the Far East

Congress of the Eastern Peoples. Colonial and semi-colonial countries occupy a decisive place in the Communist scheme of the breakdown of imperialism. Lenin held that the weakest link of the capitalist chain was in the colonies, where socialist revolutions evolve naturally from uprisings against foreign oppressors. "Geographically," Zinovev wrote in May 1919, "the proletarian revolution moves from east to west. This trend . . . is now definitely established." Fostering colonial revolution was a major activity of the Third International. "Colonial slaves of Asia and Africa," said a manifesto of the First Congress of the Comintern, "the hour of the proletarian dictatorship in Europe is also the hour of your liberation." To prove that these were no empty promises, the Soviet government notified Iran in June 1919 that it had cancelled all Iranian debts to the Russian imperial government, voided Russian concessions, and transferred to the Iranian people the Russian Bank in Persia, along with railroads, electric power stations, and the like. Capitulations were abolished. Similar policies were adopted with reference to other Asiatic countries in which imperial Russia had special rights. These moves were preparatory to the launching of a major

Communist offensive against colonialism and imperialism at the first congress of the Eastern peoples.

The congress was convened by the executive committee of the Comintern in Baku in September 1920. It was a huge ill-assorted assembly of nearly 2,000 delegates. Of this number over 200 were Turks, nearly 200 Persians, eight Chinese, eight Kurds, and three Arabs; the balance, that is, the vast majority, came from Russian central Asia and the Caucasus. Although most delegates claimed to be Communists, their actual party allegiance was in many cases uncertain. An unexpectedly much-feted delegate was Enver Pasha, one of the architects of the Turkish national revolution and of the Armenian massacres: Armenians were represented by a large delegation. The congress accomplished little of immediate consequence, except perhaps to demonstrate once more that Western and Eastern revolutionaries—a term that did not apply to many delegates—were far apart in their outlook and aspirations; it also appointed a "council of propaganda and action," which was to function in Baku and began publishing a journal. Both the council and the journal disappeared in 1921.

No second congress of the Eastern peoples was ever held, but a congress of "the toilers of the Far East," organized by the executive committee of the Comintern, met in Moscow in January 1922. This was a much smaller gathering than the Baku congress, and its resolutions did not carry much weight. In connection with the two congresses, however, concrete steps were taken to advance revolution in Eastern countries. In April 1921 a Communist University of the Toilers of the East was founded in Moscow. Instruction was offered in native languages, and by the end of the first year it had reportedly 700 students of nearly 60 nationalities. The Japanese delegates to the 1922 congress returned home with funds and instructions for the establishment of the Japanese Communist Party, which was duly founded in July 1922. These were developments pregnant with consequences for the future.

"If Marx said once that a European revolution without England would be merely a tempest in a teacup," Zinovev, who presided at both congresses, told a Halle audience in October 1920, "then I will tell you . . . that a proletarian revolution without Asia will not be a world revolution. . . . At the Baku congress we discovered . . . what is essential to the realization of world revolution. The oppressed masses of Asia must awaken. . . . I must make a confession: when I beheld in Baku hundreds of Persians and Turks joining us in singing 'The International,' I felt my eyes fill with tears and I recognized the breathing of the world revolution."

This is a romantic and exaggerated statement, yet the disintegration of the colonial empires and the inroads of Communism in the underdeveloped countries are parts of the record since World War II.

The Soviets and China. Soviet relations with China, Russia's great Far Eastern neighbor, went through a remarkable transformation. The state of turmoil prevailing in China and in the Far East until the end of the Russian civil war subsided by 1921. Sun Yat-sen, the "grand old man" of the Chinese revolution (1911), although not a Marxist, was an admirer of the Russian revolution and of Lenin's authoritarian methods. In July 1919 the Soviet government solemnly renounced all acquisitions of Chinese territories made by its predecessors and all extra-territorial rights and other privileges and declared null and void all "unequal" treaties concluded by the two countries. The declaration, which referred specifically to Manchuria and the Chinese Eastern Railway, was given an enthusiastic reception in China. The Peking government announced the resumption of control of the Chinese Eastern Railway, but this decision was not actually enforced. Outer Mongolia, which since 1915 was a Russian protectorate, reverted to Chinese rule in 1919. With the termination of the civil war, Soviet troops returned in force to these regions; Outer Mongolia was overrun by the Red Army, and a Mongolian People's Republic was set up in 1921, which concluded with Soviet Russia treaties that brought Mongolia under the total domination of Moscow (November 1921 and May 1922). This was the return to a relationship that had obtained in the closing years of the empire.

The Chinese Communist Party, founded in 1920, was small, weak, and inexperienced. In May 1921 Sun Yat-sen was installed in Canton as president of the still-disunited Chinese republic. Stalin and Bukharin (who was then Stalin's close adviser) decreed a policy of cooperation between the Chinese Communists and the nationalist Kuomintang Party, which was led by Sun Yat-sen and later, after his death in March 1925, by Chiang Kai-shek, who had studied at the Moscow military academy. At Sun's request a large group of Russian political and military advisers came to China. It was headed by Ioffe and then by L. M. Karakhan and included M. M. Borodin and General (later Marshal) V. K. Blücher (Galen). The policy of supporting Chinese nationalism and resisting sovietization of China was criticized by Trotsky and Zinovev as treason to the revolution, but for a time it worked well and Borodin's influence in China was paramount.

After the death of Sun Yat-sen, however, the situation changed. The Chinese Communists became restless and unmanageable. There were serious clashes between them and the Kuomintang, and in April 1927 Chiang Kai-shek carried out a drastic purge of his recalcitrant allies. In May the Chinese police raided the Soviet Embassy in Peking, as well as Soviet missions in Shanghai and Canton. Chiang dismissed his Russian advisers, and in 1927 the Soviet government broke diplomatic relations with China. Further complications arose in connection with the Chinese raid on the Soviet consulate in Harbin in the spring of 1929 and the arrest of the Russian employees of the Chinese Eastern Railway, but this matter was settled by negotiations before the end of the year. In 1931, with the connivance of the Comintern, a Chinese Soviet government was formed in the province of Kiangsi; the Chinese civil war was not far off.

Meanwhile the Japanese infiltrated Manchuria and at the end of 1931 landed troops in the north and, early in 1932, in the Shanghai region, where some spirited fighting took place. In March 1932 they established the "independent" state of Manchukuo. Faced with new perils, nationalist China and the Soviet Union patched up their differences, resumed diplomatic relations in December 1932, and concluded a non-aggression pact in August 1937. The Kremlin appeared to be anxious to prevent war in the Far East. It made diplomatic overtures, including offers of a non-aggression treaty, to Tokyo and after lengthy negotiations sold the Chinese Eastern Railway to Japanese interests (March 1935). The low price, representing but one-eighth of the cost of construction, was interpreted by some as a sign of weakness on the part of the USSR. Other observers, however, took the view that the Chinese Eastern Railway was useless in time of war and had become a "wasting asset" in time of peace, and that the Kremlin acted wisely in disposing of it.

Rapprochement with the West

Collective Security. The conciliatory spirit displayed by the Soviet Union in the 1930's in the Far East was also in evidence in her Western policy. The quest for security, the main theme of Soviet diplomacy in the later 1920's and 1930's, was the consequence of the failure of the international revolution and of the importance attached by Moscow to the uninterrupted growth of its planned economy. The purpose of the policy of the "united front" and, later, of the "popular front" was to combat "capitalist aggression," war, and —after Hitler's advent to power—fascism. "All the key problems of this movement," D. Z. Manuilsky told the Seventh Congress of the Comintern in 1935, "revolve around this central axis—the strengthening of the USSR as the base of the world proletarian revolution." This reformulation of the

Comintern 1928 program neatly integrated the two basic elements of Soviet policy—national and revolutionary; protection and strengthening of the USSR were a simultaneous advancement of the world revolution.

The cornerstone of the elaborate structure of non-aggression treaties erected by Litvinov was the Briand-Kellogg Pact (August 27, 1928) outlawing war—not perhaps very effectively—as an instrument of national policy. The Soviet Union had no part in negotiating the pact and was not among its original signatories, but acceded eagerly (September 6, 1928) when invited to do so. The earliest Soviet non-aggression treaties were concluded before that date: with Turkey in 1925, with Lithuania and Germany in 1926, and with Iran in 1927. The Kremlin was anxious to have non-aggression agreements with the border states, ostensibly to prevent them from joining a political combination hostile to the USSR, as it was at times rumored they might do. The negotiations proved long-drawn and laborious, because Russia's Western neighbors were suspicious, not without reason, as the events of 1939 were to show, of the Soviets' true intentions. Litvinov, however, was tireless and had it largely his own way. The Soviet Union concluded non-aggression pacts with Afghanistan in 1931, with Finland, Latvia, Estonia, Poland, and France in 1932, with Italy in 1933, and with China in 1937. There were several additional conventions stipulating conciliatory procedure.

In dealing with non-aggression Litvinov displayed great resourcefulness. In May 1931 he submitted to the Commission of Inquiry for European Union the draft of a pact of economic non-aggression, but no action was taken on it. In February 1933 he proposed to the disarmament conference in Geneva a new definition of aggression that *Izvestia* described as "the people's charter of rights to security and independence" and that prohibited not only "intervention in a country where there is a revolution, but in the name of the USSR undertook the obligation not to intervene in a country where there is a counter-revolution." This surprising renunciation by the Soviets of their revolutionary birthright was embodied in conventions concluded in July 1933 by the USSR with Afghanistan, Estonia, Latvia, Iran, Poland, Rumania, Turkey, Czechoslovakia, Yugoslavia, Lithuania, and Finland. Good care was taken to renew the various non-aggression treaties before expiration. They were all in force in 1939 and 1940, when Stalin and Hitler partitioned Poland, and the Soviet Union absorbed the Baltic states, attacked Finland, and wangled Bessarabia and Northern Bukovina from Rumania. Few, however, could have foreseen these developments in the early 1930's. The Soviet drive for collective security reached its zenith in the mutual assistance pacts with France and Czechoslovakia, both concluded in May 1935. The two pacts were similar except that the one with Czechoslovakia stipulated that provisions for mutual assistance were binding only if France gave assistance to the country attacked. When the fate of Czechoslovakia was decided in Munich in September 1938, France acquiesced in the partition of that country, and the USSR, which was not represented at Munich, did not budge.

Another aspect of the Soviet policy of collective security was the abandonment of the "united front," which meant joint action by socialists, in favor of the "people's front" or "popular front" that would comprise all elements opposed to war and fascism, irrespective of class distinctions and political allegiance. The popular front approach was adopted by the Seventh Congress of the Comintern in 1935.

Recognition by the United States. Recognition by the United States and admission to the League of Nations were elements in Moscow's policy of collective security. Desire for recognition by the United States was often voiced by Soviet leaders, but no progress was made. The American government and a large section of American opinion were repelled by the Communist doctrine, outraged by propaganda for the overthrow of American institutions, and resentful of the repudiation by the Kremlin of the obligations of its predecessors and refusal to compensate American citizens for the confiscation of their property. Negotiations with Russia's European creditors were instituted in the early 1920's but were soon broken off. While denying in principle the responsibility of a revolutionary government for the obligations incurred by the fallen regime, the Soviets agreed to discuss foreign claims bearing on the "public debt," provided "damages caused to Russia by allied intervention and blockade were recognized." The Kremlin, however, expressed its willingness to waive these counter-claims (which were quite exorbitant) in exchange for "real credits" to be placed at its disposal by the creditor powers (note of May 11, 1922). This approach offered no ground for settlement. The United States government was aware of the Soviet position and saw little practical advantage in recognition, especially because the pre-war Russo-American trade was small and the outlook for its expansion under conditions prevailing in Russia in the 1920's unpromising.

The depression of 1929, the real and rumored recovery of the Soviet Union, its recognition by the major powers, and the inherent awkwardness of the policy of non-recognition, as well as the pressure of business interests which believed in dealing with the Soviets, led to a change in American attitude. President F. D. Roosevelt favored recognition, Litvinov came to the

United States, the Soviets were officially recognized on November 16, 1933, and diplomatic relations between Washington and Moscow established. Two conditions were attached to American recognition. Litvinov formally promised the President that it would be "the fixed policy" of the USSR not to permit the formation, residence or activity on its territory "of any organization or group" which aimed at "bringing about by force a change in the political or social order . . . of the United States." This was an unmistakable reference to the Comintern. The second condition bore on negotiations for "settling all outstanding questions of indebtedness and claims." Litvinov formally expressed the hope "for the speedy and satisfactory solution of these questions . . . as soon as possible." Neither promise was fulfilled. The Communist International continued to function in Moscow, where its Seventh Congress was held in 1935. Conversations about claims dragged on for a year but in February 1935 the State Department announced that "negotiations which seemed so promising . . . must now be regarded as having come to an end." They were never resumed.

The Soviet and the League of Nations. The dual character of Soviet foreign policy was apparent in the attitude of Moscow towards the League of Nations. The 1919 program of the Communist Party, which remained in force until 1961, described the League as an "international organization of capitalists for the systematic exploitation of all the peoples of the earth and whose immediate efforts are directed to the suppression of revolutionary movements in every country." Although this ungenerous characterization was echoed by Soviet leaders, the Kremlin missed no opportunity at being represented in various commissions and conferences at Geneva, where Litvinov became a familiar figure. Events in the Far East and in Europe favored a measure of cooperation between the Soviets and the Western powers. In March 1933 Japan withdrew from the League of Nations. Hitler came to power in January 1933, and in October Germany, too, left the League. Japanese expansion in Manchuria alarmed the Soviet Union, and Hitler was militantly anti-Communist. Yet there was another side to the picture. Past experiences suggested that an accommodation between Russia and Japan in Manchuria was not precluded, and there were disturbing memories of the Soviet-German Rapallo pact (1922), which resulted in close cooperation between the Red Army and the Reichswehr, allowing the Germans to obviate the restrictive provisions of the Versailles treaty, especially in training pilots and tank crews. Whatever the reasons, Litvinov's discreet feelers this time met with ready response. The Soviet Union was invited to join the League of Nations and on September 18, 1934, was admitted as a member, with a permanent seat on the council. The final vote was 39 for, 3 against (Switzerland, Holland, and Poland), with 7 abstentions. During the next four and a half years Litvinov spoke at the League more frequently and at greater length than any other delegate. Torrents of words, however, brought no meeting of minds. Litvinov was dismissed as people's commissar for foreign affairs in May 1939, and at the end of that year the Soviet Union, then a partner of National-Socialist Germany, was expelled from the League after attacking Finland.

Years of Crisis, 1934–1938

Abyssinia, Turkey, and Spain. The five years following the admission of the Soviet Union to the League of Nations were replete with dramatic international happenings in which the Kremlin was directly or indirectly involved. The Italo-Abyssinian war, begun in October 1935, led the League of Nations to impose economic sanctions on Italy (November 1935). This unprecedented action was not uniformly popular with public opinion in the Western countries, especially with the business community. Although oil was not on the list of embargoed goods (partly because the decisions of the League were not binding on the United States, a large oil producer), massive shipments of oil by the Soviet Union to Italy were criticized as a violation of the policy of collective security: it was argued that, while Litvinov in Geneva denounced Italian aggression, Soviet oil kept Mussolini's troops and supplies moving to Africa. Thus an issue on which the West and the Soviet Union were basically in agreement—condemnation of Italian aggression in Abyssinia—created nevertheless tension and estrangement.

Soviet-Turkish relations were friendly but tended to become less intimate in the 1930's in spite of the revision of the Straits regime of which both countries approved. The Lausanne convention of 1923 provided for the demilitarization of the shores of the Bosphorus and the Dardanelles, the unimpeded circulation of merchant vessels through the Straits, and the freedom of passage for warships without distinction of flag, under certain restrictive conditions detrimental to the interests and security of the Black Sea riparian powers, that is, primarily the Soviet Union. The supervision of the application of this regime was entrusted to an International Straits Commission composed of representatives of the signatory states and responsible to the League of Nations. The Lausanne convention was a compromise between the Soviets, seeking preferential treatment, and Great Britain, demanding complete freedom of navigation. Chicherin disapproved of the convention; it was signed by Russia after a delay of three weeks and was never ratified.

The initiative for the revision of the Lausanne convention came in April 1936 from Turkey, which in the meantime had drawn closer to the Western powers and in 1932 was admitted to the League of Nations. The conference met at Montreux, Switzerland, in June 1936, and the new convention was signed in July. Again, as at Lausanne, the chief argument was between the Russians and the British. The Montreux convention altered materially the regime of the Straits. The demilitarization clauses were dropped, the International Straits Commission was abolished, and Turkey was given a large measure of control over the Dardanelles and the Bosphorus. The Black Sea powers, which in practice meant the Soviet Union, secured the right of unlimited egress for their warships to the Mediterranean, something for which Russian statesmen had been battling for over a century. The right of the non-riparian powers to enter the Black Sea continued to be restricted, although the rules of the Lausanne convention were revised. The Soviets had all reasons to be pleased: under the Montreux regime the Black Sea was controlled by the Russian fleet, as Russia acquired the freedom to send her warships through the Straits as she pleased and was protected against the possibility of a superior enemy force pursuing her into the Black Sea or threatening her southern shores. The 1936 convention, a compromise like its predecessor between the British and the Russian view, strengthened the position of the USSR as long as it continued to maintain friendly relations with Turkey.

The civil war in Spain broke out in July 1936. Since the establishment of a republic in 1931, the political situation in that country had been turbulent and confused. The left-wing parties included a large segment of anarchists and syndicalists and were in a state of continuous turmoil. The banner of revolt was raised by the conservative elements, led at first by General Sanjurjo and, after his death in an airplane accident at the beginning of the insurrection, by General Francisco Franco. A popular front republican government under Largo Caballero was formed in September—not without the encouragement of the Comintern. Fearing that the Spanish civil war might engulf other European countries, England and France (which, curiously, had herself a popular front government under Leon Blum) decided on a policy of non-intervention. An international Non-Intervention Committee was formed in London in September 1936 and was joined by the fascist powers—Germany and Italy—as well as by the Soviet Union. In spite of this official espousal of non-intervention, men ("volunteers") and supplies were poured into Franco's Spain by Germany and Italy. The Soviet Union denounced Hitler and Mussolini for violating their pledges, but itself shipped large quantities of war materials to the Spanish loyalists. The Comintern organized the International Brigade, which fought in Spain for the republic; no Russians, however, served in its ranks, and seemingly no Russian troops were used in Spain. The Soviet representative on the Non-Intervention Committee was not recalled until March 1, 1939, about three weeks before the formal termination of the Spanish civil war. The true purpose of Soviet intervention in Spain is not known and can be only surmised. It is understandable that the Kremlin should wish to prevent the establishment of fascism in Spain, but it is also likely that the enticing possibility of a Communist regime emerging from the turmoil of the civil war was not overlooked.

Germany: What Next? From the advent of national socialism to the outbreak of World War II the European scene was overshadowed by Hitler's ominous and peremptory moves. In October 1933 Germany left the League of Nations; in March 1935 came the repudiation of the disarmament provisions of the Treaty of Versailles; in March 1936, the re-occupation of the demilitarized zone of the Rhineland; in March 1938, the absorption of Austria; in September 1938, the Munich agreement and the annexation of the Sudetenland; in March 1939, the final dismemberment of Czechoslovakia and the establishment of German protectorates over Bohemia, Moravia, and Slovakia; and a few days later, the forced surrender of Memel by Lithuania. The Berlin-Rome Axis, an Italo-German alignment for the coordination of their anti-Communist policies, was created in October 1936. A month later (November 1936) a similar agreement, known as the Anti-Comintern Pact, was concluded by Germany and Japan; Italy acceded to it in November 1937, and Hungary in March 1939. The formation of the Rome-Berlin-Tokyo Axis was a matter of real concern to the USSR, especially in view of the clashes between Soviet and Japanese troops on the Manchurian and Mongolian borders in 1938 and 1939, even though their importance has been greatly overstated.

Both the West and the Soviet Union were at a loss how to deal with the unfamiliar and explosive phenomenon of fascism. The guiding motives of the Western powers are reasonably clear: ardent desire for peace and unwillingness to face the dreaded alternative of war. In London and Paris many came to feel that an arrangement with Moscow was essential in order to face the common menace, but others wondered whether the Soviet Union was a dependable partner in the quest for peace. The Comintern, rickety and ineffectual as it was, was a constant reminder that bourgeois Europe and Communist Russia, in their aspirations and objectives, were poles apart. The horrifying spectacle of the purges could not but raise grave doubts as to the soundness of the entire Soviet system, including the Red Army, which had just been shorn of a host of its commanding officers. This might well have been one of the reasons Moscow was not invited to Munich. The policy of the West failed, and "appeasement" has gone down in history as a term of opprobrium. Since the wheel of history cannot be turned back, the answer to the question whether any other approach to Hitler and Stalin would have been more successful must remain conjectural.

It is more difficult to obtain a picture of the real motivations of the Soviet leaders. They, too, wanted peace, but the Communism of the 1930's held fast to the theory that capitalism inexorably leads to war and that peace and capitalism are incompatible. Not all highly-placed Russian Communists thought in these terms, but some—we do not know how many—did. These uncertainties make the interpretation of the motives of Soviet policies difficult and unrewarding.

The Soviets Switch to Germany

Negotiations with the West. The rearmament of Germany, her unchecked territorial expansion (absorption of Austria, Czechoslovakia, and Memel), victories of fascism in Abyssinia and Spain, and the impetuous demands of the fascist powers for a place in the colonial sun—these shattered, or at least weakened, the illusions and optimism of those who trusted Hitler's reasonableness or the efficacy of collective security. Slowly and reluctantly, Western statesmen came to the tentative conclusion that an understanding with the Soviets was essential if fascist inroads were to be kept within bounds. In the middle of March 1939, immediately after the Czechoslovak *putsch,* Great Britain proposed to the Soviet Union a formal declaration by four powers (Great Britain, France, the USSR, and Poland) to the effect that they would immediately enter into consultations on any measures required to meet a threat to European peace and security. There followed conversations between England and France, on the one hand, and the Soviet Union, on the other, bearing on trade, political, and military matters. William Strang, of the London foreign office, was sent to the USSR in June, and an Anglo-French military mission reached Moscow on August 11. In the meantime, at the end of March, Great Britain gave Poland the assurance of support if the independence of that country was threatened. On

August 25, 1939, at the height of the crisis provoked by the Soviet-German pact, the "assurance" was converted into a mutual assistance treaty, which, however, did not save Poland from invasion a few days later by German and then by Russian troops.

The Anglo-French-Russian negotiations were barren of results. Formally the stumbling block was the refusal (mitigated at a later stage) of Poland and the Baltic states to authorize the passage of Soviet troops through their territory. The USSR had no common border with Germany, and the request for the right of passage was in itself reasonable, if Soviet military aid was to be made effective. But the Soviet record, policies, and doctrines being what they were, it was understandable that the border states dreaded their would-be defenders even more than they dreaded the potential assailants. The true reason for the breakdown of the negotiations was the Kremlin's decision to side with Germany, which was arrived at independently of the attitude of the border states.

The Soviet-German Pact. In spite of the seemingly irreconcilable hostility between fascism and Communism, the possibility of a Hitler-Stalin understanding had long been rumored. Abortive negotiations for a Soviet-German trade agreement were carried on in the spring and autumn of 1938 and again in the spring of 1939. The turning point in the relations of the two countries was the dismissal of Litvinov (May 3, 1939) and the appointment of Molotov, who retained the chairmanship of the Council of People's Commissars, as his successor. As a Jew and ostensibly a League of Nations man, Litvinov would be a poor choice for delicate confidential conversations with Ribbentrop and Hitler. Political negotiations between Berlin and Moscow began probably in the early summer of 1939 and were conducted in great secrecy simultaneously with those with France and Great Britain.

The Germans succeeded where the British and the French failed. A commercial agreement providing for a credit of 200 million marks for the Soviet Union was signed on August 19. At Hitler's request and with the permission of Stalin, Ribbentrop, the Reich foreign minister, flew to Moscow and on the same day (August 23, 1939) concluded with Molotov a treaty in which each government pledged itself not to attack, and not to support any attack against, the other contracting party, as well as to consult the other on all questions of common interest. A secret additional protocol dealt with the partition of the border states. Finland, Estonia, Latvia, and eastern Poland were assigned to the Russian "sphere of influence"; western Poland and Lithuania to the German. Germany disclaimed any interest in the fate of Bessarabia, which the Soviet Union wished to annex. Whether there

The Nazi-Soviet Pact, August 1939

should be "an independent Polish state" was to be determined "in the course of future political developments." The treaty would go into force "as soon as it is signed." The protocol explains the reason for Germany's success in Moscow. Great Britain and France lost not because their negotiators were not of ministerial rank, as is often suggested, but because no British or French government could have surrendered to the mercy of Stalin a half dozen independent states. The protocol also throws much light on what non-aggression, so eloquently extolled by Litvinov at Geneva, actually meant to the Kremlin.

The Soviet-German pact was the curtain-raiser of World War II. On September 1, 1939, German troops invaded Poland, and on September 3 England and France severed diplomatic relations with Germany. The war had begun.

What made Stalin enter into a partnership with Hitler? The answer to this question, as to practically all questions bearing on major Soviet issues, is speculative. The motives of the Kremlin were probably mixed: lack of confidence in the Western powers; fear of Germany; search for security in the traditional meaning of the term; crude nationalistic longing for the territories severed from Russia in 1917–1918; messianic zeal for spreading Communism in the annexed territories; security in the Communist meaning of the term—by eliminating the capitalist environment. Moreover, the pact made war practically a certainty, and revolutions, according to Lenin, grow out of wars. It has been claimed that the Stalin-Hitler pact, by postponing war with Germany, gained for the Soviet Union a much-needed breathing spell to prepare itself for the coming struggle. However, had Hitler been confronted from the very beginning with a war on two fronts, its character and course would probably have been very different from what they were, and the Soviet Union might have been saved a terrible ordeal.

PART SIX

March 1939-1968

CHRONOLOGY OF PRINCIPAL EVENTS

1940	August	Trotsky murdered in Mexico City
"	August	Lithuania, Latvia, and Estonia incorporated into the USSR
"	October 2	Tuition fees imposed in higher schools and the upper grades of secondary schools
"	October 2	Institution of labor reserves
1941		*Alexander Nevsky,* film produced by Eisenstein
"	February	Security police put under people's commissariat of state security (NKGB)
"	May	Stalin becomes chairman of the Council of People's Commissars
"	June 22	Hitler invades Russia
"	June 22–27	Italy, Rumania, Slovakia, Finland, and Hungary declare war on the Soviet Union
1941, June–1942, December		Germans advance into Russia, reaching the Caucasus
"	June 30	State Defense Committee, under Stalin, appointed
" June–1947, December		Rationing of foodstuffs and consumer goods
"	July	Stalin assumes office of people's commissar for defense
"	July 12	Anglo-Soviet mutual assistance pact
"	July 30	Soviets recognize Polish government-in-exile
"	September	Moscow subscribes to the Atlantic Charter
"	November	Germans fail to take Moscow
1942	May 26	Anglo-Soviet treaty of alliance
"	August	Churchill visits Moscow
" August–1943, February		Battle of Stalingrad
"	November	Farthest line of German penetration
	1943–1944	Dissolution of Kalmyk, Tatar, and other national republics on the ground of disloyalty
1943	January 31	von Paulus surrenders
"	March	Stalin created a marshal
"	April	Katyn massacres (1939) of Polish officers disclosed; Soviets break relations with Polish government-in-exile
"	May	Third International dissolved
"	July–August	Last major German offensive, region of Kursk
"	September	Sergius elected patriarch
"	October	Council on the affairs of the Church established
"	November	Kiev retaken by Soviets
"	November 28–	
	December 1	Teheran conference

1944	January–February	Leningrad region retaken
"	February 1	Constituent republics empowered to conduct foreign affairs and maintain armed forces
"	May	Alexis elected patriarch
"	July	Moscow recognizes Polish National Committee (Lublin) as government of Poland
"	July 8	Bonuses and decorations for mothers of large families
"	August	Soviet troops enter Poland and Rumania
"	autumn	Baltic littoral reconquered
"	September	Finland withdraws from the war
1945		*Ivan the Terrible,* Part I, film produced by Eisenstein
"	February 7–12	Yalta conference
"	April–June	Molotov at San Francisco conference, which prepares the charter of the United Nations
"	April 25	American and Soviet army units meet at Torgau, Germany
"	May 2	Soviet troops enter Berlin
"	May 8	Soviet troops enter Prague
"	June	Stalin created generalissimo
"	July 17–August 2	Potsdam conference
"	August 8–September 2	Soviet-Japanese war
"	August	Soviet treaty of friendship with the Kuomintang
"	September	State Defense Committee disbanded
1946	January–1950, December	Fourth Five-Year Plan
1946	March	People's commissariats renamed ministries
1946	September 19	Decree criticizing conditions on collective farms
	1947–1949	Imposition of Communist governments on Poland, Rumania, Bulgaria, Hungary, Czechoslovakia, and Albania
1947	February 10	Peace treaties with former enemy countries (except Germany, Austria, and Japan)
"	May	Capital punishment abolished
"	September	Cominform (Communist Information Bureau) established
"	December 14	Revaluation of the ruble; abolition of rationing
"	December 17	Decree imposing restrictions on relations with foreigners
1948	March	Soviets withdraw from Allied Control Council in Berlin

1948	June–1949, May	Berlin blockade
1949		Kamerny Theatre closed
"	January	Council for Economic Mutual Assistance (Comecon) formed
"	September	Moscow launches World Peace Movement
"	September 23	Soviets explode first atomic bomb
"	October	Eastern Germany becomes a democratic republic
"	October	Chinese Communist republic recognized by Soviets
1950	January	Capital punishment restored
"	February	Treaty of friendship with Communist China
"	April	Amalgamation of collective farms begins
"	June–1951, June	Korean war
1951	January,–1955, December	Fifth Five-Year Plan
	1952, October 5–14	Nineteenth Party Congress; Politburo replaced by enlarged presidium of the central committee
1953		Beginnings of Soviet assistance to underdeveloped countries
"		Drive for the development of virgin lands
"	March 5	Stalin dies
"	March 7	Malenkov succeeds Stalin
"	March 15	Malenkov released from position of party secretary; succeeded by Khrushchev
"	June	Anti-Communist riots in eastern Germany
"	July 10	Beria arrested
"	August	First Soviet hydrogen bomb exploded
"	September	Khrushchev appointed first secretary of party central committee
"	December	Trial, confession, and execution of Beria announced
1954		*The Thaw,* novel by Ehrenburg
"	March	Security police put under Committee of State Security (KGB)
"	October	Port Arthur returned to China
	1955–1956	Soviet economic and political assistance to Egypt
1955	February 8	Malenkov relieved of duties as chairman of the Council of Ministers; succeeded by Bulganin
"	May 14	Warsaw pact
"	May 15	Peace treaty with Austria
"	September	Soviets agree to return Porkkala base to Finland; actual surrender, January 1956
	1955, September	Relations with the Federal Republic of Western Germany established

	1956–1957	National republics dissolved in 1943–1944 restored
	1956, January– 1958, December	Sixth Five-Year Plan (discontinued)
1956	February 14–26	Twentieth Party Congress; Khrushchev exposes Stalin
"	April	Bulganin and Khrushchev visit England
"	April	Cominform dissolved
"	June 10	Tuition fees in schools abolished
"	June 26	Attachment of workers to jobs terminated
"	July 14	Old age and disability pensions and health insurance revised
"	July	Karelo-Finnish SSR reduced to status of autonomous republic; number of constituent republics declines from 16 to 15
"	summer	Soviet literary magazine rejects Pasternak's *Doctor Zhivago*
"	summer–autumn	Anti-Communist disturbances in Poland
"	October–November	Uprising in Hungary suppressed by Soviet army
"	December	Relations with Japan resumed
1957		Revaluation of the ruble; "tourist" ruble introduced
"		*Not by Bread Alone,* novel by Dudintsev
"	May 10	Economic administrative regions created; industrial federal ministries abolished
1957	spring	Compulsory subscription to state loans discontinued; payment of interest and redemption service on state loans suspended
"	June 29	"Anti-party group"—Malenkov, Kaganovich, Molotov, Shepilov—denounced by central committee
"	October	Sputnik I launched
"	October	Zhukov linked to "anti-party group" and demoted
"	November	Sputnik II, carrying dog, launched
1958		*The Cranes Are Flying,* film produced by Kalatozov
"		*Doctor Zhivago,* published abroad in 1957; Pasternak awarded 1958 Nobel prize but declines the award
"	March 31	Machine Tractor Stations abolished
"	March	Bulganin dismissed as chairman of Council of Ministers; succeeded by Khrushchev
"	December	Bulganin linked to "anti-party group"
"	December 28	Law of "Strengthening Ties Between School and Life"

	1958–1965	Seven-Year Plan
1959		Soviets support Cuban revolution
"	January–February	Twenty-first Party Congress
"	September	Khrushchev visits United States
1960	May 7	7-hour day reintroduced
"	May	U-2 incident
"	September–October	Khrushchev visits United States
1961	January	Revaluation of the ruble
	Spring	Economic administrative regions grouped into 17 major regions
"	April	Vostok I, carrying Gagarin, launched
"	April	State Committee for Coordination of Research formed
"	June 3–4	President Kennedy meets Khrushchev in Vienna
"	August	Vostok II, carrying Titov, launched
"	August 13	Berlin Wall inaugurated
"	October	Twenty-second Party Congress; new party statutes and program adopted
1962	August 11	Vostok III, carrying Andrian Nikolaev, made 63 orbits
"	August 12	Vostok IV, carrying Pavel Popovich, made 48 orbits
"	October	Crisis in Soviet-American relations over Cuba
"	"	"One Day in the Life of Ivan Denisovich," by Solzhenitsyn
	1962–1963	Socialist realism reasserted by Khrushchev
1963	February	Economic administrative regions reorganized into 47 regions
"	March	Council of the National Economy established
"	May	Castro visits Moscow
"	May	Academy of Science reorganized
"	June 14	Vostok V, piloted by Valery Bykovsky, launched; made 81 orbits
"	June 16	Vostok VI, piloted by Valentina Tereshkova, launched; made 48 orbits
1964	1964–1966	Industrial reform
	1964–1968	Deterioration of relations with Communist China
	1964–1968	Increased activity of Soviet navy in the Mediterranean
"	October 12	Voskhod I, piloted by Komarov, put into orbit
"	October 15	Khrushchev removed from office; succeeded by Brezhnev, as first party secretary, and by Kosygin, as chairman of Council of Ministers

1964	November	Party structure revised
1965	1965–1966	Agricultural reform
	1965–1966	Reform of planning
	1965–1968	Renewed emphasis on socialist realism
"	March 18	Voskhod II, carrying Beliaev and Leonov, put into orbit; Leonov walked in open space
"	October 2	Economic administrative regions dissolved; federal economic ministries restored
1966	February	Trial of the writers Siniavsky and Daniel
"	March–April	Twenty-third Party Congress; party statutes revised; Politburo restored; Brezhnev appointed general secretary of the party; Seven-Year Plan discontinued; eighth Five-Year Plan, 1966–1970, approved; United States Vietnam policy condemned
"	May	Guaranteed monthly payments to collective farmers introduced
"	June	De Gaulle visits USSR
"	November–Spring 1967	Defection of Stalin's daughter
1967	April	Launching of space ship Soyuz I ends in disaster; Komarov killed
"	May	Fourth Congress of Writers' Union
	Spring	Soviet warships in Indian Ocean
"	June	Theses on the Fiftieth Anniversary of the Revolution
"	"	Support of Arab states in war with Israel
"	"	Kosygin and President Johnson meet at Glassboro, N.J.
"	September	Rehabilitation of Crimean Tatars
"	November	Fiftieth anniversay of the revolution
"	December	Fiftieth anniversary of security agencies
"	1967–1968	Rumania's growing independence from Moscow
1968	January	Trial of Ginzburg and three other intellectuals; ineffectual protest of Soviet intelligensia
"	March	Gagarin killed in plane crash
"	April	Statute on rural and township Soviets
"	June 11	Treaty on non-proliferation of nuclear weapons, sponsored by the United States and the Soviet Union, adopted by the United Nations
"	Spring–Summer	Extreme hostility towards liberalization movement in Czechoslovakia
"	" "	Violent denunciations of the federal republic of Western Germany
"	August 20	Occupation of Czechoslovakia

24

The Soviet Union and
World War II, 1939-1945

The Soviet-German Pact in Action

Poland, the Baltic States, Finland, and Rumania. Stalin and Molotov lost no time in reaping the benefits of their bargain with Germany. While awaiting—one may surmise—with serene confidence the broader advantages which the fratricidal war of the great capitalist countries was certain to confer upon international communism and its leader, the USSR, the Moscow government proceeded to realize without delay the less ambitious but nevertheless substantial territorial and political gains bestowed upon it by the German treaty. The German troops invaded Poland on September 1, 1939, and advanced rapidly. On September 17 Molotov informed the Polish ambassador to Moscow that "the Polish state and its government have, in fact, ceased to exist. Therefore the agreements concluded between the USSR and Poland have ceased to operate." On the same day the Red Army crossed the Polish borders. A secret protocol attached to the German-Soviet boundary and friendship treaty of September 28, 1939, revised somewhat the territorial provisions of the pact of August 23: the whole of Lithuania was assigned to the Soviet sphere of influence, while the German share of Poland was extended. Under this fourth partition of Poland the Soviet Union acquired some 76,500 square miles of territory with a population of 12.8 million, of which about half were Ukrainians and White Russians. On September 19 Molotov told the German ambassador that "the original inclination entertained by the Soviet government and Stalin personally to permit the existence of a residual Poland has given way to the inclination to partition Poland" along the line agreed upon by Germany and the Soviet Union. The annexed territories were incorporated into the Soviet Ukrainian and the Soviet White Russian (Byelo-Russian) republics. Elections to the people's assemblies in the annexed provinces were held at the end of October in accordance with the familiar Soviet model, the sole candidate in each district receiving over 90 per cent of the vote. Both people's assemblies petitioned the Supreme Soviet of the USSR for incorporation into the USSR and for the nationalization of land, industry, and banking. These requests were granted on November 1, 1939.

Procedure in the Baltic states was different, but the results were similar. On September 18, 1939, the day after the Soviet troops invaded Poland, Tass, the Soviet news agency, released an announcement to the effect that "Polish submarines have taken refuge, with the connivance of the ruling circles, in the naval bases belonging to the Baltic states." Although this was denied by the Estonian authorities, the foreign ministers of the three countries were ordered to appear in Moscow and sign identical treaties of mutual assistance with the Soviet Union. The USSR was granted the right to maintain military and naval establishments on the territory of the Baltic states, but it was specifically provided that "the fulfillment of this pact must not affect in any measure the sovereign rights of the contracting parties, in particular their economic system and state organization." Simultaneously, the Soviets restored to Lithuania Vilna, which that country claimed as a part of its territory but which since 1920 had been held by Poland.

There followed a period of peace and quiet, but the respite was of short duration. The defeat of Finland (to be discussed presently) and the collapse of France and the Western front (May–June, 1940) were presumably among the reasons which led Moscow to deal the final blow to the independence of the Baltic states. In the middle of June 1940 the government of Lithuania, Latvia, and Estonia were accused by the Soviets of violating their pacts of mutual assistance. The Kremlin demanded the formation of new cabinets and free access for Soviet troops. These demands, which took the form of ultimatums, were complied with at once. The Baltic states were occupied by the Red Army, and their new governments, although not Communist, were entirely dominated by the Russians. The local legislatures were dissolved, and elections of a strictly Soviet pattern were held in the middle of

July: in each district there was but one candidate, nominated by the Union of Toiling People, who invariably obtained a very high percentage of the vote. The new parliaments decreed immediately (July 22) the nationalization of land, banks, and business enterprises. A few days later (August 1, 3, and 8, 1940, respectively) Lithuania, Latvia, and Estonia were admitted by the Supreme Soviet of the USSR into the Soviet Union with the status of Soviet socialist republics (SSR, or constituent republics). The West was shocked and refused to recognize the change, but the independence of the Baltic states was over.

The story of Finland was more dramatic and less dreary. The Finnish government was peremptorily invited to send a delegation to Moscow early in October 1939, at the time the Kremlin was negotiating with Lithuania, Latvia, and Estonia. Molotov demanded a pact of mutual assistance similar to those of the Baltic states, the leasing of the port of Hangö to the Soviet Union, the establishment of a Soviet naval base on Finnish soil, and the cession of certain territories which would necessitate the dismantling of the Finnish fortifications along the Russian border (the Mannerheim line). The Finns were offered concessions in exchange, including the right to fortify the Aland Island and a sizable slice of Russian Karelia, which, however, was of small economic or strategic value. The Finnish delegation declined the proposal and on November 13 left Moscow.

On November 26 Molotov, in a note to Helsinki, charged that Soviet troops had been fired upon by Finnish artillery. He rejected Finnish denials and an offer of an impartial inquiry and on November 28 announced that the non-aggression pact between the two countries was no longer valid. The next day the Russian troops crossed into Finland, and Helsinki was bombed from the air. Simultaneously the Soviets formed at the Finnish resort of Terijoki, near the Russian border, a Finnish people's government under Otto Kuusinen, a Finn long resident in Russia and an official of the Comintern, and recognized it as the legitimate Finnish government, which "has overthrown the Helsinki clique." The West was aroused. The council of the League of Nations was convened in a special session that Molotov refused to attend on the ground that "the Soviet Union is not at war with Finland" but "maintains peaceful relations with the Finnish democratic republic." Nevertheless the council appealed to its members to extend to Finland "all material and humanitarian aid" and declared that "by its own action the Soviet Union has expelled itself from the League of Nations." The resolution was carried without a dissenting vote, although there were several reservations (December 14, 1939). The Finnish government, hoping against hope that the Geneva institution might exercise a restraining influence on the aggressor, instructed its delegation "not to agitate for the expulsion of the USSR."

It would have been impossible, of course, for Finland to win the war against the Soviet Union, yet for two months the West watched with admiration and suspended breath the unexpected and magnificent resistance of the tiny country. The difficult terrain with its swamps, lakes, and forests, an exceptionally severe winter, but above all the courage, resourcefulness, endurance, and high sense of duty of the Finns held back the Soviet forces and inflicted heavy losses upon them. It was not until the beginning of February that the Red Army, greatly superior to its opponents in numbers and equipment, succeeded in breaking through the Finnish defenses. There was much talk about a British and French expeditionary force to Finland, but nothing came of it. By the treaty of Moscow of March 12, 1940, Finland ceded to Russia important territories, including the Karelian isthmus and the city of Viborg, and pledged herself not to take part in any anti-Soviet coalition. The war was costly and losses of human lives heavy, although estimates vary within a wide range. Probably Finland's sacrifices were not in vain. Had she submitted to the will of Stalin and Molotov as had the Baltic states, she might well have shared their fate. The territories annexed from Finland were merged with portions of Karelia previously held by Russia and became the Karelo-Finnish Soviet socialist republic, which was incorporated into the Soviet Union on March 31, 1940.

The case of Bessarabia, the last territory assigned to the USSR by the Soviet-German pact, was relatively simple. Taking advantage of the state of political confusion prevailing in Rumania, Molotov demanded on June 26, 1940, the cession "in the interest of justice" of Bessarabia and northern Bukovina. Although Bukovina, never before a part of Russia, was not mentioned in the Soviet-German pact, and Hitler and Ribbentrop were annoyed by this new Soviet exaction, they counseled Bucharest to comply with the Russian wishes; Rumania caved in, and on June 28 Soviet troops occupied both provinces. Bukovina was incorporated into the Soviet Ukraine, while most of Bessarabia became the Moldavian Soviet socialist republic and was admitted into the Soviet Union on August 2, 1940.

The formation in 1940 of five new SSR's—Karelo-Finnish, Lithuanian, Moldavian, Latvian, and Estonian—increased the number of constituent republics from 11, as provided by the 1936 constitution, to 16. They remained at that number until 1956, when the Karelo-Finnish SSR was reduced to the status of an autonomous Soviet socialist republic, and the number of constituent republics dropped to 15. The treatment meted out by the USSR to the western border states was a telling comment on what non-aggression and mutual assistance pacts actually meant to the Kremlin.

Relations with Germany, 1939–1941. During the nearly two years from the conclusion of the Soviet-German pact to the invasion of the USSR by Germany in June 1941, relations between the two countries appeared to be friendly or even cordial most of the time. The effects of one potential source of friction, the position in the Soviet-annexed Baltic territories of the German population—that traditional outpost and rampart of Germanism in eastern Europe—were mitigated, if not removed, by a confidential protocol of September 28, 1939, which provided for the organized re-settlement of national minorities. Germany's sweeping advance and conquests in southeastern Europe in the spring of 1941 created awkward and delicate situations, but no real conflict arose. Germany maintained strict neutrality during the Russo-Finnish war, accepted the sovietization of the Baltic states, and, as we know, brought pressure on Rumania to surrender Bessarabia and northern Bukovina to Moscow. Economic relations proceeded smoothly, the volume of Soviet-German trade increasing substantially under the renewed trade agreements of February 11, 1940, and January 10, 1941.

The Tripartite Pact signed by Germany, Italy, and Japan in Berlin on September 27, 1940, was reminiscent of the anti-Comintern pact and as such was not conducive to good Soviet-German relations. In the 1940 treaty the signatories undertook (Article 3) to "assist each other with all political, economic, and military means" if one of them "should be attacked by a power not at present involved in the European conflict or in the Sino-Japanese war." This provision would seem to refer to the United States and the Soviet Union. Article 5, however, stated that the treaty did not have any effect on the relations between each of the contracting parties and the USSR. In spite of this assurance the pact generated uneasiness in Moscow which the Germans were anxious to dispel. Ribbentrop, in his communications with Stalin and Molotov, argued that the chief object of the pact was to prevent Great Britain from bringing the United States into the war, as well as to promote a *rapprochement* between the Soviet Union and Japan. According to the Reich foreign minister, Hitler thought in terms of the "historic mission" of the Soviet Union, Italy, Japan, and Germany "to adopt a long-range policy and to direct the future development of their peoples into the right channels by delimitation of their interests on a world-wide scale" (October 19, 1940). The culminating point of this curious exchange was the conversations (the official German record of which has been preserved) between Molotov, on the one hand, and Ribbentrop and Hitler, on the other, held in Berlin on November 12 and 13, 1940. According to the Germans, the defeat of Great Britain was certain, and Russia was invited to associate herself with Germany, Italy, Japan, and their clients in the liquidation of the "bankrupt British estate." Molotov appeared to be favorably impressed, but no Russian version of the conversations is available. Like their predecessors in the eighteenth and early nineteenth centuries, these projects came to nought.

Evidence given at the Nuremberg trials suggests that as early as September 1940 Hitler made up his mind to attack Russia. However, trial evidence obtained under conditions such as prevailed at Nuremberg is not likely to produce exact and reliable information, and some of it is not easily reconcilable with what is known from other sources. In December 1940 Hitler wrote to Mussolini that a conflict with the Soviet Union was unlikely so long as Stalin was in power. Meanwhile the situation remained fluid. Several of the smaller countries (Hungary, Rumania, Slovakia, Bulgaria, Yugoslavia) acceded to the Tripartite Pact, while the Soviet Union signed a neutrality pact with Japan on April 13, 1941. It would be hazardous to read warlike intentions in these and similar paltry moves. The Kremlin persisted in making conciliatory gestures towards Germany. Early in May 1941 it withdrew recognition from the governments-in-exile of Belgium, Norway, and Yugoslavia, and recognized the anti-British government of Iraq, which was to last for only a few weeks. Commercial exchanges worked well. The German embassy in Moscow reported on May 15, 1941, that "the quantities of raw materials now being contracted for are being delivered punctually by the Russians, despite the heavy burden this imposes upon them, which . . . is a notable performance." Nothing was done to improve relations with the Western powers. Sir Stafford Cripps, the newly-appointed British ambassador (June 1940), was kept at arm's length, and his uncanny warning (reported by the German naval attaché on April 24, 1941) that Germany would attack the Soviet Union on June 22 was ignored.

The possibility of a war with Germany must have occurred to the Soviet leaders, but they did not seem to expect it at the time it came. In May and June, Soviet agencies repeatedly denied rumors of the impending military conflict with the Reich. In the evening of June 21, 1941, when the German declaration of war was already signed and about to be delivered, Molotov summoned the German ambassador and deplored the "indications that the German government was dissatisfied with the Soviet government." He wanted to know "what had brought about the present situation." The lengthy declaration of war, listing alleged Soviet infractions of the Soviet-German agreement, was not a good answer to Molotov's query. Hitler, perhaps, was closer to the truth when he wrote to Mussolini on June 21, 1941: "Since I struggled through to this decision, I again feel spiritually free. The partnership with the Soviet Union, in spite of the complete sincerity of the efforts to bring about a final conciliation, was nevertheless often very irksome to me, for in some way or other it seemed to be a break with my whole origin, my concepts, and my former obligations. I am happy now to be relieved of these mental agonies." He stated earlier in the same letter that "whatever may come now . . . our situation cannot become worse . . . ; it can only improve."

The Tide of War

The Invasion. In the early morning hours of June 22, 1941, the Hitler host crossed the Soviet border. Italy, Rumania, and Slovakia declared war on the Soviet Union on the same day, Finland on the 25th, and Hungary on the 27th. These countries, as well as Franco's Spain, participated in the Russian campaign. The invading army of some 3 million men comprised 69 satellite divisions: 27 Rumanian, 17 Finnish, 13 Hungaran, nine Italian, two Slovak, and one Spanish. The offensive unfolded in three main directions—Leningrad, Moscow, and Kiev—and moved inexorably forward with terrifying clock-like precision. Kiev fell in the middle of September, Kharkov and Odessa fell in October, the Crimea was occupied in November, but the naval base of Sevastopol held out until July 1942. Leningrad was virtually surrounded and gallantly withstood a siege that lasted into January 1944. In less than a month the German Panzer divisions and supporting troops had covered more than 450 miles; in November 1941 they were within a few miles of Moscow, in some localities within 20 or even 10 miles. On October 20 the Soviet government, the diplomatic corps, and foreign correspondents were evacuated to Kuibyshev (Samara) on the Volga, but Stalin remained in the Kremlin. Hitler, his successes notwithstanding, failed in his main objective—he did not capture Moscow. An offensive mounted by General G. K. Zhukov at the end of November and helped by an exceptionally severe winter, for which the invaders were not prepared, succeeded not only in stopping the advance towards the capital but in driving the enemy back to positions some 100 miles west of Moscow (March 1942).

In the spring and summer of 1942 the Germans resumed the offensive in the south. After meeting with stiff resistance east of Kharkov and at Sevastopol, they took Rostov, crossed the Don River, and occupied the oil fields of Maikop and the agricultural lands north of the Caucasian Mountains. The farthest line of German penetration was reached in November 1942. Much of the Caucasus was conquered: a triumphant swastika was flying on the snow-clad peak of Mount Elbrus (18,500 feet). On August 23, 1942, the Panzer army, having covered 275 miles in two months, broke through the Russian defenses and reached the outskirts of Stalingrad (Tsaritsyn prior to 1925; renamed Volgograd in November 1961), a sprawling city and river port on the western bank of the Volga and one of Russia's principal centers of heavy machine-building. Hitler's original objective of the southern drive was the Caucasian oil, but the resistance his troops encountered at Stalingrad altered the strategic picture.

The battle of Stalingrad lasted from August 23, 1942, to February 1, 1943. It was fought on both sides with fanatical determination and inhuman ferocity. The German mechanized armies spread over immeasurable distances and, separated from their bases by hundreds of miles of nearly impassable roads with a few inadequate railways, were short of food, spare parts, ammunition, and above all, fuel. On September 7 Stalin issued the order: "Not another step backward. . . . The Volga has now only one bank. . . ." Hitler was equally unbending and scornfully and angrily rejected the pleas of Field Marshal Friedrich von Paulus and other commanding officers who sought a tactical retreat that would save their armies from destruction. The result was (to quote Hanson W. Baldwin) that "Stalingrad, once envisaged as a means to an end—the conquest of the Caucasus—had now become an end in itself." The city, whose population was not evacuated because Stalin believed that soldiers were more likely "to fight for a live town than for an empty one," was reduced to rubble. On November 19, 1942, the Russians launched a huge offensive prepared by Generals Zhukov, Alexander Vasilevsky, and Nicholas Voronov, and supported by the armies of Generals Nicholas Vatutin and Constantine Rokossovsky. Furious fighting went on for weeks, until the total exhaustion of munition and supplies precluded further German resistance. On January 31, 1943, von Paulus surrendered. The Russians netted a large number of prisoners: 23 generals, 2,500 officers, 90,000 non-commissioned ranks, an undetermined number of Rumanians, and perhaps another 40,000 non-combatants of various nationalities. Most of them were never heard of again. The exact number of casualties is not known. An estimate quoted by Baldwin puts Soviet losses in the entire Stalingrad campaign at 400,000 and those of the Germans and their allies at 600,000. Stalingrad was a major turning point in the history of the war—and perhaps not of the war alone. The Soviets and the Western allies took heart at Hitler's first great defeat.

Meanwhile the international situation changed to the detriment of Germany. The Japanese attack on Pearl Harbor (December 7, 1941) brought the United States into the war. In November 1942 the Anglo-American expeditionary force landed in French North Africa. In July 1943 the allies invaded Sicily and in September the Italian mainland, at Salerno. The fascist government was overthrown (July 25, 1943), and Italy, no longer an asset for the axis, entered a period of civil war and overt German intervention.

The Soviets Go West. In 1943 Germany and her allies still had powerful armies in the Soviet Union, but the tide of war was turning definitely against them. The last major German offensive on the eastern front was launched in July–August 1943, in the region of Kursk. According to Soviet estimates the German high command threw into the battle 550,000 men supported by a large number of tanks and powerful artillery and air forces. The Red Army withstood the blow and, seizing the initiative for the first time, unleashed a massive offensive on a broad front. Orel, Kursk, Kharkov, and Kiev (in November) fell to the Russians. The advance was continued in 1944. In January–February the Leningrad region was freed of the enemy and the Crimea in April–May. Minsk, the capital of White Russia (Byelo-Russia) was re-taken in the summer and the littoral of the Baltic Sea in the autumn. In September Finland was forced out of the war. Meanwhile the Western allies landed in Normandy (June 6, 1944), relieving enemy pressure on the Russian front. As the Soviet territory was cleared of the invaders, the Red Army advanced into eastern and central Europe. It penetrated Poland and seized Rumania in August, occupied Bulgaria in August-September and Belgrade in October (with Tito's assistance), and approached Budapest, which, however, the Germans succeeded in holding until February 1945. The Soviet offensive in Poland was resumed in January 1945; by the middle of April the Red Army controlled virtually all of eastern Europe north of Greece, including Vienna. American and Soviet advance units met on the Elbe, at Torgau (April 25), Hitler committed suicide in the bunker under the smoldering ruins of the Reich chancellery (April 30), and the allied forces were deliberately held back in order to allow the Red Army to occupy Berlin (May 2) and Prague (May 8). With practically the entire territory of the Reich overrun by the enemy, the German government signed the act of unconditional surrender on May 8, 1945. World War II in Europe was over, with the Soviets in occupation of a large portion of the continent.

The Far East. War in the Far East was fought by the United States and Great Britain. Stalin agreed at Yalta (February 1945) to enter the war against Japan "in two or three months after Germany had surrendered." The United States dropped an atomic bomb on Hiroshima on August 6, 1945, and another on Nagasaki on August 9. The Soviet Union declared war on Japan on August 8. By that time Japan was practically defeated and on September 2, 1945, signed the unconditional surrender agreement on board the United States battleship *Missouri*. Russia's three weeks of belligerency in the Far East were rewarded by the annexation of important territories and the strengthening of her position in the Pacific area.

The Nation and the War. The war of 1941–1945 is enshrined in Soviet historiography as "The Great Patriotic War," an appellation formerly reserved for the Napoleonic invasion of 1812. The Soviet interpretation differs in two essential aspects from that of the Western historians. It is claimed by Soviet writers that the war was won practically single-handed by the USSR and that it generated in the country a spontaneous irresistible upsurge of nationalistic feelings and devotion to the socialist homeland. Neither of these contentions is supported by available evidence. Leaving aside the seemingly uncontroversial fact that the Soviet-German partnership in 1939–1941 was a decisive factor in the allied defeats during that period, Western pressure on Germany in Africa, on the high seas, from the air, and on the European continent (beginning with the landing in Italy in 1943) were essential elements in the ultimate defeat of Hitler. If the Red Army found itself in Berlin and in Prague, it was, as intimated above, by courtesy —probably misguided courtesy—of the allied statesmen and command. Disregarding the past, Churchill and Roosevelt gave the Soviet Union, beginning in August 1941, the full measure of political and economic support. The $11 billion worth of American Lend-Lease, including nearly 7,000 tanks, over 13,000 planes, 400,000 motor vehicles, 1,000 locomotives, and vast quantities of steel and consumer goods (cloth, shoes, and so on), was not a negligible contribution to the Soviet capacity to fight. It is seldom, if ever, mentioned by Soviet historians.

Dismayed by the unchecked sway of the invading armies and the poor showing of the Soviet troops during the opening months of the war, the Kremlin turned to the traditional symbols of Russian nationalism. In his oration on the anniversary of the revolution on November 7, 1941, Stalin unexpectedly and incongruously invoked, "to inspire you in this war," the princes, saints, and generals honored in pre-revolutionary Russia as great national figures. The propaganda machine took up this theme. If the appeal to crude nationalism was effective, it was not so immediately. The number of prisoners taken by the Germans during the campaigns of 1941 and 1942 was extraordinarily high. Official figures are not available but estimates of reputable historians are in terms of millions, including a large percentage of soldiers who laid down their arms. Evidence from reliable sources supports these computations. Stalin told Harry Hopkins in Teheran (1943) that "in the winter war against Finland the Soviet army had shown itself to be very poorly organized and had done very badly"; it was reorganized, "but even so, when the Germans attacked in 1941, it could not be said that the Red Army was a first-class fighting force." In July 1941 Stalin said to Hopkins in Moscow that "he would welcome American troops on any part of the Russian front under the complete command of the American army" —a truly fantastic suggestion, since the United States was not yet at war. On September 4, 1941, Stalin wrote to Churchill of the "mortal menace" facing the Soviet Union. He asked for the establishment of a second front in the Balkans or in France before the end of the year and for the delivery, beginning in October, of large quantities of aluminum, planes, and tanks. "Without these two forms of help," stated Stalin, "the Soviet Union will either suffer a defeat or be weakened to such an extent that it will lose for a long period any capacity to render assistance to the allies." On September 15 Stalin proposed the dispatch of 25 to 30 British divisions to Archangel or Iran, a request that Churchill termed an absurdity.

No less disturbing than mass surrender to the enemy and refusal to fight was the welcome extended to the Germans by a portion of the population in the occupied territories, especially in the Ukraine, the Caucasus, and the Baltic states. The policies of the occupying power, however, confused and contradictory as they were, were such as to discourage their well-wishers. Attempts at reform (reorganization of the collective farms, restoration of private ownership of land) were few and ineffectual. Racial intolerance, cruelty of the administrative methods (extermination of the Jews, public hanging of suspected partisans and saboteurs), drafting of millions of people for compulsory labor in Germany (*Ostarbeiter*), merciless exactions of raw materials and foodstuffs which occasionally resulted in local famines—all this destroyed whatever sympathy the population might have had for the Germans, whom some held at first as saviors. Nevertheless national minority groups were accused by the Soviet of disloyalty and made subject to mass persecution. The autonomous republic of the Volga Germans was dissolved in 1941, and the autonomous republics of the Kalmyk, Chechen-Ingush, Kabardino-Balkar, and Crimean Tatars, and the Karachai autonomous province, in 1943–1944. The Supreme Soviet was told in June 1946 that natives of these territories "voluntarily and together with the Germans waged an armed struggle against the Red Army." Members of these communities were "resettled elsewhere," presumably in central Asia. In 1956 and 1957 these national groups, except for the Crimean Tatars and the Volga Germans, were returned to their original places of settlement and restored to their autonomous status.

The extreme manifestations of the anti-Soviet feelings were the various military formations recruited by the Germans among prisoners-of-war and national minorities (Ukrainians, Armenians, Letts, Latvians, and so on). Factual information concerning these military groups is unreliable, but according to one estimate, their following in the autumn of 1942 numbered in the hundreds of thousands. The original plan was to merge them into a "Russian Liberation Army," which came to be associated with A. A. Vlasov, a Soviet general with a distinguished war record who took part in the defense of Moscow but was made prisoner in 1942 and turned against the Soviets. German authorities were of a divided mind as to the Russian Liberation Army, and the Vlasov movement did not gain full recognition until the end of 1944, when Germany had in effect lost the war. The objectives of the movement were not clearly formulated, except that Russia was to be liberated from Bolshevism. Vlasov is credited with a following of some 300,000, but his combatant effectives did not exceed one division, which saw practically no fighting. The number of Soviet citizens and Russian *émigrés* in German-occupied Europe was estimated at from 8 to 15 million. A comparison of these figures with those of the Vlasov army suggests that his movement did not command wide support. It may be significant that among the human flotsam gathered under his banners were many former high officials of the Soviet Communist Party and administration. Their end was pitiful. Vlasov and the other leaders of the Russian Liberation Army were handed over to the Soviets by the American authorities; they were tried and hanged in August 1946.

The partisan movement, a useful auxiliary of the armed forces, is represented by Soviet historiography as conclusive evidence of the fusion between the government and the nation in wartime. Actually, as Alexander Dallin states, it was "neither an underground movement nor a spontaneous mass rising." It was "a skillfully organized and centrally directed" arm of the government in the struggle with the invaders and disloyal elements. In addition to harassing the Germans, the partisans performed the function of absorbing and coordinating the various anti-German groups behind the lines, of which some were opposed to the Soviets. Partisan units gradually acquired political commissars, and with the growing certainty of Soviet victory they came increasingly under the control of the Communist Party.

Mass desertion, refusal to fight, defection, and the participation of large groups of Soviet citizens in anti-Soviet military formations run contrary to official theories of monolithic strength and unity of purpose. The fact remains, however, that at Stalingrad and elsewhere the Red Army fought with determination, courage, and selflessness. The imperial government dissolved under the impact of defeats far less severe than those suffered in 1941–1942 by its successor. How is the survival of Communism in face of adversity to be explained? Various considerations might be tentatively advanced: the efficiency and total ruthlessness of the security police; belief that the alliance with the Western democracies was the harbinger of a better future, although this argument could hardly have a wide appeal; crude rudimentary nationalism that comes spontaneously to the fore in wartime—it is unlikely that the invocation of thirteenth- and fourteenth-century saints and nineteenth-century generals would by itself have aroused much enthusiasm; a secular tradition of subservience; and a moral and physical exhaustion that paralyzed the will and prevented independent action. None of these explanations are comprehensive or satisfactory, even though they may offer food for thought. The retention by the Communist Party and the Soviet government through all war trials of the unchallengeable control of the nation is perhaps the most significant and puzzling feature of the Great Patriotic War.

Domestic Policies

Administrative Changes. War is not conducive to constitutional and administrative changes, except those born of necessity. A surprise development was the emergence of Stalin from the quasi-anonymity of *éminence grise* —the power behind the throne. In May 1941 he replaced Molotov as chairman of the Council of People's Commissars, Molotov retaining the post of commissar for foreign affairs. Stalin became people's commissar for defense in July 1941, marshal of the Soviet Union in March 1943, and generalissimo in June 1945. From the autumn of 1945 he was officially referred to as commander-in-chief. These changes of status, for which no reason was given, added nothing to Stalin's dictatorial and generally-recognized powers as secretary general of the Communist Party. The only perceivable difference was in his appearance: the unadorned tunic he used to wear was replaced by a snug ornate uniform with rows of medals.

On June 30, 1941, a joint decree of the presidium of the Supreme Soviet, the central committee of the Communist Party, and the Council of People's Commissars appointed a State Defense Committee, which was vested with full powers for the conduct of the war. The committee had five members (it was somewhat enlarged later) and included in addition to Stalin, who was chairman, Molotov, Voroshilov, G. Malenkov (secretary of the central committee of the party), and L. Beria (people's commissar of the interior and head of the security police). The creation of the State Defense Committee introduced no real change, for authority continued to reside, as in the past, with Stalin and the top members of the Communist hierarchy. The committee was dissolved in September 1945.

Political life, never too vigorous, came to a standstill. No elections were held during the war, the credentials of the deputies being extended from year to year by the presidium of the Supreme Soviet. The Supreme Soviet met four times in brief perfunctory sessions: once in 1942, once in 1944, and twice in 1945; that is, three of the sessions were convened when the war was nearly over; to put it differently, the Soviet parliament had no part in the organization of the war effort, although its presidium continued to meet and carried on routine work.

Two constitutional amendments of some formal significance were enacted. As stated earlier in this chapter, because of annexations, the number of constituent republics was increased in 1940 from 11 to 16. Under the constitution of 1936 foreign affairs and defense belonged exclusively to the federal government. Two decrees issued by the presidium of the Supreme Soviet on February 1, 1944, empowered the constituent republics to enter into direct relations with foreign states and to conclude international agreements, and to organize and maintain "separate military formations." The reason for this move was presumably to enhance the status of the constituent republics and to strengthen their claim to representation in the United Nations, which was then under discussion. There is no evidence that since 1944 the constituent republics have taken an independent part in international affairs (the membership of the Ukraine and White Russia in the United Nations will be examined later) or have armed forces separate from those of the USSR.

Except for these amendments the constitutional structure remained unchanged.

The discouraging performance of the Red Army during the Finnish war and in the opening phase of the German invasion called for a revision of army regulations. A decree of May 1937 had introduced in the armed forces political commissars, who shared equally with commanders responsibility for the political and moral condition of the troops, discipline, and military economy. This system did not work well, and in October 1942 the commissars were subordinated to the military commanders. There was a revival of the traditional approach to discipline and incentive. Individual military ranks, including that of marshal of the Soviet Union, had been introduced before the war by a decree of September 1935; the ranks of general and admiral were added in May 1940. After the outbreak of the war Cossack formations were restored. Beginning in 1941, units which particularly distinguished themselves in action were awarded the title of "guards" with a status reminiscent of that of their namesakes in imperial Russia. In November 1942 epaulettes, a mark of commissioned rank under the empire, were reintroduced. Numerous honorary military awards were established, some of them named after the saints, princes, and generals invoked by Stalin. In December 1943 alone, 360 officers were promoted to the rank of general. By the end of the war more than 7 million members of the armed forces were recipients of medals of one kind or another. Army bigwigs, like marshals Zhukov and Voroshilov, were plastered with them.

The Church. The war had an impact on relations between the Church and the state. Communism is hostile to religion, particularly to the Russian (Greek) Orthodox Church, which it regards as a reactionary institution. A Church council (*sobor*) of Russian clerics and laymen convened in Moscow in August 1917 and decided to restore the patriarchate, which had been abolished early in the eighteenth century. Tikhon, Metropolitan of Moscow, who was elected patriarch in November (after the Bolsheviks took power), was an avowed enemy of Communism. The separation of the Church from state and schools was proclaimed on February 5, 1918, Church properties were taken over by the government, and monasteries and Church schools were closed, but worship in the sequestered buildings was permitted if requested by groups of believers. The patriarchate lent its support to the anti-Soviet movements, relations between Church and state went from bad to worse, and in May 1922 Tikhon was arrested on counter-revolutionary charges. The administration of the Church passed temporarily into the hands of radically-minded clerics, who formed the Living Church, which cooperated with the Soviet government. Tikhon recanted, was released in June 1923, resumed his office, and urged loyalty to the Soviets. After his death in April 1925 the Church was administered by the Acting Patriarch Sergius, Metropolitan of Moscow, who together with the Synod (governing body of the Church) pledged support of the Soviet regime. These advances brought no response. Article 124 of the 1936 constitution provided for freedom of conscience guaranteed by the separation of the Church from state and schools and freedom of religious and anti-religious propaganda. Anti-religious propaganda, however, was carried on by the government and the League of Militant Godless, an officially-sponsored association that had millions of members, while the Church had to rely on its own meager resources.

The war of 1941 brought a measure of reconciliation between Church and state. The acting patriarch exhorted the believers to rally to the defense of the country and unfrocked clerics and excommunicated laymen who collaborated with the enemy. He organized and sent to the front a tank column and an air squadron named, respectively, after Dimitry Donskoy and Alexander Nevsky, two of the princely saints invoked by Stalin, whom he addressed in his messages in terms such as "the divinely appointed leader of our armed and cultural forces." Stalin began to see that religion had its good points. The anti-religious propaganda was toned down, Sergius had an audience with Stalin and Molotov (August 1943), and early in September he was elected patriarch by a council of Russian bishops. The position of the Church was regularized. A 5-man Council on the Affairs of the Orthodox Church, headed by a Communist official, was established in October 1943; the patriarchate was authorized to publish a journal and to maintain a seminary for the training of priests; teaching of religion was tolerated, although it was not permitted in the schools. Clerics who served at the front were given medals, and Metropolitan Nicholas of Kiev was appointed (November 1942) a member of a committee of 10 to investigate the crimes of the fascist invaders, which inflicted ferocious retributions on alleged war criminals.

Sergius died in May 1944, and Alexis, Metropolitan of Leningrad, was elected his successor by a large council consisting of Russian clergy and laymen and representatives of Orthodox communties abroad (January–February 1945). Alexis continued the policies of his predecessor. He was the pliable instrument of the Kremlin in forcing the return to the fold of Orthodoxy of the Uniats living in the provinces annexed from Poland and in implanting Communist dictatorships, in the guise of people's democracies, in the Orthodox Balkan lands. His efforts were appreciated. Yet coexistence between Church and state in the USSR, like any other brand of Soviet coexistence, is tenuous. "The Communist Party sees religion as an ideology which has nothing in common with science, and it cannot be indifferent or neutral towards it . . . ," says the *Large Soviet Encyclopedia* (1957). "The party considers it necessary to engage in profound, systematic, scientific-atheist propaganda among the population, without in any way offending the feelings of the believers or church ministers, or interfering administratively in the activities of the Church." How the two parts of this formula can be reconciled is not clear.

The Russian Orthodox Church, like any other church under a Communist regime, is in a tragic predicament. It has survived and has gained somewhat more elbow room, but the reprieve has been purchased at the price of the loss of moral authority resulting from cooperation with the Communist dictatorship. The Russian Church has an old tradition of subservience to the state, yet there is a basic difference between past and present: tsarism was a patron of Orthodoxy, while Communism is its avowed enemy.

War and the Economy. The German invasion inflicted on the Soviet economy truly fantastic losses, which were aggravated by the "scorched earth" policy, a re-enactment—as in 1915—of the "retreat of 1812," proclaimed by Stalin in his first wartime broadcast on July 3, 1941. According to official statistics the area overrun by the enemy accounted for 40 per cent of Russia's population, 66 per cent of her heavy industry, 38 per cent of her grain, and 30 per cent of her cattle. Between 1940 and 1942 fuel output declined by more than 50 per cent; Russia lost temporarily more than half of her steel and coal production. In the occupied territories nearly 90 per cent of the industrial plants were severely damaged, and the number of workers was reduced by over 80 per cent. The occupation destroyed completely or partially 1,700 towns, more than 7,000 villages and hamlets, 6 million buildings, 84,000 schools, 43,000 libraries, 31,000 factories, 40,000 miles of railway tracks, and 13,000 bridges. Farming paid a heavy toll: the invaders are said to have destroyed 98,000 collective farms, 1,900 state farms, and 2,900 machine tractor stations; also 49,000 combines and 137,000 tractors. Livestock suffered heavy losses amounting to 7 million horses, 17 million cattle, 20 million pigs, 27 million sheep and goats, and 110 million fowl. The aggregate direct damage was evaluated at 679 billion rubles.

These figures, which have no claim to exactness, suggest the extreme difficulties experienced by the Soviet economy in the war years. Attempts were made to relieve the situation. Some 1,360 large industrial enterprises were evacuated to the Urals, western Siberia, central Asia, and the Volga region. Industrial works which were reorganized or continued to operate were desperately short of fuel, raw materials, and labor. There was an improvement in the volume of production as the invasion rolled back and industries were restored, but it took time before the pre-war level could be reached. Except for the evacuation of enterprises to the east, which foreshadowed the post-war industrialization of these remote regions, government policies were unimaginative and stale. In agriculture there was increased interference of the authorities with the management of the collective farms as well as the raising of the number of compulsory "labor days," although the futility of this approach was long evident. Attachment of workers to their jobs, introduced in 1940, remained in force. Throughout the entire economy strong emphasis was put on "socialist emulation" organized on an "all-union scale." Official reports on the results achieved were enthusiastic but inspire little confidence. These artifices notwithstanding, recovery was slow. In 1945 the gross agricultural output was still 60 per cent of its not-too-high 1940 level.

The cost of the war to the economy was exceedingly high. It was even higher in terms of human lives. Comprehensive official figures of Soviet casualties are not available and probably do not exist, but the number of the dead alone was estimated at 7 million.

Partnership with the West

Reversal of Alignments. Hitler's attack on the Soviet Union brought about a dramatic reversal of international alignments. The USSR, an eager partner of National-Socialist Germany prior to June 22, 1941, shifted overnight into the camp of the Western powers. Churchill, grasping the significance of this momentous change, went to the microphone and, in ringing phrases appropriate to the occasion, offered "to the government of the Soviet Union any technical and economic assistance which is in our power and which is likely to be of any service to them. . . . The Russian danger is . . . our danger and the danger of the United States. . . ." He prefaced this unconditional offer with the statement that no one had been a more consistent opponent of Communism than he and added: "I will unsay no words that I've spoken about it." This pronouncement emphasized the two elements in the relations between the Soviet Union and the West: a full measure of cooperation in the war effort against the common enemy, and the absence of real mutual confidence born from the identity of views on the basic issues such as existed, for instance, between Great Britain and the

United States. The Washington government, although still a non-belligerent, associated itself with Britain's attitude towards the Soviet Union.

It was easier, however, to enunciate the policy of cooperation than to make it effective. There were many difficulties: geographical remoteness and lack of safe communications; the taxing to the limit of British economic and military capacity by the disastrous campaigns of 1940 and 1941; and the lingering suspicion both in Moscow and in London and Washington that the all-too-recent partnership might be dissolved as suddenly as it had arisen by an agreement of either the Soviet Union or of the West—as the case might be—with Hitler's Germany. The lamentable record of the Red Army during the opening phase of the campaign made Ribbentrop's statement that "the Russia of Stalin will be erased from the map within eight weeks" sound less hollow.

The British knew that the invasion of Russia would bring relief, even though perhaps a temporary one, to their hard-pressed island. On July 12, 1941, was signed the Anglo-Soviet mutual assistance pact, in which the two countries undertook not to conclude a separate peace. At the end of July, Harry Hopkins, President Roosevelt's special envoy, flew to Moscow to make preliminary arrangements for the shipment of American supplies. Hopkins' visit was followed by those of numerous Western leaders. In September the USSR subscribed to the Atlantic Charter, which had been agreed upon by Roosevelt and Churchill (August 14, 1941) and pledged the signatories to respect the right of all countries to self-determination. In August 1941 the British and the Russians jointly occupied Iran to keep open this important southern route. In May 1942 Molotov was sent to London and Washington. His mission had a three-fold objective: additional guarantees against a separate peace; establishment of a second front in Europe; and recognition by London and Washington of Russia's 1941 western frontier. He was only partly successful. A 20-year Anglo-Soviet treaty of alliance was signed (May 26, 1942) as well as a comprehensive lend-lease agreement with the United States. "Full understanding" concerning the creation of a second front in Europe in 1942 was announced, but this promise was not fulfilled. London and Washington, however, withheld recognition of the annexations made by the Soviet Union under the Stalin-Hitler pact.

In August 1942, when allied military fortunes were at low ebb, Churchill, accompanied by W. Averell Harriman, who represented President Roosevelt, paid his first visit to Moscow. His inability to give definite assurance concerning the second front and disagreements about other matters created a tense atmosphere. The Polish problem grew rapidly into a major issue dividing the allies. After the outbreak of the war Moscow annulled the Soviet-German pact and on July 30, 1941, recognized the Polish government-in-exile headed by General Wladyslaw Sikorski, with headquarters in London. The pact provided for the organization of Polish military units on Russian soil. The Sikorski government, however, insisted on the 1939 frontiers, to which the Russians would not agree. The breach between Moscow and the London Poles was precipitated by an external event. In September 1939 some 14,000 Poles, including 8,000 officers, were made prisoners by the Russians. They were never heard of again, but the Germans announced in the spring of 1943 that a mass grave containing the remnants of the prisoners was discovered in the Katyn forest, near Smolensk, and that an impartial investigation had established that they were murdered at a time when this region was held by the Russians. The disclosure created a sensation, and Sikorski demanded that the International Red Cross investigate the matter (April 1943). The Kremlin retaliated by breaking off relations with the Polish government. It is a moot question whether this decision was caused by the Katyn incident or was rather the first clear indication that Moscow would not tolerate in the border states governments not subservient to its will. The dissolution of the Comintern announced by the presidium of its Executive Committee in May 1943 was a conciliatory gesture and was widely interpreted in the West as the abandonment by Moscow of world revolution; it was actually a tactical retreat of no real consequence.

Quarrels over Poland and the inability of the Western allies to provide a second front in France brought a further deterioration in inter-allied relations. The military situation improved, however, especially in Russia, and Stalin, who had previously declined several proposals for a meeting with Roosevelt and Churchill, agreed to confer with them in Teheran, which was close to the Russian border and was under joint Anglo-Soviet occupation.

Teheran, Yalta, and Potsdam. The Teheran conference (November 28 to December 1, 1943) marked the first important diplomatic victory for the Soviet Union. According to Frances Perkins, a friend and admirer of Roosevelt, the president went to Teheran "prepared to like Stalin and determined to make himself liked." To the annoyance of the British he accepted the invitation of the Russians to stay at their Embassy compound as a guest of Stalin. The American and the British delegation labored under a double handicap: the assumption, which proved unwarranted, that the war in the Far East would be long and arduous and that Russia's participation was essential to save American and British lives; and a diffident and almost apologetic attitude towards Stalin because of the delay in establishing the second front and the contention, rubbed in by the Russians, that the Soviet Union had borne the chief brunt of the fighting. Stalin took advantage of this situation and won his major points with remarkable ease. Churchill's plan for an invasion of the Balkans was vetoed, removing the threat that Soviet penetration in eastern Europe might be checked by the allies. The United States and Great Britain undertook to launch a second front in France in the early summer of 1944. The allies accepted as the Soviet-Polish frontier the "Curzon line" (proposed by the British foreign secretary Lord Curzon in 1920), which was far more favorable to the Soviet Union than the 1921–1939 (treaty of Riga) border. Stalin, in turn, assumed the obligation to declare war on Japan after the defeat of Germany. At the closing of the conference Churchill, in a characteristic albeit somewhat incongruous ceremony, presented to Stalin, on behalf of King George, a Stalingrad sword of honor that the Communist dictator kissed, allegedly with tears in his eyes.

The Teheran accord had repercussions on Soviet-Polish relations. The Polish government in London having rejected the Curzon line, Stalin took steps which indicated what was in store for eastern Europe. In the summer of 1944, as the Russian troops were pressing into Poland, he sponsored a Communist-dominated Polish National Committee of Liberation, which, with the advance of the Red Army, moved to Lublin. In the meantime Stanislas Mikolajczyk, prime minister of the Polish government-in-exile (Sikorski had died) and a conservative peasant leader, agreed to negotiate with the Soviets on the basis of the Curzon line, but by the time he reached Moscow at the end of July 1944 Stalin had recognized the Lublin committee as the *de jure* government of Poland. The Kremlin disclaimed any intention of intervening in domestic Polish affairs and magnanimously advised Mikolajczyk to find an accommodation with the Lublin group.

On August 1, 1944 the Warsaw underground, spurred to action by the approach of the Red Army, rose against the Germans. The Poles wished to liberate their capital themselves prior to the arrival of the Muscovites. The uprising proved a ghastly failure. The Germans, instead of evacuating the city as they were expected to do, turned savagely against the insurgents, while the Russian advance stalled, at first because of temporary military reversals and then deliberately: the Soviets would not even allow the landing of British planes carrying arms, munitions, and supplies for the entrapped Poles. The Germans crushed the insurrection cruelly and methodically; there was mass executions and the city was virtually destroyed. The Warsaw

Poles were non-Communists and therefore deemed not "friendly" to the USSR. This explains Soviet action—and inaction—and the fate of Warsaw.

Teheran marked the beginning of the re-integration of the USSR into the mainstream of world affairs. The Russians were represented at the Dumbarton Oaks (October 1944) and San Francisco (April–June 1945) conferences which drafted the charter of the United Nations Organization. Stalin had his second meeting with Roosevelt and Churchill at the Yalta conference, held amidst the faded splendor of the former imperial residence in the Crimea (February 7 to 12, 1945). Yalta, like Teheran, was a victory for the Russians. The Curzon line was confirmed as the eastern frontier of Poland, that is, Russia retained a large slice of Poland, including Galicia with the city of Lvov (Lemberg), which Roosevelt and Churchill vainly tried to save for the Poles; Poland was to receive in the west territorial compensations to be determined by the future peace conference. The Polish provisional government "which is now functioning in Poland" (the Lublin committee) was recognized but was to be democratized and enlarged. Two Soviet constituent republics, the Ukraine and White Russia (Byelo-Russia) were to be admitted to the proposed United Nations Organization. Germany was to be dismembered, occupied, and jointly administered by the allies. An occupation zone was to be carved for France. There were to be reparations, Roosevelt and Stalin (but not Churchill) agreeing on $20 billion "as a basis for discussion"; half of that amount was earmarked for the Soviet Union. Reparations were to be paid by removal of industrial equipment from current production and by "the use of German labor"; the latter—a surprising provision—referred to the labor of prisoners-of-war (statement by Hector McNeil, minister of state, in the House of Commons, March 24, 1947). A secret agreement formalized the obligations assumed by Stalin in 1943 to enter the Japanese war by stipulating that Soviet intervention was to take place within three months after the termination of the German war. Russia was promised in exchange annexations and the safeguarding of her interests in the Pacific area.

Yalta produced 17 agreements; they are long complex documents, but they do not tell the whole story. The singling out of the Ukraine and White Russia as the two constituent republics (out of 16) entitled to representation in the United Nations was presumably due to the incorporation into these republics of the territories annexed from Poland. The presence of the Ukraine and White Russia among the founding members of the United Nations would have been useful to the USSR if the question of the annexation of the Polish provinces were raised in that organization, as seemed

Sovfoto

The Big Three at Teheran, November 1943

Sovfoto

Soviet troops capture Berlin

likely in 1945. The full text of the Yalta agreements was not made available until March 1947.

The Yalta accords contained customary references to the right of peoples "to enjoy democratic institutions of their own choice" and promises of non-intervention in the domestic affairs of other countries. The Soviet interpretation of these solemn undertakings was made clear by the case of the Polish Lublin committee and was confirmed by that of Rumania. In the spring of 1945 A. Vyshinsky, a Soviet emissary, ordered King Michael of Rumania to change his government within two hours and to appoint a pro-Communist prime minister. This the king did, but his compliance merely postponed his forced abdication for two years. In its sphere of influence the Soviet Union would tolerate only "friendly" governments.

The Potsdam conference (July 17 to August 2, 1945), the last of its kind, made final arrangements for the post-war world, based largely on the Yalta decisions. The leading personalities of the preceding meeting were missing. Roosevelt had died in April, and Churchill was defeated in a general election held in the middle of the conference. Their places were taken by President Harry Truman and Clement Attlee, leader of the British Labor Party and the new prime minister. The vexing question of the Polish western frontier was resolved unilaterally by Stalin before the conference met: without consulting the allies, he surrendered to the Poles the German territories east of the Oder and Neisse rivers (he had unsuccessfully advocated this course at Yalta). Truman and Attlee accepted the *fait accompli* as a "temporary" solution: Poland was to administer these lands pending the final decision, which was to be made by the peace conference, but the Potsdam accord sanctioned the expulsion of the Germans from the ceded provinces, which made things look pretty final. Provisions were made for the occupation, administration, demilitarization, democratization, and de-nazification of Germany, the punishment of war criminals, the dismantling of industry, and the collection of reparations. Each occupying power was free to administer its zone in a way that would allow it to satisfy its claims —a broad dispensation. The conference sanctioned the transfer to the Soviet Union, subject again to the subsequent approval by the peace conference, of the northern portion of East Prussia with Koenigsberg, which was speedily renamed Kaliningrad (June 1946). There was established a council of foreign ministers (United Kingdom, the USSR, China, France, and the United States), which was to prepare a peace settlement with the former enemy countries.

The Fruits of Victory. Judged by both imperial and revolutionary stand-

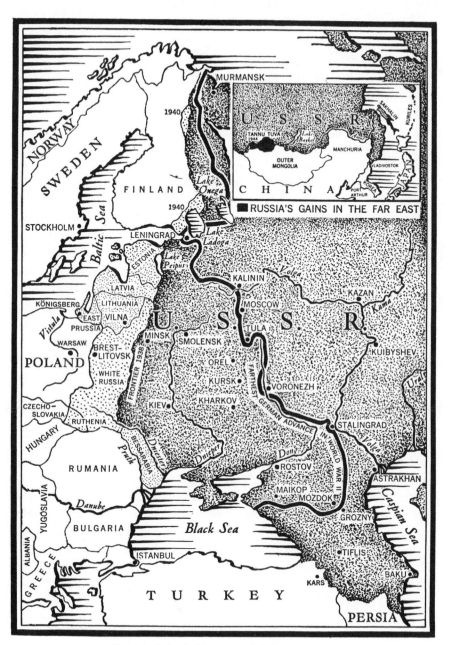

Russia's Gains in Europe and Asia, 1939–1945

ards the Soviets have reason to be satisfied with the outcome of the war. Russia not only retained the areas she had annexed under the Stalin-Hitler pact but after World War II expanded them by the incorporation of new territories. In Europe she acquired the Trans-Carpathian Ukraine from Czechoslovakia; east Karelia with Petsamo and Porkkala from Finland; and East Prussia with Koenigsberg from Germany. In the Far East she secured control of Port Arthur and Darien and annexed southern Sakhalin (ceded to Japan in 1905) and the Kurile Islands, as well as Tannu Tuva, formerly in Outer Mongolia. Russia was assured of an equal right with China in the operation of the Manchurian railways and of the safeguarding of her pre-eminent interests in Outer Mongolia and Manchuria.

Even more significant and pregnant with far-reaching consequences was the perpetuation of the Soviet occupation of half a dozen European countries. Wartime agreements bearing on military occupation, demilitarization, denazification, and dismantling of industry offered unlimited opportunities for the destruction of the social and economic framework of the former totalitarian states where affiliation, sometimes nominal, with the ruling party was mandatory for anyone in a position of prominence. The numerically weak but compact and determined Communist parties, backed by the Big Brother, stepped into the vacuum created by the relentless application of these policies. The sovietization of eastern Europe proceeded at a rapid pace, a tragic consequence of a war waged by the West in the name of self-determination and democracy. Imposed from above by a police regime dependent on foreign armies of occupation, the political and social processes set in motion in the Soviet-dominated countries were the negation of revolutionary Marxism, yet the conditions which they generated, or rather forcibly implanted, led inexorably to socialist revolutions.

The disintegration of the colonial system, which international Communism did its best to foster, provided it with possibilities for expansion which were not missed. The Soviet Union emerged from World War II as one of the world's two greatest powers—at least this is what millions of people believe—a transformation that few would have deemed possible in 1939 or 1941.

25

End of the Stalin Era, 1945-1953

Return to "Normalcy"

A Paradox? Continuity and change are present in the history of any country. In the case of Russia, however, the combination of these elements is at times so peculiar as to give it a flavor all of its own. The decade following World War II offers a notable instance of such a situation. The international position of Russia was revolutionized; she assumed new responsibilities and manifested new ambitions; she experienced and survived frightful devastation; and millions of Russian soldiers saw for the first time something of the world beyond their borders—shattered and disorganized as it was. The vast task of reconstruction was tackled with courage, determination, and, as we shall see, a measure of success. In spite of these seemingly dominant elements of novelty, the constitutional and administrative arrangements were preserved intact, and the same elderly men owing allegiance to stale, dated doctrines continued to rule by all-too-familiar methods a remarkably long-suffering and docile population. No new blood came to the top. Familiar figures—Stalin, Molotov, Mikoyan, Kaganovich, Vyshinsky, Voroshilov, Beria—ran the country as well as half a dozen foreign states. The popularity of military commanders—Zhukov, Vasilevsky, Rokossovsky, Malinovsky—if genuine it was, did not last long, and none of them played a major part in the post-war world. The final phase of the Stalin era retained in an exaggerated form the essential characteristics of the pre-war period, including those which since his death have been denounced in the Soviet Union as criminal and incompatible with Marxism-Leninism.

Foreign Relations

The Satellite Empire. A major facet of Soviet Russia's foreign policy was the consolidation of her grip over, and the implantation of Communist institutions in, the states which the fortunes of war and the optimism, myopia, and foolishness of Western statesmanship forced into the Soviet orbit. The methods used by Moscow were broadly similar to those applied in the Baltic states and in the Polish provinces annexed in 1939–1940. By the end of the war the Soviet army of occupation, with the friendly cooperation of the Moscow-trained Yugoslav Communist leader Tito, established a Communist regime in Yugoslavia, but in the other states under its domination the Kremlin in 1945 and 1946 was willing to tolerate left-wing coalition governments with the participation of peasant and independent socialist parties, provided they were "friendly" to the Soviet Union. This was a temporary arrangement that did not last long.

The elimination of non-Communist groups from the governments was carried on with great thoroughness to the accompaniment of purges, arrests, trials, and executions. Mikolajczyk, the "peasant" vice-premier of the Polish government, fled abroad in October 1947, and King Michael of Rumania was forced to abdicate in December. Bulgaria, Hungary, and Czechoslovakia were taken over by the Communists in 1947–1949. The Communist *coup* in Prague (February 1948) produced a particularly strong impression abroad, because Eduard Benes, the Czech president, and Jan Masaryk, the foreign minister, were distinguished statesmen well-known in the West. Both believed in the possibility of cooperation with Communism or, at least, tried to make it work. Both died soon after the Communist *putsch* in 1948; it was persistently rumored that Masaryk committed suicide or was murdered. In October 1949 the Soviet zone of occupation in Germany was reorganized as the German Democratic Republic. By the end of that year the sovietization of eastern Europe (except for Greece, where British influence remained pre-eminent) was complete.

Not everything, however, went according to the wishes of Moscow. Tito, his Muscovite affiliations notwithstanding, rebelled against the high-handed police methods of his former mentors, and in March–June 1948 came the formal breach between him and Stalin. "Titoism," a term implying a measure of independence from the Kremlin, became next to Trotskyism a deadly sin in orthodox Communist circles. It led to a new wave of severe purges in Hungary, Bulgaria, Albania, Czechoslovakia, and Poland: the wavering Communist leaders were replaced by unimpeachable adherents of Stalinism.

Two aspects of Soviet post-war expansion are particularly notable: the legal form given to Soviet domination and the fate of Finland. With the exception of northern Bukovina, the Trans-Carpathian Ukraine, and East Prussia, overt annexations were limited to territories formerly parts of the tsarist empire. Although the Third International proclaimed as its objective the creation of "the federation of the Soviet republics of the world," no attempt was made to bring the members of the satellite empire within the Soviet Union. Officially they are "people's democracies" or "democratic republics," and their Communist parties call themselves "united workers' parties" or some such name. Finland, the only former Russian country that has escaped incorporation in the Soviet Union, was permitted to remain outside the Soviet orbit. Nothing, of course, could have prevented the Soviet Union from crushing Finland. The explanation of Moscow's unusual magnanimity must be sought in the record of Russo-Finnish relations since the annexation of Finland at the beginning of the nineteenth century (briefly surveyed in the earlier chapters) and in that country's gallant struggle for her autonomy and, later, independence. If the federation of the Soviet republics of the world remains the ultimate objective of Communism, its leaders must have felt that the time for concrete moves in this direction was not yet ripe. An incorporation of new foreign territories would have added immeasurably to the administrative complexities of the Soviet Union which are by no means solved.

The Soviets attempted to expand in the Mediterranean area and in the Middle East. They agitated for a revision of the Montreux Straits convention (1936) that would have given Russia a base in the Dardanelles, and they demanded the trusteeship of the former Italian colony of Tripolitania. They failed in these endeavors, as they could not readily be backed by force. The occupation of Iran (jointly with Great Britain) that was instituted at the beginning of the Soviet-German war was extended by Moscow beyond the stipulated date (six months after the termination of the hostilities). Not unexpectedly, an "autonomous" pro-Soviet government appeared in the Russian-held Iranian province of Azerbaidzhan. Teheran and the West were alarmed, and it looked for a time as if the Russians were to stay. They actually agreed to withdraw in March 1946.

The Soviet Union and the West. Harry Hopkins, President Roosevelt's friend and intimate adviser, told R. E. Sherwood in 1945 that on leaving Yalta the mood of the American delegation was one of "supreme exaltation. . . . The Russians had proved that they could be reasonable and farseeing and there wasn't any doubt in the mind of the president or of any one of us that we could live with them and get along with them peacefully for as far into the future as any one of us could imagine." This was hardly an accurate forecast. Actually relations between the Soviet Union and the West deteriorated rapidly. The rickety machinery of international controls built on the foundation of Yalta and Potsdam proved unworkable. The council of foreign ministers, however, convened several times and succeeded in drafting peace treaties with Italy, Bulgaria, Hungary, Rumania, and Finland, which were debated in a large conference of 21 states in Paris (July–October 1946) and were signed at the Quai d'Orsay on February 10, 1947. The treaties adhered to the Yalta-Potsdam decisions, except that the Soviet Union and some of the minor belligerents established more definitely their claims to reparations. Negotiations for peace treaties with Austria and Germany were initiated in 1947 but ran into difficulties and were suspended.

The gap separating East and West widened. At a meeting in Poland in September 1947, representatives of the Communist parties of the Soviet Union, the satellite countries, France, and Italy set up the Communist Information Bureau, or Cominform. Its object was "to organize interexchange of experience among the parties, and if need be to coordinate their activities on the basis of mutual agreement." Unlike the Comintern, the Cominform had no statutes and did not claim to be a single Communist party. Its one important decision was the expulsion in June 1948 of Yugoslavia, which had incurred Stalin's displeasure. The formation of the Cominform was a shock to those in the West who had imagined that the dissolution of the Comintern meant the abandonment by Russia of world revolution.

Sovietization of eastern Europe forced the West to re-examine its policies. In March 1947 the United States government announced its determination to support, chiefly through economic and financial aid, "free peoples who are resisting attempted subjugation" (the Truman doctrine). The immediate reason for this pronouncement was the plight of Greece and Turkey, which were under strong Communist pressure. Allied policies towards Germany were reversed. Dismemberment, disarmament, dismantling of industry, and the proposed reduction of the country to a "pastoral condition" (the Morgenthau plan) gave way to a speedy restoration of a viable, highly industrialized, and eventually highly armed Germany. The Federal Republic of West Germany was established in March 1949; the Soviets retaliated by forming in their zone, in October 1949, the German Democratic Republic. Western defense measures against the inroads of Communism were interpreted in Moscow as aggressive action and encirclement. The European recovery program launched by George C. Marshall, American secretary of state, in June 1947 was vigorously resisted by the Kremlin. Czechoslovakia, which was still governed by a coalition, was forced to withdraw its acceptance of participation in the program.

A perennial center of discord was Berlin, which was within the Soviet zone, some 100 miles from the western border, and was administered by an allied control council. The zones of occupation of the allied powers in Berlin itself were originally intended as purely administrative subdivisions, but the Soviet zone soon became segregated from the Western sectors of the city. A dispute over the use of Eastern or Western currency in Berlin was the pretext but probably not the true cause of the sharp conflict that was soon to break out. In March 1948 the Soviets withdrew from the allied control council, and on June 24, 1948, they instituted the blockade of Berlin by closing to the allies all land and water routes leading to the city. The allies responded by organizing the air-lift, which went on until May 12, 1949, when an agreement was reached and the blockade was discontinued.

The European economic recovery program was the principal economic anti-Communist policy of the West. The North Atlantic Treaty Organization, or NATO formed on April 4, 1949, was and still is the West's chief political and military arm. The members of NATO are the United States, Canada, and 13 European countries, including Turkey and Greece, which geographically do not belong to the Atlantic community. The gist of NATO is the obligation assumed by the members that an attack against one of them will be considered an attack against them all. NATO maintains a comprehensive naval and military organization and a network of bases designed to check possible Soviet aggression. According to the West it is a purely defensive alliance, but Moscow interprets NATO as the spearhead of Western aggression against itself and other Communist countries, and much of its international action was directed to its disruption. The Soviets, in September 1949, launched with much fanfare the World Peace Movement led by the World Peace Council, which endeavors to enroll non-Communists in the service of the Communist cause and particularly to weaken and, if possible, destroy NATO.

The Far East. By the end of World War II the world shrank, overseas empires disintegrated, and the colonial powers and the United States found themselves confronted with Soviet influence in lands only recently unaware of Communism. National independence movements affiliated with extreme left-wing groups made rapid progress in Vietnam, Indonesia, Burma, Malaya, South India, and Korea. In August 1945, as a part of the Yalta-Potsdam arrangements, Moscow concluded a 30-year treaty of friendship with the Kuomintang. The Kremlin would seem to have observed its letter and spirit and to have exercised a restraining influence upon the Chinese Communists—until about the middle of 1948; but as the Communist victories mounted, the Soviet ambassador to Chiang Kai-shek was withdrawn (May 1949). A Chinese people's republic was proclaimed in October 1949 and was immediately recognized by the Kremlin. Chiang was forced to leave the mainland for Formosa (December), and a large delegation of Chinese Communists journeyed to Moscow, where they concluded with Russia a 30-year treaty of friendship and mutual assistance (February 1950). The Soviets agreed to return to China the former Japanese properties which they had taken over in Manchuria and to surrender to China not later than 1952 Port Arthur, Darien, and the Manchurian railways. Supplementary Soviet-Chinese agreements of 1952 and 1954 provided China with credits and other economic benefits but extended the term of the Soviet presence in Port Arthur until the beginning of 1955, when Russian troops were withdrawn.

A tangled situation existed in Korea. This tiny and barren land had long been a bone of contention between China and Japan, later joined by Russia. After World War II the peninsula was split into two states: the north, under a Communist regime, and the south, under a non-Communist government. After several attempts at unification had failed, the Soviets, who occupied the north, decided to withdraw (May 1948) and recognized the northern government as representative of the whole of Korea (September 1948). Evacuation of the Russian troops was completed in March 1949. The United States army, which occupied southern Korea, was withdrawn in the middle of 1949. A Communist-sponsored United Patriotic Front in north Korea issued in June 1950 an appeal for the immediate merger of the two Koreas, and when this was refused, the north Koreans crossed the 38th parallel, which formed the boundary between the two states, and invaded southern Korea (June 24). The United States came at once to its defense. The Security Council of the United Nations recommended, in the absence of the Russian delegate, military aid to south Korea and established a unified United Nations command under the United States in which 15 states participated. There followed a bitter war in which the Americans and south

Koreans were confronted with a large body of Chinese "volunteers." A cease-fire agreement was signed in June 1951, and protracted peace negotiations restored the pre-war situation. Throughout the Korean war and its aftermath the Soviet government unwaveringly supported the north Koreans. Its part in instigating the Communist attack is uncertain, but it seems clear that had it not been for the determined action of President Truman and, surprisingly, the Security Council, south Korea would have been swallowed by the Communists.

Another development in the Far Eastern situation was the consummation at a conference held in San Francisco (September 1951) of the peace treaty with Japan. The treaty was prepared by the United States government, and the various amendments moved subsequently by the Soviets were not taken into account. The treaty was signed by 49 states, 3 declined the invitation, and 3 (the USSR, Poland, and Czechoslovakia) attended but abstained.

The Atomic Bomb. It was announced on September 23, 1949, that the USSR had exploded an atomic bomb. The United States monopoly of this frightful weapon had come to an end.

Government and Economics

Government and the Party. With the termination of the war the administrative and the party machines reverted to their peacetime routine. The State Defense Committee was disbanded in September 1945, but Stalin, in his capacity as chairman of the Council of People's Commissars, remained, both in law and in fact, the head of the Soviet state. The Council of People's Commissars underwent a two-fold change. By a constitutional amendment of March 1946 the people's commissariats were renamed ministries, and the Council of People's Commissars became the Council of Ministers. No explanation for this departure from the sacred Leninist tradition was given. Perhaps Stalin, a marshal and generalissimo, preferred the new title, or the abandonment of the revolutionary appellation might have been regarded as an asset in negotiations with bourgeois governments. The second and more fundamental change was the vast increase in the number of ministries (already noted in an earlier chapter), which rose from 18 in 1936 to 58 in 1947. The ministerial structure and the structure of the administrative-territorial subdivisions were subject to continual remodeling, an instability that must have affected adversely the process of planning. Most of the ministries, unlike their namesakes in the bourgeois world, dealt with specialized economic and technical matters, as is indicated by their names. In 1950 some of the ministries were: aircraft industry, automobile and tractor industry, machine and instrument-making industry, metallurgical industry, oil industry, communications equipment industry, agricultural machinery industry, building and road-building machinery industry, and so on. Ministers, with the exception of the chairman of the council and perhaps the foreign minister, were little known by the general public and were not important political leaders. Ministerial positions were the reward of deserving party functionaries and technicians. Their appointments and dismissals were noted briefly, if at all, on the back pages of the newspapers.

The formalities of political life were revived. Elections to the Supreme Soviet of the USSR were held in February 1946 and in March 1950, and to the republican Supreme Soviets and local Soviets in 1947, 1948, and 1951. The pre-war election procedure was closely followed: in each district there was one candidate, nominated by the bloc of Communists and non-party people; everyone went to the polls and voted for the sole candidate. In the 1950 federal election 99.98 per cent of the eligible voters (111 million) voted, and 99.73 per cent cast their ballots for the candidates. Election managers have nothing to worry about except the danger of obtaining a vote of over 100 per cent, which, according to malevolent gossip, sometimes happened in districts where Stalin or other chieftains were the candidates. The percentage of Communists among the delegates to the Supreme Soviet of the USSR was high, 80 to 85 per cent, but was much lower in the newly-acquired republics: 11 per cent in Lithuania and 13 per cent in Latvia. The Supreme Soviet of the USSR met regularly twice a year, as required by the constitution; the sessions were brief and formal and adhered strictly to the pre-war pattern: leaders spoke for hours, votes were unanimous, every reference to Stalin, which no speaker omitted, was met with "stormy applause."

Victory and the passing of years brought no relaxation of the political tension. Stalin was not mellowed by adulation and age but became—as we are now officially told—increasingly suspicious and exacting. During the war, enforcement of security regulations was largely in the hands of the military. Beginning in 1947, however, the Supreme Soviet enacted measures for the protection of the state and state property. Information bearing on economic conditions, inventions, and relations with foreign states was designated as secret, except when released by the Council of Ministers. Unauthorized disclosure of such information became a criminal offense. A decree of December 17, 1947, imposed severe restrictions on relations with foreigners. The foreign minister and the minister of foreign trade were the only ones allowed to deal with foreign representatives, and that "within the limits of their authority." Shop assistants, waiters, postal and telegraph employees, and clerks selling railway and theater tickets were permitted to deal with foreigners "in so far as this is necessary for the performance of the usual functions of such persons." There should be no idle talk. Marriages between Russians and foreigners were prohibited (decree of February 17, 1947). The size of the official "Collection (*Sobranie*) of Decisions and Ordinances of the Government (changed to Council of Ministers after April 1947) of the USSR," one of the few revealing authoritative sources of information, shrank markedly after 1940, and publication was discontinued in 1949; it does not seem to have been resumed until 1955 and then on a much reduced scale.

Measures of great severity were taken against workers and farmers who failed in their duty to the Communist state. A decree of the presidium of the Supreme Soviet of May 26, 1947, abolished capital punishment and made confinement in a labor camp for 25 years the highest penalty in peacetime. The reasons given for this decision were "the loyalty of the entire population to the Soviet motherland (*rodina*) and Soviet government" during the war, and the belief that "the cause of peace may be considered secure for a long time." On January 12, 1950, however, the presidium reversed itself and reimposed capital punishment for "traitors, spies, and saboteurs." Restoration of the death penalty, according to the decree, was a response to requests addressed to the government by the national republics, trade unions, peasant organizations, and the intelligentsia—a surprising statement that, if believed, would indicate widespread subversion.

There were changes in the composition and structure of the Communist Party. The number of members increased from 2.5 million (including candidates) in 1939 to 6.9 million in March 1952. Recruitment was particularly intensive during the war, when conditions for admission were relaxed; in 1942 alone 2 million members joined the party. After the war admission was more closely regulated, and the growth of the party slowed down. Increase in membership was of more than passing significance, for it tended to transform the party from an élite into a mass organization; this process, if permitted to continue, might eventually change the party's character and, perhaps, make it more difficult to control. Although party congresses are required to meet every three years and the Eighteenth Congress convened in 1939, the Nineteenth was not held until October 1952. It changed the name of the party to Communist Party of the Soviet Union, dropping "of the Bolsheviks," and abolished the Politburo and Orgburo, replacing them by an enlarged presidium (of the central committee) that consisted of 25 members and 11 alternates. It is believed that the small secretly-appointed Bureau was the hub of the leadership. The new central committee elected by the congress had 125 members and 111 alternates and was almost twice as large as its predecessor of 1939. A committee under the chairmanship of Stalin was set up to revise the party program. It is impossible to interpret with any degree of assurance the true purpose and meaning of these changes. At the congress the key address was delivered by G. Malenkov. Both he and Stalin, who made a short speech, were enthusiastically applauded. This was the last party congress attended by Stalin.

Reconstruction and Economic Planning. At the end of the war the Soviet government was faced with the stupendous task of repairing the damages caused by the invasion. A statistical estimate of the losses suffered was given in the previous chapter. The nearly desperate economic situation was aggravated by a drought in 1946 that embraced most of the agricultural regions and was probably the most devastating since 1891. The powers of recuperation of an economy, however, are boundless. The principal official instrument of recovery was the fourth Five-Year Plan, adopted in March 1946, which followed the pattern of the pre-war plans and emphasized the development of heavy industry. The aggregate capital investment under the new plan was given as 326.5 billion rubles (at 1955 values, which precludes comparison with investment figures for the earlier period). It was claimed that the fourth Five-Year Plan was completed for industry in four years and three months; during that period 6,000 industrial enterprises, not counting the minor ones, were built or restored and put into operation, and the number of workers employed in the national economy at the end of 1950 was 39.8 million, an increase of 8.3 million over 1940. The fifth Five-Year Plan, covering the years 1951 through 1955, provided for further investments of 625.3 billion rubles (again at 1955 prices). The huge post-war capital outlays came predominantly, as before, from the turnover tax, which in 1946–1952 provided more than half of the rapidly growing total revenue. Little imagination was shown in the approach to the industrial problems. The restrictive labor legislation of 1940 remained in force. The questionable device of socialist emulation was retained and its use extended as the chief method of fostering higher productivity. Capital investment showed real results in transportation; in May 1952 there was opened for traffic the Volga-Don canal, which completed the waterway linking five seas: Baltic, White, Black, Caspian, and Azov.

Farming. Agriculture, more than any other sector of the economy, proved resistant to the entreaties of the planners. The peasants took advantage of the looser wartime controls to elude the straitjacket of collectivization. A decree issued jointly by the party and the government on September 19, 1946, disclosed a telling picture of the disarray of the *kolkhoz* system. The principal violations of the *kolkhoz* rules listed in the decree were spoliation of the public land of the collective farms by members and outsiders; wrongful allocation of labor days to the administrative personnel and non-members, a practice that imperiled the labor-day payment system; and disregard for the rules of *kolkhoz* democracy, with the consequence that no elections were held and the farms were run by appointed officials. The decree stated that "spoliation of the publicly controlled land of the farms has assumed a mass character." The subsidiary household allotments were unlawfully enlarged and became the chief interest and source of income of the collective farmers. The September decree led to the removal of half a million "superfluous" *kolkhoz* officials and to the restitution to the farmers of 5 million hectares of land which had been improperly appropriated. A Council on Collective Farms Affairs, attached to the Council of Ministers, was appointed in October 1946. Severe criticisms of the farm situation were repeated, and punitive measures provided, in several decrees issued in 1947 and 1948. Encouragement of deserving farmers took the form of incentive payments as well as medals, honorary titles, and other rewards.

In April 1950 the party and the government embarked on a policy of the amalgamation of the collective farms. Their number was reduced from 252,000 in 1949 to 93,300 in 1953, while the average size of the sown area per farm increased from 450 to 1,400 hectares, and the average number of households from 80 to 220. Nikita Khrushchev, whose influence began to be felt in the Communist hierarchy, sponsored this program. It was expected that it would increase efficiency and productivity, cut down *kolkhoz* bureaucracy, and facilitate political control. Only 15 per cent of the collective farms had primary party organs in 1949, while 80 per cent had them in 1953. Greater productivity, however, was not achieved: in 1952 the output of agriculture was practically on the 1940 level, a lack of progress that might be explained, in part, by the ravages of the war. Khrushchev's program went further and envisaged the creation of "agro-towns" (*agrogorod*), which would require mass resettlement of farmers and, incidentally, the elimination of household allotments; these were to be replaced by orchards adjoining the modern apartment houses in which the farmers were expected to live. This scheme had a utopian flavor and was not acted upon, but the elimination of household allotments has remained a feature of Khrushchev's farming policy since he succeeded Stalin. It was also about 1951 that Khrushchev

conceived the idea of the development of virgin lands in the eastern territories of the Soviet Union; its implementation came later, after Stalin's death.

Money and Rationing. Money, like agriculture, tends to elude the dictates
of planned economy. Since the Soviet government controls the volume and
prices of the goods produced as well as wages and other sources of income,
it should theoretically be possible to balance the value of the goods available
and the purchasing power in a manner that would prevent inflation. Economic theory, however, as often as not, does not agree with practice—and
this not only under socialism. Inflation has been a recurrent feature of Soviet
development. In 1941, as in 1929, the pressure of excessive purchasing power
and the shortage of goods forced the Kremlin to introduce rationing and a
multiple-price system. It was computed that in 1944 prices on the "free"
market and in state-owned "commercial" stores which sold goods without
ration cards were 40 to 50 times higher than rationed prices. This situation
created much hardship and accentuated economic inequality.

Abolition of rationing was promised immediately after the war, steps
to reduce disparity in prices were taken in September 1946, and finally on
December 14, 1947, came the decree of the party and government that dealt
with money, rationing, prices, and wages. Under its provisions all paper
currency in circulation was to be exchanged during the third week in
December 1947 for paper currency of a new pattern. Conversion was carried
at different rates. For cash it was 10 old rubles for one new ruble. The rate
for the revaluation of the deposits varied with the amount of the account.
Deposits up to 3,000 rubles were given the most privileged treatment: one
new ruble for each old ruble. Rates were less favorable for larger deposits:
three old rubles to two new ones for deposits of 3,000 to 10,000 rubles, and
two old rubles to one new one for deposits in excess of 10,000 rubles. The
rate of five old rubles to four new ones was provided for the accounts of
collective farms and other cooperative institutions. State loans were revalued
(May–August 1948) at the rate of three old rubles to one new one. Simultaneously rationing was abolished. Prices of foodstuffs were fixed, roughly, at
the level of the former rationed prices and those of manufactured goods
somewhat higher, but still one-third or one-fourth of the former "commercial
prices." Beginning in December all wages were paid in the new currency.

The revaluation of the ruble was an essential prerequisite for the abolition
of rationing and as such was welcome, but the method adopted had political
motivation. During the period of rationing, the farmers, who sold their
produce on the *kolkhoz* market—the only market where prices were not regulated—realized substantial profits. Russian peasants do not as a rule deposit

their savings in banks but keep them as cash at home; they were the principal losers under the 1947 reform, although the decree was ostensibly directed against "speculators."

Gains from Occupied Territories. Recovery was helped by reparations from Italy and the former satellites of Germany which the Soviet Union secured by virtue of the armistice agreements elaborated in the peace treaties of February 10, 1947; by the removal of large amounts of industrial equipment from western Germany and the states in the Soviet orbit, especially eastern Germany and Manchuria; by the sequestration of properties owned by German nationals in the Soviet-occupied countries; and by the operation of the joint-stock companies set up by the Soviets, usually on a 50-50 basis, in the lands under Russian control. The actual gains derived from these sources cannot be determined with any degree of precision, but they are believed to have been substantial.

With the sovietization of eastern Europe, Soviet international economic policies took a different and more benevolent turn. In January 1949 there was formed in Moscow the Council for Economic Mutual Assistance, or Comecon, an organization of European Communist states for cooperation in planning and trade. It was intended as the Communist counterpart to the Marshall Plan but showed little activity until the middle of the 1950's, and it did not secure a formal charter until December 1959.

Social Policies

Schools. Education has a high priority in the Soviet scale of values, yet progress in this area, until recently, has been hesitant and relatively slow. Lenin held that Soviet schools should provide "basic scientific knowledge of both nature and society, the world outlook of scientific materialism, communist morality, physical exercise for good health, and the close link between study and productive labor." The first people's commissar for education was Anatole Lunacharsky (1917–1929), a man of culture and imagination, an old Bolshevik, but also a playwright and literary critic. The "unified labor school" was established in October 1918 as the sole type of elementary and secondary school; it offered two consecutive sets of courses covering, respectively, five and four years. The basic principles of these schools, as defined by the Eighth Party Congress in 1919, were instruction in native languages, co-education, separation from the Church, and the linking of education with economic life. The practice of the Soviet schools in the 1920's, however, was varied, partly because of the difficulties in translating the above generalities into classroom programs and routine and partly because of Lunacharsky's aesthetic proclivities. Schools on every level taught Marxian dialectics, Communist theory, and kindred subjects regarded as essential to rear Communists. Much attention was given to the elimination of illiteracy. It was estimated that between 1920 and 1950, 50 million adults learned to read and write.

Planned economy and rapid industrialization generated a brisk demand for skilled workers and qualified employees. Attendance in elementary schools was made compulsory by a decree of July 1930. A decree of 1934 "On the Structure of Elementary and Secondary Schools" established the 7-year school as standard. The Eighteenth Congress of the party (1939) decreed that schools of this type should be organized all over the country, but the outbreak of the war prevented the implementation of this directive. Beginning in 1931 uniform curricula and traditional forms of school discipline, which were neglected during the early revolutionary period, were reinstated. Examinations and strict grading were reintroduced in August 1932, and the authority of teachers was enhanced by measures enacted in May 1934. It will be remembered that tuition fees in the upper grades of the secondary schools and in all higher schools were imposed in 1940.

The Soviet Union has a system of vocational, trade, technical, and other specialized schools that, roughly, parallels the general school system. Quantitatively, education registered substantial progress, although it slowed down in post-war years. The number of elementary and secondary schools increased from 104,000 with 10.3 million students in 1925–1926 to 198,600 with 35.5 million students in 1940–1941 and to 220,000 with 34.8 million students (a decline) in 1950–1951. There were 800 higher schools with 585,000 full-time students in 1940–1941 and 863 higher schools with 845,000 students in 1950–1951. Not all of these schools maintained high scholastic standards, but some, especially the technical schools, unquestionably did. Great emphasis was put on correspondence courses. The number of students enrolled in such courses on the higher school level rose from 227,000 in 1940–1941 to 400,000 in 1950–1951.

The Welfare State. Contrary to what might have been expected in a socialist commonwealth, social security until recently fared poorly in Soviet Russia, even though she has a comprehensive program of social benefits. Sickness and disability insurance, maternity benefits, sports and recreation facilities, and some old-age and disability pensions are classified as "social insurance" and, since the abolition of the people's commissariat of labor in 1933, are administered by the All-Russian Central Council of Trade Unions. Most of the old-age and disability pensions (including pensions of war veterans) are classified as "social security" (or "relief") and are administered by republican ministries of social security. Social insurance schemes, which are non-contributory, cover all wage-earners but not the collective farmers and members of other cooperative associations. Since 1930 there has been no unemployment insurance. Sickness and disability benefits are tied to the length of employment in one enterprise, that is, they are substantially higher for those workers who have good records of continuous employment. Budget appropriations for social insurance increased from one billion rubles in 1928–1929 to 7.4 billion in 1940 and to 18.1 billion in 1950. Budget appropriations for "social security" (as defined above) rose even more rapidly, from 107 million rubles in 1928–1929 to one billion in 1940 and to 22.4 billion in 1950 —chiefly because of war pensions. A curious decree of July 8, 1944, provided bonuses and monthly allowances for mothers of more than two children; the rates were progressive, that is, larger bonuses and larger allowances were granted for each additional child. The decree also established the "Medal of Motherhood," the badge "Glory of Motherhood," and the title "Mother Heroine"—the latter conferred on mothers of 10 or more children. In 1947, in connection with the monetary reform of that year, these benefits were cut by half. In 1950 the budget provision under this heading was 4 billion rubles. Appropriations for public health rose from 660 million rubles in 1928 to 22 billion in 1950.

Increase in appropriations should not be interpreted as conclusive evidence of a higher standard of welfare. The price and monetary situation throughout the 1930's and 1940's was chaotic, and the absence of a price index precludes meaningful comparisons between outlays in the various years. There is hardly any information on the working of social insurance and social security; even basic data, such as the number of people drawing old-age and disability pensions, are not available. The rates of some of the benefits and pensions are pitifully low. A drastic reform was long overdue and, as will appear in the next chapter, was undertaken by Khrushchev.

National Self-Determination. The USSR is a multi-national polity. The census of 1959 lists nearly a hundred nationalities living within the Soviet border, and the number of languages spoken is said to be even greater. Constitutionally the union is a federated state comprising over 50 republics and regions, which, theoretically, enjoy a measure of autonomy. The principle of national self-determination, including the right of "secession and formation of an independent state" proclaimed in the early days of the revolution, has never been repudiated. Yet in practice Soviet federalism, autonomy, and self-determination, like Soviet democracy, mean the very opposite of what these terms mean in the Western world. The interpretation put on self-determination by Stalin—that the exercise of this right must be subordinated to the interests of the revolution—has been maintained. The Supreme Soviets of the constituent and autonomous Soviet republics exercise no real power and, had they suddenly stopped meeting, few would have noticed it, except the members of these assemblies. Similarly, national self-determination is reduced to the use of local languages and the fostering of national folkways, but even these modest manifestations of nationalism are narrowly circumscribed. The national tradition of the minorities is largely derived from the history of their struggle against subjugation by Russia, a theme that lends itself to interpretations unflattering to the conquerors. The militant Russian nationalism, which became manifest in the middle 1930's, reached its apex during the war, and has retained its sway since, does not tolerate views, however artfully presented, which would mar the picture of the majestic onward march of the empire. Artists, composers, and authors belonging to national minorities must remain strictly within the bounds of Communist orthodoxy as well as avoid any possible offense to Russian nationalistic susceptibilities. Otherwise they are free, and national self-expression is greatly encouraged. This is what self-determination means in the USSR.

"The Cult of Personality"

How Could This Be True? From Stalin's personal point of view the crowning achievement of the 30 years of his dictatorship was the grotesque and fantastic ritual of which he was the center and which since the disclosures of 1956 is known as the "cult of personality." It is difficult to determine exactly when and how this extraordinary situation arose, but it is likely that the supine members of his entourage, encouraged by Stalin, endeavored to outdo one another in crude flattery until there was no way back and the real Stalin became submerged in the flood of verbal extravaganza released by the sycophants. Stalin was referred to as "the genius," "leader of the peoples," "greatest military genius of all times," "builder of the scientific foundation of Soviet foreign policy," author whose work "constitutes an era in the history of science," and so on and so forth. His opinions were never questioned. Men and women in every station in life joined lustily in the choir of unseemly adulation. The president of the Academy of Science spoke of Stalin as "our friend, teacher, and leader." The ritual was expertly organized. Every appearance of Stalin or mere reference to his name was greeted with an ovation. The purges, trials, and executions of the 1930's, of which so many Communists were the innocent victims, did nothing to dampen the party's enthusiasm for the leader. History offers no instance of hierolatry on a comparable scale.

In 1938 there appeared the *History of the All-Union Party of the Bolsheviks, A Short Course,* which, although published under the imprint of the central committee, was avowedly the work of Stalin. This clumsy, pedestrian compilation, packed with distortions of well-known facts, was acclaimed in the Soviet Union as the greatest contribution to knowledge. By 1949 no fewer than 36 million copies had been printed. Everyone, from members of the Academy of Science and high officials down to common laborers, was expected to read the *Short History;* its platitudes and untruths were disseminated in innumerable seminars and study groups, attendance of which it would have been imprudent to skip.

No one knows what went on in Stalin's tortured mind in the closing months of his life, but there is evidence that a new purge might have been in the making. In January 1953 nine well-known doctors were arrested on the charge of having in 1948 poisoned Andrew Zhdanov, head of the Leningrad party organization and an intimate of Stalin, and of plotting the destruction of other leaders. Seven of the nine were Jewish; all confessed. After Stalin's death it was announced that the confessions were obtained by improper means, and the doctors were exonerated.

The most disturbing and bewildering aspect of the "cult of personality" chapter of Soviet history is not the aberrations of Stalin, who was admittedly suffering from delusions, but the willingness of the party for years to condone this situation.

Stalin Dies. Following a stroke, Stalin died on March 5, 1953. With much pomp and circumstance his embalmed body was deposited next to that of Lenin in the Red Square mausoleum. It was announced on November 1, 1961, that his remains had been removed from the mausoleum "to the Kremlin wall."

Wide World

Stalin's bier

26

After Stalin: The First Decade

The Ascendancy of Khrushchev

Collective Leadership. Stalin's death was hardly entirely unexpected—he was 74 and was known to be in failing health—yet its impact was tremendous, particularly on party leadership. Although much has been written about the events which brought Khrushchev to power, the actual workings of the party machinery that decides such matters are not known, and conjectures and guesses, however ingenious, are of limited usefulness and not infrequently create more confusion. The presentation that follows will be limited to the few ascertainable facts.

In a surprising statement issued on March 7, 1953, the party and the government proclaimed their intention to ensure the continuity of leadership in order to prevent "disorder and panic." Malenkov succeeded Stalin as both chairman of the Council of Ministers and senior secretary of the party. Others at the top level of the official hierarchy were: Beria, minister of the interior and head of the security police; Molotov, foreign minister; Nicholas Bulganin, defense minister (who, although not an army man, was made a marshal in 1947); and Lazar Kaganovich, first deputy chairman of the Council of Ministers. The structure of the higher party organs, created by the Nineteenth Congress in October 1952, was revised. The Bureau was abolished, and the presidium of the central committee was reduced from 25 to 10 members. It comprised, in addition to the five ministers mentioned above, Khrushchev, Mikoyan, Voroshilov, and two others. There was much talk about, but little evidence of, "collective leadership." On March 15, a few days after the formation of the new administration, Malenkov was released from the position of party secretary, ostensibly at his own request. Khrushchev, a member of the secretariat since 1949, filled Malenkov's place and in September 1953 was given the title of first secretary.

Several men close to Stalin, among them Alexander Poskrebyshev, his private secretary and a member of the party secretariat, disappeared and were not heard of again—it was believed that they were executed—but developments much more sensational were in the offing. On July 10, 1953, it was announced that Beria, who had seemed all-powerful, was arrested. He was accused, among other things, of having been for 30 years an agent of British intelligence and of planning the destruction of the leading Communists in order to establish his personal dictatorship. It was officially stated in December 1953 that Beria and several accomplices were secretly tried, confessed, and were shot. The precedents of the 1930's purges were followed faithfully.

On February 8, 1955, the Supreme Soviet relieved Malenkov of the duties of chairman of the Council of Ministers. Formally, the action was taken at his own request: his statement listing his lack of experience and his responsibility for the unsatisfactory condition of agriculture was read to the Supreme Soviet in his presence but not by him. He was transferred to a minor ministerial post; in 1957 he was identified as a member of the "anti-party group" (to be discussed presently), expelled from the central committee, and sent to the Urals to become the director of a power station.

Malenkov was succeeded as chairman of the Council of Ministers by Bulganin, who for three years retained this position and was Khrushchev's companion on frequent foreign travels. Meanwhile Khrushchev greatly increased his authority by consolidating his control over the party machine, a process that eludes precise analysis. As in the days of Stalin, Soviet policies became identified with the party secretary. In May 1955 Khrushchev paid a state visit to Yugoslavia that led to the resumption of relations with that country, relations which had been broken off in 1948. On this occasion he spoke in a conciliatory vein of the right of a country to pursue its own brand of socialism. On February 25, 1956, at a closed session of the Twentieth Party Congress, Khrushchev delivered his famous speech (the text of which was never officially released) in which, with a frankness unprecedented at a Communist gathering, he presented a hair-raising factual account of the crimes of the Stalin era, although (as will be seen later in this chapter) it was not a total repudiation of Stalin. The speech had far-reaching repercussions, especially in the Communist countries and, together with Khrushchev's pronouncement (in Yugoslavia) on different roads to socialism, encouraged a spirit of independence among foreign Communists that in Poland reached the stage of almost overt revolt and in Hungary became an armed uprising (autumn 1956) that was suppressed by the Soviet army.

On June 29, 1957, the central committee of the party issued a resolution condemning the "anti-party group," which consisted of Malenkov, Kaganovich, Molotov, and Dimitry Shepilov (formerly editor of *Pravda,* member of the party secretariat, and foreign minister in 1956–1957). They were charged with flouting the party line ·on various issues (reconciliation with Yugoslavia, agricultural and industrial policies) and with trying to effect changes in the composition of the leading party organs—which presumably meant the removal of Khrushchev. The members of the "anti-party group" were expelled from the central committee and the presidium and were assigned to minor non-political posts.

At the end of March 1958 Bulganin was dismissed and was succeeded as chairman of the Council of Ministers by Khrushchev. Thus the union of the two highest party and state offices that had existed in the closing years of Stalin's rule was restored. In December 1958 Bulganin was denounced as a member of the "anti-party group" and slipped into final oblivion. Other public figures, among them Marshals Clement Voroshilov and George Zhukov, fell from grace. Voroshilov, chairman of the presidium of the Supreme Soviet and as such head of the state in 1953–1960, escaped with nothing worse than scoffing public castigation from Khrushchev; but Zhukov, a war hero and defense minister since 1953, was linked to the "anti-party group" in October 1957, expelled from the presidium and the central committee, and deprived of his offices. At the Twenty-second Congress Khrushchev referred to him as a "bankrupt factionist and scheming careerist."

These kaleidoscopic and obscure happenings reveal that of the handful of men in the front line of leadership in March 1953, all had ended in disgrace by 1958. Beria was the only top leader executed, but the chastisement of the others were severe enough. This was the startling result of "collective leadership."

Nikita Sergeevich Khrushchev. The successor of Stalin—for he is Stalin's successor in the full meaning of the term—was Nikita Sergeevich Khrushchev. A ruthless and ambitious Communist, he was not regarded in March 1953 as a serious contender for the position of leadership that he came to fill. Khrushchev was born in 1894 in the village of Kalinovka in the province of Kursk. He was the son of a miner, worked as a shepherd, locksmith, and mechanic, joined the party in 1918, fought in the civil war, and did some studying at the University of Kharkov and, later, at the industrial academy in Moscow. He spent practically his entire life in party offices and was made a member of the central committee in 1934 and of the Politburo, as a candidate in 1938 and as a full member in 1939. As already noted, he has been a member of the presidium since its reorganization in 1952, first secretary since 1953, and chairman of the Council of Ministers since 1958.

Tireless, irrepressible, and ebullient, Khrushchev, unlike Stalin, likes change. He has initiated numerous reforms, altered the structure of industry and farming, reformed schools and social security, and frequently visited foreign countries, including India, England, and the United States. In 1960 he headed the Soviet delegation to the United Nations. Khrushchev has a seemingly inexhaustible capacity for making speeches; although a man of action rather than a theorist, he has revised some of the Communist doctrines. Like Lenin, he never doubts the rightness and wisdom of his opinions and has clear-cut and unwavering views on subjects as far apart as plowing and corn growing, on the one hand, and painting, literature, and music, on the other. Khrushchev makes ritualistic references to collective leadership, but there is no evidence that party bodies exercise any more influence since he came to power than they did under his predecessor.

Constitutional Amendments

The Karelo-Finnish SSR. Under the rule of Stalin the constitution underwent no major changes. Adjustments were made to meet current exigencies, such as the shifting of boundaries of internal administrative subdivisions, the increase in the number of ministries, or the imposition of fees in the upper grades of high schools and the higher schools (the constitution of 1936 provided for free education at every level); also, in 1940 five constituent republics were added to the roster as a result of the annexation of territories. But the basic provisions of the constitution were not challenged and, indeed, came to be looked upon as immutable and nearly sacred. This is no longer the case, and, as we know, a new constitution is being drafted.

A curious constitutional change was the reduction of the Karelo-Finnish SSR to the status of an autonomous Soviet socialist republic within the

RSFSR (July 16, 1956). The initiative, according to the official version, came from the Council of Ministers of the Karelo-Finnish SSR, which, in its petition to the Supreme Soviet of the USSR, gave the following reasons: the Finnish population of the portion of the republic annexed in 1940 had emigrated to Finland and the actual population was two-thirds Russian, and the territory in question has long "historical ties" with Russia, which were allegedly strengthened by the part played by Russia in the Finnish civil war and in World War II, an argument not likely to commend itself to the Finns. The request of the Finnish government was, of course, granted by the Supreme Soviet, and the number of constituent republics was reduced from 16 to 15. The change was of small practical significance, because constituent republics are just as tightly controlled by the federal government as the autonomous republics. It is noteworthy as the only and peculiar instance of action by the legislature bearing on a federal issue. Conflict between federal and state governments over their respective rights and jurisdictions is a familiar feature of the history of federal unions, the federated states usually jealously defending their rights against infringement by the central authority. This situation has never arisen in the Soviet Union. The Karelo-Finnish SSR took the very opposite position and petitioned for the theoretical lowering of its status from independence to autonomy. The ethnic complexion of its population, the reason evoked by its government, would seem to be irrelevant in the light, for instance, of the constitutional history of the United States.

Administrative Economic Regions. Of greater practical importance was the reorganization of industrial controls by a law of May 10, 1957. This transferred the management of industry from the ministries to the economic administrative regions, governed by economic administrative councils which are appointed by the Councils of Ministers of the constituent republics. The proposed legislation, which originated with Khrushchev, was discussed for five weeks, in the Stalinist tradition, at some 500,000 meetings attended by 40 million people. The total number of economic administrative regions was 105: the RSFSR had 70; the Ukrainian SSR, 11; the Kazakh SSR, nine; the Uzbek SSR, four; and the other 11 constituent republics each constituted one economic administrative region. Simultaneously 25 of the 32 federal economic ministries were abolished, although it was not intended to bring about decentralization of controls; the true object was to establish a closer relationship between the supervising agencies and the producing enterprises. The planning bodies were remodeled and their powers actually extended. The reform, said Khrushchev, embodied "the basic Leninist principle of democratic centralism and planned management," not perhaps a very helpful formula. It has been suggested that the dismantling of the ministries might have had a political object—dispersal of centers of opposition to Khrushchev among the bureaucrats cluttered in Moscow—but these surmises cannot be verified.

Apparently "democratic centralism" did not work well. The economic administrative councils were widely criticized for their parochial approach that tended to sacrifice broader interests to those of their particular regions. A decree of April 24, 1958, established the "disciplinary, material, and criminal responsibility" of the leaders of enterprises for failure to carry out planned deliveries "to other economic regions of constituent republics." Punitive measures alone did not seem to bring satisfactory results. It was argued that the economic administrative regions were too small to allow effective economic planning. In 1961 they were grouped into 17 major economic regions, each under a coordinating council. The RSFSR had 10 such regions; the Ukrainian SSR, three; the Kazakh SSR made up one region; and there were three major regions embracing the other constituent republics, except for White Russia and the Moldavian SSR, which for reasons not made clear were left out of the scheme.

Problems of economic organization were discussed at great length by the plenary session of the central committee in November 1962. A resolution of that body recognized the necessity "to reorganize the leading party agencies from bottom to top on the basis of the production principle and thereby to ensure more concrete guidance of industry and agriculture"— as recommended in a report by Khrushchev. The revised scheme put into operation in February 1963 divided the USSR into 47 economic regions, each under an economic council. The regions are of uneven size. The Northeastern region, covering the northeastern portion of Siberia, is territorially by far the largest; it comprises the huge area of 4.3 million square kilometers but has one of the smallest populations—800,000 people.

The above changes suggest that after 35 years of economic planning, no satisfactory solution has been found for the institutional control of a socialized economy.

There were other amendments to the constitution, such as the restoration of the provision guaranteeing free education at all levels, which was revived after the abolition of tuition fees in 1956.

The Party

Statutes and Program, 1961. Under the direction of Khrushchev the Communist Party increased outwardly its participation in public affairs. Party congresses were convened more frequently: the Twentieth in February 1956, the Twenty-first in January–February 1959, and the Twenty-second in October 1961. As in the past, congresses offered no opportunity for genuine debate, the first secretary—now Khrushchev—dominating the proceedings. In the summer of 1957, in connection with the expulsion of the "anti-party group," the presidium was enlarged from 10 to 15 members. Between the Twenty-first and Twenty-second Congresses party membership rose from 7.2 million to 9.7 million. During the same period 200,000 members were expelled. The Twentieth Congress became a landmark in the party history because of Khrushchev's denunciation of Stalin; the Twenty-first confirmed the "target figures" for the Seven-Year Plan; and the Twenty-second approved the party statutes and program. The statutes introduced no major changes in the structure of the party, except, perhaps, that they endeavored to inject new blood into party organs by providing that a specified proportion of new members should be elected at each election and by restricting membership in the presidium and other agencies to three successive terms. This rule, however, could be waived "in consideration of the political and work qualities of an individual"—a thoughtful provision to protect the tenure of the VIP's. The party congresses were to meet at least once every four years.

The party program is a more interesting and revealing document. Commissions for the preparation of the new program were appointed by the Eighteenth Congress in 1939 and by the Nineteenth in 1952. Stalin was the chairman of both, but no progress was made and the program of 1919 theoretically continued in force. The 1961 program—a long, wordy, and complicated document—bears the imprint of Khrushchev. While retaining the phraseology of revolutionary Marxism, it introduces certain novel elements. World Communism remains the immutable objective. Appropriately, Part I of the program, entitled "The Transition from Capitalism to Communism—the Road of Development of Mankind," deals with the "historical inevitability of the transition from capitalism to socialism." Contrary to the previously-accepted view, however, the program holds that "in the present-day conditions in a number of capitalist countries the working class headed by its vanguard has the possibility . . . of uniting the majority of the people, winning state power without civil war and ensuring the transition of the basic means of production to the hands of the people." This is the theoretical basis of coexistence, even though the Communist parties remain "the vanguard of the world revolutionary movement."

The program unfolds an enticing picture of the economic advancement and social and cultural betterment in the conditions of the people over a period of 20 years. The dictatorship of the proletariat is to be replaced by "social democracy." The withering away of the state will be achieved through the transfer of functions formerly performed by state agencies to public organizations—trade unions, cooperatives, the Young Communist League, and the like. "Transition to communism," says the program, "means the fullest development of personal freedom and the rights of Soviet citizens." If the promises of the program are fulfilled, the future should be indeed different from the past and the present. This the Communists do not doubt. Says the program: "The Communist Party, which . . . possesses knowledge of the laws of social development, ensures correct leadership in all the work of communist construction, giving it an organized, planned, and scientific character."

De-Stalinization. A few paragraphs later the program states that "the cult of the individual and related violations of the collective leadership, inner-party democracy, and socialist legality are not compatible with the Leninist principles of party life." The two statements just quoted do not go well together. How is the infallibility of the party to be reconciled with the fact that the "cult of personality," which permeated every aspect of Russian life, went on, according to Mikoyan for 20 years, but actually longer? Khrushchev's denunciation of Stalin, for all its vitriolic ardor, was not a total and unconditional repudiation. He said at the Twentieth Congress that "Stalin doubtlessly performed great services to the party, to the working class, and to the international workers' movement." The fantastic accusations against Trotsky and Trotskyism have not been rescinded, and Khrushchev did not even mention the extermination of the *kulaks* in the 1930's. More recently (March 8, 1963) Khrushchev said that "we believe even today that Stalin was devoted to communism; he was a Marxist, and this cannot and must not be denied. . . . At Stalin's funeral many people, myself among them, had tears in their eyes. Although we did know of some of Stalin's personal shortcomings, we still believed in him."

Stalin's body was removed from the Mausoleum in Red Square, and Stalingrad became Volgograd, yet the departed leader dominates the Communist world. His image is untarnished in Communist China and Albania and probably in many factions of the Communist parties in other lands. The "cult of personality" is far from dead. The adulation of Lenin is even more extravagant than was Stalin's, and although Khrushchev holds that "since the Twentieth Congress . . . Leninist principles . . . of collective leadership have been restored in the party," there is not a single instance on record of anyone so much as implying publicly that Nikita Sergeevich might be wrong.

As a political leader close to the top, Khrushchev had a heavy share of responsibility for Stalin's misrule. The reasons which made him launch the de-Stalinization drive can only be conjectured. His objective was presumably to promote his own advancement, and in this he fully succeeded; the true story of how his ambition was achieved will probably never be told.

Social Policies

Schools. A determined effort was made in post-Stalin Russia to improve the cultural and material standards of the people. Tuition fees in the upper grades of the secondary schools and in all higher schools (introduced in 1940) were abolished by a law of June 10, 1956. "The citizens of the USSR have the right to education," says Article 121 of the constitution, as amended in December 1958. "This right is ensured by universal compulsory 8-year education; by the extensive development of secondary general polytechnic education, technical vocational schools, and specialized higher and secondary schools on the basis of a link between training, and life and production; by instruction in schools in native languages; and by the organization at plants and at state and collective farms of free training—production, technical, and agronomic—of the working people." The amended version of Article 121 was based on the "Law for Strengthening Ties Between School and Life and Further Developing the Public Education System of the USSR," adopted by the Supreme Soviet on December 24, 1958. The object of the law was to eradicate the contemptuous attitude towards manual labor common among the bureaucracy and the intelligentsia and to encourage children of peasant families to enter higher schools.

Under the new dispensation, admission to higher schools is determined by merit attested by public organizations, such as the trade unions and the Young Communist League. Only candidates with at least two years of practical work in industry or agriculture are admitted to the schools teaching law and social sciences. The law encouraged practical on-the-job instruction on secondary and advanced levels, which was to be organized at places of work. The curricula of the two basic types of schools—the 7-year school and the 9-year school—were to be extended by one year, that is, to 8 and 10 years. The transition to the 8-year school was expected to be completed in 1962–1963. In 1960 the standards for obtaining higher degrees were tightened, and educational authorities were empowered to revoke the degrees of unworthy recipients. Another novel departure was the boarding schools for boys and girls established in 1956. Their student body in 1956–1957 was 56,000; by 1961, according to Khrushchev's estimate at the Twenty-second

Congress, it had risen to 600,000 and was expected to reach 2.5 million by 1965. Expenses of these students are paid by the government. The number of students in elementary and secondary schools declined somewhat from the 1950–1951 level, 34.8 million, to 33.4 million in 1959–1960. The student body of the higher schools, including students taking evening and correspondence courses, increased from 1.2 million in 1950–1951 to 2.3 million in 1959–1960. In 1961 about 4 million students in higher, secondary, and elementary schools received government fellowships and were provided with lodgings. The total number of students at every level—elementary, secondary, and higher—in 1958–1959 was 36.4 million; the corresponding figure for the United States was 46.1 million, but the population of the USSR was larger (209 million) than that of the United States (180 million). However, in 1958 the Soviet Union graduated 94,000 engineers, almost three times the number in the United States. The entire student body of the Soviet "general education system" in 1963 was estimated at 41 million.

Viewed as a whole, the progress of education in the USSR, substantial as it was, was less spectacular than is often imagined. It seems clear that the implications of the 1958 law "For Strengthening Ties Between School and Life" are revolutionary, and the law, if enforced, is likely to preclude the resurgence of a class society.

Old Age, Disability, and Health Insurance. The long-overdue overhauling of old age, disability, and health insurance was effected by a law of July 14, 1956. It covers workers, employees, servicemen, and students in higher and specialized schools, as well as families which have been deprived of their breadwinner. Old age pensions are from 300 to 1,200 rubles per month, the actual amount being based on the average earnings of the recipient over the last 12 months or over a statutory period. The qualifying age is 60 for men and 55 for women, and the required period of employment, respectively, 25 and 20 years. If these conditions are not met, the amount of the pension can be reduced. It is increased for continuous employment at one place of work, for mothers of five or more children, and for workers employed in underground, arduous, or dangerous occupations. Qualifications for disability (temporary or permanent) and sickness benefits differ from those for old age pensions, but the actual amount, again, depends on the length of employment at one place of work. Twelve years of continuous employment in one enterprise are required to establish claim to full benefit; it may be reduced by as much as 50 per cent for injured or sick persons whose record of employment at one place of work was three years or less. As under the earlier legislation, the social insurance schemes are non-contributory, that is, no deduction is made from the payroll, but the employing agencies (enterprises) make payments to the treasury on account of social security; in 1958 the amount of these payments varied from 4 to 9 per cent of the payroll. Any deficit is met from public funds.

As during the earlier period, information on social security is scant and difficult to interpret. Khrushchev said at the Twenty-second Party Congress that "payments and benefits received by the population out of public funds" increased from 4.2 billion rubles in 1940 to 24.5 billion rubles in 1960, that 20 million people were receiving pensions, and that 7 million mothers were drawing state allowances. According to another official source, appropriations for old age and disability pensions in 1963 were 6.4 billion rubles (this figure should be multiplied by 10 to make it comparable with those for the pre-1961 period; see below, pp. 600–601). These are large but hardly revealing figures. The law of 1956 has no doubt improved the position of the beneficiaries under the social insurance schemes, although it is believed that coverage remains incomplete and the level of benefits low.

Industrial Labor. The legal status and economic position of industrial labor have improved since 1953. Attachment to jobs was terminated by a law of April 25, 1956, and all persons detained under the decree of June 26, 1940, were set free. Workers could leave their jobs after giving a two-week notice and were permitted to move about as they pleased. The only survival of the past was the provisions which linked the amount of social benefits to the length of employment at one place of work. It is likely that attachment to jobs was never fully enforced. Nevertheless, its repeal was a major event: it restored the workers to the status of freemen.

There were important economic changes. Wages were raised and wage differentials reduced. The minimum monthly wage in industry, construction, transport, and communications was increased to 300 rubles for urban, and 270 rubles for rural workers (law of September 1956). The Twenty-first Congress (1959) ordered a further raise in wages to a minimum of 400 to 500 rubles in 1959–1962 and 500 to 600 rubles in 1963–1965. Workers were both to earn more and to work shorter hours. The Twentieth Party Congress (1956) approved the restoration of the 7-hour day (for which the 8-hour day had been substituted in 1940) and of the 6-hour day in dangerous and strenuous occupations. The change was to be made effective over an unspecified period. A law of May 7, 1960, decreed the general introduction of the 7-hour day before the end of that year; the complete transition to the 40-hour week by 1962; and the changeover to the 30- to 35-hour week beginning in 1964. The 1961 party program spoke of the 6-hour day "within the coming 10 years," and Professor S. Strumilin, a venerable and obliging Soviet economist, predicted that automation under Communism would reduce "obligatory work" to 4 hours per day.

If many consumer goods were still in short supply, factory buildings unsanitary and grim, and housing facilities overcrowded and almost unobtainable, one could always look with hope, if not necessarily with confidence, to the future. The party program stated that "the primary task of historical importance" was "to ensure a living standard in the Soviet Union higher than that of any capitalist country." The income of the workers in the lower brackets will increase three times during the next 10 years. Poverty will disappear, and comforts and even luxuries will be available to the Soviet people by the end of the second decade. This is a heartening prospect that, if one believes it, should make more palatable the hardships, drudgery, ugliness, and discomforts of the present.

Yes the fact remains that the improvement in the position of labor in the 1950's was real.

Planning, Farming, and Finance

The Seven-Year Plan. The urge for reforms invaded the field of planning. The fifth Five-Year Plan, introduced in 1951, was completed in 1955 and was followed in 1956 by the sixth Five-Year Plan, which was brought to an end in 1958 and was superseded by the Seven-Year Plan covering the period 1959 through 1965. The discontinuance of the Five-Year Plans, which for three decades had been the symbol of Soviet economic development, was officially motivated by the creation of the economic administrative regions, which "necessitated radical changes" in the system of planning, the discovery of new raw materials, and the formulation of a program for the development of synthetic fibers and plastics, for which no provision had been made in the sixth Five-Year Plan. In view of the flexibility of the earlier plans and the frequent revisions of their targets, this explanation seems disingenuous. It has been suggested that the quotas set in the sixth Five-Year Plan were too high and that its abandonment offered a convenient way out of an embarrassing situation, but this contention would be difficult to prove, and Soviet statistical procedure is sufficiently fluid to allow the invariable overfulfillment—at least on paper—of planned assignments. The general trend of Soviet thinking in this area is in the direction of long-term planning, and this may well be the true reason for the shift to the Seven-Year Plan.

The quantitative achievements of planning are impressive, although the mechanics of the Soviet statistical procedure are not accessible to outsiders. According to an official report approved by the Twenty-first Party Congress (1959), "gross industrial output in 1958 was 36 times as great as in 1913, the production of means of production—the foundation of the national economy—83 times, and the output of machine building and metal working 240 times." The actual figures of output were described by Khrushchev, with some justification, as "majestic." Khrushchev said at the Twenty-second

OUTPUT OF SELECTED COMMODITIES, 1950, 1955, AND 1962 *

	1950	1955	1962
Pig iron, million tons	19.2	33.3	55.3
Steel, " "	27.3	45.3	76.3
Coal, " "	261.1	391.0	517.0
Oil, " "	37.9	70.8	186.0
Paper, thousand tons	1,193.0	1,862.0	2,800.0
Leather footwear, million pairs	203.4	274.3	456.0

* For the output of these commodities in 1913, 1928, and 1938, see p. 504.

Congress that between 1956 and 1961, state investment in the national economy came to 156 billion rubles, which is more than the aggregate investment during the entire period of the Soviet regime prior to the Twentieth Congress (1956). The rapid rate of industrial expansion continues under the Seven-Year Plan, which has set very high targets. The emphasis is still on the production of means of production, which grows more rapidly than that of consumer goods. Khrushchev stated at the plenary session of the central committee in November 1962 that "more than 3,700 large state industrial enterprises began operating in the first four years of the Seven-Year Plan. In industry the new productive capacity that was created exceeds the capacity created in all the years of the pre-war Five-Year Plans."

Economic Growth. These very impressive figures do not tell the entire story. Devastating criticisms of production methods coming from authoritative Soviet sources are numerous and revealing, even though they invariably end with the triumphant assertion that the plan has been overfulfilled. The cost of industrialization has been very high; errors in planning were many and onerous; the quality of the goods produced was often poor, and the percentage of defective production exorbitant; recurrent shortages of fuel and raw materials have caused grievous interruptions in production. These factors cannot be left out of account in appraising the performance of the Soviet economy. The obvious truth, only too often ignored by the economists (who should know better), is that a country's economic development cannot be accurately measured by a few index numbers, especially when they are based on statistics as unrevealing as those of the Soviet Union. Professor Raymond J. Saulnier, former Chairman of the President's Council of Economic Advisers, noted after a recent visit to Russia that "one familiar with statistics of Soviet economic growth will be astonished to see so little evidence of the growth that these statistics proclaim" (*Fortune*, May 1962). It is a truism among a large segment of Western economists that the rate of growth is faster in the Soviet Union than in the United States. However, Professor G. Warren Nutter, in a careful and well-documented study prepared under the auspices of the National Bureau of Economic Research —America's most authoritative organization—reached the conclusion that "over the Soviet era as a whole the Soviet industries have generally lost historical ground to their American counterparts—the lags have generally increased—in terms of both total and per capita output. That is, the growth from the same level of output has been slower in Soviet than in American industry." Disagreement of this magnitude among the authorities indicates that the rate of growth, especially when used for comparison of countries as far apart in their economic organization and tradition as the United States and the Soviet Union, is not a trustworthy and reliable tool.

Dissatisfaction with the methods of planning is suggested by frequent revisions of the structure of planning agencies. In March 1963 there was created the Council of the National Economy (attached to the Council of Ministers of the USSR) "as the supreme state agency for guiding industry and construction." The State Planning Committee (Gosplan) was subordinated to the new council. D. F. Ustinov was appointed its chairman and, simultaneously, first vice chairman of the Council of Ministers.

It seems that until recently there was no definite theory of Soviet planning. Since the middle 1950's, however, Soviet economists showed interest in mathematical economics, especially in input-output analysis, which involves the use of computers. It is believed that this approach is being applied to planning. A computer center was established in Moscow in April 1963. However, mathematical economics, their appearance of exactness notwithstanding, are still in an experimental stage, and their usefulness in solving the practical problems of planning remains to be proved.

Farming. The position of agriculture at the time of Stalin's death was wholly unsatisfactory. The yield per hectare was persistently low, and the *kolkhoz* system did not function well. Khrushchev addressed himself to the problem of farm reorganization with energy and enthusiasm. The program of farm amalgamation that he sponsored under Stalin was continued. By 1959 the number of collective farms was reduced to 55,000, while the average sown area per farm increased to 2,300 hectares and the number of households to 340. The basic goal was higher productivity. The easiest and least costly method of augmenting the supply of marketable agricultural commodities was to encourage the cultivation of household allotments and the expansion of the privately-owned livestock. This policy, although running contrary to Khrushchev's views, was adopted as a temporary expedient. Produce of household allotments was given tax relief and reduction of delivery quotas. Some of these concessions, which were believed to be successful, were withdrawn in 1957. Prices paid to the farmers by the state were increased in 1953 and again in 1956. Compulsory deliveries, the farmers' greatest financial burden, were curtailed in 1954 and discontinued in 1958; however, the farms were still obligated to sell to the state a specified amount of agricultural produce per hectare—which looked suspiciously like compulsory deliveries in a different guise. Simultaneously the entire system of multiple prices was abolished, and all state purchases were made at a single price, differentiated only according to region. Although the revised prices were several times as high as the former compulsory delivery prices (in the case of potatoes, for instance, ten times as high), it was estimated that they were still lower than the average cost of production, and while the earnings of the farmers rose considerably, they remained below those of industrial workers, in spite of the marked acceleration in the flow of agricultural investments.

On March 31, 1958, the Supreme Soviet passed a law abolishing the machine tractor stations (MTS). The proposed measure, according to Khrushchev, was discussed, from March 1 to March 25, at 576,000 meetings attended by 50 million people who listened to 3 million speeches. Some 126,000 men and women wrote to the newspapers and radio and TV stations expressing their admiration for Khrushchev's proposal. The law provided for the sale to the collective farms of the heavy agricultural machinery owned by the MTS, which were to be retained, at least temporarily, as repair and technical service stations (RTS). By the middle of 1959 the collective farms, assisted by large state credits, purchased over 20 billion rubles worth of agricultural machinery. It was officially explained that the abandonment of the political control formerly exercised by the MTS was made possible by the reduction in the number of collective farms and their higher level of political leadership. Some 230,000 Communists were sent to the rural communities between 1954 and 1958. The elimination of the MTS was expected to increase efficiency by removing the dual control formerly exercised by the officials of the MTS and the farm administration. As a preliminary measure, the methods of planning were liberalized in 1955 by giving the management of the farms a larger part than before in deciding what their assignments should be.

The drive for bringing under cultivation the virgin lands of Kazakhstan, Siberia, and the Volga and Urals regions was dramatically announced by Khrushchev in 1953. "The development of the virgin lands," he told the Twenty-second Party Congress, "is a great feat that our heroic people have performed in building communism, an achievement that will live through the ages." There was much resounding propaganda, and various inducements were offered, especially to the young people, to join in the opening of Russia's frontier. As in industrial planning, the quantitative results achieved are impressive. In 1961 some 41.8 million hectares of virgin lands were under cultivation, which was over 20 per cent of the aggregate sown area. It is this expansion in a record time and on an unprecedented scale that accounts for the increase of the gross harvest of all grain crops from 5 million tons in 1953 to 9 million in 1962. Most of the virgin lands, however, are situated in the semi-arid zone, which is subject to devastating droughts and where the growing season is short. They had poor harvests in 1955, 1956, and 1957. In the long run climate and rainfall might prove crucial, and it is the sustained performance of the virgin lands that will decide whether the increase of 70 per cent in agricultural output required by the Seven-Year Plan will be achieved.

A by-product of the virgin land program was the revival of interest in the *sovkhozy*—the state farms. All the farms in the newly-developed regions belong to this type. Their number increased from 4,900 in 1953 to 6,500 in 1959, when they accounted for over one-quarter of the total sown area and for more than one-third of the State grain procurement. The state farms, which have no household allotments and are run by hired labor, employed 4 million people in 1958. Recently there has been a tendency to bring the collective farms closer to the state farms, for instance, by substituting regular monetary payments for the distribution of proceeds among the farm members on the basis of labor days. If this trend persists, the *kolkhozy* may well be doomed. Hostility to the farm program was one of the charges levied against the "anti-party group."

It will appear from the above that as Soviet Russia is approaching the half-century mark, her agriculture is still in a state of flux. The economic position of the farmers was somewhat improved in the post-Stalin era, but no solution of the problems of socialized agriculture would seem to be in sight.

Public Finance. The picture of Soviet finance is not one of unmitigated bliss. In the post-war era state revenue continued to rise, from 180.2 billion rubles in 1940 to 302 billion in 1945, to 422.8 billion in 1950, to 564.3 billion in 1955, and to 819 billion in 1962 (the official figure of revenue in 1962, expressed in rubles of post-1960 value, is 81.8 billion rubles; see below, this section). In the 1950's and early 1960's the turnover tax remained the principal single source of revenue, although its share of the total revenue declined to about 45 per cent, as compared with 70 and 60 per cent in the 1930's and the 1940's. Correspondingly, revenue from other sources, of which the largest is withholding from the profits of nationalized industries, was increased.

Wage earners, like collective farmers, were given a measure of tax relief. Beginning in October 1960 taxes on wages and salaries were scaled down, and their total elimination for taxpayers in the lower income brackets is scheduled for 1965. The reform, which is attractively publicized as "an abolition of taxes on the population," leaves intact the existing system of taxation of the "socialist sector," from which comes the bulk of the revenue. Direct taxes play a minor part in Soviet finance, which relies on indirect taxation, and abolition of direct taxes will make little difference to the treasury or the taxpayers. Under capitalism reliance on indirect taxation is the earmark of underdeveloped countries, but this would not be true of a socialist economy.

Prior to 1957 state loans were a steady source of public revenue. Subscription to loans was free in theory but in practice was compulsory, with industrial enterprises and farms regularly investing in state securities a specified proportion of the earnings of their employees or members. The practice of forced loans was discontinued in the spring of 1957. Simultaneously, payment of interest on and redemption service of the state debt of some 260 billion rubles were suspended for 20 to 25 years. It is not likely that they will ever be resumed. The announcement, which wiped out the savings of millions of people, was received without a murmur and, indeed, was wildly cheered in Soviet representative assemblies. At the same time the ruble was devalued by the curious device of adding 6 rubles to the official rate of 4 rubles to the dollar, that is, the rate of exchange for current expenditure in the USSR became 10 "tourist" rubles to the dollar.

Another monetary reform was announced in May 1960 and was put into effect on January 1, 1961. The paper currency in circulation was exchanged during a 3-month transition period for a paper currency of a new pattern at the rate of 10 old rubles to one new ruble. Simultaneously all prices were cut down to one-tenth of their former level. The theoretical gold content of the ruble was increased four-fold (to .987 gm), which resulted in a new *at par* rate of $1 = .9 ruble; thus the ruble acquired a higher international value than the dollar. The reform eliminated the dual rate of exchange of the ruble—"official" and "tourist"—and added to the international standing of the Soviet currency. The merit of this policy is debatable, and there is nothing in the record of the ruble to indicate that it is a sound currency or that the Soviet planned economy is immune against inflation.

Coexistence, the Later Phase

Doctrine Revised? The death of Stalin was greeted with a sigh of relief by a great many people in the Soviet Union and throughout the world. New faces—Malenkov, Bulganin, Khrushchev—and new ideas, especially a fresh emphasis on coexistence, appeared to promise a better future. Malenkov's tenure of office was too brief and precarious to leave any imprint on foreign relations, but the Bulganin-Khrushchev team visited India, Belgium, France, England, and other countries. After Bulganin's elimination Khrushchev continued on his own, at times accompanied by his family and kin, as on his first visit to the United States, where he came twice, in 1959 and again in 1960. An imposing array of VIP's, headed by West German Chancellor Konrad Adenauer, the British prime minister Harold Macmillan, and the vice president of the United States Richard Nixon, took the road to Moscow. The aloofness of the Kremlin, where Stalin, like the Muscovite tsars, dwelt in a state of near-ritualistic immobility and reticence, gave place to boisterous activities, with Khrushchev dashing from place to place and talking interminably. The change not only was one of form but affected some of the essentials of Soviet foreign policy. The elements which determined the new course were: the weakening and disorganization of the West; the disintegration of the political and colonial system, which invited subversive activities; the strengthening of the Soviet economy, permitting foreign aid that formerly was outside Russian reach; and the rapid growth of nuclear armaments, which brought the belief that war—even a successful war—would be suicidal.

The Communist leaders made explicit what they meant by coexistence. "Peaceful coexistence of states with different social systems does not mean a reconciliation between the socialist and the bourgeois ideologies," said a resolution of a conference of 81 Communist parties (December 1960). "On the contrary, it implies an intensification of the struggle of the working class and all communist parties for the triumph of the socialist ideas." The resolution added that "peace is the true ally of socialism, for time is working for socialism and against capitalism." Separate Soviet international moves should be interpreted in the light of this statement.

Soviet Policies. The real difference between the Stalin and post-Stalin policies is their scope. The main objective—the elimination of the capitalist environment—has not and cannot be altered (for it is ordained by the immutable laws of history), nor have the ingredients of Soviet policies changed. Under the banner of the struggle for peace, the Kremlin works for the systematic weakening of the position of the Western powers in the colonial and underdeveloped countries; the undermining of NATO and of its Eastern counterparts, SEATO (South East Asia Treaty Organization, founded in 1954) and CENTO (Central Treaty Organization, established in 1955 as the Baghdad Pact and renamed in 1959 after the Iraqi revolution of 1958 and the withdrawal of that country); the prevention of the unification of Germany on terms acceptable to the West; the fostering of the perennial conflict over Berlin, accompanied by threats of a separate peace with the German Democratic Republic; the maintenance of total domination over the countries in the Soviet orbit; the indefinite prolongation of disarmament and nuclear tests negotiations; and—on a different level—promotion of East-West trade and expansion of cultural exchanges and personal contact among the leaders.

Soviet disruptive activities are flexible and are carried on by a variety of means: missile threats; military aid and assistance in the organization of the armed forces and guerrilla warfare in the former colonial countries; training of Communists destined to lead Communist revolutions in their native lands; political revolutions and assassinations; technical and economic assistance (India, United Arab Republic, Guinea, Cuba) on an ever-widening scale; disparaging of Western values and undermining of Western institutions; disruption of Western trade. A recent manifestation of the latter policy is the building of a vast system of pipelines and the spectacular rise of Soviet oil exports to the free world at prices far below those charged by the USSR to satellite countries ($1.56 and $3.01 average per barrel, respectively, in 1960, according to the American Petroleum Institute). The execution of predatory policies in the colonial countries is facilitated by the fact that Russia never was a colonial power in the traditional meaning of the term. Inevitably, the interests of the Soviet Union and of the West are in conflict in many parts of the world.

Soviet policies are characterized by rapid shifts from conciliatory moves to aggressive actions and threats. To the admission of the Federal Republic of Germany in NATO (May 1955) the Kremlin responded by the annulment of the Anglo-Soviet and the Franco-Soviet wartime treaties of friendship and by the formation of the Warsaw Pact military alliance comprising Soviet Russia and her seven European satellites (May 14, 1955), which is the Communist counterpart of NATO. Simultaneously the Soviets, reversing themselves, agreed to a peace treaty with Austria that ended Soviet occupation and guaranteed Austrian neutrality. In the summer of 1955 an inconsequential summit meeting was held in Geneva (President Eisenhower, Bulganin, and the British and French prime ministers, Anthony Eden and Edgar Faure). In August 1955 the Soviets joined the Inter-Parliamentary Union, and in September they established diplomatic relations with the Federal Republic of Germany and returned the Porkkala base to Finland; at the same time they concluded with that country a 20-year treaty of friendship. In April 1956 the Cominform was dissolved—to placate Tito, with whom Moscow sought a reconciliation and who resented Yugoslavia's expulsion in 1948. In the Far East the Russians signed a treaty with China and agreed to withdraw from Port Arthur and to dissolve the mixed companies (October 1954). In 1956 diplomatic relations with Tokyo were restored. The Kremlin has maintained a consistently hostile attitude towards the European Common Market and other institutions for the economic integration of Europe which the Russians interpret as the tools of "German revanchists" and American "monopolies."

The relaxation of pressure in the satellite empire led to anti-Soviet riots in eastern Germany (June 1953). More serious disturbances in Poland, in the summer and autumn of 1956, brought back to power Wladyslaw Gomulka, a Communist leader removed in 1948 for "nationalistic deviations" and kept in prison for several years. Even more violent outbreaks occurred in Hungary in October–November 1956 and were suppressed by Soviet armed force. The Communist prime minister Imre Nagy, who had faltered in his allegiance to Moscow, was executed by the Russians. The Hungarian tragedy, which the West watched helplessly from the sideline, demonstrated Moscow's determination to uphold Communist rule in the countries in its orbit.

There was a great expansion of Soviet activity in the Far, Middle, and

"De-Stalinization" in Hungary, October 1956

Khrushchev and Mao

Near East. An important landmark was the Afro-Asian conference at Bandung, Indonesia, in April 1955, the first major gathering of this nature since the Baku meeting in 1920; although it was not an avowedly Communist undertaking, the Communist influence was strong. In the Near East the Soviets, beginning in 1955, supplied Egypt with arms and encouraged Gamal Abdel Nasser to nationalize the Suez Canal (July 1956). Throughout the ensuing crisis the Kremlin stood firmly behind Egypt and against Great Britain, France, and Israel. In the middle 1950's the Council for Mutual Economic Assistance (CEMA) emerged from the state of hibernation in which it had lingered since its founding in 1949. It has been increasingly active since then and has played a part in coordinating Communist foreign aid, which, although not as massive as American aid, has been extended to a large and growing number of underdeveloped countries. The Soviet Union did not enter this field until 1953. Among the more ambitious projects sponsored by Moscow are a large steel plant in India and the Aswan High Dam in Egypt. Loans and grants, technical assistance, and trade expansion are effective tools for spreading Soviet influence, which has been particularly marked in the key regions—strategically and economically—such as the oil lands of the Middle East.

In the Far East, in spite of the ideological differences between Moscow and Peking, the Soviets have staunchly supported Communist China against the Chinese national government of Chiang Kai-shek, presumably instigated Communist attacks on the nationalist-held off-shore islands of Quemoy and Matsu in 1958 and 1959, and have pressed for the admission of Communist China in the United Nations.

In 1959 and 1960 relations between the Soviet Union and the West appeared to be less tense. Khrushchev came to the United States, and a summit conference was to be held in Paris in the summer of 1960 but went by default because an American U-2 reconnaissance plane was brought down while flying over Soviet territory. Nevertheless President Kennedy and Khrushchev met in Vienna in the summer of 1961, but their conversations, like the previous summit meeting, produced no tangible results. On August 13, 1961, the East Germans inaugurated the Berlin wall, which they built at record speed and which cut Berlin in two. The immediate object of this extraordinary step was to check the mass flight of East Germans to the Federal Republic.

The Soviets secured a footing in the Western hemisphere. The Cuban revolution of 1959 was consistently supported by the Kremlin, and the discovery of Soviet missile sites on the island in October 1962 caused a crisis in Soviet-American relations, which was resolved peacefully, however, by Soviet withdrawals of the offensive weapons. Cuba is believed to be the Soviet jumping-off board for infiltration in South and Central America. Fidel Castro was given a hero's welcome in Moscow in May 1963, and Khrushchev accepted an invitation to visit Cuba.

There have been serious fissures in the Communist bloc, Yugoslavia and then Albania and China refusing to follow blindly the dictates of Moscow. Chinese Communists are critical of the partial revision of Stalinism and of the emphasis on peaceful coexistence with the capitalist countries. Whether these disagreements are sufficiently grave to impair the basic unity of the bloc, it is impossible to say.

Coexistence, in so far as it is a barrier against war, can only be welcome, but the West must keep constant vigilance to protect its vital interests and fight Communist infiltration. Since World War II Soviet influence has grown alarmingly. The suppression of the Hungarian uprising, the Berlin wall, and the 100 vetoes interposed by the Soviet delegation at the United Nations are tangible evidence of what coexistence means in Moscow.

Ten Years After

A Reflection. Khrushchev, who is not given to understatement, said at the Twenty-second Party Congress (1961) that "for our party, for the Soviet people, and all mankind" the six years which has elapsed since the Twentieth Congress "have been of extraordinary, one may say, world-historic, significance." There may seem to be some apparent justification for this statement. The Communist doctrine that governs Soviet foreign and domestic policies has been amended. Khrushchev stated at the 81-Communist-party conference (December 1960) that the transition to socialism need not be linked in every case to "armed uprising and civil war," but he added that "in those countries where capitalism is still strong . . . the transition to socialism will inevitably take place under the conditions of sharp class struggle." The change in doctrine is thus more apparent than real: violent revolutions will be bypassed if capitalism surrenders to Communism, a course of action not likely to commend itself to Western democracies. Claims of "majestic" technical and economic advance are corroborated by notable achievements in space exploration and by statistics of economic growth showing the expansion of industrial production and of sown area, but not by the performance of the economy as a whole. After Stalin's death the improvement in the status of both workers and peasants was real, although not striking or epoch-making. The police regime was believed to be less stringent, a generalization that does not rest on concrete evidence. Khrushchev stated at the Twenty-second Congress that 200,000 Communists —a large number—were expelled from the party during the previous six years "for various reasons." He did not explain what these were, and no one, of course, asked him any questions. Literature, music, and art were closely controlled. The "cult of personality" was officially gone, but party congresses, allegedly the nation's élite, greeted with "stormy applause" every crudity of Khrushchev, just as they greeted those of his predecessor. At the end of the first decade after the death of Stalin, Soviet Russia was different—but not vastly different—from what she was under his rule.

27

"Collective Leadership," 1964-1968

The Fall of Khrushchev

A Palace Revolution. The unexpected eclipse of Khrushchev was highly dramatic in its apparent simplicity. Having successfully disposed of his potential rivals, and seemingly in full control of the summit of the Communist Party, Khrushchev was generally regarded as the Soviet Union's undisputed master. It was presumably during his stay in the Crimea that the plot—for there must have been a plot—to unseat him was hatched in Moscow. On October 15, 1964, a plenary session of the central committee of the party and the presidium of the Supreme Soviet released him from the duties of the party's first secretary and those of chairman of the USSR Council of Ministers. Ostensibly this was done at Khrushchev's own request because of his "advanced age and ill health." Ironically the decree terminating Khrushchev's chairmanship of the Council of Ministers was signed by A. Mikoyan, his junior by a few months.

Unlike other deposed Soviet leaders—Beria, Malenkov, Bulganin, Molotov, Kaganovich—no criminal charges or accusation of anti-party activity were brought against Khrushchev. He was permitted to live, presumably unmolested, in a Moscow apartment or a *dacha* near the capital, and was reported in the foreign press to have voted in the local elections of March 1965 and to have attended a play in Moscow in May 1968. But his name never appears in the Soviet press. Nevertheless his indictment was unmistakably spelled out in generalized terms in a *Pravda* editorial of October 18, 1964: "The Leninist party is an enemy of subjectivism and drift in Communist construction. Harebrained scheming (*prozhektorstvo*); half-baked conclusions and hasty decisions . . .; bragging and bluster; lust for rule by fiat; disregard for practical and scientific experience—these are alien to our party. The building up of Communism . . . does not tolerate armchair methods, one-man decisions, disregard for the practical experience of the masses." This line of argument was closely followed by Soviet leaders and organs of public opinion, and "subjectivism" has gained acceptance as a term of opprobrium and the standard explanation of the failing of Soviet policies under Khrushchev.

The unprecedented magnanimity towards a fallen leader displayed by the Kremlin in the case of Khrushchev has its counterpart in the nearly total absence of persecution of the members of his *entourage*. Alexis Adzhubei, his son-in-law, was dismissed from the post of editor of *Izvestia* and a few other men particularly close to Khrushchev were sent into retirement; but none of them, so far as it is known, were deported or suffered other punishments.

Brezhnev and Kosygin. The actual mechanics that brought about Khrushchev's downfall are not known. It is notable that the men who, no doubt, contributed to his undoing and succeeded him were his associates of long standing. With the dismissal of Khrushchev the office of chairman of the Council of Ministers and that of first secretary of the party, which he held simultaneously, were separated. Leonid Brezhnev (born in 1906), who succeeded Khrushchev as first secretary of the party, was a party member since 1931 and had held various high posts in the Communist hierarchy, including that of member of the presidium of the central committee. He and Khrushchev had long worked together.

Alexis Kosygin (born in 1904), the new chairman of the Council of Ministers, had been a party member since 1927; he had filled important positions in economic agencies and was deputy chairman of the Council of Ministers when Khrushchev headed that body. The Brezhnev-Kosygin team —the kernel of "collective leadership"—is rather drab and lacks the element of excitement and popular appeal that was provided by their predecessor. The days when an ebullient Nikita Sergeevich took his family on much-publicized junkets in foreign lands was over. Brezhnev and Kosygin travel a great deal but their manner is unemotional and distant, and foreign relations tend to revert to the frigid anonymity of the Stalin era.

The intimate link between Khrushchev and his successors suggests that the explanation of his removal given in the *Pravda* editorial quoted above may well be the true one. It is reasonable to assume that Khrushchev's "subjectivism," that is, personal rule, was not to the liking of his associates. However, as will be seen later in this chapter, the disagreements between Khrushchev and other Communist leaders went further than suggested by *Pravda* and, after his elimination, led to some drastic revisions of policy, especially domestic policy. It is a striking and puzzling feature of the Soviet scene that members of the Communist hierarchy who unanimously and unreservedly acclaim certain policies one day, just as unanimously and unreservedly repudiate them the next.

The Party

Plenary Sessions of the Central Committee, 1964–1966. No time was lost in revising the policies of which the new leadership disapproved. The principal agency for carrying out the changes was the Communist Party, especially its central committee. As already noted, it was the plenary session of the central committee that, jointly with the presidium of the Supreme Soviet, removed Khrushchev from office on October 15, 1964. A month later (November 16, 1964) a plenary session of the central committee abrogated a measure that it itself had enacted, at Khrushchev's behest, two years earlier (November 1962) when party agencies below the republican level were split into two separate sets of institutions, one concerned exclusively with industry and the other with agriculture. This reorganization necessitated a reconstruction of the higher party bodies based, again, on specialization in one of the two main fields of economic activity. In November 1964 the two sets of institutions were merged and the pre-1962 scheme of party organization restored, a move praised in *Pravda* (November 18, 1964) as a major event that "would ensure correct guidance of the entire work of building Communism."

The plenary session of March 1965 decreed important changes in farming and that of September 1965 in industry. The session of February 1966 prepared the directives for the new Five-Year Plan. The measures enacted by the party Twenty-third Congress and by the Supreme Soviet were actually the acceptance and elaboration of the proposals made by the central committee. They will be examined below.

The Twenty-third Congress. The Twenty-third Congress of the Communist Party met in Moscow from March 29 to April 8, 1966. It was a large assembly—4,943 delegates, of whom all but one were present at the opening session. The proceedings followed the firmly established pattern: mercilessly long reports by the first secretary (Brezhnev) and the chairman of the Council of Ministers (Kosygin), endorsement of official proposals by a few leaders and by a small number of rank-and-file delegates, and the invariably unanimous acceptance of these proposals by the assembly. The rule of unwavering unanimity established in the days of Stalin was maintained.

According to an official report published on the occasion of the fiftieth anniversary of the revolution, party membership on January 1, 1967, was 12,684,000, including 549,000 candidate members. Slightly more than half of the members (51.5 per cent) were under 41, slightly less than half (48 per cent) had been in the party for less than ten years, and about one-fifth (20.9 per cent) were women. In 1962–1966 38.4 per cent of the members were white-collar workers (*sluzhashchie*), 14 per cent were collective farmers, and 47.6 per cent were workers employed in industry, transportation, commerce, on state farms, and so on. In 1967 16.5 per cent of the members had complete and 2.5 per cent incomplete higher education, and 31.5 per cent were graduates of secondary schools. On July 1, 1967, there were 344,500 primary party organs which, according to Brezhnev, functioned "in nearly every enterprise and organization." Between 1961 and 1967 party membership increased by 3,400,000; the number of members expelled during this period was not disclosed.

Revision of Party Statutes, 1966. These figures indicate an influx of new blood which, although desirable, had its disadvantages. Brezhnev said that because of the laxity of the admission procedure "unprepared and immature people" had been granted admission. To meet this criticism the rules governing acceptance of new members were made more stringent. The provisions of the 1961 party statutes stipulating that a specific proportion of new members should be elected to party agencies at each election, and restricting the tenure of party offices to three consecutive terms, were repealed on the ground that "they have not justified themselves." Communist office holders may look to the future with renewed confidence. The first secretary of the central committee became the general secretary; Brezhnev was elected to fill the new post. Among other amendments of the statutes adopted in 1966 were the provisions that party congresses should be convoked at least once every four (instead of every three) years, and the revival of the Politburo, which took over the functions of the presidium of the central committee. This was a reversal of the decision of the Nineteenth Congress (1952), which abolished the Politburo and substituted for it the enlarged presidium. According to Brezhnev, "the name Politburo expresses more fully the nature of the activities of the party's highest political body." The Politburo appointed by the central committee in April 1966 had 11 full members, including Brezhnev and Kosygin, and eight candidate members. They are, presumably, the true rulers of the Soviet Union.

Government and Administrative Reforms

The Ministries. The economic administrative regions introduced by Khrushchev in 1957 (see p. 588) came under criticism while he was still in office. The revival of the pre-1957 "branch agencies of control," or ministries, was regarded by his successors as essential to a better working of the economy. A number of "state committees" attached to the federal Council of Ministers and resembling the former ministries were created. In March 1965 six of them (for aviation industry, defense industry, electronic technology, and so on) were reorganized as ministries. At the September 27, 1965, plenary session of the central committee Kosygin presented a lengthy report on "improving the management of industry, perfecting planning, and strengthening economic incentives in industrial production." His report was, of course, unanimously approved by the plenary session and became the foundation of the subsequent industrial policy of the party and the government. The administrative and constitutional changes involved in the implementation of this policy were enacted by a law of October 2, 1965, passed by the Supreme Soviet. The agencies governing the economic administrative regions, including the councils of national economy, were abolished and their functions were transferred to 20 federal economic ministries, revived or newly created. Simultaneously eight of the existing state committees were reorganized as ministries, while several new such committees were set up. Under the law of 1965 the reconstructed federal Council of Ministers (which comprised ministers, chairmen of the state committees, heads of several other departments, and chairmen of the councils of ministers of the 15 constituent republics) had 80 members. Several new economic ministries were created in later years.[1] The constitutional structure of the 15 constituent republics was re-

---

[1] For instance, four ministries dealing with construction (different types) were organized in February and the ministry of medical industry in April 1967, and the ministry of machine-building in February 1968.

modeled along similar lines and the planning agencies, both federal and republican, were revised to meet the new situation. In July 1967 the General Statute of the USSR Ministries, a lengthy and complex document, was enacted by a resolution of the federal Council of Ministers. The statute defined a USSR ministry as "the central agency of state administration that exercises the management of the respective branch of national economy." Its function is "to carry on the planned management of the branch on a scientific basis," not a simple assignment in view of the present state of the science of economics. The minister, says the statute, "bears personal responsibility" for the successful fulfillment of the "tasks and duties imposed on the ministry."

The remodeling of the agencies of industrial control, although it contained few new ideas, actually amounted to a managerial revolution and the difficulties in implementing it were great. For instance, the 1966 budget and economic plan for that year were adopted by the Supreme Soviet in December 1965 on the basis of "materials and proposals" submitted by the regional administrative economic councils. Both had to be thoroughly revised to fit the new situation but the readjusted version was approved by the federal Council of Ministers as late as June 1966. How the planned economy functioned during the first half of that year remains unclear.

Other elements of the Kosygin plan for industrial reforms will be presented later in this chapter.

The Soviets. Under the regime of "collective leadership" the Soviet system continued to operate as it did in the days of Stalin and Khrushchev. Elections to the Supreme Soviet were held on June 12, 1966. The results presented little surprise. As in the past, the electorate was large and docile. Of the 144 million registered voters 143.9 million, or 99.94 per cent, voted in the election. In each of the 15 constituent republics the vote for the sole candidate was in excess of 99 per cent of the ballots cast. Seven hundred and sixty-seven deputies were elected to the Council of the Union and 750 to the Council of Nationalities. All deputies were candidates of the bloc of Communist and non-party people.

Elections to the republican and local Soviets were held in some of the constituent republics on March 12, and in others on March 19, 1967. Of the 146,076 thousand voters 146,014 thousand, or 99.96 per cent, cast ballots. The number of delegates elected to Soviets of various types was well over two million; in each territorial subdivision the sole candidate received, as in the elections to the Supreme Soviet, more than 99 per cent of the votes cast. However, in 129 districts the candidates to the local Soviets "did not receive an absolute majority of votes and were not elected." In ten districts "elections were not held because of the withdrawal of the candidates," and, finally, in three districts "elections were declared invalid because of the violation of the law." The official report published in *Pravda* (March 26, 1967) from which this information is taken does not explain these odd happenings. From 50 to 70 per cent of the deputies in the various Soviets were party members.

Proceedings in Soviet assemblies, like elections, adhered to a familiar pattern: sessions were short, lasting two or three days; most of the time was taken up by long reports by Brezhnev, Kosygin, and a few other leaders; debate was perfunctory and dreary; and the vote was invariably unanimous. Stalin and Khrushchev are gone; but Soviet democracy, like the leopard, cannot change its spots.

A novel constitutional development were the standing committees, which originated in the decisions of the Twenty-third Congress of the Communist Party. They were organized by Soviets at every level, from the village Soviet up, and were said to run into many thousands. Their chief object was to give the deputies the opportunity to take an active part in economic and cultural work. According to the Statute on Standing Committees of the USSR Supreme Soviet (published on October 13, 1967), the committees "were formed for the preliminary examination and preparation of questions pending before the Supreme Soviet" and for assisting that body in implementing its decisions.

Other attempts were made to inject new life into the amorphous mass of lower Soviets. Early in 1967 the central committee of the party passed a resolution on improving the work of rural and township Soviets. These directives, elaborated and amplified, were formalized in the decree On Basic Rights and Duties of Rural and Township Soviets, issued by the Supreme Soviet on April 8, 1968. The effectiveness of these innovations remains to be seen.

Rehabilitation of the Crimean Tatars. The Khrushchevian policy of rehabilitating the victims of Stalin's purges was continued. New names were added to the long list of former leaders unwarrantably persecuted and condemned. A decree of the presidium of the Supreme Soviet of September 5, 1967, stated that "after the liberation of the Crimea . . . in 1944, instances of active collaboration with the German invaders were groundlessly attributed to the entire Tatar population . . . (see p. 552). These sweeping accusations against all the citizens of Tatar nationality who resided in the Crimea must be withdrawn." A concurrent resolution of the presidium of the Supreme Soviet explained that "citizens of Tatar nationality who formerly resided in the Crimea and members of their families have the right . . . to live anywhere on the territory of the Soviet Union" like any other Soviet citizens.

The decision of the presidium is a notable instance of the abandonment of the theory of "guilt by association" of which the Crimean Tatars were the innocent victims for nearly a quarter of a century.

A New Constitution Still in the Making? In December 1964 Brezhnev replaced Khrushchev as chairman of the commission for the drafting of a new constitution that was appointed by the Supreme Soviet in 1962. In the middle of 1968 the work of the commission was not yet completed and, indeed, little was heard of it.

The Police Regime

Public Order. There is evidence that the rigidities of the Stalinist police regime were somewhat mitigated under Khrushchev. This more magnanimous attitude was retained, with some reservations, by his successors. The police, nevertheless, continued to play an important part in the life of Soviet citizens. Like other countries the USSR was faced, after World War II, with the mounting tide of anti-social behavior, especially among young people. Liability for hooliganism, a term used in the Soviet Union to denote a variety of minor offenses, was substantially increased by a decree of the presidium of the Supreme Soviet of July 26, 1966. Sentences were to be made stiffer, judges and prison wardens were to show less leniency, and the prosecution procedure was simplified. Public organizations and agencies, such as Komsomol (Young Communist League) were to take an active part in this campaign, which was to be directed by the newly created ministry for the protection of public order.

State Security. The state security committee (KGB) of the Council of Ministers took over the functions of the ministry of internal affairs (MVD), which was disbanded in 1960, and was given broad powers in dealing with the more important cases, particularly those involving the safety of the state. This agency was responsible for several much-publicized trials of Soviet citizens and foreign nationals accused of espionage or subversive activities.

The fiftieth anniversary of the state security agencies was the occasion for a remarkable tribute to this hardly popular branch of public administration. A joint message addressed by the central committee of the party, the presidium of the Supreme Soviet, and the Council of Ministers to "the workers of the Soviet state security agencies" (published on December 21, 1967) stated that "the Cheka's glorious traditions are now being continued by the state security agencies." They were praised for their "heightened revolutionary vigilance and perfection of Chekist proficiency." The message closed with

wishes of "new successes" in "the difficult, responsible and noble task" of the
security police and proclaimed "honor and glory to the Soviet Chekists." The
Soviet press duly elaborated this theme. According to *Izvestia* (December
21, 1967), "the Cheka activities accord with the whole democratic spirit of
Soviet rule." The paper pictured the Chekist—and his successor—as "the
image of a passionate revolutionary, a man of pure honesty and great personal courage, implacable in the struggle against enemies, stern in the name
of duty, humane, and prepared to sacrifice himself for the sake of the people's
cause to which he has dedicated his life." Other alleged characteristics of the
security police are "devotion to the cause of the revolution, unshakable loyalty to the party and the Soviet rule, fortitude in the struggle against class
enemies, and lofty proletarian humanism." This verbal extravaganza, accompanied by a shower of medals bestowed upon the members of the security
service, augured ill for the liberalization of the police regime.

Pravda (December 18, 1967) chose that time to remind its readers that
under a decree of the Supreme Soviet of January 13, 1960, Soviet citizens were
not criminally liable for accepting service with a foreign intelligence agency,
provided they did not actually engage in treasonable or subversive activities
and kept Soviet authorities informed. "This law," said *Pravda,* "is of exceptional importance for protecting Soviet citizens against the base machinations
of enemy agents."

Svetlana. The stifling atmosphere of the police regime was the basic cause
of the defection of Stalin's daughter to the West. Svetlana Alliluyeva, who
uses her mother's maiden name, was Stalin's daughter by his second wife.
She was married three times and had two children. In November 1966 she
flew to India, with the permission of the Soviet government, accompanying
the ashes of her third husband, an Indian Communist who had died in the
Soviet Union. In the spring of 1967 she decided not to return to the USSR
and traveled instead to Switzerland and then to the United States. Svetlana's
defection, her interviews and writings, especially her book *Twenty Letters to
a Friend* (1967), created a sensation. From the historian's point of view, however, her statements so far have been disappointing. Svetlana offered glimpses
of conditions in and about the Kremlin, made clear that Stalin died a natural
death (there had been occasional reports that he was murdered), but added
next to nothing to what was generally known. Her sincerity seems genuine
but her interpretations—for instance, the responsibility of Beria for Stalin's
crimes—were not convincing. Her writings are those of an emotional, high-
strung, and mystically inclined woman. Nevertheless, Svetlana's renunciation of the Soviet Union and her preference for the religious and intellectual

freedom of the West produced a profound impression and probably have left a lasting imprint on the relations between the Kremlin and the non-Communist world. Soviet reaction to her defection was one of intense hatred and scorn. Yet, commenting on the success of Svetlana's book, *Pravda* (May 27, 1967) admitted that "this occasion is of no small importance."

Industrial Reform

The Background. In the 1960's the Kremlin was faced with a host of urgent problems inherent in the stage then reached by the Soviet economy. Over a period of three or four decades the USSR has built up, at the price of heavy sacrifices, a huge machinery of production, an achievement usually evaluated in terms of rates of economic growth. However, as noted in an earlier chapter, rates of economic growth do not tell the whole story and, indeed, can be misleading. In the Soviet Union, after the recovery from the devastation of World War II, the real issue was not so much how to produce more but how to do it better, that is, the effective control of productive capacity. Debates in party and state assemblies and the press provided numerous instances of the unsatisfactory work of productive enterprises, accumulation in warehouses of large stocks of defective or unwanted and therefore unsalable goods, and failures to improve industrial techniques. The Directives for the new Five-Year Plan drafted by the February 1966 plenary session of the central committee and approved by the Twenty-third Congress summed up some of the drawbacks revealed in carrying out the plan for 1959–1965. "The output plans for certain types of heavy industry were not fulfilled," said the Directives. "New capacities were brought up to full production slowly, equipment was poorly used at a number of enterprises, and losses of working time remained great. The rate of growth of labor productivity is insufficient. Many enterprises turn out products that are technically obsolete and of low quality. The achievements of science and technology are being introduced into the national economy but slowly." These failures were ascribed to setbacks suffered by agriculture (to be discussed presently), to inadequacies of planning and management, and to "subjectivism," that is, arbitrary decisions.

Greater Independence for the Enterprise. The industrial reform devised by the September 1965 plenary session of the central committee and sanctioned by the Twenty-third Congress comprised three elements: restoration of the "branch agencies of control," or ministries; a measure of independence for the productive enterprise in its relations with both the planning bodies and the consumers; and incentive payments to foster exertion by managers, em-

ployees, and workers. It was argued by Communist leaders and Soviet economists that the restoration of the economic ministries (outlined above) was
not a return to the pre-1957 structure of industrial management because of
the revised status of the enterprise, its closer ties with consumers and lesser
dependence on supervising and planning agencies.

The legislation enacted in 1965–1966 was influenced by the theoretical
views of several economists, of whom the best known is Yevsei Liberman,
professor at the University of Kharkov. Their writings about the reform are
abstruse, enmeshed in technicalities and Marxian metaphysics, and difficult to
summary. Yet the basic idea as expounded in pertinent legislation is simple:
centralized planning was to be combined with a wide margin of autonomy
for the productive enterprise; or, as an American student put it, let the enterprise decide *how* to produce, once the planners have told it *what* to produce.
The performance of the enterprise should be measured by profits, not by the
volume of output as was the Soviet practice. It was held that profits under
socialism were the difference between the selling price of goods and the cost
of producing them, and that therefore they were totally unlike profits in a
capitalist society. Socialist profits were said to be a reliable indicator of the
efficiency of an enterprise, and conditions were to be created to encourage
industrial managers and workers to strive to achieve profits by allowing the
enterprise to retain a portion of the gains resulting from efficient management. The assortment of the goods produced by an enterprise was to be determined by direct contractual relations between the enterprise and the distribut-
ing (wholesale and retail) agencies, and should not be dictated by the
planning bodies as was formerly the case. Communist leaders and economists
denied any intention to restore private enterprise, as alleged by some Western
commentators.

The new methods of industrial management were first tried in July 1964—
that is, when Khrushchev was still in office—in the garment manufacturing
concerns Bolshevichka and Mayak. Their managers were empowered to
draw their own production plans after consultation with the appropriate sales
organizations. The guiding principle was that the volume and grades of the
goods produced should be such as to meet the demand of the consumers.
Planning was to begin not at the top but at the bottom, by ascertaining consumer preferences; then production programs would move up through the
various planning agencies until they reached the State Planning Committee,
which made the final decision. The experiment in "direct relationship" was
declared a success. Kosygin stated in September 1965 that "in 1964 and 1965

the new methods of planning . . . had been introduced in a number of enterprises of the clothing, footwear, and textile industries." They were rapidly extended to other fields.

Planning Procedure Revised. "In present conditions great flexibility and efficiency are required in the management of production and planning," Kosygin said in September 1965. "It is extremely important to take prompt account of the changing economic situation: to maneuver resources, to coordinate production skillfully—not only from above but also from below—with the growing requirements of the population; to apply scientific and technical achievements in production quickly, and to find the best methods for solving economic tasks in the concrete conditions of the enterprise. All this can be achieved only when centralized planned guidance is combined with economic initiative of the enterprise. . . ." Under the new procedure the multiplicity (actually hundreds) of indices formerly imposed on an enterprise from above were reduced to eight, of which the most important were the volume of output sold, basic assortment, wage fund, amount of profits and level of profitability (ratio of the profits to the value of basic assets). Matters not covered by these indices were decided by the enterprise independently. Economic accountability (*khozraschet*), that is, the strict balancing of the accounts of an enterprise or section thereof, was to be strengthened. Management, employees, and workers were given a direct interest in the profitability of an enterprise. There was to be formed in each enterprise a material incentive fund as well as a fund for social and cultural measures—both derived from profits—of which the personnel were the beneficiaries.

The purpose of the reform was not to eliminate planning but to make it somewhat less rigid. Article 29 of the Statute on the Socialist State Production Enterprise (1965) states that "the non-fulfillment (by the enterprise) . . . of the plan and assignments constitutes a gross violation of the state discipline and entails the responsibility of the guilty officials." The independence of the enterprise was thus to be kept within narrow limits.

A Tentative Appraisal. Soviet leaders attached great importance to the reform and no effort was spared to give it wide application. According to the official report on the fulfillment of the economic plan for 1967, at the end of that year 7,000 industrial enterprises, responsible for about 40 per cent of the total industrial output and yielding about one-half of industrial profits, had been transferred to the new system of planning and economic incentive. One-third of all industrial workers were employed in these enterprises. A wide range of industries was brought within the purview of the reform. They included plants engaged in manufacturing machine tools, automation and control systems; consumer goods—clothing, cotton, silk and wool fabrics, and leather footwear; also sugar refineries. "The enterprises working in the new conditions," says the report, "overfulfilled the increased sales and profit plans they had accepted."

This official evaluation was, perhaps, somewhat too optimistic. The quasi-omnipotent bureaucracy of the planning agencies would not be likely to accept meekly a drastic curtailment of the powers it had exercised for decades. In an article published simultaneously with the report just quoted (*Planovoe khoziastvo,* January 1968) Professor Liberman noted the many difficulties involved in the application of the reform, including "groundless administration by fiat and disregard for the economic interests of the enterprise" by the supervising and planning bodies.

There were other and no less formidable difficulties. The 1965–1966 reform did not tackle the vital question of prices. Kosygin announced at the September 1965 plenary session the appointment of a state committee on prices. He added, however, that "experience has shown that calculations of the level of wholesale prices for all types of output and the preparation of new price lists for all branches of industry will require considerable time. It would seem that the introduction of new prices may be effected in 1967–1968." The committee completed its work in time to make effective in 1967 revised wholesale prices for light and heavy industry. The change required the recalculation of indices of the 1967 budget and economic plan. It was simultaneously announced that the revision of wholesale prices would not affect the level of retail prices and would cause no serious loss to the collective farmers.

Ironically, the industrial revolution of 1965–1966 had a strong conservative flavor; indeed, none of the measures enacted was really new. Official denials notwithstanding, the revival of ministries was a return to the pre-1957 practice. Incentive wages, bonuses, funds for the benefit of the employees financed from profits, and devices for fostering productivity such as "socialist emulation," which were much in the picture in the 1960's, are as old as Soviet planning. The new leeway to enterprise brings to mind NEP, with the important difference that in the early 1920's Soviet planning was still in its infancy. The crux of the matter is that no satisfactory way had been found to control and direct efficiently the huge machinery of socialist industry. It remains uncertain whether planning of the Soviet type is compatible with the even narrowly circumscribed independence of productive enterprise.

Agriculture

A Disappointing Record. "In the development of our country's economy an especially important rôle belongs to agriculture," said Kosygin at the Twenty-third Congress. "It largely determines the growth of the other branches of the national economy and the advance in the material well-being of the working people." Historically, however, farming has proved to be the most recalcitrant and unmanageable segment of the economy. Its failures have been recurrent and many. "We are faced with the fact that in the last few years agriculture has slowed in its development, and our plans for an upsurge in agricultural production have remained unfulfilled," Brezhnev told the March 1965 plenary session of the central committee. "According to the control figures, the gross output of agriculture during the Seven-Year Plan (1959–1965) should have risen 70 per cent; in fact, during the first six years the increase came to only 10 per cent." He ascribed the disappointing performance to poor planning, unsound economic and administrative policies, and frequent and unwarranted reorganizations. At the Twenty-third Congress Brezhnev stated that the rates of growth of the more essential agricultural products "in the five years just elapsed were substantially lower than in the preceding five-year period." The reasons, according to Brezhnev, were "unjustified reorganizations of agricultural agencies, the imposition from above of stereotyped policies, and the underestimation of science and practical experience." The conditions of animal husbandry were particularly unsatisfactory in 1963 when they marked a sharp decline, and in 1965 the number of pigs, sheep, goats, and fowl were still below the 1962 level.

The Remedies. As we know, the farming situation was tackled by the March 1965 plenary session of the central committee. Its decisions were immediately made effective by decrees of the federal Council of Ministers and were endorsed by the Twenty-third Congress. The general objectives of the revised policy were to increase the productivity of farm labor, to bring higher yields, and to raise the living standards of the rural population. Its essential features were as follows. The volume of annual purchases of grain and other agricultural commodities by the state under the procurement system (that is, obligatory sales to government agencies by collective farms and state farms) was lowered. In the case of grain, the reduction was from 4,000 million poods to 3,400 million poods (55.7 million tons). The annual figure of procurement was to remain "fixed and unalterable" through 1970. The basic procurement prices for grain, meat, and other agricultural commodities were raised. For grain the increase, which varied from region to region, was from 50 to 100 per cent. Basic procurement prices were further increased for sales to the state in excess of the planned quotas; for wheat and rye the increment was 50 per cent. The object of the revised price policy was to foster higher output by making every branch of husbandry profitable. Farm administration was to expand the area under grass. The reduction of the volume of grain procurement, by easing the pressure of the demand for grain, should facilitate this objective. Within the framework of the national procurement plan local party and state agencies were to prepare detailed annual plans covering the period 1966–1970 for the sale to the state of specific amounts of agricultural commodities. These plans were to be determined by the conditions of each agricultural enterprise—soil, climate, economic features, and so on. Such plans, after they had been adopted, were not subject to change and had the force of law. According to Brezhnev, "when we say that the plan has the force of law, then it is mandatory for every one. It cannot be changed and it cannot go unfulfilled." This is a more rigid attitude than was Stalin's 35 years earlier (see p. 500), although Stalin spoke not of yearly plans but of plans for a longer period.

There were other important financial provisions. The technical base of farming was to be strengthened by the investment of 71,000 million rubles under the 1966–1970 Five-Year Plan. Production of agricultural machines was to be greatly increased. The entire farm indebtedness of 2,130 million rubles was written off. The collective farm income tax was revised and its rates cut down by nearly 50 per cent. Additional incentives for farm workers and officials were provided by a revised system of bonuses for the fulfillment and over-fulfillment of the plan. The prices of goods widely used in the countryside were lowered. Payment of labor on the collective farms, said Kosygin at the Twenty-third Congress, "will increasingly approximate the level and forms that have evolved on state farms. It is planned that monthly guaranteed payments for labor of the collective farmers will be gradually introduced everywhere." By a joint resolution of the central committee and the Council of Ministers (published May 18, 1966) collective farmers were guaranteed payments in cash and in kind, at least once a month, beginning July 1, 1966. The amount of the monthly payment was to be "based on the rates of pay of corresponding categories of state farm workers." Special funds were to be set by farm management to meet the guaranteed payments to the collective farmers and, in case of necessity, appropriate credits were to be provided by the state bank. This measure appeared as an important step toward the often rumored elimination of the collective farms, but the party and the government had no such intention at that time. "It must be assumed," said Brezhnev in March 1965, "that these two forms of farming [collective and state] will continue to exist and develop for a long time to come" and he deprecated the "unwarranted conversion" of many collective farms that had taken place in recent years. A commission was indeed appointed (January 1966) to revise the Collective Farm Statute of 1935; in mid-1968 its report was still pending.

Russia has long been a grain-exporting country. It is noteworthy that farm disorders and poor harvests allegedly due to inclement weather conditions in 1963 and 1965 forced the Soviet Union to import large amounts of grain, which in 1963–1966 were estimated at 22 million tons. Moscow had also concluded with Canada a contract calling for the purchase between 1966 and 1969 of 9 million tons of wheat worth $800 million. However, Soviet exports of wheat to Eastern Europe and Cuba were believed to be larger over the three-year period than imports from Canada. Foreign grain was presumably paid for by shipments of Soviet gold.

Planning

The Five-Year Plan Again. The mid-1960's brought a revision of the methods of Soviet planning. Among the discarded features was Khrushchev's Seven-Year Plan. Kosygin said at the Twenty-third Congress that "the Twentieth Congress (1956) . . . approved the directives for the sixth Five-Year Plan; three years later the Twenty-first Congress adopted control figures for the development of the national economy 1959–1965. This entire period comprises two Five-Year Plans. Thus our country has carried out in all seven Five-Year Plans." Therefore the plan for 1966–1970 adopted by the Twenty-third Congress became the eighth Five-Year Plan.

As already noted, the structure of the planning agencies was readjusted to meet the situation created by the restoration of the economic ministries. It was also noted that plans, as finally approved, continued to be binding on both industrial and agricultural enterprises. The novel element was the more active participation of enterprises in framing the plan and the less detailed assignments they received from the planning agencies.

The Plan, 1966–1970. The tasks set by the plan for 1966–1970 were, as Kosygin put it, "enormous and majestic." They were formulated in the Directives prepared by the February 1966 plenary session of the central committee, were elaborated in the reports of Brezhnev and Kosygin, and were approved by the Twenty-third Congress. The eighth Five-Year Plan was "to ensure a substantial advance . . . along the road of building up Communism, further development of the material and technical base, and the strengthening of the country's economic and defensive might. . . ." More concretely, it was intended to attain "further significant growth of industry and a high stable rate of industrial development" which would lead to "a substantial rise in the people's standard of living and full satisfaction of their material and cultural needs." The plan called for a 40 per cent increase in the gross social product, and a 50 per cent increase in the fixed production assets, including 60 per cent in industry and 90 per cent in agriculture. National income was expected to rise by 38 to 41 per cent and the real per capita income of the working people by 30 per cent. It was claimed that the plan had "a firm economic and scientific foundation."

The chief task set for farming was to increase substantially the output of field and livestock products and to ensure a high and stable rate of growth. The average annual output of all agricultural products was to increase by 25 per cent over the average annual output in the preceding five years. The average annual grain harvest, according to the plan, was to rise by 30 per cent and reach 167 million tons. Improved farm equipment and greater incentives were expected to result in an increase in labor productivity of 20 to 45 per cent.

The targets set for industry were no less exacting. During the five-year period the volume of industrial output was to increase 47 to 50 per cent, including 49 to 52 per cent in industries producing means of production, and 43 to 46 per cent in those producing consumer goods. The traditional primacy of industries producing means of production was thus maintained but the spread between the rates of growth of the heavy and the light industry was narrowed down, as it was under the earlier plans. A few concrete examples may give an idea of the scope of the proposed expansion. The figures that follow indicate respectively the actual output in 1965 and the targets for 1970; oil, 243 million tons and 345-355 million tons; coal, 578 million tons and 665-675 million tons; steel, 91 million tons and 124-129 million tons; motor vehicles, 616,400 and 1,360,000-1,510,000; leather shoes, 486 million pairs and 610-630 million pairs; radios and radio phonographs, 5.2 million and 7.8-8.0 million; television sets, 3.7 million and 7.5-7.7 million; household refrigerators, 1.7 million and 5.3-5.6 million.

The aggregate capital investment over the five-year period was planned at 310,000 million rubles or 47 per cent more than in 1961-1965. Of this amount, 152,000 million were earmarked for industry, transport, and communication; 71,000 million, as already stated, for farming; and 75,000 million for housing, cultural needs, and services to the population. Wages of industrial workers were to increase by at least 20 per cent and incomes of the collective farmers by 34 to 40 per cent, thus narrowing the difference in the earnings in industry and agriculture. The minimum wage was to be raised, according to Brezhnev, to 60 rubles a month. There was to be a massive increase in pensions and the benefits to which workers were entitled. A shift was to be made to the five-day week (five working days and two days off) without however reducing the established number of hours per week. It was expected that these measures would increase the productivity of industrial labor by 33 to 35 per cent.

Science and Planning. These were impressive assignments, much in line with those of the earlier plans. To reach the targets set by the plan the Soviet leaders depended primarily on science. The eighth Five-Year Plan called for "the acceleration of scientific and technical progress on the basis of the broad development of scientific research, the rapid application of its results in production, and the use of inventions." Special attention should be paid to "the development of research in theoretical and applied mathematics, ensuring the wide application of mathematical methods in the various branches of science and technology." Similar provisions were made for nuclear physics, geology, chemistry, and so on. The social sciences were not overlooked. The plan stated that in economics "attention should be focused on the further elaboration of the theory of planned guidance of the national economy on the basis of profound study and utilization of the economic laws of socialism; on the determination of the ways and methods of raising the effectiveness of social production; and on the application of economic incentives in the development of production."

Kosygin said at the Twenty-third Congress that "a special feature of the new Five-Year Plan is the provision for the rapid technical re-equipment of the entire national economy, the progressive changing of its structure, and the prompt replacement of obsolete products with new and better ones. In this connection the Five-Year Plan should envisage the more rapid development of fundamental theoretical and applied scientific research . . . which should promptly provide production with clear long-range prospects and suggest progressive solutions." In connection with the 1965–1966 reform, said Kosygin, "new and higher demands are being made on our economists. . . . Scientists will have to solve a number of urgent problems of scientific planning and management of the economy. . . . This requires a deep and thorough study of economic processes and the preparation of scientifically valid recommendations for improving the practice of building up the economy."

Brezhnev expressed similar views. "Scientific research should be inseparably linked with the interests of the further development of production . . . ," he said. "The task is to ensure a high rate of growth of labor productivity and the profitability of production. Party and economic agencies, scientists and specialists, and all workers in industry must devote their energy to achieve this objective. The principal source of higher labor productivity should be a rise in the technical level of production on the basis of the development of new machinery and progressive technical processes, the broad utilization of integrated mechanization and automation, greater specialization and improved cooperation of enterprises in production."

Advanced technology based on the extensive use of computers was to play an increasingly important part in the management of the economy. Kosygin discussed electronic computers in his address before the Twenty-third Congress. "These machines," he said, "will perform various functions in engineering, economic and financial calculations, and will automate accounting to a substantial degree. The introduction of this equipment in the system of management is an important national-economic task." M. V. Keldysh, president of the USSR Academy of Sciences, told the congress that "electronic computer equipment, which appeared after the war and has been developing rapidly, is penetrating increasingly all branches of the national economy and is becoming one of the main levers of technical progress and economic development. The level we have achieved in developing and applying electronic computer equipment is inadequate at the present stage." He noted, however, considerable improvement in recent years, and added that "economic research has always been based on economic information and mathematical elaborations. The development of electronic computer technology has opened new and unprecedented possibilities. It is incumbent upon economic science to make fuller use of such means for raising the level of management and planning. . . . Methods must be worked out that will make it possible to choose the maximum variant of the plan."

Soviet interest in computer technique was entering the stage of large-scale practical application. A resolution of the party central committee and the Council of Ministers "on the introduction in the economy of computer technology and automatic control systems" was issued in March 1966. It stated that "the creation, development, and introduction of computer technology into the system of planning, accounting, and control" was a highly important task but that this technique is not being used widely enough. The All-Union Design and Installation Association was established "to engage in the designing, installation, adjustment, and putting into operation of automated control systems." Simultaneously the Academy of Sciences was directed to work out, jointly with other agencies, "scientific bases of a unified system of optimal planning, accounting, and control."

Not all Soviet economists, however, share the official faith in the virtues of automation. "Some economists hope that the miscalculations and mistakes of maximal centralized planning can be avoided by creating a ramified network of computer centers, to be unified in a system harnessed to a kind of electronic plan," Professor Liberman, one of the authors of the 1965 reform, told a correspondent of *Komsomolskaia Pravda* (April 24, 1966). "It is highly doubtful however whether any single center, even armed to the teeth with up-to-date electronics, can direct so complex an organism as the national economy today. I have little faith in push-button economics." This was a sound warning. Unlike electronics and space studies, mathematical economics is not an exact science. Liberman's statement is also notable as one of the rare instances (perhaps the only one on record) when an economic policy approved by the government was permitted to be openly criticized.

In April 1968 *Izvestia* held a "round table" or seminar on mathematical methods for optimum planning. The participants, all high planning officials or mathematicians, agreed on the crucial importance of mathematical economics for optimum planning but noted the many difficulties inherent in the application of this method. "Optimum planning is just taking its first step," was *Izvestia*'s terse summary of the discussion.

Some Results. The report of the Central Statistical Administration of the Council of Ministers on the fulfillment of the economic plan for 1967—the second year of the eighth Five-Year Plan—presented the familiar opaque and unrevealing picture of over-fulfillment of planned targets in practically every field of endeavor. The only—but important—exception was agriculture. The grain crop in 1966 was 171.2 million tons, that is, in excess of the 167 million target set by the plan, but declined to 147.6 million tons in 1967, ostensibly because of unfavorable weather conditions. The 1967 harvest was still 13 per cent above the yearly average for 1961–1965 (130.3 million tons) but these were admittedly very poor years. The "high and stable" rate of growth predicated by the plan was not achieved in the case of grain. Other branches of rural husbandry fared better. Nevertheless, the report noted that "there are shortcomings in the work of collective and state farms. Crop yields and livestock productivity in a number of areas are still low. On many collective and state farms labor productivity is rising slowly, and production costs are not decreasing enough. Although the state farms as a whole finished the year with a profit, many of them did not fulfill the profit plan, and some suffered losses." These gloomy observations suggest that the sanguine expectations raised by the reform were not justified.

The state of education offered a more heartening picture. It was reported that in 1967 about 76 million people were engaged in various types of study —most of them, presumably, in correspondence courses—and 4.3 million were enrolled in higher schools, while the population, as of January 1, 1968, stood at 237 million.

"Coexistence" Continued

The Doctrine. The October 1964 plenary session of the central committee, which decreed the removal of Khrushchev, is officially rated as a "turning point" in Soviet history. It was not followed, however, by any significant revision of the Communist doctrine. The party program of 1961, although of Khrushchevian inspiration, was retained as the depository of ultimate verity. Its basic principles—including those bearing on foreign relations—were reiterated with but minor modifications in the subsequent resolutions of the central committee and in the pronouncements of Soviet leaders. According to the lengthy (some 20,000 words) *Theses on the Fiftieth Anniversary of the Revolution* issued by the central committee in June 1967, "capitalism is doomed. The cause of the revolutionary rejuvenation of the world, begun by the October revolution and fostered by the triumph of socialism in the USSR, has been continued by the victories of socialist revolutions in other countries. The formation of the world socialist system is one of the most important historical events since the victory of the great October socialist revolution." The large number of countries that established socialist regimes after World War II "was the striking confirmation of the Marxist-Leninist theory of the inevitable triumph of the new order." The October revolution "has dealt a crushing blow to the whole system of imperialist colonial rule and has given a powerful stimulus to the development of national liberation movements." The inevitable transition to socialism may be peaceful or violent; its character will depend in each case on "the balance of class forces, the degree of organization and political maturity of the working class, the authority and ability of its vanguard [the Communist party], the degree of resistance offered by the ruling class, and the world situation." Meanwhile "the struggle between socialism and imperialism has become the pivot of all world politics." The socialist countries are striving for peace but "the menace of predatory wars will remain as long as imperialism remains." Moreover, "Marxism-Leninism regards as just and gives support to wars in defense of people's rights against imperialist aggression and for national liberation. . . ." The Communist Party of the USSR "considers support of international revolutionary forces as an indivisible part of its activity," because "only Communism can solve the fundamental problems of social development, deliver mankind from oppression and exploitation, from hunger and poverty, from militarism and wars, and establish on our planet democracy, peace, friendship among peoples and a life in keeping with the dignity of man. . . ." This is an enticing picture, but it bears little resemblance to Soviet reality.

Brezhnev has discussed repeatedly the Communist doctrine and its international implications. He told the Twenty-third Congress that "the capitalists will never surrender their rule voluntarily. The working class and the laboring masses will achieve victory only in the course of stubborn class battles." There is no doubt that "the peoples who have entered the path of struggle for independence will carry it out to a victorious end." They can count on the support of nearly 90 Communist parties with an aggregate membership approaching 50 million. Although the Soviet state "extends all possible help to countries fighting for their liberation," the Kremlin invariably "has pursued a policy of relaxation of tension, of strengthening of peace, of peaceful coexistence of states with different social systems, of creating conditions that would enable each country to develop freely along the path of national and social progress." The Soviet Union, said Brezhnev, "has repeatedly declared its willingness to develop relations with the United States, and still adheres to this position," but a major obstacle was the war in Vietnam. Moreover, "there could be no peaceful coexistence when it comes to internal processes of class struggle and national-liberation struggle in the capitalist countries or in the colonies." In spite of these reservations "interstate relations with the capitalist countries," according to Brezhnev, "should not only be peaceful but should also provide the broadest possible mutually advantageous economic, scientific, and cultural ties." Brezhnev quoted Lenin's statement to the effect that "a socialist state exerts its chief influence on the international revolution through its economic policy."

In his address on the fiftieth anniversary of the revolution (November 1967) Brezhnev recalled Lenin's dictum that foreign policy questions must be dealt with "from the standpoint of conditions that are best for the development and consolidation of the socialist revolution that had already begun." But he also held that "Marxist-Leninists have always understood that socialism cannot be carried from one country to another by military force, but is the outcome of the internal development of each given society. They firmly believe . . . in the advantages of the socialist system and are convinced that for it to be victorious there is no need to resort to war between states." The Soviet government, he said, "attaches serious significance to the United Nations and will strive . . . to turn it into an effective organ of international cooperation . . . and will support mutually advantageous collaboration of states with different social systems on the basis of . . . principles of peaceful coexistence." Brezhnev claimed that the Soviet Union, in spite of her military might, "advocates renunciation of attempts at settling questions of relations between the two social systems by military means," and he spoke approvingly of reaching understandings with "sober-minded representatives of the bourgeoisie."

It follows that coexistence, with the reservations indicated above, retained its place as a guiding principle of Soviet foreign policy. The main objectives of the Kremlin remained the same as under Khrushchev, although practical policies were influenced by novel factors, of which the more important were the cleavage in the international Communist movement, the intensification of the war in Vietnam, and the Israel-Arab war.

UPI

Leonid Brezhnev

Relations with the Communist Bloc. The assumed monolithic unity of the Communist movement, which was an element in the Communist claim to an inevitable victory over capitalism, came under attack after World War II, especially following Stalin's death and, again, in the 1960's. As indicated in an earlier chapter, the first socialist countries to regain a measure of independence from Moscow were Yugoslavia, Albania, and China; there were abortive anti-Soviet outbreaks in East Germany, Poland, and Hungary. In the 1960's the difficulties of the Kremlin with its Communist partners became more pronounced and assumed a different form. Soviet hegemony over eastern Europe—and beyond—was threatened by two sets of developments reflecting opposite trends. On the one hand, there appeared an extreme left-wing movement represented by the followers of Mao Tse-tung, the Trotskyites, and the anarchists; on the other hand, a tendency towards the liberalization of Communist methods which, if permitted to grow, might eventually lead to democratic regimes of the western type.

The chief proponent of the left-of-Soviet-Communism orientation was China. Frictions with the Chinese went back as far as the 1920's but they did not assume importance until after Stalin's death. Mao-Tse-tung, the unchallengeable master of the Chinese People's Republic, is dogmatic, rigid, and unbending. He accepted, although at times not without misgivings, the leadership of Stalin, but was critical of his successors on the grounds of both ideology and practical policy. The Chinese Communist leaders resented the partial reconciliation between the Soviets and Yugoslavia (1955) and de-Stalinization; they rejected the Soviet thesis of the possibility of peaceful transition to socialism and its concomitant, the notion of coexistence of states with different social systems. These divergencies of views arose while Khrushchev was still in office, but they became sharper and indeed virulent after his removal. Moreover, Mao was revered by the Chinese Communists as "the greatest Marxist-Leninist of our era" and therefore Stalin's successor as the true leader of world Communism. The Soviets were accused of "revisionism," "betrayal of socialism," and "cooperating" with the United States in the Vietnamese war. Moscow retaliated in kind. A resolution of the central committee of the Soviet Communist Party (August 31, 1966) asserted that "the Chinese leadership has given the approval of its anti-Soviet line the form of an official policy of the Chinese Communist Party." Brezhnev said (November 1967) that "events in China have fully laid bare the ideological and political degradation of some of the leaders of the Communist Party of China."

The Chinese "cultural revolution" that began in 1966 introduced a novel element of discord. Its object was to wipe out the existing order, especially state and party bureaucracy, and—as a Western commentator put it—"the sheer experience of rebellion." The latter notion appealed strongly to a restless postwar generation and led to the founding—or strengthening—in many countries of hosts of extreme left-wing groups which challenged the authority of official communist parties. These groups were presumably responsible for the tide of student rebellion, accompanied by seizures of university buildings, which in the spring and summer of 1968 swept first over France and then over other western European countries, the United States, Latin America, Africa, and, indeed, the world. Yugoslavia and Czechoslovakia were affected but not the USSR. On June 12, 1968, the French government ordered the dissolution of 11 militant organizations, chiefly those of students of Maoist, Trotskyist, and anarchist persuasion. The aloofness of the Soviet youth was notable. It will be recalled that Russian pre-1917 universities had a long revolutionary tradition. Should the fact that in 1968 Soviet higher schools were not affected by a world-wide revolutionary movement be interpreted as evidence of their students' support of the official Communist doctrine and satisfaction with the existing conditions? Or should it be credited to the efficacy of segregation from the intellectual currents of the West and, perhaps, the vigilance of the security police? There is no doubt, however, that Soviet Communism was faced with a strong challenge from the left.

The trend towards liberalization manifested itself in different degrees in several eastern European states and, from the Soviet standpoint, was all the more disturbing because it affected countries that were members of the Warsaw Pact (1955)—the Communist counterpart of NATO (North Atlantic Treaty Organization). Rumania was among the first to show some independence from the dictations of Moscow. In January 1967 she established diplomatic relations with West Germany, contrary to the policy prescribed by the Kremlin and in March of that year abstained from attending (as did Yugoslavia, Albania, and the Communist parties of three non-socialist European states) the Communist conference at Karlovy Var (see below), as well as the one held in Moscow in June of the same year to devise a common policy in the Israel-Arab crisis. Rumania, again, was not represented at the consultative meeting of the Communist parties in Budapest in February-March 1968. Czechoslovakia, too, became recalcitrant. Antonin Novotny, a staunch supporter of the USSR, was removed from the position of first secretary of the Czech Communist Party in January 1968 and in March from the presidency of the republic; in May 1968 he was expelled from the central committee. These developments and the simultaneous moves towards the liberalization of the Czechoslovak regime imposed a great strain on Soviet-Czech relations and led to the occupation, on August 20, 1968, of Czechoslovakia by the troops of the Soviet Union and of four other members of the Warsaw Pact (Poland, East Germany, Bulgaria, and Hungary). Communist Cuba was another country to falter in its allegiance to Moscow.

The Kremlin endeavored to reassert its leadership by organizing a world Communist conference that would be linked to similar conferences in Moscow in 1957 and 1960. The proposal was launched at the end of 1966. A five-day meeting of the preparatory committee was held in Budapest in April 1968. It was attended by the representatives of 54 parties and 15 more expressed their intention to attend the conference. However, only 14 of the ruling Communist parties were present. The conference was to meet in Moscow in November-December 1968 but was postponed. It seemed likely that several of the Communist parties, among them some of the key ones—those of Yugoslavia, Rumania, and perhaps Hungary and Czechoslovakia—would not send delegates.

East and West. The implementation of the policy of coexistence led to increased contacts with many lands. Even more than in the Khrushchevian era, VIP's from near and far flocked to Moscow. Some of them—surprisingly—were hereditary rulers while others were elected heads of states. The royalties who came to the USSR as guests of the Soviet government were the shah and empress of Iran (June 1965), the king and queen of Afghanistan (August 1965), King Hassan of Morocco (October 1966), and Emperor Haile Selassie of Ethiopia (February 1967). Most of the countries of western Europe and of the Near and Far East sent to Moscow their presidents, prime ministers, ministers of foreign affairs, and other high officials. Outstanding among these visitors were the president of Pakistan, Marshal Ayub Khan (April 1965 and September 1967); L. B. Shastri (May 1965) and Mrs. Indira Gandhi (July 1966), the two successive prime ministers of India; and Harold Wilson, prime minister of Great Britain (February and July 1966 and January 1968). The apparently most successful guest of the Soviet government was the president of France, General Charles de Gaulle (June 1966). His militant anti-American and anti-British policy in every field—international politics, trade, and finance—and his not entirely unsuccessful efforts to undermine NATO made him a valuable ally of Soviet Communism. Several economic, cultural, and technical agreements were concluded between Moscow and Paris. Even his vitriolic attack on "totalitarian Communism" in his radio interview (June 7, 1968) given at the height of the French internal crisis and reported in Soviet newspapers, did not seem to have affected unfavorably his standing with the Kremlin. Harold Wilson fared less well. His endorsement of the United

States Vietnamese policy and, perhaps, the decline of Great Britain's international position, precluded any real improvement in Soviet-British relations.

The main topics of discussion between the Soviet leaders and their non-Communist guests were the extension of trade, cultural exchanges, and measures for the preservation of peace. On the latter issue, which involved the entire field of international relations, agreement was seldom, if ever, reached or even in sight.

Close and often intimate ties were maintained by the Kremlin with the friendly states of Communist persuasion and with the Communist parties in the capitalist countries. States engaged in a "liberation" struggle naturally turned for help to Moscow, unless they relied entirely on Mao's China. For instance, a delegation of the Liberation Front of South Vietnam negotiated in the Soviet capital with Kosygin in June 1965.

Brezhnev, Kosygin, and other Soviet leaders, usually accompanied by delegations of state and party officials, frequently visited capital cities throughout

UPI

Pope Paul VI and Soviet President Podgorny at the Vatican

the world, from London and Paris to Pyongyang, North Korea, and Hanoi, North Vietnam, where Kosygin made brief appearances in February 1965. At times the Moscovites turned up in unexpected places: for instance, in January 1967 N. V. Podgorny, chairman of the presidium of the Supreme Soviet, had an audience in the Vatican with Pope Paul VI.

Somewhat earlier the Soviet Union assumed the unaccustomed rôle of peacemaker. Following the United Nations' action in the autumn of 1965 to stop the India-Pakistan war, the two antagonists accepted the invitation of the Soviet government to have the issue negotiated, under the chairmanship of Kosygin, in Tashkent in January 1966. The Kosygin mediation was successful and the Tashkent Declaration provided a settlement acceptable to both parties.

In July 1966 a conference of the Warsaw Pact states—the USSR, Bulgaria, Czechoslovakia, East Germany, Hungary, Poland, and Rumania—met in Bucharest and issued a declaration of predominantly Soviet inspiration. It called for an all-European conference (the United States was not to be represented) that would establish a Europe unified both politically and economically. NATO and the Warsaw Pact organization were to be dismantled as well as the European Economic Community (The Common Market) and its Communist counterpart, Comecon, and the Western powers were to recognize the independent republic of East Germany. There was, of course, no chance of this program being accepted by the West. Another attempt at concrete action was the Communist conference at Karlovy Var, Czechoslovakia, in March 1967. It is believed that its original object was to organize a united Communist front against China, but it actually limited itself to an elaboration of the Budapest Declaration dealing with European issues.

Meanwhile the Soviet Union continued the policy of making its presence felt in the strategically, politically, and economically important area of the Mediterranean and the Middle East. Oil, the elimination of the remnants of colonialism, and the eventual withdrawal of the United States navy were the principal objectives of this policy. The most favored country was the United Arab Republic. Its president, Gamal Abdel Nasser, was fêted in Moscow in August 1965, and its vice-president and deputy commander of the armed forces, Marshal Abdel Hakum Amer, in November 1966. In May 1966 Kosygin spoke at a rally held at Aswan to celebrate the progress of the Aswan High Dam, the building of which was made possible by Soviet financial and technical assistance. A large number of Soviet engineers and technicians were employed in building the dam. According to the United States department of state, Soviet economic aid to the United Arab Republic in 1954-1966 amounted to over $1,000 million, or slightly less than one fifth of the aggregate Soviet aid to 33 countries during that period. India was the only country to receive larger Soviet aid (nearly $1,600 million in 1954–1966).

The Soviet Union has long been hostile to Israel, which she regarded as a client of the United States and the western European powers. Moscow had armed Syria and especially the United Arab Republic but there is no evidence that it actually encouraged, or even contemplated, war between the Arab states and Israel, although a war victorious for the Arabs would, no doubt, be welcome in Moscow. The lightning defeat of Nasser and his allies (June 1967) was a severe shock to the Kremlin and a blow to its prestige, but the Soviet Union did not intervene directly. Instead she joined the United States in the security council of the United Nations in calling for a cease-fire. The Arab defeat had its advantages from the Soviet standpoint. Arab governments, in their disappointment and frustration, decreed the nationalization of oil and other important Western interests and broke off diplomatic relations with the West. These moves the Kremlin welcomed if it did not inspire them. Nor did it abandon its defeated clients. It is known that within a few months the Soviet Union shipped to the United Arab Republic, Syria, and their allies enough aircraft and other war materiel to make good the losses they had suffered in the war of June 1967.

The Arab-Israeli war revealed a potentially important and hitherto neglected factor—the emergence of the Soviet Union as an incipient naval power. Soviet warships first began to appear in the Mediterranean in significant numbers in 1964. They were heavily reinforced during the crisis of June 1967, but the strength of the Soviet squadron was still greatly inferior to United States forces in these waters. According to a Western expert "the Russians could not stand up to the Sixth and Seventh fleets for half an hour." Nevertheless, the strengthening of the Soviet navy and the new willingness to use it in distant waters was unmistakable; it was demonstrated by the appearance of Soviet warships in the Indian Ocean in the spring of 1967. As an English journal put it, "the Russian bear learns to swim"—at the very time when Great Britain was drastically cutting down her overseas commitments. The combination of a large Soviet army and air force with a fast-growing navy could profoundly affect the international situation.

The Soviets and the United States. Soviet policies towards the United States reflected the complexities and contradictions inherent in the Communist doctrine and the position of the USSR in the midst of an unsettled and rapidly changing world. The doctrine, as stated above, preached peaceful coexistence of states with different social systems, "willingness to develop

Soviet missile-carrying destroyer cruising off the coast of Turkey

relations with the United States," and understanding "with sober-minded representatives of the bourgeoisie" (Brezhnev). But it also held that the advent of socialism was inevitable, and that it was the primary duty of the Soviet state "to extend all possible help to countries fighting for their liberation." What actually mattered, however, were not so much the niceties of revolutionary theory as their translation in terms of practical policies.

In the post-Khrushchev era the policy of expanding trade relations and cultural exchanges was continued on a modest scale. Cultural exchanges were often marred by outbreaks of xenophobia in the Soviet Union and by mutual charges of subversive activities. Soviet accusations of espionage and subversion were directed not only against the Americans but also against British, German, and other foreign visitors. A more promising development was the launching of the first Soviet trans-Atlantic liner *Alexander Pushkin,* a 19,800-ton vessel built in East Germany which made its first crossing to Quebec in April 1966. The purpose of the liner, it was officially stated, was to increase exchanges between the Soviet Union and North America.

The principal immediate causes of discord between the Soviet Union and the United States were Vietnam, Germany, and Israel. The basic reason for American intervention in Vietnam was the belief that it was in the interest of the United States to prevent the imposition of Communist rule on the unwilling population of South Vietnam. What was originally a program of relatively modest economic and military aid grew into large-scale military intervention. The Soviet government never accepted the American interpretation. The situation was made worse by the beginning of extensive American bombing of North Vietnam early in 1965, at the very time when Kosygin was visiting Hanoi. The Soviet view was stated with extreme violence in a resolution of the Twenty-third party Congress (April 1966). "The entire Soviet people. . . ," said the resolution, "angrily and indignantly condemns the barbarous aggression of the United States of America against the fraternal Vietnamese people." American imperialists "are endeavoring to suppress the national-liberation struggle of the South-Vietnamese people and other peoples of Southeast Asia. . . . The American military is using the most savage inhuman methods." The contention that the United States was defending freedom and counteracting Communist expansion was branded as "a lie." The United States, said the resolution, "has covered itself with eternal shame." The Soviets demanded "the cessation of United States aggression . . . and the withdrawal of all troops," and announced that "the aggressor will encounter ever-growing support for Vietnam on the part of the Soviet Union." The South Vietnam Liberation Front must be recognized as the sole legitimate representative of South Vietnam. The resolution closed with a dramatic appeal to "all friends of progress and democracy, all honest men and women to whom peace, justice, freedom, and independence of peoples are dear . . . to oppose the aggressive action of the United States imperialists. . . ."

The Soviet government consistently adhered to this program. The many appeals of President Johnson for Soviet mediation of the Vietnamese war met with no response. Kosygin, who came to New York in connection with the Middle East crisis, met President Johnson twice, on June 23 and 27, 1967, at Glassboro, N.J. On both principal issues discussed—the Middle East and Vietnam—the conference disclosed, according to the official communiqué, "profound divergencies" in the position of the two countries. Patriarch Alexis of Moscow, always subservient to the wishes of the government, organized in the town of Zagorsk, near the Soviet capital, a conference of the international Christian Movement for the Defense of Peace (April 1966). A resolution of the conference stated that "the imperialist aggressive war

UPI

Kosygin and Johnson at Glassboro

in South Vietnam has nothing in common with a just battle for freedom and the defense of human rights."

There were probably several reasons for Soviet intransigence in dealing with Vietnam. On the assumption that the Communist movement in that country was a genuine liberation movement, its defense was clearly in agreement with the Communist doctrine. The desire to counteract Chinese denunciations of the Soviets as stooges of American imperialism and their effect, especially in Southeast Asia, was probably another reason. From the Communist point of view, the prolongation, due to Soviet help, of the Vietnamese war had several advantages. It was likely to weaken the United States in the long run economically and militarily and created serious friction with America's allies, and much unrest and opposition in the country itself. For many people in the United States and elsewhere who had nothing to do with Communism intensely disliked the Vietnamese war.

The disagreement between Moscow and Washington on the Middle East issue, although fraught with grave danger, was kept reasonably under control. There was much friction over West Germany, her rôle in NATO, and the potential use of nuclear weapons. The Kremlin protested frequently West Germany's alleged "revanchism" but the nostalgic Berlin question remained quiescent until June 1968 when the East German government imposed visa restrictions on West Germans travelling to Berlin by road, that is, through East German territory, as well as a tax on commercial vehicles taking the same route. The resulting situation contained elements of a major crisis. The United States, Great Britain, and France protested to Moscow on the ground that the East German action was a violation of existing treaties and inimical to the policy of coexistence. However, since the three powers were not directly involved, strong retaliatory action on their part did not seem likely.

There were instances when peaceful coexistence produced tangible results. A Soviet-American consular treaty, which had been under negotiation for several years and was opposed in the United States on the grounds that it gave immunity to consular staff and therefore increased the danger of espionage, was approved after long delays by the United States Senate in March 1967; the instruments of ratification were exchanged in Washington on June 13, 1968, and the treaty took effect a month later.

Of broader significance was the draft treaty on the non-proliferation of nuclear weapons, the text of which was agreed, after a lengthy negotiation, by the Soviet Union and the United States and, on June 11, 1968, was adopted by the general assembly of the United Nations by a very large majority. Under the provisions of this treaty the nuclear powers undertook not to transfer the possession or control of nuclear weapons to other states, while the non-nuclear powers undertook not to accept nuclear weapons and not to seek to produce them. Soviet and American representatives had the leading rôle in piloting the treaty through the general assembly. The treaty, which would not become effective until ratified by 40 states, was attacked by the Chinese Communists as a shameless instance of the determination of the great powers to retain the monopoly of nuclear arms. The successful cooperation of Moscow and Washington in reaching an agreement on the complex and controversial issue of non-proliferation would seem to indicate that peaceful coexistence contains possibilities of fruitful development.

The Outlook. The longing for peace essential to the accomplishment of the tasks set for themselves by the Communists, the mountainous economic difficulties facing Moscow, the haunting memories of World War II, and the frightfulness of a nuclear war suggest that, barring unforeseeable developments, the policy of peaceful coexistence might continue for an indefinite and, perhaps, protracted period.

28

Letters, Arts, And Science, 1917-1968

Impact of the Revolution

Immediate Effects of War and Revolution. "Let us go to work," Lenin wrote in 1905. "We are faced with a difficult and novel but great and rewarding task—the organization of the vast, many-sided, varied literary effort in close and indissoluble cooperation with the social-democratic labor movement. All social-democratic literature must be party literature." It took 15 years after the advent of the Bolsheviks to power before this directive, which embraced all forms of cultural and artistic endeavor, was fully applied.

War and revolution are not, as a rule, conducive to the advancement of the arts, even though *La Marseillaise,* a truly great revolutionary song written by Rouget de l'Isle in 1792 in the midst of a military campaign, was the product of revolutionary inspiration. But this was the exception rather than the rule. World War I, with its disorganization and shortages and the drafting into the armed forces of many artists and writers, drastically curtailed cultural activities. Hardships of every nature increased greatly with the outbreak of the revolution and civil war: the struggle for survival rather than for self-expression was what artists and writers had to contend with during these bleak years. Moreover, many of the leading personalities in literature and the arts were non-Bolsheviks and found it impossible to continue to work under the new conditions. Some perished in the civil war, died from hunger and privations, or were exterminated by the security police. Others emigrated abroad. This was a grievous blow, because Russia's cultural élite was small, and it took years before the loss was made good. Some of it proved irreparable.

The destruction or attrition of cultural forces, however, was gradual. It will be remembered that on the eve of World War I "art for art's sake," symbolism, futurism, cubism, impressionism, post-impressionism, and various brands of abstract painting were favored in Russian vanguard literary and art circles. The Russian theater, including the ballet, gained world-wide recognition for its bold and brilliant experimentation with novel methods of stagecraft. Quite a few representatives of the vanguard movements welcomed enthusiastically the fall of the *ancien régime* and believed that the revolution opened limitless horizons for the triumphant progress of the most daring forms of artistic expression. These expectations were soon to be disappointed.

A curious episode was Lenin's plan for "propaganda by monuments" (*monumentalnaia propaganda*) to which he attached great importance (decree of April 13, 1918). Monuments, emblems, and memorial tablets commemorating tsars and pre-revolutionary events and personalities were to be removed and replaced by others "reflecting the ideas and feelings of revolutionary workers' Russia." According to Lunacharsky, people's commissar for education, who drafted the decree and was in charge of its implementation, the results were unsatisfactory, especially in Moscow. For instance the whims of the sculptor (whose name Lunacharsky does not disclose) represented Marx and Engels plodding through a basin, with the unintended result that the founders of scientific socialism became popular with the Muscovites as "the bearded bathers." Bakunin, a theorist of anarchism, fared even less well. His effigy, says Lunacharsky, was that of a demented man, and immediately after its unveiling, it was smashed by irate anarchists who saw in the memorial an insult to their leader. Only a few of the proposed "propaganda" memorials were actually erected, and since most of them were made of plaster and other perishable materials ill-adapted to the rigors of the climate, they soon fell apart—much to the relief of the public, one may surmise.

During the opening years of the Bolshevik regime the vanguard movements were active. An important center was *Proletkult*—a federation of militant "proletarian" associations concerned with the advancement of science, art, and especially literature. *Proletkult* was formed in September 1917, shortly before the advent of the Bolsheviks, and for a time enjoyed considerable popularity: in 1919 it had about 100 divisions in the provinces. The program of *Proletkult* called for independence from the authorities, especially from the people's commissariat of education, which was in charge of cultural affairs; held that industrial workers alone—to the exclusion of peasants and intellectuals—were capable of creating a truly proletarian culture; and rejected Russia's cultural heritage. These contentions led to a conflict with the government, which was sponsoring collaboration (*smychka*) between workers and peasants. Moreover, far from rejecting the heritage of the past, Lenin held (1919) that "one must take all the culture which capitalism has left behind and use it to build up socialism." In spite of these basic disagreements *Proletkult* was tolerated, although its path was beset with mounting difficulties. Throughout the 1920's there was still a great diversity of cultural movements in every field—literature, painting, music, architecture, the theater, cinematography—which may be partly explained by the proclivities of Lunacharsky, who remained people's commissar for education until 1929.

Socialist Realism. By the end of the 1920's Stalin had eliminated all opposition within the party, and his dictatorship was firmly entrenched. The turn of literature and the arts came next. A decree of the central committee "On the Reconstruction of the Literary and Art Organizations" (April 13, 1932) abolished the existing associations of writers, artists, and musicians. Their number was considerable; in Moscow alone there were 14 associations of painters. For the various groupings there were substituted the Union of Soviet Writers, the Union of Soviet Composers, and the Union of Soviet Artists, highly centralized associations under the direct control of the party and the government. The first congress of the Union of Soviet Writers was held in July 1934, and its statutes were confirmed by the government on February 17, 1935. The members of the union were requested "to participate actively in socialist construction." They were to be guided, said the statutes, by "socialist realism, the basic method of Soviet belles-lettres and literary criticism, which requires from the writer truthful, historically concrete representation of reality in its revolutionary development. Moreover, the truthfulness of the historico-concrete artistic representation of reality must be combined with the objective of the spiritual transformation and re-education of the working people in the spirit of socialism." Similar obligations were imposed on the members of the other unions.

Socialist realism was the negation of "art for art's sake," formalism, and cosmopolitanism. It has been officially defined (1948) as "ideological chastity —Soviet patriotism, defense of the motherland, happiness of the free life of toil, love for the great leader Stalin." The last requirement was soft-pedaled after 1953 and dropped in 1956, but the others remain. Moreover any work of art—literature, painting, or music—must be expressed in a medium accessible to the masses, which excludes all vanguard movements. For practical purposes socialist realism may be said to have made literature and the arts into tools of Soviet propaganda. No deviation from the approved pattern is tolerated. Soviet intellectuals, even the most prominent, are being frequently chastised for deviation from the party line; they are forced to recant if they wish to continue their work. These are not conditions under which letters, arts, and science can develop successfully and freely. The levels of artistic production, with perhaps the exception of music and pure science, have been exceedingly low. Control of artists and writers was greatly tightened during the rule of Andrew Zhdanov (1896–1948), who became head of the Leningrad party organization in 1935 and a member of the Politburo in 1939. An ardent devotee of the Stalin brand of Communist orthodoxy, he was very influential in the 1940's and relentless in exterminating "cosmopolitan" deviations. As will appear in the closing section of this chapter, socialist realism has been retained by Stalin's successors.

Literature and the Theater

Belles Lettres. The revolution deprived Russia of a number of established and prospective authors. Among those who emigrated were: Ivan Bunin, the first Russian to be awarded the Nobel prize for literature, Alexander Kuprin, Michael Artsybashev, Leonid Andreev, Dimitry Merezhkovsky, Zinaida Hippius, Constantine Balmont, Mark Aldanov (Landau, 1886–1957), and Vladimir Nabokov (1899–   ). Many remained, however, including the symbolist poets Valery Briusov, Andrew Bely, and Alexander Block, who for a time held their ground. *The Twelve* (1918) by Block is the only near-great work in verse that came from the revolution. Flamboyant propaganda poems were written by the talented writers Demian Bedny (Efim Pridvorov, 1883–1945) and Vladimir Mayakovsky. Serge Esenin (1895–1925) was a young gifted poet; he came of peasant stock, wrote "imaginist" verse, was briefly married to the American dancer Isadora Duncan (1922), and soon thereafter committed suicide. Several promising writers of non-proletarian origin who believed that literature must be free formed a group known as the Serapion Brothers. Among the members of this organization were the novelists, well-known later, Constantine Fedin (1892–   ), Boris Pilniak (1894–1942), and Vsevolod Ivanov (1895–   ). The more important novels written in the 1920's were Dimitry Furmanov's *Chapaev* (1923), Fedor Gladkov's *Cement* (1925), and Michael Sholokhov's *The Quiet Don* (1926–1940), an epic of the civil war. These books were largely in the tradition of Russia's nineteenth-century realism. Later Sholokhov wrote *The Virgin Soil Upturned* (1932 and 1959–1960), a very long novel about collectivization, strictly in accordance with the rules of socialist realism. Viewed as a whole, literature in the 1920's retained a measure of vitality and independence.

The two leading Soviet authors, Maxim Gorky and Alexis N. Tolstoy (1885–1945), had established their literary reputations prior to the revolution. It will be remembered that Gorky came from a working-class family and had connections of long standing with the Bolsheviks. His principal literary work after the revolution was a 4-volume family chronicle *The Life of*

Sovfoto

Vladimir Mayakovsky

Klim Samgin (1927–1936), which remained unfinished, as well as a volume of literary reminiscences. Gorky was active in the Union of Soviet Writers and after his death in 1936 was held as the father of socialist realism. Alexis N. Tolstoy, a count and kin of Leo Tolstoy, was a poet and a novelist and had to his credit several books prior to 1917. He opposed the Bolshevik revolution, fought against the Reds in the civil war, emigrated after the defeat of the anti-Soviet forces, but in 1923 returned to Russia. Tolstoy's most important book is the long historical novel *Peter the First,* the publication of which began in 1929 but which remained unfinished. Other fictional works enjoying popularity were Nicholas Ostrovsky's novel *How Steel Is Tempered* (1935) and fictional biographies of historical and literary personalities—Pushkin, Radishchev, Field Marshal Kutuzov, Dimitry Donskoy—by various authors, and written in a supra-patriotic vein. The effects of the Zhdanov regime were indeed deadly. Lenin's wish that all literature should be party literature was fulfilled.

Encouragement was, and is, given to literature of national minorities, provided local nationalism does not infringe on Soviet (great-Russian) patriotism. Works of this group follow closely the rules of socialist realism; their number is large, but they have little intrinsic merit.

The Theater. The evolution of the theater broadly paralleled that of literature. A few actors and some of the leading producers emigrated. Nicholas Evreinov, a master of stagecraft and founder of the satirical theater *Twisted Mirror,* left Russia in 1920. Nikita Baliev, a talented and resourceful producer, revived in Paris his Petrograd company *The Bat,* which specialized in highly stylized short sketches; it had a long and successful career abroad. Meanwhile vanguard movements were gaining ground in Russia. Theaters were nationalized and were placed under the direction, first, of the theater department of the people's commissariat of education and in the 1930's of the department of arts. The former imperial theaters, the Moscow Art Theater and the Kamerny Theater, were designated as academic theaters and were given assurance of continuity and special government protection. The leading theaters displayed at first a spirit of independence; they stuck to their traditional repertories or claimed the right to experiment with new methods. An influential innovator was Vsevolod Meyerhold, who joined the Communist Party, was the first director of the theater department, and announced the "theatrical October," or "revolution in the theater," which was to do away with conventions. He was a partisan of "constructivism" and then of "biomechanics," which necessitated special physical training for the actors. His productions, which combined the elements of the legitimate theater, circus, and musical comedy, employed at times very large casts and were striking and unconventional. Many new theaters were founded under the auspices of local authorities, trade unions, and the army. The leading new theaters were the Leningrad Great State Drama Theater (1918), the Second Moscow Art Theater, the Meyerhold Theater (1920), and the Vakhtangov Theater (1922). For about 10 years these, as well as the provincial theaters which followed their lead, showed remarkable creative activity and a ceaseless quest for new forms.

Lunacharsky, whose plays Meyerhold produced and who as commissar for education was responsible for the leeway allowed to the theaters, soon found himself in difficulties with the authorities. Beginning in 1921 the party voiced disapproval of the "bourgeois-aesthetic and decadent" trend in the theater. At first restrictions applied rather to the contents of the plays than to methods of production. Playwrights were to conform to the approved pattern: they were to deal with revolutionary themes and to present idealized images of heroic and virtuous Communists contrasted with the unrelieved villainy of the enemies of the Soviets (M. Bulgakov, *The Days of the Turbins,* 1926; Yuri Olesha, *Conspiracy of Feelings,* 1929), but a measure of freedom was still permitted in staging these uninspiring offerings. In 1929 Lunacharsky was dismissed, and in the 1930's socialist realism came inexorably to the fore. The central committee of the party ordered the liquidation of the "formalist-aesthetic experimentations" of the vanguard directors. The Second Moscow Art Theater was closed in 1936 and the Meyerhold Theater in 1938. In 1939 Meyerhold was arrested and died three years later in a concentration camp. Stanislavsky, the Moscow Art Theater director, died in 1938. Socialist realism was made mandatory for the provincial stage. The relaxation of controls during and immediately after the war proved short-lived. The Kamerny Theater was closed in 1949 because of "alien ideology and formalism." Its director, Tairov, died soon thereafter.

The number of theaters was greatly increased. In 1960 there were 500 urban theaters and another 500 on the collective farms, as well as children's (about 100) and army theaters. It is believed that in spite of the stifling party control, some of the younger directors show imagination and promise and that the "Stanislavsky method" ("psychological realism") is generally followed, even in the provinces.

The Ballet. The story of the ballet is different. The Russian ballet, of necessity a relatively small group, lost as a consequence of the revolution a large proportion of its leading dancers and choreographers. Serge Diaghilev, who was responsible for the transformation of the Russian ballet and who introduced it to Europe in 1909, emigrated in 1918, and his ballet company danced in Europe, the United States, and South America until his death in 1929. The Diaghilev company comprised Russia's greatest dancers—Anna Pavlova, Tamara Karsavina, Vaslav Nijinsky (until 1913)—as well as the outstanding choreographers Michael Fokin, George Balanchine, Leonid Massin, and Bronislava Nijinska. These artists continued their fruitful work abroad, but they did not return to Russia. In spite of this loss the technical levels of the Leningrad and Moscow ballet have showed no marked decline, because the Soviets have retained the state-sponsored ballet school, which provides the ballet with a steady flow of highly-trained dancers.

A subtle art, the ballet did not respond readily to the pressures of socialist realism. The first ballet on a revolutionary theme, *The Red Poppy*, with a score by Reinhold Gliere, was produced in 1927 and was followed by others in the same vein, but this trend was not exclusively pursued. *The Fountain of Bakhchisarai* (based on a poem by Pushkin, score by Boris Asafiev, choreography by Rostislav Zakharov), 1934, as well as three ballets by Prokofiev, *Cinderella, Romeo and Juliet,* and *The Stone Flower,* dealt with non-revolutionary subjects. It has been suggested by Western critics that the new Soviet ballets tend towards over-elaborate plots and a proliferation of folk-dance elements that is a departure from classical tradition. Otherwise the Leningrad and the Moscow companies are essentially conservative. Of the numerous ballets by Fokin, who revolutionized choreography, only *Les Sylphides* (known in Russia by its original name *Chopiniana*) is part of the Soviet repertory, while old classics such as *Swan Lake* are frequently given, imaginatively produced, and extremely well-danced. The caliber of the performers is high. The leading ballerinas—Galina Ulanova, Maya Plisetskaya—and their male partners are talented and accomplished dancers. The Soviet ballet is not a progressive art, but art it is.

Cinematography. The Soviet motion picture industry had to begin from scratch. The personnel of the seven studios which existed in 1917 was dispersed by war and revolution, and many of the motion picture houses foundered in the turmoil. On August 27, 1919, the photographic and cinematographic industry was nationalized and placed under the control of the people's commissariat of education. Although Lenin held that "for us the most important art is the cinema," progress in reorganizing the industry was slow. A training school was founded, and short "agitation films" were turned out. The leading motion picture producers were Serge Eisenstein (1898–1948), Vsevolod Pudovkin (1893–1953), and Alexander Dovzhenko (1894–1956). The first full-length film on a revolutionary subject was *The Hammer and Sickle,* directed by V. R. Gardin in 1921. In the 1920's the Soviet cinema produced several notable pictures: *Battleship Potemkin,* 1925, directed by Eisenstein; *Mother,* 1926, a dramatization of Gorky's novel and directed by Pudovkin; and *Arsenal,* 1929, and *Earth,* 1930, directed by Dovzhenko. The film directors, however, found themselves in difficulties with the authorities and were accused of "formalistic" errors. Socialist realism was applied to the film industry with such rigor that the volume of motion picture production in the 1930's was far below the plan

Sovfoto

Ulanova in *Swan Lake*

and, indeed, remained close to the 1917 level. The subjects of the pictures were Soviet patriotism and the glorious deeds of traditional national heroes. The social contents and artistic merits of these films were low, but there were exceptions: the striking *Alexander Nevsky,* 1941, directed by Eisenstein, and his monumental *Ivan the Terrible,* of which Part I was released in 1945 and Part II not until 1958. Among the later films the more notable were *Othello,* produced by Serge Yutkevich, and *Don Quixote* and *The Cranes Are Flying,* 1958, produced respectively by G. N. Kozintsev and M. K. Kalatozov. Since the war the artistic and technical (if not thematic) levels of the motion picture industry have greatly improved. The All-Union State Institute of Cinematography maintains high standards, and preliminary training of five years is required prior to appointment to technical or creative departments in the industry, which has grown tremendously. In 1960 there were 35 motion picture studios; the number of projecting installations increased from 1,500 in 1914 to 28,000 in 1941, and to 91,000 in 1960; and annual attendance from 300 million in the 1920's to 3 billion in 1957.

Visual Arts and Music

Painting. Painting, which never did well in Russia, gained nothing by the revolution. Among the numerous artists who emigrated were Alexander Benois, Mstislav Dobuzhinsky (1875–1957), Constantine Korovin, Nicholas Roerich, and Serge Sudeykin. The vanguard movements which had gained a footing in Russia prior to 1914 were revitalized by the revolution. Non-objective painters, later to achieve prominence outside Russia—Naum Gabo (1890–   ), Anton Pevzner (1886–1962), Marc Chagall (1889–   ), and Wassily Kandinsky (1866–1944)—believed that the revolution would favor their endeavors. They had studied abroad but were in Russia at the time of the revolution, Chagall from 1914 to 1922 and Kandinsky from 1914 to 1921. Kandinsky was already well known, his book *On the Spiritual in Art* (1910) having laid the theoretical foundation of non-objective art. After the advent of the Bolsheviks, he was director of the Museum of Pictorial Culture in Moscow, a founder of the Institute of Artistic Culture and of the Academy of Artistic Science, and professor of art at Moscow University. Kandinsky and the other leading non-objective painters left Russia in the early 1920's because of the hostility of the party and the government towards their art.

There was much disagreement among the various factions of the vanguard movement, which was opposed by the Association of Artists of Revolutionary Russia on the ground that art must deal with contemporary themes and be accessible to the masses. Following the decision of the central committee of the party of April 13, 1932, the various associations of artists were merged into the Communist-controlled Union of Soviet Artists. Under the ensuing regime of socialist realism the creation of "the image of the positive Soviet hero" became the principal objective of Russian art.

Museum of Modern Art

I and the Village, painting by Marc Chagall, 1911

Portraits and group portraits with Lenin, Stalin, and Voroshilov as central figures were among the favorite themes. The origins of socialist realism were traced to the "social" school of painting sponsored by the Circular Exhibitions movement of the nineteenth century. The effects of official tutelage were calamitous. Commenting on an exhibition of Soviet graphic art held in London, a left-wing English journal (*New Statesman and Nation*) wrote in 1945: "Those who believe . . . in the importance of environment would expect from the USSR an art remarkably unlike our own. And in fact what we get is an art like that of our most academic and genteel practitioners, and art that, coming from any one else, would be labeled dismally bourgeois." Among the better-known Soviet painters were: I. I. Brodsky (1883–1939), president of the Leningrad Academy of Fine Arts; Igor Grabar, once an impressionist, portrait painter, and art historian; and Alexander Gerasimov (1881–   ), portrait painter, elected chairman of the Union of Soviet Artists in 1952. In spite of the efforts of the artists to comply with the requirements of socialist realism, accusations of "formalism" are frequent.

As in literature, encouragement is given to the art of national minorities, provided it remains strictly within the bounds of Communist orthodoxy.

Sculpture and Architecture. Russian sculpture and architecture, like painting, had an undistinguished record and gained little by the revolution. A few sculptors (N. A. Altman, V. A. Tatlin) attempted some daring experimentation stemming from cubism and futurism and known as "constructivism." Technically their work was a combination of various materials —steel, glass, concrete, wrought iron, paper—the use of which was intended to suggest the many-sidedness of human experience. An example of this type of art, if art it is, was Tatlin's projected monument to the Third International, which was never built. Experimentation soon gave way to stark realism and grandiosity; there were created numerous statues of heroic dimensions, particularly those of Lenin and Stalin, worker and peasant, partisan and farmer, executed in a strictly realistic manner. Two of the leading sculptors were Serge Merkulov (1881–1952) and Ivan Shadr (Ivanov, 1887–1941). A prominent sculptor active in the 1960's is Eugene Vuchetich (1908–   ), who designed the Soviet memorial in Berlin and, in collaboration with the architects G. Zakharov and M. Posokhin, the monumental architectural ensemble for Poklonnaya Hill, near Moscow, which is to commemorate the victory over Germany. Vuchetich was awarded the Grand Prix at the International Exhibition in Brussels in 1958 and must be regarded as a sculptor of international reputation. Yet his memorials are open to criticism on many grounds. Both—that in Berlin and especially the proposed one in Moscow—are exceedingly large structures loaded with patriotic symbolism, ornate and pretentious; they are indeed characteristic of the notion of grandeur that Stalin endeavored to implant.

Architecture, like other arts, went through severe trials and a period of experimentation. World War I and the revolution did relatively little harm to architectural monuments, but damages caused by the German invasion during World War II were grave. Many ancient buildings in Kiev, Novgorod, and other localities were razed to the ground or partly destroyed, as were the less ancient but quaint and charming imperial residences around Leningrad and palaces and public buildings in the former capital. In spite of skillful and painstaking restoration, much of this damage is irreparable.

In architecture, as in other arts, rebels against tradition exercised some influence from 1917 to 1932–1935. The prevalent approach to building was experimentalism and an international modernist style. A striking example of this type of architecture was the Soviet Army Theater (completed in 1940), which is shaped like a 5-point star. Khrushchev, a staunch conservative in art, described this structure (March 8, 1963) as "an example of unwise enthusiasm for form in architecture . . . probably the most unwise building we have put up," and as "a stupid idea, the result of an immature notion about the beautiful and the intelligent in art and life." The building was designed by Karo Alabyan (1897–　) and V. N. Simbirtsev (1901–　) and the plan approved by Stalin on the recommendation of Kaganovich.

Outbursts against architects, such as Khrushchev's, were unusual. Unlike authors and composers, architects were not publicly castigated, ordered to renounce their errors, or imprisoned. Nevertheless, they saw the writing on the wall, abandoned experimental ways, and in the 1930's reverted to Russian (and other) national styles and to nineteenth-century neo-classicism. There was also a tendency to emulate American skyscrapers. Such, for instance, is the building of the University of Moscow (completed 1953, architects L. V. Rudnev and others), which is remarkably like the Chicago Tribune building. Mention should be made of a small structure, the Lenin Mausoleum in Red Square, which was erected according to plans by A. V. Shchusev, first of wood in 1924 and rebuilt in stone in 1930.

No new type of architecture emerged from the Soviet revolution. One characteristic of the new buildings is a tendency toward grandiosity and excessive ornamentation.

Music. Music, which had made good progress in Russia since the middle of the nineteenth century, had to adapt itself, like the other arts, to the ways of the Communist state. War and revolution disorganized musical life. Many distinguished musicians emigrated, among them Rachmaninoff, Glazunov, Alexander Ziloti, A. T. Grechaninov, Igor Stravinsky, Alexander Cherepnin, Igor Markevich, Nicholas Nabokov, and Vladimir Dukelsky (Vernon Duke), to mention only a few. Nevertheless music held its own. Gliere, Nicholas Miaskovsky (1881–1950), Yuri Shaporin (1887–   ), and other composers and teachers of the older generation stayed on. Serge Prokofiev went abroad in 1918 but returned to Russia in 1932 and did not leave again. The principal composers who began their professional careers under the Soviets were Dimitry Shostakovich (1906–   ), Aram Khachatur-yan (1903–   ), Dimitry Kabalevsky (1904–   ), Tikhon Khrennikov (1913–   ), and Ivan Dzerzhinsky (1909–   ). That Soviet music schools have maintained the traditional high level of instruction is indicated by the distinguished company of Soviet-trained instrumentalists: the pianists Sviatoslav Richter (1914–   ), Emil Gilels (1916–   ), and Lev Oborin (1907–   ); the violinists David Oistrakh (1908–   ) and Leonid Kogan (1924–   ); and the cellist Daniel Shafran (1924–   ). It would be easy to add other names to this list.

Facilities for enjoying music have been greatly expanded. The USSR has a large number of opera houses, many symphony orchestras and choral societies, and innumerable recitals by individual artists. In two respects Soviet musical life differs from that of other countries. Soviet composers, including the most eminent, such as Prokofiev and Shostakovich, are from time to time accused of "formalism" or some other sin against the party line. They usually recant their errors, and things return to normal until the next mishap. The second element of difference is the abundance of operas and choral compositions. Hundreds of operas and many more pieces for voice, none of them outstanding, have been written in recent years. This peculiarity may be explained, partly, by the emphasis on local music, for which operas and choral works provide a convenient vehicle, and partly, perhaps, by the desire to avoid charges of "formalism." Instrumental music by its very nature lends itself to a variety of interpretations. An opera or cantata may obviate this difficulty by loudly spelling out the required obeisance to Soviet patriotism. It usually helps.

Science

Academy of Science of the USSR. Science holds a high priority in the Soviet design for living. In the first decade of the twentieth century Russian science, if quantitatively weak, had qualitatively caught up with western European countries and was second to none in various fields (chemistry, biology, physiology, mathematics). The impact of the revolution of 1917 was severe, many scientists fleeing the country, while others perished in the upheaval. At the end of the civil war scientific work was at a very low level but recovered rapidly. In 1925 the Imperial Academy of Science was reorganized as the Academy of Science of the USSR and was given the status of the highest scholarly institution, subordinated directly to the Council of People's Commissars (later Council of Ministers). It was enlarged in 1929 to include engineers and in 1934 was transferred from Leningrad to Moscow. Scientific work expanded substantially in 1924–1935, and fairly close relations were established with Western institutions. This situation was reversed following the refusal of the Soviet government in 1934 to allow Peter Kapitsa, a Soviet citizen and distinguished physicist on the faculty of Cambridge University, to return to England. About that time prominent Soviet pro-Western scholars disappeared, and Western scientists working in Russia left the Soviet Union. Russian science was again isolated from the West.

With the outbreak of the Soviet-German war the academy was moved to Kuibyshev (Samara), and its numerous institutes were scattered through various eastern towns. Much of the building and scientific equipment was destroyed. It took about 10 years for restoration to be completed. The reconstructed facilities of the academy have the advantage of being up to date and equipped with modern appliances. The chief characteristics of the years following the end of the war, in addition to the reconstruction of the destroyed scientific establishments, were work on the atomic bomb and missiles and isolation from the West. The membership of the academy, which in 1960 consisted of 160 full and 350 corresponding members, was divided into nine sections: physics and mathematics; chemistry; biology; geology and geography; technical science; history; economics, philosophy, and law; literature and linguistics; and the Siberian section, which comprises members of the academy working in Siberia and in the Far East. The academy maintained over 160 institutes and independent laboratories and sections, which carry on research and graduate teaching, and it has the authority to confer higher degrees. A State Committee for Coordination of Research was created in April 1961, and a thorough reorganization of the academy was decreed in May 1963. Its object was to increase the usefulness of the academy as an agency for carrying out technical assignments. The constituent republics have their own academies of science; that of the Ukraine was established in 1919 but the others in the 1940's and 1950's. The number of universities in 1961 was given as 40; these institutions, however, must differ considerably in their scholastic standards and the size of their student bodies.

Failures and Achievements. The performance of Soviet science, and it is performance that really counts, is uneven. The social sciences and, surprisingly, certain disciplines that would seem to be non-political (linguistics, genetics) were doing poorly, while mathematics and especially technology scored notable successes. History, economics, government, philosophy, and literature were forced into the straitjacket of dialectical materialism, which many of those who wrote on these subjects understood but imperfectly. No interpretative studies of any importance have appeared in these fields; Russian history in the twentieth century, especially since 1917, is being incessantly rewritten to meet the whims of the central committee of the Communist Party or, more likely, its secretary. It is a shocking situation. Linguistics, unexpectedly, became a controversial subject, because Professor Nicholas Marr (1864-1934), an orientalist and philologist, invented a doctrine that purportedly established a direct link between the development of languages and the evolution of material culture and economy. The endorsement by Stalin and the party of these views, which were interpreted as Marxist, led to the practical destruction of philology and linguistics in the Soviet Union, for no one was permitted to express dissenting opinions publicly; in 1950, however, Marr's theories were criticized in *Pravda* and in 1952 by Stalin. They are no longer mandatory.

The much over-written case of genetics was similar, but its consequences graver. After World War I Russia was the leading center of research in genetics; the recognized Russian authority in this field was Professor Nicholas Vavilov (1887-1943), director of the All-Russian Academy for Plant Study (1924-1940). Trofim Lysenko (1898-   ), a biologist, elaborating the views of a practical plant-breeder I. V. Michurin, held that characteristics acquired through environmental influences could be inherited, a theory that ran contrary to the doctrine of heredity held by Western geneticists and by Vavilov. Seemingly this was an academic controversy, even though it had practical implications in so far as plant-breeding was concerned. However, the Communist Party and Stalin personally espoused the Lysenko theory. Vavilov was dismissed and deported to a camp beyond the Arctic Circle, where he died. Geneticists who shared his views were denounced as "bourgeois idealists," and a week-long conference in August 1948 ended in proclaiming the Lysenko brand of genetics as the "true science." It is unlikely that Stalin and the central committee had an understanding of genetics, a highly specialized subject, but Vavilov shared the views of Western scientists, and this was fatal. "This policy decision," says Professor John Turkevich, "affected other branches of science . . . and they underwent thorough search for any evidence of idealism, non-appreciation of Soviet achievements, and pro-Westernism. During the Stalin period many prominent scientists were arrested. . . . Communication between Soviet science and the rest of the world was for all practical purposes non-existent." This situation has changed since 1953, and some of the missing scientists have reappeared, but in 1962–1963 Lysenko was still ruling Soviet genetics. In December 1962 he expanded his views at length before a conference "on guiding the heredity of agricultural plants," held at the Academy of Plant Breeding, of which he was president, and in March 1963, *Kommunist,* the party's leading theory journal, unreservedly endorsed his views.

Pure science and technology have a better record. The Soviets are not given to publicity about their defense plans, but it would seem that they began to work on the atomic bomb, missiles, and space exploration imme-

Vostok spacecraft

Cosmonaut Vladimir Komarov

Cosmonaut Yuri Gagarin

diately after the war, under the direction of Beria. Progress was fast. The first Soviet atomic bomb was exploded in September 1949 and the first hydrogen bomb in August 1953. In October 1957 Sputnik I was launched, followed in November of the same year by Sputnik II, which carried the first living creature to enter celestial regions—the dog Laika. A new phase in space exploration was inaugurated with the launching in April 1961 of Vostok I, carrying Major Yuri Gagarin, and in August of that year of Vostok II, with Major German Titov aboard. On August 11, 1962, Vostok III, with Andrian Nikolaev, and on August 12 Vostok IV, with Pavel Popovich, went into orbit. Vostok III stayed up for 95 hours and made 63 orbits; Vostok IV, 71 hours and 48 orbits. They came down within a few minutes of each other. This impressive record was bettered in 1963. On June 14 Lieutenant Colonel Valery F. Bykovsky, piloting Vostok V, and on June 16 the first woman cosmonaut Lieutenant Valentina V. Tereshkova, piloting Vostok VI, were launched into outer space. Both landed safely on June 19 in Kazakhstan within a short distance from one another. Bykovsky remained afloat for nearly 5 days and completed 81 orbits; Tereshkova's flight lasted 71 hours and orbited the earth 48 times.

On October 12, 1964, Voskhod I, piloted by Vladimir M. Komarov and carrying two passengers—a scientist and a physician, was put into orbit. The spacemen wore no special air clothing because of the total airtightness of the capsule. The flight lasted 24 hours. Voskhod II carrying Pavel I. Beliaev and Alexis A. Leonov was launched on March 18, 1965. Leonov, wearing a space suit, left the capsule and remained in open space for ten minutes. The duration of the flight was 26 hours.

The Soviet space program is diversified, comprehensive, and massive. Some Soviet satellites orbit the earth, others aim at the moon, Venus, and Mars. Molnia communication satellites were placed in orbit in 1965. They were used to relay remote television broadcasts, radio communications, and two-way radio and telephone communications. The first successful soft landing on the moon was achieved by Luna 8 in December 1965; this program continued to be developed. From 1962 to 1967 180 space stations of the Cosmos program were put into orbit around the earth. An important step forward was the creation in 1965 of the powerful Proton rocket-space system, with a maximum effective power exceeding 60 million h.p., that is, three times as great as that of the Vostok rocket.

These were extraordinary exploits which prove a high degree of technical proficiency. The Soviet Union, like Great Britain and the United States, uses the services of German space experts, but there is no reason for attaching to this fact any special significance in the case of Russia. The high standards of mathematical studies in the Soviet Union, a discipline in which the Russians have held their place well since the days of Nicholas Lobachevsky (1792–1856), might have something to do with the success of the space program. Incidentally, Soviet mathematics are said to be computer-oriented, and this may presage significant developments in this important and forbidding field.

The success of the program was marred and, perhaps, jeopardized by grievous losses of personnel. S. P. Korolev, fellow of the Academy of Sciences and an outstanding designer of space-rocket systems, died in January 1966 after a severe illness at the relatively early age of 60. Komarov, 20 years his junior, who had piloted in 1964 the first multimanned ship Voskhod, perished in April 1967 in the crash-landing of the latest and most promising spaceship Soyuz I, which he took on a test flight. In March 1968 Gagarin, the first man to orbit the earth, and Colonel Vladimir S. Seregin were killed in the crash of a plane which Gagarin was piloting on a training flight. He was only 34. Special commissions were appointed to investigate the causes of both disasters but their findings were not made public.

An annual event is the award of Lenin prizes for achievements in science, technology, letters, arts, and music. The Lenin prizes were established in 1925, but in 1935 the name was changed to Stalin prizes; the original appellation was restored in 1956 as a part of Khrushchev's de-Stalinization program. Annually 50 prizes of 75,000 rubles each are awarded on the anniversary of Lenin's birth. A large proportion of the awards go to scientists, but letters and arts are always represented. Many of the prize winners, even in the division of literature and the arts, are unknown in the West.

Since 1953

The "Thaw." The death of Stalin generated among a section of the Soviet intelligentsia a movement to escape from the straitjacket of socialist realism. There was evidence—or promise—of a relaxation of the severity of party and government controls. As already noted, contacts with foreign scientific institutions were resumed. Russian delegations participated in the 1955 and 1958 Geneva conferences for the peaceful use of atomic energy. Closer relations with foreign countries were encouraged. The long dormant VOKS, the All-Union Society for Cultural Relations with Foreign Countries, created in 1925, was replaced in 1957 by the State Committee for Cultural Relations with Foreign Countries, which, unlike its predecessor, is officially a "public" and not a "state" agency. It has negotiated agreements with a number of countries, including the United States, for exchanges of students, artists, orchestras, theatrical companies, and delegations of professional people. New hotels were built, and the staff and facilities of Intourist, the Soviet travel agency, have been greatly expanded.

Censorship became less rigid. Vera Panova's novel *The Four Seasons,* Leonid Zorin's play *The Guests,* and Ilia Ehrenburg's novel *The Thaw,* all three published in 1954, contained pessimistic reflections on Soviet conditions which would have been unthinkable before 1953. One swallow, however, does not make the spring: Zorin's play was closed after one performance, and Panova and Ehrenburg were severely taken to task by the critics. At the second congress of Soviet writers in December 1954, party leaders staunchly upheld socialist realism. The effect on Russian letters of Khrushchev's anti-Stalin campaign at the Twentieth Congress (1956) was similar to that in Poland and Hungary. Daniel Granin's story *Personal Opinion,* 1956, and Vladimir Dudintsev's *Not by Bread Alone,* 1957, were critical of bureaucratic controls. *Not by Bread Alone* was translated into several foreign languages and enjoyed great popularity at home and abroad. It was criticized by the party, but seemingly no harm came to the author. In the

Wide World

Khrushchev and Cosmonaut Gagarin, Red Square, 1961

summer of 1956 Boris Pasternak (1890–1960), a poet and novelist who for two decades published little except philosophical verse and translations, offered a Soviet literary magazine his novel *Doctor Zhivago,* a melancholy account of the experiences of an intellectual during the revolution. The novel was rejected but was published abroad in 1957 and Pasternak was awarded in 1958 the Nobel prize which, because of the extremely hostile reaction of Soviet authorities, he declined. Official criticism of authors suspected of "formalism" was sharpened after the Polish and Hungarian events of 1956. There was a relaxation in 1959, followed by renewed attacks in 1962 and particularly in the spring of 1963, when a major campaign for ideological purity was in progress.

Khrushchev's Attitude, 1963. Particularly outspoken and revealing was a lengthy speech by Khrushchev at a meeting of party and government leaders with workers in literature and art, on March 8, 1963. Somewhat earlier, commenting on the Twenty-second Congress, *Pravda* took pains to explain (November 21, 1961) that "in condemning the cult of the individual, Marxism-Leninism by no means denies the role of the outstanding organizers and leaders of the party. . . . V. I. Lenin was such a leader. . . . It would be wrong and harmful to confuse leaders' authority with the cult of the individual. . . ." The expected liberalization of the regime has often been identified with Ehrenburg's novel *The Thaw,* but Khrushchev did not encourage these speculations. He included *The Thaw* among the books which give "an incorrect, one-sided interpretation of the events and developments connected with the cult of the individual." According to Khrushchev "skepticism, weakness of will, slackness, pessimism, and a nihilistic attitude to reality are alien to the Soviet people." He expressed astonishment that so many books, films, and plays should reflect the negative aspects of Soviet life and spread a feeling of despondency. A. Solzhenitsyn's story "One Day in the Life of Ivan Denisovich," depicting conditions in a Stalin labor camp, and Ehrenburg's memoirs *People, Years, and Life,* belong to this class of writing. "I can say from personal experience, as a participant in those years that are sometimes presented in somber colors and gray tones, that these were happy, joyous years, years of struggle and victory, of triumph of communist ideas"—a statement not easy to reconcile with the picture he himself has traced repeatedly of Stalin's rule. Khrushchev spoke not only of literature but of music, painting, architecture, and films. "Our policy in art," he declared, "the policy of firm rejection of abstract art, formalism and any other bourgeois distortions, is a Leninist policy that we unswervingly have applied, are applying, and will apply." Khrushchev stated that when he listens to Glinka—a very conservative composer—"tears of joy always come" to his eyes, but he objected strenuously to jazz and modern dances.

These views are not different from those held throughout the world by a large number of conservative people who abhor Communism. The difference between the West and the Soviet Union is that in Russia they are inexorably enforced. Said Khrushchev: "We adhere to class positions in art and are resolutely opposed to the peaceful coexistence of socialist and bourgeois ideologies." And again: "The Communist Party of the Soviet Union is the guiding force of socialist society. It expresses the will of the entire Soviet people. The party enjoys the people's confidence, which it has earned with its struggle, with its blood. And the party will remove from the path of communist construction everything that stands in the way of

UPI

Boris Pasternak

the people's interest." This is a plain statement on which Stalin could hardly have improved. In the same speech, however, Khrushchev said that "magazines and publishing houses are flooded with manuscripts about the life of persons in exile, in prison, in the camps"—something that could not have happened prior to 1953. Yet the protest was hesitant, roundabout, and weak; its restraint and mildness confirm the conclusion of Chapter 26: "At the end of the first decade since the death of Stalin, Soviet Russia is different—but not vastly different—from what she was under his rule."

After Khrushchev. The more liberal attitude towards arts and letters that

Sovfoto

Ancient Scythian monuments

many in the West expected to follow the removal of Khrushchev did not materialize. Communist orthodoxy was maintained intact and the few attempts at challenging official views were ruthlessly suppressed. A slight relaxation was noticeable in the field of the arts. In December 1966 an exhibition of drawings and ceramics by Pablo Picasso was held at the Pushkin Museum of Fine Arts in Moscow. *Izvestia* gave it a brief noncommittal notice.

Efforts were made to familiarize the West with Russian art. An exhibition held in Paris in 1960 was limited to Russian painters of the nineteenth century, an unexciting and unimaginative period. A more ambitious and better-organized retrospective show of Russian art was opened at the Grand Palais in Paris at the end of 1967. Its more interesting and successful section was the one devoted to prehistoric, primarily Scythian, art; early religious

Sovfoto

Scythian vase

Russia, a painting by Ilia Glazunov

Russian Icarus, a painting by Ilia Glazunov

paintings were revealing and popular while works of the later period, not surprisingly, failed to impress most of the critics. Nearly 400 modern Soviet paintings by 200 artists were exhibited in Cannes, South of France, in the spring of 1968. They belonged to the conventional school and showed the influence of the French impressionists.

A surprising tolerance was displayed by Soviet authorities toward the unorthodox work, partly in the surrealist manner, by Ilia Glazunov, an artist still in his thirties. After some ups and downs in his brief career, he gained a measure of recognition both in the Soviet Union and abroad, painted the portraits of several Western notables of the diplomatic and art worlds, and was sent on a mission to North Vietnam where he made some 140 drawings, which were exhibited in Hanoi and in Moscow. In the summer of 1968 he had a comprehensive show in Paris. Glazunov's case, however, was quite exceptional and should not be interpreted as an abandonment, or even a weakening, of socialist realism.

The partial rehabilitation of Stalin was evidence of the persistence of traditional thinking. The Stalin Museum at Gori, his birthplace, which was closed during the de-Stalinization drive, was reopened in 1965. The history of World War II was rewritten once more to depict Stalin as a military leader in a favorable light. Professor Nekrich, an anti-Stalin historian of note who had blamed the purges of the 1930's for Russia's staggering defeats in 1941, was expelled from the party. The case of the former dictator was sponsored by the influential journal *Oktiabr*. The young poet F. Chuyev toured the provinces reciting poems with the refrain "put Stalin back on his pedestal." He was reportedly decorated on the occasion of the fiftieth anniversary of the revolution.

A theme incessantly expounded in official pronouncements and in the statements of Soviet leaders was socialist realism. "The art of socialist realism," said a *Pravda* editorial of January 9, 1965, "is extending the frontiers of artistic perception of the world and is opening up new opportunities for the emotional and esthetic influence of man." But "there is not and there cannot be peaceful coexistence" between the (allegedly) progressive Soviet art and the reactionary bourgeois art which "is striving to disarm the peoples in their struggle for freedom, peace, and socialism." Brezhnev, following in the footsteps of Khrushchev, voiced similar views. "The struggle against bourgeois ideology must under all circumstances be uncompromising," he told the Twenty-third Party Congress, "for this is a class struggle, a struggle for man, for his dignity and freedom, for the consolidation of the position of socialism and communism; it is a struggle in the interest of the international working class." The *Pravda* editorial ominously argued that "there cannot be concessions of principle or compromises in evaluating works containing errors of an ideological nature."

The party's watchdog of ideological purity in literature was the Writers' Union. Its first congress met in 1934, the second in 1954, the third in 1959, and the fourth in May 1967. The message addressed to the fourth congress by the central committee on the Communist Party restated forcibly the official view of the nature of literary work and the duties of writers. "The congress," said the message, "is an important landmark in the development of the literature of socialist realism, a significant event in the entire spiritual life of our society." The message held that "Soviet literature opened a new stage in the development of the culture of mankind." The duties of authors were sharply defined: "Literature's militant task is the patriotic and international upbringing of the working people. . . . Literature strengthens man's conviction in the triumph of the ideas of Communism and his boundless love for our socialist homeland. It is called upon to instill in young people pride in our victories and achievements . . . and forge in the young generation the qualities of fighters for the construction of the new society." And again: "The writer has a lofty mission in socialist society. To be a man of letters in the land of the Soviets means to remain a staunch party fighter at all times and in all ways, to discover heroic communist activity and wage an implacable struggle against all manifestations of bourgeois ideology."

In 1967 the Writers' Union had 6,600 members; 525 delegates were elected to the fourth congress. The chief task of the Union, it was officially stated, was "guidance of the Soviet Union's entire multinational literature." The debate at the conference was heavily tinged with optimism characteristic of socialist realism. For instance, according to one report, "our entire life is marked by serene confidence in the rightness of our cause, the heroic scope of the people's labor, and the sober calculations of our plans and a strict scientific approach to every social and national-economic problem." M. A. Sholokhov who only recently was awarded the Nobel prize for literature (1965) unkindly reminded the assembly that while 71 per cent of the delegates at the first writers' congress were under 40, at the fourth only 12 per cent were in that age group.

Renewed emphasis on socialist realism and the duties of a writer were probably, in part, the consequence of the sensational trial of Siniavsky and Daniel for which these doctrines provided the ideological background. Andrew Siniavsky and Yuri Daniel were tried in Moscow on February 10–13, 1966. Both were 40 and were of good standing in Soviet literary circles.

Siniavsky was an author of fiction, a literary critic, an official of the Institute of World Literature of the USSR Academy of Sciences, and a member of the Writers' Union. Daniel was a poet and a translator. Both were charged under Article 70 of the criminal code of the Russian republic which deals with "agitation or propaganda conducted for the purpose of undermining or weakening the Soviet rule . . . or the circulation . . . of slanderous publications that defame the Soviet state or social system, as well as the preparation, or possession of such literature." It was admitted that beginning in 1956 Siniavsky, and somewhat later Daniel, surreptitiously sent abroad articles and stories which appeared in foreign and emigré bourgeois publications. Siniavsky used the pseudonym Abram Tertz and Daniel that of Nikolai Arzhak. The first story of Tertz was published abroad in 1959. It is notable that it took the security police, so lavishly praised on its fiftieth anniversary, seven years to discover who were the authors of the incriminated publications. Both defendants were found guilty. Siniavsky was given the heaviest sentence provided by the law: seven-year imprisonment in a strict regime labor camp, and Daniel a similar five-year sentence. According to the official Soviet view, the writings the two authors sent abroad were "anti-Soviet calumnies" devoid

Trial of writers Siniavsky and Daniel

of literary merit. An eminent American student of Soviet letters (Edward J. Brown) took a different view. Writing before the identity of Tertz was disclosed, he stated that while Tertz's stories contained "many pages of excellent writing" they "are not successful artistically"; he concluded that "Tertz will remain an anomaly and a riddle even if his identity should come to light." The odd behavior of Siniavsky-Tertz at his trial, which at times looked like a debate in a small-town literary society, would seem to confirm this judgment.

Another case that attracted world-wide attention was the trial of four young intellectuals—A. I. Ginzburg, Y. T. Galaskov, A. A. Dobrovosky, and V. I. Lashkova—which took place in Moscow in January 1968. They were accused of subversive activities and given prison sentences ranging from seven to two years.

The two trials differed in some aspects from the political trials of the earlier period. Proceedings were held in open court although access to the court room was restricted and closely controled; the defendants—unlike their predecessors of the Stalin era—made no confessions and, indeed, insisted on their innocence. Yet their conviction was a foregone conclusion. Another unprecedented development was a minor movement of protest in the USSR against both trials, the manner in which they were conducted, and the severity of the sentences. It was believed that such protests were signed by several hundred members of the intelligentsia. Among them was Paul Litvinov, grandson of Stalin's minister of foreign affairs, Maxim Litvinov. The party and the government took strong retaliatory measures. Some of the signatories were expelled from the party, pressure was brought on others to recant and withdraw their signatures. All were silenced, and socialist realism continued to rule Soviet arts and letters.

The Fiftieth Anniversary of the Revolution. "In 50 years absolutely everything in the life of our people has changed," said Brezhnev in his anniversary oration in November 1967. "We have built a totally new world, a world of new social relations, a world of the new Soviet man. . . . Renewed and transformed by socialism, our country has appeared before mankind in all its might and grandeur, in all the brilliance of its remarkable people's talent." Celebrations of historical anniversaries are not conducive to moderation, yet this was a truly fantastic claim unrelated to the record.

CONCLUDING REMARKS

An Afterthought. There are problems of historiography which inevitably present themselves to the student who casts a glance over the long span of centuries covered by a book that attempts to describe and analyze a thousand years of a nation's history. None of them, perhaps, is more challenging than the question of continuity and change that has been touched upon in connection with the various aspects of the earlier discussion. Is the familiar adage—*plus ça change, plus c'est la même chose*—true? Does the knowledge of the past offer a key to an understanding of the present or to a reasonable appraisal of the future? Historians have addressed themselves frequently to these questions. It seems clear that no political regime can entirely divest itself of its past, and the temptation of finding elements of continuity even where none exists is great. ". . . During the first years of the regime, while the revolutionary impetus continued to predominate," writes E. H. Carr, "familiar features of the Russian landscape and the Russian outlook slowly emerged from beneath the revolutionary flood." [1] He believes that " 'socialism in one country' was a repetition of what has happened countless times before in Russian history," meaning by this striking statement that "innovation undertaken in time of emergency under the inspiration of the West was reabsorbed into a national setting, and took a spe-

[1] Edward Hallett Carr, *A History of Soviet Russia: Socialism in One Country, 1924–1926,* vol. I (New York: Macmillan, 1958), p. 21.

[675]

cifically national colour." [2] This was a bold assertion even for the early period of Soviet history with which Carr deals—when the revolution was still too young to offer firm ground for generalizations.

A striking instance of the continuity of Russia's historical tradition is the feebleness of the elements of self-government and the persistence of those of police and bureaucratic omnipotence. The situation in this respect has not greatly changed since the unification of Russia under the rule of Moscow in the fourteenth and fifteenth centuries. The failure of the various local government reforms, beginning with those of Ivan IV and including Alexander II's *zemstvo* and municipal government acts (important as they were), to create institutions of self-government capable of representing and defending local interests against bureaucratic arbitrariness is a permanent salient feature of Russian history that is being retained under the Soviets. Administrative trappings and phraseology have changed, but the essence has not been altered, and this is why Gogol's *The Inspector General* has lost none of its appeal and its timeliness. The stern rule of the imperial police, "do not get together" (*"ne skopliatsia"*), has been reversed, and countless multitudes obedient to party orders, assemble at short notice to acclaim Stalin, Malenkov, Beria, or Khrushchev, to denounce American or British imperialism, to cheer Castro, or to applaud the fulfillment figures of the plans. But after the revolution—as before—official guidance is invariably present.

In some respects, however, the situation has greatly changed. Russia never had truly representative assemblies, advisory or legislative, but such as they were—the boyar duma, the *zemskii sobor*, Catherine II's legislative commission, the State Duma—they were no mere rubber stamps. Debate was often lively and disagreement sharp. This is not true of Soviet assemblies, which, like the docile crowds which foregather in Red Square, are always of one mind. The secret of this unprecedented unanimity, which had its counterpart in the fascist states, is, of course, the party. The German dictum *Und der König absolut, wenn er unsern Willen tut*—the king has absolute powers if he does what we tell him to do—has been reversed. In the modern totalitarian states the people have absolute power, provided they do what the party tells them to do. This is the true meaning of Soviet democracy. Under the Communist regime the total control of all means of public communication by far exceeds the most daring dreams of imperial censorship in the darkest periods of Russian history.

In no field is the change more pronounced than in foreign relations. Since World War II the USSR has been a world power. Soviet foreign policy

[2] *Ibid.,* p. 15.

is governed by the Communist doctrine, which is predicated on the inevitability of world communism. It is a grievous, albeit common, error to see in Soviet annexations during and after World War II a continuation of the policies of the imperial regime. Both the objectives and the methods of the two are different. Some of Russia's eighteenth- and nineeenth-century rulers—Catherine II, Paul, Alexander I, perhaps Nicholas I—at times contemplated "projects" of world domination, but they never had the means to implement these foolish schemes, which remained in the discussion stage. Moreover, annexation by imperial Russia meant a change in political regime but not in the social structure, while the Communist system was imposed on the territories annexed by Soviet Russia or comprised in her orbit. This is a major element of difference from the past. The execution of these policies is assisted by the international Communist movement, which—in spite of China, Albania, and Yugoslavia—the Soviet Union largely controls. This, again, is a novel situation, and there is no evidence that the "familiar features of the Russian landscape and Russian outlook" (to quote Carr's observation about a much earlier period) are emerging "from beneath the revolutionary flood." Half a century is too short a period to form a definite judgment, yet one may be justified in drawing the tentative conclusion that the elements of continuity tend to decline and those of change to increase. The world, indeed, is confronted with a situation for which history offers no precedent.

SELECTED BIBLIOGRAPHY

SELECTED BIBLIOGRAPHY

This bibliography comprises exclusively books in the English language, easily available, which may be useful to general readers, teachers, and students. By a process of careful elimination the bibliography has been deliberately kept short. Those interested in more detailed and specialized bibliographical information are referred to the comprehensive bibliographies in my *Russia: A History and An Interpretation*, 2 volumes (New York: Macmillan, 1953), and *Towards an Understanding of the USSR*, revised edition (New York: Macmillan, 1951).

ALLEN, W. E. D. *The Ukraine: A History*. New York: Cambridge U.P., 1941.
ALLILUYEVA, SVETLANA. *Twenty Letters to a Friend*. New York: Harper and Row, 1967.
ANTSIFEROV, A. N., BILIMOVICH, A. D., *et al. Russian Agriculture During the War*. New Haven, Conn.: Yale U.P., 1930.
BADDELLEY, JOHN F. *Russia, Mongolia, and China*. 2 volumes. London: Macmillan, 1919.
BAIN, R. N. *The Daughter of Peter the Great*. Westminster, England: Constable, 1899.
———. *The Pupils of Peter the Great*. Westminster, England: Constable, 1897.
———. *Peter III, Emperor of Russia*. New York: Dutton, 1902.
BARGHOORN, FREDERICK C. *Soviet Russian Nationalism*. New York: Oxford U.P., 1956.
BARON, SALO W. *The Russian Jew Under Tsars and Soviets*. New York: Macmillan, 1964.
BAYKOV, ALEXANDER. *Development of the Soviet Economic System: An Essay on the Experience of Planning in the USSR*. Cambridge, England: The University Press, 1950.

BELOFF, MAX. *The Foreign Policy of Soviet Russia,* Volume I: 1929–1936; Volume II: 1936–1941. New York: Oxford U.P., 1947–1949.

BERDIAEV, NICHOLAS. *The Origins of Russian Communism.* London: G. Bles, 1937.

BERGSON, ABRAM. *The Real National Income of Soviet Russia Since 1928.* Cambridge, Mass.: Harvard U.P., 1961.

———. *The Structure of Soviet Wages.* Cambridge, Mass.: Harvard U.P., 1944.

———, editor. *Soviet Economic Growth, Conditions and Perspectives.* Evanston, Ill.: Row, Peterson, 1953.

BIENSTOCK, G., SCHWARZ, S., and YUGOW, M. *Management in Russian Industry and Agriculture.* New York: Oxford U.P., 1944.

BLACK, CYRIL E. *Rewriting Russian History: Soviet Interpretation of Russia's Past.* New York: Praeger, 1956.

BROWN, EDWARD J. *Russian Literature since the Revolution.* New York: Collier Books, 1969.

BROWN, EMILY CLARK. *Soviet Trade Unions and Labor Relations.* Boston: Harvard U.P., 1966.

BUCHANAN, SIR GEORGE W. *My Mission to Russia and Other Diplomatic Memories.* 2 volumes. London: Cassell, 1923.

BUNYAN, JAMES, and FISHER, H. H. *The Bolshevik Revolution, 1917–1918: Documents and Materials.* Stanford, Calif.: Stanford U.P., 1934.

BYRNES, JAMES F., *Speaking Frankly.* New York: Harper, 1947.

The Cambridge History of Poland, Sir. A. W. Ward, editor. Cambridge, England: Cambridge U.P., 1941.

CAMPBELL, ROBERT W. *Soviet Economic Power.* Boston: Houghton Mifflin, 1960.

CARR, EDWARD HALLETT. *A History of Soviet Russia.* 7 volumes. New York: Macmillan, 1951–1964.

CHAMBERLIN, WILLIAM HENRY. *The Russian Revolution, 1917–1921.* 2 volumes. New York: Macmillan, 1952 (1935).

CHERNOV, VICTOR M. *The Great Russian Revolution.* New Haven, Conn.: Yale U.P., 1936.

CHURCHILL, WINSTON SPENCER. *The Second World War.* 6 volumes. Boston: Houghton Mifflin, 1948–1954.

———. *The World Crisis, Volume II: 1915.* London: Butterworth, 1923.

Current Digest of the Soviet Press, a weekly journal. New York and Ann Arbor, Mich., 1949–

CURTISS, JOHN S. *Church and State in Russia, 1900–1917.* New York: Columbia U.P., 1940.

———. *The Russian Church and the Soviet State, 1917–1950.* Boston: Little, Brown, 1953.

DALLIN, ALEXANDER. *German Rule in Russia, 1941–1945: A Study of Occupation Policies.* New York: St. Martin's Press, 1957.

DANIELS, ROBERT. *Red October: The Bolshevik Revolution of 1917.* New York: Scribner, 1967.

DEUTSCHER, ISAAC. *The Prophet Armed: Trotsky, 1897–1921.* New York: Oxford U.P., 1954.

———. *The Prophet Unarmed: Trotsky, 1921–1929.* New York: Oxford U.P., 1959.

———. *The Prophet Outcast: Trotsky, 1929–1940.* New York: Oxford U.P., 1963.

———. *Soviet Trade Unions: Their Place in Soviet Labour Policy.* London: Royal Inst. of International Affairs, 1950.

———. *Stalin: A Political Biography.* New York: Oxford U.P., 1949.

DOBB, MAURICE H. *Soviet Economic Development Since 1917.* London: Routledge and Kegan Paul, 1948.

DULLES, FOSTER RHEA. *The Road to Teheran, The Story of Russia and America, 1781–1943.* Princeton, N.J.: Princeton U.P., 1944.

FAINSOD, MERLE. *How Russia Is Ruled.* Cambridge, Mass.: Harvard U.P., 1963 (1953).

FEIS, HERBERT. *Churchill, Roosevelt, and Stalin.* Princeton, N.J.: Princeton U.P., 1957.

FIELD, MARK G. *Soviet Socialized Medicine: An Introduction.* New York: Free Press, 1967.

FISCHER, LOUIS. *The Soviets in World Affairs: A History of the Relations Between the Soviet Union and the Rest of the World, 1917–1929.* Abridged by the author. New York: Vintage Books, 1960.

FISHER, J. R. *Finland and the Tsars, 1809–1899.* London: Arnold, 1899.

FLORINSKY, MICHAEL T. *The End of the Russian Empire.* New Haven, Conn.: Yale U.P., 1931; New York: Collier Books, 1961.

———. *Russia: A History and an Interpretation.* 2 volumes. New York: Macmillan, 1961 (1953).

———. *Towards an Understanding of the USSR.* Revised edition. New York: Macmillan, 1951.

———. *World Revolution and the USSR.* New York: Macmillan, 1933.

FRANKLAND, MARK. *Khrushchev.* New York: Stein and Day, 1967.

GANKIN, OLGA H., and FISHER, H. H. *The Bolsheviks and the World War: The Origins of the Third International.* Stanford, Calif.: Stanford U.P., 1940.

GOLDER, FRANK A. *Documents of Russian History, 1914–1917.* New York: Century, 1927.

———. *Russian Expansion on the Pacific, 1641–1850.* Cleveland: A. H. Clark, 1914.

GOLDMAN, MARSHALL I. *Soviet Foreign Aid.* New York: Praeger, 1967.

GOLOVINE, NICHOLAS N. *The Russian Army in the World War.* New Haven, Conn.: Yale U.P., 1931.

GOOCH, GEORGE P. *Catherine the Great and Other Studies.* New York: Longmans, Green, 1954.

GORDON, MANYA. *Workers Before and After Lenin.* New York: Dutton, 1941.

GRAHAM, STEPHEN. *Ivan the Terrible: Life of Ivan IV of Russia, Called the Terrible.* New Haven, Conn.: Yale U.P., 1933.

———. *Tsar of Freedom: The Life and Reign of Alexander II.* New Haven, Conn.: Yale U.P., 1935.

GRONSKY, PAUL P., and ASTROV, NICHOLAS J. *The War and the Russian Government.* New Haven, Conn.: Yale U.P., 1929.

GRUNWALD, CONSTANTINE DE. *Peter the Great.* New York: Macmillan, 1956.

———. *Tsar Nicholas I.* London: D. Saunders, 1954.

HARCAVE, S., editor. *Readings in Russian History.* 2 volumes. New York: Crowell, 1962.

———. *First Blood: The Russian Revolution of 1905.* New York: Macmillan, 1964.

HAYWARD, MAX, editor. *On Trial: The Soviet State Versus "Abram Terz" and "Nikolai Arzhak."* New York: Harper and Row, 1966.

HENDERSON, W. O. *The Industrial Revolution in Europe, 1815–1914.* Chicago: Quadrangle Books, 1961.

HILDT, J. C. *Early Diplomatic Negotiations of the United States with Russia.* Baltimore: Johns Hopkins, 1906.

HILGER, GUSTAV, and MEYER, ALFRED G. *The Incompatible Allies: A Memoir-History of German-Soviet Relations, 1918–1941.* New York: Macmillan, 1953.

HRUSHEVSKY, MICHAEL. *A History of Ukraine.* New Haven, Conn.: Yale U.P., 1941.

HUNT, R. N. CAREW. *The Theory and Practice of Communism—An Introduction.* New York: Macmillan, 1957.

IZVOLSKY, A. P. *Recollections of a Foreign Minister.* Garden City, N.Y.: Doubleday, 1921.

JUVILER, PETER H., and MORTON, HENRY W., editors. *Soviet Policy Making.* New York: Praeger, 1967.

KAYDEN, EUGENE M., and ANTSIFEROV, ALEXIS N. *The Cooperative Movement in Russia During the War.* New Haven, Conn.: Yale U.P., 1929.

KERENSKY, ALEXANDER F. *Russia and History's Turning Point.* New York: Duell, 1965.

KLIUCHEVSKY, V. O. *A History of Russia.* 5 volumes. London: J. M. Dent, 1911–1931.

———. *Peter the Great.* New York: St. Martin's Press, 1958.

KOKOVTSOV, COUNT V. N. *Out of My Past.* Stanford, Calif.: Stanford U.P., 1935.

KORNILOV, ALEXANDER A. *Modern Russian History.* New York: Knopf, 1948.

LANGER, WILLIAM L. *The Diplomacy of Imperialism, 1890–1902.* 2 volumes. New York: Knopf, 1935.

———. *European Alliances and Alignments, 1871–1890.* New York: Knopf, 1931.

———. *Franco-Russian Alliance, 1890–1894.* Cambridge, Mass.: Harvard U.P., 1929.

LASERSON, MAX M. *The American Impact on Russia.* New York: Macmillan, 1950.

The Letters of the Tsaritsa to the Tsar, 1914–1916, with an introduction by Sir Bernard Pares. London: Duckworth, 1923.

The Letters of the Tsar to the Tsaritsa, 1914–1917. London: J. Lane, 1929.

LIDDELL HART, B., editor. *The Red Army.* New York: Harcourt, Brace, 1956.

LINDE, CARL A. *Khrushchev and the Soviet Leadership, 1957–1964.* Baltimore: John Hopkins, 1966.

LOBANOV-ROSTOVSKY, A. *Russia in Asia.* Ann Arbor, Mich.: G. Wahr, 1951.

———. *Russia in Europe, 1789–1825.* Durham, N.C.: Duke U.P., 1947.

———. *Russia in Europe, 1825–1878.* Ann Arbor, Mich.: G. Wahr, 1954.

LORD, ROBERT H. *The Second Partition of Poland, A Study in Diplomatic History.* Cambridge, Mass.: Harvard U.P., 1915.

Lowe, C. *Alexander III of Russia, 1895.* London: Macmillan, 1895.

Lyashchenko, P. I. *History of the National Economy of Russia to the 1917 Revolution.* New York: Macmillan, 1949.

McGraw-Hill Encyclopedia of Russia and the Soviet Union, Michael T. Florinsky, editor. New York: McGraw-Hill, 1961.

Mackintosh, Malcolm. *Juggernaut: A History of the Soviet Armed Forces.* New York: Macmillan, 1967.

Massie, Robert K. *Nicholas and Alexandra.* New York: Atheneum, 1967.

Mavor, James. *An Economic History of Russia.* 2 volumes. New York: Dutton, 1925.

Maynard, Sir John. *Russia in Flux.* London: V. Gollancz, 1941.

Meisel, J., and Kozera, E. S. editors. *Materials for the Study of the Soviet System.* Ann Arbor, Mich.: G. Wahr, 1953.

Memoires of Catherine the Great. New York, 1955.

Meyer, Alfred G. *Communism.* New York: Random House, 1960.

———. *Leninism.* Cambridge, Mass.: Harvard U.P., 1957.

Michelson, A. M., Apostol, Paul N., and Bernatzky, Michael W. *Russian Public Finance During the War,* New Haven, Conn.: Yale U.P., 1928.

Miliukov, P. N. *Outlines of Russian Culture.* 3 volumes. Philadelphia: Univ. Pennsylvania P., 1942.

———. *Russia and Its Crisis.* Chicago: Univ. Chicago P., 1962 (1905).

Miller, Margaret S. *The Economic Development of Russia, 1905–1914.* London: P. S. King, 1926.

Mirsky, D. S. *A History of Russian Literature* (rev. ed.). New York:Knopf, 1949.

———. *Russia, A Social History.* London: Cresset, 1952.

Moore, Harriet L. *Soviet Far Eastern Policy, 1931–1945.* Princeton, N.J.: Princeton U.P., 1945.

Morton, Henry W. *Soviet Sport.* New York: Collier Books, 1963.

Mosely, Philip E. *Russian Diplomacy and the Opening of the Eastern Question in 1838 and 1839.* Cambridge, Mass.: Harvard U.P., 1934.

———, editor. *The Soviet Union, 1922–1962.* New York: Praeger, 1963.

Nazi-Soviet Relations, 1939–1941, Documents from the Archives of the German Foreign Office, edited by Raymond James Sontag and James Stewart Beddie. Washington, D.C.: Department of State, 1948.

Nicolson, Sir Harold. *The Congress of Vienna, a Study in Allied Unity: 1812–1822.* London: Constable, 1947.

Nolde, Baron Boris E. *Russia in the Economic War.* New Haven, Conn.: Yale U.P., 1928.

Nove, Alec. *The Soviet Economy, An Introduction.* New York: Praeger, 1963 (1961).

Nutter, G. Warren, assisted by Israel Borenstein and Adam Hofman. *Growth of Industrial Production in the Soviet Union.* Princeton, N.J.: Princeton U.P., 1962.

Odinetz, D. I. and Novgorotsev, P. J. *Russian Schools and Universities in the World War.* New Haven, Conn.: Yale U.P., 1929.

Okune, S. B. *The Russian-American Company.* Cambridge, Mass.: Harvard U.P., 1951.

PALEOLOGUE, MAURICE. *The Enigmatic Czar: The Life of Alexander I of Russia.* London: H. Hamilton, 1938.

PARES, SIR BERNARD. *The Fall of the Russian Monarchy: A Study of Evidence.* London: J. Cape, 1939.

PAVLOVSKY, G. *Agricultural Russia on the Eve of the Revolution.* London: G. Routledge, 1930.

PIPES, RICHARD. *The Formation of the Soviet Union: Communism and Nationalism, 1917–1923.* Cambridge, Mass.: Harvard U.P., 1954.

PLATONOV, S. F. *History of Russia.* New York: Macmillan, 1925.

POKROVSKY, M. N. *Brief History of Russia from the Earliest Times.* 2 volumes. New York: International Publ., 1933.

POLNER, TIKHON J., *et al. Russian Local Government During the War and the Union of Zemstvos.* New Haven, Conn.: Yale U.P., 1930.

RADKEY, OLIVER H. *The Agrarian Foes of Bolshevism: Promise and Default of the Russian Socialist Revolutionaries, February to October, 1917.* New York: Columbia U.P., 1958.

———. *The Election to the Russian Constituent Assembly of 1917.* Cambridge, Mass.: Harvard U.P., 1950.

RAEFF, MARC. *Michael Speransky: Statesman of Imperial Russia, 1772–1839.* The Hague: Nijhoff, 1957.

VON RAUCH, GEORGE. *A History of Soviet Russia.* New York: Praeger, 1957.

ROBINSON, GEROID T. *Rural Russia Under the Old Regime.* New York: Macmillan, 1949 (1932).

RODZIANKO, M. C., *The Reign of Rasputin: An Empire's Collapse.* London: A. M. Philpot, 1927.

ROMANOV, B. A. *Russia in Manchuria, 1892–1906.* Ann Arbor, Mich.: J. W. Edwards, 1952.

ROSTOVTZEFF, MICHAEL. *Iranians and Greeks in Southern Russia.* Oxford: Clarendon Press, 1922.

The Russian Provisional Government, 1917, documents selected and edited by R. P. Browder and Alexander F. Kerensky. 3 volumes. Stanford, Calif.: Stanford U.P., 1961.

RYWKIN, MICHAEL. *Russia in Central Asia.* New York: Collier Books, 1963.

SALISBURY, HARRISON E., editor. *The Soviet Union: Fifty Years.* New York: Harcourt, Brace, 1967.

SAZONOV, S. D. *Fateful Years, 1909–1916.* London: J. Cape, 1928.

SCHAPIRO, LEONARD. *The Communist Party of the Soviet Union.* London: Eyre & Spottiswoode, 1960.

———. *The Government and Politics of the Soviet Union.* New York: Random House, 1965.

SCHWARTZ, HARRY. *Russia's Soviet Economy.* Englewood Cliffs, N.J.: Prentice-Hall, 1960.

SCHWARZ, SOLOMON. *Labor in the Soviet Union.* New York: Praeger, 1951.

SETON-WATSON, HUGH. *The Decline of Imperial Russia, 1855–1914.* London: Methuen, 1952.

——. *From Lenin to Khrushchev: The History of World Communism.* New York: Praeger, 1962.

——. *The Russian Empire, 1801–1917.* New York: Oxford U.P., 1967.

SHERWOOD, ROBERT E. *Roosevelt and Hopkins, an Intimate History.* New York: Harper, 1948.

SHOTWELL, JAMES T., and DEAK, FRANCIS. *Turkey at the Straits.* New York: Macmillan, 1940.

SHULMAN, MARSHALL D. *Stalin's Foreign Policy Reappraised.* Cambridge, Mass.: Harvard U.P., 1963.

SIMMONS, ERNEST J., editor. *Through the Looking Glass of Soviet Literature: Views of Russian Society.* New York: Columbia U.P., 1953.

SLONIM, MARC L. *The Epic of Russian Literature from Its Origins Through Tolstoy.* New York: Oxford U.P., 1950.

——. *Modern Russian Literature from Chekhov to the Present.* New York: Oxford U.P., 1950.

SOLOVEYCHIK, GEORGE. *Potemkin: A Picture of Catherine's Russia.* London: Butterworth, 1939.

STETTINIUS, EDWARD R. *Roosevelt and the Russians: The Yalta Conference,* edited by Walter Johnson. Garden City, N.Y.: Doubleday, 1949.

STRUVE, GLEB. *Russian Literature.* Norman, Okla.: Univ. Oklahoma P., 1951.

SUKHANOV, NICHOLAS. *The Russian Revolution, 1917: A Personal Record.* New York: Oxford U.P., 1955.

SUMNER, B. H. *Peter the Great and the Emergence of Russia.* London: English Universities P., 1950.

——. *Russia and the Balkans, 1870–1880.* Oxford: Clarendon Press, 1937.

TARACOUZIO, T. A. *War and Peace in Soviet Diplomacy.* New York: Macmillan, 1940.

TARLE, E. V. *Napoleon's Invasion of Russia, 1812.* New York: Oxford U.P., 1942.

TEMPERLEY, H. *England and the Near East: The Crimea.* London: Longmans, Green, 1936.

TOWSTER, JULIAN. *Political Power in the USSR, 1917–1947.* New York: Oxford U.P., 1948.

TREADGOLD, DONALD W., editor. *Soviet and Chinese Communism: Similarities and Differences.* Seattle: Univ. Washington P., 1967.

TROTSKY, LEON. *History of the Russian Revolution.* 3 volumes. Ann Arbor, Mich.: Univ. Michigan P., 1957 (1932).

——. *My Life.* New York: Scribner's, 1930.

TURIN, S. P. *From Peter the Great to Lenin: The History of the Russian Labour Movement with Special Reference to Trade Unionism.* London: P. S. King, 1935.

VERNADSKY, G. *The Origins of Russia.* Oxford: Clarendon Press, 1959.

——, and KARPOVICH, M. *A History of Russia.* 4 volumes. New Haven, Conn.: Yale U.P., 1946–1959.

VOLIN, LAZAR. *A Survey of Soviet Russian Agriculture.* Washington, D.C.: U.S. Government Printing Office, 1951.

WALISZEWSKI, K. *Paul the First of Russia, the Son of Catherine the Great*. London: W. Heinemann, 1913.

———. *Peter the Great*. New York: D. Appleton, 1897.

———. *The Romance of an Empress: Catherine II of Russia*. New York: D. Appleton, 1895.

WEBSTER, SIR CHARLES K. *The Congress of Vienna, 1814–1815*. London: Thames, 1963 (1919).

WHEELER-BENNETT, JOHN W. *The Forgotten Peace: Brest-Litovsk, March 1918*. New York: Morrow, 1939.

WITTE, SERGE. *The Memoirs of Count Witte*. Garden City, N.Y.: Doubleday, 1921.

WOLFE, BERTRAM D. *Khrushchev and Stalin's Ghost*. New York: Praeger, 1957.

ZABRISKIE, E. H. *American Russian Rivalry in the Far East, 1895–1914*. Philadelphia: Univ. Pennsylvania P., 1946.

ZAGORSKY, S. O. *State Control of Industry in Russia During the War*. New Haven, Conn.: Yale U.P., 1928.

———. *Wages and Regulations of Conditions of Labour in the USSR*. Geneva: World Peace Foundation, 1930.

ZALESKI, EUGENE. *Planning Reforms in the Soviet Union, 1962–1966*. Chapel Hill: Univ. North Carolina P., 1967.

ZAUBERMAN, ALFRED. *Aspects of Planometrics*. London: The Atheneum Press, Univ. London, 1967.

ZEMAN, Z. A. B. *Germany and the Revolution in Russia, 1915–1918*. New York: Oxford U.P., 1958.

INDEX